The
National
Underwriter
Company *a division of ALM Media, LLC*

P9-BZQ-509

**NATIONAL SOCIAL
SECURITY ADVISOR** SM

Does your team have the knowledge and education to be a trusted resource for the 78 million baby boomers maturing into Social Security?

The National Underwriter Company and NSSA® can help!

The National Underwriter Company in partnership with National Social Security Association is offering a limited-time opportunity to earn the National Social Security Advisor (NSSA®) Certificate at a discounted group rate.

Your instructors, Marc Kiner, CPA, and Jim Blair, are Social Security experts and co-authors of 2019 Social Security and Medicare Facts.

Marc and Jim will travel to your facility and provide live training and support for your team!

Increasing Advisor Value With NSSA® Certificate Training

Advisors who earn the NSSA® Certificate will:

- Increase their credibility as a Social Security professional
- Gain confidence in educating others about Social Security
- Be a trusted resource to the millions of baby boomers who have questions about Social Security

Among the topics covered by the NSSA® program:

- Benefit Computations
- Retirement Benefits
- Medicare
- Spousal Elections
- Surviving Spousal Benefits
- Lump Sum Death Payments
- WEP/GPO
- Benefits Taxation
- COLA
- Case Studies
- ...and much more

For more information on providing training and certification for your team of advisors, please contact Mark Kiner at mkiner@mypremierplan.com or 513-218-8505 (cell) or 513-247-0526.

THE NATIONAL UNDERWRITER COMPANY

a division of ALM Media, LLC

2019 SOCIAL SECURITY & MEDICARE FACTS

Michael D. Thomas, J.D., Author
Marc Kiner, CPA, NSSA, and Jim Blair, NSSA, Contributing Authors

2019 Social Security & Medicare Facts is a one-stop guide for attorneys, CPAs, and retirement and financial planning professionals to advise on tax and policy changes affecting Social Security and Medicare. Organized in a unique and convenient Q&A format, this book helps professionals find exactly what they're looking for quickly and easily to solve clients' important planning issues in a timely manner.

The 2019 edition has been fully revised, featuring:

- New question & answers sections on the Windfall Elimination Provisions to the Social Security Act and Government Pension Offset

- Additional information regarding Delayed Retirement Credits and Self-Employment Insurance

- Expanded coverage of disability benefits, mother and father's benefits, spousal and surviving spouse benefits, children's benefits

- Updated status of the Medicaid expansion under the Affordable Care Act

- Additional coverage of rights and benefits for same-sex marriages

- Case studies illustrating real-life scenarios of how maximization of benefits strategies can be applied

- The effect of "Excess Earnings" on benefits for Social Security recipients

- 2019 inflation-adjusted numbers for Social Security and COLA increases

- Significant expansion of coverage of Railroad Retirement benefits and benefits for federal government employees, including new questions relating to FERS and Civil Service Retirement program

- Additional coverage of Military Retirement including addition of coverage of new Blended Retirement program, military disability pay, and coverage for National Guard and Reservists

- Expanded coverage of disability benefits for Social Security, military, government, and railroad worker

- Expanded coverage of Medicare Advantage, as well as Medigap insurance, included the elimination of the popular "Plan F"

This new edition continues to deliver completely up-to-date answers to over 840 Social Security and Medicare benefits questions, covering:

- Retirement & disability benefits
- Filing for benefits
- Loss of Social Security benefits due to "excess" retirement earnings
- Social Security taxes
- Railroad retirement benefits
- Benefits for federal government employees
- Medicare Part A, Hospital Insurance
- Medicare Part B, Medical Insurance
- Medicare Part C, Medicare Advantage
- Medicare Part D, Prescription Drug Insurance
- Medigap insurance
- Medicaid
- How to submit Medicare claims as well as filing appeals
- Social Security coverage
- Benefit computation
- Taxation of Social Security benefits
- Wages & self-employment income
- Benefits for service members & veterans

Authored by retirement planning and estate planning experts, *2019 Social Security & Medicare Facts* is the practical, comprehensive reference you can rely on.

Related Titles Also Available:

- *The Tools & Techniques of Trust Planning*
- *The Tools & Techniques of Estate Planning for Modern Families*
- *Tax Facts on Insurance & Employee Benefits*
- *Tax Facts on Investments*
- *Tax Facts on Individuals & Small Business*
- *Health Savings Accounts Facts*
- *The Tools & Techniques of Employee Benefit & Retirement Planning*
- *Field Guide to Estate Planning, Business Planning & Employee Benefits*
- *Healthcare Reform Facts*

For customer service questions or to place orders for any of our products, please call 1-800-543-0874 or email customerservice@nuco.com.

2019 SOCIAL SECURITY & MEDICARE FACTS

• Retirement and Disability Coverage • Medicare Benefits • Filing for Benefits • Computation of Benefits • Loss of Benefits and Benefit Reduction • Delayed Retirement Credits • Government Pension Offset and Windfall Elimination Provision • Changes in Medigap Plans • Taxation of Benefits • Benefits for Service Members and Veterans • Government Retirement Benefits • Railroad Retirement • Social Security Case Studies and Benefit Maximization • Medicaid • Medicare Advantage

Michael D. Thomas, J.D., Author
Marc Kiner, CPA, NSSA®, Contributing Author
Jim Blair, NSSA®, Contributing Author

Circular 230 Notice – The content in this publication is not intended or written to be used, and it cannot be used, for the purposes of avoiding U.S. tax penalties.

ISBN 978-1-949506-21-1

Copyright © 2019

The National Underwriter Company
a division of ALM Media, LLC
4157 Olympic Blvd., Suite 225
Erlanger, KY 41018

Printed in U.S.A.

The National Underwriter Company publishes the following Social Security/Medicare publications:

Social Security & Medicare Facts
Social Security Planner
Medicare Planner

A12007252 380

ABOUT THE NATIONAL UNDERWRITER COMPANY
a division of ALM Media, LLC

For over 110 years, The National Underwriter Company, *a division of ALM Media, LLC* has been the first in line with the targeted tax, insurance, and financial planning information you need to make critical business decisions. Boasting nearly a century of expert experience, our reputable Editors are dedicated to putting accurate and relevant information right at your fingertips. With *Tax Facts, Tools &Techniques, National Underwriter Advanced Markets, Field Guide, FC&S®, FC&S Legal* and other resources available in print, eBook, CD, and online, you can be assured that as the industry evolves National Underwriter will be at the forefront with the thorough and easy-to-use resources you rely on for success.

Update Service Notification

This National Underwriter Company publication is regularly updated to include coverage of developments and changes that affect the content. If you did not purchase this publication directly from The National Underwriter Company, *a division of ALM Media, LLC* and you want to receive these important updates sent on a 30-day review basis and billed separately, please contact us at (800) 543-0874. Or you can mail your request with your name, company, address, and the title of the book to:

The National Underwriter Company
a division of ALM Media, LLC
4157 Olympic Boulevard
Suite 225
Erlanger, KY 41018

If you purchased this publication from The National Underwriter Company, *a division of ALM Media, LLC*, directly, you have already been registered for the update service.

Contact Information

To order any National Underwriter Company title, please

- call 1-800-543-0874, 8-6 ET Monday – Thursday and 8 to 5 ET Friday

- online bookstore at www.nationalunderwriter.com, or

- mail to Orders Department, The National Underwriter Company, *a division of ALM Media, LLC*, 4157 Olympic Blvd., Ste. 225, Erlanger, KY 41018

ACKNOWLEDGEMENTS AND DEDICATION

I would like to take this opportunity to extend my gratitude to the editorial and production staff, especially Connie Jump, Patti O'Leary, Emily Brunner, and Rick Cline of the National Underwriter Company – without their efforts, this book would not be possible.

I also would like to dedicate this book to my children, Caitlin and Caleb, and my wife Rita, who are my support and foundation. In addition, I posthumously dedicate this book to my parents, Donald and Angeline Thomas – whose decades of tireless work afforded me the opportunity to gain the education and skills to undertake this work.

Michael D. Thomas

PREFACE TO 2019 SOCIAL SECURITY AND MEDICARE FACTS

The 2019 edition of *Social Security and Medicare Facts* is designed to provide you with all the information needed to help your clients plan for retirement and to make the most of their Social Security and Medicare benefits. Our goal is to supply you with a hands-on reference tool administering not only the basic information about Social Security and Medicare, but also answers to some of the more complex and confusing aspects and issues associated with these tools.

For the 2019 edition we have expanded our coverage of this topic by updating information on planning techniques to help your clients maximize their Social Security benefits. Especially important in this area is the explanation of the changes wrought by the 2015 Bi-Partisan Budget Act which implemented sweeping changes to the ability of individuals to utilize "file and suspend" and "restricted application" to maximize their retirement benefits. In addition, there are new sections covering how benefits can be reduced or lost though the Windfall Elimination Provision, and the Government Pension Offset. There is expanded coverage on important topics such as Delayed Retirement Credits, Self-Employment Income, and additional and updated materials regarding reduction of benefits because of the effect of "excess" earnings. We have reviewed our Case Studies component of the publication illustrating dozens of examples of how certain actions will affect the amount that your clients collect – or do not collect – from Social Security during their retirement years. In addition to reviewing the existing questions, we have added nearly 140 new questions expanding our coverage of nearly every topic as well as updating benefits amounts and costs to 2019 values. In addition, we have addressed changes and updates to Medicare, Medicare Advantage, Medigap policies and Medicaid, including the Medicaid expansion under the Affordable Care Act. In addition, we have greatly expanded our coverage of benefits relating to military pensions, government pensions and railroad retirement.

Whether your clients work in the private sector, for the government (federal, state, or local), in connection with the railroad industry, or in the military, this book has information on their retirement, disability, and survivor benefits. Using this reference tool can help you present your clients with the knowledge they need to know what to expect in retirement, when they die, or if they should unexpectedly become disabled.

I want to thank my contributing authors, Marc Kiner and Jim Blair who created the Case Studies and who are truly experts in how individuals can assure themselves of gaining maximum advantage of their Social Security benefits. My thanks also extend to everyone at National Underwriter Company/ALM Media who have worked so hard to help me with this 2019 edition, especially Patti O'Leary, Emily Brunner, Rick Cline and especially Connie Jump who kept me mostly on schedule.

Mike Thomas
November 2018

ABOUT THE AUTHOR

Michael D. Thomas is an author and consultant and has served as the Manager of Online Product Development and a Senior Editor with the National Underwriter Company, a division of ALM Media. In addition, Mike serves as a consultant to the State of Ohio, Department of Medicaid and as a writer for "The Digital Broker Podcast", which focuses on insurance technology and operations. In addition to co-authoring the *2019 Social Security & Medicare Facts* and the *2019 Healthcare Reform Facts*, Mike has been responsible for the editorial process and development of other healthcare and insurance publications including: *Advisor's Guide to Long Term Care 2nd Edition, ERISA Facts*, and *Health Savings Accounts Facts* for The National Underwriter Company, as well as designing, implementing, and managing the *NUPro Healthcare Reform* online service. Mike has also authored numerous articles on healthcare reform, Social Security, Medicare, and Insurance issues. In addition, he has developed, hosted and taught webinars on Healthcare Reform and Social Security, including "*The Affordable Care Act and the Employer Mandate*", "*The Affordable Care Act and the Cadillac Tax — Use the Delay for Your Advantage!*", "*How to Successfully Navigate the Latest Changes to the Affordable Care Act*", and "*The Impact of Social Security on Retirement Plans*".

Prior to joining National Underwriter, Mike spent over twenty-five years with LexisNexis®, where he was responsible for the editorial content and new product development of new online and traditional legal products, including *Health Law, Insurance Law, Social Security Law, Labor & Employment Law, Family Law*, as well as other legal research tools. In addition, he worked as a Field Agent for Knights of Columbus Insurance specializing in life, health, disability income, long-term care insurance as well as annuity sales.

Mike has a Bachelor of Arts from Tufts University and a Juris Doctorate from the University of Dayton.

ABOUT THE CONTRIBUTING AUTHORS

Marc Kiner is the President of Premier Social Security Consulting, LLC, and has thirty years' experience in public accounting. Marc's primary areas of service are to privately-held businesses and to individuals. He consults with clients on a variety of complex tax and business issues. Marc obtained his Bachelor of Science degree in Accounting and Finance and a master's degree from the University of Cincinnati. He is licensed to practice as a CPA in the State of Ohio.

Jim Blair is the lead Social Security consultant at Premier Social Security Consulting, LLC. A former Social Security Administrator, Operations Supervisor and a District Manager, Mr. Blair has over thirty-five years' experience in helping individuals manage their Social Security benefits, retirement, survivors, disability, and health insurance.

About the Publisher

Richard H. Cline, J.D., is the Manager, Tax, and Insurance Content for the Practical Insights Division of the National Underwriter Company, an ALM Media company. He is responsible for both the print and online versions of Tax Facts as well as developing new tax products for our customers.

Richard joined the company in 2013 but has over twenty-five years of tax editing and publishing experience. Prior to joining our team, Richard worked for Lexis-Nexis, CCH, Inc., and PricewaterhouseCoopers.

He has a B.S. degree from Franklin and Marshall College in Lancaster, Pennsylvania, and earned his law degree from Tulane University in New Orleans, Louisiana.

Editorial Services

Connie L. Jump, Senior Manager, Editorial Operations

Patti O'Leary, Senior Editorial Assistant

Emily Brunner, Editorial Assistant

SUMMARY TABLE OF CONTENTS

PART I: SOCIAL SECURITY

PART II: MEDICARE

APPENDICES

LIST OF QUESTIONS
PART I: SOCIAL SECURITY
UNDERSTANDING AND PLANNING FOR SOCIAL SECURITY

19. Can individuals that are not U.S. citizens get a Social Security number?

20. What types of Social Security cards are issued?

21. What documents are required to get a Social Security number?

22. Can individuals with Deferred Action Status and employment authorization get a Social Security number?

23. Under what circumstances can a non-citizen be eligible for SSI?

24. How are Social Security numbers verified?

25. How long does it take to get a Social Security number and card for a newborn baby?

26. How are Social Security numbers assigned?

27. How can a person check on his Social Security earnings record and receive an estimate of future Social Security benefits?

28. What will happen to Social Security benefit payments when the Trust Fund becomes insolvent?

29. Where and how does a person apply for Social Security benefits?

30. Where and how does a person apply for Social Security benefits if they live overseas?

31. Which government agency issues a beneficiary's Social Security payment?

32. When does a Social Security beneficiary receive a monthly direct deposit?

33. To whom is a benefit payment made payable and how are benefits received?

34. If a husband and wife are both receiving monthly benefits, do they receive one or two monthly payments?

35. If several children are entitled to benefits, will each child receive a separate payment?

36. Can a power of attorney be granted for the purpose of collecting and managing payments?

37. Can Social Security benefits be assigned?

38. Can Social Security benefits be attached for the beneficiary's debts?

39. Are Social Security benefits subject to federal taxes?

40. What happens when a Social Security overpayment is made to a Social Security beneficiary by mistake?

41. Can individuals request a copy of a deceased individual's Social Security number application?

RETIREMENT AND DISABILITY BENEFITS

64. How are childhood disabilities classified?

65. What is a compassionate allowance?

66. Which illnesses currently qualify for compassionate allowances?

67. What is the definition of a medically determinable impairment?

68. Can a child qualify for disability benefits?

69. What disability benefits are available for Wounded Warriors?

70. Does blindness qualify a person for disability benefits?

71. At what age can a person receive disability benefits?

72. What is the waiting period for disability benefits?

73. When must an application for disability benefits be filed?

74. What is the process used to determine disability?

75. What is the amount of a disability benefit?

76. Is a person entitled to disability benefits regardless of wealth?

77. Can a disabled person receive disability benefits even though his spouse is employed?

78. Can a disabled person return to work while getting Social Security benefits?

79. What is the trial work period?

80. What amount of earnings trigger a trial work period?

81. What is the trigger amount of income which indicates a person is engaged in Substantial Gainful Activity?

82. What is the re-entitlement period?

83. Can a person become entitled to disability benefits after becoming entitled to some other type of Social Security benefit?

84. Will a disabled person lose benefits by refusing to accept rehabilitation services?

85. What are the special rules for disability benefits when alcoholism or drug addiction is involved?

86. When do a person's disability benefits end?

87. Are benefits payable to the family of a disabled worker?

88. If an individual is already collecting a disability benefit, can they suspend their benefits at Full Retirement Age and earn delayed retirement credits?

Same-Sex Marriages

Spouse's Benefit

Child's Benefits (Child of Retired or Disabled Worker)

110. Is a child of a retired or disabled parent entitled to Social Security benefits?

111. Who is considered a "child" of a retired or disabled worker for benefit purposes?

112. Must a child be dependent upon the worker to qualify for child's benefits?

113. Is a child considered to be dependent upon his father or mother regardless of actual dependency?

114. Under what circumstances is a child considered to be dependent upon a stepparent?

115. Can a child receive benefits based on one parent's Social Security account even though the other parent is working and furnishing support?

116. When is a child a full-time elementary or secondary school student?

117. Is the disabled child of a retired or disabled worker entitled to benefits past age twenty-two?

118. What is the amount of the benefit for a retired or disabled worker's child?

119. Can a child lose his benefits by working?

120. If the retired or disabled parent loses benefits, will the child lose benefits also?

121. Will a child lose his or her benefits if he or she marries?

122. When does a child's benefit end?

123. If a child is neither disabled nor a full-time elementary or secondary student, when does the benefit end?

124. Who files application for a child's benefits?

125. Can a child receive their own benefits?

Survivor's Benefits

126. What benefits are payable to the survivors of a deceased insured worker?

Mother's or Father's Benefit

127. Is the surviving spouse of an insured worker entitled to a monthly mother's or father's benefit at any age?

128. Is there an exception to the rule that the surviving spouse be married for at least nine months?

129. Can a divorced spouse qualify for a survivor's benefit?

130. Must a worker be fully insured at death to qualify for the mother's or father's benefit?

Child's Benefit (Child of Deceased Worker)

Widow(er)'s Benefit

Disabled Widow(er)'s Benefit

Parent's Benefits

Lump-Sum Death Payment

Prisoners

COVERAGE

Qualification

192. How does someone obtain a quarter of coverage as an employee?

193. How does someone obtain a quarter of coverage as a self-employed person?

194. What calendar quarters cannot be counted as quarters of coverage even though the earnings requirement has been met?

195. How do the requirements of the Social Security Protection Act of 2004 (SSPA) affect insured status?

196. Who is an alien worker under the SSPA?

197. How does work performed in a foreign country get taken into consideration for determining insured status?

198. With which countries does the United States have totalization agreements?

Fully Insured

199. How does a person become fully insured?

200. Are there other ways of becoming fully insured?

201. Must a person be fully insured to qualify for retirement benefits?

202. How do you determine the number of quarters of coverage needed for a person to be fully insured for retirement benefits?

203. Can a person be fully insured for retirement benefits even though not working in covered employment for many years?

204. Can a person become fully insured after retirement age?

205. How do you determine the number of quarters of coverage needed for a person to be fully insured at death?

206. When is someone deemed to be fully insured?

207. How many credits are necessary to be deemed fully insured?

Currently Insured

208. What benefits are payable if a person is only currently insured at death?

209. When is a person currently insured?

Insured Status for Disability Benefits

210. What insured status requirements must be met to qualify a person for disability benefits?

Computing Benefits

211. In general, how are Social Security benefits determined?

FILING FOR BENEFITS

General Information

212. What procedure should be followed to determine if a person is eligible for Social Security benefits?

213. At what point should the survivors of a deceased worker file for survivor's benefits?

214. When should an application for disability benefits be filed?

215. When should a person file an application for the lump-sum death payment?

Proof Required

216. What proofs are required before survivors' and retirement benefits can be paid?

217. What are acceptable proofs of death?

218. What are the best forms of proof of age and family relationship?

Right to Appeal

219. Is there a review procedure available if a person is disappointed with the Social Security Administration's initial determination regarding benefits?

220. How can a person appeal the reconsideration determination?

221. How is a hearing request made and how long will it take from the request to the actual hearing?

222. How long are the average delays in Social Security Hearing offices?

223. What will a hearing cost?

224. If an individual disagrees with the hearing decision, may they ask for a review?

225. May a person file a civil action in the United States District Court?

226. Are there situations where the Social Security Administration may not recover an overpayment to a beneficiary?

227. When is an individual considered to be "without fault" for getting an overpayment?

228. What are the factors considered by the Social Security Administration to determine whether a person is "at fault" or "without fault?"

229. When is an individual considered to be "at fault" for getting an overpayment?

BENEFIT COMPUTATION

MAXIMIZATION OF BENEFITS

Year of Retirement

305. Could both husband and wife file a restricted application for the other's spousal benefit?

306. Could you file and suspend at sixty-two to allow a nonworking spouse who is in ill health to collect one-half of benefit?

307. In a situation where a husband is aged sixty-six and working, could he file and suspend? Assuming his wife is age sixty – two and has earned forty credits, could she have then waited until she was seventy to begin benefits or should she have filed a restricted application at her own FRA?

308. After filing a restricted application, does one have to wait until reaching age seventy to begin their own benefit?

309. Is it safe to assume that a single person could only use the File and Suspend strategy but not the restricted application?

310. If a spouse filed and suspended by April 29, 2016 and delays collecting until age seventy, will the other spouse get an amount equal to half of the income based on the Delayed Retirement Credits or based on the Full Retirement Age (FRA) benefit?

311. What if a person dies after filing and suspending but before receiving benefits? Can the widow collect that lump sum?

312. If a husband filed and suspended and the wife takes spousal benefits at age sixty-two, will the wife get a stepped-up spousal benefit if the husband dies at age seventy-two after delaying his benefit until age seventy?

313. Can a working couple both at Full Retirement Age (FRA) claim both file and suspend and file restricted applications in order to receive two Social Security checks?

314. What is the best strategy in a situation where the husband is age sixty-six, with an income of $150,000 per year, and the wife is age sixty-eight, with an income of $50,000 per year?

315. What is a good strategy in a situation where the husband is age sixty-six with an income of $150,000 per year and the wife is age sixty-eight, with an income of $50,000 per year and the wife has already filed for benefits?

316. What option might one use if there is a significant difference in ages between spouses, for example, if the husband is twelve years older than wife?

317. What are the limitations of the "do-over" as an option?

LOSS OF BENEFITS BECAUSE OF "EXCESS" EARNINGS

Retirement Test

318. Can a person lose some or all Social Security benefits by working?

319. What are the components of the "Earnings Test"?

TAXATION OF SOCIAL SECURITY BENEFITS

343. Are Social Security benefits subject to federal income taxation?

344. What are the base amounts?

345. What portion of Social Security benefits are subject to income taxes?

346. Why is nontaxable interest income included in a taxpayer's adjusted gross income?

347. Are workers' compensation benefits included in the definition of Social Security benefits for tax purposes?

348. How are overpayments and lump-sum retroactive benefits taxed?

349. What reporting requirements must be met by the Social Security Administration?

350. Are Social Security benefits subject to income tax withholding?

351. If a recipient of Social Security benefits elects Medical Insurance (Part B) under Medicare and the premiums are deducted from the individual's benefits, is the whole benefit, before the deduction, a Social Security benefit?

SOCIAL SECURITY TAXES

352. What are the Social Security and Medicare tax rates for employers and employees?

353. If an employee works for two employers during the year and more than the maximum tax is paid on his or her wages, will the overpayment be refunded to the employee and his or her employers?

354. Does an employer receive an income tax deduction for Social Security tax payments?

355. Must Social Security taxes be paid on cash tips?

356. How are uncollected Social Security and other taxes collected?

357. How does an individual report Social Security taxes for domestic help?

358. What is the rate of Social Security and Medicare tax for a self-employed person?

359. If a self-employed person also receives wages as an employee, what portion of income is subject to tax as self-employment income?

360. Must a Social Security beneficiary who works pay Social Security and Medicare taxes?

361. How does a life insurance agent pay Social Security taxes on first-year and renewal commissions?

362. Must the self-employment tax be included in a person's estimated tax return?

363. What is the federal income tax deduction for medical expense insurance premiums?

WAGES AND SELF-EMPLOYMENT INCOME

364. What earnings are subject to Social Security tax and are counted in computing Social Security benefits?

365. For Social Security purposes, what is meant by the term "wages"?

366. Are only payments in cash counted as wages?

367. Are employer payments for group life insurance covered wages?

368. Are vacation pay and severance pay wages?

369. Are payments on account of sickness or accident disability counted as wages for Social Security purposes?

370. Are payments made under a deferred compensation plan counted as wages?

371. Are payments made to or from a qualified pension or annuity plan counted as wages?

372. If a teacher takes a reduction in salary to provide funds for a tax-sheltered annuity, how are his or her wages computed for Social Security purposes?

373. Are cash tips considered wages?

374. Are noncash tips considered wages?

375. Do prizes and awards from someone not an employer count as wages?

376. Do taxes withheld from pay count as a beneficiary's wage?

377. Do expense reimbursements and travel expenses count as wages?

378. Are payments made to a disabled former employee counted as wages?

379. Do wages include the portion of an employee's Social Security taxes paid by an employer?

380. Are a salesperson's commissions considered to be wages?

381. Under what circumstances are the first-year and renewal commissions of a life insurance agent treated as wages?

382. Is the value of meals and lodging furnished by an employer to an employee considered wages for Social Security taxation purposes?

Self-Employment Income

383. What is taxable and creditable self-employment income?

384. How is the amount of self-employment income figured if a person has both wages and net earnings from self-employment in the same year?

385. In general, what constitutes net earnings from self-employment?

RAILROAD RETIREMENT

Employee and Spousal Annuities

Railroad Retirement Benefits

Applying for Railroad Benefits

Survivor Benefits

Railroad Retirement Taxes

BENEFITS FOR SERVICE MEMBERS AND VETERANS

Military Retirement – Generally

Military Retirement Plans – High-3 and Blended Retirement

Government Life Insurance
Servicemembers' Group Life Insurance

510. Who is eligible to be insured automatically under Servicemembers' Group Life Insurance (SGLI)?

511. What is the SGLI Online Enrollment System?

512. What can Service members do in SOES?

513. Can reservists and National Guard members with part-time SGLI also access their coverage online?

514. Can service members automatically enroll in Veteran's Group Life Insurance through SOES?

515. What is the amount and nature of the coverage?

516. When is coverage terminated and can the policy be converted?

517. Who pays the cost of SGLI?

518. How does a person designate a beneficiary?

519. Does payment TSGLI reduce the amount of SGLI payable at the time of the service member's death?

520. Will SGLI pay if the service member is killed wearing privately purchased body armor or helmets?

521. Will SGLI pay if the service member is in a motor vehicle accident, an airline accident or a motorcycle accident and is not wearing seat belts or helmets?

522. Does SGLI cover Reservists and National Guard members?

523. Does SGLI cover deaths as of the result of a terrorist attack?

Veterans' Group Life Insurance

524. Who is eligible for Veterans' Group Life Insurance (VGLI)?

525. What is the amount of Veterans' Group Life Insurance and the enrollment and eligibility periods?

526. How is the beneficiary designated under Veterans' Group Life Insurance?

527. What are the premium rates for Veterans' Group Life Insurance?

528. How is Veterans' Group Life Insurance converted to an individual policy?

529. Will SGLI pay benefits if an insured dies while wearing privately-owned body armor or helmet?

BENEFITS FOR FEDERAL GOVERNMENT EMPLOYEES

Introduction

Federal Employees' Retirement System

Basic Annuity

Survivor Benefits

Annuity Eligibility Requirements

570. Who is eligible for a survivor annuity?

Computing the Survivor Annuity

571. How is the survivor annuity computed?

Lump-Sum Death Benefit

572. When does the lump-sum death benefit become payable?

Annuity Payments

573. How are annuity payments made?

Disability Retirement

574. When is an annuity payable for disability retirement?

Cost-of-Living Adjustments

575. Is there a cost-of-living adjustment to CSRS annuities?

Refund of Contributions

576. Is there a refund of contributions if an employee leaves government service?

Life Insurance Benefits

577. In general, what life insurance benefits are available to federal civil service employees?

578. How does an employee designate the beneficiary or beneficiaries?

579. When does insurance coverage cease?

580. Can an employee convert to an individual policy?

581. What is the cost of basic insurance?

582. What optional insurance coverages are available to the civil service employee?

583. May a retiring employee continue life insurance coverage?

584. How are State and Local Government employees covered under Social Security and Medicare?

585. What is a Section 218 Agreement?

586. What types of coverage are provided under a Section 218 agreement?

587. Is Social Security and Medicare Hospital Insurance coverage mandatory or voluntary?

PART II: MEDICARE

INTRODUCTION

PART A: HOSPITAL INSURANCE

Eligibility

Administration

Financing Part A (Hospital Insurance)

Benefits

Qualified Medicare Beneficiaries

Inpatient Hospital Services

1036. What special provisions apply to care in Religious Nonmedical Health Care Institutions (RNHCI)?

1037. Can patients choose their own hospitals?

1038. How is it certified that hospitalization is required?

1039. What must a hospital do to qualify for Medicare payments?

Hospice Care

1040. What is hospice care?

1041. How is hospice care covered under Part A (Hospital Insurance)?

1042. What is not covered under Part A (Hospital Insurance) in regard to hospice?

1043. What is the hospice benefit period?

1044. What does the patient pay for hospice care?

1045. How is respite care covered?

Skilled Nursing Facility Care

1046. What is a qualified skilled nursing facility?

1047. Does Part A (Hospital Insurance) pay for custodial care in a skilled nursing facility?

1048. Do most nursing home residents qualify for Part A (Hospital Insurance) coverage?

1049. Under what circumstances does a patient qualify for skilled nursing facility benefits under Part A (Hospital Insurance)?

1050. What items and services generally are (and are not) covered under Part A (Hospital Insurance) when provided in a participating skilled nursing facility?

1051. What provisions are made under Part A (Hospital Insurance) for care in a skilled nursing facility?

1052. How much does the patient pay for skilled nursing facility care?

1053. When can payment be made for skilled nursing care under Part A (Hospital Insurance)?

Home Health Care

1054. When are post-institutional home health services covered under Part A (Hospital Insurance)?

1055. What conditions must be met for Part A (Hospital Insurance) to cover home health visits?

1056. What post-institutional home health services are covered under Part A (Hospital Insurance)?

1057. How does Medicare pay the costs of home health services?

General Information

PART B: MEDICAL INSURANCE

Eligibility

Financing Part B (Medical Insurance)

1075. How are "approved charges" for covered medical services determined under Part B (Medical Insurance)?

1076. How are Part B (Medical Insurance) payments made?

1077. How can a person find out if a doctor accepts assignment of all Medicare claims?

1078. What are Medicare providers and Medicare suppliers?

1079. What portion of the cost must be borne by the patient?

1080. How does a patient find out how much Medicare will pay on a claim?

Benefits

1081. What doctors' services are covered under Part B (Medical Insurance)?

1082. What outpatient hospital services are covered under Part B (Medical Insurance)?

1083. When are outpatient physical therapy and speech-language pathology services covered under Part B (Medical Insurance)?

1084. Are partial hospitalization services connected to mental health services covered?

1085. Are certified nurse-midwife services covered under Part B (Medical Insurance)?

1086. Is dental work covered under Part B (Medical Insurance)?

1087. What medical equipment is covered under Part B (Medical Insurance)?

1088. Is ambulance service covered by Part B (Medical Insurance)?

1089. How much will Medicare Part B (Medical Insurance) pay for outpatient treatment of mental illness?

1090. What mental health services does Medicare Part B cover?

1091. When is the cost of vaccines covered?

1092. Is the cost of antigens covered under Part B (Medical Insurance)?

1093. When are organ transplants covered under Part B (Medical Insurance)?

1094. Can Part B (Medical Insurance) help pay for outpatient services at a comprehensive out-patient rehabilitation facility?

1095. Are home health services covered under Part B (Medical Insurance)?

1096. Are independent clinical laboratory services covered under Part B (Medical Insurance)?

1097. Are screening pap smears and pelvic exams covered by Part B (Medical Insurance)?

Medicare Coverage of Blood

Private Contracts

PART C: MEDICARE ADVANTAGE

Definition

Eligibility, Election, and Enrollment

Benefits and Beneficiary Protections

Premiums

Contracts with Medicare Advantage Organizations

1163. How does a plan become part of the Medicare Advantage program?

Medigap Insurance Program

1164. What rules apply regarding Medigap insurance and Medicare Advantage plans?

1165. What are the special rules regarding Medigap protections under the Medicare Advantage program?

Medicare Advantage Marketing Rules

1166. What are the rules about the marketing of Medicare Advantage plans?

1167. What are the pros and cons of Medicare Advantage plans?

PART D: PRESCRIPTION DRUG INSURANCE

1168. What is Medicare Part D?

1169. When did Medicare Part D become effective?

1170. Who is eligible for Medicare Part D?

1171. What does the Part D (Prescription Drug Insurance) cost?

1172. What benefits does Part D (Prescription Drug Insurance) provide?

1173. What notice must an employer who maintains a prescription drug plan provide to Medicare-eligible individuals?

Prescription Drug Marketing Rules

1174. What are the rules about the marketing of Medicare Part D (Prescription Drug Insurance) plans?

MEDIGAP INSURANCE

1175. What is Medigap Insurance?

1176. Is there an open enrollment period for Medigap policies?

1177. Does a Medicaid recipient need Medigap insurance?

1178. Are there Federal standards for Medigap policies?

1179. What else should be known about Medigap policies?

1180. Do Medigap policies cover medical expenses outside of the United States?

HOW TO SUBMIT CLAIMS AND APPEALS

Claims Procedure

Appeals Procedure

Long-Term Care

State LTC Partnership Program

Exempt Income and Resources

Spousal Impoverishment

Medicaid Transfer Rules

Trusts

INTRODUCTION TO THE 2019 EDITION

Social Security & Medicare Facts provides the reader with a description of Social Security, Medicare, benefits for federal government employees, benefits for service members and veterans, and benefits for workers covered under the Railroad Retirement System.

Social Security is administered by the Social Security Administration and provides Old Age, Survivors, and Disability benefits. Medicare provides hospital and medical insurance for the aged and disabled and is administered by the Centers for Medicare & Medicaid Services.

The Social Security Act was signed into law on August 14, 1935, by President Franklin D. Roosevelt. Originally the Social Security Act of 1935 was named the "Economic Security Act" but the title was changed during Congressional debate. The original program created a social insurance program that was created to pay retirees some income after the age of sixty-five. Registration of employers and workers began in November 1936, through the United States Post Office to begin allowing workers to acquire credits beginning in January 1937. A man named John David Sweeney, Jr. from New Rochelle, NY was the first person to be assigned a Social Security account but the honor of the lowest Social Security number "001-01-0001" went to Grace Dorothy Owen of New Hampshire. By July 1937, The Social Security Board had issued over 30 million SS cards. FICA contributions began in January 1937. The Social Security Administration reports that since the inception of the program, over $8.9 trillion dollars has been paid into the Trust Fund and more than $7.6 million has been paid out.

From 1937 to 1940, Social Security payments were a single lump-sum payment, with the smallest payment being for five cents and the average payment being about $58. The first monthly retirement check was issued to Ida May Fuller of Ludlow, VT for $22.54. Miss Fuller was a retired legal secretary who collected benefits from age sixty-five until her death in 1975 at the age of 100 – collecting nearly $23,000 in benefits.

The original Social Security Act provided only retirement benefits for wage and salary earners. In 1939, amendments to the law added dependents benefits for family members after the worker's death or retirement. Most amendments have expanded the scope of the Social Security program – by extending coverage to more groups of persons, by increasing benefits, by creating new benefits (such as disability), by liberalizing requirements for benefits, or by increasing the wage base for taxes and benefits. The 1939 amendments also increased benefit amounts and advanced the start of monthly payments from 1942 to 1940.

In 1946, the three-person Social Security Board was replaced by the Social Security Administration. In 1950, there were significant amendments to the Social Security law – including the potential of annual increases in benefits – known as COLAs or Cost-of-Living Allowances. Benefits were increased in 1950 and again in 1952. These increases were not automatic – it literally took an "Act of Congress" to increase the retirement benefit. In 1956, additional amendments created a Disability Insurance program with benefits being provided to disabled workers from fifty to sixty-four and to disabled adult children. By 1960, the disability coverage extended to disabled workers of any age as well as their dependents. Additional amendments in 1961 allowed men to retire at a reduced benefit at sixty-two (women had this right for a few years before).

In 1965, on July 30 – President Lyndon B. Johnson signed Medicare into law by presenting the first Medicare card to former President Harry Truman. By 1968, almost twenty million people were signed up for Medicare. In 1972, the Social Security Administration took responsibility for the Supplemental Security Income (SSI) which had been state-run but partially federally funded. The same 1972 amendments passed automatic Cost-of-Living Allowances which were implemented in 1975, tied to the increase in consumer prices. These amendments also created increased Social Security benefits for widows and widowers, a minimum retirement benefit, adjusted the early retirement benefit formula for men, to make it consistent with that for women, extended of Medicare to those who have received disability benefits for at least two years and to those with Chronic Renal Disease; simplified the Retirement Test; and created "Delayed Retirement Credits" for those that work past Full Retirement Age until age seventy.

Amendments in 1977 were to address the funding shortfall of the program. Amendments raised the payroll tax from 6.45 percent to 7.65 percent and separated the wage adjustment from the COLA and effectively restored solvency of the program for about fifty years. Amendments passed in 1983 brought more changes – including taxation of Social Security benefits, coverage of Federal employees under Social Security and an increase in the Full Retirement Age.

The nineties brought additional changes – including the *Contract with America Advancement Act of 1996* changed benefits of the Disability benefit – disallowing eligibility for benefits if drug addiction or alcoholism was the cause of the disability. This law also doubled the earnings limit for retired beneficiaries. *The Personal Responsibility and Work Opportunity Reconciliation Act of 1996* ended SSI eligibility for most non-citizens. The *Omnibus Consolidated Rescissions and Appropriations Act of 1996* required direct deposit of all federal checks by 1999. The *Department of Defense Appropriations Act, 1997* made sponsorship agreement legally enforceable and established federal standards for birth certificates and required a Social Security card that was harder to counterfeit. The century ended with the *Ticket to Work and Work Incentives Improvement Act of 1999* which intended to change the Disability Insurance program from benefits to focusing on rehabilitation and enabling the disabled to become productively employed. The Senior Citizens' Freedom to Work Act of 2000 eliminated the Retirement Earnings Test for beneficiaries at or over Full Retirement Age (FRA), a sea change to the Social Security program which had required that beneficiaries be "substantially retired" to collect full benefits.

The next major change in the program was enacted on December 8, 2003 with the *Medicare Prescription Drug, Improvement, and Modernization Act of 2003* which amended Title XVIII to provide for the creation of Part D – the voluntary prescription drug program. During the Obama Administration, we saw the American Recovery and Reinvestment Act of 2009 which allocated an additional $1 billion to the SSA. In 2015, the Bi-Partisan Budget Act severely curtailed the use of the "restricted application" and eliminated the "file and suspend" benefit.

Today, the largest and most common programs under the Social Security Act and its amendments are:

(1)   Federal Old-Age (Retirement), Survivors, and Disability Insurance (OASDI),

(2)   Temporary Assistance for Needy Families (TANF),

(3)   Health Insurance for Aged and Disabled (Medicare),

(4)   Grants to States for Medical Assistance Programs for low income citizens—(Medicaid),

(5)   State Children's Health Insurance Program for low income citizens—(SCHIP), and

(6)   Supplemental Security Income (SSI).

Today, one of seven Americans receives a Social Security benefit, and more than 90 percent of US jobs fall under the system.

This new 2019 edition of *Social Security & Medicare Facts* includes new discussions of planning techniques designed to maximize benefits, especially for married couples. There is also information on the ability of same-sex couples to receive benefits, a discussion of the ability to pay future benefits, as well as the impact of federal government gridlock on benefits received through the Social Security system. In addition, there is a section detailing methods and practices for maximizing benefits, as well as Case Studies of a variety of situations detailing how various actions can help to maximize benefits collected under the Social Security program even in light of the changes imposed by Section 831 of the 2015 Bi-Partisan Budget Act.

PART I
SOCIAL SECURITY

UNDERSTANDING AND PLANNING FOR SOCIAL SECURITY

1. What is the Social Security Act?

The Social Security Act has established numerous programs which provide supplemental income for insured individuals and their families in the event of disability, when they retire, or at death. This supplemental income acts as a safety net – especially in old age – and keeps an estimated 22 million elderly Americans out of poverty.[1]

Congress passed the Social Security Act and President Franklin D. Roosevelt signed the measure into law on August 14, 1935 and the retirement benefits program went into effect on January 1, 1937. The law has been amended many times since its original enactment.

There have been many changes in Social Security and the United States since 1935. In 1935 the life expectancy was only age sixty, while today it is 78.7 years. Therefore, in 1935 most people would not have lived long enough to collect Social Security retirement benefits. Today, many retirees are concerned that they will outlive their retirement savings.

In 1935, Social Security was designed to supplement a retiree's retirement income. Today, Social Security provides about 40 percent of the average retiree's income. This statistic worries many analysts who contend that workers rely too much on Social Security and should save more.

In 1949, the worker/retiree ratio was about 160:1. By 2013, it had fallen to 2.8:1.[2] This is expected to fall to 2.2:1 by 2035. Part of this is due to the continuing retirement of baby boomers as well as the increase in life expectancy. When the program began, Social Security paid out about $35 million in benefits annually. Today it pays out over $675 billion annually.[3] It is projected that by 2030, the ratio will be down to 2.3:1.

Finally, in 1935, the poverty rate for seniors exceeded 50 percent. As measured in 2016, the poverty rate for seniors was approximately 9.3 percent nationwide.[4]

Nearly 90 percent of Americans over the age of sixty-five receive some Social Security income and approximately 35 percent of that same group relies almost entirely on Social Security payments alone. With longer life expectancy, and the recent issues with the economy it has become increasingly important to understand and plan for Social Security benefits. With a thorough understanding of the program and useful strategies for applying for and receiving Social Security, most recipients can increase the amount of benefits they would receive if they simply apply for Social Security at Full Retirement Age (FRA) – also referred to as Normal Retirement Age.

---

1. https://www.cbpp.org/research/social-security/social-security-keeps-22-million-americans-out-of-poverty-a-state-by-state (Last accessed September 24, 2018).
2. https://www.ssa.gov/history/ratios.html (Last accessed September 24, 2018).
3. http://www.ssa.gov/history/ratios.html (Last accessed September 24, 2018).
4. https://www.kff.org/report-section/how-many-seniors-are-living-in-poverty-national-and-state-estimates-under-the-official-and-supplemental-poverty-measures-in-2016-data-note/ (Last accessed September 24, 2018).

2. What are the stated purposes of Social Security?

The basic purposes of the Social Security Act is to establish programs that will:

- provide for the material needs of individuals and families;
- protect aged and disabled persons against the expenses of illnesses that may otherwise use up their savings;
- keep families together; and
- give children the chance to grow up healthy and secure.

3. What programs are covered by the Social Security Act?

The original Social Security Act (1935) and the current version of the Act, as amended, encompass several social welfare and social insurance programs.

The following programs are covered by the Social Security Act:

- Social Security
  - Retirement insurance
  - Survivors insurance
  - Disability insurance
- Medicare
  - Hospital and medical insurance for the aged, disabled, and those with end-stage renal disease
  - Prescription drug benefits
  - Extra help with Medicare Prescription Drug costs
- Unemployment insurance
- Black lung benefits
- Supplemental Security Income (SSI)
- Special Veterans benefits
- Public assistance and welfare services, including
  - Aid to needy families with children
  - Medical assistance
  - Maternal and child health services
  - Child-support enforcement
  - Family and child welfare services

- Food stamps

- Energy assistance

The Federal Old-Age (Retirement), Survivors, and Disability Insurance program (OASDI) is the main program that people think of when they think of the term "Social Security". You will also hear this program referred to as the Old-Age, Survivor, Disability and Health Insurance (OASDHI) program, as well as the Retirement, Survivor, Disability, and Health Insurance (RSDHI) program. This program covers workers and their dependents.[1]

4. Who is covered by Social Security?

Most workers are covered by Social Security and if they work long enough (and accrue enough credits) will be entitled to retirement benefits and/or disability.

An individual is NOT covered if they were:

- A Federal civilian employee who was hired before 1984. There is an exception for anyone that changed to the Federal Employee Retirement System during the 1987 transition period (see Q 485). The Federal civilian employees not covered by Social Security are instead covered under the Civil Service Retirement System (see Q 511). However, all Federal civilian employees are covered under the Medicare Part A hospital insurance program.

- Individuals covered under the Railroad Retirement System, which is governed by the Railroad Retirement Act (see Q 393).

- Employees of a state or local government entity that is not part of their employer's retirement system and not covered by a voluntary State/Federal Social Security agreement.

- Certain farm workers, workers of a family business, or domestic workers.

5. In general, who can receive Social Security?

Who Can Receive Social Security Benefits

- A disabled insured worker under the age of sixty-five.

- A retired insured worker at age sixty-two or over.

- The spouse of a retired or disabled worker entitled to benefits who:

  - is age sixty-two or over; OR

  - has in care a child under age sixteen (or over age sixteen and disabled), who is entitled to benefits on the worker's Social Security record.

- The divorced spouse of a retired or disabled worker entitled to benefits if age sixty-two or over and married to the worker for at least ten years.

---

1. 42 U.S.C. 402.

- The divorced spouse of a fully insured worker who has not yet filed a claim for benefits if both are age sixty-two or over, were married for at least ten years, and have been finally divorced for at least two continuous years.

- The dependent, unmarried child of a retired or disabled worker entitled to benefits, or of a deceased insured worker if the child is:

  - under age eighteen; OR

  - under age nineteen and a full-time elementary or secondary school student; OR

  - aged eighteen or over but under a disability that began before age twenty-two.

- The surviving spouse (including a surviving divorced spouse) of a deceased insured worker if the widow(er) is age sixty or over.

- The disabled surviving spouse (including a surviving divorced spouse in some cases) of a deceased insured worker, if the widow(er) is age fifty to fifty-nine and becomes disabled within a specified period.

- The surviving spouse (including a surviving divorced spouse) of a deceased insured worker, regardless of age, if caring for an entitled child of the deceased who is either under age sixteen or disabled before age twenty-two.

- The dependent parents of a deceased insured worker at age sixty-two or over.

In addition to monthly survivor benefits, a lump-sum death payment is payable upon the death of an insured worker.

For explanation of these benefits and eligibility requirements, see RETIREMENT AND DISABILITY BENEFITS, Q 42 to Q 187.

6. What do the phrases "Normal Retirement Age" (NRA) and "Full Retirement Age" (FRA) mean?
Normal Retirement Age and Full Retirement Age

For many years "Normal Retirement Age" (NRA) meant the age at which someone was eligible for benefits that were not reduced for taking early benefits (see Q 251 and Q 299). But recently this phrase has come to mean, among planners and the general public, the age when many people "normally" apply for benefits, which is often when they are generally first eligible — at age sixty-two. According to the Social Security Administration, 34.3 percent of people begin collecting Social Security benefits at age sixty-two, when they first become eligible. For those that do not begin collecting at age 62, the following is the breakout of the age that people begin collecting:

- Age 63: 6.3 percent

- Age 64: 6.4 percent

- Age 65: 10.3 percent

- Age 66: 18.1 percent

- Ages 67 to 69: 3.9 percent

- Age 70: 3.7 percent

- The remaining 17 percent of Social Security is collected by those under 65 who qualify for disability.

As a result of this shift in language, a new phrase has developed among planners and the public to describe the age when unreduced benefits may be received – "Full Retirement Age" (FRA). As may seem obvious, FRA refers to the age at which a person qualifies for full Social Security benefits. This age is now determined by a person's year of birth and for those born during 1960 or later it is age sixty-seven. The prevailing definition by the Social Security Administration (SSA) at their website is that the normal retirement age (NRA) is the age at which retirement benefits are equal to the "primary insurance amount", (unreduced benefits), although the SSA still uses both phrases to describe when unreduced benefits may be taken.

For the 2019 edition of *Social Security & Medicare Facts* the phrase "Normal Retirement Age" is used in the place of the phrase "Full Retirement Age" to describe the age at which unreduced benefits may be taken. Below is listed how the Normal Retirement Age varies by year of birth.[1]

Normal Retirement Age

Year of birth	Age
1937 and prior	65
1938	65 and 2 months
1939	65 and 4 months
1940	65 and 6 months
1941	65 and 8 months
1942	65 and 10 months
1943-54	66
1955	66 and 2 months
1956	66 and 4 months
1957	66 and 6 months
1958	66 and 8 months
1959	66 and 10 months
1960 and later	67

Notes:

1. Persons born on January 1 of any year should refer to the normal retirement age for the previous year.
2. For the purpose of determining benefit reductions for early retirement, widows and widowers whose entitlement is based on having attained age 60 should add 2 years to the year of birth shown in the table.

---

1. Normal Retirement Age, https://www.ssa.gov/oact/progdata/nra.html (Last accessed October 24, 2018).

7. Does Social Security accept donations for the solvency of the trust fund?

The Social Security trust funds have a combined balance of $2.890 trillion dollars as of late 2018, down from $2.890 trillion in 2017.[1] The Social Security Administration does accept voluntary donations to the trust fund. If inclined, donations can be made to extend the fund's solvency. Visit the Social Security website area dealing with donations[2] for additional information. Voluntary donations can be made via check or money order or by will. Voluntary donations are deductible on Schedule A as a casualty or theft loss.

Since 2011 the program has received the following donations:

2011	$1,000,000
2012	$1,000
2013	0
2014	$5,000
2015	0
2016	0
2017	0
2018	0

8. Are same-sex couples eligible to receive spousal Social Security benefits?

Yes. The Social Security Administration now recognizes same-sex marriages in all states and some marital legal relationships such as civil unions and domestic partnerships for the purposes of determining entitlement to Social Security, Medicare, and Supplemental Security Income. The SSA is also recognizing same-sex marriages and some non-martial legal relationships entered into in foreign jurisdictions as well.[3] Social Security is now processing some retirement, surviving spouse and lump-sum death payment claims for same-sex couples in nonmarital legal relationships and paying benefits where they are due. In addition, the Social Security Administration considers same-sex marriage when determining SSI eligibility and benefit amounts.

On June 26, 2015, the United States Supreme Court issued a decision in *Obergefell v. Hodges*,[4] holding that same-sex couples have a constitutional right to marry in all states. This decision enables same-sex couples to be married in one state and have their marriage recognized by all other states. As a direct result of this decision, more same-sex couples will be recognized as being married for the purposes of determining their entitlement to Social Security benefits and as well as Supplemental Security Income (SSI) payments. The Social Security Administration recommends that someone who is the spouse, divorced spouse, or surviving spouse or a same-sex marriage

1. Operations of the Combined OASI and DI Trust Funds in Current Dollars – 2018 https://www.ssa.gov/OACT/TR/2018/lr6g8.html (Last accessed September 24, 2018).
2. https://www.ssa.gov/agency/donations.html Last accessed September 24, 2018).
3. SSA Publication No. 05-10014, January 2017, What Same-Sex Couples Need to Know, https://www.ssa.gov/pubs/EN-05-10014.pdf (Last accessed September 24, 2018).
4. 576 U.S. ___, 135 S.Ct. 2587, 192 L.Ed.2d 609 (2015).

or other legal same-sex relationship to immediately apply for benefits. Immediate applying will preserve the filing date, which can affect benefits.

This had been a developing area of law. In June 2013, the Supreme Court ruling in *United States v. Windsor*,[1] had established that same sex couples who were married in a jurisdiction where same-sex marriages are recognized were eligible for spousal benefits, such as the spousal survivor benefit, the spousal retirement benefit, and the lump sum death benefit. At that time, the Social Security Administration reviewed its own policies regarding same-sex marriage after the Supreme Court decision and concluded that same-sex couples who are legally married in one state remain married for federal tax purposes even if they reside in a state that does not recognize their marriage.[2] Of course, the Obergefell case made that issue moot.

9. Will Social Security adjust the Income Related Monthly Adjustment Amounts for an individual who filed a tax return as "single" but has now amended it to "married" for prior years in a same-sex marriage?

In many cases — yes. If an amended return is filed and it changes the income counted to determine the IRMAA, Social Security will change it. The filer will need to provide:

- The amended return; and

- The acknowledgment receipt from the Internal Revenue Service.

Social Security will update the records as necessary.

10. Can a same-sex couple place both their names on the child's Social Security record?

Yes.

Regardless of the sex of the partners, both parents' names can be placed the child's Social Security number record.

Both parents will need to provide proof that they are the legal parents of the child. The following documents are considered proof the legal parentage of the child:

- Original or amended birth certificate

- final adoption decree

- Court determination of paternity (also referred to as a court order of parentage)

All documents must be originals or certified copies from the issuing agency. Photocopies or notarized copies are not acceptable.

---

1. 570 U.S. 744, 133 S.Ct. 2675, 186 L.Ed. 808 (2013).
2. Rev. Rul. 2013-17.

11. Should couples in a same-sex marriage or civil union or other non-marital legal relationship inform Social Security if one or the other are receiving Social Security benefits or Supplemental Security Income (SSI)?

A same-sex marriage, civil union or other non-marital legal relationship may affect entitlement to benefits. Individuals in a civil union or other non-marital legal relationship need to report this status to the Social Security Administration. The Social Security Administration now recognizes same-sex marriages in all states and foreign jurisdictions, as well as some nonmarital legal relationships such as civil unions and domestic partnerships, including those established in foreign jurisdictions for purposes of determining entitlement to Social Security benefits, Medicare, and SSI.

In the case of separation, divorce or annulment, as well as becoming a parent, this information must be reported as well as it can affect eligibility and or payment amounts.

In addition, a spouse's income and resources may affect SSI eligibility or the payment amount.

12. Increasingly, the government has experienced the threat of, or actual shutdowns of services. What happens to Social Security benefits during government shutdowns?

The threat of a government shutdown remains a highly-charged political issue that emerges frequently due to stop-gap funding efforts. Funding is often through short-term spending bills. To date, the policy during a government shutdown or the threat of a government shutdown has been to insure that benefit payments continue without interruption. Although payments continue without interruption, some services provided at regional offices are curtailed. When a government shutdown is anticipated, see the Social Security Administration website (www.ssa.gov) for announcements of curtailment of services. Office closings are specifically addressed at http://www.ssa.gov/agency/emergency/.

13. What federal agency administers the Social Security or OASDI program?
The Social Security Administration

The central office is located in Baltimore, Maryland. The administrative offices and computer operations are housed at this location.

The Social Security Administration is an independent agency in the executive branch of the federal government. It is required to administer the retirement, survivors, and disability program under the Social Security and the Supplemental Security Income (SSI) programs. The commissioner of the Social Security Administration is appointed by the President and approved by the Senate and serves a term of six years.

In recent years, the Social Security has increasingly provided services through its website at www.ssa.gov. Many of the services that were traditionally carried out through local Social Security offices or through the mail can now be done online at http://www.ssa.gov/onlineservices/.

These services allow a person to apply for benefits, get a Social Security Statement, appeal a decision, find out about qualifying for benefits, estimate future benefits, and do other activities related to the management of benefits.

Alternatively, the local Social Security office is the place where a person can apply for a Social Security number, check on an earnings record, apply for Social Security benefits, black lung benefits, SSI, and Hospital Insurance (Medicare Part A) protection, enroll in Medical Insurance (Medicare Part B), receive assistance in applying for food stamps, and get full information about individual and family rights and obligations under the law. Also, a person can call the Social Security Administration's toll-free telephone number, 1-800-772-1213, to receive these services. This toll-free telephone number is available from 7:00 a.m. to 7:00 p.m. any business day. From a touch-tone phone, recorded information and services are available twenty-four hours a day, including weekends and holidays. People who are hearing-impaired may call 1-800-325-0778 between 7:00 a.m. and 7:00 p.m. Monday through Friday.

Regular visits to outlying areas are made by the Social Security office staff to serve people who live at a distance from the city or town in which the office is located. These visits that are made to locations are called contact stations. A schedule of these visits may be obtained from the nearest Social Security office. If because of illness or disability, an SSA representative can make a visit to a person's home if they are unable to reach an office or a contact station.

Social Security Administration regional offices are located in Atlanta, Boston, Chicago, Dallas, Denver, Kansas City, New York, Philadelphia, San Francisco, and Seattle. Approximately 1,230 Social Security offices throughout the United States, Puerto Rico, the Virgin Islands, Guam, and American Samoa deal directly with the public. Each region also has a number of teleservice centers located primarily in metropolitan areas. These offices handle telephone inquiries and refer callers appropriately. To find a local office, visit the Social Security Administration website at http://www.ssa.gov/agency/contact/.

The Office of Hearings and Appeals administers the nationwide hearings and appeals program for the Social Security Administration. Administrative law judges, located in or traveling to major cities throughout the United States, hold hearings and issue decisions when a claimant or organization has appealed a determination affecting rights to benefits or participation in programs under the Social Security Act. The Appeals Council, located in Falls Church, Virginia, may review hearing decisions. (See FILING FOR BENEFITS, Q 212 to Q 226.)

The Social Security Administration maintains program service centers in Birmingham, AL; Chicago, IL: Kansas City, MO; New York, NY; Philadelphia, PA; and Richmond, CA. These offices – in addition with the Office of International Operations and the Office of Disability Operations, located in Baltimore, MD are the locations which house and service the records of individuals collecting benefits.

The Office of Central Operations maintains records of an individual's earnings and prepares benefit computations. These offices are located in Salinas, CA and Wilkes-Barre, PA. Data processing operations occur at the Office of Systems in Baltimore.

14. Where can I get forms related to Social Security and disability?

The Social Security Administration provides many, though not all, of its forms online at https://www.ssa.gov/forms/. Increasingly, the Social Security Administration encourages people to go online to download, fill out, and submit forms. All forms are free, but the SSA cautions that not all forms are listed on the website – however as of October 2018, there were 146 forms listed. These forms, however, can still be obtained from the local Social Security Office during regular business hours.

For a list of Forms available, see Appendix M.

15. How does a person obtain a Social Security number?

By filling out Form SS-5[1] (Application for a Social Security Card) and submitting evidence of age, identity, and citizenship or alien status.

Parents applying for a Social Security number for their children under age seven will need to furnish only a birth record if no other record of age or identity has been established for the child.

Applicants eighteen and older must apply in person at a Social Security office. Applicants will need to provide two documents proving age, identity, and U.S. citizenship (or lawful employment-authorized immigrant status). Other documents may be required for noncitizens that are lawfully in the United State without Department of Homeland Security employment-authorization.

A Social Security number is needed not only for Social Security purposes, but also for income tax purposes. The Internal Revenue Service uses this number as a Taxpayer Identification Number (TIN) for processing tax returns and controlling the interest and dividend reports of banks and other financial institutions. Failure to put a valid Social Security number on a tax return may mean a delay or reduction in any refund claimed.

A Social Security number is also needed by persons age one or older who are claimed as dependents on someone's federal income tax return. All income tax returns claiming dependents (whether taxpayer's children or others) one year old or older must show the dependent's Social Security number. Failure to include a dependent's Social Security number on a tax return could result in the Internal Revenue Service disallowing related items such as the personal exemption, child tax credit, child care credit, or earned income credit.

A person must have a Social Security number in order to receive Social Security benefits. Those lacking a Social Security number are required to apply for one. Beneficiaries on the Social Security rolls prior to May 10, 1989, are not required to have a Social Security number. However, as a practical matter, Social Security numbers are also commonly used by many nongovernmental entities, such as health care providers or banks, for tracking and security purposes.

Foreign-born applicants of any age must submit evidence of United States citizenship or alien status.

---

1. See Form SS-https://www.ssa.gov/forms/ss-5.pdf. (Last accessed September 24, 2018).

Form SS-5 can be obtained from any local Social Security office or online from the Social Security Administration's website. Forms must be either mailed to or presented to a local Social Security office.

Some businesses advertise that they can provide Social Security cards or name changes for a fee. There is no need to use such a business. Getting a Social Security number is free through the Social Security Administration.[1]

16. What do you do if you need a replacement Social Security card or need to make changes?

If the Social Security card is lost, a person can apply for a duplicate card by filling out another Form SS-5[2] and showing a driver's license, voter registration card, school identification card, or other official proof of identity. The new card will have the same number as the one that was lost. There is no charge for a lost Social Security card.

You can use a Social Security account to request a replacement Social Security card online if you:

- Are a U.S. citizen aged eighteen years or older with a U.S. mailing address;

- Are not requesting a name change or any other change to your card; and

- Have a driver's license or a state-issued identification card from one of the following states: AZ, AR, CA, DE (Driver License only), DC, FL, ID, IL, IN, IA, KY, ME, MD, MA, MS, MI, NE, ND, NM, PA, SD, TX, VA, WA, WI (Driver License only).

- Online service is not available using the following state identifications: AL, AK, CT, GA, HI, KS, MN, NV, NH, NJ, NC, OH, OK, OR, SC, TN, UT, VT, WV

There is a limit on the number of replacement Social Security Cards. An individual can request THREE PER YEAR and is limited to TEN in a lifetime. Changes in legal name or changes to a restrictive legend (validity to work notation, etc.) do not count for the lifetime ten or three annual cards.

17. How can you change or correct your name or other information on a Social Security card?

If a person wishes to correct or update the identifying information given on the original application for a Social Security number, a new Form SS-5 must be submitted. The applicant will need to submit documents supporting whatever changes need to be made. A change in name (for example, upon marriage) should always be reported.

---

1. See www.ssa.gov/ssnumber. (Last accessed September 24, 2018).
2. https://www.ssa.gov/ssnumber/. (Last accessed October 15, 2018).

18. If someone is a victim of identity theft, can they get a new Social Security number?

Perhaps. The Social Security Administration MAY issue a new Social Security number if someone is using an individual's number and it cannot be stopped. The Social Security Administration offers advice regarding identity theft as related to an SSN in their publication "Identity Theft and Your Social Security Number"[1]

19. Can individuals that are not U.S. citizens get a Social Security number?

Generally not. Only individuals with permission to work from the Department of Homeland Security can get a Social Security number if they are not a U.S. citizen.

20. What types of Social Security cards are issued?

There are three kinds of Social Security cards.

1.   The first type of Social Security card is the basic one. It lists name and Social Security number and allows work without restriction. These cards are issued to

   •   U.S. citizens and

   •   Noncitizens to whom the Department of Homeland Security (DHS), which oversees immigration, has given permission to live and work in the United States permanently. These include green-card holders as well as refugees and people granted political asylum.

2.   The second type of card carries the words "valid for work only with DHS authorization". It is issued to people who have permission to live and work here only for temporary periods.

3.   The third type has the words "not valid for employment". This type is issued to noncitizens who do not have work permission but need a Social Security number for other reasons, such as to apply for government benefits or services.

21. What documents are required to get a Social Security number?

Regardless of whether the applicant is an American citizen or a foreigner, the following information needs to be provided to Social Security in order to apply:

   •   **Evidence of age:** Usually a birth certificate will suffice. Other proof of age consists of a record of birth from a U.S. hospital, a U.S. passport, or an adoption record.

   •   **Evidence of identity:** Documents must show legal name and, preferably, include a photograph and physical description such as height, weight, hair, and eye color. The document must be a U.S. driver's license, a U.S. state-issued nondriver identity card, or a U.S. passport. For non-citizens, Social Security will need current immigration documents and a foreign passport.

---

1. https://www.ssa.gov/pubs/EN-05-10064.pdf (Last accessed October 24, 2018).

- **Evidence of U.S. citizenship:** These documents include a U.S. birth certificate, a U.S. passport, a certificate of naturalization, or a consular report of birth.

- **Evidence of immigration status.** For non-citizens, the documents issued by DHS showing immigration status and authorization to work in the United States.

All documents must be originals or certified copies from the agency that issued the document. Photocopies or notarized copies are not accepted.

22. Can individuals with Deferred Action Status and employment authorization get a Social Security number?

Probably. If the U.S. Citizenship and Immigration Services grants an individual Deferred Action status and employment authorization, they may be eligible for a Social Security number.

If the U.S. Citizenship and Immigration Services (USCIS) approves the request for Deferred Action for Childhood Arrivals and the application to work in the United States, the individual may be eligible for a Social Security number. After getting the (I-766) Employment Authorization Card, the application can be submitted for a Social Security number.

23. Under what circumstances can a non-citizen be eligible for SSI?

A non-citizen (also called an "alien" for immigration purposes) may be eligible for Supplemental Security Income (SSI) if he or she meets the requirements of the laws for non–citizens that went into effect on August 22, 1996. In general, beginning August 22, 1996, in order to be potentially eligible for SSI most non-citizens must:

1. be in a **qualified alien** category; and

2. meet a condition that allows qualified aliens to get SSI.

Note that a non-citizen must also meet all of the other rules for SSI eligibility, including the limits on income and resources.

24. How are Social Security numbers verified?

Employers, organizations, or third-party submitters can verify Social Security numbers for wage reporting purposes only. Social Security offers the following options to verify Social Security numbers:

1. **The Social Security Verification Service** – This free online service allows registered users to verify that the names and Social Security numbers of hired employees match Social Security's records.

2. **The Consent Based Social Security Number Verification Service** – This fee-based Social Security number verification service is available to enrolled private companies, state and local government agencies to provide instant automated verification and can handle large volume requests.

25. How long does it take to get a Social Security number and card for a newborn baby?

Times vary, but generally the card will be mailed within an average of two weeks of the infant's birth. In some instances, it may take as long as a month.

26. How are Social Security numbers assigned?

On June 25, 2011, the Social Security Administration changed the method in which Social Security numbers are issued to a process referred to as "randomization." This new method was developed to help protect the integrity of the SSN and to extend the longevity of the nine-digit SSN.

The SSA began assigning the nine-digit SSN in 1936 to track workers' earnings over the course of their lifetimes in order to pay benefits. The SSN has always been comprised of the three-digit area number, followed by the two-digit group number, and ending with the four-digit serial number. Since 1972, the area number reflected the state, as determined by the ZIP code in the mailing address of the application.

There are approximately 420 million numbers available for assignment. The previous assignment process limited the number of SSNs available for issuance to individuals by each state.

SSN randomization affected the SSN assignment process in the following ways:

- It eliminated the geographical significance of the first three digits of the SSN, referred to as the area number, by no longer allocating the area numbers for assignment to individuals in specific states.

- It eliminated the significance of the highest group number and, as a result, the High Group List is frozen in time and can only be used to see the area and group numbers SSA issued prior to the randomization implementation date.

- Previously unassigned area numbers were introduced for assignment excluding area numbers 000, 666 and 900-999.

27. How can a person check on his Social Security earnings record and receive an estimate of future Social Security benefits?

The Social Security Statement containing both an estimate of benefits and a record of earnings is available either online or by the mail. To access the statement online, a person must create a "*my Social Security*" account at www.ssa.gov/myaccount/. This account also allows a person to manage personal information such as changing an address or the way in which a direct deposit is received.

To receive the statement by mail, a person should fill out Form SSA-7004[1] (Request for Social Security Statement). The form is available at the Social Security Administrations website

---

1. *See* Request for Social Security Statement at https://www.ssa.gov/hlp/global/hlp-statement-7004.htm (Last accessed September 29, 2018).

at www.ssa.gov, at any Social Security office, or by calling the Social Security Administration's toll-free number, 1-800-772-1213. A statement of total wages and self-employment income credited to the earnings record and an estimate of current Social Security disability and survivor benefits and future Social Security retirement benefits will be mailed to the individual.

If all earnings have not been credited, the individual should contact a Social Security office and ask how to correct the records. The time limit for correcting an earnings record is set by law. An earnings record can be corrected at any time up to three years, three months, and fifteen days after the year in which the wages were paid or the self-employment income was derived. "Year" means calendar year for wages and taxable year for self-employment income. An individual's earnings record can be corrected after this time limit for a number of reasons, including to correct an entry established through fraud; to correct a mechanical, clerical, or other obvious error; or to correct errors in crediting earnings to the wrong person or to the wrong period.

The Social Security Administration must provide individuals, age twenty-five or older, who have a Social Security number and have wages or net self-employment income, with a Social Security account statement upon request. These statements must show:

(1)   the individual's earnings;

(2)   an estimate of the individual's contributions to the Social Security program (including a separate estimate for Medicare Part A Hospital Insurance); and

(3)   an estimate of the individual's current disability and survivor benefits and also future benefits at retirement (including spouse and other family member benefits) and a description of Medicare benefits.

Earnings and benefit estimates statements are automatically mailed on an annual basis to all persons age twenty-five or over who are not yet receiving benefits.

This earnings and benefit estimates statements contain the following information:

(1)   The individual's Social Security taxed earnings as shown by Social Security Administration records as of the date selected to receive a statement.

(2)   An estimate of the Social Security and Medicare Part A Hospital Insurance taxes paid on the individual's earnings.

(3)   The number of credits (i.e., quarters of coverage, not exceeding forty) that the individual has for both Social Security and Medicare Hospital Insurance purposes, and the number the individual needs to be eligible for Social Security benefits and also for Medicare Hospital Insurance coverage.

(4)   A statement as to whether the individual meets the credit (quarters of coverage) requirements for each type of Social Security benefit, and also whether the individual is eligible for Medicare Hospital Insurance coverage.

(5)   Estimates of the monthly retirement, disability, dependents' and survivors' insurance benefits potentially payable on the individual's record if he meets the credits (quarters of coverage) requirements. If the individual is age fifty or older, the estimates will include the retirement insurance benefits he could receive at age sixty-two (or his current age if he is already over age sixty-two), at full retirement age (currently age sixty-six to sixty-seven, depending on year of birth) or at the individual's current age if he is already over full retirement age, and at age seventy. If the individual is under age fifty, the Social Security Administration may provide a general description, rather than estimates, of the benefits that are available upon retirement.

(6)   A description of the coverage provided under the Medicare program.

(7)   A reminder of the right to request a correction in an earnings record.

(8)   A remark that an annually updated statement is available upon request.

28. What will happen to Social Security benefit payments when the Trust Fund becomes insolvent?

Social Security and disability benefits are financed through the payroll tax. In 2018, the revenue collected by this tax went to pay out benefits that were due. The payroll tax was insufficient to pay out all benefits, so the balance was made up by interest payments due on government bonds held in the Social Security trust funds.

Over the eighty-two years of Social Security, the program has brought in approximately $19.9 trillion and paid out $17.1 trillion, with an asset reserve of $2.9 trillion as of June 30, 2018. The asset reserves have grown by $47 billion since 1986. The Bipartisan Budget Act of 2015, effective in November 2015 was supposed to have postponed the exhaustion of the Social Security Disability Trust Fund from 2016 to 2022, by temporarily reallocating some of the payroll tax from the Old Age and Survivors Insurance Trust Fund to the Disability Insurance Trust Fund but the Trustees are now estimating some success, stating that the DI Fund should remain solvent an additional five years until 2028. Part of this success is due to the decline in the number of applications and awards of Disability Insurance.

The Trustees project that the combined fund asset reserves of OASI and DI Trust Funds, at the beginning of each year will exceed that year's projected cost through 2029. The Trustees project that the combined trust funds will be depleted in 2034, the same year projected in the 2017 report. Social Security's total income is projected to exceed its total cost through 2021, as it has since 1982. The 2018 surplus of total income relative to cost was $34.4 billion. However, when interest income is excluded, Social Security's cost is projected to exceed its non-interest income throughout the projection period, as it has since 2010. It is projected that annual non-interest deficit will average approximately $51 billion between 2017 and 2020 and begin to rise dramatically after that as the number of beneficiaries continue to grow at a faster and faster rate. After 2021, the Trustees project that interest income and redemption of trust fund asset reserves from the US Treasury's General Fund will offset Social Security's annual deficits until 2034.

In 2034, the OASDI reserves will be depleted – with estimated payments from Social Security taxes being sufficient to cover about 75 to 77 percent of scheduled benefits through the end of the projection period in 2091.

The Trustees current projections indicate that annual costs of Social Security benefits as a share of taxable earnings will increase from 13.7 percent in 2016 to roughly 17.0 percent in 2038. This percentage will begin to decline slightly until 2051 and then begin to increase. The Trustees also compare program costs to Gross Domestic Product – noting that Social Security costs constituted 5.0 percent of GDP during 2016 with an anticipated increase to 6.1 percent by 2037, and then decline to 5.9 percent by 2050, after which the costs measured against GDP will increase back to 6.1 percent by 2091.

The Trustees acknowledge that projections for the combined funds are less positive than 2016 even with the projection for the DI Trust Fund being a little rosier. However, the Trustees acknowledge that the depletion of the combined fund has not changed from the estimated date of 2034. At that point, the reserves will be exhausted according to the intermediate assumptions of the Office of the Chief Actuary in the Social Security Administration and other funding sources will be necessary.[1]

29. Where and how does a person apply for Social Security benefits?

A person can apply for Social Security benefits online at www.ssa.gov, by mail, by telephone (at 1-800-772-1213), or by visiting one of 1,230 Social Security field offices. The online application for benefits is the most efficient way to apply for benefits, and increasingly the Social Security Administration is encouraging people to apply using this method. The Social Security Administration estimates that completing the application online will take only ten to thirty minutes.

30. Where and how does a person apply for Social Security benefits if they live overseas?

Someone who does not live in the United States should consult the Social Security Administration's website resource on International Programs and Resources at www.ssa.gov/international for general information. The Office of International Operations (OIP) provides online instructions for how to apply for benefits if living overseas at www.ssa.gov/foreign/index.html. A person may also contact a U.S. embassy or consulate for information.

If the claimant lives overseas, the SSI payments are handled based on the following:

- Blind or Disabled Child of Military Parent(s) stationed overseas: this type of claim is handled by the Social Security office in Cumberland, Maryland

- Students overseas temporarily: this type of claim is handled by ANY Social Security office

---

1. THE 2017 ANNUAL REPORT OF THE BOARD OF TRUSTEES OF THE FEDERAL OLD-AGE AND SURVIVORS INSURANCE AND FEDERAL DISABILITY INSURANCE TRUST FUNDS, https://www.ssa.gov/OACT/TR/2018/ (Last accessed September 29, 2018).

- Any other claimant living overseas: this claim is handled by the Office of International Operations of the Office of Disability and International Operations (ODIO)

Outside of the United States is defined as being physically outside the fifty states, the District of Columbia, Puerto Rico, the U.S. Virgin Islands, Guam, the Northern Mariana Islands, and American Samoa. There is a tool at the Social Security website to help beneficiaries determine if they can receive Social Security benefits outside the United States.[1]

31. Which government agency issues a beneficiary's Social Security payment?

Social Security benefit payments are issued, and electronic deposits are made by the Treasury Department – not by program service centers. However, questions about a missing direct deposit should be directed to a Social Security office or by calling 1-800-772-1213 between 7:00 a.m. and 7:00 p.m. Monday through Friday.

On March 1, 2013, the government required that all beneficiaries for Social Security or Supplemental Security Income receive payments electronically. Prior to that, a person could have received a check through the mail. The electronic payment must be made either through a direct deposit to a bank account or to a Direct Express® Debit MasterCard® card. The Direct Express® Debit MasterCard® is a prepaid debit card payment option for those who do not have a bank account.[2]

In some limited circumstances, a person can still seek a waiver and receive a check by using FS Form 1201 W. The Treasury Department provides the following exception:[3]

- Check recipients living in remote areas without sufficient banking infrastructure may apply for a waiver, as well as check recipients for whom electronic payments would impose a hardship due to a mental impairment. Automatic waivers are granted to people born on or before May 1, 1921, and people who qualify for this waiver do not need to submit an application.

- For more information or to request a waiver, call 855-290-1545. You may also print and fill out a waiver form and return it to the address on the form.

32. When does a Social Security beneficiary receive a monthly direct deposit?

For persons who started receiving benefits on or before May 1, 1997, Social Security benefits are direct deposited into the specified account on the third day of the month following the month for which the payment is due. For example, payments for January are delivered on February 3rd.

---

1. https://www.ssa.gov/international/payments_outsideUS.html (Last accessed September 30, 2018).
2. Social Security: Get Your Payments Electronically https://www.ssa.gov/pubs/EN-05-10073.pdf (Last accessed September 30, 2018).
3. See http://www.ssa.gov/deposit/EFT%20Waiver%20Form.pdf (Last accessed September 30, 2018).

If the third day of the month falls on a weekend or federal holiday, deposits are made on the first day preceding the third of the month that is not a Saturday, Sunday, or federal holiday. For example, if the third is a Saturday or Sunday, deposits are made on the preceding Friday.

Persons who began receiving Social Security benefits after May 1, 1997, will be paid on a different monthly schedule than that described above. The payment day will be selected, based on the day of the month on which the insured individual was born.

- Insured individuals born on the first through the tenth of the month will be paid on the second Wednesday of each month.

- Insured individuals born on the eleventh through the twentieth of the month will be paid on the third Wednesday of each month.

- Insured individuals born after the twentieth of the month will be paid on the fourth Wednesday of each month.

- New beneficiaries living in foreign countries will have deposits made on the third day of the month. Note, however, that deposits cannot be made in some countries. See the International Programs section of the Social Security Administration's website at www.socialsecurity.gov/international/payments.html for more information.

If a direct deposit is not made, then report the nonreceipt by calling 1-800-772-1213 (TTY 1-800-325-0778) between 7:00 a.m. and 7:00 p.m., Monday through Friday. The following information will be needed to report the nonreceipt:

(1)   The Social Security claim number on which the benefit is being paid

(2)   The period of payment covered by the missing deposit

(3)   The name and account number of the bank where the deposit was to be made

A change in the direct deposit account to which benefits are deposited should be reported promptly to the Social Security Administration through your online *my Social Security* account, by telephone, or in writing, signed by the payee. Promptly reporting a change of in the bank account will avoid having the deposits going to an incorrect or old account.

33. To whom is a benefit payment made payable and how are benefits received?

Payment is made through direct deposit to a beneficiary's account with a financial institution, or to a representative payee if the beneficiary is incapable of managing finances.

All beneficiaries with accounts in financial institutions will have their benefit checks deposited directly into those accounts instead of mailed to their homes. A financial institution may be a bank, trust company, savings and loan association, or a federal or state-chartered credit union. The beneficiary continues to be responsible for notifying the Social Security Administration of any changes that affect eligibility to receive benefits. Beneficiaries without accounts in financial institutions will receive a payment to a Direct Express® Debit MasterCard®. The Direct Express® Debit MasterCard® is a prepaid debit card payment option for those who do not have a bank account.

A minor child (a child under eighteen years of age) is ordinarily considered incapable of managing benefit payments and a representative payee (usually a parent, close relative, or legal guardian) will be selected to receive payments on the child's behalf.

However, payment will be made directly to a child over eighteen, or to a child under eighteen if there is no indication that the child is immature or unstable and it appears to be in the minor's best interest to make direct payment.

Also, if alcoholism or drug addiction is a contributing factor in determining that an individual is entitled to disability benefits, the benefits must be paid through a representative payee.

For a beneficiary outside the United States, direct deposit may be available into a bank or financial institution in the country where they live.

34. If a husband and wife are both receiving monthly benefits, do they receive one or two monthly payments?

If a husband and wife have both worked, they will each be paid their own Social Security benefit by direct deposit to their designated bank account.

However, monthly benefits payable to a husband and wife who are entitled on the same Social Security record and are living at the same address are usually combined in one payment.

35. If several children are entitled to benefits, will each child receive a separate payment?

No. Social Security benefit payments for minor children in one family unit are usually combined into one payment. Where the children customarily reside in different households, separate payments will be issued to each family group.

36. Can a power of attorney be granted for the purpose of collecting and managing payments?

Yes. If payments are to be deposited in an account at a United States financial institution, completion of SF-1199A (Direct Deposit Sign-Up Form) is required. This form can be obtained on the Social Security Administration's website.[1] If payments are to be directed to a foreign financial institution, Standard Form 233 (Power of Attorney by Individual to a Bank for the collection of checks drawn on the Treasury of the United States) must be completed.[2]

---

1. https://www.irs.gov/pub/irs-utl/sf-1199-a_dirdeposit.pdf. (Direct Deposit Sign-Up Form). (Last accessed September 30, 2018).
2. https://www.fiscal.treasury.gov/fsservices/gov/pmt/chkClaims/form_233.pdf (Power of Attorney). (Last accessed September 30, 2018).

37. Can Social Security benefits be assigned?

No. The provision in the Social Security Act (Section 207)[1] prohibiting assignment of benefits or subjecting them to the operations of bankruptcy laws may not be superseded by another law unless the other law does so by express reference to Section 207. Some bankruptcy courts have considered Social Security benefits listed by the debtor to be income for purposes of bankruptcy proceedings and have ordered the Social Security Administration to send all or part of a debtor's benefit payment to the trustee in bankruptcy. Such orders are not appropriate.

The following exceptions to assignment have been allowed:

1. Garnishment of benefit payments for child support or alimony; Under Section 659 of the Act,[2] garnishment of benefit payments for the purpose of collecting amounts owed for child support or alimony is permitted.

2. Garnishment of benefit payments for victim restitution: Garnishment of benefit payments to recover court-ordered victim restitution is permitted under 18 USC 3613(a), 3663, 3663A, and 3664.

3. Levy for unpaid federal taxes: The IRS can place a levy on benefit payments to recover unpaid federal taxes under 26 USC 6331 and 6334.

38. Can Social Security benefits be attached for the beneficiary's debts?

Benefits are not subject to levy, garnishment, or attachment, except in very restricted circumstances, such as by court order for the collection of child support or alimony, or by the Internal Revenue Service for unpaid federal taxes.

*   Enforcement of child support and alimony obligations under Section 459 of the Social Security Act.[3]

*   Collection of civil penalties under the Mandatory Victim Restitution Act.[4]

*   Under a Notice of Levy to collect overdue federal taxes under Section 6334(c) of the Internal Revenue Code.

*   Collection via the Federal Payment Levy Program to collect overdue federal taxes by levying up to 15 percent of each monthly payment until the debt is paid under Section 1024 of the Taxpayer Relief Act of 1997.[5]

*   Nontax debt owed to an agency under the Debt Collection Improvement Act of 1996.[6]

1. 42 USC 407.
2. 42 USC 659.
3. 42 U.S.C. 659.
4. 18 U.S.C. 3613.
5. Public Law 105-34.
6. Public Law 104-134.

A U.S. District Court reaffirmed the right of the Internal Revenue Service to seize Social Security benefits to collect overdue taxes. The plaintiff owed the IRS over $100,000. The IRS sent a notice of levy to the Social Security Administration, garnishing the plaintiff's entire Social Security benefit for one month and approximately half of his benefit for each month thereafter. The plaintiff sought reimbursement of the benefit garnished by the IRS and a judgment declaring future benefits exempt from collection. The court ruled that Social Security benefits are subject to levy by the IRS, and that the IRS may garnish the plaintiff's Social Security benefits until his federal income taxes and assessed penalties are paid.[1]

39. Are Social Security benefits subject to federal taxes?

Up to one-half of the Social Security benefits received by taxpayers whose incomes exceed certain base amounts are subject to income taxation.[2]

The base amounts are $32,000 for married taxpayers filing jointly, $25,000 for unmarried taxpayers, and zero for married taxpayers filing separately who did not live apart for the entire taxable year.[3]

There is an additional tier of taxation based upon a base amount of $44,000 for married taxpayers filing jointly, $34,000 for unmarried taxpayers, and zero for married taxpayers filing separately who did not live apart for the entire taxable year.[4]

The maximum percentage of Social Security benefits subject to income tax increases to 85 percent under this second tier of taxation.[5] (The rules listed in the paragraph above continue to apply to taxpayers not meeting these thresholds.)

After the end of the year, Form SSA-1099 (Social Security Benefit Statement)[6] is sent to each beneficiary showing the amount of benefits received. A worksheet (IRS Notice 703)[7] is enclosed for figuring whether any portion of the Social Security benefits received is subject to income tax.

For a detailed explanation of taxation of benefits, see TAXATION OF SOCIAL SECURITY BENEFITS, Q 343 to Q 351.

40. What happens when a Social Security overpayment is made to a Social Security beneficiary by mistake?

An overpayment made to a beneficiary is normally recovered from a beneficiary by withholding future payments until the overpayment is paid back.[8] If a beneficiary receives an overpayment, he should contact the Social Security Administration directly as soon as possible to

---

1. *Leining v. U.S.*, 97-1 USTC ¶50,254 (D. Conn. 1996). Also see https://www.ssa.gov/OP_Home/rulings/oasi/41/SSR79-04-oasi-41.html (Last accessed September 30, 2018).
2. IRC Sec. 86.
3. IRC Sec. 86(c)(1).
4. IRC Sec. 86(c)(2).
5. IRC Sec. 86(a)(2).
6. http://www.irs.gov/pub/irs-pdf/p915.pdf (Last accessed September 30, 2018).
7. IRS Notice 703 (2014) http://www.irs.gov/pub/irs-prior/n703–2014.pdf (Last accessed September 30, 2018).
8. See http://www.ssa.gov/pubs/EN-05-10098.pdf (Last September 30, 2018).

make the SSA aware of the overpayment. If a beneficiary received a notice of overpayment and believes the notice is incorrect, then he should file Form SSA-561, *Request for Reconsideration*, which is available on the Social Security Administration's website.[1]

41. Can individuals request a copy of a deceased individual's Social Security number application?

Social Security can provide information about a Social Security number record but will charge a fee when an individual asks for information for a purpose that does not directly relate to the administration of a Social Security program, such as genealogy research. The fee depends upon the format of the information, and whether or not the Social Security number is known.[2]

Social Security can send you a photocopy of an original *Application for a Social Security Card* (Form SS-5) or a computer extract of information from the form. Social Security has recorded information from the original SS-5s onto computer record and can furnish computer extracts instead of photocopies.

---

1. See http://www.socialsecurity.gov/forms/ssa-561.html (Last accessed September 30, 2018).
2. Request for Deceased Individual's Social Security Record, https://secure.ssa.gov/apps9/eFOIA-FEWeb/internet/main.jsp (Last accessed September 30, 2018) or Form SSA-711 https://www.ssa.gov/forms/ssa-711.pdf. (Last accessed September 30, 2018).

RETIREMENT AND DISABILITY BENEFITS

42. What Social Security benefits are available for retired or disabled workers and their families?

There are different types of benefits available for workers and their dependents. The following benefits are available for workers and their families while the worker is still alive:

- A monthly Retirement benefit for a retired worker

- A monthly Disability benefit for a disabled worker

- A monthly Spouse's benefit for a retired or disabled worker's spouse if:

    (1) at least sixty-two years old; or

    (2) caring for at least one child (under age sixteen, or over age sixteen and disabled (if disability began before age twenty-two)) of the retired or disabled worker

- A monthly Child's benefit for a retired or disabled worker's child if the child is:

    (1) under age eighteen;

    (2) age eighteen and a full-time high school or elementary school student; or

    (3) age eighteen or over and disabled, if the disability began before age twenty-two

43. What is the date that benefits are paid?

Benefits are paid based on the recipient's birthdate. See schedule below:

Date of Birth	Benefit Paid
1 - 10	2nd Wednesday (following month)
11 - 20	3rd Wednesday (following month)
21 - 31	4th Wednesday (following month)

If the payment date falls on a weekend, then the benefit will be paid on the previous Friday. If the payment date falls on a holiday, the benefit will be paid the business day previous to the holiday. Social Security benefits are paid a month in arrears. Recipients must survive the entire previous month to earn a check in the current month.

Example: if John passes away on June 29, either he will not receive a July benefit – or – if the Social Security benefit is deposited in July, it will be reversed. His estate will keep the June benefit as it was based on surviving all of May.

Retirement Benefits

44. In general, what requirements must be met to qualify a person for retirement benefits?

An individual is entitled to a retirement benefit if he or she:

(1)   is fully insured;

(2)   is at least age sixty-two throughout the first month of entitlement; and

(3)   has filed an application for retirement benefits.[1]

45. Must a person be fully insured to qualify for retirement benefits?

Yes, however, a small monthly benefit is payable to some men who reached age seventy-two before 1972 and some women who reached age seventy-two before 1970.[2]

46. What is the earliest age at which a person can start to receive retirement benefits?

Age sixty-two.

A retired worker who is fully insured can elect to start receiving a reduced benefit at any time between ages sixty-two[3] and Full Retirement Age (FRA) (which is gradually increasing from sixty-five to sixty-seven; see Q 8 and subsequent explanation) when he or she would receive the full benefit rate. A person is not required to be completely retired to receive retirement benefits. A person is considered "retired" if the retirement test is met. (See LOSS OF BENEFITS BECAUSE OF "EXCESS" EARNINGS, Q 318 to Q 336.)

The retirement age when unreduced benefits are available (previously age sixty-five) increased by two months per year for workers reaching age sixty-two in 2000 through 2005. It is age sixty-six for workers reaching age sixty-two in 2006 through 2016. It will increase again by two months per year for workers reaching age sixty-two in 2017 through 2022. Finally, the retirement age will be age sixty-seven for workers reaching age sixty-two after 2022 (i.e., reaching age sixty-seven in 2027).[4] See Q 251 for more detailed information about the increase in the full retirement age.

The Full Retirement Age (FRA) for spouse's benefits (also previously age sixty-five) moves upward in exactly the same way as that for workers. The Full Retirement Age for widow(er)'s benefits also rises but in a slightly different manner (beginning for widow(er)s who attain age sixty in 2000 and reaching a full retirement age of sixty-seven in 2029).

Reduced benefits will continue to be available at age sixty-two, but the reduction factors are revised so that there is a further reduction of up to a maximum of 30 percent for workers

---

1. 42 U.S.C. 402(a).
2. 42 U.S.C. 428.
3. 42 U.S.C. 402(a)(2).
4. 42 U.S.C. 416.

entitled at age sixty-two after the retirement age is increased to age sixty-seven (rather than only 20 percent for entitlement at age sixty-two under previous law). See Q 253.

47. Must a person file an application for retirement benefits?

Yes. Retirement benefits are not automatic. An application MUST be filed in order to collect. A person can file an application within three months before the first month in which he becomes entitled to benefits. The earliest date for filing would be three months before the month of attaining age sixty-two.

As evidence of age, a claimant must ordinarily submit one or more of the following:

- Birth certificate

- Church record of birth or baptism

- Census Bureau notification of registration of birth

- Hospital birth record

- Physician's birth record

- Family Bible

- Naturalization record

- Immigration record

- Military record

- Passport

- School record

- Vaccination record

- Insurance policy

- Labor union or fraternal record

- Marriage record

- Other evidence of probative value

Note that if a public or religious record was not made before the claimant was age five, they must produce at least two other documents that prove age, such as a:

- birth certificate recorded after age five;

- school record;

- State census record;

- vaccination record;

- insurance policy;

- hospital admission record, etc.

Preference is given to the oldest documents.

If a person is receiving Social Security disability benefits for the month before the month he reaches full retirement age, no application is required; the disability benefit ends and the retirement benefit begins automatically. For an explanation of how to file for benefits, see FILING FOR BENEFITS, Q 212 to Q 226.

48. What is the amount of a retirement benefit?

A retirement benefit that starts at Full Retirement Age (FRA) (see Q 46) equals the worker's Primary Insurance Amount (PIA).[1]

A worker who elects to have benefits start before Full Retirement Age will receive a monthly benefit equal to only a percentage of the PIA. The PIA will be reduced by:

- 5/9 of 1 percent for each of the *first thirty-six months* the worker is under FRA when payments commence;

- and by 5/12 of 1 percent for each such month *in excess of thirty-six*.[2] (See Table 10 for reduced retirement benefits.)

As a general rule, a person taking reduced retirement benefits before FRA will continue to receive a reduced rate after normal retirement age.

An individual can obtain higher retirement benefits by working past FRA to the age of seventy. (See Q 300.)

49. What is the financial effect of early retirement?

This table illustrates the financial effect of early retirement, for both a retired worker and his/her spouse, assuming a $1,000 primary insurance amount. With this primary insurance amount and both the primary and spouse retiring at their respective normal retirement ages, the primary would receive $1,000 per month and his/her spouse would receive $500 per month. The table shows that retirement at age sixty-two results in substantial reductions in monthly benefits. Very few people actually being receiving a benefit at exactly age sixty-two because a person must be sixty-two throughout the first month of retirement. Most early retirees begin at age sixty-two and one month.

---

1. 20 CFR §404.201.
2. https://www.ssa.gov/oact/quickcalc/earlyretire.html (Last accessed September 30, 2018).

Primary and spousal benefits at age 62

(benefits based on a $1,000 primary insurance amount)

Year of birth[1]	Normal (or full) retirement age	Number of reduction months[2]	Primary		Spouse	
			Amount	Percent reduction[3]	Amount	Percent reduction[4]
1937 or earlier	65	36	$800	20.00%	$375	25.00%
1938	65 and 2 months	38	791	20.83%	370	25.83%
1939	65 and 4 months	40	783	21.67%	366	26.67%
1940	65 and 6 months	42	775	22.50%	362	27.50%
1941	65 and 8 months	44	766	23.33%	358	28.33%
1942	65 and 10 months	46	758	24.17%	354	29.17%
1943-1954	66	48	750	25.00%	350	30.00%
1955	66 and 2 months	50	741	25.83%	345	30.83%
1956	66 and 4 months	52	733	26.67%	341	31.67%
1957	66 and 6 months	54	725	27.50%	337	32.50%
1958	66 and 8 months	56	716	28.33%	333	33.33%
1959	66 and 10 months	58	708	29.17%	329	34.17%
1960 and later	67	60	700	30.00%	325	35.00%

1 If birthday is January 1, use the prior year of birth.

2 Applies only if born on the second of the month; otherwise the number of reduction months is one less than the number shown.

3 Reduction applied to primary insurance amount ($1,000 in this example). The percentage reduction is 5/9 of 1 percent per month for the first 36 months and 5/12 of 1 percent for each additional month.

4 Reduction applied to $500, which is 50 percent of the primary insurance amount in this example. The percentage reduction is 25/36 of 1 percent per month for the first thirty-six months and 5/12 of 1% for each additional month.

50. What is the first month for which a retired person receives a retirement benefit?

A monthly benefit is available to a retired worker when he reaches age sixty-two, provided he is fully insured.

Workers and their spouses (including divorced spouses) do not receive retirement benefits for a month unless they meet the requirements for entitlement throughout the month. The major effect of this provision is to postpone, in the vast majority of cases, entitlement to retirement benefits for persons who claim benefits in the month in which they reach age sixty-two to the next month. Only in the case of a person who attains age sixty-two on the first or second day of a month can benefits be paid for the month of attainment of age sixty-two. Note that a person attains his age on the day preceding the anniversary of his birth. For example, if an individual was born on May 2, 1957, he is considered sixty-two years old on May 1, 2019.

Most entitlement requirements (other than the entitlement of the worker) affecting young spouses or children of retired or disabled workers are deemed to have occurred as of the first of the month in which they occurred. However, in the case of a child who is born in or after the first month of entitlement of a retired or disabled worker, benefits are not payable for the month of birth (unless born on the first day of the month).

Retroactive benefits are usually prohibited if permanently reduced benefits (as compared with what would be payable for the month the application is filed) would occur in the initial month of eligibility. However, retroactive benefits may be applied for if:

(1)   with respect to widow(er)'s benefits, the application is for benefits for the month of death of the worker, if filed for in the next month; and

(2)   retroactive benefits for any month before attaining age sixty are applied for by a disabled widow(er) or disabled surviving divorced spouse.

51. Can a person receive retirement benefits regardless of the amount of his wealth or the amount of his retirement income?

Yes, a person is entitled to retirement benefits regardless of how wealthy he is. Also, the amount of retirement income a person receives (e.g. dividends, interest, rents, etc.) is immaterial. A person is subject to loss of benefits only because of excess earnings arising from his personal services (earned income).

See Q 52 and LOSS OF BENEFITS BECAUSE OF "EXCESS" EARNINGS, Q 318 to Q 336).

52. Can a person lose retirement benefits by working?

Yes, a person can lose some or all monthly benefits if he or she is under the Full Retirement Age (FRA) (see Q 46) for all of 2019 and his or her earnings for the year exceed $17,640.[1] A person may lose benefits if he or she reaches full retirement age in 2018 and if he or she earns over $46,920, but only those earnings earned before the month he or she reaches FRA count towards the $46,920 limit. The amount of loss depends on the amount of earnings in excess of these earnings limits. In no case will a person lose benefits for earnings earned after reaching FRA. For the initial year of retirement of a person who is under the Full Retirement Age for all of 2018, the monthly earnings limit is $1,460.

For purposes of this test, "earnings" include not only earnings in covered employment, but also earnings in noncovered employment in the United States. As to noncovered employment outside the United States, benefits are lost for any month before reaching FRA when so employed for more than forty-five hours, regardless of the amount of earnings. It should be noted that benefits are not truly "lost" as benefits at full retirement age will be increased to account for benefits withheld due to later earnings.

---

1. *See* 42 U.S.C. 403.

The dollar exempt amounts mentioned above will be increased automatically after 2016 as wage levels rise.

See LOSS OF BENEFITS BECAUSE OF "EXCESS" EARNINGS, Q 318 through Q 336.

See Q 253 for a discussion of the increase in the Full Retirement Age.

53. Do unemployment benefits affect Social Security benefits?

Social Security does not count unemployment benefits as earnings. They do not affect retirement benefits.

However, income received from Social Security may reduce your unemployment compensation. Different states may apply the reduction differently.

54. When do retirement benefits end?

Retirement benefits end at the worker's death. No retirement benefit is paid for the month of death regardless of the date of death, even if the worker dies on the last day of the month. With benefits being directly deposited, the Social Security Administration will reach into the account and withdrawal the last month's deposit.

Disability Benefits

55. In general, what requirements must be met to qualify a person for disability benefits?

A worker is entitled to disability benefits if he:

(1) is insured for disability benefits;

(2) has not attained retirement age;

(3) has been disabled for twelve months, or is expected to be disabled for at least twelve months, or has a disability that is expected to result in death;

(4) has filed an application for disability benefits; and

(5) has completed a five-month waiting period or is exempted from this requirement.[1]

Determinations of disability are generally made by Disability Determination Services (DDS), which are agencies of each individual state. The Social Security Administration makes disability insurance determinations for persons living outside the United States (and for a few other applicants whose cases are specifically excluded from the federal-state regulations). Disability claims and supporting evidence are sent to the DDS located in the state where the claimant resides. The evaluation team makes every reasonable effort to obtain medical evidence from the claimant's treating sources. This team is composed of a medical consultant and a lay disability evaluation specialist, and is responsible for making the disability determination.

---

1. 42 U.S.C. 423.

The Social Security Administration's Office of Program and Integrity Reviews may reverse a DDS finding that no disability exists, or, on the basis of evidence in the folder, reverse an allowance of disability.

The claimant may request a reconsideration of the claim and submit new evidence, if available. A reconsideration determination as to disability is generally handled by the DDS that made the original determination, and is reviewed by a special group in the Office of Disability Operations. In a further appealed case, an administrative law judge or the Appeals Council of the Office of Hearings and Appeals may issue an independent decision.

The Social Security Administration uses a multistep process to determine whether someone is eligible for disability benefits. These steps are as follows:

Step 1: Is the individual engaging in substantial gainful activity? If yes, benefits are denied. If no, continue to Step 2.

Step 2: Does the individual have a severe medically determinable physical or mental impairment? If no, benefits are denied. If yes, continue to Step 3.

Step 3: Does the individual have an impairment included in the Listing of Impairments? If yes, benefits are allowed. If no, continue to Step 4.

Step 4: Does the impairment prevent the individual from doing past relevant work? If the individual is able to do work that was done in the past, then benefits are denied. If not, continue to Step 5.

Step 5: Does the impairment prevent the individual from doing any other work? If yes, benefits are allowed, if no, benefits are denied.

The Social Security Administration (SSA) issued a final rule on March 20, 2015, that changed several of the Social Security Regulations related to EVIDENCE in Social Security Disability Insurance ("SSDI") and Supplemental Security Income ("SSI") disability claims. These changes require that someone applying for disability benefits is now required to inform or submit *ALL* evidence to SSA, *regardless of whether it helps establish disability*. This is a big change from the prior Social Security Regulations that only requires that only "material" evidence be submitted to SSA that *shows* you are disabled. The changes to the Social Security Regulations were effective April 20, 2015. However, since the changes provide a continuing obligation to disclose information or evidence to SSA, any decisions not made prior to April 20, 2015 will be impacted as pending claims.

In the Regulations that were in effect until April 19, 2015, sections 404.900 and 416.1400 included text indicating that "you may present any information you feel is *helpful* to your case," and sections 404.1512 and 416.912 stated that an individual is only required to bring attention to everything that *shows* SSA that the individual is disabled.

Under the revised Regulations sections 404.900 and 416.1400 remove the sentences that indicate that an individual may present any information they feel is *helpful*, and sections 404.1512 and 416.912 now indicate that an individual *must* inform SSA or submit to SSA *all* evidence that they are aware of that *relates* to whether they are disabled. This means that where in the past a person applying for benefits only had to give evidence that helped prove they are disabled, they will now also be required to provide information or submit evidence that shows they are not disabled.[1]

Summary of Rule Changes

Must submit ALL evidence "relates" to a disability claim

- Includes favorable *and unfavorable* evidence even if not "material"

Privileged communications – Exceptions

- Confidential communications between claimant and attorney or nonattorney representative are protected unless waived

  - Factual information is not covered

  - Oral communication with a medical personnel IS covered as well as notes taken

- Work product can be withheld

The duty is to submit "ALL" evidence received in "entirety"

- Exception: exact "same" evidence which was "previously submitted" or if agency instructs "otherwise"

There is a duty to inform about evidence NOT submitted – "ALL" evidence is not LITERAL

- Example – there is no duty to take notes, identify people with knowledge, provide information about adverse witnesses

The duty to submit and inform is a continuing one

See Q 503 for additional information on disability claims.

56. What insured status is required for disability benefits?

Generally, a person is insured for disability benefits if he:

(1)   is fully insured; and

(2)   has worked under Social Security for at least five of the ten years (twenty-out-of-forty quarters) just before becoming disabled.

EXCEPTION: If disability begins before age thirty-one but after age twenty-four, for at least one-half of the quarters after reaching age twenty-one and before becoming disabled (but not fewer than six).

---

1. *See* Submission of Evidence in Disability Claims https://www.federalregister.gov/articles/2015/03/20/2015-05921/submission-of-evidence-in-disability-claims (Last accessed September 30, 2018).

If a person becomes disabled before the quarter in which he attains age twenty-four, he must have six quarters of coverage in the twelve quarter period ending with the quarter in which the disability began.[1]

However, a person who had a period of disability that began before age thirty-one, who subsequently recovered and then became disabled again at age thirty-one or later, is again insured for disability benefits if he has one quarter of coverage for every two calendar quarters elapsing after age twenty-one and through the quarter in which the later period of disability began (up to a maximum of twenty quarters of coverage out of the last "countable" forty calendar quarters), but excluding from such elapsed quarters any quarters in the previous period of disability which were not quarters of coverage. Quarters acquired during the first period of disability are excluded in counting the "elapsed" quarters, however, and the quarters of coverage must be acquired during the measuring period. This provision provides relief to those workers who could otherwise not get disability benefits because they did not have time following recovery from an earlier disability to work long enough before a second disability to meet the twenty-out-of-forty quarters insured status test.

57. How disabled must a person be to qualify for disability benefits?

Disability is defined as the inability to engage in any substantial gainful activity by reason of any medically determinable physical or mental impairment, which can be expected to result in death or that has lasted or can be expected to last for a continuous period of not less than twelve months.[2] A person must be not only unable to do his previous work but cannot (considering age, education, and work experience) engage in any other kind of substantial work that exists in the national economy. It is immaterial whether such work exists in the immediate area, or whether a specific job vacancy exists, or whether the worker would be hired if he applied for work.

The worker's impairment or impairments must be the primary reason for his or her inability to engage in substantial gainful activity, although age, education, and work experience are also taken into consideration in determining the worker's ability to do work other than previous work.

The term "substantial gainful activity" is used to describe a level of work activity that is both substantial and gainful. Substantial work activity involves the performance of significant physical or mental duties, or a combination of both, which are productive in nature. Gainful work activity is activity for remuneration or profit, whether or not a profit is realized. For work activity to be substantial it need not necessarily be performed on a full-time basis; work activity performed on a part-time basis may also be substantial.

Illegal activities can constitute substantial gainful activity. For example, tax fraud is an illegal activity that can be both substantial and gainful because of the possibility of significant mental activity and potential gain involved.

---

1. 42 U.S.C. 423(c).
2. 42 U.S.C. 423(d).

Impairments related to the commission of a felony for which the individual is subsequently convicted or related to confinement in a correctional facility for conviction of a felony, may not be used to establish a disability for Social Security benefits.

58. What is a medically determinable impairment?

Disability is defined as the inability to engage in any substantial gainful activity. A medically determinable physical or mental impairment is an impairment that results from anatomical, physiological, or psychological abnormalities that can be shown by medically acceptable clinical and laboratory diagnostic techniques. The medical evidence must establish that an individual has a physical or mental impairment; a statement about the individual's symptoms is not enough.

59. How is a disability evaluated?

Disability evaluations are based solely on medical evidence under both the title II and title XVI programs. The claimant is responsible for providing medical evidence showing an impairment(s) and the severity of the impairment(s).

The Social Security Administration (SSA), with the claimant's permission, will help the claimant get medical evidence from his or her own medical sources who have evaluated, examined, or treated the claimant for his or her impairment(s). SSA will also request copies of medical evidence from hospitals, clinics, or other health facilities when appropriate.

60. What is the procedure in a disability evaluation?

The evaluation is essentially a three-step process as detailed below:

Step One: Establishment of Existence of an impairment

By law, SSA needs specific medical evidence to establish that a claimant has an impairment. SSA regulations require "objective medical evidence" from an "acceptable medical source" to establish that a claimant has a medically determinable impairment. The regulations define these terms.

Step Two: Determination of Severity

Once the existence of an impairment is established, SSA considers all evidence from all medical and nonmedical sources to assess the extent to which a claimant's impairment(s) affects his or her ability to function in a work setting; or in the case of a child, the ability to function compared to that of children the same age who do not have impairments. Nonmedical sources include, but are not limited to: the claimant, educational personnel, public and private social welfare agency personnel, family members, caregivers, friends, neighbors, employers, and clergy.

Step Three: Consultative Examinations

If the evidence provided by the claimant's own medical sources is inadequate to determine if he or she is disabled, additional medical information may be sought by recontacting the medical source for additional information or clarification, or by arranging for a consultative examination (CE). A claimant's own medical source(s) is the preferred source to perform the needed examination or test, and SSA will pay the authorized fee for the CE. However, SSA may use an independent medical source other than the claimant's own medical source(s) to conduct the CE in several situations, such as:

- the claimant's own medical source(s) prefers not to perform the examination;

- the claimant's own medical source(s) does not have the equipment to provide the specific data needed;

- there are conflicts or inconsistencies in the file that cannot be resolved by going back to the claimant's own medical source(s);

- the claimant prefers another source and has good reason for doing so;

- SSA knows from prior experience that the claimant's own medical source(s) may not be a productive source; or

- the claimant's own medical source(s) is not qualified, as is defined by regulation.

In developing evidence of the effects of symptoms on a claimant's ability to function, SSA investigates all avenues presented that relate to the complaints. These include evidence about:

- the claimant's daily activities;

- the location, duration, frequency, and intensity of the pain or other symptom;

- precipitating and aggravating factors;

- the type, dosage, effectiveness, and side effects of any medication;

- treatments, other than medications, for the relief of pain or other symptoms;

- any measures the claimant uses or has used to relieve pain or other symptoms; and

- other factors concerning the claimant's functional limitations due to pain or other symptoms.

In assessing the claimant's pain or other symptoms, SSA considers all of the above-mentioned factors. It is important that medical sources address these factors in the reports they provide.

61. What are the responsibilities of the claimant in the process of disability determination?

A claimant must inform SSA about or submit all evidence known to him or her that relates to whether or not he or she is blind or disabled. This duty is ongoing and requires the claimant to disclose any additional related evidence about which he or she becomes aware throughout the administrative review process. The evidence must be complete and detailed enough for SSA to determine:

- the nature and severity of the claimant's impairment(s),

- how long the claimant has experienced the impairment(s), and

- whether the claimant can still do work-related physical and mental activities with the impairment(s).

62. What is contained within the Consultative Examination Report?

A complete Consultative Examination report will involve all the elements of a standard examination in the applicable medical specialty and should include the following elements:

- The claimant's major or chief complaint(s).

- A detailed description, within the area of specialty of the examination, of the history of the major complaint(s).

- A description, and disposition, of pertinent "positive" and "negative" detailed findings based on the history, examination, and laboratory tests related to the major complaint(s), and any other abnormalities or lack thereof reported or found during examination or laboratory testing.

- Results of laboratory and other tests (for example, X-rays) performed according to the requirements stated in the Listing of Impairments (see Part III of this guide).

- The diagnosis and prognosis for the claimant's impairment(s).

- In claims for adults, a statement about what a claimant can still do despite his or her impairment(s) and whether the claimant has one or more impairment-related limitations or restrictions in the following abilities:

  - The ability to perform physical demands of work activities, such as sitting, standing, walking, lifting, carrying, pushing, pulling, or other physical functions (including manipulative or postural functions, such as reaching, handling, stooping, or crouching)

  - The ability to perform mental demands of work activities, such as understanding; remembering; maintaining concentration, persistence, or pace; carrying out instructions; or responding appropriately to supervision, co-workers, or work pressures in a work setting

  - The ability to perform other demands of work, such as seeing, hearing, or using other senses

  - The ability to adapt to environmental conditions, such as temperature extremes or fumes.

- In claims for children under age eighteen, a statement about the child's impairment-related limitations and restrictions (as compared to children his or her age who do not have impairments) in:

- acquiring and using information;

- attending and completing tasks;

- interacting and relating with others;

- moving about and manipulating objects;

- caring for yourself; and

- heath and physical well-being.

- The consultant's consideration, and some explanation or comment on, the claimant's major complaint(s) and any other abnormalities found during the history and examination or reported from the laboratory tests. The history, examination, evaluation of laboratory test results, and the conclusions will represent the information provided by the consultant who signs the report.

63. How are adult disabilities classified?

The following sections detail the classification of impairments in adults age eighteen and over and that may apply to the evaluation of impairments in children under age eighteen if the disease processes have a similar effect on adults and younger children.

- Musculoskeletal Systems

- Special Senses and Speech

- Respiratory Disorders

- Cardiovascular system

- Digestive system

- Genitourinary disorders

- Hematological disorders

- Skin disorders

- Endocrine disorder

- Congenital disorders that affect multiple body systems

- Neurological disorders

- Mental disorders

- Cancer (Malignant Neoplastic Diseases)

- Immune System disorders

64. How are childhood disabilities classified?

The following sections detail the classification of impairments in children under the age of eighteen.

- Low Weight Birth and Failure to Thrive

- Musculoskeletal System

- Special Senses and Speech

- Respiratory Disorders

- Cardiovascular system

- Digestive system

- Genitourinary disorders

- Hematological disorders

- Skin disorders

- Endocrine disorders

- Congenital disorders that affect multiple body systems

- Neurological disorders

- Mental disorders

- Cancer (Malignant Neoplastic Diseases)

- Immune System disorders

65. What is a compassionate allowance?

Compassionate allowances allow expediting of Social Security Disability Insurance (SSDI) and Supplemental Security Income (SSI) applications for people whose medical conditions are so severe that their conditions obviously meet Social Security's definition of disability. Compassionate allowances are a way to quickly identify diseases and other medical conditions that, by definition, meet Social Security's standards for disability benefits.

These conditions primarily include certain cancers, adult brain disorders, and a number of rare disorders that affect children. The CAL initiative helps reduce waiting time to reach a disability determination for individuals with the most serious disabilities.

The Compassionate Allowances program identifies claims where the applicant's disease or condition clearly meets Social Security's statutory standard for disability. The SSA can easily identify potential compassionate allowances to quickly make decisions. The Social

Security Administration (SSA) uses the same rules to evaluate CAL conditions when evaluating either Social Security Disability Insurance (SSDI) or Supplemental Security Income (SSI) programs.

66. Which illnesses currently qualify for compassionate allowances?

Acute Leukemia

Adrenal Cancer - with distant metastases or inoperable, unresectable or recurrent

Adult Non-Hodgkin Lymphoma

Adult Onset Huntington Disease

Aicardi-Goutieres Syndrome

Alexander Disease (ALX) - Neonatal and Infantile

Allan-Herndon-Dudley Syndrome

Alobar Holoprosencephaly

Alpers Disease

Alpha Mannosidosis - Type II and III

ALS/Parkinsonism Dementia Complex

Alstrom Syndrome

Alveolar Soft Part Sarcoma

Amegakaryocytic Thrombocytopenia

Amyotrophic Lateral Sclerosis (ALS)

Anaplastic Adrenal Cancer - Adult with distant metastases or inoperable, unresectable or recurrent

Angelman Syndrome

Angiosarcoma

Aortic Atresia

Aplastic Anemia

Astrocytoma - Grade III and IV

Ataxia Telangiectasia

Atypical Teratoid/Rhabdoid Tumor

Batten Disease

Beta Thalassemia Major

Lissencephaly

Liver Cancer

Lowe Syndrome

Lymphomatoid Granulomatosis - Grade III

Malignant Brain Stem Gliomas – Childhood

Malignant Ectomesenchymoma

Malignant Gastrointestinal Stromal Tumor

Malignant Germ Cell Tumor

Malignant Multiple Sclerosis

Malignant Renal Rhabdoid Tumor

Mantle Cell Lymphoma (MCL)

Maple Syrup Urine Disease

Marshall-Smith Syndrome

Mastocytosis - Type IV

MECP2 Duplication Syndrome

Medulloblastoma - with metastases

Megacystis Microcolon Intestinal Hypoperistalsis Syndrome (Effective 8/20/2018)

Megalencephaly Capillary Malformation Syndrome (Effective 8/20/2018)

Menkes Disease - Classic or Infantile Onset Form

Merkel Cell Carcinoma - with metastases

Merosin Deficient Congenital Muscular Dystrophy

Metachromatic Leukodystrophy (MLD) - Late Infantile

Mitral Valve Atresia

Mixed Dementias

MPS I, formerly known as Hurler Syndrome

Bilateral Optic Atrophy- Infantile

Bilateral Retinoblastoma

Bladder Cancer - with distant metastases or inoperable or unresectable

Breast Cancer - with distant metastases or inoperable or unresectable

Canavan Disease (CD)

CACH–Vanishing White Matter Disease-Infantile and Childhood Onset Forms

Carcinoma of Unknown Primary Site

Cardiac Amyloidosis- AL Type

Caudal Regression Syndrome - Types III and IV

Cerebro Oculo Facio Skeletal (COFS) Syndrome

Cerebrotendinous Xanthomatosis

Child Lymphoblastic Lymphoma

Child Lymphoma

Child Neuroblastoma - with distant metastases or recurrent

Chondrosarcoma - with multimodal therapy

Chronic Idiopathic Intestinal Pseudo Obstruction

Chronic Myelogenous Leukemia (CML) - Blast Phase

Coffin-Lowry Syndrome

Congenital Lymphedema

Congenital Myotonic Dystrophy

Cornelia de Lange Syndrome - Classic Form

Corticobasal Degeneration

Creutzfeldt-Jakob Disease (CJD) – Adult

Cri du Chat Syndrome

Degos Disease - Systemic

MPS II, formerly known as Hunter Syndrome

MPS III, formerly known as Sanfilippo Syndrome

Mucosal Malignant Melanoma

Multicentric Castleman Disease

Multiple System Atrophy

Myoclonic Epilepsy with Ragged Red Fibers Syndrome

Neonatal Adrenoleukodystrophy

Nephrogenic Systemic Fibrosis

Neurodegeneration with Brain Iron Accumulation - Types 1 and 2

NFU-1 Mitochondrial Disease

Niemann-Pick Disease (NPD) - Type A

Niemann-Pick Disease-Type C

Nonketotic Hyperglycinemia

Non-Small Cell Lung Cancer

Obliterative Bronchiolitis

Ohtahara Syndrome

Oligodendroglioma Brain Cancer- Grade III

Ornithine Transcarbamylase (OTC) Deficiency

Orthochromatic Leukodystrophy with Pigmented Glia

Osteogenesis Imperfecta (OI) - Type II

Osteosarcoma, formerly known as Bone Cancer - with distant metastases or inoperable or unresectable

Ovarian Cancer – with distant metastases or inoperable or unresectable

Pallister-Killian Syndrome

Pancreatic Cancer

Paraneoplastic Pemphigus

DeSanctis Cacchione Syndrome

Dravet Syndrome

Early-Onset Alzheimer's Disease

Edwards Syndrome (Trisomy 18)

Eisenmenger Syndrome

Endometrial Stromal Sarcoma

Endomyocardial Fibrosis

Ependymoblastoma (Child Brain Cancer)

Erdheim Chester Disease

Esophageal Cancer

Esthesioneuroblastoma

Ewing Sarcoma

Farber Disease (FD) – Infantile

Fatal Familial Insomnia

Fibrodysplasia Ossificans Progressiva

Fibrolamellar Cancer (Effective 8/20/2018)

Follicular Dendritic Cell Sarcoma - metastatic or recurrent

Friedreichs Ataxia (FRDA)

Frontotemporal Dementia (FTD), Picks Disease -Type A – Adult

Fryns Syndrome

Fucosidosis - Type 1

Fukuyama Congenital Muscular Dystrophy

Fulminant Giant Cell Myocarditis

Galactosialidosis - Early and Late Infantile Types

Gallbladder Cancer

Gaucher Disease (GD) - Type 2

Giant Axonal Neuropathy

Glioblastoma Multiforme (Brain Cancer)

Glioma Grade III and IV

Glutaric Acidemia - Type II

Head and Neck Cancers - with distant metastasis or inoperable or unresectable

Patau Syndrome (Trisomy 13)

Pearson Syndrome

Pelizaeus-Merzbacher Disease-Classic Form

Pelizaeus-Merzbacher Disease-Connatal Form

Peripheral Nerve Cancer - metastatic or recurrent

Peritoneal Mesothelioma

Peritoneal Mucinous Carcinomatosis

Perry Syndrome

Phelan-McDermid Syndrome

Pleural Mesothelioma

Pompe Disease – Infantile

Primary Central Nervous System Lymphoma

Primary Effusion Lymphoma

Primary Progressive Aphasia

Progressive Bulbar Palsy

Progressive Multifocal Leukoencephalopathy

Progressive Supranuclear Palsy

Prostate Cancer - Hormone Refractory Disease – or with visceral metastases

Pulmonary Atresia

Pulmonary Kaposi Sarcoma

Retinopathy of Prematurity - Stage V

Rett (RTT) Syndrome

Revesz Syndrome

Rhabdomyosarcoma

Rhizomelic Chondrodysplasia Punctata

Roberts Syndrome

Salivary Cancers

Sandhoff Disease

Schindler Disease - Type 1

Seckel Syndrome

Severe Combined Immunodeficiency - Childhood

Heart Transplant Graft Failure

Heart Transplant Wait List - 1A/1B

Hemophagocytic Lymphohistiocytosis (HLH) - Familial Type

Hepatoblastoma

Hepatopulmonary Syndrome

Hepatorenal Syndrome

Histiocytosis Syndromes

Hoyeaal-Hreidarsson Syndrome

Hutchinson-Gilford Progeria Syndrome

Hydranencephaly

Hypocomplementemic Urticarial Vasculitis Syndrome

Hypophosphatasia Perinatal (Lethal) and Infantile Onset Types

Hypoplastic Left Heart Syndrome

I Cell Disease

Idiopathic Pulmonary Fibrosis

Infantile Free Sialic Acid Storage Disease

Infantile Neuroaxonal Dystrophy (INAD)

Infantile Neuronal Ceroid Lipofuscinoses

Inflammatory Breast Cancer (IBC)

Intracranial Hemangiopericytoma

Jervell and Lange-Nielsen Syndrome

Joubert Syndrome

Junctional Epidermolysis Bullosa - Lethal Type

Juvenile Onset Huntington Disease

Kidney Cancer - inoperable or unresectable

Kleefstra Syndrome

Krabbe Disease (KD) – Infantile

Single Ventricle

Sinonasal Cancer

Sjogren-Larsson Syndrome

Skin Malignant Melanoma with Metastases

Small Cell Cancer (Large Intestine, Prostate or Thymus)

Small Cell Cancer of the Female Genital Tract

Small Cell Lung Cancer

Small Intestine Cancer - with distant metastases or inoperable, unresectable or recurrent

Smith Lemli Opitz Syndrome

Soft Tissue Sarcoma - with distant metastases or recurrent

Spinal Muscular Atrophy (SMA) - Types 0 and 1

Spinal Nerve Root Cancer-metastatic or recurrent

Spinocerebellar Ataxia

Stiff Person Syndrome

Stomach Cancer - with distant metastases or inoperable, unresectable or recurrent

Subacute Sclerosing Panencephalitis

Superficial Siderosis of the Central Nervous System (Effective 8/20/2018)

Tabes Dorsalis

Tay Sachs Disease - Infantile Type

Tetrasomy 18p (Effective 8/20/2018)

Thanatophoric Dysplasia - Type 1

Thyroid Cancer

Transplant Coronary Artery Vasculopathy

Tricuspid Atresia

Ullrich Congenital Muscular Dystrophy

Ureter Cancer - with distant metastases or inoperable, unresectable or recurrent

Usher Syndrome - Type I

Kufs Disease - Type A and B	Ventricular Assist Device Recipient - Left, Right, or Biventricular
Large Intestine Cancer - with distant metastasis or inoperable, unresectable or recurrent>	Walker Warburg Syndrome
Late Infantile Neuronal Ceroid Lipofuscinoses	Wolf-Hirschhorn Syndrome
Leigh's Disease	Wolman Disease
Leiomyosarcoma	X-Linked Lymphoproliferative Disease
Leptomeningeal Carcinomatosis	X-Linked Myotubular Myopathy
Lesch-Nyhan Syndrome (LNS)	Xeroderma Pigmentosum
Lewy Body Dementia	Zellweger Syndrome
Liposarcoma - metastatic or recurrent	

67. What is the definition of a medically determinable impairment?

A medically determinable physical or mental impairment is an impairment that results from anatomical, physiological, or psychological abnormalities that can be shown by medically acceptable clinical and laboratory diagnostic techniques. The medical evidence must establish that an individual has a physical or mental impairment; a statement about the individual's symptoms is not enough.[1]

68. Can a child qualify for disability benefits?

A child under age eighteen will be considered disabled if he or she has a "medically determinable" physical or mental impairment or combination of impairments that causes marked and severe functional limitations, and that can be expected to cause death or that has lasted or can be expected to last for a continuous period of not less than twelve months.[2]

69. What disability benefits are available for Wounded Warriors?

Social Security pays disability benefits through the Social Security disability insurance program or through the Supplemental Security Income (SSI) program to military members or veterans who meet Social Security's definition of disability. If a military member or veteran sustained an illness, injury, or wound while on active duty status on or after October 1, 2001, they will receive expedited processing of their disability claim, regardless of how or where the disability occurred. Social Security pays disability benefits through two programs: 1) the Social Security disability insurance program, which pays benefits to the beneficiary and certain members of their family if insured (worked enough quarters and paid Social Security taxes; and 2) the Supplemental Security Income (SSI) program, which pays benefits based on financial need.

---

1. https://www.ssa.gov/OP_Home/cfr20/404/404-1529.htm (Last accessed October 24, 2018).
2. https://www.ssa.gov/OP_Home/cfr20/404/404-1529.htm (Last accessed October 24, 2018).

70. Does blindness qualify a person for disability benefits?

A special definition of "disability" is provided for an individual age fifty-five or over who is blind. Such an individual is disabled for the purpose of disability benefits, if he is unable to engage in substantial gainful activity requiring skills or abilities comparable to those of any gainful activity in which he has previously engaged with some regularity and over a substantial period of time.

A person who is not statutorily blind and is earning (in 2019) more than $1,220 a month (net of impairment-related work expenses) is ordinarily considered to be engaging in substantial gainful activity. This represents an increase of $30 from the 2018 level of $1,180 per month.

The Social Security Act has established a higher substantial gainful activity amount for statutorily blind individuals. The monthly substantial gainful activity amount for blind individuals is $2,040 (in 2019). Also, under SSDI, this condition has to have lasted or be expected to last at least twelve months. There is no duration requirement for blindness under SSI.

Blindness, for Social Security purposes, means either central visual acuity of 20/200 or less in the better eye with the use of a correcting lens, or a limitation in the fields of vision such that the widest diameter of the visual field subtends an angle of twenty degrees or less. However, no benefits will be payable for any month in which the individual engages in substantial gainful activity.

71. At what age can a person receive disability benefits?

At any age under the normal retirement age (see Q 46).[1] If a person is receiving disability benefits when reaching normal retirement age, the disability benefit automatically ends and the retirement benefit begins. It should be noted that children can collect disability benefits.

72. What is the waiting period for disability benefits?

Yes, there is a full five-month waiting period.[2] Generally, benefits will start with the sixth full month of disability. However, if an application is not made until later, benefits are payable retroactively for up to twelve months, beginning with the first month after the waiting period.

Ordinarily, no benefits are payable for the first five full months of disability. Under some circumstances, however, where the person has had a prior period of disability, benefits will begin with the first full month of disability.

Benefits will begin with the first full month of disability in two situations:

REINSTATED BENEFITS

(1)   the new disability arises within five years after the previous one ended; and

(2)   the new disability is expected to last for at least twelve months, or to result in death.

---

1. 42 U.S.C. 423(a)(1)(B).
2. 42 U.S.C. 423(c)(2).

DEPENDENT BENEFITS

The benefits are for the child of a disabled worker.

73. When must an application for disability benefits be filed?

An application for disability benefits may be filed before the first month for which the person can be entitled to benefits. An application filed before the first month in which the applicant satisfies the requirements for disability benefits is valid only if the applicant satisfies the requirements at some time before a final decision on his application is made. If the applicant is found to satisfy the requirements, the application is deemed to have been filed in the first month in which he satisfied the requirements. An application for disability benefits may be made retroactively effective for as many as twelve months before the one in which the application is filed. For an explanation of how to file for benefits, see FILING FOR BENEFITS, Q 212 to Q 226.

Social Security disability benefits may be reinstated without a new disability application if, during the fifteen-month period following a trial work period, a person who has not recovered medically no longer engages in substantially gainful activity. (See Q 86.)

74. What is the process used to determine disability?

Ordinarily disability claims are initially processed through a local Social Security field offices and State agencies (referred to as Disability Determination Services, or DDSs). Subsequent appeals of unfavorable determinations may be decided in the DDSs or by Administrative law judges in SSA's Office of Disability Adjudication and Review (ODAR).

- SSA Field Offices

    - Application may be online, in person or by telephone or mail

    - Application and forms provide information about:

    - The impairment

    - Names, addressed and telephone numbers of medical sources

    - Field office will verify the NONMEDICAL eligibility requirement including age, employment, marital status, residency, citizenship, income, resources, as well as living arrangements

    - Field office then sends the case to a DDS for determination of disability

- Disability Determination Services (DDSs)

    - These are state agencies fully funded by the Federal Government

    - Responsibilities include developing the medical evidence and coming to an initial determination regarding whether the claimant is disabled or blind

- Claimant's medical sources are contacted – if not sufficient, the DDS may request a Consultative Examination (CE) to get additional information

- DDS makes a disability determination through an adjudicative team consisting of a medical or psychological consultant and a disability examiner. The case might be referred to a state vocational rehabilitation agency if appropriate

- After decision – the case is returned to the field office

- If the claimant is found to be disabled, the field office will complete the paperwork and begin paying benefits

- If the claimant is found to not be disabled, the file is retained pending any appeal.

- Appeals are handled in a similar fashion to the initial claim (other than a different DDS adjudicative team does the review and reconsideration)

- Office of Disability Adjudication and Review

  - Claimants who are denied disability benefits can request a hearing before an Administrative Law Judge (ALJ) in ODAR. Additional evidence can be submitted and the ALJ will make a decision.

75. What is the amount of a disability benefit?

The amount of a disabled worker's benefit generally equals his Primary Insurance Amount (PIA), determined as if the worker were at Full Retirement Age (FRA) and eligible for retirement benefits in the first month of his waiting period.[1]

However, the formula for determining a disabled worker's Average Indexed Monthly Earnings (AIME) and PIA differs from the formula used for a retiring worker. (See Primary Insurance Amount, Q 231 to Q 242.) There are also different limits on the amount of family benefits that can be paid to a disabled worker and his family. (See Maximum Family Benefits, Q 243 to Q 246.)

Disability benefits may be reduced before the worker attains Full Retirement Age (FRA) (see Q 46) to fully or partially offset a workers' compensation benefit or disability benefit under a federal, state, or local public law. This reduction will be made only if the total benefits payable to the worker (and dependents) under both programs exceed either 80 percent of his "average current earnings" before the onset of disability, or the family's total Social Security benefit, whichever is higher.

"Average current earnings" is defined as the highest of:

(1) the "average monthly wage" used for computing primary insurance amounts for some beneficiaries, even though not used for this particular one; or

---

1. 42 U.S.C. 423(a)(2).

(2)   the average monthly earnings from covered employment during the highest five consecutive years after 1950; or

(3)   the average monthly earnings based on the one calendar year of highest earnings from covered employment during a period consisting of the year in which disability began and the five preceding years.

Note that the "highest earnings" in items (2) and (3) are determined *without* considering the maximum taxable earnings base.

Different factors are used in determining whether there is an offset and the amount of the offset. The factors used are determined by the date the worker first became disabled and the date the worker first became entitled to benefits. For workers who first became disabled after February 1981, and who first became entitled to disability benefits after August 1981, benefits paid as workers' compensation and received under a federal, state, or local public program will be considered in determining the amount of the offset.

Specifically excluded are all VA disability benefits, needs-based benefits, federal benefits based on employment covered for Social Security purposes, and state and local benefits based on covered state and local employment. Private pension or insurance benefits will also not be considered in determining the amount of the offset. The offset of benefits will continue until the worker reaches normal retirement age.

For a worker disabled and receiving benefits prior to the above dates, only benefits paid as workers' compensation are considered in determining the amount of the offset. The offset of benefits stops when the worker reaches age sixty-two (rather than normal retirement age).

The amount of the reduction is the amount by which Social Security benefits plus workers' compensation, and, where applicable, public disability benefits exceeds 80 percent of the average current earnings. The combined payments after the reduction will never be less than the total Social Security benefits were before the reduction. However, the amount of Social Security benefits can fluctuate based on the decrease or increase in the amount of workers' compensation. In addition, the amount of the reduction is adjusted periodically to take into account increases in national earnings levels (as applied to the initially-determined average current earnings), but this adjustment will never decrease the amount of benefits payable on the worker's earnings record.

When a state workers' compensation law, and, where applicable, a federal, state, or local public disability benefit law or plan, *generally* provides for periodic payments but permits a lump-sum settlement, either in the form of a commutation or compromise agreement that discharges the liability of the insurer or the employer, such settlement is a substitute for periodic payments and is subject to the offset provisions. In this situation, the lump sum is prorated to reflect, as accurately as possible, the monthly rate that would have been paid had the lump sum award not been made. Medical and legal expenses incurred by the worker in connection with the workers' compensation/public disability benefit claim may be excluded from computing the offset.

In Oregon, when prorating a lump-sum award or settlement made under Oregon workers' compensation law for a permanent disability, the Social Security Administration will treat the lump sum as a substitute for periodic payments and will calculate the offset rate on a monthly basis by dividing the lump sum by the number of months between the date of the award and the date the worker reaches age sixty-five. However, if a workers' compensation award expressly establishes an offset rate under the Oregon statutory scheme, the Social Security Administration will prorate the lump-sum award according to that expressly stated offset rate.[1]

Workers' compensation payments for loss of bodily function, in addition to wage loss, can be used to offset Social Security disability insurance benefits. In a New Hampshire case, the claimant applied for, and was found entitled to, Social Security disability benefits. However, these benefits were offset because he also received New Hampshire workers' compensation payments, including a permanent impairment lump-sum award. After unsuccessfully appealing his case through administrative channels, the claimant appealed to the district court, claiming that the portion of his lump-sum settlement representing compensation for permanent impairment was not subject to offset. The district court held that permanent impairment payments under workers' compensation were to compensate an individual for loss of bodily function (not loss of wages), and thus could not be used to offset Social Security disability benefits.

The U.S. Court of Appeals for the First Circuit reversed the decision of the district court, holding that, although permanent impairment awards may be paid regardless of any actual loss of wages, the awards were never intended to be a departure from, or an exception to, the wage-loss principle. Permanent impairment benefits under New Hampshire workers' compensation law are for compensable disability under a state workers' compensation law and, therefore, are subject to offset against Social Security disability benefits.[2]

76. Is a person entitled to disability benefits regardless of wealth?

Yes, benefits are not payable on a "needs" basis. If a person meets the requirements for entitlement, disability benefits are payable regardless of wealth.

77. Can a disabled person receive disability benefits even though his spouse is employed?

Yes, if the person is entitled to benefits based on his own earnings record. Entitlement to benefits as a worker is entirely independent of a spouse's employment.

78. Can a disabled person return to work while getting Social Security benefits?

Yes, Social Security allows what is referred to as a "trial work period" to see if an individual is able to return to work. These periods can last up to nine months.

---

1. Social Security Acquiescence Ruling 95-2(9) https://www.ssa.gov/OP_Home/rulings/ar/09/AR95-02-ar-09.html (Last accessed October 1, 2018).
2. *Davidson v. Sullivan*, 942 F.2d 90, 34 Soc.Sec. Rep. Serv. 389 (1st Cir. 1991).

79. What is the trial work period?

A trial work period is provided as an incentive for personal rehabilitation efforts for disabled workers, disabled widow(er)s and childhood disability beneficiaries who are still disabled but return to work. It allows them to perform services in as many as nine months (within a sixty-consecutive-month period if nine months of services were not completed before January 1992) without affecting their right to benefits during the trial work period, if their impairment does not improve during this period. (Because benefits will continue for the month the disability is determined to have ceased and the two months after that, benefits may be paid for at least twelve months during which the individual works.)

A person is generally entitled to a trial work period if receiving disability insurance benefits, child's benefits based on disability, or widow(er)'s or surviving divorced spouse's benefits based on disability.

The trial work period begins with the month in which the person becomes entitled to:

(1)   disability insurance benefits; or

(2)   child's benefits based on disability; or

(3)   widow(er)'s or surviving divorced spouse's benefits based on disability.

It cannot begin before the month in which the person files an application for benefits.

The trial work period ends with the close of whichever of the following calendar months is earlier:

(1)   The ninth month (whether or not the months have been consecutive) in which the person has performed services if that ninth month is prior to January 1992.

(2)   The ninth month (whether or not the months have been consecutive and whether or not the previous eight months of services were prior to January 1992) in which the person has performed services within a rolling sixty-month period if that ninth month is after December 1991.

(3)   The month in which new evidence, other than evidence relating to any work the person did during the trial work period, shows that the person is not disabled, even though the person has not worked a full nine months. The Social Security Administration may find that the disability has ended at any time during the trial work period if the medical or other evidence shows that the person is no longer disabled.

A person is not entitled to a trial work period if:

(1)   the person is entitled to a period of disability but not to disability insurance benefits, child's benefits based on disability, or widow(er)'s or surviving divorced spouse's benefits based on disability; or

(2) the person performs work demonstrating the ability to engage in substantial gainful activity during any required waiting period for benefits; or

(3) the person performs work demonstrating the ability to engage in substantial gainful activity within twelve months of the onset of the impairment(s) that prevented him from performing substantial gainful activity and before the date of the decision awarding him disability benefits; or

(4) the person performs work demonstrating the ability to engage in substantial gainful activity at any time after the onset of the impairment(s) that prevented him from engaging in substantial gainful activity but before the month he files his application for disability benefits.

80. What amount of earnings trigger a trial work period?

During a trial work period, a beneficiary receiving Social Security disability benefits may test his or her ability to work and still be considered disabled. The SSA does not consider services performed during the trial work period as showing that the disability has ended until services have been performed in at least nine months (not necessarily consecutive) in a rolling sixty-month period. During 2017, any month in which earnings exceeded $840 was considered a month of services for an individual's trial work period. In 2018, this monthly amount increased to $850 and will increase to $880 for 2019.

Amount of monthly earnings that initiate a trial work period

Year	Monthly earnings
1978 and before	$50
1979 through 1989	75
1990 through 2000	200
2001	530
2002	560
2003	570
2004	580
2005	590
2006	620
2007	640
2008	670
2009	700
2010	720
2011	720
2012	720
2013	750
2014	770

2015	780
2016	810
2017	840
2018	850
2018	880

81. What is the trigger amount of income which indicates a person is engaged in Substantial Gainful Activity?

To be eligible for disability benefits, a person must be unable to engage in substantial gainful activity (SGA). A person who is earning more than a certain monthly amount (net of impairment-related work expenses) is ordinarily considered to be engaging in SGA. The amount of monthly earnings considered as SGA depends on the nature of a person's disability. The Social Security Act specifies a higher SGA amount for statutorily blind individuals; Federal regulations specify a lower SGA amount for non-blind individuals. The amount is set annually based on the national average wage index.

Amounts for 2019

The monthly SGA amount for statutorily blind individuals for 2019 is $2,040. For non-blind individuals, the monthly SGA amount for 2019 is $1,220. SGA for the blind does *not* apply to Supplemental Security Income (SSI) benefits, while SGA for the non-blind disabled applies to Social Security and SSI benefits. See historical series of SGA amounts below.

Historical SGA Amounts

Year	Blind	Non-blind
1975	$200	$200
1976	230	230
1977	240	240
1978	334	260
1979	375	280
1980	417	300
1981	459	300
1982	500	300
1983	550	300
1984	580	300
1985	610	300
1986	650	300
1987	680	300
1988	700	300
1989	740	300

1990	780	500
1991	810	500
1992	850	500
1993	880	500
1994	930	500
1995	940	500
1996	960	500
1997	1,000	500
1998	1,050	500
1999	1,110	700[a]
2000	1,170	700
2001	1,240	740
2002	1,300	780
2003	1,330	800
2004	1,350	810
2005	1,380	830
2006	1,450	860
2007	1,500	900
2008	1,570	940
2009	1,640	980
2010	1,640	1,000
2011	1,640	1,000
2012	1,690	1,010
2013	1,740	1,040
2014	1,800	1,070
2015	1,820	1,090
2016	1,820	1,130
2017	1,950	1,170
2018	1,970	1,180
2019	2,040	1,220

82. What is the re-entitlement period?

The re-entitlement period is an additional period after nine months of trial work during which a person may continue to test their ability to work if they have a disabling impairment. A person will not be paid benefits for any month after the second month following the month disability ceased due to substantial gainful activity in this period in which they did substantial gainful activity. A person will be paid benefits for months in which they did not do substantial gainful activity.

If anyone else is receiving monthly benefits based on a disabled person's earnings record, that individual will not be paid benefits for any month for which the disabled person cannot be paid benefits during the re-entitlement period. If a disabled person's benefits are stopped because he or she does substantial gainful activity, the benefits may be started again without a new application and a new determination of disability if the person discontinues doing substantial gainful activity during this period. In determining, for re-entitlement benefit purposes, whether a person does substantial gainful activity in a month, the Social Security Administration considers only work in or earnings for that month. It does not consider the average amount of work or earnings over a period of months. (See Q 86.)

83. Can a person become entitled to disability benefits after becoming entitled to some other type of Social Security benefit?

Yes. For example, a person who is receiving a reduced retirement benefit before Full Retirement Age (FRA) can become entitled to disability benefits. However, the disability benefit is actuarially reduced for the months that the person has already received retirement benefits.

84. Will a disabled person lose benefits by refusing to accept rehabilitation services?

Yes, a person will lose the disabled worker's benefit by refusing without good cause to accept vocational rehabilitation services.

Good cause for refusing vocational rehabilitation services exists if, for example, the person is a member of any recognized church or religious sect that teaches reliance solely upon prayer or spiritual means for the treatment of any impairment, and refusal to accept vocational rehabilitation services is based solely on adherence to these teachings.[1]

85. What are the special rules for disability benefits when alcoholism or drug addiction is involved?

An individual is not considered disabled if alcoholism or drug addiction is a contributing factor material to the Social Security Administration's determination that the individual is disabled.

Since 1996, a claimant cannot get Social Security disability insurance (SSDI) or SSI benefits for alcoholism or drug addiction alone. Disability benefits for damage caused by alcohol or drug abuse, such as liver damage, emotional problems, cardiovascular disease, or cancer ARE available, with a caveat – the claimant must no longer have a drinking problem or be abusing drugs unless the condition is so severe that the damage is not reversible. However, if the SSA determines that illness of a claimant would go away if they stopped the abuse of alcohol or drugs, the SSA can deny the claim. Social Security does not consider substance abuse to be disabling until it causes irreversible medical conditions. Social Security agrees that some medical and mental conditions from abuse cannot be reversed merely by abstaining from continuing the abuse. Most chronic

---

1. See SSR 64-13: SECTION 222(b). – DISABILITY – DEDUCTION FOR REFUSAL TO ACCEPT VOCATIONAL REHABILITATION SERVICES https://www.socialsecurity.gov/OP_Home/rulings/di/02/SSR64-13-di-02.html (Last accessed October 1, 2018) and SSR 78-24: DISABILITY — REFUSAL TO ACCEPT VOCATIONAL REHABILITATION SERVICES https://www.socialsecurity.gov/OP_Home/rulings/di/02/SSR78-24-di-02.html (Last accessed October 1, 2018).

substance abusers have irreversible medical or mental problems because of the changes in their body from the abuse.

Social Security no longer has a specific list of items used to qualify for drug addiction.

Up until 2017, there was a listing for substance addiction disorders that could be used to determine if the claimant had suffered specific changes in behaviors or physical health due to regular abuse of any prescription or illegal drugs affecting the central nervous system. However, a claimant can still qualify for disability benefits by meeting the criteria for the following conditions:

- brain damage (neurocognitive disorder)

- liver damage

- pancreatitis

- gastritis

- peripheral neuropathy

- seizures

- anxiety disorders

- major clinical depression

- personality disorder

A beneficiary who qualifies for disability benefits on a basis other than alcoholism or drug addiction, but is determined by the Social Security Administration to have an alcohol or drug addiction and to be incapable of managing the disability benefits, must have the disability benefit paid to a representative payee. The Social Security Administration must notify the beneficiary that benefits are being deposited to a representative payee because of alcoholism or drug addiction. In addition, the Social Security Administration must refer these individuals to the appropriate state agency administering the state plan for substance abuse treatment services.

The Social Security Administration determines whether drug addiction or alcoholism is a contributing factor material to the determination of disability by evaluating which physical and mental limitations would remain if the disabled person stopped using drugs or alcohol. If the Social Security Administration determines that the disabled person's remaining limitations are not disabling, the Social Security Administration will find that drug addiction or alcoholism is a contributing factor material to the determination of disability and deny disability benefits.[1]

86. When do a person's disability benefits end?

The last month of entitlement to a disabled worker's benefit generally is whichever of the following occurs earliest:

---

1. http://www.ssa.gov/OP_Home/cfr20/416/416-0935.htm (Last accessed October 1, 2018).

(1)   the second month after the month in which the disability ceases;

(2)   the month before the month the worker attains Full Retirement Age (at which time benefits are automatically converted to retirement benefits); or

(3)   the month before the month in which the worker dies.

However, there are certain conditions under which benefits may continue or re-entitlement to benefits may be established after disability ceases:

1.   ***Benefits for persons in vocational rehabilitation programs.*** Benefits for disabled and blind workers participating in a vocational rehabilitation program may continue until completion of the program, or for a specified period of time in certain situations where disability ceases prior to completion of the program. This provision applies only to disabled individuals who have medically recovered, who began the vocational rehabilitation program before disability ceased, and for whom the Social Security Administration has determined that continued participation in the vocational rehabilitation program would increase the likelihood of permanent removal from the disability benefit rolls.[1]

2.   ***Extended period of eligibility for re-entitlement to benefits following trial work period.*** Individuals who continue to have a disabling impairment receive an extended period of eligibility immediately following the completion of a nine-month trial work period. If disability ceased because of work activity and earnings subsequently fall below the level considered substantial gainful activity within a specified period, benefits may be reinstated without the need for a new application and disability determination. This re-entitlement period to disability benefits is thirty-six months. Benefits for the family of the worker are suspended during this period if the worker's benefits are suspended.[2]

Example 1. A disabled person completes the trial work period in December 2014. He is then working at the substantial gainful activity level and continues to do so throughout the thirty-six months following completion of his trial work period and thereafter. The disabled person's termination month is January 2018, which is the thirty-seventh month—that is, the first month in which the disabled person performed substantial gainful activity after the thirty-sixth month following his trial work period.

Example 2. A disabled person completes the trial work period in December 2014 but she is not able to work at the substantial gainful activity level until March 2018, three months after the last month of his re-entitlement period. The disabled person's termination month is June 2018 – that is, the third month after the earliest month he or she performed substantial gainful activity.

The Social Security Administration may use a "medical improvement standard" to terminate disability benefits. Benefits can be terminated only if:

---

1. See, Vocational Rehabilitation Cost Reimbursement Program http://www.ssa.gov/work/vocational_rehab.html. (Last accessed October 1, 2018).
2. See DI 13010.210 Extended Period of Eligibility (EPE) – Overview https://secure.ssa.gov/poms.nsf/lnx/0413010210 (Last accessed October 1, 2018) and 20 C.F.R. 404.1592a.

(1)   there is substantial evidence that there has been medical improvement in the individual's impairment or combination of impairments (other than medical improvement which is not related to the person's ability to work), *and* the individual is able to engage in substantial gainful activity (see Q 57);

(2)   there is substantial evidence demonstrating that, although there is no medical improvement, the person has benefited from advances in medical or vocational therapy or technology related to the ability to work, *and* the person is now able to perform substantial gainful activity;

(3)   there is substantial evidence that, although there is no medical improvement, the person has benefited from vocational therapy, *and* the beneficiary can now perform substantial gainful activity;

(4)   there is substantial evidence that, based on new or improved diagnostic techniques or evaluations, the person's impairment or combination of impairments is not as disabling as it was considered to be at the time of the prior determination, and therefore the individual is able to perform substantial gainful activity;

(5)   there is substantial evidence, either in the file at the original determination or newly obtained, showing that the prior determination was in error;

(6)   there is substantial evidence that the original decision was obtained by fraud; or

(7)   if the individual is engaging in substantial gainful activity and fails without good cause to cooperate in the review or follow prescribed treatment or cannot be located.

87. Are benefits payable to the family of a disabled worker?

Yes.

See SPOUSE'S BENEFIT and CHILD'S BENEFIT, immediately following.

88. If an individual is already collecting a disability benefit, can they suspend their benefits at Full Retirement Age and earn delayed retirement credits?

Yes. They can suspend at Full Retirement Age (FRA) to earn Delayed Retirement Credits. The beneficiary needs to realize, however, that any benefits being paid off their record will also be suspended.

Same-Sex Marriages

89. Are same-sex couples eligible for the same Social Security benefits as opposite-sex couples?

Yes. The Social Security Administration fully recognizes same-sex marriages in all states and some marital legal relationships such as civil unions and domestic partnerships for the purposes of determining entitlement to Social Security, Medicare and Supplemental Security Income. The SSA is also recognizing same-sex marriages and some nonmartial legal relationships entered into in foreign jurisdictions as well.[1] Social Security is now processing some retirement, surviving spouse and lump-sum death payment claims for same-sex couples in nonmarital legal relationships and paying benefits where they are due. In addition, the Social Security Administration considers same-sex marriage when determining SSI eligibility and benefit amounts.

BACKGROUND

On June 26, 2015, the United States Supreme Court issued a decision in *Obergefell v. Hodges*,[2] holding that same-sex couples have a constitutional right to marry in all states. This decision enables same-sex couples to be married in one state and have their marriage recognized by all other states. As a direct result of this decision, more same-sex couples will be recognized as being married for the purposes of determining their entitlement to Social Security benefits and as well as Supplemental Security Income (SSI) payments. The Social Security Administration recommends that someone who is the spouse, divorced spouse, or surviving spouse or a same-sex marriage or other legal same-sex relationship to immediately apply for benefits. Immediate applying will preserve the filing date, which can affect benefits.

This had been a changing area of law. In June 2013, the Supreme Court ruling in *United States v. Windsor*,[3] had established that same sex couples who were married in a jurisdiction where same-sex marriages are recognized were eligible for spousal benefits, such as the spousal survivor benefit, the spousal retirement benefit, and the lump sum death benefit. At that time, the Social Security Administration reviewed its own policies regarding same-sex marriage after the Supreme Court decision, and concluded that same-sex couples who are legally married in one state remain married for federal tax purposes even if they reside in a state that does not recognize their marriage.[4]

90. Does a person qualify for a benefit as a spouse (or surviving spouse) if in a civil union, a domestic partnership, or other non-marital legal relationship?

Social Security is now processing some retirement, surviving spouse, and lump-sum death payment claims for same-sex couples in non-marital legal relationships (such as some civil unions and domestic partnerships) and paying benefits where they are due. The best action would be to apply immediately for benefits, which will protect the filer against loss of any potential benefits.

91. Does being in a same sex marriage affect Supplemental Security Income (SSI) payments?

Possibly. The assets of the spouse and the spouse's resources could affect both eligibility and payment amount.

---

1. SSA Publication No. 05-10014, January 2017, What Same-Sex Couples Need to Know, https://www.ssa.gov/pubs/EN-05-10014.pdf (Last accessed October 1, 2018).
2. 576 U.S. ___, 135 S.Ct. 2587, 192 L.Ed.2d 609 (2015).
3. 570 U.S. ___, 133 S.Ct. 2675, 186 L.Ed. 808 (2013).
4. Rev. Rul. 2013-17. https://www.irs.gov/pub/irs-drop/rr-13-17.pdf (Last accessed October 1, 2018).

92. Does the Supreme Court case legalizing same-sex marriage affect Medicare?

Medicare is managed by the Centers for Medicare & Medicare Services (CMS). The Social Security Administration works with CMS by determining eligibility for and enrolling people in Medicare.

93. How can someone in a same-sex marriage be sure if he/she is eligible for benefits?

The best way is simply to apply immediately and get a determination. In addition, it will preserve the filing date that is used to determine the start date of benefits.

94. Must an individual that is receiving Social Security benefits tell the Social Security Administration that they are in a civil union or other non-marital legal relationship?

Yes. An individual's status in a civil union or other non-marital legal relationship may affect their entitlement to benefits.

95. Can same-sex partners with a child put both of their names on a Social Security number record?

Yes. regardless of the sex of either partner, SSA can place both parents' names on the child's Social Security number record. Both parents need to provide proof of being the legal parents of the child. The following documents will provide proof that you and your partner are the child's legal parents.

- Original or amended birth certificate

- The final adoption decree

- Court determination of paternity (also referred to as a court order of parentage)

96. Does an individual in a same-sex marriage tell Social Security of the marriage?

Yes. An individual must informa the SSA of their status as married, separated, or divorced, or if a marriage was annulled. This information could affect SSI eligibility or payment amount.

97. If the Internal Revenue Service (IRS) recognizes a same-sex marriage and allows an individual to file as "married filing jointly", can that individual have their Income-Related Monthly Adjustment Amounts (IRMAA) removed?

Yes. Any life-changing event, such as marriage, can create eligibility for a new determination. The individual must provide proof of marriage and estimated income for the tax year. If a tax return is amended and it changes the income used to determine the income-related monthly adjustment amounts, this information needs to be provided, including the amended return and the receipt of acknowledgement from the IRS.

98. Will the Social Security Administration recognize a same-sex marriage that was celebrated in a foreign country?

Yes. The SSA is now recognizing some foreign same-sex marriages for purposes of determining entitlement to benefits.

Spouse's Benefit

99. Is the spouse of a retired or disabled worker entitled to benefits?

Yes, an individual is entitled to spouse's benefits on a worker's Social Security record if:[1]

- the worker is *entitled* to retirement or disability benefits;

- the individual has *filed* an application for spouse's benefits;

- the spouse is *not entitled* to a retirement or disability benefit based on a primary insurance amount equal to or larger than one-half of the worker's primary insurance amount; and

- the spouse is either *age sixty-two* or over, or has in their care a *child under age sixteen, or disabled*, who is entitled to benefits on the worker's Social Security record.

The spouse of a worker must also meet *one* of the following conditions:

(1)   The spouse must have been married to the worker for at least one year just before filing an application for benefits.

(2)   The spouse must be the natural mother or father of the worker's biological child.

(3)   The spouse was entitled or potentially entitled to spouse's, widow(er)'s, parent's, or childhood disability benefits in the month before the month of marriage to the worker.

(4)   The spouse was entitled or potentially entitled to a widow(er)'s, parent's, or child's (over eighteen) annuity under the Railroad Retirement Act in the month before the month of marriage to the worker.

A spouse is "potentially entitled" if he or she meets all of the requirements for entitlement other than the filing of an application and attaining the required age.

100. What is meant by having a child "in care"?

Having a child in care is a basic requirement for spouse's benefits when the spouse is under age sixty-two and for mother's and father's benefits (see Q 127 to Q 141).[2]

"In care" means that the mother or father:

---

1. 42 U.S.C. 402(b), 402(c).
2. 42 U.S.C. 402(b)(1)(B), 402(c)(1)(B).

(1) exercises parental control and responsibility for the welfare and care of a child under age sixteen or mentally incompetent child aged sixteen or over; or

(2) performs personal services for a disabled but mentally competent child aged sixteen or over.

The mother or father may exercise parental control and responsibility or perform personal services alone or together.

A claimant for mother's/father's, surviving divorced mother's/father's, or spouse's (under age sixty-two) benefits must have in-care an entitled child of the wage earner. To receive an unreduced benefit, a spouse age sixty-two to full retirement age (FRA) must have a child of the wage earner in their care.

The in-care child must meet **all** of the following:

- be entitled to a child's insurance benefit,

- meet the conditions for entitlement,

    - For mother's/father's or spouse's (age sixty-two to FRA) benefits, the child may be entitled on any earnings record.

    - For surviving divorced mother's/father's and spouse's benefits (under age sixty=two), the child must be entitled on the wage earner's earning record.)

- meet the relationship requirements to be considered a child of the deceased NH; and

- be under age sixteen (age eighteen prior to September 1981) or, be disabled.

- Child-in-care also applies when the child was entitled to childhood disability benefits (CDB) prior to age twenty-two termination and became re-entitled to a new period of disability as a CDB after age twenty-two.

A mother/father must have in-care an entitled child of the wage earner when:

- he or she files an application for benefits; or

- he or she seeks entitlement within the retroactive period; or

- converting a spouse's benefit to a mother's/father's benefit.

101. Is the divorced spouse of a retired or disabled worker entitled to a spouse's benefits?

The spouse is entitled to a divorced spouse's benefit on the worker's Social Security record if:[1]

---

1. 42 U.S.C. 402(b)(1), 402(c)(1).

(1)   the worker is entitled to retirement or disability benefits;

(2)   the spouse has filed an application for divorced spouse's benefits;

(3)   the spouse is not entitled to a retirement or disability benefit based on a primary insurance amount that equals or exceeds one-half the worker's primary insurance amount;

(4)   the spouse is age sixty-two or over;

(5)   the spouse is not married; and

(6)   the spouse was married to the worker for at least ten years before the date the divorce became final.

A divorced spouse who is age sixty-two or over and who has been divorced for at least two years is able to receive benefits based on the earnings of a former spouse who is eligible for retirement benefits, regardless of whether the former spouse has retired or applied for benefits. This two-year waiting period for independent entitlement to divorced spouse's benefits is waived if the worker was entitled to benefits prior to the divorce. A spouse whose divorce took place after the couple had begun to receive retirement benefits, and whose former spouse (the worker) returned to work after the divorce (thus causing a suspension of benefits), will not lose benefits on which he or she had come to depend.

102. What is the amount of a spouse's benefit?

If the spouse of a retired or disabled worker is caring for the worker's child under age sixteen or disabled child, the monthly benefit equals half of the worker's PIA, regardless of his age.[1] If the spouse is not caring for a child, monthly benefits starting at full retirement age likewise equal half of the worker's PIA; but if the spouse chooses to start receiving benefits at or after age sixty-two, but before full retirement age, the benefit is reduced. (See Table 10 for spouse's reduced benefits.)

If the spouse chooses to receive, and is paid, a reduced spouse's benefit for months before full retirement age, the spouse is *not entitled to the full spouse's benefit rate upon reaching full retirement age.* A reduced benefit rate is payable for as long as the spouse remains entitled to spouse's benefits. (But see Q 259, Recomputation of Benefits.)

A spouse will not always receive a spouse's full benefit; under the following circumstances a spouse will receive a smaller amount:

(1)   If the total amount of monthly benefits payable on the worker's Social Security account exceeds the Maximum Family Benefit, all benefits (except the worker's benefit) will be reduced proportionately to bring the total within the family maximum limit. (See BENEFIT COMPUTATION, Q 226 to Q 259.)

---

1. 42 U.S.C. 402(b)(2), 402(c)(2).

(2)   If a spouse who is not caring for a child elects to start receiving a spouse's benefit at age sixty-two (or at any time between age sixty-two and full retirement age), the benefit will be reduced by 25/36 of 1 percent for each of the first thirty-six months that the spouse is under full retirement age when benefits commence, and by 5/12 of 1 percent for each such month in excess of thirty-six months.

(3)   If the spouse is entitled to a retirement or disability benefit that is smaller than the spouse's benefit rate, the spouse will receive a spouse's benefit equal to only the difference between the retirement or disability benefit and the full spouse's benefit rate.

(4)   The amount of a spouse's monthly benefit is usually reduced if the spouse receives a pension based on his or her own work for a federal, state, or local government that is not covered by Social Security on the last day of such employment. However, the Social Security Protection Act of 2004 generally requires that a person work in a situation covered by Social Security for five years to be exempt from this Government Pension Offset (GPO). See Q 108 for more information on the GPO.

If a spouse is entitled to a retirement or disability benefit that is larger than the spouse's benefit rate, he or she will receive only the retirement or disability benefit.

103. What is the amount of a divorced spouse's benefit?

The amount of a divorced spouse's benefit is the same as a spouse's benefit amount.[1] As a general rule, it will equal half of the beneficiary's former spouse's PIA and will be reduced if he or she elects to start receiving benefits before Full Retirement Age. However, a divorced spouse's benefit is paid independently of other family benefits. In other words, it will not be subject to reduction because of the family maximum limit and will not be considered in figuring the maximum limit for the former spouse's family.

104. What is the impact of the 2015 Bi-Partisan Budget Act on divorced spouses and their ability to collect?

The Bi-Partisan Budget Act DOES impact divorced individuals. Individuals divorced for greater than two years are considered an *Independently Entitled Divorced Spouse* and can collect a benefit from an ex-spouse even if the ex-spouse is not receiving any benefit. If divorced for two years or fewer the ex-spouse must be receiving a retirement or disability benefit or have filed and suspended benefits by April 29, 2016 for the other ex-spouse to collect.

The Social Security Administration provided guidance during 2016 when a benefit is being paid to an ex-spouse as the other ex is either receiving a retirement or disability benefit and they have not divorced for greater than two years. This situation, if the ex-spouse from whose account is being drawn decides to suspend benefits, then spousal benefit payable to the ex-spouse will continue.

---

1. 42 U.S.C. 402(b)(2), 402(c)(2).

105. Must a spouse be dependent upon the worker for support to be eligible for a spouse's benefits?

No, a spouse is entitled to benefits if the worker is receiving benefits and the spouse is otherwise qualified. A spouse need not be dependent upon the worker and may be independently wealthy.

106. May a spouse lose benefits if the worker works or if the spouse works?

Yes, a spouse can lose some or all of his or her monthly benefits if the worker is under the full retirement age for the entire year and earnings exceed $17,640.[1] A spouse may also lose benefits in the year the worker reaches full retirement age if the worker earns over $46,920 (in 2019), but only earnings earned before the month the worker reaches full retirement age count towards the $46,920 limit. Similarly, if the spouse is under full retirement age for the entire year and has earnings of over $17,640 (or earnings of over $46,920 in the year that full retirement age is attained), some or all benefits can be lost. (See LOSS OF BENEFITS BECAUSE OF "EXCESS" EARNINGS, Q 318 to Q 336.) See Q 253 for a discussion of the increase in the full retirement age.

When both the worker and the spouse have earnings in excess of the earnings limitation:

(1)   50 percent of the worker's "excess" earnings are charged against the total monthly family benefits if the worker is under the full retirement age, and 33⅓ percent in the year the worker is to reach the full retirement age; and then

(2)   the spouse's "excess" earnings are charged against his or her own benefits in the same manner, depending upon the age of the spouse, but only to the extent that those benefits have not already been charged with the worker's excess earnings.

Example. Mr. Smith, age sixty-two on January 1, 2018, is entitled to a monthly retirement benefit of $346, and his wife, also age sixty-two on January 1, 2018, is entitled to a monthly spouse's benefit of $162. Mr. Smith had earnings that were $4,064 in excess of the earnings limitation. His wife had earnings that were $1,620 in excess of the earnings limitation. Mr. Smith's earnings are charged against the total monthly family benefit of $508 ($346 + $162), so neither Mr. Smith nor his wife receives payments for January through April (50 percent of $4,064 = $2,032, and 4 × $508 = $2,032). The wife's excess earnings are charged only against her own benefit of $162. As her benefits for January through April were charged with the worker's excess earnings, the charging of her own earnings cannot begin until May; she thus receives no benefits for May through September (50 percent of $1,620 = $810, and 5 × $162 = $810).

Exception. The excess earnings of the worker do not cause deductions from the benefits of an entitled divorced spouse who has been divorced from the worker at least two years or whose former spouse was entitled to benefits before the divorce.

107. When does a spouse's benefit end?

A spouse's benefits end when:

(1)   the spouse dies;

---

1. See 42 U.S.C. 403(b)(1).

(2)   the worker dies (in this case, the spouse will be entitled to widow(er)'s, mother's, or father's benefits);

(3)   the worker's entitlement to disability benefits ends and he or she is not entitled to retirement benefits (unless the divorced spouse meets the requirements for an independently entitled divorced spouse);

(4)   the spouse is under age sixty-two and there is no longer a child of the worker under sixteen or disabled who is entitled to child's benefits;

(5)   the spouse becomes entitled to retirement or disability benefits and his or her PIA is equal to or larger than one-half of the worker's PIA;

(6)   the spouse and the worker are divorced before the spouse reaches age sixty-two and before the spouse and worker had been married for ten years; or

(7)   the divorced spouse marries someone other than the worker. However, the divorced spouse's benefit will not be terminated by marriage to an individual entitled to widow(er)'s, mother's, father's or parent's monthly benefits, or to an individual age eighteen or over who is entitled to childhood disability benefits.

A spouse is not entitled to a spouse's benefit for the month in which any of the above events occurs. The last payment will be the payment for the preceding month.

108. Will a spouse's benefit be reduced if the spouse is receiving a government pension?

Social Security benefits payable to spouses – including surviving spouses and divorced spouses – are reduced (but not below zero) by two-thirds of the amount of any governmental (federal, state, or local) retirement benefit payable to the spouse based on *his or her own earnings* in employment not covered by Social Security, if that person's last day of employment was not covered by Social Security (but see below for the SSPA of 2004). Thus, for the affected group, the spouse's benefit is reduced two dollars for every three dollars of the government pension.[1] For example, if the monthly civil service pension is $600, then two-thirds or $400 will be used to offset benefits.

The Social Security Protection Act of 2004 (SSPA 2004) requires a person to work in covered employment for the last sixty months (instead of one day) of employment to be exempt from the Government Pension Offset (GPO). This change will not apply to someone whose last day of government service was before July 1, 2004. Also, the required sixty months will be reduced for each month of government service that was covered by Social Security before the enactment of SSPA 2004. These reduced months of service must be performed after enactment.

This offset against Social Security benefits did not apply prior to December 1977, or if the individual:

---

1. Social Security Publication No. 05-10007 https://www.socialsecurity.gov/pubs/EN-05-10007.pdf. (Last accessed October 1, 2017).

(1)   met all the requirements for entitlement to Social Security benefits that existed and were applied in January 1977; and

(2)   received or was eligible to receive a government pension between December 1977 and December 1982.

In addition, it does not apply to those first eligible to receive a government pension prior to July 1983 if they also meet the one-half support test.

Generally, federal workers hired before 1984 are part of the Civil Service Retirement System (CSRS) and are not covered by Social Security. Most Federal workers hired after 1983 are covered by the Federal Employees' Retirement System Act of 1986 (FERS), which includes coverage by Social Security. The FERS law provided that employees covered by the CSRS could – from July 1, 1987 to December 31, 1987 – make a one-time election to join FERS (and thereby obtain Social Security coverage). Thus, a CSRS employee who switched to FERS during this period immediately became exempt from the government pension offset. Also, an employee who elected FERS on or before December 31, 1987 is exempt from the government pension offset, even if that person retired from government service before his FERS coverage became effective.

However, federal employees who elect to become covered under FERS during any election period which may occur on or after January 1, 1988, are exempt from the government pension offset only if they have five or more years of federal employment covered by Social Security after January 1, 1988. This rule also applies to certain legislative branch employees who first become covered under FERS on or after January 1, 1988.

Pensions based wholly on service performed as a member of a uniformed service, whether on active or inactive duty, are excluded from the offset.

109. In the event of several marriages, which one will the Social Security Administration consider to be valid?

Generally, the most recent (latest in time) marriage will be the one considered to be valid unless there is direct evidence of its invalidity, such as bigamy or a court order dissolving or invalidating the marriage.

Child's Benefits (Child of Retired or Disabled Worker)

110. Is a child of a retired or disabled parent entitled to Social Security benefits?

Yes, if:

(1)   the parent is entitled to retirement or disability benefits;

(2)   the child is (or was) dependent upon the parent (but see Q 112 to Q 115);

(3)   the child is under age eighteen, or between the ages of eighteen and nineteen and a full-time elementary or high school student, or eighteen or over and under a disability that began before age twenty-two;

(4)   the child is unmarried (but see Q 121); and (5) an application for the child's benefit has been filed.

A **grandchild or step-grandchild** is considered the child of the worker in the following certain circumstances:

(1)   The grandchild's natural or adoptive parents are deceased or disabled: (1) at the time the worker became entitled to retirement or disability benefits or died, or (2) at the beginning of the worker's period of disability, which continued until the worker became entitled to disability or retirement benefits.

(2)   The grandchild was legally adopted by the worker's surviving spouse in an adoption decreed by a court, and the grandchild's natural or adopting parent or stepparent was not living in the same household and making regular contributions to the child's support at the time the insured worker died.

The grandchild or step-grandchild also must be dependent on the insured. (See Q 112.)

An **illegitimate child** is eligible for child's benefits if the worker:

(1)   has acknowledged in writing that the child is his or her son or daughter;

(2)   has been decreed by a court to be the father or mother of the child;

(3)   has been ordered by a court to contribute to the support of the child because the child is his or her son or daughter; or

(4)   has been shown to be the child's father or mother by other satisfactory evidence and was living with the child or contributing to the child's support when the child's application is filed (in life cases) or when the worker died (in survivor cases).

111. Who is considered a "child" of a retired or disabled worker for benefit purposes?

The term "child" includes the worker's:

(1)   legitimate child, or any child who would have the right under applicable state law to inherit intestate personal property from the worker as a child;

(2)   stepchild, under certain circumstances;

(3)   legally adopted child;

(4)   illegitimate child, under certain circumstances (see Q 110); and

(5)   grandchild or step-grandchild, under certain circumstances (see Q 110).

A stepchild-stepparent relationship arises when the worker marries the child's natural parent or marries the child's adopting parent after the adoption. Death of the stepparent does not end the relationship. If the stepparent and the child's natural parent are divorced, the stepparent-stepchild relationship ends. However, in either case, there is no termination of a stepchild's existing established entitlement to child's benefits as a child of a stepparent. A stepchild must have been a stepchild of the parent on whose Social Security record the claim for benefits is filed for at least one year before the day the child's application is filed (if the parent is alive).

112. Must a child be dependent upon the worker to qualify for child's benefits?

Yes. A child must be dependent upon the worker to qualify for benefits on the worker's Social Security record. The factors that determine whether a child is dependent upon a worker vary, depending upon whether the worker is the natural parent (see Q 113), the legally adopting parent, the stepparent (see Q 114), or the grandparent (see below).

To be dependent on the worker, a grandchild or step-grandchild must have:

(1)   begun living with the worker before the grandchild became eighteen years old; and

(2)   lived with the worker in the United States and received at least one-half support for the worker.

The support test is met if the worker provides one-half of the support:

(1)   for the year before the month the worker became entitled to retirement or disability benefits or died; or

(2)   if the worker had a period of disability that lasted until he or she became entitled to benefits or died, for the year immediately before the month in which the period of disability began.

113. Is a child considered to be dependent upon his father or mother regardless of actual dependency?

Yes, a child is deemed to be dependent upon his parent (father or mother). The fact that the parent and child are not living together, or the parent is not contributing to the child's support, is not a factor unless the child has been adopted by another person.

114. Under what circumstances is a child considered to be dependent upon a stepparent?

The child is considered dependent upon a stepparent if the stepparent is contributing at least one-half of the child's support, or if the child is living with the stepparent.

115. Can a child receive benefits based on one parent's Social Security account even though the other parent is working and furnishing support?

Yes. A good example would be where the child is entitled to benefits due to the death of his or her mother who was a covered worker. The fact that the child's father was supporting him or her would not matter.

116. When is a child a full-time elementary or secondary school student?

A child may be eligible for child's benefits if she is a full-time elementary or secondary school student.[1]

A child is a full-time elementary or secondary school student if she attends a school that provides elementary or secondary education as determined under the law of the state or other jurisdiction in which it is located. Participation in the following programs also meets the requirements:

(1) *Home Schooling.* The child is instructed in elementary or secondary education at home in accordance with a home-schooling law of the state or other jurisdiction in which the child resides. Students in these types of situations include a wide range of individuals. For example, home-schooling students may be in that situation for religious reasons or because the parents do not agree with the local school curriculum.

(2) *Independent Study.* The child is in an independent study elementary or secondary education program in accordance with state law or other jurisdiction in which she resides, which is administered by the local school or school district jurisdiction. Students in independent study programs may include those individuals who cannot take advantage of the traditional school setting, such as hard-to-keep-in-school students (unable to adjust or delinquents), single mothers, or expectant mothers.

A child must be in full-time attendance in a day or evening course of at least thirteen weeks duration and must be carrying a subject load which is considered full-time for day students under the institution's standards and practices. If a child is in a home-schooling program, the child must be carrying a subject load that is considered full-time for day students under standards and practices set by the state or other jurisdiction in which the child resides.

To be considered in full-time attendance, a child's scheduled attendance must be at the rate of at least twenty hours per week. If a child is in an independent study program, the number of hours spent in school attendance are determined by combining the number of hours of attendance at a school facility with the agreed-upon number of hours spent in independent study.

A child may still be considered in full-time attendance if the scheduled rate of attendance is below twenty hours per week if the Social Security Administration finds that:

---

1. 20 C.F.R. 404.367.

(1)   the school attended does not schedule at least twenty hours per week and going to that particular school is the child's only reasonable alternative; or

(2)   the child's medical condition prevents him or her from having scheduled attendance of at least twenty hours per week. To prove that a child's medical condition prevents scheduling twenty hours per week, the Social Security Administration may request that the child provide appropriate medical evidence or a statement from the school.

A child enrolled solely in correspondence courses is not a full-time elementary or secondary school student. The student is not being paid by an employer who has requested that the student attend the school. In addition, the student must be in grade twelve or below.

Benefits paid to students age eighteen who attend elementary or secondary schools on a full-time basis end with the last month they are full-time students or, if earlier, the month before the month they become age nineteen.

117. Is the disabled child of a retired or disabled worker entitled to benefits past age twenty-two?

Yes, if the disability began before the child reached age twenty-two and continued until the filing date of the application. The definition of "disability" is the same as for a worker applying for disability benefits (see Q 57).

118. What is the amount of the benefit for a retired or disabled worker's child?

The child of a retired or disabled worker is entitled to a monthly benefit equal to 50 percent of his parent's PIA. Usually this is an amount equal to one-half of the worker's benefit, but if the worker has elected to receive a reduced retirement benefit before full retirement age (see Q 46), the child's benefit will be based on one-half of his parent's PIA, not on one-half of the reduced benefit. If the worker receives a larger benefit than the PIA due to delayed retirement beyond full retirement age, the child's benefit is still only 50 percent of the PIA.

Although a child's full benefit is equal to one-half his parent's PIA, in many cases the benefit actually paid to a child will be smaller because of the "family maximum" limit. Thus, if the total amount of benefits based on the parent's Social Security account exceeds the family maximum, all benefits (except the worker's benefit) will be reduced to bring the total within the family maximum. (See Q 243, Maximum Family Benefits and Table 11.)

Notice that the benefit for a retired or disabled worker's child is less than the benefit for a deceased worker's child. The child of a deceased worker is entitled to a benefit equal to 75 percent of his deceased parent's PIA (see Q 144, Child's Benefit, Child of Deceased Worker).

119. Can a child lose his benefits by working?

Yes, a child can lose some or all of his benefits if he or she works and earns over $17,640 in 2019.

See LOSS OF BENEFITS BECAUSE OF "EXCESS" EARNINGS, Q 318 to Q 336.

120. If the retired or disabled parent loses benefits, will the child lose benefits also?

Yes. For example, if a disabled worker loses his benefits because he refuses to accept rehabilitation services, his child's benefits will also be discontinued. Or, if the disabled worker recovers and is no longer entitled to benefits, the child's benefits will end.

121. Will a child lose his or her benefits if he or she marries?

Yes, with one exception: a disabled child aged eighteen or over will not lose his or her benefits because of marriage to another disabled child aged eighteen or over who is receiving child's benefits, or because of marriage to a person entitled to retirement, widow(er)'s, mother's, father's, parent's, disability, or spouse's benefits.

122. When does a child's benefit end?

A child's benefits end when:

(1) the child dies;

(2) the child marries (but not if the child is a disabled child over eighteen and the child marries another Social Security beneficiary);

(3) the child's parent is no longer entitled to disability benefits, unless entitlement ended because the insured parent became entitled to retirement benefits or died; or

(4) the child reaches age eighteen and is neither under a disability nor a full-time student. Benefits for full-time elementary or secondary school students end when the child reaches age nineteen. Entitlement to childhood disability benefits ends when the child over age eighteen ceases to be under a disability, which began before age twenty-two, unless the child is age eighteen to nineteen and a full-time elementary or secondary school student.

The beneficiary is not entitled to child's insurance benefits for the month in which any of the above events occur, except that a disabled child's benefits will end with the second month following the month in which the child ceases to be under a disability.

Also, if the benefits of a stepchild are based on the wages or self-employment income of a stepparent who is subsequently divorced from the child's natural parent, the stepchild's benefit ends the month after the month in which the divorce becomes final.

A child's benefit may also end if the child is missing. In 1993, the Social Security Administration suspended benefits for a child who disappeared mysteriously and was missing for five years. Further payment of benefits was suspended until the beneficiary's whereabouts and continuing eligibility for benefits were determined.[1]

---

1. Social Security Ruling SSR 93-3. https://www.ssa.gov/OP_Home/rulings/oasi/09/SSR93-03-oasi-09.html (Last accessed October 1, 2018).

123. If a child is neither disabled nor a full-time elementary or secondary student, when does the benefit end?

When the child reaches age eighteen, unless the child marries before then. The last benefit is the benefit for the month preceding the month when the child reaches age eighteen.

124. Who files application for a child's benefits?

If the child is at least age eighteen and physically and mentally competent, the child must file the application form. Otherwise, an application may be filed on the child's behalf by a legal guardian or by the person (e.g., parent or relative) who is caring for the child. (See FILING FOR BENEFITS, Q 212 to Q 229.)

125. Can a child receive their own benefits?

It depends. Ordinarily, a representative payee, such as a parent or relative, will be appointed to receive the child's benefits. However, if the child is over age eighteen and competent, payment will be made directly to the child. Also, if the child is under eighteen, away from home (e.g., in the Army), and is deemed mature enough to handle the benefit, payment may be made directly to the child.

Survivor's Benefits

126. What benefits are payable to the survivors of a deceased insured worker?

- Mother's or Father's benefit (monthly benefit for widow(er), regardless of age, who is caring for at least one child, under sixteen or disabled before age twenty-two, of the deceased worker) – see Q 127 to Q 141.

- Child's benefit monthly benefit for each child who is:

  (1) under age eighteen;

  (2) over age eighteen and disabled before age twenty-two; or

  (3) under age nineteen and attending a full-time elementary or high school – see Q 144 to Q 156.

    - Widow(er)'s benefit (monthly benefit for widow(er), or surviving divorced widow(er), age sixty or older) – see Q 159 to Q 173.

    - Disabled Widow(er)'s benefit (monthly benefit for a disabled widow(er), age fifty to sixty) – see Q 174.

    - Parent's benefit (monthly benefit for parent age sixty-two or older who was dependent upon deceased worker for support) – see Q 175 to Q 184.

    - Lump sum death payment – see Q 185 to Q 187.

Mother's or Father's Benefit

127. Is the surviving spouse of an insured worker entitled to a monthly mother's or father's benefit at any age?

Yes, if caring for a child of the deceased worker under age sixteen or disabled before age twenty-two. Otherwise, a surviving spouse is not eligible for benefits until age sixty (age fifty if disabled).

The surviving spouse of a fully or currently insured worker is entitled to a mother's or father's benefit at any age if:

(1)   he or she is caring for a child of the deceased worker under age sixteen or disabled before age twenty-two who is entitled to a child's benefit on the deceased worker's account;

(2)   he or she is not married;

(3)   he or she is not entitled to widow(er)'s benefits;

(4)   he or she is not entitled to a retirement benefit based on his or her own work record that is equal to or larger than the amount of the unadjusted mother's or father's benefit; and

(5)   he or she has filed an application for benefits.

One of the following requirements must also be met:

(1)   the surviving spouse was married to the deceased worker for at least nine months before the worker died (see exception below);

(2)   the surviving spouse is the biological parent of the worker's child;

(3)   the surviving spouse legally adopted the worker's child during their marriage and before the child reached age eighteen;

(4)   the surviving spouse was married to the worker when they both legally adopted a child under age eighteen;

(5)   the worker legally adopted the surviving spouse's child during their marriage and before the child reached age eighteen; or

(6)   the surviving spouse was entitled or potentially entitled to spouse's, widow(er)'s, father's, mother's, parent's, or childhood disability benefits in the month before the month the surviving spouse married the deceased worker.

A surviving spouse is "potentially entitled" if he or she meets all requirements for entitlement, other than the filing of an application and attainment of the required age.

128. Is there an exception to the rule that the surviving spouse be married for at least nine months?

Yes. There is an exception to the requirement that the surviving spouse be married to the deceased worker for at least nine months before the worker died. The rule is waived if the worker's death was accidental, or if it occurred in the line of duty while a member of a uniformed service serving on active duty, or if the surviving spouse who was married to the worker at the time of death was previously married to and divorced from the worker and the previous marriage had lasted nine months. The worker's death is defined as accidental only if the worker received bodily injuries solely through violent, external, and accidental means and, as a direct result of the bodily injuries and independent of all other causes, died within three months after the day the injuries were received. The exception does not apply if, at the time of the marriage, the worker could not reasonably have been expected to live for nine months.

129. Can a divorced spouse qualify for a survivor's benefit?

Yes, a person is entitled to mother's or father's benefits as a surviving divorced spouse of a worker who died fully or currently insured if he or she:

(1)   is the parent of the worker's child, or was married to the worker when either of them adopted the other's child or when both of them adopted a child and the child was then under eighteen;

(2)   filed an application for these benefits;

(3)   is not married;

(4)   is not entitled to a widow(er)'s benefits, or to a retirement benefit that is equal to or larger than the mother's or father's full benefit; and

(5)   has in care the worker's child who is entitled to child's benefits based on the worker's earnings record. The child must be under age sixteen or disabled.

130. Must a worker be fully insured at death to qualify for the mother's or father's benefit?

No. The mother's or father's benefit is payable if the worker was *either* fully or currently insured.

See Q 205 to Q 209.

131. What is the amount of a mother's or father's benefit?

The amount of a mother's or father's benefit is equal to 75 percent of the deceased spouse's Primary Insurance Amount (PIA). However, because of the "family maximum" limit, the monthly benefit actually received by the surviving spouse may be less. If the total benefits payable on one worker's Social Security account exceed the family maximum, all benefits are reduced proportionately to bring the total within the family maximum. (See Maximum Family Benefits, Q 243.) A surviving divorced mother's or father's benefit is the same amount. However, benefits paid to a divorced mother or father will not be reduced because of the limit on total family benefits, and such benefits are not counted in figuring the total benefits payable to others on the basis of the deceased worker's account.

If the surviving spouse is entitled to a smaller retirement or disability benefit based on his own earnings record, he will receive the benefit based on his own account, and will receive as a mother's or father's benefit only the difference between the mother's or father's benefit rate and the other benefit rate.

132. What are the differences between a mother's or father's benefit and a widow's or widower's benefit?

A *mother's or father's* benefit is payable to a surviving spouse *at any age*, but he or she must be caring for at least one child under age sixteen or a disabled child of the deceased spouse. A *widow's or widower's* benefit is not payable until the surviving spouse *reaches age sixty* unless the surviving spouse is disabled, in which case benefits may begin at age fifty.

A surviving spouse will qualify for a *mother's or father's* benefit if the deceased spouse was either fully or currently insured at death. However, a surviving spouse will not qualify for a *widow's or widower's* benefit unless the deceased spouse was fully insured at death.

A full *mother's or father's* benefit is equal to only 75 percent of the deceased spouse's PIA. A full *widow's or widower's* benefit (at the Full Retirement Age, see Q 46) is equal to 100 percent of the deceased spouse's PIA.

133. Is a mother's or father's benefit payable regardless of the surviving spouse's need?

Yes, if the surviving spouse meets the necessary qualifications (see Q 127), he or she will receive benefits regardless of wealth or income.

134. Can a surviving spouse lose some or all of the benefits by working?

Yes, in 2019, by earning over $17,640 a year if under the full retirement age (see Q 46) for the entire year. In the year the surviving spouse reaches full retirement age, benefits may be lost by earning over $46,920. However, only earnings earned before the month the surviving spouse reaches full retirement age count toward the $46,920 limit. The loss of benefits by a surviving spouse will not cause the children to lose their benefits.

See LOSS OF BENEFITS BECAUSE OF "EXCESS" EARNINGS, Q 318 to Q 336.

135. If the only child in a surviving spouse's care loses benefits by working, will this cause the child's mother or father to lose benefits?

No.

See LOSS OF BENEFITS BECAUSE OF "EXCESS" EARNINGS, Q 318 to Q 336.

136. Must a surviving spouse file an application for a mother's or father's benefit?

Yes, unless receiving a spouse's benefit before the worker's death. The application should be filed within six months after the worker's death, because no more than six month's benefits will be paid retroactively.

137. When do a mother's or father's benefits begin?

If a surviving spouse qualifies, benefits will begin with a payment for the month in which his or her spouse died (but see Q 136).

138. When do a mother's or father's benefits end?

Mother's or father's benefits end when:

(1)   there is no longer a child of the deceased under age sixteen or disabled in the parent's care;

(2)   in the case of a surviving divorced father or mother, no natural or legally adopted child of the surviving spouse under age sixteen or disabled is entitled to a child's benefit on the deceased worker's earnings record;

(3)   the surviving spouse becomes entitled to a widow(er)'s benefit;

(4)   the surviving spouse dies;

(5)   the surviving spouse becomes entitled to retirement benefits in an amount equal to or greater than three-fourths of the deceased spouse's PIA; or

(6)   the surviving spouse marries. However, if the surviving spouse marries a person entitled to retirement, disability, divorced spouse's, widow(er)'s, father's, mother's, parent's, or childhood disability benefits, the marriage has no effect on entitlement (unless marriage is to a child under age eighteen or a full-time student under the age nineteen, in which case both benefits terminate).

If the subsequent marriage ends, the surviving spouse may be reentitled to mother's or father's benefits on the prior deceased spouse's (or former spouse's) earnings record, beginning with the month the subsequent marriage ends.

The surviving spouse can receive no further benefits until he or she becomes entitled to a widow(er)'s benefit at age sixty (or a disabled widow's or widower's benefits at age fifty). The period during which the surviving spouse is entitled to no benefits is known as the *black-out period*. The fact that a child's benefits will continue after age sixteen does not entitle the child's mother or father to a continuation of benefits.

139. Will a mother's or father's benefit be reduced if he or she is receiving a government pension?

Social Security benefits payable to spouses – including surviving spouses and divorced spouses – are reduced (but not below zero) by two-thirds of the amount of any governmental (federal, state, or local) retirement benefit payable to the spouse based on *his or her own earnings* in employment not covered by Social Security if that person's last day of employment is not covered by Social Security. Thus, for the affected group, the spouse's benefit is reduced two dollars for every three dollars of the government pension. However, the Social Security Protection Act of 2004 generally requires that a person work in covered employment for five years (instead of one day) to be exempt from this Government Pension Offset (GPO). See Q 108 and Q 171 for more information on the GPO.

This offset against Social Security benefits does not apply if the individual:

(1)   met all the requirements for entitlement to Social Security benefits that existed and were applied in January 1977; and

(2)   received or was eligible to receive a government pension between December 1977 and December 1982.

Pensions based entirely on service performed as a member of a uniformed service, whether on active or inactive duty, are excluded from the offset.

140. Will a mother's or father's benefits stop when the youngest child (or only child) reaches age sixteen?

Yes (unless the child is disabled and was disabled before age twenty-two), and he or she will not become eligible for widow(er)'s benefits until age sixty. The time when a surviving spouse is not entitled to any Social Security benefits is commonly called the *black-out period*. But if the surviving spouse is caring for a disabled child whose disability began before age twenty-two, mother's or father's benefits will not stop so long as the child continues to be disabled and entitled to a child's benefits. If the surviving spouse is disabled, he or she may qualify for a disabled widow(er)'s benefit at age fifty. (See Q 173.)

141. Does a mother or father continue to receive benefits until the youngest child (or only child) is age twenty-two if the child is attending school?

No. A mother's or father's benefits are payable only so long as the child in his or her care is under age sixteen or disabled. See Q 116.

142. What documentation is needed to apply for mother or father's benefits?

The following documentation may be requested by the Social Security Administration in order to determine eligibility for benefits for a child that is in care.

- Proof of the worker's death

- Applicant's birth certificate or other proof of birth

- Proof of U.S. citizenship or lawful alien status if you were not born in the United States

  - Most normal documentation is accepted of most applicants born in the U.S.

  - Applicants who are U.S. citizens born outside of the country should provide:

    - U.S. consular report of birth,

    - U.S. passport,

    - Certificate of Naturalization, or

    - Certificate of Citizenship.

  - Applicants who are not U.S. citizens need to produce their Department of Homeland Security (DHS) documents, including form I-551 (Permanent Resident Card, with 9-digit Alien Registration Number (A-Number)). In addition, the applicant should produce their DHS form I-94, Admission-Departure Record.

- U.S. military discharge paper(s)

- W-2 form(s) and/or self-employment tax returns for last year

- Proof of marriage

- Final divorce decree if applying as a surviving divorced mother or father

- Child's birth certificate or other proof of birth

143. What information will be asked of individuals applying for mother or father's benefits?

- Your name and Social Security number

- The deceased worker's name, date of birth, gender, and Social Security number

- The deceased worker's date of death and place of death

- Applicant's name at birth (if different) and any other names used

- Date and place of birth (City, State, and/or foreign country)

- Whether a public or religious record was made of applicant's birth before age five

- Applicant's citizenship status

- Any other Social Security number used

- Whether applicant or anyone else has ever filed for Social Security benefits, Medicare, or Supplemental Security Income on behalf of the applicant

- Whether the deceased worker ever filed for Social Security benefits, Medicare, or Supplemental Security Income

- Whether applicant or the deceased worker were ever in the active military service before 1968 or ever worked for the railroad industry

- Whether applicant became unable to work because of illnesses, injuries, or conditions at any time within the past fourteen months

- Whether the deceased worker was disabled at the time of death

- Whether the deceased worker has a surviving parent who was dependent on the worker for one-half of his or her support at the time of the worker's death

- Whether applicant or the deceased worker have earned Social Security credits under another country's Social Security system

- Whether the deceased worker was a civilian employee of the Federal Government in January 1983

- Whether applicant qualified for or expects to receive a pension or annuity based on employment with the Federal government of the United States or one of its States or local subdivisions

- The names, dates of birth (or age) and Social Security numbers (if known) of former spouses or and the deceased worker's former spouses

- The dates and locations of applicant's marriages, and for marriages that have ended, how, when, and where they ended

- The dates of the deceased worker's marriages and how, when, and where they ended

- The names of the deceased worker's children under eighteen, eighteen to nineteen and attending secondary school, or disabled before age twenty-two;

- The names and Social Security numbers of the deceased worker's unmarried children under sixteen or sixteen and older and disabled before age twenty-two in applicant's care and the months the child lived with applicant

- Whether the deceased worker had earnings (and the amount) last year or this year

- The amount of applicant's earnings for this year, last year, and next year

- Whether applicant and the deceased worker were living together at the time of death

- If applicant is within three months of age sixty-five, a decision needs to be made on whether to enroll in Medicare Part B (Medical Insurance)

Child's Benefit (Child of Deceased Worker)

144. Is a child of a deceased worker entitled to Social Security benefits?

If a worker dies either fully *or* currently insured, each child who meets the relationship requirements is entitled to a child's benefit if:

(1) under age eighteen, or over age eighteen and disabled by a disability that began before age twenty-two, or under age nineteen and a full-time elementary or secondary school student;

(2) not married;

(3) dependent upon the deceased parent; and

(4) an application has been filed for benefits.

The Social Security Administration agreed to pay a survivor's benefit to a child who was conceived through artificial insemination after her father's death. An administrative law judge ruled in 1995 that the child was entitled to $700 a month in Social Security child's benefits.

145. Must a parent be fully insured at death to qualify the child for a child's benefits?

No, the child is eligible for benefits on the parent's Social Security account, if the parent was either fully or currently insured at death.

See Q 205 to Q 209.

146. Must a child have been dependent upon the deceased parent to be eligible for a child's benefit?

Yes, the child must have been dependent upon the deceased worker.

The factors that determine whether a child is dependent upon a worker vary, depending upon whether the worker is the natural parent, the legally adopting parent, the stepparent, or the grandparent.

A child is "deemed" dependent upon the worker if the child has not been legally adopted by someone other than the worker and:

(1) is the legitimate child of the worker;

(2)   an illegitimate child who would have the right under applicable state law to inherit intestate property from the worker as a child;

(3)   the child of a void or voidable marriage;

(4)   the child of an invalid ceremonial marriage; or

(5)   the legally adopted child of the worker adopted prior to the worker's death.

147. Under what circumstances is a child considered dependent upon a grandparent, step-grandparent, great-grandparent, or step-great-grandparent?

A child is dependent upon a grandparent, step-grandparent, great-grandparent, or step-great-grandparent if the child:

(1)   began living with the worker before he or she reached age eighteen; and

(2)   lived with the worker in the United States and received at least one-half support from the worker.

The support test is met if the worker provides one-half of the support:

(1)   for the year before the month the worker died; or

(2)   if the worker had a period of disability that lasted until he or she became entitled to benefits, for the year immediately before the month in which the period of disability began.

148. Under what circumstances is a child considered dependent upon a stepfather or stepmother?

The child is considered dependent upon a stepfather or stepmother if the stepfather or stepmother is contributing at least one-half of the child's support. The child is not required to live with the stepfather or stepmother.

A stepchild must have been the stepchild of the insured worker for at least nine months immediately preceding the day the worker died, unless the worker and the child's natural or adopting parent were previously married, divorced, and then remarried at the time of the worker's death, and the nine-month-duration-of-relationship requirement was met at the time of the divorce. If the death of the worker was accidental or occurred in the line of duty while a member of a uniformed service serving on active duty, the nine-month requirement may be considered satisfied, unless at the time of the marriage, the worker could not have been expected to live for nine months. A child who was not legally adopted by the worker will nevertheless be treated as a legally adopted child if the child was living in the worker's home or receiving at least one-half of his support from the worker at the time of the worker's death, and the child is adopted by the worker's surviving spouse after the worker's death (but only if adoption proceedings were instituted by the worker before his death or adoption by the surviving spouse occurs within two years after the worker's death). However, such a child will not be treated as the worker's legally adopted child if at the time of the worker's death he was receiving regular contributions toward his support from someone other than the worker or the worker's spouse or a public or private welfare organization.

A child is eligible for benefits based on his parent's Social Security earnings record, even if the child was supported by a stepparent when the parent died.

149. Can a child receive benefits based on a deceased parent's Social Security account, even though the other parent is still living and supporting the child?

Yes.

150. Is a child age eighteen or over entitled to benefits if attending school?

A child may be eligible for child's benefits if she is under age nineteen and a full-time elementary or secondary school student.[1]

Benefits paid to a student age eighteen who attends elementary or secondary schools on a full-time basis end with the last month that the student is a full-time student or, if earlier, the month before the month the student becomes age nineteen.

A child is a full-time elementary or secondary school student if she attends a school that provides elementary or secondary education, as determined under the law of the state or other jurisdiction in which it is located. Participation in one of the following programs also meets the following requirements:

(1)   The child is instructed in elementary or secondary education at home in accordance with a home-schooling law of the state or other jurisdiction in which the child resides. Students in these types of situations include a wide range of individuals. For example, home-schooling students may be in that situation for religious reasons or because the parents do not agree with the local school curriculum.

(2)   The child is in an independent study elementary or secondary education program in accordance with state law or other jurisdiction in which she resides, which is administered by the local school or school district jurisdiction. Students in independent study programs may include those individuals who cannot take advantage of the traditional school setting, such as hard-to-keep-in-school students (unable to adjust or delinquents), single mothers, or expectant mothers.

A child must be in full-time attendance in a day or evening course of at least thirteen weeks duration and must be carrying a subject load that is considered full-time for day students under the institution's standards and practices. If a child is in a home-schooling program, the child must be carrying a subject load that is considered full-time for day students under standards and practices set by the state or other jurisdiction in which the child resides.

---

1. 20 C.F.R. 404.367 https://www.ssa.gov/OP_Home/cfr20/404/404-0367.htm (Last accessed October 1, 2018).

To be considered in full-time attendance, a child's scheduled attendance must be at the rate of at least twenty hours per week. If a child is in an independent study program, the number of hours spent in school attendance are determined by combining the number of hours of attendance at a school facility with the agreed-upon number of hours spent in independent study.

A child may still be considered in full-time attendance if the scheduled rate of attendance is below twenty hours per week if the Social Security Administration finds that:

(1)   the school attended does not schedule at least twenty hours per week, and going to that particular school is the child's only reasonable alternative; or

(2)   the child's medical condition prevents him or her from having scheduled attendance of at least twenty hours per week. To prove that a child's medical condition prevents scheduling twenty hours per week, the Social Security Administration may request that the child provide appropriate medical evidence or a statement from the school.

A child enrolled solely in correspondence courses is not a full-time elementary or secondary school student. A child does not qualify as a student if being paid by an employer to attend school.

151. What is the amount of the monthly benefit for a child of a deceased worker?

The surviving child's benefit is equal to 75 percent of the deceased parent's primary insurance amount. However, because of the "family maximum" limit, the monthly benefit actually received by the child may be less. If the total amount payable in benefits based on one worker's Social Security account exceeds the "family maximum," all benefits are reduced proportionately to bring the total within the "family maximum." (See Maximum Family Benefits, Q 243 to Q 246.)

A child entitled to benefits based on more than one worker's record will receive the benefit based on the record that provides the highest amount, if the payment does not reduce the benefits of any other individual who is entitled to benefits based on the same earnings record.

152. Will a child lose benefits if the child works or the child's parent works?

The child can lose part or all of his benefits if he earns over $17,640 in 2019. However, none of the child's benefits will be lost because his surviving parent works. Also, the child's work will not affect the parent's benefits.

See LOSS OF BENEFITS BECAUSE OF "EXCESS" EARNINGS, Q 318 to Q 336.

153. If a child is entitled to benefits on more than one person's Social Security account, will the child receive both benefits?

No, the child will receive only ONE benefit, but it will be the HIGHER one. (But see Q 257.) In no circumstances does an individual receive more than one benefit under Social Security but is always entitled to the larger one.

154. When does a child's benefit begin?

Ordinarily, the first benefit is payable for the month in which the parent died. However, unless the child was receiving benefits before the parent's death, an application should be filed within six months after death. Benefits will be paid retroactively for up to but not more than six months.

155. When does a child's benefit end?

A child's benefit ends:

(1)   at death;

(2)   at age eighteen (age nineteen if a full-time elementary or secondary school student);

(3)   when disability ceases if benefits are received only because the child was disabled before age twenty-two (but further benefits may be available if disability occurs again within seven years after childhood disability benefits terminate); or

(4)   when married. However, marriage of a disabled child age eighteen or over to another Social Security beneficiary over age eighteen (other than to a person receiving child's benefits under age eighteen or age eighteen as a full-time elementary or secondary school student) will ordinarily not terminate the child's benefits.

The benefits of a childhood disability beneficiary, regardless of sex, continue after the child's spouse is no longer eligible for benefits as a childhood disability beneficiary or disabled worker beneficiary.

The child is not entitled to a payment for the month in which any of the foregoing events occur, but benefits will be continued through the second month after the month that a disabled child's disability ceases.

A child's benefit may end if the child is missing. In 1993, the Social Security Administration suspended benefits for a child who disappeared mysteriously and was missing for five years. Further payment of benefits was suspended until the beneficiary's whereabouts and continuing eligibility for benefits could be determined.[1]

156. Will a child's benefits end if the child marries?

Yes, as a general rule. However, marriage of a disabled child over age eighteen to another Social Security beneficiary over age eighteen will ordinarily not terminate the child's benefits (see Q 155).

157. What documents will be needed to apply for a child's benefits?

- •   The applicant's birth certificate or other proof of birth

- •   The child's birth certificate or other proof of birth or adoption

---

1. Social Security Ruling SSR 93-3. https://www.ssa.gov/OP_Home/rulings/oasi/09/SSR93-03-oasi-09.html (Last accessed October 1, 2018).

- The applicant's proof of marriage to the worker

- Proof of U.S. citizenship or lawful alien status if applicant was not born in the United States

- U.S. military discharge paper(s)

- W-2 forms(s) and/or self-employment tax returns for last year

158. What information will be needed to apply for a child's benefits?

- Applicant's name and Social Security number

- The worker's name and Social Security number

- The date of birth, Social Security number and relationship to the worker (i.e., legitimate child, adopted child, stepchild, dependent grandchild, other) of each child listed on the application

- The child's citizenship status

- Whether any child seventeen years of age or older is a student or is disabled

- If any child is the worker's stepchild, when and where the worker and the child's parent married

- Whether applicant is the child's natural or adoptive parent

- Whether any child has a legal guardian

- Whether any child has been adopted by someone other than the worker

- Whether the children live with applicant and whether they lived with the worker during each of the last thirteen months

- Whether any child has ever been married and, if so, the dates and locations of the marriages, and how, when, and where they ended

- Whether applicant or anyone else has ever filed for Social Security benefits, Medicare, or Supplemental Security Income on behalf of the child(ren)

- The amount of each child's earnings for this year, last year and next year

- The dates of adoption for any children adopted by the worker

- Whether applicant has ever been convicted of a felony if applying to be a representative payee

- Whether applicant ever served as a representative payee for someone's Social Security benefits

If the worker is deceased, Social Security will also need the following information:

- The worker's date of birth and his or her name at birth (if different)
- The worker's date of death and the place of death
- The State or foreign country of the worker's fixed permanent residence at the time of death
- Whether the worker was unable to work because of illnesses, injuries, or conditions at any time during the 14 months before his or her death
- Whether the worker was in the active military service before 1968 or ever worked for the railroad industry
- Whether the worker earned Social Security credits under another country's Social Security system
- Whether the worker was employed or self-employed in all years from 1978 through last year
- How much the worker earned in the year of death and the year before death
- Whether the worker ever filed for Social Security benefits, Medicare, or Supplemental Security Income
- Whether each child was living with the worker at the time of death

Widow(er)'s Benefit

159. Is the widow(er) of an insured worker entitled to benefits if there are no children in his or her care?

A widow(er) is entitled to a widow(er)'s benefit based on the deceased spouse's earnings if:

(1)   the widow(er) is age sixty or over, or is at least age fifty but not age sixty and is disabled;

(2)   the worker died fully insured;

(3)   the widow(er) is not entitled to a retirement benefit that is equal to or larger than the worker's primary insurance amount;

(4)   the widow(er) has filed an application for widow(er)'s benefits; and

(5)   the widow(er) is not married except under special circumstances discussed below.

In addition, *one* of the following conditions must be met:

(1)   the widow(er) was married to the deceased worker for at least nine months immediately prior to the worker's death (see exceptions below);

(2)   the widow(er) is the biological mother or father of the worker's child (this require-
        ment is met if a live child was born to the worker and the widow(er), although the
        child need not still survive);

(3)   the widow(er) legally adopted the worker's child during their marriage and before
        the child reached age eighteen;

(4)   the widow(er) was married to the worker when they both legally adopted a child
        under age eighteen;

(5)   the worker legally adopted the widow(er)'s child during their marriage and before
        the child reached age eighteen; or

(6)   the widow(er) was entitled (or potentially entitled) to spouse's, widow(er)'s,
        father's (based on the record of a fully insured individual), mother's (based on
        the record of a fully insured individual), parent's, or childhood disability benefits,
        or to a widow(er)'s, child's (age eighteen or over) or parent's annuity under the
        Railroad Retirement Act, in the month before the month the widow(er) married
        the deceased worker.

A widow(er) is "potentially entitled" if he or she meets all requirements for entitlement,
other than filing of an application and attainment of the required age.

The nine-month duration of marriage requirement is waived if the worker's death was accidental or it occurred in the line of duty while a member of a uniformed service serving on active
duty, or if the widow(er) who was married to the worker at the time of death, was previously
married to and divorced from the worker and the previous marriage had lasted nine months.

The worker's death is "accidental" if he or she received bodily injuries solely through violent,
external, and accidental means and, as a direct result, died within three months after the day
the injuries were received. The exception to the nine-month duration of marriage requirement
does not apply if, at the time of marriage, the worker could not reasonably have been expected
to live for nine months.

An application for widow(er)'s benefits is not required if the person was age sixty-five or
over and entitled to spouse's benefits for the month immediately preceding the month in which
the worker died, or if the person was entitled to mother's or father's benefits for the month
immediately preceding the month in which age sixty-five was attained. If an entitled spouse is
between ages sixty-two and sixty-five when the worker dies and the spouse is not also entitled
to a disability or retirement benefit, the spouse's benefits will automatically be converted to
widow(er)'s benefits.

160. What is the impact of the 2015 Bi-Partisan Budget Act on the ability of a widow or widower to collect from a deceased spouse?

The Bi-Partisan Budget Act signed into law on November 2, 2015 does not impact surviving
spouse benefits as "deemed filing" does NOT apply to widows and widowers. Thus, surviving

spouses can receive the survivor's benefit as early as age sixty (or age fifty if disabled) and switch to their own benefits anywhere from age sixty-two through age seventy.

In the alternative, a surviving spouse may begin collecting their own benefit as early as age sixty-two and switch to the survivor's benefit at their Full Retirement Age. The Full Retirement Age for surviving spouses born between 1943 and 1944 is sixty-six and represents the age that a surviving spouse can collect 100 percent of survivor's benefit.

161. Must the worker be fully insured at death to qualify the widow(er) for a widow(er)'s benefit?

Yes, the widow(er) will not be entitled to a widow(er)'s benefit at age sixty or over if the worker was only currently insured at death (see Q 132, Q 208, and Q 209).

162. Can the divorced spouse of a deceased worker qualify for a widow(er)'s benefit?

A widow(er) is entitled to surviving divorced spouse's benefits on the worker's Social Security record if:

(1)   the surviving divorced spouse was married to the worker for at least ten years prior to the date the divorce became final;

(2)   the surviving divorced spouse is age sixty or over, or is at least age fifty but not age sixty and is disabled;

(3)   the deceased spouse died fully insured;

(4)   the surviving divorced spouse is not married (but see Q 165 below);

(5)   the surviving divorced spouse is not entitled to a retirement benefit that is equal to or greater than the deceased worker's primary insurance amount (PIA); and

(6)   the surviving divorced spouse has filed an application for widow(er)'s benefits.

A surviving divorced spouse meets the ten-year marriage requirement, even if, within the ten-year period, they were divorced, provided they remarried each other no later than the calendar year after the year of the divorce.

163. What are the requirements for a divorced spouse to be able to file for spousal benefits from the former spouse?

These requirements include:

(1)   an application must actually be filed;

(2)   the marriage must have lasted ten years or longer;

(3)   if the divorce was less than two years ago, the ex-spouse upon whose record the benefits are being paid must have also filed an application; and

(4)   each party must be at least sixty-two years of age.

164. What is the earliest age at which a widow(er) can receive a widow(er)'s benefit?

A widow(er) can elect to start receiving a reduced widow(er)'s benefit at age sixty (see Q 165). A disabled widow(er) can start receiving benefits at age fifty.

165. What is the monthly rate of a widow(er)'s benefit?

The monthly amount someone would get is a percentage of the deceased's basic Social Security benefit. It depends on their age and the type of benefit they would be eligible to receive.

A widow(er) who is eligible for a widow(er)'s benefit may apply for a reduced benefit at any time between sixty and full retirement age, or may wait until Full Retirement Age (FRA) to receive a full widow(er)'s benefit. If the widow(er) is Full Retirement Age or older when benefits commence, the monthly benefit is equal to 100 percent of the deceased worker's PIA (the amount the worker would have been entitled to receive upon retirement at Full Retirement Age), plus any additional amount the deceased worker was entitled to because of delayed retirement credits (the delayed retirement credit is discussed at Q 169 and Q 253). If the worker was actually receiving benefits that began before Full Retirement Age, the widow(er) would be entitled to an amount equal to the reduced benefit the worker would have been receiving had he lived (but not less than 82.5 percent of the PIA).

If the widow(er) chooses to receive, and is paid, a reduced widow(er)'s benefit for months before full retirement age, he or she is not entitled to the widow(er)'s full benefit rate upon reaching full retirement age. A reduced benefit is payable for as long as he or she remains entitled to widow(er)'s benefits.

If the widow(er)'s full retirement age is sixty-five, the widow(er)'s benefit is reduced by 19/40 of 1 percent for each month that the widow(er) is under age sixty-five when the benefits commence. A benefit beginning at age sixty will equal 71.5 percent of the deceased worker's PIA. If the widow(er)'s Full Retirement Age is more than sixty-five, the 71.5 percent at age sixty will remain unchanged, but the reduction factor will be different (based on 71.5 percent at age sixty and 100 percent at full retirement age).

The monthly payment amount of a widow(er) who remarries after attaining age sixty is not reduced.

If there are other survivors entitled to benefits based on the deceased worker's earnings record, the widow(er) could receive a smaller benefit because of the family maximum limit. (See Maximum Family Benefits, Q 243 to Q 246, and Table 11.)

If the widow(er) has in care the deceased spouse's child, under sixteen or disabled, who is entitled to child's benefits, for some months while he or she is under sixty-five, his or her widow(er)'s benefits are not reduced for those months below 75 percent of the deceased spouse's PIA.

The surviving divorced spouse's benefit is the same amount as a widow(er)'s benefit. However, it is paid independently of benefits for the former spouse's family. In other words, it is not subject to reduction because of the family maximum limit, and does not affect the family maximum for the former spouse's family.

A widow(er) who files an application for actuarially reduced widow(er)'s benefits in the calendar month following the month his or her spouse died is entitled to one month of retroactive benefit payments.

166. How much will a spouse, aged sixty-four, collect when an older spouse dies at age sixty-nine before filing or receiving benefits?

The spouse is eligible for 100 percent of what the deceased was eligible for in the month of death. If the full retirement age benefit was $2,000 and the spouse died at age sixty-eight, the deceased spouse would have earned twenty-four percent Delayed Retirement Credits, then the surviving spouse's benefit is based on $2,000 plus 16 percent. However, if the surviving spouse takes the benefit at age sixty-four, it will be reduced because of age.

167. How does remarriage affect a widow(er)'s benefits?

The remarriage of a widow(er) or surviving divorced spouse after age sixty, or the remarriage of a disabled widow(er) or disabled surviving divorced spouse after age fifty and after the date he or she became disabled, will not prevent that individual from becoming entitled to benefits on his or her prior deceased spouse's Social Security record.

A widow(er) or a surviving divorced spouse's remarriage before age sixty will prevent entitlement unless the subsequent marriage ends, whether by death, divorce, or annulment. If the subsequent marriage ends, the widow(er) or surviving divorced spouse may become entitled or reentitled to benefits on the prior deceased spouse's earnings record beginning with the month the subsequent marriage ends.

A widower is entitled to benefits even when remarriage takes place prior to the death of the former spouse.

There is a distinct advantage in being able to receive the widow(er)'s benefit instead of the spouse's benefit. Part or all of a spouse's benefit could be lost if the new spouse is under full retirement age and loses benefits by working and earning more than the Social Security earnings limit. The widow(er)'s benefit, on the other hand, will be unaffected by the new spouse's work.

168. If a widow(er) is entitled to a retirement benefit and a widow(er)'s benefit, will the widow(er) receive both benefits?

No, the widow(er) will receive the retirement benefit plus the difference if the widow(er)'s benefit is greater. In other words, the widow(er) will receive only the larger benefit. (See also Reduction in Benefits, Q 251 to Q 255.) The Social Security Administration does not allow "double-dipping" in that a beneficiary will always be paid the larger entitled benefit, but not more than one benefit.

However, it is possible to take a widow(er)'s benefit for a period of time (such as starting at age sixty), and then later apply for a full retirement benefit at full retirement age. It is also possible to take a retirement benefit for a period of time (such as starting at age sixty-two), and then later apply for a full widow(er)'s benefit at the full retirement age.

169. How does the Delayed Retirement Credit affect a widow(er)'s benefit?

A widow(er) whose spouse reaches age sixty-five after 2007 receives an increase in benefits equal to 8 percent, for each year (2/3 of 1 percent per month) in which the spouse deferred retirement benefits between age sixty-five and age seventy.

For spouses' reaching age sixty-five prior to 2008, the increases per year of deferring retirement were as follows:

- Age sixty-five in 2006-2007, 7.5 percent

- Age sixty-five in 2004-2005, 7 percent

- Age sixty-five in 2002-2003, 6.5 percent

- Age sixty-five in 2000-2001, 6 percent

- Age sixty-five in 1998-99, 5.5 percent

- Age sixty-five in 1996-97, 5 percent

- Age sixty-five in 1994-95, 4.5 percent

- Age sixty-five in 1992-93, 4.0 percent

- Age sixty-five in 1990-91, 3.5 percent

- Age sixty-five in 1982-89, 3 percent

- Age sixty-five before 1982, 1 percent

The Delayed Retirement Credit is based on the year of attainment of age sixty-two (not the year of work), and it can be earned only after full retirement age. (See Q 253 for further information.)

A surviving divorced spouse is entitled to the same increase that had been applied to the benefit of the deceased worker or for which the deceased worker was eligible at the time of death.

170. Can a widow(er) lose benefits by working?

Yes. Although benefits are payable regardless of how wealthy the widow(er) is, the widow(er) will lose some or all benefits if she is under the normal retirement age (see Q 46) for the entire year and her earnings exceed $17,640 in 2019. In the year the widow(er) reaches normal retirement age, the widow(er) will lose some or all benefits if her earnings exceed $46,920 in 2019.

However, only earnings earned before the month that normal retirement age is reached count towards the $46,920 limit.

See LOSS OF BENEFITS BECAUSE OF "EXCESS" EARNINGS, Q 322 to Q 336.

171. Will a widow(er)'s benefits be reduced if the widow(er) is receiving a government pension?

Social Security benefits payable to spouses – including surviving spouses and divorced spouses – are reduced (but not below zero) by two-thirds of the amount of any governmental (federal, state, or local) retirement benefit payable to the spouse based on *his or her own earnings* in employment not covered by Social Security if that person's last day of employment was not covered by Social Security. Thus, for the affected group, the spouse's benefit is reduced two dollars for every three dollars of the government pension. However, the Social Security Protection Act of 2004 generally requires that a person work in covered employment for five years to be exempt from this Government Pension Offset (GPO). See Q 108 for more information on the GPO.

This offset against Social Security benefits does not apply if the individual:

(1)   met all the requirements for entitlement to Social Security benefits that existed and applied in January 1977; and

(2)   received or was eligible to receive a government pension between December 1977 and December 1982.

Generally, federal workers hired before 1984 are part of the Civil Service Retirement System (CSRS) and are not covered by Social Security. Federal workers hired after 1983 are covered by the Federal Employees' Retirement System Act of 1986 (FERS), which includes Social Security coverage. Legislation provided an opportunity for federal employees covered by CSRS to join FERS in 1987 (and thereby obtain Social Security coverage). Thus, a CSRS employee who switched to FERS during this period immediately became exempt from the government-pension offset.

Federal employees who switch from CSRS to FERS during any election period on or after January 1, 1988, are exempt from the government-pension offset only if they have five or more years of federal employment covered by Social Security beginning January 1, 1988. This rule also applies to certain legislative branch employees who first become covered under FERS on or after January 1, 1988.

Pensions based wholly on service performed as a member of a uniformed service, whether on active or inactive duty, are excluded from the offset.

172. How is the effect of public employee pension income on how Social Security benefits calculated?

There are TWO factors that come into play.

Firstly, the **Windfall Elimination Provision (WEP)** – which affects Social Security benefits based upon what you can receive on your own work record because of pensions from a job which did NOT contribute to Social Security. Under the WEP, the Social Security benefit reduction is capped at one-half of the amount of the pension from noncovered employment, which substantially reduces the WEP penalty and prevents the WEP adjustment from falling disproportionately on households in the lowest earnings category. Social Security benefits are based on the worker's average monthly earnings adjusted for inflation. This average is separated into three brackets: The first is 90 percent of the first $926 of a person's average wage. With WEP, the 90 percent can be as low at 40 percent. The fact sheets on WEP and GPO from Social Security provide further reference – Publication Numbers 05-10045 (WEP)[1] and 05-10007 (GPO).[2]

Secondly, the **Government Pension Offset (GPO)**, reduces Social Security benefits paid to spouses or survivors when the spouse or survivor earned a pension from a government job that was not covered by Social Security. The GPO reduction equals two-thirds of the amount of the pension payment from noncovered government work.

Efforts to repeal the Windfall Elimination Provision and the Government Pension Offset have thus far been unsuccessful.

173. When do widow(er)'s benefits end?

Widow(er)'s benefits end when:

(1)   the widow(er) dies; or

(2)   the widow(er) becomes entitled to a retirement benefit which is as large as or larger than the deceased worker's primary insurance amount; or

(3)   the widow(er)'s disability ceases.

If a widow(er)'s disability ceases, the last month of entitlement is the second month after the month in which the disability ceased, except that entitlement continues if the widow(er) becomes age sixty-five on or before the last day of the third month after the disability ends.

Disabled Widow(er)'s Benefit

174. Is a disabled widow(er) entitled to benefits starting before age sixty?

A disabled widow(er) (or surviving divorced widow(er)) who otherwise qualifies for a widow(er)'s benefit can start receiving a disabled widow(er)'s benefit at any time after attaining age fifty and before attaining age sixty. The monthly benefit will be based on 100 percent of the deceased spouse's PIA, but will be reduced by 28.5 percent so that the benefit equals 71.5 percent of the deceased spouse's PIA at age sixty. The monthly benefit remains at 71.5 percent of the deceased spouse's PIA for disabled widow(er)'s between ages fifty and fifty-nine. Once established, the benefit rate remains the same; it will not be increased when the widow(er) reaches age sixty or full retirement age.

---

1. See Publication No. 05-10045 Windfall Elimination Provision (2018) http://www.ssa.gov/pubs/EN-05-10045.pdf (Last accessed October 1, 2018).
2. See Publication 05-10007 Government Pension Offset (2018) https://www.socialsecurity.gov/pubs/EN-05-10007.pdf (Last accessed October 1, 2018).

Disabled widow(er)'s benefits are payable to a disabled widow(er) or surviving divorced spouse age fifty to fifty-nine if the individual:

(1) meets the definition of disability for disabled workers,

(2) became disabled no later than seven years after the month the worker died or seven years after the last month the widow(er) was previously entitled to benefits on the worker's earnings record,

(3) has been disabled throughout a waiting period of five consecutive full calendar months, except that no waiting period is required if the widow(er) was previously entitled to disabled widow(er)'s benefits, and

(4) meets the nondisability requirements for a surviving spouse or a surviving divorced spouse.

The first month of entitlement to disabled widow(er)'s benefits is the *latest* of the following months:

(1) either the sixth consecutive calendar month of disability, where a waiting period is required, or the first full calendar month of disability, if a waiting period is not required;

(2) the month the insured spouse died;

(3) the twelfth month before the month the widow(er) applied for benefits; or

(4) the month the widow(er) attains age fifty.

Widow(er)s must meet the definition of disability used to determine if workers are entitled to disability benefits. In other words, the widow(er) must be unable to engage in any substantial gainful activity by reason of physical or mental impairment. The impairment must be medically determinable and expected to last for at least twelve months or result in death.

If benefits to a widow(er) who is disabled based on drug addiction or alcoholism are terminated after thirty-six months of benefits, that person cannot become entitled again to widow(er)'s benefits if drug addiction or alcoholism is a contributing factor material to the later determination of disability. See Q 85.

Parent's Benefits

175. Under what circumstances is a deceased worker's parent entitled to benefits?

The parent of a deceased insured person is entitled to a parent's benefit if:

(1) the insured person was fully insured at the time of death;

(2) the parent files an application for parent's benefits;

(3)   the parent has reached age sixty-two;

(4)   the parent is not entitled to a retirement benefit that is equal to or larger than the amount of the unadjusted parent's benefit after any increase to the minimum benefit;

(5)   the parent was receiving at least one-half support from the insured person;

(6)   evidence that the support requirement was met has been filed with the Social Security Administration within the appropriate time limit; and

(7)   the parent has not remarried since the insured person's death.

The support requirement must be met at:

(1)   the time that the insured person died; or

(2)   the beginning of a period of disability that was established for the deceased if it continued up until the month in which he or she died.

Evidence of support must be filed within the two-year period:

(1)   after the date of the death of the insured person, if that point is being used; or

(2)   after the month in which the insured person had filed an application to establish a period of disability, if that point is being used. Evidence of support must be filed within the appropriate period, even though the parent may not be eligible for benefits at that time (e.g., has not reached retirement age). The time limit may be extended for good cause.

The insured provided one-half of a parent's support if:

(1)   the insured made regular contributions for the parent's ordinary living costs;

(2)   the amount of these contributions equaled or exceeded one-half of the parent's ordinary living costs; and

(3)   any income (from sources other than the insured person) for support purposes was one-half or less of the parent's ordinary living costs.

The insured was not providing at least one-half of the parent's support unless the insured had done so for a reasonable period of time. Ordinarily, the Social Security Administration will consider a reasonable period to be the twelve-month period immediately preceding the time when the one-half support requirement must be met.

176. Who is a parent for the purpose of receiving a parent's benefit?

One of the following conditions must be met:

(1)   the parent is a natural parent and would be eligible under the law of the state of the worker's domicile to share in the intestate property of the worker as the worker's father or mother;

(2)   the parent has legally adopted the insured person before the insured person attained age sixteen; or

(3)   the person claiming benefits became the deceased's stepparent by a marriage entered into before the deceased had attained age sixteen.

177. What is the amount of a parent's monthly benefit?

A parent's benefit is equal to 82.5 percent of the deceased worker's Primary Insurance Amount (PIA), if there is only one eligible parent. If two parents are entitled to benefits, the benefit for each is 75 percent of the worker's PIA. The full benefit is payable at age sixty-two. However, because of the maximum family limit, the monthly benefit actually received by a parent may be less. If total monthly benefits payable on the basis of one worker's earnings record exceeds the family maximum, all benefits are reduced proportionately, to bring the total within the family maximum.

See Maximum Family Benefits, Q 243 to Q 246.

178. Can a parent receive benefits, even if the worker's widow(er) and children are eligible for benefits?

Yes, but benefits payable to a parent may reduce the benefits payable to the worker's widow(er) and children. See Q 179.)

179. May benefits payable to a parent reduce the benefits payable to the worker's widow(er) and children?

Yes, because the total amount of monthly benefits based on one worker's Social Security account is limited by a maximum family benefit ceiling. If total benefits computed separately exceed this limit, all benefits are reduced proportionately to bring the total within the family maximum. (See Maximum Family Benefits, Q 243 to Q 246.)

180. Is a parent's benefit starting at age sixty-two smaller than one starting at age sixty-five?

No, the full parent's benefit is payable (to a father or mother) at age sixty-two.

181. If a person is entitled to a parent's benefit and a retirement benefit, will he receive both full benefits?

If the parent is also eligible for a retired worker's benefit based on his own earnings record, he will receive the retired worker's benefit if it equals or exceeds the parent's benefit. However, he is not compelled to take a reduced retired worker's benefit before Full Retirement Age (see Q 46). He can receive the parent's benefit and then switch to a full retired worker's benefit at

Full Retirement Age. The Social Security Administration always pays the higher benefit to which the individual is entitled but not more than one benefit.

182. Can a person lose a parent's benefit by working?

Yes, a person will lose some or all benefits if the person is under normal retirement age for the entire year and his earnings exceed $17,640 in 2019. In the year the person reaches normal retirement age (see Q 52), he will lose some or all benefits if his earnings exceed $46,920 in 2019. However, only earnings earned before the month that he or she reaches normal retirement age count toward the $46,920 limit.

See LOSS OF BENEFITS BECAUSE OF "EXCESS" EARNINGS, Q 318 to Q 336.

183. When do a parent's benefits end?

When the parent dies, marries (but see Q 184), or when the parent becomes entitled to a retirement benefit or disability benefit equal to or larger than the amount of the unadjusted parent's benefit.

184. If a parent remarries after the worker's death, will the parent lose benefits?

Yes, unless the marriage is to a person entitled to monthly Social Security benefits as a divorced spouse, widow(er), mother, father, parent, or a disabled child aged eighteen or over.

Lump-Sum Death Payment

185. What is the amount of the Social Security lump-sum death payment?

A lump-sum death benefit of $255 is paid upon the death of an insured worker, provided he is survived by a spouse who was living in the same household as the deceased at the time of death, or a spouse or dependent child eligible to receive Social Security benefits for the month of death based on his earnings record. This benefit was established by the Omnibus Budget Reconciliation Act of 1981 which made two changes to lump-sum death benefit:

1. Previously if no spouse or child of the deceased worker was eligible for receipt of the lump-sum death benefit, a funeral home or other party who was responsible for the funeral expenses could sometimes claim the benefit. After the 1981 changes, the only people eligible for the lump-sum death benefit are

   a. a spouse who was living with the worker at the time of his/her death, or

   b. a spouse or child who is receiving monthly benefits on the worker's record.

2. The second change in the 1981 law eliminated the minimum benefit guarantee of previous law. To prevent lump-sum death benefits from being lower than $255 the law provides that the provisions of the 1981 OBRA act which eliminated the minimum benefit are not considered when computing the lump-sum death benefit

a. current law provides that the benefit is three times the PIA, or $255, which-
    ever is less. The PIA is computed as if the minimum benefit repeal provision
    of the 1981 law had never been passed.

Also, the lump-sum death benefit is paid to a spouse when the widow(er) and the deceased
customarily lived together as husband and wife in the same residence. While temporary separations do not necessarily preclude the Social Security Administration from considering a couple
to be living in the same household, extended separations (including most that last six months
or more) generally indicate the couple was not living in the same household.

"Living in the same household" requires a male and female living together as husband and
wife in the same residence. The couple may be considered to be living in the same household
although one of them is temporarily absent from the residence. An absence is considered
temporary if:

(1) it was due to service in the United States Armed Forces;

(2) it was six months or less and neither spouse was outside of the United States dur-
     ing this time, and the absence was due to business, employment, or confinement
     in a hospital, nursing home, other medical institution, or a penal institution;

(3) it was for an extended separation, regardless of the duration, due to the confine-
     ment of either spouse in a hospital, nursing home, or other medical institution, if
     the evidence indicates that the spouses were separated solely for medical reasons
     and the spouses otherwise would have resided together;

(4) it was based on other circumstances, and it is shown that the spouses could have
     expected to live together in the near future.

The lump-sum death payment is paid in the following order of priority:

(1) The widow(er) of the deceased wage earner who was living in the same household
     as the deceased wage earner (or customarily lived together as husband and wife in
     the same residence) at the time of death

(2) The widow(er) (excluding a divorced spouse) who is eligible for or entitled to
     benefits based on the deceased wage earner's record for the month of death

(3) Children who are eligible for, or entitled to, benefits based on the deceased wage
     earner's record for the month of death

If no surviving widow(er) or child as defined above survives, no lump sum is payable.

However, if an otherwise eligible widow(er) dies before making application for the
lump-sum death payment or before negotiating the benefit check, the legal representative
of the estate of the deceased widow(er) may claim the lump-sum payment. Where the legal
representative of the estate is a state or political subdivision of a state, the lump-sum death
benefit is not payable.

The lump-sum death benefit is not payable to an otherwise ineligible child of the wage earner after the wage earner's widow, who applied for the benefit, died before it could be paid.[1]

No part of the lump-sum benefit is taxable.[2]

186. Is the lump-sum death benefit payable only if the worker was fully insured at death?

No, it is payable if the worker was either fully or currently insured.

187. Must an application be made for the lump-sum death benefit?

An application need not be made by the widow(er) if he or she was receiving a spouse's benefit when the insured person died. Otherwise, an application must be filed within two years after the insured person's death unless good cause can be shown why the application was not filed within the two-year period.

Prisoners

188. Can imprisoned individuals get Social Security or SSI payments?

Both Social Security and Supplemental Security Income prohibit payments to most prisoners.

Social Security benefits are suspended if an individual is confined to a jail, prison or other penal institution for more than thirty continuous days due to a criminal conviction. Social Security WILL continue to pay benefits to a dependent spouse or children as long as they remain eligible.

SSI recipients will have payments stopped after month of imprisonment.

Social Security and SSI benefits can be reinstated with the month of release if the pre-release procedures are followed, however SSI recipients who are confined twelve consecutive months or longer, must reapply for SSI and again be approved.

189. How does the No Social Security Benefits for Prisoners Act of 2009 affect prisoners?

The Act prohibits payment of any retroactive Title II or Title XVI payments to a current or terminated beneficiary or recipient who is subject to suspension because he or she is:

- a prisoner,

- confined in a public institution based on a court order for a criminal act (CPICO);

- a fugitive felon (FF); or

- in violation of probation or parole (PPV).

---

1. Social Security Ruling 85-24a, 20 CFR 404.392, October 1985. https://www.ssa.gov/OP_Home/rulings/oasi/17/SSR85-24-oasi-17.html (Last accessed October 2, 2018).
2. See Publication 915. https://www.irs.gov/pub/irs-pdf/p915.pdf (Last accessed October 2, 2018).

When the NSSBP was enacted in 2009, Congressional intent was to prohibit any payments of Social Security benefits to prisoners, even retroactive payments. Therefore, under NSSBP, the SSA will not pay retroactive benefits until the beneficiary is no longer a prisoner, probation or parole violator, or fugitive felon. The law also prohibits paying death underpayments on the record of a deceased beneficiary or recipient to a surviving beneficiary or recipient who is not eligible for monthly benefits or payments based on being a prisoner, confined in a public institution based on a court order for a criminal act, a fugitive felon, or parole violator.

Under the No Social Security Benefits for Prisoners Act, Social Security benefit payments are held until an individual is released from incarceration. The benefits are suspended if an individual is convicted of a criminal offense and sent to jail or prison for more than thirty continuous days. Benefits are not suspended if the person is awaiting trial or pleas or not yet convicted.

Payment will be suspended beginning with the month in which the individual was first incarcerated after being convicted and sentenced. Benefits payments would not be received if the individual was confined by court order and at public expense to an institution because of being found to be incompetent to stand trial or found guilty by reason of insanity or mental disease.

190. What are the pre-release procedures for Social Security or SSI payments?

If the institution has a prerelease agreement with the local Social Security office, when the prisoner knows their release date they will need to notify someone at their facility that they want to start SSI payments or Social Security benefits. The institution then will notify Social Security that the individual is likely to meet the requirements for benefits. Social Security will start an application several months before the anticipated release and begin processing the application. Benefits can start as soon as possible after your release.

If the institution does not have a prerelease agreement with the local Social Security office then the prisoner will need to call Social Security at 1-800-772-1213 when they know their anticipated release date. Social Security will set up an appointment with the local Social Security office.

COVERAGE

Qualification

191. How does someone become qualified for retirement, survivor, and disability benefits under Social Security?

By becoming "insured". Most types of benefits are payable if the person is *fully* insured. Some types of benefits are payable if the person is either *fully* or *currently* insured. A special insured status is required for disability benefits (see Q 210).

A person becomes insured by acquiring a certain number of *quarters of coverage*.

192. How does someone obtain a quarter of coverage as an employee?

For 2019, an employee receives one quarter of coverage for each $1,360 of earnings up to a maximum of four quarters.[1]

> *Example.* Mrs. Hall works for two months in 2019 and earns $2,720. She is credited with two quarters of coverage for the year because she receives one quarter of coverage for each $1,360 of earnings, up to a maximum of four. In order to receive four quarters of coverage in 2018, Mrs. Hall would have needed earnings totaling $5,440 ($1,360 × 4 = $5,440).

This method of determining quarters of coverage will also be used for years after 2014, but the measure of earnings ($1,360 in 2019) will automatically increase each year, to take into account increases in average wages.

However, see Q 194 for quarters that cannot be counted as quarters of coverage, regardless of whether the earnings requirement has been met.

193. How does someone obtain a quarter of coverage as a self-employed person?

For 2019, a person who is self-employed receives one quarter of coverage for each $1,360 of earnings from self-employment, up to a maximum of four quarters.[2]

Note that earnings from self-employment are gross receipts minus expenses in the business. Therefore, if the business suffers a loss or if profits are low for a particular year, the self-employed person could earn less than four quarters of coverage.

> *Example.* Mr. Smith is self-employed. His gross receipts for the year are $50,000, but his expenses for the year are $48,000. Because his earnings from self-employment are only $2,000 he earns only one quarter of coverage. If Mr. Smith had incurred expenses in excess of $48,640 he would not have earned any quarters of coverage ($50,000 − $48,640 = $1,360).

---

1. See Generally 20 CFR 404.
2. See Generally 20 CFR 404.

194. What calendar quarters cannot be counted as quarters of coverage even though the earnings requirement has been met?

A calendar quarter cannot be counted as a quarter of coverage if:

- it begins after the calendar quarter in which the person died;

- it has not started yet;

- it is within a period of disability that is excluded in figuring benefit rights (see BENEFIT COMPUTATION, Q 230 to Q 259). (However, the beginning and ending quarters of a prior disability period may be counted as quarters of coverage if the earnings requirement is met in these quarters.)

    Example. Mr. Smith dies on June 24, 2019, after having earned $132,900 (the maximum earnings base for 2019). Normally he would be credited with four quarters of coverage for that year (see Q 192). However, he is credited with only two because the quarters after his death cannot be counted.

195. How do the requirements of the Social Security Protection Act of 2004 (SSPA) affect insured status?

Alien workers, who had Social Security numbers assigned on or after January 1, 2004, must meet ONE of the following additional requirements to become either fully or currently insured and to establish eligibility under Social Security or Medicare.[1] These requirements affect members of the family of the alien worker as well.

(1)   The alien worker must have been issued a Social Security Number for work purposes at any time on or after January 1, 2004; or

(2)   The alien worker must have been admitted to the United States as a nonimmigrant visitor for business (B-1 visa) or as an alien crewman (D-1 or D-2 visa).

Without meeting either of these requirements, the alien worker is not fully insured nor is currently insured – regardless of whether the alien has the required number of Social Security credits. For greater detail on requirements for alien workers, see Additional Requirements for Alien Workers – Social Security Protection Act of 2014.[2]

196. Who is an alien worker under the SSPA?

An alien worker, as defined by the Social Security Protection Act of 2004, is a worker who is not a citizen of the United States as spelled out by the Immigration and Nationality Act, Section 301 through 310.

---

1. Social Security Protection Act of 2004, Section 211.
2. Social Security Program Operations Manual System (POMS) https://secure.ssa.gov/poms.nsf/lnx/0300301102.

197. How does work performed in a foreign country get taken into consideration for determining insured status?

If someone worked under the social security system of a foreign country, those periods of work might be taken into consideration toward meeting Social Security insured status if:

(1)   a social security agreement between the United States and the other country (referred to as a totalization agreement) covers the overseas coverage;

(2)   the worked has at least six credits under U.S. Social Security;

(3)   the worker would not gain insured status without taking the foreign employment into consideration.

If an individual qualifies for coverage because of foreign employment, the amount payable is based on the United State Primary Insurance Amount only, not the foreign earnings.

Unless there is some means of coordinating Social Security coverage, people who work outside their native country may find themselves covered under the systems of two countries simultaneously for the same work. Generally, in this situation, both countries generally require the employer and employee or self-employed person to pay Social Security taxes.

Dual Social Security tax liability is a widespread problem for U.S. multinational companies and their employees because the U.S. Social Security program covers expatriate workers–those coming to the United States and those going abroad—to a greater extent than the programs of most other countries. U.S. Social Security extends to American citizens and U.S. resident aliens employed abroad by American employers without regard to the duration of an employee's foreign assignment, and even if the employee has been hired abroad. This frequently results in dual tax liability for the employer and employee. This dual tax liability can also affect U.S. citizens and residents working for foreign affiliates of American companies.

Foreign workers in the United States may also face dual coverage. U.S. law provides compulsory Social Security coverage for services performed in the United States as an employee, regardless of the citizenship or country of residence of the employee or employer, and irrespective of the length of time the employee stays in the United States. Unlike many other countries, the United States generally does not provide coverage exemptions for non-resident alien employees or for employees who have been sent to work within its borders for short periods. For this reason, most foreign workers in the United States are covered under the U.S. program.

Paying dual Social Security contributions is especially costly for companies that offer "tax equalization" arrangements for their expatriate employees. A firm that sends an employee to work in another country often guarantees that the assignment will not result in a reduction of the employee's after-tax income. Employers with tax equalization programs, therefore, typically agree to pay both the employer and employee share of host country Social Security taxes on behalf of their transferred employees.

The intent of U.S. totalization agreements is to eliminate dual Social Security coverage and taxation while maintaining the coverage of as many workers as possible under the system of the country where they are likely to have the greatest attachment, both while working and after retirement. Each agreement seeks to achieve this goal through a set of objective rules.

A misconception about U.S. agreements is that they allow dually-covered workers or their employers to elect the system to which they will contribute. This is not the case. The agreements, moreover, do not change the basic coverage provisions of the participating countries' Social Security laws—such as those that define covered earnings or work. They simply exempt workers from coverage under the system of one country or the other when their work would otherwise be covered under both systems.

198. With which countries does the United States have totalization agreements?

The following is the list of nations that the United States currently has agreements and the date the agreement went into force:

(1)   A social security agreement between the United States and the other country (referred to as a totalization agreement) covers the overseas coverage

(2)   The worked has at least six credits under US Social Security

(3)   The worker would not gain insured status without taking the foreign employment into consideration.

If an individual qualifies for coverage because of foreign employment, the amount payable is based on the United State Primary Insurance Amount only, not the foreign earnings.

As of 2019, the countries with agreements in place include:

Countries with Social Security Agreements

Country	Entry into Force
Italy	November 1, 1978
Germany	December 1, 1979
Switzerland	November 1, 1980
Belgium	July 1, 1984
Norway	July 1, 1984
Canada	August 1, 1984
United Kingdom	January 1, 1985
Sweden	January 1, 1987
Spain	April 1, 1988
France	July 1, 1988
Portugal	August 1, 1989

Country	Entry into Force
Netherlands	November 1, 1990
Austria	November 1, 1991
Finland	November 1, 1992
Ireland	September 1, 1993
Luxembourg	November 1, 1993
Greece	September 1, 1994
South Korea	April 1, 2001
Chile	December 1, 2001
Australia	October 1, 2002
Japan	October 1, 2005
Denmark	October 1, 2008
Czech Republic	January 1, 2009
Poland	March 1, 2009
Slovak Republic	May 1, 2014
Hungary	September 1, 2016

Fully Insured

199. How does a person become fully insured?

A person becomes fully insured by acquiring a sufficient number of quarters of coverage to meet either of these two tests:[1]

(1)   A person is fully insured if they have forty quarters of coverage (a total of ten years in covered work). Once a person has acquired forty quarters of coverage, they are fully insured for life, even if they spend no further time in covered employment or covered self-employment.

(2)   A person is fully insured if:

(a) they have at least six quarters of coverage; and

(b) have acquired at least as many quarters of coverage as there are years elapsing *after* 1950 (or, if later, after the year in which the person reaches age twenty-one) and *before* the year of death, becoming disabled, or reaching (or will reach) age sixty-two, whichever occurs first. (However, if a year, or any part of a year, falls within an established period of disability, that year need not be counted.)

Note that prior to 1975, there is a transition period in effect for men. See Q 202 and Q 205.

---

1. 42 U.S.C. 414.

The two tests above serve only to determine the *number* of quarters of coverage needed to be fully insured. It is immaterial when these quarters of coverage were acquired (however, they can be acquired only after 1936). Also, in applying Test Number Two, it is not necessary that the quarters of coverage be acquired during the elapsed period. All quarters of coverage, whether within or outside the elapsed period, are counted to determine whether the person has the required number.

For method of determining fully insured status for retirement benefits, see Q 199 to Q 204. For method of determining fully insured status for survivors' benefits, see Q 205. For method of determining fully insured status for disability benefits, see Q 210.

200. Are there other ways of becoming fully insured?

A person becomes fully insured if they are:

(1)   a male born before January 2, 1911 (needs one credit for each year after 1950 up to the year before the year that occurs first as listed below);

    a.   turned age sixty-five;

    b.   died; or

    c.   became disabled;

(2)   a male born from January 2, 1911 through January 1, 1913 (needs one credit for each year after 1950 up to the year before the year that occurs first in the list);

    d.   1975;

    e.   year of death; or

    f.   became disabled.

201. Must a person be fully insured to qualify for retirement benefits?

Yes, in addition to other requirements (see RETIREMENT AND DISABILITY BENEFITS, Q 42 to Q 187), a person must be fully insured.

202. How do you determine the number of quarters of coverage needed for a person to be fully insured for retirement benefits?

To make this determination, count the number of years *after* 1950 (or, if later, after the year in which the person attained age twenty-one), and *before* attaining age sixty-two. Do not count any part of a year which was in an established period of disability. Generally, this is the minimum number of quarters of coverage a person will need to be fully insured. However, the person must have at least six quarters of coverage to be fully insured, and a person is fully insured in any event if the person has forty or more quarters of coverage.[1]

---

1. 42 U.S.C. 414.

See APPENDIX A, TABLE 2, for minimum numbers of quarters of coverage needed to be fully insured for retirement benefits.

Example 1. Mr. Jones applies for retirement benefits in 2018; he attained age sixty-two in 2017. He needs forty quarters of coverage to be fully insured (there are over forty years between 1976 and 2017, the year he attained age sixty-two).

Example 2. Miss Johnson applies for retirement benefits in 2019, the year she attains age sixty-five. She needs forty quarters of coverage to be fully insured (there are over forty years between 1975 and 2016, the year she attained age sixty-two).

Example 3. Mr. Jackson was born in 1957 and will be sixty-two in 2019. Normally, he would need forty quarters of coverage to be fully insured for retirement benefits. However, Mr. Jackson had a period of disability lasting from August 1992 to February 1994. Therefore, he would need only thirty-seven quarters of coverage to be fully insured for retirement benefits (the three years, 1992-1994, would not be counted in determining the number of quarters of coverage required.)

203. Can a person be fully insured for retirement benefits even though not working in covered employment for many years?

Yes. To be fully insured for retirement benefits, a person needs at least as many quarters of coverage as there are years after 1950 (or, if later, the year of the person's twenty-first birthday) and before the year when the person reaches age sixty-two. However, it is immaterial when these quarters of coverage were acquired.

Example. Mrs. Luck was born in 1954. In 2019 (at age sixty-five), she applied for retirement benefits. She needs forty quarters of coverage to be fully insured (one quarter of coverage for each year between 1975 and 2016). Mrs. Luck worked in covered employment for ten years (acquiring forty quarters of coverage) prior to her thirty-fifth birthday in 1989. Mrs. Luck is fully insured — she has the required forty quarters of coverage.

204. Can a person become fully insured after retirement age?

Yes. A person can acquire (or continue to acquire) quarters of coverage after age sixty-two or even after Full Retirement Age.

205. How do you determine the number of quarters of coverage needed for a person to be fully insured at death?

Count the number of years *after* 1950 or, if later, after the year in which the person reached age twenty-one and *before* the year the person died. (But do not count any part of a year of which was in an established period of disability.) A person needs at least this many quarters of coverage to be fully insured at death. However, no person can be fully insured with fewer than six quarters of coverage; and a person is fully insured in any event with forty quarters of coverage.

NOTE: A person born in 1929 reached age twenty-one in 1950. Consequently, for persons born in 1929 or before, count the years after 1950 and before the year of death. For persons born after 1929, see APPENDIX A, TABLE 4 for year of twenty-first birthday.

Example 1. Mr. Smith, who was born in 1957, dies in 2019. He is fully insured if he has forty quarters of coverage (there are forty years between 1977, the year he reached age twenty-one, and 2019, the year in which he died, so that the maximum of forty quarters of coverage applies).

Example 2. Mr. Jones, who was born in 1977, dies in 2019. He is fully insured if he has twenty quarters of coverage (there are twenty years between 1998, the year in which he reached age twenty-one, and 2019, the year in which he died).

The above rule applies to persons who die before age sixty-two. If a person dies after reaching age sixty-two, count only the years between 1950 (or the year of attainment of age twenty-one, if later) and age sixty-two.

206. When is someone deemed to be fully insured?

A person is deemed to be fully insured if they are:

(1)   at least fifty-five years old on January 1, 1984;

(2)   an employee of a nonprofit (noncovered) employer on January 1, 1984; and

(3)   the employer did not have a waiver certificate under Internal Revenue Code section 312(k)[1] in effect on January 1, 1984.

207. How many credits are necessary to be deemed fully insured?

The number of credits necessary for being deemed fully insured depends upon age as of January 1, 1984:

If sixty years old or older on January 1, 1984:	six credits are required
If fifty-nine years old but less than sixty years old on January 1, 1984:	eight credits are required
If fifty-eight years old but less than fifty-nine years old on January 1, 1984	twelve credits are required
If fifty-seven years old but less than fifty-eight years old on January 1, 1984:	sixteen credits are required
If fifty-five years old but less than fifty-seven years old on January 1, 1984:	twenty credits are required

Currently Insured

208. What benefits are payable if a person is only currently insured at death?

Child's benefits, mother's or father's benefits, and the lump-sum death payment. Benefits for a widow(er) age sixty or over, and benefits for a dependent parent, are payable only if the worker was *fully insured* at death.

209. When is a person currently insured?

A person is currently insured when having at least six quarters of coverage during the full thirteen-quarter period ending with the calendar quarter in which:

---

1. IRC section 312 https://www.law.cornell.edu/uscode/text/26/312 (Last accessed October 2, 2018).

(1)   death occurred; or

(2)   most recently became entitled to disability benefits; or

(3)   became entitled to retirement benefits.[1]

The six quarters of coverage need not be consecutive, but they must be acquired *during* the thirteen-quarter period. As insured status is based on quarters of coverage, one can work for as little as two months in two different years and be currently insured. (Calendar quarters, any part of which are in an established prior period of disability, are not counted in figuring the thirteen-quarter period, except that the first and last quarters of the disability period are counted if they are quarters of coverage.)

> *Example.* Mrs. Smith, who reached age twenty-one in 2014, dies in February 2019. Mrs. Smith had started to work in covered employment on October 1, 2016 and worked until her death. During that period, she acquired nine quarters of coverage (four in 2017, because her earnings in October-December were at least $5,200; four in 2018, because her earnings in the year were at least $5,200; and one in 2019, because her earnings in January and February were at least $1,360). Mrs. Smith was currently insured at death because she had more than the required six quarters of coverage in the thirteen-calendar-quarter period.

Insured Status for Disability Benefits

210. What insured status requirements must be met to qualify a person for disability benefits?

A person is qualified for disability benefits fully insured (see Q 205) and has at least twenty quarters of coverage during a forty-quarter period ending with the quarter in which the person is determined to be disabled.[1]

In order to meet the twenty-out-of-forty-quarters requirement, the twenty quarters of coverage need not be consecutive, but they must all be acquired during the forty-quarter period. (A quarter any part of which was included in a prior period of disability is not counted as one of the forty quarters, unless it was a quarter of coverage and was either the first or last quarter of the period.) Generally speaking, this requirement is met if the person has worked five years in covered employment or covered self-employment out of the last ten years before disability.

Special insured status is needed by individuals who are disabled before age thirty-one to qualify for disability benefits or to establish a period of disability. The special insured-status requirements are met if, in the quarter that disability is determined to have begun or in a later quarter, a person:

(1)   is disabled before the quarter in which age thirty-one is attained; and

(2)   has credits in one-half of the quarters, during the period beginning with the quarter after the quarter in which the person attained age twenty-one and ending with the quarter in which the person became disabled.

---

1. 42 U.S.C. 423(c).

The credits must be earned in this period. If the number of elapsing quarters is an odd number, the next lower even number is used, and a minimum of six credits is required. If a person became disabled before the quarter in which age twenty-four is attained, the person must have six quarters of coverage in the twelve-quarter period ending with the quarter in which the disability began.

A special insured status can apply to disabled individuals over age thirty-one who had a previous period of disability established prior to the attainment of age thirty-one; had then met, and currently meet, the special insured requirements (as set out above); and who do not currently meet the 20/40 rule or fully insured status requirements.

To qualify for entitlement to disability benefits, fully insured status is required for a person who meets the statutory definition of blindness.

If a disability period is established for a person, the earnings records are frozen, and the period of disability may be excluded in determining insured status when either becoming eligible for retirement benefits or dying. The disability period may also be excluded in figuring the Primary Insurance Amount for benefit purposes (see Computing Benefits). The same insured status is required to qualify a person for a disability "freeze" as is required for disability benefits.

Computing Benefits

211. In general, how are Social Security benefits determined?

Benefits payable under the retirement, survivors, and disability benefits program are almost always based on the insured's Social Security earnings since 1950. (Under some circumstances – where an individual has little or no earnings since 1950 – benefits may be computed based on earnings since 1937.)

The wage indexing formula is used to compute benefits if disability, death, or age sixty-two occurs after 1978. (See Q 232).

If disability, death, or age sixty-two occurred before 1979, benefits are determined using the simplified old-start benefit computation method. (See Q 230.)

A transition period took place from 1979 through 1983. A worker who became sixty-two, or a worker who died after reaching age sixty-two during this period, is guaranteed that the method producing the larger benefit will be used.

To be eligible for the guarantee, the worker must:

(1)   have had income credited for one year prior to 1979; and

(2)   must not have been disabled prior to 1979.

The transitional guarantee does not apply to disability computations – even if disability occurs after reaching age sixty-two. It does, however, apply to benefits for survivors if the insured becomes sixty-two – then dies – during the transition period. (See Q 247.)

FILING FOR BENEFITS

General Information

212. What procedure should be followed to determine if a person is eligible for Social Security benefits?

An application must be filed for a person to become entitled to benefits, including Medicare, or to establish a period of disability under the retirement, survivors, and disability programs. The easiest and quickest way for most people to apply for benefits is by filling out an application on the Social Security Administration's website, www.ssa.gov. The process normally takes between ten and thirty minutes.

Alternatively, a person can apply by phone, the mail, or by visiting one of the Social Security Administration's 1,230 field offices.[1]

Since a person age sixty-five or older who is entitled to monthly benefits under Social Security or Railroad Retirement is automatically entitled to Medicare Part A Hospital Insurance and Part B Medical Insurance, no separate application is required. However, a person who is *eligible* for monthly Social Security benefits and is at least age sixty-five may apply for Hospital Insurance and Medical Insurance without applying for Social Security benefits. Also, an application is necessary for persons age sixty-five or older who have no Social Security coverage or other entitlement, but who wish to file for Hospital Insurance and Medical Insurance, and who are willing to pay the monthly premiums involved.

Prompt filing of an application is generally advantageous, even if the person is still working. Delay may result in fewer payments, since monthly benefits cannot be paid retroactively in some instances and not for more than twelve months (depending on the situation) before the month in which the application is filed.

A person may be entitled to monthly benefits retroactively for months before the month in which he filed an application for benefits. Retirement and survivor claims may be paid for up to six months retroactively and benefits may be paid in certain cases involving disability up to twelve months retroactively. The claimant is entitled to benefits beginning with the first month in the retroactive period in which all the requirements for entitlement to benefits are met (except for the filing of an application). For example, if a man reaches age sixty-six in March 2019 and is then fully insured but does not file an application for retirement benefits until March 2020, he may be entitled retroactively beginning with the month of September 2019.

Retroactive benefits for months prior to attainment of full retirement age are not payable to a retired worker, a spouse, or a widow(er), if this would result in a permanent reduction of the monthly benefit amount. However, there are exceptions to this rule, which permit payment of retroactive benefits even though it causes an actuarial reduction in benefits. This limitation

---

1. See https://www.ssa.gov/org/ (Last accessed October 2, 2018).

does not apply if the applicant is a surviving spouse or surviving divorced spouse who is under a disability and could be entitled to retroactive benefits for any month before attaining age sixty.

A widow(er) or surviving divorced spouse who files an application in the month after the month of the worker's death may be entitled to benefits in the month of his or her death if otherwise eligible in that month.

Regulations issued by the Social Security Administration establish deemed filing dates for applications filed by persons who have received misinformation about eligibility from the Social Security Administration. The Social Security Administration may establish an earlier filing date when there is evidence that the Social Security Administration gave the claimant misinformation, which caused the claimant not to file an application at the appropriate time.

> *Example.* Mr. Smith contacts a Social Security office at age sixty-two to inquire about applying for retirement benefits. He is told by an employee of the Social Security Administration that he must be age sixty-five to be eligible for retirement benefits. This information is incorrect and causes Mr. Smith to delay filing an application for retirement benefits for three years. When he reaches age sixty-five, he contacts the Social Security Administration and is told that he could have received reduced retirement benefits at age sixty-two. After filing an application for retirement benefits, Mr. Smith provides information to show that a Social Security Administration employee provided misinformation and requests a deemed filing date based on the misinformation he received when he was age sixty-two.

If the Social Security Administration determines that a person failed to apply for monthly benefits because it gave the person incorrect information about eligibility for such benefits, the Social Security Administration will deem an application for such benefits to have been filed with the Social Security Administration on the later of:

(1)   the date on which the misinformation was provided to the person; or

(2)   the date on which the person met all of the requirements for entitlement to the benefits, other than the requirement for filing an application for benefits.

Preferred evidence that misinformation was given by the Social Security Administration includes a notice, letter, or other document issued by the Social Security Administration and addressed to the claimant, or the Social Security Administration's record of the claimant's letter, phone call, or visit to an office of the Social Security Administration. In the absence of preferred evidence, the Social Security Administration will consider statements by the claimant about misinformation and other evidence. The claimant's statements, however, must be supported by other evidence in order for the Social Security Administration to find that the claimant was given misinformation.

A person may make a claim for benefits based on misinformation at any time. The claim must be in writing and must contain the information that was provided by the Social Security Administration and why this information resulted in the person not filing an application for Social Security benefits.

A person cannot receive more than one full monthly benefit. If eligible for more than one monthly benefit, the amount payable will be equal to the largest one for which the person is eligible.

Each application form is clearly worded to show its scope as an application for one or more types of benefits. For example, the present applications for entitlement to Medicare Part A Hospital Insurance protection, or for monthly Social Security benefits, may be applications for all benefits that a claimant may be entitled to on any Social Security earnings record. The scope of any application may, however, be expanded or restricted, as the claimant desires, if appropriate remarks are added in writing prior to adjudication. The Social Security Administration will use the application to make an *initial determination* regarding the amount of benefits, if any.

213. At what point should the survivors of a deceased worker file for survivor's benefits?

An application should be filed immediately in the month of death by or for *each* person who is entitled to a benefit as a survivor of a deceased worker.

An application for the lump-sum death payment must be filed within the two-year period after the worker's death by the person eligible for the lump sum, unless the eligible person is the widow(er) of the deceased worker and was entitled to spouse's benefits for the month before the month in which the worker died. In the latter case, no application for the lump sum is required.

214. When should an application for disability benefits be filed?

An application for the establishment of a period of disability may be filed before the first day this period can begin. In these circumstances, the application will be effective if the person actually becomes eligible for the benefit, or for the period of disability, at some time before a final decision on the application is made.

When a person applies for monthly disability benefits, he simultaneously applies for a "disability freeze" (see Q 258).

215. When should a person file an application for the lump-sum death payment?

An application for the lump-sum death payment must be filed within a two-year period by the person eligible for the lump sum, unless the eligible person is the widow(er) of the deceased worker and was entitled to spouse's benefits for the month before the month in which the worker died. In the latter case, no application for the lump sum is required.

An application filed after the two-year period will be deemed to have been filed within the two-year period if there is good cause for a failure to file the application in time. Good cause means that the claimant did not file the lump-sum death payment application within the time limit because of:

(1) circumstances beyond the claimant's control, such as extended illness, communication difficulties, etc.;

(2) incorrect or incomplete information given the claimant by the Social Security Administration;

(3)   efforts to get the evidence to support the claim, not realizing she could file the application within the time limit and submit the supporting evidence later; or

(4)   unusual or unavoidable circumstances that show that the claimant could not reasonably be expected to have been aware of the need to file the application within a specified period.

Proof Required

216. What proofs are required before survivors' and retirement benefits can be paid?

Social Security survivors' and retirement benefits cannot be paid until satisfactory proofs have been furnished. Claimants must prove their identity and that they have met all the requirements to be entitled to the benefits which are being claimed. Evidence usually required to be submitted to the Social Security Administration in claims for monthly benefits is summarized below:

- *Insured person*: evidence of age. If disability is involved, evidence to establish disability.

- *Spouse (sixty-two or over)*: evidence of age and marriage.

- *Spouse under sixty-two (child in care)*: evidence of marriage and child in care.

- *Divorced spouse (sixty-two or over)*: evidence of age, marriage and divorce.

- *Child*: evidence of age, parent-child relationship, dependency or support, school attendance (if eighteen to nineteen years old and not disabled), and death of the worker in survivor claims. If disability is involved, evidence to establish disability.

- *Widow(er) (sixty or over, fifty or over if disabled)*: evidence of age, marriage, and death of worker. If disability is involved, evidence to establish disability.

- *Surviving divorced spouse*: evidence of age, marriage, divorce, and death of worker. If disability is involved, evidence to establish disability.

- *Widow(er) under sixty-two or surviving divorced mother or father (child in care)*: evidence of marriage, divorce (surviving divorced mother or father only), parent-child relationship, child in care, and death of worker.

- *Parent*: evidence of age, parent-child relationship, dependency or support, and death of worker.

217. What are acceptable proofs of death?

Evidence of death may consist of:[1]

---

1. Social Security Handbook, Section 1720, Evidence of Death. http://www.ssa.gov/OP_Home%2Fhandbook/handbook.17/handbook-1720.html (Last accessed October 2, 2018).

(1)   a certified copy of a public record of death;

(2)   a Statement of Death[1] by a funeral director;

(3)   a statement of death by the attending physician or the superintendent, physician, or intern of the institution where the person died;

(4)   a certified copy of the coroner's report of death or the verdict of the coroner's jury;

(5)   a certified copy of an official report of death or finding of death, made by an agency or department of the United States government that is authorized or required to make such report or finding in the administration of any law of the United States;

(6)   if death occurred outside the United States (U.S.), an official report of death by a U.S. Consul or other employee of the State Department; or a copy of the public record of death in the foreign country.

Note that obituaries are NOT considered proof of death, but can be used as leads to gain acceptable proof.

If none of the above can be obtained, one can submit statements from two or more persons (preferably not related to the claimant) who saw the body. These statements must be complete and indicate the following:

(1)   why none of the types of evidence above can be obtained;

(2)   the date and place of death;

(3)   the date and place of viewing the body;

(4)   the cause of death, if known;

(5)   the occupation, age, sex, and race of the deceased;

(6)   the relationship of the deceased, if any, to the person making the statements; and

(7)   the basis for identification of the body.

Recent court cases have held that a claimant had to show only that the missing person had been absent for seven years, and that the Social Security Administration had the burden of proving that the individual was still alive, or an explanation to account for the individual's absence in a manner consistent with continued life.

Social Security Administration regulations conform with the court cases, by providing that the presumption of death arises when a claimant establishes that an individual has been absent from his residence and not heard from for seven years. Once the presumption arises, the burden

---

1. Form SSA-721, Statement of Death by Funeral Director https://www.socialsecurity.gov/forms/ssa-721.pdf (Last accessed October 2, 2018).

then shifts to the Social Security Administration to rebut the presumption, either by presenting evidence that the missing individual is still alive or by providing an explanation to account for the individual's absence in a manner consistent with continued life rather than death.

The regulations also state that the presumption of death can be rebutted by evidence that establishes that the person is still alive or explains the individual's absence in a manner consistent with continued life. Two examples are provided. In one, evidence in a claim for surviving child's benefits showed that the worker had wages posted in his earnings record in the year following his disappearance. It was established that the wages belonged to the worker and were for work done after he was supposed to have disappeared. The presumption of death is rebutted by evidence (wages belonging to the worker) that the worker is still alive. In a second example, evidence showed that the worker left the family home shortly after a woman, whom he had been seeing, also disappeared. The worker phoned his wife a few days after he left home to tell her he was starting a new life in California. The presumption of death is rebutted in this case, because the evidence explains the worker's absence in a manner consistent with continued life.

No one *convicted* of the felonious and intentional homicide of the worker can be entitled to benefits on the worker's earnings record. Further, the convicted person is considered not to exist in deciding the rights of other persons to benefits on the worker's record.

218. What are the best forms of proof of age and family relationship?

Proof of age is required when age is a factor in determining benefit rights. A public record of birth or a religious record of birth or baptism established or recorded before the individual's fifth birthday must be submitted as proof of age, if available. Where such a document is unavailable, the individual must submit another document or documents that may serve as the basis for a determination of date or birth, provided the evidence is corroborated by other evidence or by information in the records of the Social Security Administration.

Some records that may be submitted are listed below; these records must show the individual's date of birth or age:

(1)   School record

(2)   Census record

(3)   Bible or other family record

(4)   Religious record of confirmation or baptism in youth or early adult life

(5)   Insurance policy

(6)   Marriage record

(7)   Employment record

(8)   Labor union record

(9)   Fraternal organization record

(10) Military record

(11) Voting record

(12) Vaccination record

(13) Delayed birth certificate

(14) Birth certificate of child, showing age of parent

(15) Physician's or midwife's record of birth

(16) Passport

(17) Immigration record

(18) Naturalization record

A person should obtain, and file among his or her valuable papers, the most acceptable form of proof of the ages and relationships of all members of his or her family. This will save time, effort, and money later, when Social Security benefits become payable.

A natural legitimate parent-child relationship may be shown by the child's birth or baptismal certificate if it shows the worker to be the child's parent. If the child is illegitimate, he or she may be considered the worker's child for Social Security purposes if he or she is legitimated, or can inherit the worker's intestate personal property under applicable state law. The evidence required would depend on state law requirements for legitimation or inheritance rights.

The legal adoption of a child may be provided by an amended birth certificate issued as the result of an adoption.

A step-relationship is proved by:

(1) first proving the relationship between the child and the natural (or adopting) parent; and

(2) then proving the marriage between the natural (or adopting) parent and the stepparent.

Evidence of full-time school attendance is required if a child age eighteen to nineteen is not under a disability. Necessary information is obtained from the child and verified by the school or schools involved.

A ceremonial marriage may be proved by:

(1) a certified copy of the public record of the marriage;

(2) a certified copy of the religious record of the marriage; or

(3) the original marriage certificate.

Evidence to prove a common-law marriage in those states that recognize such marriages must, where obtainable, include:

(1)   if the husband and wife are living, a statement from each and a statement from a blood relative of each;

(2)   if either the husband or wife is dead, a statement from the surviving widow or widower and statements from two blood relatives of the decedent; and

(3)   if both a husband and wife are dead, a statement from a blood relative of the husband and from a blood relative of the wife.

Evidence of termination of a marriage may be required if the claimant's right to benefits depends upon the validity of a subsequent marriage or the termination of a prior marriage. The termination of a marriage may be established by:

(1)   a certified copy of the divorce decree;

(2)   a certified copy of the annulment decree;

(3)   a certified copy of the death certificate; or

(4)   if none of the above is available, any other evidence of probative value.

Evidence that a child is in a claimant's care usually consists of:

(1)   statements by the claimant;

(2)   where the claimant and the child are living apart, statements by the person with whom the child is living or by an official of the school which the child is attending, or both; and

(3)   statements of other people who know the facts, if necessary.

Evidence of support includes a statement from the claimant, and whatever other evidence may be necessary to substantiate the claimant's statements concerning support.

Evidence of United States citizenship may be required in certain cases (for instance, to determine coverage status of people working in foreign countries or the applicability of the alien nonpayment provision). The most acceptable evidence is a birth certificate showing birth within the United States. Other acceptable evidence includes:

(1)   Certificate of Naturalization;

(2)   Citizenship Certificate issued by the Immigration and Naturalization Service to United States citizens who derived their citizenship through another person;

(3)   a United States passport issued by the Department of State;

(4)   Consular report of birth issued by the Department of State;

(5)   proof of marriage to a male United States citizen before September 22, 1922;

(6)   a card of identity and registration as a United States citizen, or an official communication from an American Foreign Service post indicating the individual is registered there as a United States citizen; or

(7)   Form I-197 (United States Citizen Identification Card).[1]

Right to Appeal

219. Is there a review procedure available if a person is disappointed with the Social Security Administration's initial determination regarding benefits?

There is an administrative review process for a person who is dissatisfied with the Social Security Administration's action concerning a claim for benefits. After the Social Security Administration makes an initial determination, further review may be requested by the person or his representative. The administrative review process consists of several steps that must be requested in writing, usually within specified time periods, and in the following order:

(1)   *Reconsideration:* The person or representative may request that the initial determination be reconsidered. A reconsideration is a reexamination of the administrative records that results in another determination.

(2)   *ALJ Hearing:* If there is still disagreement with the reconsidered determination, the person or representative may request a hearing before an Administrative Law Judge of the Office of Hearings and Appeals.

(3)   *Appeals Council Review:* If the person disagrees with the administrative law judge's decision or dismissal, he may request a review by the Appeals Council of the Office of Hearings and Appeals, which has the authority to deny or grant review or dismiss the request for any reason for which the administrative law judge could have dismissed. Also, the Appeals Council may, on its own motion, review an administrative law judge's decision.

(4)   *Federal Court Action – United States Distict Court:* After Appeals Council review (or denial of review), a person who is still dissatisfied may file a civil action in a federal district court.

An initial determination becomes final unless reconsideration is requested within sixty days from the date notice of the initial determination is received by the person or the person's representative. In counting the sixty days, it is presumed that the Notice of Decision is received FIVE DAYS after mailing.

Reconsideration is the first step in the administrative review process that is provided if there is dissatisfaction with the initial determination. The request for reconsideration may be made

---

1. U.S. Citizen Identification Card https://www.uscis.gov/i-9-central/133-list-c-documents-establish-employment-authorization (Last accessed October 2, 2018).

by the claimant, by another person whose benefit rights are affected by the determination, or by the appointed representative of either. The reconsideration must be requested in writing by the person (or the person's representative).

The reconsideration process is an independent reexamination of all evidence on record related to the case by the Social Security Administration. It is based on evidence submitted for the initial determination, plus any additional information that the claimant or representative may submit in connection with the reconsideration. The reconsideration is not limited to the issues raised by the claimant. A reconsideration is made by a member of a different staff from the one that made the initial determination and who is specially trained in the handling of reconsiderations. The claimant receives a personalized notice detailing the basis for the determination in his case.

When a person can demonstrate that he failed to appeal an adverse decision because of reliance on incorrect, incomplete, or misleading information provided by the Social Security Administration, his failure to appeal may not serve as the basis for denial of a second application for any Social Security benefit. This protection applies to both initial denials and reconsiderations. The Social Security Administration is required to include, in all notices of denial, a clear, simple description on the effect of reapplying for benefits rather than filing an appeal.[1]

The Social Security Administration issued a ruling in 1995 on establishing good cause for late filing of a request for administrative review, for a claimant who received an initial or reconsideration determination notice that did not state that filing a new application instead of a request for administrative review could result in the loss of benefits. The Social Security Administration will make a finding of good cause for late filing of a request for administrative review for a claim, if the claimant received an initial or reconsideration determination notice and demonstrates that, as a result of the notice, he did not timely request such review. Notices covered by this ruling include only those dated prior to July 1, 1991, that did not state that filing a new application for benefits instead of a request for review could result in the loss of benefits. If the adjudicator determines that good cause exists, the Social Security Administration will extend the time for requesting administrative review and take the action that would have been appropriate had the claimant filed a timely request for administrative review.[2]

220. How can a person appeal the reconsideration determination?

A hearing before an Administrative Law Judge may be requested by the person or appointed representative who disagrees with the reconsidered determination, or by a person who can show that the reconsidered determination will harm the person's rights under the Social Security Act.

The person and/or person's representative may appear in person, submit new evidence, examine the evidence used in making the determination under review, give testimony, and present and question witnesses. If a person properly waives the right to an oral hearing, the Administrative Law Judge will ordinarily make a decision on the basis of the evidence already submitted or otherwise obtained by the person or any other party to the hearing.

---

1. Publication 05=10058 Your Right to Question the Decision Made on Your Claim https://www.ssa.gov/pubs/EN-05-10058.pdf July 2017 edition (Last accessed October 2, 2018).
2. Social Security Ruling SSR 95-1p. https://www.ssa.gov/OP_Home/rulings/oasi/33/SSR95-01-oasi-33.html (Last accessed October 2, 2018).

If the claim is about the amount of Part A Hospital Insurance benefits under Medicare, the amount in question must be $100 or more. Carriers review complaints about the amount of Medical Insurance benefits under Medicare.

A person may also be able to use an expedited appeals procedure, if he or she has no dispute with the findings of fact of the reconsideration determination beyond a contention that a section of the applicable statute is unconstitutional. (For further details, see Q 224.)

Notice of time and place of the hearing is sent by the Administrative Law Judge to the parties to the hearing at least twenty days before the date set for the hearing. The hearing is usually held in the area where the person requesting the hearing resides, although the person may be required to travel up to seventy-five miles. (Travel expenses are paid by the government, if travel over seventy-five miles is required.)

At times, the Administrative Law Judge will examine the evidence and certify a case to the Appeals Council with a recommended decision. (See Q 224.)

221. How is a hearing request made and how long will it take from the request to the actual hearing?

A request for a hearing is made by filling out Form HA-501, "Request for Hearing by Administrative Law Judge,"[1] or by writing a letter to the nearest Social Security office, a presiding officer, or with the Appeals Council. If the hearing request is for disability benefits, then the appeal may be made online.

The request for a hearing must be made within sixty days after the date that the notice of the reconsidered decision is received and must include:

(1) the name and Social Security number of the individual;

(2) the reason for disagreeing with the reconsidered or revised determination;

(3) a statement of additional evidence that will be submitted; and

(4) the name and address of the individual's representative, if any. The sixty-day time limit can be extended if there is a good reason. Note that the SSA presumes receipt of the notice of decision is five days after mailing.

A beneficiary of disability benefits has the option of having his benefits continued through the hearing stage of appeal if there was a determination of medical improvement (also called medical cessation). But where benefits are adversely affected because of the performance of substantial gainful activity (also called work cessation) benefits may not be continued. If the earlier unfavorable determinations are upheld by the administrative law judge, the benefits that were received during the appeal process are subject to recovery by the Social Security Administration. (If an appeal is made in good faith, recovery may be waived.) Medicare eligibility is also continued, but Medicare benefits are not subject to recovery.

---

1. Form HA-501 Request for Hearing By Administrative Law Judge http://www.ssa.gov/fodrms/ha-501.pdf (Last accessed October 2, 2018).

In recent years, the Social Security Administration has come under criticism for its backlog of hearings. In the 2008 fiscal year, the average processing time was 514 days. It had decreased to 415 days by June 2010. Since then, the Social Security Administration has devoted efforts to decrease the processing times. Processing times were reduced to 353 days by the end of 2012, but climbed to 378 for 2013, 437 for 2014, 477 for 2015 and 544 2016. Figures reported on August 25, 2017 show an average backlog of 602 days – ranging from 154 days in the Mayaguez office to a staggering 854 days in San Juan, PR.[1]

222. How long are the average delays in Social Security Hearing offices?

The following is a list of Office of Disability Adjudication and Review (ODAR) with the average number of days until final disposition of hearing requests. The average shown is combined average of all cases completed in that particular office. This can be helpful estimating time until final disposition.

Rank	Hearing Office	Region	Average Processing Time
1	MAYAGUEZ	2	154
2	PROVIDENCE	1	359
3	FORT SMITH	6	382
4	HOUSTON NORTH	6	415
5	OKLAHOMA CITY	6	416
6	MANCHESTER	1	422
7	BOSTON	1	424
8	SHREVEPORT	6	432
9	ALEXANDRIA	6	441
10	DALLAS NORTH ODAR	6	453
11	MIDDLESBORO	4	458
12	LITTLE ROCK	6	467
12	PORTLAND ME	1	467
14	METAIRIE	6	468
15	FORT WORTH	6	479
16	SPRINGFIELD MA	1	480
17	HONOLULU	9	492
18	ANCHORAGE	10	494
18	HARTFORD	1	494
20	DAYTON	5	509
20	NASHVILLE	4	509
22	DETROIT	5	516
22	FORT MYERS FL	4	516

1. Hearing Office Average Processing Time Ranking Report for Fiscal Year Ending August 31, 2018. https://www.ssa.gov/appeals/DataSets/ 05_Average_Processing_Time_Report.html (Last accessed October 2, 2018).

Rank	Hearing Office	Region	Average Processing Time
24	TULSA	6	518
25	LIVONIA MI	5	522
26	NEW ORLEANS	6	527
26	SAN ANTONIO	6	527
28	NEW HAVEN	1	530
29	FARGO	8	535
30	AKRON OH	5	540
30	DALLAS DOWNTOWN	6	540
30	KINGSPORT	4	540
33	JACKSON	4	541
34	PEORIA	5	542
35	LAWRENCE MA	1	548
36	MONTGOMERY	4	549
37	OAK PARK	5	550
38	FORT WAYNE	5	551
39	CLEVELAND	5	555
40	CHATTANOOGA	4	556
41	TOPEKA KS	7	557
42	ALBUQUERQUE	6	561
43	SPOKANE	10	563
44	CHICAGO	5	564
44	TOLEDO OH	5	564
46	FRANKLIN TN	4	567
47	KANSAS CITY	7	568
48	LAS VEGAS	9	569
48	TALLAHASSEE FL	4	569
50	RENO	9	570
50	SACRAMENTO	9	570
52	TACOMA	10	572
53	FLORENCE	4	574
53	MINNEAPOLIS	5	574
55	LANSING	5	575
56	KNOXVILLE	4	576
57	SPRINGFIELD MO	7	580
58	ST PETERSBURG FL	4	581
59	DENVER	8	583

Rank	Hearing Office	Region	Average Processing Time
59	MOBILE	4	583
59	OAK BROOK	5	583
62	ORANGE	9	585
63	BILLINGS	8	588
64	ORLAND PARK	5	589
64	PORTLAND OR	10	589
66	LOS ANGELES DOWN-TOWN	9	591
67	LEXINGTON	4	592
68	EVANSVILLE	5	593
69	MCALESTER	6	597
69	STOCKTON	9	597
71	WICHITA	7	598
72	COLUMBIA MO	7	599
72	HOUSTON-BISSONNET	6	599
74	MACON	4	600
74	MEMPHIS	4	600
76	SAN BERNARDINO	9	603
77	MADISON	5	605
77	SANTA BARBARA	9	605
79	COLORADO SPRINGS	8	607
80	SEATTLE	10	609
81	NORWALK	9	610
81	SAN FRANCISCO	9	610
83	OMAHA	7	611
83	RIO GRANDE VALLEY TX	6	611
85	ATLANTA NORTH	4	612
85	EVANSTON	5	612
87	NORFOLK	3	614
88	TUPELO	4	615
89	INDIANAPOLIS	5	617
89	SALT LAKE CITY	8	617
91	CHARLOTTESVILLE	3	618
92	MILWAUKEE	5	621
93	TUCSON	9	622
93	WEST DES MOINES	7	622

Rank	Hearing Office	Region	Average Processing Time
95	BIRMINGHAM	4	624
96	FLINT	5	626
97	DOVER	3	628
97	SAVANNAH	4	628
99	CINCINNATI	5	629
99	HATTIESBURG	4	629
99	SYRACUSE	2	629
102	PADUCAH	4	630
102	PHOENIX	9	630
104	ORLANDO	4	631
105	MT PLEASANT MI	5	632
105	RALEIGH	4	632
107	SEVEN FIELDS	3	635
108	CREVE COEUR	7	636
109	COVINGTON GA	4	637
110	PHOENIX NORTH	9	639
111	FAYETTEVILLE NC	4	641
112	GRAND RAPIDS	5	642
113	COLUMBUS	5	644
114	MORENO VALLEY CA	9	647
115	BALTIMORE	3	648
116	OAKLAND	9	649
116	SAN JOSE	9	649
116	SAN RAFAEL	9	649
119	HARRISBURG	3	650
120	JACKSONVILLE	4	651
121	HUNTINGTON WV	3	652
122	RICHMOND	3	653
123	COLUMBIA SC	4	655
124	WASHINGTON	3	656
125	ALBANY	2	657
125	LOUISVILLE	4	657
125	PASADENA	9	657
128	NEW YORK VARICK	2	660
128	WILKES BARRE	3	660
130	CHARLESTON WV	3	661

Rank	Hearing Office	Region	Average Processing Time
131	EUGENE	10	664
131	SAN DIEGO	9	664
133	TAMPA	4	666
133	VALPARAISO IN	5	666
135	LOS ANGELES WEST	9	669
136	CHARLESTON SC	4	673
137	ELKINS PARK	3	674
138	ST LOUIS	7	677
139	FT LAUDERDALE	4	678
140	ATLANTA DOWNTOWN	4	685
140	FRESNO	9	685
142	LONG BEACH	9	690
143	MORGANTOWN	3	691
144	GREENVILLE	4	692
145	WHITE PLAINS	2	693
146	PHILADELPHIA EAST	3	698
147	JERSEY CITY	2	700
147	PITTSBURGH	3	700
149	CHARLOTTE	4	702
150	NEWARK	2	709
151	LONG ISLAND	2	712
152	JOHNSTOWN	3	715
152	ROCHESTER	2	715
154	GREENSBORO	4	724
155	ROANOKE	3	727
156	NEW YORK	2	730
157	BRONX	2	736
158	PHILADELPHIA	3	737
159	QUEENS	2	741
160	BUFFALO	2	750
161	SOUTH JERSEY	2	757
162	MIAMI	4	759
163	PONCE	2	808
164	SAN JUAN	2	854

223. What will a hearing cost?

There is no charge for a hearing. If counsel represents an individual, there will, of course be attorney's fees. There are also travel expenses, which are not reimbursed, unless the hearing is held more than seventy-five miles from the individual's home. If the hearing is more than seventy-five miles from the person's home, there are reimbursed for reasonable travel expenses.

224. If an individual disagrees with the hearing decision, may they ask for a review?

Yes. A review of the hearing by the Appeals Council of the Office of Hearings and Appeals must be in writing and must be filed within sixty days from the date the person or the person's representative receives notice of the administrative law judge's action.

Within sixty days from the date of the administrative law judge's decision or dismissal, the Appeals Council may on its own initiative decide to review the action that was taken. Notice of this review is mailed to all parties at the last known address.

The Appeals Council will review a hearing decision or dismissal where:

(1)   there appears to be an abuse of discretion by the administrative law judge;

(2)   there is an error of law;

(3)   the presiding officer's action, findings, or conclusions are not supported by substantial evidence; or

(4)   there is a broad policy or procedural issue that may affect the general public interest.

The Appeals Council will notify the person whether it will review the case. If the Appeals Council decides to review the case, the claimant or representative may request an appearance before the Appeals Council for the presentation of oral arguments. If the Appeals Council determines that a significant question of law or policy is presented, or that oral arguments would be beneficial in rendering a proper decision, the appearance will be granted. The claimant may also file written statements in support of his claim. The Appeals Council will notify the claimant of its action in the case.

The Appeals Council may deny or dismiss a party's request for review, or it may grant the request and either issue a decision or remand the case to an administrative law judge. If the Appeals Council denies a request for review of a decision by an administrative law judge, the administrative law judge's decision becomes a final decision of the Social Security Administration, subject to judicial review (except when judicial review is precluded in certain Medicare cases). If the Appeals Council grants a request for review and issues a decision, that decision also becomes a final decision of the Social Security Administration, subject to judicial review except in certain Medicare cases.

If an administrative law judge makes a decision in favor of a person in a disability case and the Appeals Council does not render a final decision within 110 days, interim disability benefits are provided to the person. (Delays in excess of twenty days caused by or on behalf of the claimant do not count in determining the 110-day period.) These benefits begin with the month before the month in which the 110-day period expires, and are not considered overpayments if the final decision is adverse, unless the benefits are fraudulently obtained.

225. May a person file a civil action in the United States District Court?

Yes, a person dissatisfied with the decision of the Appeals Council or denial of the request for review of the Administrative Law Judge's decision by the Appeals Council may bring suit in a federal district court. To file a civil action regarding the amount of Part A Hospital Insurance benefits under Medicare, however, the amount in question must be $1,000 or more. The Social Security Act does not provide for court review of a determination concerning the amount of benefits payable under Medicare Part B Medical Insurance.

The civil action in the court must be filed within sixty days from the date notice of the Appeals Council decision or denial of the request for review is received by the person or appointed representative. This time limit may be extended by the Appeals Council for good reason.

The court may issue a decision on the record or remand for further development. There is no right to court action where the Appeals Council has dismissed a request for review or denied a request for review of an Administrative Law Judge's dismissal.

A person may be able to advance directly from a reconsideration determination to a federal district court by filing a claim contending that the applicable statute of the Social Security Act is unconstitutional. This procedure, known as expedited appeals process, is allowable when:

(1)   the individual has presented a claim at the reconsideration level;

(2)   the only issue is the constitutionality of the statutory requirement;

(3)   the claim is neither invalid or cognizable under a different section of the Social Security Act; and

(4)   the amount in controversy is $1,000 or more.

In order to reach a federal district court after a reconsideration determination, the Social Security Administration must determine that the claim raises a constitutional question and is appropriate for treatment under the expedited appeals procedure. After this is done, the Social Security Administration and the person must sign an agreement that identifies the constitutional issue involved and explains the final reconsideration determination.

A person must file for expedited judicial review within sixty days after the date of receipt of notice of the reconsideration determination. An extension of time is available if good cause is established for not filing on time.

Should the Social Security Administration determine that a claim is not appropriate for expedited judicial review before a federal district court, its decision is final and not subject to administrative or judicial review. It is required, however, to notify the person filing the claim of its decision, and to treat the person's request as a request for a reconsideration, a hearing, or an Appeals Council review (whichever is appropriate).

The Supreme Court has held that the Social Security Act does not permit a person to have subject-matter jurisdiction to the federal district courts to review a decision of the Social Security Administration not to reopen a previously adjudicated claim for Social Security benefits. The Court found that, unless the claim was based on a constitutional challenge, the Act did not authorize judicial review to reopen a final decision on disability benefits after the sixty-day limit for a review by civil action had terminated.[1]

226. Are there situations where the Social Security Administration may not recover an overpayment to a beneficiary?

Yes, the Social Security Administration is barred from recovering an overpayment if recovery is "against equity and good conscience." According to the Social Security regulations, recovery of an overpayment is "against equity and good conscience" under three conditions:

(1)   if the beneficiary has changed his or her position for the worse;

(2)   if the beneficiary relinquished a valuable right because of reliance upon a notice that a payment would be made or because of the overpayment itself; or

(3)   if the beneficiary was living in a separate household from the overpaid person or the eligible spouse, and did not receive the overpayment.

The Ninth Circuit Court of Appeals has broadened the definition of "against equity and good conscience."[2] The case involved a former inmate who had been in prison from 1963 to 1985 on a felony conviction, and who had been receiving Social Security disability benefits while in prison. Although the Social Security Act was amended in 1980 to prohibit payment of disability benefits to certain incarcerated felons, he continued to receive benefits until 1982 and was unaware of the change in the law. After learning about the change in the law, the inmate informed the Social Security Administration of his situation. The Social Security Administration requested repayment. The inmate requested a waiver of recovery for the overpayment; a personal conference with a government representative was held in 1984, but no decision was issued at that time. The inmate was released from prison in 1985 and spent his overpayment.

The Ninth Circuit held that requiring the former inmate to repay the overpayment was against equity and good conscience because Congress intended a broad concept of fairness to apply to waiver requests, one that takes into account the facts and circumstances of each case. The court noted that the former inmate had no material goods, no means of transportation, no income, and had only worked in a few temporary jobs. Also, the court pointed to the presence of a psychological impairment as a factor in favor of waiver of recovery of the overpayment.

Social Security regulations address the rights of individuals regarding overpayment and waiver determinations. The rules follow policy established as a result of a series of court decisions.

---

1. *Califano v. Sanders*, 430 U.S. 99 (1977).
2. *Quinlivan v. Sullivan*, 916 F.2nd 524 (9th Cir. 1990).

Whenever an initial determination is made that more than the correct amount of payment has been made, and the Social Security Administration seeks adjustment or recovery of the overpayment, the individual involved must be immediately notified.

The notice must include:

(1)   the overpayment amount, and how and when it occurred;

(2)   a request for full, immediate refund, unless the overpayment can be withheld from the next month's benefit;

(3)   the proposed adjustment of benefits if refund is not received within thirty days after the date of the notice and adjustment of benefits is available;

(4)   an explanation of the availability of a different rate of withholding;

(5)   an explanation of the right to request waiver of adjustment or recovery, and the automatic scheduling of a file review and prerecoupment hearing if a request for waiver cannot be approved after initial paper review;

(6)   an explanation of the right to request reconsideration of the fact and/or amount of the overpayment determination;

(7)   instructions about the availability of forms for requesting reconsideration and waiver;

(8)   an explanation that, if the individual does not request waiver or reconsideration within thirty days of the date of the overpayment notice, adjustment or recovery of the overpayment will begin;

(9)   a statement that a Social Security Administration office will help the individual complete and submit forms for appeal or waiver requests; and

(10) a statement that the individual receiving the notice should notify the Social Security Administration promptly if reconsideration, waiver, a lesser rate of withholding, repayment by installments, or cross-program adjustment is wanted.

There can be no adjustment or recovery in any case where an overpayment has been made to an individual who is without fault, if adjustment or recovery would either defeat the purpose of the Social Security Act or be against equity and good conscience.

If an individual requests waiver of adjustment or recovery within thirty days after receiving a notice of overpayment, no action will be taken until after the initial waiver determination is made. If an individual requests waiver of adjustment or recovery more than thirty days after receiving a notice of overpayment, the Social Security Administration will stop any adjustment or recovery actions until after the initial waiver determination is made.

When waiver is requested, the individual should provide the Social Security Administration with information to support the contention that the individual is without fault in causing the overpayment, and that adjustment or recovery would either defeat the purpose of the Social

Security Act or be against equity and good conscience. That information, along with supporting documentation, is reviewed to determine if waiver can be approved. If waiver cannot be approved after this review, the individual is notified in writing and given the dates, times, and place of the file review and personal conference. The file review is always scheduled at least five days before the personal conference.

At the file review, the individual and the individual's representative have the right to review the claims file and applicable law and regulations with the decision maker or another Social Security Administration representative who is prepared to answer questions.

At the personal conference, the individual is given the opportunity to:

(1)   appear personally, testify, cross-examine any witnesses, and make arguments;

(2)   be represented by an attorney or other representative, although the individual must be present at the conference; and

(3)   submit documents for consideration by the decision maker.

The decision maker:

(1)   explains the provisions of law and regulations applicable to the issue;

(2)   briefly summarizes the evidence already on file;

(3)   ascertains from the individual whether the information presented is correct and understandable;

(4)   allows the individual and the individual's representative to present the individual's case;

(5)   allows each witness to present information and allows the individual and the individual's representative to question each witness;

(6)   ascertains whether there is any further evidence;

(7)   reminds the individual of any evidence promised by the individual that has not been presented;

(8)   allows the individual and the individual's representative to present a proposed summary or closing statement;

(9)   explains that a decision will be made and the individual will be notified in writing; and

(10) explains repayment options and further appeal rights in the event the decision is adverse to the individual.

The Social Security Administration will issue a written decision, specifying the findings of fact and conclusions in support of the decision to approve or deny waiver and advising of the individual's right to appeal the decision. If waiver is denied, adjustment or recovery of the overpayment begins, even if the individual appeals.

If the individual is dissatisfied with the initial determination, reconsideration is the first step in the administrative review process. If dissatisfied with the reconsidered determination, the individual may request a hearing before an administrative law judge.

227. When is an individual considered to be "without fault" for getting an overpayment?

An individual is considered to be without fault for an overpayment did not result due to lack of care of the person receiving payment, including:

- not providing full and accurate information;

- not complying with annual earning reporting and other reporting requirement; and

- returning payments believed not to be earned.

The individual has the responsibility to show lack of fault, even if the Social Security Administration caused the check to be issued or the deposit to be made.

228. What are the factors considered by the Social Security Administration to determine whether a person is "at fault" or "without fault?"

Factors considered include:

- understanding of reporting requirements;

- understanding of obligation to return payments not due or owed;

- actual knowledge of events that should have been reported;

- opportunities to comply with reporting requirements and efforts made to report;

- ability to comply with reporting requirements, including any mental or physical limitations.

229. When is an individual considered to be "at fault" for getting an overpayment?

An individual is considered to be at fault for an overpayment which resulted from:

- willful misstatement;

- obscuring of facts which caused the overpayment, whether directly or indirectly;

- failure to furnish or disclose information which was known to be important or should have been known to be important;

- accepting payments that were known to be incorrect or should have been known to be incorrect.

BENEFIT COMPUTATION

230. How are benefits computed under the simplified old-start benefit computation method?

The simplified old-start benefit computation[1] method must be used if disability, death, or age sixty-two occurred before 1979.

Step I. Count the number of years elapsed after 1950 (or after year the insured reached age twenty-one, if later) and before (not including) the year of death, disability, or year of attaining age sixty-two (sixty-five for a worker born before 1911, sixty-four if born in 1911, sixty-three if born in 1912).

Step II. Subtract five. (Also subtract any years that fell wholly or partly in a period of disability.) The result is the number of years of earnings (but not less than two) to be used in computing Average Monthly Earnings (AME).

Step III. List earnings for each year starting with 1951 and including the year in which the worker died – or the year *prior* to disability or application for old-age benefits. Earnings listed cannot exceed the maximum earnings base for that particular year (see Q 234).

Step IV. From this list, select years of highest earnings (same number found in Step I).

Step V. Total the earnings in the selected years – divide by the number of months in those years (drop cents). This is the worker's AME.

A worker's AME are subject to recalculation, if earnings in his year of retirement or year of disability are higher than the lowest year of earnings used in the original calculation. Earnings in the last year are substituted for earnings in the lowest year if this results in higher AIME.

Step VI. Determine the insured's Primary Insurance Amount (PIA).

Primary Insurance Amount

231. What is the Primary Insurance Amount (PIA)?

The Primary Insurance Amount (PIA) is the basic unit used to determine the amount of each monthly benefit payable under Social Security. It applies to both the old and new method of computing benefits.

A disabled worker – or a retired worker whose retirement benefits start at normal retirement age – receives monthly benefits equal to the PIA.[2] Retired workers who are fully insured and whose retirement benefits start *after* full retirement age also receive an additional delayed retirement credit. (See Q 253.)

---

1. 20 C.F.R. 404.241 1977 simplified old-start method.
2. 42 U.S.C. 402(a); 20 CFR §404.201.

Monthly benefits for members of an insured worker's family (dependent's and survivor's benefits) are all figured as percentages of the worker's PIA. (See Appendix A, Table 1.)

The total amount of monthly benefits payable on a worker's Social Security account is limited by a "maximum family benefit," which is also related to the worker's PIA.

In some instances, monthly benefits will be reduced if the insured elects to receive benefits before a specified age. (See Q 300.)

The retirement benefit is reduced if the retired worker elects to start receiving a benefit at or after age sixty-two but before full retirement age. The benefit for the spouse of a retired worker is also reduced if received before full retirement age. (See Q 255, Q 300, and Appendix A, Table 10.)

The benefit for a widow(er) is reduced if he or she elects to start receiving benefits at or after age sixty but before full retirement age. (See Q 256 and Appendix A, Table 11.)

Disabled widow(er)'s benefits are payable beginning at age fifty for disability occurring before age sixty and are always reduced from what would have been payable at full retirement age. (See Q 174.)

The law provides a minimum benefit for insured workers and for survivors of insured workers when the worker had many years of coverage. (See Q 248 and Q 249.)

"Wage Indexing" Benefit Computation Method

232. In general, how is the PIA computed under the "wage indexing" method?

It is based on "indexed" earnings over a fixed number of years after 1950. (Indexing is a mechanism for expressing prior years' earnings in terms of their current dollar value.) Previous computations used actual earnings and a PIA Table. The "wage indexing" method uses a formula to determine the PIA.

Step I. Index the earnings record

Step II. Determine the Average Indexed Monthly Earnings (AIME)

Step III. Apply the PIA formula to the AIME

233. Who should use the "wage indexing" benefit computation method?

The "wage indexing" method applies where first eligibility begins after 1978. First eligibility is the earliest of:

(1)   the year of death;

(2)   the year disability begins; or

(3)   the year the insured reaches age sixty-two.

However, if the worker was entitled to a disability benefit before 1979, and that benefit terminated more than twelve months before death, another disability, or age sixty-two, the new method will be used in determining the PIA for the subsequent entitlement. (See Q 242.)

234. What earnings are used in computing a person's Average Indexed Monthly Earnings (AIME)?

The AIME is based on Social Security earnings for years after 1950. This includes wages earned as an employee and/or self-employment income. (For an explanation of the terms wages and self-employment income, see WAGES AND SELF-EMPLOYMENT INCOME, Q 364 to Q 392.)

Only earnings credited to the person's Social Security account can be used and the maximum earnings creditable for specific years are as follows:

$132,900 for 2019	$37,800 for 1984
$128,700 for 2018	$35,700 for 1983
$127,200 for 2017	$32,400 for 1982
$118,500 for 2016	$29,700 for 1981
$118,500 for 2015	$25,900 for 1980
$117,000 for 2014	$22,900 for 1979
$113,700 for 2013	$17,700 for 1978
$110,100 for 2012	$16,500 for 1977
$106,800 for 2011	$15,300 for 1976
$106,800 for 2010	$14,100 for 1975
$106,800 for 2009	$13,200 for 1974
$102,000 for 2008	$10,800 for 1973
$97,500 for 2007	$9,000 for 1972
$94,200 for 2006	$7,800 for 1971
$90,000 for 2005	$7,800 for 1970
$87,900 for 2004	$7,800 for 1969
$87,000 for 2003	$7,800 for 1968
$84,900 for 2002	$6,600 for 1967
$80,400 for 2001	$6,600 for 1966
$76,200 for 2000	$4,800 for 1965
$72,600 for 1999	$4,800 for 1964
$68,400 for 1998	$4,800 for 1963
$65,400 for 1997	$4,800 for 1962
$62,700 for 1996	$4,800 for 1961
$61,200 for 1995	$4,800 for 1960
$60,600 for 1994	$4,800 for 1959

$57,600 for 1993	$4,200 for 1958
$55,500 for 1992	$4,200 for 1957
$53,400 for 1991	$4,200 for 1956
$51,300 for 1990	$4,200 for 1955
$48,000 for 1989	$3,600 for 1954
$45,000 for 1988	$3,600 for 1953
$43,800 for 1987	$3,600 for 1953
$42,000 for 1986	$3,600 for 1951

235. How is the earnings record indexed for the AIME computation?

The AIME is based on the earnings record after wages have been indexed.[1] Indexing creates an earnings history that more accurately reflects the value of the individual's actual earnings in comparison to the national average wage level at the time of eligibility. Earnings for each year are indexed up to the "indexing year" – the second year before the worker reaches age sixty-two – or dies or becomes disabled before age sixty-two.

Wages are indexed by applying a ratio to the worker's earnings for each year beginning with 1951. The ratio is the "indexing average wage" for the second year before the year of the worker's eligibility for benefits or death, divided by the "indexing average wage" for the year being indexed. Thus, indexed earnings for each year are computed as follows:

Worker's Actual Earnings (Up to the Social Security Maximum) for Year to be Indexed $\times$ $\dfrac{\text{Average Earnings of All Workers in Indexing Year (Second year before Eligibility or Death)}}{\text{Average Earnings of All Workers for Year being Indexed}}$

Example. Mr. Martin earned $15,000 in 1992 and reached age sixty-two in 2018. The indexing average wage for 2016 (his "indexing year") was $48,642.15 and the indexing average wage for 1992 was $22,935.42. Indexed earnings for 1991 are computed as follows:

$$\$15,000 \times \frac{\$48,642.15}{\$22,935.42} = \$31,812,47$$

Indexed earnings of $31,827.23 are used in place of actual earnings for 1992 in Mr. Martin's AIME computation.

The indexing formula must be applied to earnings in each year after 1950 – up to, but not including, the "indexing year." Actual earnings are used for the indexing year and all later years.

The list below shows the indexing average wages for each year beginning with 1951. These amounts must be used in 2017 to index earnings from 1951 through the "indexing year."

---

1. 20 CFR 404.210.

1964	$4,576.32	1978	$10,556.03	1991	$21,811.60	2004	$35,648.55
1965	$4,658.72	1979	$11,479.46	1992	$22,935.42	2005	$36,952.94
1966	$4,938.36	1980	$12,513.46	1993	$23,132.67	2006	$38,651.41
1967	$5,213.44	1981	$13,773.10	1994	$23,753.53	2007	$40,405.48
1968	$5,571.76	1982	$14,531.34	1995	$24,705.66	2008	$41,334.97
1969	$5,893.76	1983	$15,239.24	1996	$25,913.90	2009	$40,711.61
1970	$6,186.24	1984	$16,135.07	1997	$27,426.00	2010	$41,673.83
1971	$6,497.08	1985	$16,822.51	1998	$28,861.44	2011	$42,971.61
1972	$7,133.80	1986	$17,321.82	1999	$30,469.84	2012	$44,321.67
1973	$7,580.16	1987	$18,426.51	2000	$32,154.82	2013	$44,888.16
1974	$8,030.76	1988	$19,334.04	2001	$32,921.92	2014	$46,481.52
1975	$8,630.92	1989	$20,099.55	2002	$33,252.09	2015	$48,098.63
1976	$9,226.48	1990	$21,027.98	2003	$34,064.95	2016	$48,642.15
1977	$9,779.44					2017	$50,321.89

Each year, before November 1, the Social Security Administration publishes the indexing average wage for the next indexing year. The indexing average wage for 2017 – the "indexing year" for those reaching age sixty-two or dying or becoming disabled before age sixty-two in 2019 is $50,321.89 an increase of 3.45 percent over 2016.

It is important to remember that the "indexing year" is related to the year of first *eligibility* and not necessarily to the year of *entitlement*. A person filing for a retirement benefit in 2019 at age sixty-four is first *eligible* in 2017 (at age sixty-two) and the earnings record will be indexed based on the indexing year 2015 (two years prior to first eligibility).

236. How is the Average Indexed Monthly Earnings (AIME) determined?

Earnings listed in the records of the Social Security Administration – up to the annual wage limitation – are the basis for computing the AIME.

Step I. Count the *number* of years *after* 1950 (or after year person reached age twenty-one, if later) and *up to* (not including) the year of attaining age sixty-two (or the year of disability or death, if before age sixty-two). The number of years counted is the number of *computation elapsed years*.

Step II. Subtract five from the number of computation elapsed years when computing the AIME for *retirement* or *death benefits*. The number remaining (if less than two, use two) is the *number of computation base years* to be used in computing the AIME.

Example 1. An insured worker attained age sixty-two on December 2, 2018 and filed his application for retirement benefits on January 3, 2019. There are forty elapsed years, counting the years from age twenty-two (1978) through 2017. The number of computation years is thirty-five (forty minus five).

Example 2. An insured worker died on November 3, 2019, at the age of fifty-nine. The widow filed a claim for mother's benefits on November 10, 2019. There are thirty-seven elapsed years beginning with 1982 (age twenty-two) through 2018. There are thirty-two computation years (thirty-seven minus five).

The number of years to be subtracted for *disability benefits* is scaled accordingly to the worker's age, under the following schedule:

Worker's Age in year of disability	Number of dropout years
Under 27	0
27 through 31	1
32 through 36	2
37 through 41	3
42 through 46	4
47 and over	5

Example 3. An insured woman attained age forty in January 2019 and is found entitled to disability benefits. It is determined that her waiting period began on March 1, 2019. The elapsed years run from 2001 (age twenty-two) through 2018 and total eighteen. Because the woman is forty years old, there are fifteen computation years (eighteen minus three).

Step III. List Social Security earnings in the *computation base years*. (See Q 234 for Social Security earnings limits.) Computation base years are years *after* 1950, up to and *including* the year of death, or the year *before* entitlement to retirement or disability benefits. (A person is not entitled to benefits until an application for benefits is filed.)

Notice that the year of death is included as a computation base year, but the year in which an application is made for retirement or disability benefits is not included. However, for benefits payable for the next year after an application is made for retirement or disability benefits, the AIME for retirement or disability benefits will be recomputed, and earnings for this final year substituted for the lowest year if the result is a higher AIME.

Where benefits are estimated for entitlement at some future time, use anticipated earnings (but not over the Social Security maximum) for future computation base years.

Step IV. Index earnings in each computation base year up to, but not including, the "indexing year." (See Q 235 for instructions on how to index earnings.)

Step V. From the list of indexed earnings (and nonindexed earnings for and after the "indexing year"), select years of highest earnings (same number as found in Step II). Selected years need not be in consecutive order.

Step VI. Total indexed and nonindexed earnings for the selected years are divided by the number of months in the number of years found in Step II, dropping cents. This is the person's AIME.

If a person does not have earnings covered by Social Security in as many years as are required to be used as benefit computation years, total earnings must nevertheless be divided by the number of months in the required number of years. In other words, one or more years of zero earnings must be used. (See Q 237.)

AIME for Widow(er)'s Benefits. In computing aged widow(er)'s benefits for the spouse of a worker who died before age sixty-two, the deceased worker's earnings are indexed to wages up to the earliest of:

(1)   two years before the worker would have reached age sixty-two;

(2)   two years before the survivor becomes eligible for aged widow(er)'s benefits; or

(3)   two years before the survivor becomes eligible for disabled widow(er)'s benefits. This computation applies only if it results in a higher benefit than the standard computation above (including applicable cost-of-living adjustments for the deferred period before benefits start). It will provide higher benefits for many widow(er)s whose spouses died before age sixty-two and will assure that the widow(er)'s initial benefit reflects wage levels prevailing nearer the time that he or she comes on the rolls.

Examples

In each of the three examples provided below, the worker earned at least the Social Security maximum each year. See Q 233 for the Social Security maximum for a particular year.

Example I. Computation of AIME for person entitled to retirement benefits.

Mr. Smith, born in 1956, reaches age sixty-two on November 1, 2018. On November 1, he retires and applies for retirement benefits. Earnings and months in thirty-five years must be used in computing his AIME (forty computation elapsed years, 1979–2018, minus five). Mr. Smith has worked in covered employment and earned at least the Social Security maximum in every year after 1976. Earnings are indexed from 1979–2016. Mr. Smith's earnings in 2017, his "indexing year" and the next two years are not indexed.

Indexed earnings that apply to each example in-whole or in-part are as follows:

1964	$48,753.43	1983	$108,889.31	2002	$118,677.68
1965	$47,891.12	1984	$108,893.33	2003	$118,711.23
1966	$62,121.44	1985	$109,416.18	2004	$114,611.27
1967	$58,843.69	1986	$112,703.16	2005	$113,207.14
1968	$61,515.21	1987	$110,487.04	2006	$113,283.30
1969	$61,515.21	1988	$108,185.79	2007	$112,161.72
1970	$58,606.82	1989	$111,003.13	2008	$114,699.85
1971	$55,802.89	1990	$113,396.63	2009	$121,936.38
1972	$58,641.07	1991	$113,797.85	2010	$119,120.95
1973	$66,225.27	1992	$112,477.75	2011	$115,501.89
1974	$76,400.75	1993	$115,738.28	2012	$115,465.31
1975	$75,935.06	1994	$118,583.64	2013	$117,735.92

1976	$77,078.94	1995	$115,112.40	2014	$117,000.00
1977	$78,424.23	1996	$112,464.40	2015	$118,500.00
1978	$77,938.67	1997	$110,839.77	2016	$118,500.00
1979	$92,724.47	1998	$110,158.60	2017	$127,200.00
1980	$96,206.11	1999	$110,750.77	2018	$128,700.00
1981	$100,231.69	2000	$110,151.19	2019	$132,900.00
1982	$103,638.15	2001	$113,514.47		

Mr. Smith's highest AIME is obtained by selecting the highest thirty-five years of the forty years from 1978 to 2017. His AIME is $9,474 ($3,979,314.48 ÷ 420).

His AIME will later be recomputed to include earnings in 2018 and, if this results in a higher AIME, the higher benefit will be paid beginning the following year. Thus, if Mr. Smith earned at least $128,700.00 in 2018, the recomputation will be based on the highest thirty-five years of the forty-one years from 1979 to 2019, giving him an AIME of $9,531 ($4,002,876.33 ÷ 420).

Example II. Computation of AIME for disability benefits.

Mr. Jones, born in February 1973, is disabled as a result of an accident on October 15, 2019. He applies for disability benefits on December 1, 2019. In computing his AIME for disability benefits, twenty benefit computation years must be used (twenty-four years in 1995–2018, less four). Mr. Jones has worked in covered employment every year since 1992 and in each year (including the year in which he became disabled) was paid at least the maximum Social Security earnings base for that year.

Earnings in 1995–2016 are indexed. Earnings in 2017–2019 are not adjusted because they were paid in and after his "indexing year" (2017).

Mr. Jones' highest AIME is obtained by selecting the highest twenty years of the twenty-four years from 1995 to 2016. His AIME is $10,550 ($2,532,104.24 ÷ 240).

The AIME will be recomputed to include earnings in 2017 and, if this results in a higher AIME, the higher benefit will be paid beginning the following year. If Mr. Jones earned at least $128,700 in 2017, the recomputation will be based on the highest twenty years of the twenty-five years from 1996 to 2017, giving him an AIME of $10,601 ($2,544,191.84 ÷ 240).

Example III. Computation of AIME for person who dies before retirement age.

Mr. Martin dies in November 2019, at age sixty (he was born in February 1959). In computing his AIME, thirty-three benefit computation years must be used (thirty-eight years in 1981–2017, less five). Mr. Martin has worked in covered employment every year since 1979 and in each year (including the year of death) was paid at least the maximum Social Security earnings base for that year. Earnings in Mr. Martin's computation base years through 2016 are indexed. Actual earnings in 2017–2019 are not adjusted because 2017 is his "indexing year."

Mr. Martin's highest AIME is obtained by selecting the highest thirty-three years of the thirty-eight years from 1981 to 2019. Mr. Martin's AIME is $9,658 ($3,824,574.35 ÷ 396).

237. How are Average Indexed Monthly Earnings (AIME) computed for a self-employed individual whose self-employment came under Social Security after 1951?

The same formula and starting date (1951) are used as in the computation for employees. In many cases, this will mean that years of zero earnings must be used in the AIME contribution.

> *Example.* Dr. Smith, a physician, came under Social Security in 1965. He applies for retirement benefits in 1995 when he reaches age sixty-two. Earnings and months in thirty-five years must be used in computing his AIME (forty elapsed years, 1955–1994, less five). Social Security earnings in his elapsed years are at the- maximum creditable amount in 1965–1994.

> Although Dr. Smith has covered earnings in only thirty years before 1995, the total earnings for these thirty years must be divided by the number of months in thirty-five years (420). His AIME is computed by indexing his earnings from 1965–1992, adding actual earnings in 1993 and 1994 to total indexed earnings, and dividing by 420. Thus, his AIME is $3,127 ($1,313,559 ÷ 420).

> Recomputation to include Dr. Smith's earnings in 1995 (assuming they are at least $61,200) will give him an AIME of $3,273.

238. An individual is considering early retirement at age fifty-five. If she retires at fifty-five with NO earned income for the next seven years, how will this affect her benefits at age sixty-two?

Benefits are based on the highest thirty-five years of indexed earnings. The effect in this case is generally that the highest earning years are often the last years of employment, therefore benefits may not be as high as estimated by the Social Security Administration.

239. Do Social Security benefits increase by continuing to work and contributing to social security?

It depends. When benefits are computed, Social Security uses the highest thirty-five years of indexed earnings. If the current earnings exceed the lowest year used in the computation, the benefits will increase. If the current earnings are less, then there will be no change.

240. How is the Primary Insurance Amount (PIA) for a person who first becomes eligible in 2019 determined?

The Primary Insurance Amount (PIA) is determined by applying a formula to the person's Average Indexed Monthly Earnings (AIME). Where first eligibility is in calendar year 2019, the PIA is the sum of three separate percentages of portions of the AIME. It is found by taking 90 percent of the first $926 or less of the AIME, 32 percent of the AIME in excess of $926 through $5,583, and 15 percent of the AIME in excess of $5,583.

If the resulting PIA is not an even multiple of ten cents, it is rounded to the next lower multiple of ten cents.

The percentage figures and the dollar figures in the PIA formula will remain constant for computations and recomputations where first eligibility is in 2019, no matter when entitlement is established.

The PIA is subject to cost-of-living increases beginning with the year of first eligibility. (See Q 297.)

Example 1. Mr. Bell, born May 10, 1955, filed an application for retirement benefits on May 1, 2019. His AIME is $6,500. His PIA is calculated as follows:

$$90\% \text{ of } \$926 \quad = \quad \$833.40$$
$$32\% \text{ of } \$4,657 = \quad \$1490.24$$
$$15\% \text{ of } \$967 \quad = \quad \$145.05$$
$$\$926 + \$1490.24 + \$145.05 = \text{PIA of } \$2,561.29$$

Example 2. Mr. Jones, born February 13, 1957, filed an application for retirement benefits on February 10, 2019. His AIME is $600. His PIA is $540 (90 percent of $600 = $540).

Note, however, that the PIA is calculated differently if eligibility begins before 2019. The percentages in the PIA formula remain constant but the dollar amounts differ each year. The dollar amounts in the formula since 1979 are as follows:

Eligibility Begins	AIME Dollar Amounts
1979	$180 and $1,085
1980	$194 and $1,171
1981	$211 and $1,274
1982	$230 and $1,388
1983	$254 and $1,528
1984	$267 and $1,612
1985	$280 and $1,691
1986	$297 and $1,790
1987	$310 and $1,866
1988	$319 and $1,922
1989	$339 and $2,044
1990	$356 and $2,145
1991	$370 and $2,230
1992	$387 and $2,333
1993	$401 and $2,420
1994	$422 and $2,545
1995	$426 and $2,567
1996	$437 and $2,635
1997	$455 and $2,741

Eligibility Begins	AIME Dollar Amounts
1998	$477 and $2,875
1999	$505 and $3,043
2000	$531 and $3,202
2001	$561 and $3,381
2002	$592 and $3,567
2003	$606 and $3,653
2004	$612 and $3,689
2005	$627 and $3,779
2006	$656 and $3,955
2007	$680 and $4,100
2008	$711 and $4,288
2009	$744 and $4,483
2010	$761 and $4,586
2011	$749 and $4,517
2012	$767 and $4,624
2013	$791 and $4,768
2014	$816 and $4,917
2015	$826 and $4,980
2016	$856 and $5,157
2017	$885 and $5,336
2018	$896 and $5,399
2019	$926 and $5,583

Example 3. Mr. Smith, born March 12, 1943, filed an application for retirement benefits on August 19, 2008. His AIME was $4,200. As he became eligible for retirement benefits in 2006 (the year he reached age sixty-two), his PIA is calculated as follows:

$$90 \text{ percent of } \$656 \quad = \quad \$590.40$$
$$32 \text{ percent of } \$3,299 = \quad \$1,055.68$$
$$15 \text{ percent of } \$245 \quad = \quad \$36.75$$
$$\$590.40 + \$1,055.68 + \$36.75 = \$1,682.83 = \text{PIA of } \$1,682$$

This amount was subject to a 3.3 percent increase in December 2006, a 2.3 percent increase in December 2007, a 5.8 percent increase in December 2008, no increases in December 2009 or 2010, a 3.6 percent increase in December 2011, a 1.7 percent increase in December 2012, a 1.5 percent increase in December 2013, a 1.7 percent increase in December 2014, no increase in December 2015, a 0.3 percent increase in December 2016, and a 2.0 percent increase in 2017 a 2.0 percent increase in 2018, and a 2.8 percent increase in 2019. Thus, his PIA is $1,737 for December 2006, $1,776 for December 2007, $1,880 for December 2008, 2009, and 2010, $1,947 for December 2011, $1,980 for December 2012, $2,009 for December 2013, $2,043 for December 2014 and 2015, $2,049 for 2016, $2,090 for 2017, $2,032 for 2018, and $2,192 for 2019.

Formula for Workers Receiving a Pension from Work Not Covered by Social Security

If a worker receives a pension from a job not covered by Social Security, and the worker also has enough Social Security credits to be eligible for retirement or disability benefits, a different formula may be used to figure the Social Security benefit. This formula results in a lower benefit. But the worker's pension from the job not covered by Social Security is not affected by this change.

The reason a different formula is used is that Social Security benefits are weighted in favor of low earners (i.e., low earners' benefits represent a higher percentage of their prior earnings than do the benefits of workers with higher earnings). If the benefits of people who work for only a portion of their careers in jobs covered by Social Security were computed as if they had been long-term, low-wage workers, these individuals would receive the advantage of the weighted benefit formula. Instead, a modified formula eliminates this unintended windfall.

The modified formula does not affect survivor benefits. It affects only workers who reach age sixty-two or become disabled after 1985 and first become eligible after 1985 for a monthly pension based in whole or in part on work not covered by Social Security. A worker is considered eligible to receive a pension if he meets the requirements of the pension, even if he continues to work.

The modified formula does not apply if:

- the worker is a federal worker hired after December 31, 1983;

- the worker was employed on January 1, 1984, by a nonprofit organization that was mandatorily covered under Social Security on that date;

- the worker has thirty or more years of substantial earnings under Social Security;

- the worker's only pension from work not covered by Social Security is based solely on railroad employment;

- the worker's only work not under Social Security was before 1957.

The modified formula is used in figuring the Social Security benefit beginning with the first month for which the worker receives both a Social Security benefit and a pension from work not covered under Social Security.

Social Security benefits are normally based on the worker's AIME. In figuring benefits, the first part of the average earnings is multiplied by 90 percent; the second part is multiplied by 32 percent; and any part of the AIME remaining is multiplied by 15 percent. In the modified benefit formula, the 90 percent used in the first factor is reduced.

Benefits for workers first eligible in 2019 who use the modified formula are determined by taking 40 percent of the first $926 of Average Indexed Monthly Earnings; 32 percent of AIME from $926 to $5,583; and 15 percent of AIME above $5,583.

The reduction was phased in gradually for workers who reached sixty-two or became disabled in 1986 through 1989. The phase-in applies as follows:

Year Person Became 62 or Disabled	First Factor
1986	80 percent
1987	70 percent
1988	60 percent
1989	50 percent
1990 or later	40 percent

Workers with thirty or more years of substantial Social Security coverage are not affected by the modified benefit formula. Workers with twenty-one to twenty-nine years of Social Security coverage (as defined in Q 248) will have the first factor reduced as follows:

Years of Coverage	First Factor
30 or more	90 percent
29	85 percent
28	80 percent
27	75 percent
26	70 percent
25	65 percent
24	60 percent
23	55 percent
22	50 percent
21	45 percent
20 or less	40 percent

In this formula, a worker is credited with a year of coverage if earnings equal or exceed the figures shown for each year in the following chart.

Year	Earnings	Year	Earnings
1937-50	$900	1993	10,725
1951-54	900	1994	11,250
1955-58	1,050	1995	11,325
1959-65	1,200	1996	11,625
1966-67	1,650	1997	12,150
1968-71	1,950	1998	12,675
1972	2,250	1999	13,425
1973	2,700	2000	14,175
1974	3,300	2001	14,925

Year	Earnings	Year	Earnings
1975	3,525	2002	15,750
1976	3,825	2003	16,125
1977	4,125	2004	16,275
1978	4,425	2005	16,725
1979	4,725	2006	17,475
1980	5,100	2007	18,150
1981	5,550	2008	18,975
1982	6,075	2009	19,800
1983	6,675	2010	19,800
1984	7,050	2011	19,800
1985	7,425	2012	20,475
1986	7,875	2013	21,075
1987	8,175	2014	21,750
1988	8,400	2015	22,050
1989	8,925	2016	22,050
1990	9,525	2017	23,625
1991	$9,900	2018	23,850
1992	10,350	2019	not yet available

A guarantee is provided to protect workers with relatively low "noncovered" pensions. It provides that the reduction in the Social Security benefit under the modified formula cannot be more than one-half of that part of the pension attributable to earnings after 1956 not covered by Social Security. Effective for benefits based on applications filed in or after November 1989, the amount of the pension considered when determining the windfall guarantee is the amount payable in the first month of concurrent entitlement to both Social Security and the pension from noncovered employment.

241. How is the Primary Insurance Amount (PIA) determined after 2017?

For individuals who attain age sixty-two or become disabled or die before age sixty-two in any calendar year after 2016, the PIA will be determined by formulas using the same percentage amounts listed in Q 240 above. However, the bend points (dollar amounts) will be adjusted yearly as average wages rise or fall.

On or before November 1 of each year, the Social Security Administration must publish in the Federal Register the bend points (dollar amounts) that will be used in computing the PIA for those eligible in the year after publication. The bend for 2018 are $895 and $5,397 and the bend points for 2019 are $926 and $5,583.

Remember that the bend points used in calculating an individual's PIA are determined from the year the individual first became *eligible* for the benefits and not necessarily the year first *entitled* to benefits.

242. How is the PIA computed for an individual who was previously entitled to a disability benefit?

The PIA is not always computed under the "wage indexing" benefit computation method when a worker reaches age sixty-two or becomes disabled. Other benefit computations may be required if the worker was previously entitled to a disability benefit.

The PIA will be computed or recomputed under the simplified old-start benefit computation method if the individual was entitled to a disability benefit before 1979 and fewer than twelve months have passed between the prior entitlement to the disability benefit and current entitlement to benefits.

If an individual has been entitled to a disability benefit either before or after 1979 – but within twelve months of current entitlement to retirement, disability, or death benefits – the PIA is the largest of the following:

(1)   The PIA (including one computed under the simplified old-start benefit computation method) that was used in figuring the individual's previous disability benefit – increased by any cost-of-living or general benefit increases that occurred since the individual was last entitled

(2)   The special minimum PIA

(3)   A recomputation of the former PIA, to consider earnings after the disability entitlement ended

If an individual's entitlement to a disability benefit ended more than twelve months before his current entitlement to benefits, a new PIA must be computed under the "wage indexing" method. The PIA will be the higher of the recalculated PIA or the individual's PIA during the last month of his former entitlement to disability benefits (without regard to any interim cost-of-living increases).

243. How is the Maximum Family Benefit determined under the wage indexing method in 2019?

The following formula determines the Maximum Family Benefit for those reaching age sixty-two or dying before age sixty-two in 2019:

(1)   150 percent of the first $1,184 of PIA; plus

(2)   272 percent of PIA over $1,184 through $1,708; plus

(3)   134 percent of PIA over $1,708 through $2,228; plus

(4)   175 percent of PIA over $2,228.

The result is the family maximum. (The final figure should be rounded to the next lower multiple of $.10 if not an even multiple of $.10.) The Maximum Family Benefit is subject to cost-of-living increases beginning with the year of first eligibility. (See Q 297.)

The Maximum Family Benefit is calculated differently if eligibility begins before 2015. The percentages in the Maximum Family Benefit formula remain constant, but the dollar amounts differ each year. The dollar amounts in the formula since 1979 are as follows:

Eligibility Begins	PIA Dollar Amounts
1979	$230, $332, and $433
1980	$248, $358, and $467
1981	$270, $390, and $508
1982	$294, $425, and $554
1983	$324, $468, and $610
1984	$342, $493, and $643
1985	$358, $517, and $675
1986	$379, $548, and $714
1987	$396, $571, and $745
1988	$407, $588, and $767
1989	$433, $626, and $816
1990	$455, $656, and $856
1991	$473, $682, and $890
1992	$495, $714, and $931
1993	$513, $740, and $966
1994	$539, $779, and $1,016
1995	$544, $785, and $1,024
1996	$559, $806, and $1,052
1997	$581, $839, and $1,094
1998	$609, $880, and $1,147
1999	$645, $931, and $1,214
2000	$679, $980, and $1,278
2001	$717, $1,034, and $1,349
2002	$756, $1,092, and $1,424
2003	$774, $1,118, and $1,458
2004	$782, $1,129, and $1,472
2005	$801, $1,156, and $1,508
2006	$838, $1,210, and $1,578
2007	$869, $1,255, and $1,636
2008	$909, $1,312, and $1,711
2009	$950, $1,372, and $1,789
2010	$972, $1,403, and $1,830
2011	$957, $1,382, and $1,803
2012	$980, $1,415, and $1,845

Eligibility Begins	PIA Dollar Amounts
2013	$1,011, $1,459, and $1,903
2014	$1,042, $1,505, and $1,962
2015	$1,056, $1,524, and $1,987
2016	$1,093, $1,578, and $2,058
2017	$1,131, $1,633, and $2,130
2018	$1,145, $1,652, and $2,155
2019	$1,184, $1,708, and $2,228

Disability

For a disabled worker and family, benefits may not exceed the lesser of 85 percent of the Average Indexed Monthly Earnings (AIME) on which the worker's disability benefit is based, or 150 percent of the disability benefit payable to the worker alone. However, in no case will a family's benefit be reduced below 100 percent of the benefit that would be payable to the worker alone.

This limit on family disability benefits applies to workers who first become entitled to disability benefits after June 30, 1980. A worker who first becomes entitled to disability benefits in the first six months of 1980 will compute the maximum family benefit in the same manner as those who reach age sixty-two or die in 1980.

> *Example.* Mr. Smith becomes entitled to disability benefits on October 1, 2017. His AIME is $2,000 and he would be eligible to receive $1,136 a month in disability payments on his own. However, Mr. Smith also has a wife and a 10-year-old child. His maximum family benefit is the lesser of 85 percent of his AIME (85 percent × $2,000 = $1,700), or 150 percent of his disability benefit (150 percent × $1,136 = $1,704). As 150 percent of his disability benefit is more than 85 percent of his AIME, his maximum family benefit is $1,700.

244. How is the Maximum Family Benefit determined under the simplified old-start benefit computation method?

Maximum Family Benefits applicable under the law in December 1978 remain in effect for those individuals who attained age sixty-two, became disabled, or died before January 1979. Maximum Family Benefits – based on the worker's Average Monthly Earnings (AME) – are listed in the June 1978 benefit table of the Social Security Administration.

See Table 13. Consumer Price Index increases after June 1978 must be applied to Maximum Family Benefits listed in Table 13.

245. How are individual benefit rates reduced to bring the total amount payable within the family maximum limit?

Adjustment of individual benefit rates because of the family maximum limit is required, whenever the total monthly benefits of all the beneficiaries payable on *one* Social Security account exceed the family maximum that can be paid on that record for the month. All the benefit rates, except the retirement or disability benefit and benefits payable to a divorced spouse or surviving divorced spouse, must be reduced to bring the total monthly benefits payable within the family maximum. This means that, even though a beneficiary's benefit rate is originally set by law as a percentage of the insured person's PIA, the actual benefit paid may be less when the total monthly benefits payable on one earnings record exceed the family maximum prescribed by law.

The entitlement of a divorced spouse to a spouse's benefit or a surviving divorced spouse's benefit does not result in reducing the benefits of other categories of beneficiaries. Likewise, the entitlement of a legal spouse where a deemed spouse is also entitled will not affect the benefit of other beneficiaries entitled in the month. The other dependents or survivors' benefits are reduced for the maximum, not considering the existence of the divorced spouse, surviving divorced spouse, or the legal spouse. Nor are the benefits of the divorced spouse, surviving divorced spouse, or the legal spouse ever reduced because of the family maximum. (See Q 103 and Q 167.)

Adjustment for the family maximum is made by proportionately reducing all the monthly benefits subject to the family maximum on the Social Security earnings record (except for retired worker's or disabled worker's benefits) to bring the total monthly benefits payable within the limit applicable in the particular case.

The individual reduced benefit rates are figured as follows:

(1)   If the insured person is alive, the insured person's benefit is subtracted from the applicable family maximum amount. Any remainder is divided among the other persons entitled to benefits on the insured person's Social Security earnings record.

(2)   If the insured worker is dead and all monthly benefits are based on the same percentage (e.g., all are based on 100 percent of the PIA, or all are based on 75 percent), the applicable family maximum is divided equally among all those who are entitled to benefits on the Social Security earnings record.

(3)   If the insured person is deceased and some benefits are based on 100 percent, some on 82.5 percent, and some on 75 percent of the PIA, each beneficiary is paid a proportionate share of the applicable family maximum based on that beneficiary's original benefit rate.

This adjustment is made after any deductions that may be applicable. Thus, where: (1) reduction for the family maximum is required, and (2) a benefit payable to someone other than the worker must be withheld, the reapportionment for the maximum is made as if the beneficiary whose benefit must be withheld were not entitled to the amounts withheld.

Example 1. Mr. Edwards dies before age sixty-two in 2018, leaving a widow age thirty-five and two small children. His AIME is $2,500, and his PIA is $1,296. The full benefit for the widow and each child is $972 (75 percent of $1,296). However, the sum of the full benefits is $2,916 (3 × $972), which exceeds $2,192 – the maximum family benefit for a PIA of $1,296. Thus, the benefit actually payable to each beneficiary is $730 (1/3 of $2,192).

When a person is entitled to benefits based on two different earnings records, only the amount of benefits actually paid on a record is considered in determining how much to reduce monthly benefits because of the family maximum. Any amount not paid because of a person's entitlement on another earnings record is not included. The effect of this provision is to permit payment of up to the full maximum benefits to other beneficiaries who are not subject to a deduction or reduction.

> *Example 2.* Mr. Smith, his wife, and two children are entitled to benefits. Mr. Smith's PIA is $1,250 and his family maximum is $2,066. Due to the maximum limit, the monthly benefits for his wife and children must be reduced to $272 each ($816 ÷ 3). Their original rates (50 percent of Mr. Smith's benefit) are $625 each. Mr. Smith's children are also entitled to benefits on their own records. One child is entitled to $390 per month and the other child is entitled to $280 per month. This causes a reduction in the benefit to the first child to $118, and the benefit to the second child to $7.

In computing the total benefits payable on Mr. Smith's record, only the benefits actually paid to the children, or $125, are considered. This allows payment of an additional amount to Mrs. Smith, increasing her benefit to $625.00 (50 percent of her husband's benefit). This is how the calculation works:

(1)   The amount available under the family maximum for the wife and children is $816 $2,066 − $1,250 = 816).

(2)   Subtract the amount that is due the children after a reduction due to entitlement to their own benefits ($125).

(3)   The amount available for Mrs. Smith is $816 ($2,066 − $1,250 = 816).

(4)   The amount payable to Mrs. Smith is $625, which is the lesser of $625 and $691.

246. If one or more members of a family cease to be entitled to benefits, will the benefits of the remaining beneficiaries be increased?

Yes, if their benefits have been reduced because of the family maximum limit.

> *Example.* Mr. Jones dies in 2018, leaving a widow and two children, aged six and twelve, entitled to survivor's benefits. His AIME is $1,800; his PIA, $1,072; and the maximum family benefit is $1,608. As the full benefit for each family member is $804 (75 percent of $1,072), the total of all three benefits exceeds the family maximum of $1,608 (3 × $804 = $2,412). Initially then, each beneficiary receives only $536 (1/3 of $1,608, rounded to the next lowest dollar). Eventually, the older child reaches age eighteen, and his benefits end. The widow and younger child then receive their full benefits (the widow until the child attains age sixteen, and the child until attaining age eighteen or, if enrolled in a full-time elementary or secondary school program, upon attaining age nineteen) because the sum of these two benefits does not exceed the maximum family benefit.

Transitional Guarantee Benefit Method

247. What does the transitional guarantee benefit method work?

To provide a degree of protection for workers nearing retirement when decoupling was implemented, those who reach age sixty-two after 1978 and before 1984 are guaranteed a retirement benefit no lower than they would have received under the simplified old-start benefit computation method as of December 1978. The benefit computed under this method is known as the transitional guarantee PIA.

Those eligible for retirement benefits in the transition period are eligible for the larger of the PIA under the "wage indexing" benefit computation method or the transitional guarantee method.

The PIA under the transitional guarantee method is based on the June 1978 benefit table. (See Table 13.) The benefit table will not be subject to future automatic benefit increases, but an individual's retirement benefits will automatically increase beginning with age sixty-two for cost-of-living adjustments.

To be eligible for the guarantee, an individual must:

(1)   have had income credited for one year prior to 1979; and

(2)   must not have been disabled prior to 1979.

The transitional guarantee does not apply to disability computations, even when the disability begins after age sixty-two. It does apply to survivors of individuals who attain age sixty-two in the transition period and who die in or after the month they reach age sixty-two.

The transitional guarantee method is basically the same as the simplified old-start benefit computation method, but earnings in the year in which the worker reached age sixty-two and any year thereafter may not be included in the benefit computation.

> *Example.* Mr. White, born 1917, reaches age sixty-two on October 7, 1979. He retires one day later and applies for retirement benefits. Earnings and months in twenty-three years must be used in computing his AME (twenty-eight computation elapsed years, 1951–1978, less five). Mr. White has worked in covered employment and earned at least the Social Security maximum in every year after 1950. Social Security earnings in his computation base years are therefore as follows: $3,600 (1951–1954); $4,200 (1955–1958); $4,800 (1959–1965); $6,600 (1966–1967); $7,800 (1968–1971); $9,900 (1972); $10,800 (1973); $13,200 (1974); $14,100 (1975); $15,300 (1976); $16,500 (1977); $17,700 (1978). Mr. White's highest AME is obtained by selecting the twenty-three years 1956–1978. His AME is $678 ($187,200 ÷ 276), and his PIA is $486.10.

The PIA computed above under the transitional guarantee method will be used if it is higher than Mr. White's PIA computed under the "wage indexing" method.

The PIA under the transitional guarantee method is subject to cost-of-living increases beginning with the month applicable for the year of first eligibility. A worker who attains age sixty-two in 1982 is entitled to a transitional guarantee PIA determined from the PIA Table printed in 1978. The PIA was not affected by cost-of-living benefit increases in 1979, 1980, or 1981, but the June 1982 cost-of-living increase and subsequent increases apply.

Minimum and Maximum Single Benefits Increase in Benefits

248. Do benefits increase when the cost-of-living increases?

The Social Security Act provides for automatic increases in benefits and in the maximum earnings base (earnings subject to Social Security taxes) due to changing economic conditions.

The automatic increases in benefits are determined by increases in the Consumer Price Index for All Urban Wage Earners and Clerical Workers prepared by the Department of Labor. (But see Q 299) The increases in the maximum earnings base are determined from increases in average nationwide wages, if there has been a cost-of-living increase in benefits for the preceding December. (See Q 365).

Benefits have been raised by the following percentages since 1977:

Month/Year	Increase in Benefits
July 1977	5.9%
July 1978	6.5%
July 1979	9.9%
July 1980	14.3%
July 1981	11.2%
July 1982	7.4%
January 1984	3.5%
January 1985	3.5%
January 1986	3.1%
January 1987	1.3%
January 1988	4.2%
January 1989	4.0%
January 1990	4.7%
January 1991	5.4%
January 1992	3.7%
January 1993	3.0%
January 1994	2.6%
January 1995	2.8%
January 1996	2.6%
January 1997	2.9%
January 1998	2.1%
January 1999	1.3%
January 2000	2.5%
January 2001	3.5%
January 2002	2.6%
January 2003	1.4%
January 2004	2.1%
January 2005	2.7%
January 2006	4.1%
January 2007	3.3%
January 2008	2.3%
January 2009	5.8%
January 2010	0.0%
January 2011	0.0%
January 2012	3.6%

Month/Year	Increase in Benefits
January 2013	1.7%
January 2014	1.5%
January 2015	1.7%
January 2016	0.0%
January 2017	0.3%
January 2018	2.0%
January 2019	2.8%

There can be no cost-of-living computation quarter in any calendar year if, in the year prior to that year, a general benefit increase has been enacted or become effective.

The amount of excess earnings that results in loss of benefits will be increased whenever there is an automatic cost-of-living benefit increase and nationwide average wages have risen (the increase is based on the rise in average wages). (See Q 320).

249. Who is entitled to a cost-of-living benefit increase?

Individuals using the "wage indexing" benefit computation method are entitled to cost-of-living increases, beginning with the year of first eligibility (the year of attaining age sixty-two, or disability or death before age sixty-two). The PIA is calculated for the year of first eligibility and the cost-of-living increases in that year and subsequent years will be added. As long as eligibility exists in any month of the year, the PIA will be increased by the automatic-benefit increase percentage applicable to the check sent in January of the following year.

> *Example.* Mr. Johnson attains age sixty-two in November 2017 and waits until January 2019 to apply for benefits. The PIA is calculated and will be increased by the automatic cost-of-living benefit increases applicable to December 2017 and December 2018. The resultant PIA will be payable in the benefit paid for January 2019.

The automatic cost-of-living increase provisions in effect in December 1978 continue to apply for those who reached age sixty-two, became disabled, or died before January 1979. A revised benefit table is published each year by the Social Security Administration. (See Table 13.) These revised tables are *not* applicable to individuals who become eligible for benefits *after 1978*, except those using the transitional guarantee.

Beneficiaries using the transitional guarantee will also receive cost-of-living increases beginning with the year of first eligibility. (See Q 247).

250. How will the cost-of-living stabilizer affect future cost-of-living benefit increases?

The Social Security Amendments of 1983 include a provision designed to protect the system from the kinds of trust-fund depletions that occur when price increases outpace wage gains. This stabilizer provision goes into effect if reserves in the trust fund providing retirement, disability, and survivor benefits fall below 20 percent of what is needed to provide benefits for a year. When the stabilizer takes effect, automatic cost-of-living benefit increases are based on the lower of the percentage increase in the Consumer Price Index (CPI) or the percentage rise in the nationwide average wage.

Later, if the fund reserves exceed 32 percent of what is estimated to be needed for a year, recipients will be entitled to extra cost-of-living increases, to compensate for losses in inflation protection resulting from having benefit increases tied to wage levels in the past (if this occurred).

Reduction in Benefits

251. When a person elects to start receiving a retirement benefit before full retirement age, how is the benefit reduced?

A fully insured worker can start receiving retirement benefits the month after she reaches age sixty-two (or the month she reaches age sixty-two if his or her birthday is on the first or second of the month), or for any month thereafter. (See Q 50.) However, if the worker elects to start receiving benefits before full retirement age, the benefit is reduced.

In making the reduction, the worker's PIA must first be determined. The PIA is then reduced by 5/9 of 1 percent (1/180) for each of the first thirty-six months that the worker is under full retirement age when the benefits commence and by 5/12 of 1 percent (1/240) for each such month in excess of thirty-six. (The amount of the reduction, if not an even multiple of ten cents, is increased to the next higher multiple of ten cents.) For example, if the worker's PIA is $1,000, and he elects to retire and start receiving benefits twenty-four months before his full retirement age, his benefit will be reduced by $133.33 (24 × 1/180 × $1,000), giving him a monthly benefit of $866.67. Ordinarily, he will continue to receive the reduced benefit even after full retirement age (but see Recomputation of Benefits, Q 259).

252. If the spouse of a retired worker starts receiving a spouse's benefit before full retirement age, how is the benefit reduced?

First, the spouse's full benefit is determined. This is one-half of the retired worker's PIA. (Where the retired worker is receiving a reduced retirement benefit starting before full retirement age, the spouse's full benefit is computed as 50 percent of the retired worker's PIA, not 50 percent of the reduced benefit.) The spouse's full benefit is then reduced by 25/36 of 1 percent (1/144) for each of the first thirty-six months that the spouse is under full retirement age when benefits commence and by 5/12 of 1 percent (1/240) for each month in excess of thirty-six. (The amount of the reduction, if not an even multiple of ten cents, is increased to the next higher multiple of ten cents.)

For example, suppose that the retired worker's PIA is $1,000, and the spouse's full benefit is $500 (1/2 of $1,000). If the spouse takes the benefit exactly twenty-four months before his full retirement age, the full benefit will be reduced by $83,33 (24 × 1/144 × $500), giving the spouse a monthly benefit of $416.67 ($500 − $83.33). If a spouse starts receiving benefits for the month thirty-six months before full retirement age, the benefit under this formula will be 75 percent of the full benefit, or 37.5 percent of the retired worker's PIA. Ordinarily, the spouse will continue to receive the reduced benefit even after normal retirement age (but see Recomputation of Benefits, Q 259). (See also Table 10.)

253. If a widow(er) elects to start receiving a widow(er)'s benefit before full retirement age, how is the benefit reduced?

The widow(er)'s full benefit must first be determined. The full benefit (to which he would be entitled by waiting until full retirement age) is 100 percent of the deceased spouse's PIA. When the full retirement age was sixty-five, this benefit was reduced by 19/40 of 1 percent (19/4000) for each month that the widow(er) was under full retirement age when benefits began.

For example, suppose that the deceased spouse's PIA was $1,000. The widow(er)'s full benefit would have been $1,000. However, if the widow(er) elected to receive benefits starting with the month of his sixtieth birthday (sixty months before age sixty-five), the full widow(er)'s benefit would have been reduced by $285 (60 × 19/4000 × $1,000), resulting in a benefit of $715 ($1,000 − $285). The amount of the reduction, if not an even multiple of ten cents, is increased to the next higher multiple of ten cents. A benefit beginning with the month of a widow(er)'s sixtieth birthday accordingly will equal 71.5 percent of the spouse's PIA.

When the full retirement age is more than sixty-five, the 71.5 percent reduction at age sixty remains unchanged, but the reduction factor will be different (based on 71.5 percent at age sixty and 100 percent at full retirement age). Ordinarily, the widow(er) will continue to receive the reduced benefit, even after full retirement age (but see Recomputation of Benefits, Q 259). (See Table 11 for widow(er)'s reduced benefits.)

If the widow(er)'s deceased spouse started receiving benefits before full retirement age, the widow(er)'s benefit cannot exceed the deceased spouse's reduced benefit or, if larger, 82.5 percent of his PIA.

The benefit of a disabled widow(er) who starts receiving benefits before age sixty is equal to 71.5 percent of his spouse's PIA. (See Q 174.)

254. How do the benefit reduction rules affect a high-earning spouse who dies after reaching Full Retirement Age (FRA) with a surviving spouse who is younger than Full Retirement Age?

The "Reduction Factor" depends upon the year that the widow attains Full Retirement Age (FRA). If the FRA is age sixty-six, the reduction factor is the original benefit multiplied by the number of months that benefits are taken before FRA multiplied by 19 multiplied by .01 divided by 48.

For example: if the original benefit is $2,000 and the widow takes benefits at age sixty:

- $2,000 × the Reduction Factor (RF) times 19 multiplied by .01 /48 = $570

- The spouse will receive $1340 as a result of the Reduction Factor. ($2,000 − $570 = $1,340)

255. How are benefits figured if a beneficiary starts receiving a reduced retirement benefit and later becomes entitled to a larger spouse's benefit?

The beneficiary will continue to receive the retirement benefit reduced in the regular manner. (See Q 251.) When he becomes entitled to the larger spouse's benefit, he will receive, in addition, a partial spouse's benefit. This benefit will be based on the difference between a spouse's full benefit (1/2 of his spouse's PIA) and the beneficiary's PIA. If he becomes entitled to the spouse's benefits at or after full retirement age, the spouse's benefit will equal this difference. If he becomes entitled to the spouse's benefit before full retirement age, this difference must be reduced by 25/36 of 1 percent (1/144) for each of the first thirty-six months that he is under full retirement age when the spouse's benefits commence, and 5/12 of 1 percent (1/240) for each month in excess of thirty-six.

Recomputation of Benefits

256. Under what circumstances are benefits recomputed?

Automatic recomputation of benefits is provided each year to take account of any earnings a beneficiary might have that would increase his benefit amount. Also, the recomputation takes into account the final year's earnings in the case of retirement and disability benefits. The recomputation for a living beneficiary is effective with January of the year following the one in which the earnings were received. A recomputation affecting survivor's benefits is effective with the month of death.

The "wage indexing" computation method must be used to recompute the PIA for an individual who has earnings after 1978, if the PIA was originally computed (or could have been computed) under this method.

The actual dollar amounts in the records of the Social Security Administration for the year of entitlement and each later year will annually be compared with the earnings in the base years that were used in the last computation. Higher earnings in any year that was not used in the last computation will be substituted for one or more years of lower earnings that were used, and the PIA will be recomputed.

The PIA will be recomputed using the same "bend points" and "indexing year" that applied when current eligibility was established. (See Q 240.) Recomputation must result in a PIA increase of at least one dollar to be effective.

A PIA computed using the transitional guarantee benefit computation method or the simplified old-start benefit computation method – based on eligibility after 1978 – cannot be recomputed to include earnings in or after the year of current eligibility.

257. If a person is simultaneously entitled to two or more benefits, which benefit will be paid?

A person may be entitled to more than one Social Security benefit at the same time. For example, a woman may be entitled to a parent's benefit on her deceased child's account and to a spouse's benefit on her husband's account. However, only the highest benefit will be paid, except when one of the benefits is a retirement or disability benefit. The lower benefit cannot be paid, even though the higher benefit is not payable for one or more months. But if the higher benefit is terminated, the lower benefit will be reinstalled automatically.

If a person is entitled to retirement or disability benefits and to a higher benefit, he or she will receive the retirement or disability benefit plus the difference between this benefit and the higher one. Payment, however, may be made in a single check. If one benefit is not payable for one or more months, the other benefit may be payable. For example, if a spouse's benefit is not payable for some months because of the worker's excess earnings, he or she will nevertheless receive a retirement benefit.

A child may be entitled to child's benefits on more than one earnings record, for example, his father's record and his mother's record. A child can receive the benefit based on the PIA that will result in the highest original benefit. However, if the highest original benefit is payable on the lowest PIA, he is paid on this account only if it would not reduce (after the reduction for the family maximum) the benefit of any beneficiary because of his entitlement.

Disability Freeze

258. How does a period of disability affect retirement and survivor's benefits?

A person who has an established period of disability will have his or her earnings record "frozen" during the period of disability. This means that the years of disability need not be included in computing his or her AIME. Otherwise, if the worker died or recovered and returned to work before he or she reached retirement age, the years of zero earnings in his or her period of disability might reduce his or her PIA for retirement or survivors' benefits. In figuring the number of years that must be used in computing the worker's AIME, a year which fell wholly or partly within a period of disability is not counted. However, a year that is partly within a period of disability will be used as a computation base year, if inclusion of earnings for that year will produce a higher AIME.

Calculating the Exact Benefit Amount

259. In calculating the exact amount of each monthly benefit, how must the figures be rounded?

Benefits for members of a worker's family, if not an even multiple of one dollar, are rounded (after deducting the premium for Medical Insurance under Medicare, if any) to the next lower multiple of one dollar. For example, if the PIA of a deceased worker is $444.30, a child's survivor benefit is figured as $333.23 (75 percent of $444.30). However, this amount will be rounded to $333.00 (the next lower multiple of one dollar).

Government Pension Offset and Windfall Elimination Provision

260. What is the Government Pension Offset?

The Government Pension Offset (GPO) is a reduction in the Social Security dependent benefits paid to the spouse (including the surviving spouse or, in certain circumstances, divorced spouse) of a Social Security contributor. Some of an employee's spousal Social Security benefit may be offset if the employee has a government pension from work not covered by Social Security.

The offset does not apply to the employee's own Social Security benefit, only the benefit that comes from a spouse's employment. If the Government Pension Offset applies, the spousal Social Security benefit will be reduced by two-thirds of any Federal pension based on employment not covered by Social Security. It applies to a spouse who also receives a federal, state, or local government pension based on the spouse's own earnings for which no Social Security taxes were paid.

Some employees are exempt from the Government Pension Offset. They are employees who are automatically covered by the Federal Employees Retirement System (FERS), Civil Service Retirement System (CSRS) Offset, and those who elected to transfer to the FERS before January 1, 1988, or during the belated transfer period that ended June 30, 1988. Employees who were covered by the CSRS and who elected FERS coverage after June 30, 1988 must have five years of Federal employment covered by Social Security to be exempt from the offset.

261. Who does the GPO affect?

There are three general criteria:

- **First**, you work or worked for a State or local government in non-SS-covered employment.

- **Second**, you are entitled to a government pension from that employment. SSA deems you to be "entitled to a pension" when you file an application for the pension and a benefit is payable.

- **Third**, you are entitled to a Social Security survivor/dependent benefit from a marriage that lasted ten years or longer.

The GPO reduces Social Security survivor/dependent benefits by two-thirds of the person's public pension. It can cause a total loss of Social Security benefits.

262. Does the Government Pension Offset reduce an individual's Social Security benefit from their own work?

No. The GPO affects a person's dependent/survivor benefit only. The Windfall Elimination Provision reduces the Social Security benefit the individual earned from Social Security covered employment.

263. Does the Government Pension Offset affect a disability benefit?

Yes. If an individual is entitled to a dependent/survivor benefit based on a spouse's disability, the GPO applies.

264. Can the GPO reduce a dependent or survivor benefit to zero?

Yes. This is referred to as a "total GPO offset."

265. Does ineligibility for a dependent or survivor benefit affect Medicare eligibility?

No. An individual is still eligible for Medicare at age sixty-five based on a spouse's Social Security covered employment if the individual is not eligible for it from their own employment.

266. If an individual has a government pension from a non-Social Security military reserve pension, is it subject to the GPO?

No. Congress exempted that type of service from the GPO.

267. What happens to an individual that retires from non-Social Security employment and begins to draw a government pension and then begins work in a Social Security eligible position?

The SSA will still reduce survivor/dependent benefit by the applicable amount.

268. What happens to an individual that takes a government pension from non-Social Security employment as a lump sum?

The SSA will determine how much the government pension would be if it were paid monthly and then reduce the monthly survivor/dependent benefit accordingly.

269. Can both the Government Pension Offset and the Windfall Elimination Provision reduce Social Security benefits?

Yes. The Social Security retirement that was earned as well as dependent/survivor benefit may be reduced if:

- the individual has some Social Security covered work and non-Social Security covered work, and

- the individual is or was married.

> *Example:* During Barry's career, he works both in the private sector, where he was covered by Social Security, and for a government agency in a non-Social Security position. Barry's wife spends her entire career in employment covered by Social Security. Barry reaches the age at which he can draw a Social Security benefit. He goes to the local SSA office to apply for his benefits and learns that because of the WEP, Barry's Social Security benefit is reduced unless he had thirty or more years of Social Security coverage. Because of the GPO, Barry's dependent benefit from his wife is either reduced or eliminated. If Barry had not worked in the non-Social Security role for the government agency, the reductions would not have applied.

270. What was the rationale for the GPO?

In 1977, Congress studied the Social Security Act and took note of the dual entitlement rule, which forbids an individual from receiving both a Social Security benefit from his/her own work and a Social Security dependent/survivor benefit.

Congress decided that someone with both a government pension and a survivor/dependent benefit violated the dual entitlement rule. The rationale for this conclusion was reached by equating the government pension with a Social Security retirement benefit. Congress could have just as easily determined that the government pension was analogous to a pension from a private sector employment or Social Security covered work for a state or local government, in which case no dual entitlement would arise, but did not.

271. What is an example of a partial offset?

Under the GPO, the SSA reduces dependent/survivor benefit by two-thirds of the person's government pension. The GPO lowers the dependent/survivor benefit by $2 for every $3 received from a government pension.

> *Example:* Brendt works in non-Social Security-covered employment for a government agency. He will receive a government pension from the job of $1,200 per month. His wife, Caitlin, works in Social Security covered employment. She is entitled to a dependent benefit from his work of $900 per month before the SSA applies the GPO. To calculate the GPO, SSA does the following:
>
> $1,200 is multiplied by two-thirds (1,200 × 2/3 = $800)
>
> $800 is subtracted from the $900 dependent benefit (900 – 800 = $100)
>
> The result is that Caitlin receives a dependent or survivor benefit of $100 per month. This is called a partial GPO offset.

272. What is a government pension?

It is any periodic or lump sum benefit that is based upon your own non-SS-covered employment for a SLG. The government pension is payable because you qualify for either

- a retirement benefit based on age and length of service; or

- a permanent disability, that is, a condition which is expected to continue throughout your lifetime and precludes return to work. A government pension does not include such payment as:

    - a Social Security retirement or disability benefit;

    - a payment from an optional savings plan, e.g., a 403(b) or 457 plan, which is separate from the retirement plan and yields only the amount the employee paid in (plus interest) rather than an amount calculated based upon certain conditions such as age, earnings and length of service;

    - an early incentive retirement payment, e.g., a bonus paid as an incentive to retire early; or

    - a survivor annuity from a spouse's government pension.

273. Does the GPO have exceptions?

Yes. The GPO does not apply for persons who:

- worked the last five years of a state or local government job in a position covered both by Social Security and the same government pension as the non-Social Security position;

- receive a government pension from state or local government employment that is not based on their own earnings (such as a survivor's annuity from a deceased spouse);

- were eligible for a dependent/survivor benefit before December 1, 1977;

- were eligible to receive a government pension from non-SS-covered employment before December 1, 1982, and met the requirements for a dependent/survivor benefit in effect in January 1977; or

- receive a government pension from non-SS-covered military reserve service.

274. What was the Congressional intent in establishing survivor and disability benefits?

Congress enacted the survivor benefit as part of the Social Security Act. It recognized that a worker's family requires financial support if the worker dies. Even in cases where the surviving spouse has always worked, the loss of the deceased worker's income reduces the family's total income. Congress realized a few years later that the retirement or disability of a worker also affects household income. While a Social Security benefit may be adequate for the retiree or disabled person to live on, the amount is insufficient, especially when the retired or disabled worker was the family's principal breadwinner. In 1939, therefore, Congress provided a dependent benefit, payable to the spouse and minor children of a retired or disabled worker.

275. Is an individual eligible for both a survivor benefit and a benefit based on their own work record?

No. The Social Security Act does not permit an individual to receive a Social Security benefit from his/her own work and also a survivor/dependent benefit. This "dual entitlement rule" allows an individual to receive only the higher of the two benefits.

276. What is the Windfall Elimination Provision (WEP)?

The WEP is a penalty imposed on one's own Social Security retirement benefit when one begins to collect a pension from a public agency that did not collect FICA taxes during your employment. The WEP reduces the Social Security benefit for retired and disabled workers receiving pensions from non-SS-covered employment.

277. What is the rationale for the Windfall Elimination Provision (WEP)?

SSA uses a formula for computing Social Security benefits that provides individuals with low average lifetime wages a proportionally higher rate of return on their contributions to Social Security than individuals with relatively high average lifetime wages. Those who have spent most of their careers in non-Social Security employment with a state or local government and a minimal amount of time in SS-covered employment will appear to SSA as lower-paid workers. Congress enacted the WEP in the belief that one should not receive a Social Security benefit as a low-paid worker, plus receive a government pension from non-Social Security covered employment.

278. What is the argument that WEP is unfair?

It is argued that the WEP penalizes those who have had two jobs:

- One job that entitles them to a Social Security retirement or disability benefit from work that paid the required Social Security taxes.

- A second job that did not pay Social Security taxes, but instead entitled them to a pension from a separate pension system.

The argument is that these pensions were earned separately and differently from Social Security, yet they are used to reduce the amount of Social Security benefits that a worker receives during retirement. When participation is required by both Social Security and also State and local pensions, the public pension is earned and collected separately.

279. How many people are affected by the GPO and WEP?

According to federal figures released in 2015, about 652,100 Social Security beneficiaries or about 1 percent of all beneficiaries, had their benefits reduced by the GPO. Of those people penalized by the GPO, approximately 73 percent lose their entire Social Security benefit.

According to the Social Security Administration data as of December 2015, approximately 1.7 million Social Security beneficiaries were penalized by the WEP. These affected workers constitute about 3 percent of all Social Security beneficiaries.

280. If the GPO and WEP offsets were eliminated, what would be the cost to Social Security?

It is estimated that the total cost of repealing of both the Government Pension offset and the Windfall Elimination Program would be approximately 1.5 percent of the the total amount of Social Security expenditures each year.

281. How does the WEP work?

The WEP reduces the factor by which average earnings are multiplied to determine Social Security benefits. The amount of reduction depends on when the person retires and how many years of earnings he or she has accumulated. The reduction may be no more than one-half of the government pension to which the person is entitled in the initial month of entitlement to the pension.

282. Who does the WEP affect?

The WEP affects persons who:

- work or worked for a state or local government in non-Social-Security-covered employment;

- are entitled to a government pension from that employment; and

- are also entitled to a Social Security retirement or disability benefit from Social-Security covered work.

283. What are the exceptions to the WEP?

The WEP does not apply for persons who:

- Have thirty or more years of coverage under Social Security.

- Those with twenty-one to twenty-nine years of coverage are eligible for a partial exemption; or

- Have a government pension from non-SS-covered military reserve service.

284. When do the offsets begin?

The trigger is receipt of the pension from non-Social Security covered employment.

MAXIMIZATION OF BENEFITS

285. When is the best time to apply for Social Security retirement benefits, and what are some of the ways of maximizing Social Security Benefits over time?

Many individuals treat deciding which benefits to collect and when to collect as a one-time choice. However, there are a few cases that offer opportunities to switch between different types of benefits over time. Two strategies, File and Suspend and Restricted Application were impacted by the 2015 Bi-Partisan Budget Act. Through this Act, Congress included Section 831 titled "Closure of Unintended Loopholes". Section 831 phased out these strategies over time. The benefits of the "file and suspend" strategy such as the payment of spousal and children benefits while the wage earner's benefits have been suspended are only available if the application was filed by April 29, 2016. The opportunity to file a restricted application is only available for folks turning age sixty-two by January 1, 2016.

Before the law changed, an individual who qualified for both individual and spousal and who was at least Full Retirement Age (FRA – also called Normal Retirement Age (NRA)) when filing for benefits was able to choose which benefits to collect. This option allowed him or her to collect spousal benefits (which are highest at FRA) while allowing his or her own benefits to receive Delayed Retirement Credits (DRCs). Unfortunately, the law passed in November 2015 phases out this strategy referred to as Restricted Application. Only individuals turning age sixty-two by January 1, 2016 can file a Restricted Application at Full Retirement Age. This strategy is still available for some individuals. If the age requirement is met the individual can then file for his or her own benefits later, potentially as late as age seventy, and claim increased individual benefits. The major benefit is the receipt of a spousal benefit from ages sixty-two through seventy. Assuming a spousal benefit of $1,000, if the recipient files a Restricted Application they will receive $48,000. As a reminder, to collect "spouse only" benefits, the individual cannot have filed for his or her own individual benefits. Therefore, at any given time, only one spouse may be collecting spousal benefits.

Prior to the change in the law, individuals reaching Full Retirement Age had the opportunity to file and suspend allowing for the payment of spousal and children benefits while the worker's Social Security benefits have been suspended. The wage earner is earning Delayed Retirement Credits while spousal benefits are paid to the spouse and or children.

The Restricted Application and File and Suspend strategies are only available at Full Retirement Age. FRA for folks born between 1943 and 1954 is age sixty-six. These strategies together and individually represent the "Coordination of Spousal Benefits". Use of these strategies will greatly increase the total Social Security benefits paid to a married couple.

In addition, an individual who qualifies for both individual and survivor benefits can choose which benefits to collect. This option enables him or her to collect survivor benefits, potentially as early as age sixty, while allowing his or her own benefits to increase and potentially receive DRCs. The individual can then switch to his or her own benefits later, potentially as late as age seventy, and claim higher individual benefits. On the other hand, the individual could also elect to collect his or her individual benefits early and switch to the survivor benefits later. It is important to note that Deemed Filing does not apply to surviving spouse benefits, thus permitting the opportunity to switch among benefits.

For working examples of maximization of benefits, see Case Studies Used in Planning for Social Security Maximization.

286. What was the "file and suspend" strategy in regard to applying for Social Security benefits?

The File and Suspend strategy was only available for individuals filing and suspending by April 29, 2016. "File and Suspend" (also referred to as "Claim and Suspend") was a strategy that allowed the primary earner to delay and grow benefits at a guaranteed eight percent per year while the lower-earning spouse collects a spousal benefit every month. The primary earner could file for benefits, making the spouse eligible to begin collecting the spousal benefit, and the primary earner could then immediately request that the retirement benefit be suspended. The person requests to receive no checks, and that triggers an eight percent growth per year. The primary earner can then elect to begin drawing Social Security benefits later.

Filing and suspending also allowed an individual to retroactively change his or her mind about suspending and start collecting as if he or she had not suspended. For example, if an individual filed and suspended at age sixty-six and then decided at age sixty-nine that he or she should have begun collecting at age sixty-six, he or she can retroactively reverse the decision. The SSA will send the individual a lump-sum payment of the benefits he or she would have collected without the suspension and, going forward, will pay monthly benefits based on beginning collection at age sixty-six.

See Case Studies illustrating use of "File and Suspend" planning.

287. What is a "restricted application" strategy for maximizing Social Security benefits?

Another concept in Social Security planning strategy was the Restricted Application. This strategy was used to maximize Social Security benefits for a married couple or for an ex-spouse. One spouse filed a Restricted Application to receive a spousal benefit. While receiving a spousal benefit the worker will earn Delayed Retirement Credits of 8 percent annually. If we assume that the wife's PIA is $1,250 and that she was eligible to file a restricted application at her Full Retirement Age as she turned age sixty-two by January 1, 2016. She would have filed a restricted application at her FRA and began to collect a spousal benefit of $1,000 per month. At age seventy, she would file for her own benefits and receive a monthly benefit of $1,650 after earning Delayed Retirement Credits of 32 percent. In this situation, she not only received $48,000 in spousal benefits but also her own monthly benefit has grown by 32 percent. A restricted application could be appropriate when husband and wife PIAs are similar or when there is a disparity in earnings.

Another variation of the restricted application was that the lower earner could file an application for retirement benefits. In this instance, the higher earner will file a "restricted application" for spousal benefits on the spouse's earnings record. The higher earner then delays

Social Security to age seventy to get the full thirty-two percent growth. DRCs of 32 percent were available to individuals with an FRA of age sixty-six. Folks with FRAs between age 66 and two months to age seventy would receive decreased Delayed Retirement Credits. This allowed the higher earner to collect half of the spouse's retirement benefit until turning age seventy without adversely affecting delayed earnings.

See Case Studies illustrating use of "Restricted Application" planning.

288. Are there differences in strategies for maximizing Social Security benefits for a married couple depending upon the earnings history of the couple?

Yes. Depending on whether the members of the couple had a significant difference in earnings or similar earnings, there will generally be different considerations.

Married Couple – Large Difference in Benefits

This collection strategy, often referred to as the Hybrid Approach, tends to work best for couples who are around the same age with one individual entitled to benefits that are more than double those of the other spouse.

This approach entails the lower earner claiming individual benefits early to start the flow of income and adding adjusted spousal benefits later, with the higher earner deferring, which maximizes benefits as well as potential survivor benefits. The lower earner would file at age sixty-two and collect individual benefits. When the lower earner reaches full retirement age, assuming the higher earner is also at least Full Retirement Age (FRA), the higher earner would file for benefits to allow spousal benefits to be paid but suspend collecting until reaching age seventy. Due to Congressional changes, this strategy was only available to individuals that filed and suspended by April 29, 2016.

By filing for benefits when the lower earner reaches FRA, the higher earner enables the spouse to collect unreduced adjusted spousal (spousal boost) benefits in addition to the lower earner's reduced individual benefits. The higher earner deferring collection to age seventy allows for the highest possible benefits to be paid not only during the higher earner's lifetime, but also as survivor benefits when the higher earner passes.

Married Couple – Small Difference in Benefits

This collection strategy, sometimes referred to as a "Two High Earners strategy", tends to work best for couples who are entitled to similar benefits.

This approach entails the lower earner claiming spousal benefits at FRA and switching to individual benefits at age seventy, while the higher earner defers until age seventy, maximizing potential survivor benefits. When the lower earner reaches FRA, assuming the higher earner is also at least FRA, the higher earner would file for benefits to allow spousal benefits to be paid but suspend collecting until reaching age seventy. The April 29, 2016 deadline applied in this situation.

By filing for benefits when the lower earner reaches FRA, the higher earner enables the spouse to collect unreduced spousal benefits. Since the lower earner has attained FRA, the lower earner can choose to collect "spouse only" benefits (which are their highest at FRA) and defer collecting individual benefits until later when benefits have accumulated delayed retirement credits. The collection of a spousal benefit only is referred to as restricting the scope of the Social Security application and is known as filing a Restricted Application. Recent law changes limit the use of the Restricted Application to folks turning age sixty-two by January 1, 2016. The higher earner deferring collection to age seventy allows for the highest possible benefits to be paid not only during the higher earner's lifetime, but also as survivor benefits when the higher earner passes.

See Case Studies illustrating situations such as Married Couples with Large Differences in Benefits, Married Couples with Small Differences in Benefits, and Sole Breadwinner.

Other factors include:

- estimated life expectancy of each spouse;

- effect that timing of filing will have on widow's/widower's benefits;

- effect of Government Pension Offset (GPO) and Windfall Elimination Provision (WEP).

289. Are there any strategies a widow or widower can use to maximize benefits?

Yes. A potential for strategic collection occurs when a widow or widower is entitled to survivor benefits as well as his or her own individual benefits. Since survivor benefits can be collected earlier than other benefits (as young as age sixty or age fifty if disabled) and are highest at Full Benefit Age, a common strategy involves the widow or widower collecting survivor benefits beginning at age sixty while deferring collecting individual benefits until age seventy when they are at their highest. Another strategy available to surviving spouses is to collect their own benefit at age sixty-two and then switch to the surviving spouse benefit at Full Benefit Age.

Collecting survivor benefits early starts the flow of income while allowing the individual to defer collecting his or her own benefits until they are higher.

Surviving spouses have greater latitude regarding structuring of their benefits because Deemed Filing does not apply to surviving spouses. Deemed Filing applies to worker and spousal benefits but NOT to surviving spouses.

See Case Studies for illustrations of strategies that a widow or widower can use.

290. Can both spouses receive retirement benefits?

Yes. If each is entitled to receive benefits based on their own earnings record, each can receive retirement benefits independently of the other's benefits. However, a spouse who is entitled to a retirement benefit AND a spouse's benefit cannot receive both in full. (For details of how a spouse's benefit is determined, see Q 102.)

See Case Studies for illustrations of situations where married couples have used planning to maximize benefits.

291. What kind of planning can be done regarding when Social Security benefits are started?

People today are much more interested in how they can maximize benefits. In dealing with clients now, it is more than just a question of "When should I take benefits?" Married couples can engage in planning, especially if both have worked and paid into Social Security for most of their careers. Ex-spouses also have claiming options. These planning techniques include taking a spousal benefit for a certain period of time and then switching to a benefit on the worker's own record. Or, a worker filing for benefits, but then electing not to take the benefits so that a spouse can take benefits. These strategies are known as "Restricted Application" and "File and Suspend". In November 2015, Congress passed the 2015 Bi-Partisan Budget Act which limits the use of the strategies and over time will completely phase out these options. Do not dismiss these strategies. Many of your clients are still able to utilize the Restricted Application, thereby maximizing their Social Security benefits. Please keep in mind that the use of following strategies listed below are subject to the deadlines identified in the 2015 Bi-Partisan Budget Act.

Among the strategies available for married couples are:

- Both Husband and Wife file for retirement benefits at age sixty-two.

- Wife files for retirement benefits at age sixty-two. Husband files for spousal benefits at age sixty-six (FRA). Husband files for retirement benefits on his own at age seventy.

- Wife takes retirement benefits at age sixty-two. Husband files for retirement benefits at his full retirement age and suspended his benefits by April 29, 2016. Wife files for spousal benefits at this time. Husband reinstates his benefits at age seventy. This is often called, "File & Suspend" (see Q 286).

- Wife takes retirement benefits at her full retirement age Husband takes spousal benefits at his full retirement age. Husband files for retirement benefits at age seventy. This is often referred to as "Restricted Application" (see Q 287).

- Wife files for retirement benefits at her full retirement age. Husband files for retirement benefits at his full retirement age and suspended his benefits by April 29, 2016. Wife files for spousal benefits when husband files at his full retirement age. Husband reinstates his retirement benefits at age seventy.

- Husband files for retirement benefits at his full retirement age and suspended his benefits by April 29, 2016. Wife files for spousal benefits at her full retirement age. Husband reinstates his retirement benefits at age seventy and Wife files for her own retirement benefits at age seventy.

- Wife files for retirement at her full retirement age and suspends benefits by April 29, 2016. Husband files for spousal benefits at his full retirement age. Wife reinstates her retirement benefits at age seventy and Husband files for his own retirement benefits at age seventy.

- Husband takes retirement benefits at age sixty-two. Wife files for spousal benefits at her full retirement age; Wife files for her own retirement benefits at age seventy.

Please remember that wife must have been born on before January 1, 1954 to file a Restricted Application. Of course, if not desiring to file a Restricted Application, wife will be subject to the Deemed Filing rules.

- Recent law changes may encourage the higher wage earner to claim benefits at FRA, to allow the payment of spousal benefits to spouse. Assume that Husband is eligible for $2,000 at FRA. One option is to wait to age seventy, thereby maximizing his benefit due to the receipt of Delayed Retirement Credits. His wife has not earned forty credits and is not eligible to her own Social Security benefits. Wife is only eligible for a spousal benefit. If Husband delays to age seventy, then Wife will miss out on four years of spousal benefits. If Husband begins at FRA, then Wife will be eligible for spousal benefits sooner. Thus, the decision by Husband on when he begins his benefits will have a direct impact to the timing of spousal benefits by Wife.

- In the case of a married couple, the Husband's PIA is $2,250 and Wife's PIA is $1,000. One strategy is for Wife to begin her benefit at age sixty-two. At age sixty-two, Wife will receive $750 per month. Husband waits to age seventy to begin his benefits thereby receiving the maximum in DRCs. Wife will "step into the shoes" of her husband upon his death as she will be eligible for a survivor's benefit. This strategy makes sense as Wife will most likely collect as a surviving spouse. In the meantime, she receives her benefit albeit at a reduced amount. If Wife waits to age seventy to begin her benefit, she will receive $1,320. But she will only receive this higher amount until Husband passes away. It might be best for Wife to begin her benefit at age sixty-two. Wife will of course be subject to the Annual Earnings Test. Husband, if born on or before January 1, 1954 can file a Restricted Application.

As Deemed Filing does not apply to surviving spouses the following strategies are still available for widows or widowers:

- Widow/Widower takes the higher benefit at the earliest time; thus, she would take Widows/Widowers benefits at age sixty or retirement benefits at age sixty-two.

    o   Widow/Widower takes surviving spouse benefits at age sixty, then begins benefits on own retirement at full retirement age.

    o   Widow/Widower takes surviving spouse benefits at age sixty, then begins benefits on own retirement at age seventy.

    o   Widow/Widower takes her own retirement at age sixty-two, and then begins Widows/Widowers benefits at full benefit age.

See Case Studies which illustrates situational planning resulting in maximization of benefits.

292. In a situation where there is a lower earning spouse aged sixty-two and a higher earning spouse aged sixty-six – can the lower earning spouse claim benefits at age sixty-two and then switch to a spousal benefit when the higher earning spouse applies at age seventy?

Technically – no. A sixty-two-year-old cannot simply switch to a spousal benefit when the spouse begins to receive. The younger spouse may be eligible for the spousal boost in additional to their own benefit. The spousal boost is equal to 50 percent of the higher earner's PIA, (Primary Insurance Amount), minus the PIA of the younger lower earning spouse. The spousal boost is added to the younger spouse's own benefit. If the spouse aged sixty-two took their own benefits prior to FRA, then he / she will never receive 50 percent of spouse's PIA. Once someone takes a reduced benefit on their own work record, it remains reduced. An erroneous misunderstanding is that a wife can begin her benefits at age sixty-two (reduced by 25 percent) and then switch to 50 percent of husband's PIA when eligible.

See Case Studies for illustration of situations where one spouse has significantly lower earnings than the other spouse.

293. Can you file for spousal benefits only at FRA if your spouse is only sixty-two and has not filed?

No. You can only file the Restricted Application at Full Retirement Age (FRA) if your spouse is sixty-two is receiving retirement benefits or receiving disability benefits or filed and suspended by the April 2016 deadline. If receiving disability benefits, the spouse you are collecting from may be under age sixty-two. The individual must have turned age sixty-two by January 1, 2016 to file a restricted application at Full Retirement Age.

See Case Studies illustrating where spousal benefit is claimed and also where the restricted application is used.

294. If a person files for a spousal benefit before age seventy and then begins receiving monthly benefits at age seventy, do they get BOTH the spousal amount plus the age seventy monthly benefit?

No, they get the higher benefit of the two.

See Case Studies illustrating situations where people filed for spousal benefits.

295. When is the best time to file for Social Security retirement benefits?

The decision on when to apply for Social Security retirement benefits depends on a number of factors. Taking benefits early (before Full Retirement Age) will result in a permanent reduction of benefits. Taking retirement benefits later can result in a higher benefit amount, but a shorter life may result in collecting lower total benefits. The Social Security Administration provides a Benefits Planners on its website which includes a number of calculators to help a person determine the right time to file for benefits and the effect on benefits of filing early or late.[1]

However, the federal government does allow an individual a "re-do" if he or she decides that the application for retirement benefits was made too early. By filing Form SSA-521,[2] an individual can request that the original application for retirement benefits be withdrawn and a new application date be substituted. The catch is that the individual must pay back all retirement benefits received up to the date of the withdrawal. However, the federal government does not

---

1. Benefits Planners, https://www.ssa.gov/planners/index.html (Last accessed October 24, 2018).
2. Form SSA-521 Request for Withdrawal of Application, Social Security Administration http://www.ssa.gov/forms/ssa-521.pdf (Last accessed October 24, 2018).

charge a penalty or interest for filing a Form SSA-521, but the individual must have the cash to repay the federal government. Note that a "re-do" can only be done within one year of first filing for benefits.

Another consideration to be considered as to when to take retirement benefits is how much income will be earned in the year for which benefits are applied. Too much earned income can result in a loss of benefits (see Q 318).

Additionally, since Social Security benefits may be subject to income taxation (see Q 343), the individual's income and tax situation should be considered.

A person should access the Social Security Administration's website or contact a Social Security office two or three months before reaching age sixty-two. The website and/or the Social Security office will furnish the information needed to decide whether or not to file an application for retirement benefits at that time. Because of the rules regarding retroactive benefits, a person should consider filing for benefits on January 1 of the year that he attains full retirement age, which may actually be older than age sixty-five (see Q 46).

If a worker does not file an application, he should contact the Social Security office again:

(1)   two or three months before retirement;

(2)   as soon as the worker knows that he will neither earn more than the monthly exempt amount in wages nor render substantial services in self-employment in one or more months of the year, regardless of expected total annual earnings; or

(3)   two or three months before the worker reaches Full Retirement Age (FRA), even if still working.

It may be advantageous to delay filing an application for benefits where: (1) the person is under the FRA and wishes to wait and receive an unreduced benefit at FRA but benefits are not payable because of earnings (application at or near retirement may provide higher benefits in the year of retirement), or (3) the person would lose benefits payable under some other program.

See Case Studies for illustration of situations detailing the best time to file for Social Security benefits.

296. When should a person file for retirement benefits?

In the past, the Social Security Administration suggested that a person contact a Social Security office within two months of reaching age sixty-two (or the age in which they wanted to begin collecting retirement benefits.) This suggestion was before the advent of computers and online filing – at this point the person can file the application in the month they want benefits to begin.

It may be advantageous to delay filing an application for benefits where:

(1)   the person is under the Full Retirement Age (FRA) and wishes to wait and receive an unreduced benefit at FRA;

(2)   the person is at the FRA, but benefits are not payable because of earnings (application at or near retirement may provide higher benefits in the year of retirement); or

(3)   the person would lose benefits payable under some other program.

Year of Retirement

297. If age sixty-two is the computation age, is there any advantage to waiting until Full Retirement Age (FRA) to collect benefits?

Yes, the full PIA is payable at Full Retirement Age (FRA), (see Q 251), with a reduced amount paid in case of an earlier retirement age. Age sixty-two is used to determine elapsed years but earnings are counted to full retirement age.

Early retirement usually affects the benefit in two ways:

- the PIA usually will be smaller (because fewer years of possibly higher earnings will be used in computing the AIME); and

- the lower PIA will be subject to reduction (5/9 of 1 percent per month for the first thirty-six months under the full retirement age and 5/12 of 1 percent per month for any additional months under the full retirement age).

See Case Studies for illustrations of advantages of waiting until Full Retirement Age (FRA) or later.

298. Can a person obtain higher retirement benefits by working past full retirement age?

Yes, in two ways.

First, workers who continue on the job receive an increase in retirement benefits for each year they work between full retirement age and age seventy. Note that this is *not* an increase in the worker's PIA. Other benefits based on the PIA, such as those payable to a spouse or children, are not affected.

This delayed retirement credit is also payable to a worker's surviving spouse receiving a widow(er)'s benefit.

Beginning in 1990, the delayed retirement credit payable to workers who attain age sixty-two after 1986 and who delay retirement past the full retirement age, the full-benefit age (gradually rising from age sixty-five to age sixty-seven) is gradually increased. The delayed retirement credit is increased by one-half of 1 percent every other year until reaching 8 percent per year in 2009 or later. The higher delayed retirement credits are based on the year of attaining age sixty-two and are payable only at and after full retirement age.

Delayed Retirement Credit Rates

Attain Age 62	Monthly Percentage	Yearly Percentage
1979-1986	1/4 of 1%	3%
1987-1988	7/24 of 1%	3.50%
1989-1990	1/3 of 1%	4%
1991-1992	3/8 of 1%	4.50%
1993-1994	5/12 of 1%	5%
1995-1996	11/24 of 1%	5.50%
1997-1998	1/2 of 1%	6%
1999-2000	13/24 of 1%	6.50%
2001-2002	7/12 of 1%	7%
2003-2004	5/8 of 1%	7.50%
2005 or after	2/3 of 1%	8%

Workers, who became age sixty-five before 1990 (and after 1981) and continued on the job, received an increase in retirement benefits usually equal to 3 percent for each year (1/12 of 3 percent for each month) they worked between age sixty-five and seventy. (The factor was only 1 percent for workers who became age sixty-five before 1982.)

Second, working past the full retirement age may result in a larger PIA due to higher earnings. The reason: In figuring the earnings to be used in the thirty-five calculations the Social Security Administration will compare recent earnings to the lowest earnings level used and if higher the recent earnings will replace a lower year resulting in increased benefits.

Assume that Paul, age sixty-two, has paid in the maximum SS tax resulting in the maximum benefit. Paul decides to work from age sixty-two to age sixty-six. Paul's higher earnings will replace the prior earnings years used in the calculating resulting in a $20 increase to his PIA. Paul would have paid around $28,000 in FICA taxes. Breakeven point is 100 years or age 166. (See Q 236).

See Case Studies for illustrations of advantages of working past Full Retirement Age (FRA).

299. Will the retirement age at which unreduced benefits are available ever be increased?

Yes, the Social Security Amendments of 1983 increased the full retirement age (the age at which unreduced benefits are available), by two months per year for workers reaching age sixty-two in 2000-2005 – to age sixty-six; maintained age sixty-six for workers reaching age sixty-two in 2006-2016; increased by two months a year the retirement age for workers reaching age sixty-two in 2017-2022; and maintained age sixty-seven for workers reaching age sixty-two after 2022. It does not change the age of eligibility for Medicare.

The 1983 amendments do not change the availability of reduced benefits at sixty-two (sixty for widow(er)s), but revise the reduction factors so that there is a further reduction (up to a maximum of 30 percent for workers entitled at age sixty-two after the full retirement age is increased to age sixty-seven, rather than only up to 20 percent for entitlement at age sixty-two under prior rules). There is no increase in the maximum reduction in the case of widow(er)s, but some increases in the reduction occur at ages over sixty and under full retirement age.

Effects of Retirement-Age Provision in Social Security Amendments of 1983*

Year of Birth	Attainment of Age 62	Full retirement age (Year/Months)	Date of Attainment of Full retirement age[1]	Age-62 Benefit as Percent of PIA[2]
1938	2000	65/2	March 1, 2003	79.2
1939	2001	65/4	May 1, 2004	78.3
1940	2002	65/6	July 1, 2005	77.5
1941	2003	65/8	September 1, 2006	76.7
1942	2004	65/10	November 1, 2007	75.8
1943-1954	2005-2016	66/0	January 1, 2009-2020	75.0
1955	2017	66/2	March 1, 2021	74.2
1956	2018	66/4	May 1, 2022	73.3
1957	2019	66/6	July 1, 2023	72.5
1958	2020	66/8	September 1, 2024	71.7
1959	2021	66/10	November 1, 2025	70.8
1960 and after	2022 and after	67/0	January 1, 2027 and after	70.0

* Full retirement age is for worker and spouse benefits only. Full retirement age for widow(er)s is based on attainment of age 60 in 2000 or later, so that Full retirement age is age 67 beginning 2029.

[1] Birth date assumed to be January 2 of year (for benefit-entitlement purposes, the Social Security Administration considers a person to reach a given age on the day before the anniversary of his birth, thus, someone born on the 1st of the month is considered to reach a given age on the last day of the previous month). For later months of birth, add number of months elapsing after January up to birth month.

[2] Applies present-law reduction factor (5/9 of 1 percent per month) for the first 36 months' receipt of early retirement benefits and new reduction factor of 5/12 of 1 percent per month for additional months.

300. How are a beneficiary's benefits figured when he is entitled to a reduced retirement benefit and a larger spouse's benefit simultaneously?

The beneficiary will receive the retirement benefit, reduced in the regular manner. (See Q 251.) That is, the PIA is reduced by 5/9 of 1 percent (1/180) for each of the first thirty-six months that he is under Full Retirement Age (FRA) when benefits commence, and 5/12 of 1 percent (1/240) for each month in excess of thirty-six. The beneficiary will also receive a spouse's benefit based on the difference between the (1/2 of his or her spouse's PIA) and his or her PIA. This spouse's benefit is reduced by 25/36 of 1 percent (1/144) for each of the first thirty-six months that he is under Full Retirement Age (FRA) when benefits commence, and 5/12 of 1 percent (1/240) for each month in excess of thirty-six. (See Q 255.)

301. What were the advantages and disadvantages of using file and suspend?

Prior to recent changes by Congress, there were two advantages and one disadvantage.

The advantages included:

1) If you file and suspend, you allowed anyone else eligible on your work record (i.e., spouse or child) to draw their benefits.

2) You also created a safety net so if at some point before you reach age seventy, you can request your benefits all the way back to when you filed (i.e., age sixty-six).

The disadvantage to file and suspend was that there were limitations on having a Health Savings Account (HSA) – if you file and suspend, you will at least have Part A of Medicare. Participating in Medicare precludes you from contributing to a Health Savings Account.

The benefits discussed above are only available if an individual filed and suspended by April 29, 2016.

302. How does a "restricted application" differ from "file and suspend"?

"File and Suspend" is the action of filing for benefits on your own work record but suspending payment. You will earn delayed retirement credits and create the "safety net". Prior to recent law changes the main benefit of the strategy was the payment of a spousal benefit while the high-income earner's benefits were suspended. Due to the recent change, auxiliary benefits such as to a spouse or children will also be suspended.

A "Restricted application" is filing for spousal benefits. You will still earn Delayed Retirement Credits (DRC) on your own work record but draw benefits as a spouse at the same time.

See Case Studies for illustrations of using "File and Suspend" and for using "Restricted Application".

303. Can both spouses "file and suspend" at the same time?

Assuming the April 2016 deadline had been met, both spouses could have filed and suspended at the same time.

Caution – in this situation it might have been beneficial for one of the spouses to file a restricted application at Full Retirement Age (FRA) if they reached age sixty-two by January 1, 2016.

304. Was it possible to file and suspend and file a restricted application?

No. You could only do one. Of course, you needed to meet the deadlines outlined in the Bipartisan Budget Act of 2015.

305. Could both husband and wife file a restricted application for the other's spousal benefit?

No. To file a restricted application, the other spouse must have already filed for retirement or disability benefits or filed and suspended by April 29, 2016 on their own work record.

306. Could you file and suspend at sixty-two to allow a nonworking spouse who is in ill health to collect one-half of benefit?

No, you could not file and suspend until Full Retirement Age (FRA). Due to changes in the law, an individual must have filed and suspended by April 29, 2016.

307. In a situation where a husband is aged sixty-six and working, could he file and suspend? Assuming his wife is age sixty – two and has earned forty credits, could she have then waited until she was seventy to begin benefits or should she have filed a restricted application at her own FRA?

It depends. If the husband was able to file and suspend by the April 2016 deadline, then he would have been to utilize this strategy. If he turned FRA after May 1, 2016, then, no – the file and suspend strategy is not available.

The wife can wait until age seventy, however if she turned age sixty-two by January 1, 2016, then she should have considered the restricted application at her own Full Retirement Age, thereby receiving spousal benefits while her benefits are increasing. Unfortunately, for the wife to draw a spousal benefit the husband must be receiving a benefit or have filed and suspended by the April 29, 2016 deadline.

308. After filing a restricted application, does one have to wait until reaching age seventy to begin their own benefit?

No. A person is not locked in until age seventy but can begin benefits at any time.

309. Is it safe to assume that a single person could only use the File and Suspend strategy but not the restricted application?

Yes, unless they have an ex-spouse and were married to them for over ten years. One of the benefits to filing and suspending was the accumulation of a cash reserve. Due to the changes from the 2015 Bipartisan Budget Act, the opportunity to build a cash reserve while benefits have been suspended has been terminated. Thus, the incentives to suspend benefits have been greatly reduced.

See Case Studies for an illustration of individuals with ex-spouses.

310. If a spouse filed and suspended by April 29, 2016 and delays collecting until age seventy, will the other spouse get an amount equal to half of the income based on the Delayed Retirement Credits or based on the Full Retirement Age (FRA) benefit?

The spousal benefit is based on Primary Insurance Amount (PIA). The PIA represents the amount of Social Security benefits at Full Retirement Age (FRA). A current spouse does not receive any advantage of the delayed retirement credits. Of course, the opposite is also true. If the husband took his benefit at age sixty-two and took the 25 percent reduction, his spouse is still eligible for a spousal benefit based on his PIA at her Full Retirement Age (FRA).

311. What if a person dies after filing and suspending but before receiving benefits? Can the widow collect that lump sum?

No. Only the person filing the application can request the lump sum benefit. The widow would still get the Delayed Retirement Credits, which results in a higher monthly benefit.

312. If a husband filed and suspended and the wife takes spousal benefits at age sixty-two, will the wife get a stepped-up spousal benefit if the husband dies at age seventy-two after delaying his benefit until age seventy?

Yes. The spouse taking a reduced benefit, either on their own or as a spouse, does not affect the survivor's benefit. If the surviving spouse is Full Benefit Age when their spouse dies, they will get 100 percent of what the deceased was receiving or was eligible to receive.

313. Can a working couple both at Full Retirement Age (FRA) claim both file and suspend and file restricted applications in order to receive two Social Security checks?

To file and suspend, husband and wife must have filed by April 29, 2016. However, it would have been a mistake for both spouses to have filed and suspended by the April 2016 deadline. Filing and suspending does not allow the payment of spousal benefit. The payment of a spousal benefit is accomplished by filing a restricted application. In the situation above, either spouse would file and suspend allowing the other spouse to file a restricted application. Both spouses cannot file restricted applications to receive only spousal benefits. Both can file and suspend, but only one can do the restricted application. You cannot do both and you cannot file on another's record unless they have also filed.

314. What is the best strategy in a situation where the husband is age sixty-six, with an income of $150,000 per year, and the wife is age sixty-eight, with an income of $50,000 per year?

This depends on the PIA of each and when the husband turned FRA. Assuming that the husband has the higher PIA and turned FRA by May 1, 2016, he should have filed and suspended by the April 29, 2016, deadline allowing the wife to file a restricted application. This will ensure the maximization of benefits.

See Case Studies for illustrations of couples where one spouse had significantly more income than the other spouse.

315. What is a good strategy in a situation where the husband is age sixty-six with an income of $150,000 per year and the wife is age sixty-eight, with an income of $50,000 per year and the wife has already filed for benefits?

It is difficult determining the best strategy regarding Social Security benefits as many factors need to be considered. However, in this situation a strategy to consider is the husband filing a restricted application to receive a spousal benefit at FRA delaying receipt of his benefits to age seventy. This strategy makes sense if the wife filed over a year ago as she cannot withdraw her application.

See Case Studies for illustrations of high earners filing Restricted Applications.

316. What option might one use if there is a significant difference in ages between spouses, for example, if the husband is twelve years older than wife?

Normally in this case, the older individual (in this case, the husband) is looking at the same options as a single person; however, unlike the single person, they DO want to maximize survivor benefits. For example, the older spouse takes benefits at age seventy and the younger spouse takes benefits at age sixty. This works because based on life expectancies, the younger spouse will collect survivor benefits for many years.

See Case Studies for illustrations of planning where one spouse is significantly older than the other.

317. What are the limitations of the "do-over" as an option?

The "do-over" still exists, with limitations. It must be done within the first year of entitlement and can only be done once. If an individual begins benefits in July, the last day to file Form SSA-521 is June 30th of the following year.

LOSS OF BENEFITS BECAUSE OF "EXCESS" EARNINGS

Retirement Test

318. Can a person lose some or all Social Security benefits by working?

Yes, if the person is under Full Retirement Age (FRA) (see Q 46) for all of 2019 and earns over $17,640; or in the year the person reaches Full Retirement Age he or she earns over $46,920, except that only earnings earned before the month he or she reaches Full Retirement Age count towards the $46,920 limit.[1] An alternative test applies in the initial year of retirement if it produces a more favorable result (see the last "bullet" of Q 320). See Q 255 for a discussion of the Full Retirement Age.

The annual exempt amounts will be increased each year as wage levels rise.

A beneficiary who is older than the Full Retirement Age can earn any amount without losing benefits. Regardless of how much earnings are in the year of attaining Full Retirement Age, no benefits are withheld for the month in which Full Retirement Age is reached, or for any subsequent month. Also, earnings in and after the month in which a person attains Full Retirement Age will not be included in determining total earnings for the year.

The retirement test does not apply to individuals entitled to benefits because of their disability or to beneficiaries outside the United States whose work is not covered by Social Security.

Annual Exempt Amounts

Year	Year Retirement Age Reached	Under Retirement Age
1985	$7,320	$5,400
1986	7,800	5,760
1987	8,160	6,000
1988	8,400	6,120
1989	8,880	6,480
1990	9,360	6,840
1991	9,720	7,080
1992	10,200	7,440
1993	10,560	7,680
1994	11,160	8,040
1995	11,280	8,160
1996	11,520	8,280

---

1. 42 U.S.C. § 403(f).

Year	Year Retirement Age Reached	Under Retirement Age
1997	13,500	8,640
1998	14,500	9,120
1999	15,500	9,600
2000	17,000	10,080
2001	25,000	10,680
2002	30,000	11,280
2003	30,720	11,520
2004	31,080	11,640
2005	31,800	12,000
2006	33,240	12,480
2007	34,440	12,960
2008	36,120	13,560
2009-2011	37,680	14,160
2012	38,880	14,640
2013	40,080	15,120
2014	41,400	15,480
2015-2016	41,880	15,720
2017	44,880	16,920
2018	45,360	17,040
2019	46,920	17,640

319. What are the components of the "Earnings Test"?

The "Earnings Test" is also commonly referred to as the "Retirement Test" and is used to:

(1)   measure the extent of a person's retirement;

(2)   determine any amount that needs to be deducted from monthly benefits (if any); and

(3)   measure the work activity of any other individuals entitled to collect from a person's record and the amount due to them.

320. What are the general rules for loss of benefits because of excess earnings?

When the beneficiary is older than the Full Retirement Age (FRA) (see Q 46), no benefits are lost because of his earnings. If he is under the Full Retirement Age, the following rules apply:[1]

- If no more than $46,920 is earned in 2019 by a beneficiary who reaches the Full Retirement Age in 2018, no benefits will be lost for that year.

---

1. 42 U.S.C. 403(f).

- If more than $46,920 is earned in 2019 before the month the beneficiary reaches Full Retirement Age, one dollar of benefits will ordinarily be lost for each three dollars of earnings over $46,920.

- If not more than $17,640 is earned in 2019 by a beneficiary who is under the Full Retirement Age for the entire year, no benefits will be lost for that year.

- If more than $17,640 is earned in 2019 by a beneficiary who is under the Full Retirement Age for the entire year, one dollar of benefits will ordinarily be lost for each two dollars of earnings over $17,640.

- No matter how much is earned during 2019, no *retirement* benefits in the *initial year of retirement* will be lost for any month in which the beneficiary neither: (1) earns over $1,470 as an employee if retiring in a year prior to the year he reaches Full Retirement Age, nor (2) renders any substantial services in self-employment.

The initial year of retirement is the first year in which he is both entitled to benefits and has a month in which he does not earn over the monthly exempt wage amount (as listed previously) and does not render substantial services in self-employment.

When the monthly earnings test applies, regardless of the amount of annual earnings, the beneficiary gets full benefits for any month in which earnings do not exceed the monthly exempt amount, and the beneficiary does not perform substantial services in self-employment.

The attainment of Full Retirement Age in a year determines which test applies. The Full Retirement Age test applies if the beneficiary attains Full Retirement Age on or before the last day of the taxable year involved. The "under Full Retirement Age" test applies if the beneficiary does not attain Full Retirement Age on or before the last day of the taxable year. See Q 255 for a discussion of the increase in the Full Retirement Age.

> *Example 1.* Dr. James, who reports his earnings on a calendar year basis, reaches Full Retirement Age (sixty-six years old) on June 18, 2019. The under Full Retirement Age test ($17,640 for 2019) applies for calendar year 2019, and the Full Retirement Age test ($46,920) applies for calendar year 2018. However, none of Dr. James earnings earned in June through December 2018 count towards the $46,920 limit.

> *Example 2.* Miss Norton, who reports her earnings on the basis of a fiscal year ending June 30, attains Full Retirement Age (sixty-six years old) on September 15, 2019. The under Full Retirement Age test ($17,640) applies for her fiscal year July 1, 2018 through June 30, 2019. The Full Retirement Age test ($46,920) applies for her next fiscal year; however, only earnings earned in July and August, 2018 count towards the $46,920 limit.

321. What is the monthly exempt amount?

The monthly exempt amount that applies to earnings from employment is as follows:

(1) For years 2015, and 2016,–

    (a) Prior to reaching Full Retirement Age: $1,310

    (b) After reaching Full Retirement Age: $3,490

(2)   For 2017 —

(a) Prior to reaching Full Retirement Age: $1,410

(b) After reaching Full Retirement Age: $3,740

(3)   For 2018 —

(a) Prior to reaching Full Retirement Age: $1,420

(b) After reaching Full Retirement Age: $3,780

(4)   For 2019 —

(a) Prior to reaching Full Retirement Age: $1,470

(b) After reaching Full Retirement Age: $3,910

322. How are "excess" earnings charged against benefits?

In determining the amount of benefits for a given year that will be lost, two factors must be taken into consideration:

(1)   the amount of the person's "excess" earnings for the year; and

(2)   the months in the year that can actually be charged with all or a portion of the excess earnings potentially chargeable in the initial year of retirement.[1]

Both wages earned as employee and net earnings from self-employment are combined for purposes of determining the individual's total earnings for the year. Only "excess earnings" are potentially chargeable against benefits. If a person is under the Full Retirement Age (FRA) for the entire year and earns $17,640 or less (in 2019) for the year, there are no "excess earnings." If earnings for the year are more than $17,640, one-half of the amount over $17,640 is "excess earnings." In the year a person reaches the Full Retirement Age, he or she can earn up to $46,920 (in 2019) before losing benefits. However, only earnings earned before the month the person reaches Full Retirement Age count toward the $46,920 limit. See Q 253 for a discussion of the Full Retirement Age.

Excess earnings are charged against retirement benefits in the following manner. They are charged first against all benefits payable on the worker's account for the first month of the year. If any excess earnings remain, they are charged against all benefits payable for the second month of the year, and so on until all the excess earnings have been charged, or no benefits remain for the year. However, a month cannot be charged with any excess earnings and must be skipped if the individual:

(1)   was not entitled to benefits for that month;

(2)   was over Full Retirement Age in that month;

---

1. 20 CFR Part 404, Subpart E.

(3)   in the initial year of retirement, he or she did not earn over $1,470 (using 2019 figures) if he or she retires in a year before the year he or she reaches Full Retirement Age; or

(4)   he or she did not render substantial services as a self-employed person in that month.

If the excess earnings chargeable to a month are less than the benefits payable to the worker and to other persons on his account, the excess is chargeable to each beneficiary in the proportion that the original entitlement rate of each bears to the sum of all their original entitlement rates.

Example 1. Dr. Brown partially retires in January 2019 at the age of sixty-two. Based on his earnings history and the age he starts receiving benefits, his Social Security benefit is $1,200 per month. He practices for three months in 2019 and earns $30,000. The remainder of his initial year of retirement is spent in Florida playing golf. Despite the fact that Dr. Brown has excess earnings in 2019 that would, under the annual test, cause a benefit loss of $7,140, he will lose only the $3,600 in benefits for the three months during which he performed substantial services in self-employment, because 2019 is his initial year of retirement.

Example 2. Dr. Smith, who partially retired in 2018 at age sixty-two, practices for four months in 2018 and earns $32,000. As 2019 is his second year of retirement, the monthly-earnings test does not apply. His benefit will be reduced by $1 for each $2 of earnings over $17,640. This means that Dr. Smith's benefits in 2019 will be reduced by $7,480 (one-half of the amount in excess of $17,640).

Example 3. Mr. Martin is sixty-six years old and has not retired. He earns $46,000 a year. Mr. Martin receives Social Security retirement benefits of $700 a month. Because he is over the Full Retirement Age, he loses none of his benefits by working.

The annual exempt amount is not prorated in the year of death. In addition, the higher exempt amount applies to persons who die before their date of birth in the year that they otherwise would have attained Full Retirement Age.

323. Can a person who is receiving dependent's or survivor's benefits lose benefits by working?

Yes, if the person is under the Full Retirement Age (FRA) for the entire year and earns over $17,640 (in 2019), or in the year the person reaches Full Retirement Age he earns over $46,920. Only earnings earned before the month the person reaches Full Retirement Age count toward the $46,920 limit.[1] The same "retirement test" applies as applies to retirement beneficiaries (see Q 320). However, the excess earnings of a person receiving dependent's or survivor's benefits are not charged against the benefits payable to other dependents or survivors. For example, a child's excess earnings are not chargeable against a mother's benefits. A retirement beneficiary's excess earnings, on the other hand, *are* chargeable against a dependent's benefits, as those benefits are based on the retirement beneficiary's Social Security account.

324. If a widow's benefits are withheld because of work, will this necessarily reduce the total amount of benefits payable to the family?

No. Where there are several children, all survivor benefits may have to be reduced to come within the maximum family benefit. Even though the mother works and loses her benefits, the

---

1. 42 U.S.C. § 403(f).

maximum may still be payable to the children. In many cases, however, loss of the mother's benefits will reduce the total amount of benefits payable to the family.[1]

> *Example 1.* Mr. Smith dies in 2018, leaving a widow and four small children. His PIA is $700. If it were not for the maximum family limit, the widow and each child would be entitled to a survivor's benefit of $525 (75 percent of $700). However, because the maximum family benefit for a PIA of $700 is $1,050, each beneficiary receives only $210 (one-fifth of $1,050, rounded to the next lower even dollar). Mrs. Smith goes to work and earns an amount sufficient to eliminate her mother's benefits ($1 is withheld for every $2 of excess earnings). Nevertheless, the family still receives $1,050 in benefits, because each child's benefit is raised to $262 (one-fourth of $1,050, rounded to the next lower even dollar).

> *Example 2.* Mr. Jones dies in 2018, leaving a widow and two small children. His PIA is $800, and the maximum family benefit is $1,200. If it were not for the maximum family limit, the widow and each child would be entitled to a monthly benefit of $600 (75 percent of $800). Because of the family maximum limit, however, each receives only $400 (one-third of $1,200, rounded to the next lower even dollar). Mrs. Jones goes to work and earns an amount sufficient to eliminate her widow's benefits. Each child then receives a full benefit of $600.

325. Which beneficiaries are not subjected to the Earnings Test?

The "Earnings Test" will not apply if the individual:

(1)   has reached Full Retirement Age (FRA);

(2)   has become eligible to collect benefits based on disability;

(3)   is living outside of the United States AND the work performed is not covered by Social Security; or

(4)   is a divorced spouse of the earner whose month of entitlement is prior to the month of the divorce.

326. What is the benefit amount when the monthly earnings test applies?

When the monthly earnings test applies, the individual will receive fully benefits for any month that they did not:

(1)   exceed the monthly exemption amount; and

(2)   perform substantial services in self-employment.

327. How is the loss of benefits figured for the year in which the worker reaches full retirement age?

In the year in which a person reaches Full Retirement Age (FRA), his earnings in and after the month in which he reaches Full Retirement Age will not be included in determining his total earnings for the year.[2]

---

1. See 20 CFR Part 404, Subpart E.
2. 42 U.S.C. 403(f).

328. What kinds of income will not count under the Earnings Test and will not cause loss of benefits?

The following types of income are *not* counted as "earnings" for purposes of the retirement test:[1]

- Any income from employment earned in or after the month the individual reaches Full Retirement Age (FRA). (Self-employment income earned in the year is not examined as to when earned, but is prorated by months, even though actually earned after Full Retirement Age.) See Q 253 for a discussion of Full Retirement Age.

- Any income from self-employment received in a taxable year after the year the individual becomes entitled to benefits, but not attributable to significant services performed after the first month of entitlement to benefits. This income is excluded from gross income only for purposes of the earnings test.

- Damages, attorneys' fees, interest, or penalties paid under court judgment or by compromise settlement with an employer based on a wage claim. However, back pay recovered in such proceedings counts for the earnings test.

- Payments to secure release of an unexpired contract of employment.

- Certain payments made under a plan or system established for making payments because of the employee's sickness or accident disability, medical or hospitalization expenses, or death.

- Payments from certain trust funds that are exempt from income tax.

- Payments from certain annuity plans that are exempt from income tax.

- Pensions and retirement pay.

- Sick pay, if paid more than six months after the month the employee last worked.

- Payments-in-kind for domestic service in the employer's private home, for agricultural labor, for work not in the course of the employer's trade or business, or the value of meals and lodging furnished under certain conditions.

- Rentals from real estate that cannot be counted in earnings from self-employment because, for instance, the beneficiary did not materially participate in production work on the farm, the beneficiary was not a real estate dealer, etc.

- Interest and dividends from stocks and bonds (unless they are received by a dealer in securities in the course of business).

---

1. 20 CFR Part 404, Subpart E.

- Gain or loss from the sale of capital assets, or sale, exchange, or conversion of other property that is not stock in trade or includable in inventory.

- Net operating loss carryovers resulting from self-employment activities.

- Loans received by employees, unless the employees repay the loans by their work.

- Workers' compensation and unemployment compensation benefits.

- Veterans' training pay.

- Pay for jury duty.

- Prize winnings from contests, unless the person enters contests as a trade or business.

- Payments for length of service awards or achievement awards.

- Tips paid to an employee that are less than twenty dollars a month or are not paid in cash.

- Payments by an employer that are reimbursements specifically for travel expenses of the employee and that are so identified by the employer at the time of payment.

- Payments to an employee as a reimbursement or allowance for moving expenses, if they are not counted as wages for Social Security purposes.

- Royalties received in or after the year in which a person reaches Full Retirement Age, to the extent that they flow from property created by the person's own personal efforts that she copyrighted or patented before the taxable year in which she reached Full Retirement Age. These royalties are excluded from gross income from self-employment only for purposes of the earnings test.

- Retirement payments received by a retired partner from a partnership, provided certain conditions are met.

- Certain payments or series of payments paid by an employer to an employee or any of his or her dependents on or after the employment relationship has terminated because of death, retirement for disability, or retirement for age and paid under a plan established by the employer.

- Payments *from* Individual Retirement Accounts (IRAs) and Keogh Plans.

In other words, a person can receive almost any amount of investment or passive income without loss of benefits.[1]

---

1. https://www.ssa.gov/OP_Home%2Fhandbook/handbook.18/handbook-1812.html (Last accessed October 8, 2018).

329. Which earnings will count under the Earnings Test and potentially cause loss of benefits?

Generally, *Wages* received as an employee and net *earnings* from self-employment. Bonuses, commissions, fees, and earnings from all types of work, whether or not covered by Social Security, count for the retirement test. For example, earnings from family employment are counted – even though such employment is not covered by Social Security. Earnings above the Social Security "earnings base" are counted. Income as an absentee owner counts as "earnings" for the retirement test.[1] If the person renders substantial services as a self-employed person (even in another business), such income also will count as "earnings" for the taxable year in the initial year of retirement.

Specifically, the following types of earnings count for purposes of the earnings test:

- Wages for employment covered by Social Security

- Cash pay (even if not considered as "wages" under the cash-pay test) for:

  - Agricultural work

  - Domestic work in a private home, or

  - Service not in the course of the employer's trade or business

- All pay, cash and noncash, for work as a homeworker or for a nonprofit organization whether or not the $100 per year test is met

- Cash tips that equal or exceed $20 a month

- All pay for work not covered by Social Security, if the work is done in the U.S., including pay for:

  - Family employment

  - Work by students, student nurses, interns, newspaper, and magazine vendors

  - Work by Federal or State or foreign governments or instrumentalities; or

  - Word covered by the Railroad Retirement Act

- All net earnings from self-employment

- All pay for incentive, suggestion, and outstanding work awards

- All pay for occasional and regular bonuses

- All pay from a "cafeteria" plan if the payments meet the definition of wages and the plan is not a "qualified benefit"

---

1. 42 U.S.C. 403(f).

- All pay from a non-qualified deferred compensation plan/system

- All pay by an employer for educational assistance

- All pay from federally sponsored economic and human development programs only if payments are wages

- All pay for non-work periods including idle time, standby, and subject to call related payments

- All pay for prizes, awards, and gratuities only if it is part of the salesperson's wage structure

- All pay from television, radio, and motion picture residuals if the performer was an employee at the time of the original performance

330. How does the Annual Earnings Test work?

If you take Social Security benefits before reaching Full Retirement Age (FRA), and you earn income in excess of the annual earnings limit, your Social Security benefit will be reduced. Only "earned income" applies – NOT investment income. The annual earnings test limits (in 2019) earnings to $17,640. If your earnings exceed $17,640, Social Security will withhold one dollar of benefits for each two dollars that exceeds the earnings test limit.

During the year you reach Full Retirement Age, and up until the month you reach Full Retirement Age, Social Security will deduct one dollar for every three dollars you earn over the annual earnings limit, however you can earn up to (in 2019) $46,920 during the year you reach Full Retirement Age.

Once you reach Full Retirement Age, you are no longer subject to the annual earnings limit; you can earn as much as you like without incurring a reduction in your Social Security benefits. Your social benefits may however still be subject to income taxes.

331. How are total earnings computed?

Earnings, for the taxable year, as computed under the Earnings Test are:

(1)   the sum of wages for services performed during the taxable year; plus

(2)   all net earnings from self-employment for the taxable year; minus

(3)   any net loss from self-employment for the taxable year.

332. Are earnings counted even if the earner was not entitled to benefits for the entire year?

Yes. Earnings for the entire year are counted regardless of when during the year the individual became eligible for benefits.

333. Are earnings counted when the earner reaches Full Retirement Age (FRA)?

No. Earnings are not counted if earned in the month when the individual reaches Full Retirement Age (FRA) or any month thereafter.

334. What is meant by "substantial services" in self-employment?

Whether a self-employed beneficiary is rendering "substantial services" in the initial year of retirement is determined by the actual services rendered in the month. Each month is considered individually in determining if there are substantial services. The test is whether the person can reasonably be considered retired in the month. In applying the test, consideration is given to such factors as:

(1) the amount of time devoted to the business (including all time spent at the place of business or elsewhere) in any activity related to the business (including the time spent in planning and managing, as well as doing physical work);

(2) the nature of the services;

(3) the relationship of the activities performed before retirement to those performed after retirement; and

(4) other circumstances, such as the amount of capital the beneficiary has invested in the business, the type of business establishment, the presence of a paid manager, partner, or family member who manages the business, and the seasonal nature of the business.[1]

Generally, services of forty-five hours or less in a month are not considered substantial. However, as few as fifteen hours of service a month could be substantial if, for instance, they involved management of a sizeable business or were spent in a highly skilled occupation. Services of fewer than fifteen hours a month are never considered substantial.

There ARE limited instances in which regardless of the time devoted to business, services are not substantial if:

(1) the person's monthly earnings are readily determinable (e.g. personal service type self-employment involving no significant investment),

(2) the person's gross earnings, figured on a time basis, for services in a month are equal to or less than the monthly exempt amount, and

(3) there is no evidence to the contrary.

This exception to the forty-five-hour rule has limited application since in most self-employment, the monthly earnings are not easily determined.

---

1. 20 CFR Part 404, Subpart E.

The amount of earnings is not controlling. High earnings do not necessarily mean that substantial services were rendered, nor do low or no earnings mean that they were not rendered.

The Social Security Administration Program Operations Manual System (POMS) provides some illustrative examples of "substantial" and "not substantial":[1]

Services of More Than Forty-five Hours per Month Not Substantial

Example 1: A minister retires from a large church. He accepts appointment to a small church for monthly income which is equal to or less than the monthly exempt amount (including the value of parsonage he receives). Considering that the earnings do not exceed the monthly exempt amount, it would be reasonable to find that the services are not substantial even though the time he devotes to his ministry exceeds forty-five hours in a calendar month.

Example 2: An individual worked as an employee January through April and became entitled in May. He again works as an employee in November and December and the monthly earnings test applies to these months. He states he was self-employed from June through September and furnishes a contract with a company stating the services, he, as a self-employed individual, was to provide as a grounds keeper. The contract calls for payment on an hourly basis. Development shows the beneficiary was validly self-employed. In each of the months June through September he rendered over forty-five hours of service, but, because of the modest hourly fee paid for his services he earned less than the monthly test amount in each of the months. Based on the contract, his monthly earnings could be readily determined since he was paid an hourly rate and his earnings depended solely on his personal services. He had no significant investment in a "business." Therefore, it was determined that work deductions would not apply for June through September even though he exceeded forty-five hours of service in each of the months.

Services from Fifteen through Forty-five Hours
A Month That Are Substantial

The beneficiary devotes fifteen hours or more per month to managing a large business or engages in a highly skilled occupation. In such cases, the services could be considered substantial. In SSR 71-13c, an experienced engineer who, as a member of the board of directors of a loan association, inspected properties for a high fee but worked less than forty-five hours per month. Court determined services were substantial.[2]

NOTE: The "substantial services" test is used only for the initial year of retirement. After that, the amount of earnings alone determines whether benefits will be lost.

335. Must a Social Security beneficiary report earnings to the Social Security Administration?

The Social Security Administration uses earnings information for workers that has been reported by employers on W-2 income tax forms – or income reported by the self-employed on their tax forms. For most beneficiaries, the process is totally automated, with the Social Security Administration receiving and processing earnings information reported for tax purposes and using that information to adjust the Social Security benefits payable accordingly.

---

1. https://secure.ssa.gov/poms.nsf/lnx/0302505065.
2. *deVilla v. Finch*, U.S.D.C., S.D. Indiana (1/2/70) (CCH, UIR, Vol. 1A Fed. para 15,835.

Benefits will be stopped for the number of months necessary to offset excess earnings. If too much has been withheld, the beneficiary will receive a check for the underpayment. If too little, the overpayment will be withheld from future benefits or must be refunded.

336. How are a life insurance agent's first-year and renewal commissions treated for purposes of the retirement test?

Whether original (first year) and renewal commissions from the sale of life insurance policies are wages or earnings from self-employment depends upon the status of the agent when the sale of the policy was completed. If the agent was an employee when the sale of the policy was consummated, both original and renewal commissions from that policy are wages. If the agent was self-employed when the sale of the policy was completed, both the original and renewal commissions from the policy are earnings from self-employment.[1]

Each insurance company normally furnishes its agents with sufficient information identifying policies on which commission payments are made, amounts of payments that are regular commissions, the commuted value of the renewals, service fees, efficiency income, etc., to enable a beneficiary to figure how much the earnings are for Social Security purposes.

A life insurance agent will receive retirement benefits for the month in which Full Retirement Age (FRA) is reached, and for every month thereafter, regardless of whether still working and regardless of how much is earned.

Moreover, in the *initial year of retirement*, and regardless of the amount of earnings for the taxable year, benefits will not be lost for any month in which the individual neither:

(1)   earns more than $1,470 (if under Full Retirement Age) as an employee; nor

(2)   renders substantial services in self-employment. See Q 253 for a discussion of the Full Retirement Age.

It is necessary to determine whether the agent was an employee or a self-employed person when the policy was sold. (For status of a life insurance agent as an employee or as a self-employed person under Social Security, see Q 392.) The reason is that, for retirement test purposes, "wages" of an employee are treated as earnings in the year in which they are earned. But net earnings for self-employment are treated as earnings in the year in which they are received.

Original (first-policy-year) commissions are earnings for purposes of the retirement test for the month and year in which an employee-agent completed the sale of the policy. As a rule, an employee-agent is paid the original commission on a policy according to the way the insured person pays the premium. The entire original commission is earnings for the month in which the agent completed the sale of the policy, regardless of whether the commission is received on a monthly, quarterly, semi-annual, or annual basis.

---

1. 20 CFR Part 404, Subpart E.

Renewal commissions of an employee-agent are earnings for purposes of the retirement test for the month in which the employee completed the sale of the life insurance policy and are includable in total earnings for the taxable year. They are deferred compensation for services rendered in completing the sale.

All of the renewal commissions that an employee-agent anticipates receiving from a life insurance policy sold while an employee must be reported as earnings for purposes of the retirement test for the month and year in which the original sale of the policy was completed. If the anticipated renewal commissions fail to materialize (thus making incorrect the total annual or monthly earnings), any benefit previously withheld but now due the beneficiary will be paid.

An employee-agent beneficiary must include the following in figuring total earnings for purposes of the retirement test for a taxable year:

- All original commissions on life insurance policies sold during the year.

- All anticipated renewal commissions on life insurance policies sold in the year. If the agent-beneficiary cannot determine the exact amount of anticipated renewals from such policies, as a last resort it should be assumed that they equal the amount of the original commission.

- Insurance service fees, persistency fees, and the like earned during the year.

- All renewal commissions received in the taxable year from policies sold in prior years while self-employed.

- All remuneration classified as earnings from other jobs, trades, or business.

Thus, renewal commissions on business in past years are not "earnings" for retirement test purposes when received by the agent-beneficiary if he was an employee when the policies were sold.

An employee-agent earns commission on a life insurance policy in the month in which the last act required for entitlement to the commission is performed. The acts to be performed before entitlement to commissions are usually set out in the agent's contract with the company, or can be determined from the company's regulations, rules, or practices. The agent should submit a copy of the contract or other evidence if there is any doubt about the last act required.

The month in which the company approves the policy is not the month in which the commission was earned, unless it happens to coincide with the last act required of the agent (for instance, if later in that month the agent forwarded the first premium due on the approved policy and this qualified for the commission). Similarly, the month in which the agent delivered the policy and collected the initial premium is not the month in which the commission was earned if the agent qualified for the commission when the customer signed the policy application.

This same rule applies to converted policies. If the conversion of the life insurance policy resulted in new commissions, the commissions are earned in the month in which the agent performed the last act that qualified for those new commissions. In the latter case, it is immaterial that the conversion was accomplished with the help of another agent through the insistence of the purchaser of the policy; some action (even if it is only the signature) was required of the selling agent in order to be entitled to the new rate of commissions.

If the life insurance agent is a self-employed person when the policy is sold, first-year and renewal commissions are treated as earnings for purposes of Social Security taxes for the taxable year in which they are received. When a policy is sold, there should be reported in the year of sale only the first-year commission received on the policy in that year. Renewal commissions on such a policy will be treated as earnings for purposes of Social Security taxes in the year when received. Renewal commissions received in a year after the year of entitlement to Social Security benefits are not included as earnings for purposes of the retirement test, if they were the result of services rendered in or prior to the initial month of entitlement.

A self-employed agent includes the following in figuring total earnings for a particular taxable year for purposes of the retirement test:

- Original commissions received during the year.

- Renewal commissions received during the year from policies sold while a self-employed agent, if the policies were sold after the initial month of entitlement to Social Security benefits, but not for such policies sold in or before such initial month. Further, there will be excluded all renewal commissions received from policies sold in prior years while an employee. Also excluded will be anticipated renewal commissions on policies sold during the current year while self-employed.

- All net earnings from self-employment derived during the year in the form of insurance service fees, persistency fees, etc.

- All remuneration classified as earnings from other jobs, trades, or businesses.

- Any net loss from other self-employment during the year.

Are Self-Employed Earnings Subject to Social Security Retirement Test?

Time of Sale	Commissions Received In	
	Year of First Entitlement*	Year After Year of First Entitlement*
Prior to Year of First Entitlement	Yes	No
In Year of First Entitlement		
(1) Sold in months through month of First Entitlement	Yes	No
(2) Sold in months after month of First Entitlement	Yes	Yes
After Year of First Entitlement	Yes	Yes

* Entitlement means (a) being eligible by virtue of age and insured status (i.e., having the required number of quarters of coverage), and (b) having filed a claim for benefits.

The receipt of renewal commissions in the initial year of retirement on policies sold by a self-employed agent will not necessarily result in a loss of benefits, even though they exceed the earnings limit for the taxable year. The reason is that such "self-employment" earnings cannot be charged against benefits for any month in the initial year of retirement in which the agent-beneficiary does not render any substantial services in self-employment. Even large amounts of renewal commissions will not cause loss of any benefits if the agent-beneficiary renders no substantial services in self-employment during the taxable year in which the commissions are received.

Generally, repeat commissions paid on casualty insurance policies (e.g., accident and health) differ from renewal commissions in the life insurance field. This is true even though the repeat commissions are sometimes called "renewal" commissions. Each repeat commission is, in fact, for a policy written for a new and different term.

Ordinarily, the rate of commission on these repeats is the same regardless of how many times the insurance is extended for a new term. In life insurance renewals, on the other hand, there is a limit on the number of years for which renewal commissions are paid on the same life insurance policy. Regardless of the amount of work done by an agent when a casualty insurance policy is extended, the commission paid is for the new term only. It is not additional compensation for the original term of the policy. For these reasons, repeat commissions from accident and health policies are normally earned in the month in which the policy is extended. Thus, they are wages for the month and year if the agent then was an employee. If the agent then was self-employed, they may be included as earnings from self-employment for the year in which they are received.

337. What is the Foreign Work Test?

The "foreign work test" is a separate retirement test that applies to beneficiaries who engage in employment (or self-employment) outside of the United States that is not covered by the Social Security system. The foreign work test is based only on the amount of time in which the beneficiary was employed or self-employed and is not based on the amount of earnings or losses by the beneficiary. The intention was to make it unnecessary to convert earnings or losses from non-US currency into specific dollar amounts.

338. When are benefits withheld under the Foreign Work Test?

Under the "foreign work test", monthly benefits are withheld for each calendar month that an individual (or a person entitled to benefits on that individual's work record) works:

- outside of the United States;

- performing work for pay not covered by Social Security;

- for more than forty-five hours.

The test applies only to persons who have not reached Full Retirement Age. Benefits are not withheld for anyone over Full Retirement Age.

If a benefit holder works and loses benefits for one or more months – it should be noted that family benefits are withheld for those same months. These benefits would include:

- benefits payable to spouse or children based on the earnings record; and

- benefits payable to a spouse on earnings as disabled child, mother, or father.

NOTE: A divorced spouse, divorced at least two years, is not subject to withholding because of the beneficiary's work.

339. What constitutes "work outside of the United States"?

Work outside of the United States is any work that takes place outside of the territorial boundaries of the fifty United States, the District of Columbia, Puerto Rico, the U.S. Virgin Islands, Guam, American Samoa, and the Commonwealth of the Northern Mariana Islands.

NOTE: Self-employment by resident aliens in Puerto Rico, the U.S. Virgin Islands, Guam, American Samoa, and the Commonwealth of the Northern Mariana Islands IS considered to be outside of the United States, unless the nonresident alien is a resident of a State, the District of Columbia, Puerto Rico, the U.S. Virgin Islands, Guam, American Samoa, and the Commonwealth of the Northern Mariana Islands.

The foreign work test does not apply to activity which would, if carried on in the U.S., result only in income which is specifically excepted from coverage such as:

- rentals from real estate

- capital gains

- dividends or interest

- retirement pay to partners who rendered no services; or

- limited partnership income

340. What is "noncovered work for pay" under the foreign work test?

Noncovered work for pay includes work:

- outside of the United States in a job not covered by Social Security; OR

- being self-employed outside the United States in a trade or business where your income is not subject to the Social Security tax; OR

- being a self-employed owner or part-owner or a trade or business outside the United States not subject to the Social Security tax – where the owner or part-owner holds themselves out to work for more than forty-five hours a month, regardless of whether that much work is performed.

341. Does work performed outside the United States have to be reported?

Yes. If the beneficiary is under Full Retirement Age and receives retirement or disability benefits as a worker, spouse, survivor or dependent of a worker, a report must be filed with the Social Security Administration if the worker becomes employed for forty-five or more hours per month or becomes self-employed outside of the United States.

Employment must be reported to the nearest United States Embassy or Consulate if outside of the United States. The report must be filed before the receipt of the second month's benefit after work began.

342. What is the penalty for failure to report foreign work?

Penalty deductions may be imposed for failure to report the following:

(a)   For the first time to fail to report: a penalty of one month's benefit is withheld. This is regardless of the number of months worked before reporting.

(b)   For the second time to fail to report: two months benefits can be withheld.

(c)   For the third and subsequent times that there is a failure to report: three additional months benefits can be withheld.

These penalties are in addition to the monthly benefits lost because of the application of the Foreign Work Test.

TAXATION OF SOCIAL SECURITY BENEFITS

343. Are Social Security benefits subject to federal income taxation?

Social Security retirement, survivor, and disability benefits may be subject to federal income taxes in some cases. The person who has the legal right to receive the benefits must determine if the benefits are taxable. For example, if a parent and child both receive benefits, but the payment for the child is made to the parent's account, the parent must use only the parent's portion of the benefits in figuring if benefits are taxable. The portion of the benefits that belongs to the child must be added to the child's other income to see if any of those benefits are taxable.

If the only income a person receives is Social Security benefits, the benefits generally are not taxable and he probably does not need to file a tax return. However, if a person has other income in addition to benefits, he may have to file a return (even if none of the benefits are taxable).

If the total of a person's income plus half of his or her benefits is more than the *base amount*, some of the benefits are taxable. Included in the person's total income is any tax-exempt interest income, excludable interest from United States savings bonds, and excludable income earned in a foreign country, United States possession, or Puerto Rico. [1]

Voluntary federal income tax withholding is allowed on Social Security benefits. Recipients may submit a Form W-4V[2] if they want federal income tax withheld from their benefits. Beneficiaries are able to choose withholding at 7 percent, 10 percent, 12 percent, or 22 percent of their total benefit payment. Note that Form W4-V has been updated as of February 2018 due to tax law changes.

344. What are the base amounts?

The base amount is as follows, depending upon a person's filing status:[3]

- $32,000 for married couples filing jointly

- $0 for married couples filing separately and who lived together at any time during the year

- $25,000 for other taxpayers

If a person is married and files a joint return, the person and his spouse must combine their incomes and their Social Security benefits when figuring if any of their combined benefits are taxable. Even if the spouse did not receive any benefits, the person must add the spouse's income to his when figuring if any of his benefits are taxable.

> *Example.* Jim and Julie Smith are filing a joint return for 2019 and both received Social Security benefits during the year. Jim received net benefits of $6,600, while Julie received net benefits of $2,400.

1. IRC Sec. 86.
2. Form W-4V https://www.irs.gov/pub/irs-pdf/fw4v.pdf (Last accessed October 8, 2018).
3. IRC Sec. 86(c)(1).

Jim also received a taxable pension of $10,000 and interest income of $500. Jim did not have any tax exempt interest income. Jim and Julie's Social Security benefits are not taxable for 2018 because the sum of their income ($10,500) and one-half of their benefits ($9,000 ÷ 2 = $4,500) is not more than their base amount ($32,000).

Any repayment of Social Security benefits a person made during the year must be subtracted from the gross benefits received. It does not matter whether the repayment was for a benefit the person received in that year or in an earlier year.

345. What portion of Social Security benefits are subject to income taxes?

The amount of benefits to be included in taxable income depends on the person's total income plus half his or her Social Security benefits. The higher the total, the more benefits a person must include in taxable income. Depending upon a person's income, he or she may be required to include either up to 50 percent or up to 85 percent of benefits in income.

50 Percent Taxable

If a person's income plus half of his Social Security benefits is more than the following *base amount* for his filing status, up to 50 percent of his or her benefits will be included in his or her gross income:[1]

- $32,000 for married couples filing jointly

- $0 for married couples filing separately and who lived together at any time during the year

- $25,000 for all other taxpayers

85 Percent Taxable

If a person's income plus half of his or her Social Security benefits is more than the following *adjusted base amount* for his or her filing status, up to 85 percent of his or her benefits will be included in his or her gross income:[2]

- $44,000 for married couples filing jointly

- $0 for married couples filing separately and who lived together at any time during the year

- $34,000 for other taxpayers

If a person is married filing separately and *lived with* his or her spouse at any time during the year, up to 85 percent of his or her benefits will be included in his or her gross income.

---

1. IRC Sec. 86(c)(1).
2. IRC Sec. 86(c)(2).

346. Why is nontaxable interest income included in a taxpayer's adjusted gross income?

Nontaxable interest income is included in income to limit opportunities for manipulation of tax liability on benefits. Individuals whose incomes consist of different mixes of taxable and nontaxable income are treated the same as individuals whose total income is taxable for federal income tax purposes.

347. Are workers' compensation benefits included in the definition of Social Security benefits for tax purposes?

Yes, also included in the definition of Social Security benefits for tax purposes are workers' compensation benefits, to the extent they cause a reduction in Social Security and Railroad Retirement Tier I disability benefits.[1] This is intended to assure that these social insurance benefits, which are paid in lieu of Social Security payments, are treated similarly for purposes of taxation. For additional details, see Publication 05-10018.[2]

If a person receives workers' compensation or other public disability benefits, AND Social Security disability benefits, the total amount of these benefits can't exceed 80 percent of your average current earnings before the disability occurred.

Social Security disability benefits, including benefits payable to your family members, are added together with workers' compensation and other public disability payments. If the total amount of these benefits exceeds 80 percent of average current earnings, the excess amount is deducted from your Social Security benefit.

The Social Security benefit will be reduced until the month the beneficiary reaches age sixty-five, or the month your other benefits stop, whichever comes first. Starting December 19, 2015, due to a change in the law, benefits will continue to be reduced until you reach your full retirement age.

Average Current Earnings is calculated by the highest of three computation methods:

- High-1 Average Current Earnings

    - highest yearly earnings from the year of current onset and the five previous years and divide the yearly total by twelve months and round to the next lower dollar amount.

- High-5 Average Current Earnings or

    - Sum of the five consecutive years after 1950 with the highest unindexed earnings and divided by sixty months and round to the next-lowest dollar amount.

---

1. IRC Sec. 86(d)(3).
2. https://www.ssa.gov/pubs/EN-05-10018.pdf (July 2017 edition) (Last accessed October 3, 2018).

- Average Monthly Wage (AMW)

  - Divide the total unindexed earnings for the computation years (dividend) by number of months in the computation years (divisor) and round to the next-lowest dollar amount.

348. How are overpayments and lump-sum retroactive benefits taxed?

Special rules are provided for dealing with overpayments and lump-sum retroactive benefit payments.[1] Benefits paid to an individual in any taxable year are reduced by any overpayments repaid during the year. Taxpayers who received a lump-sum payment of retroactive benefits may treat the benefits as wholly payable for the year in which they receive them or may elect to attribute the benefits to the tax years in which they would have fallen had they been paid timely. No benefits for months before 1984 are taxable, regardless of when they are paid.

> *Example 1.* Ms. Jones is single. In 2018, she applied for Social Security disability benefits but was told she was ineligible to receive them. She appealed the decision and won her appeal. In 2019, she received a lump-sum payment of $6,000, which included $2,000 for 2018. She has two choices. She can use her 2019 income to figure the taxable part of the entire $6,000 payment, or she can use her 2018 income to figure the taxable part of the $2,000 received for 2018. In the latter case, for 2018 she would include only the $4,000 attributable to 2019.

> *Example 2.* Assume that Mr. Jackson receives a $1,000 Social Security benefit in 2018, $400 of which is attributable to 2017. Assume also that the $1,000 benefit would increase Mr. Jackson's 2017 gross income by $500 (i.e., by the full 50 percent), but that the $400 would have increased his 2017 gross income by only $150, and the remaining $600 would have increased his 2017 gross income by $300. He may limit the increase in 2017 gross income to only $450, the sum of the increases in gross income that would have occurred had the $400 been paid in 2016.

349. What reporting requirements must be met by the Social Security Administration?

The Commissioner of Social Security must file annual returns with the Secretary of the Treasury setting forth the amounts of benefits paid to each individual in each calendar year, together with the name and address of the individual. The Commissioner of Social Security must also furnish similar information to each beneficiary by January 31 of the year following the benefit payments. The statement will show the total amount of Social Security benefits paid to the beneficiary, the total amount of Social Security benefits repaid by the beneficiary to the Social Security Administration during the calendar year, and the total reductions in benefits to offset workers' compensation benefits received by the beneficiary.

350. Are Social Security benefits subject to income tax withholding?

Voluntary federal income tax withholding on Social Security benefits is allowed. Recipients may submit a Form W-4V[2] if they want federal income tax withheld from their

---

1. IRC Secs. 86(d)(2), 86(e).
2. Form W-4V Voluntary Withholding Request https://www.irs.gov/pub/irs-pdf/fw4v.pdf (Revised February 2018) (Last accessed October 8, 2018).

benefits. Recipients may choose withholding at 7 percent, 10 percent, 12 percent, or 22 percent of their total benefit payment.

The following are **not** subject to VTW:

- Title XVI payments,

- Black Lung payments,

- Lump Sum Death Payments,

- returned check reissuances, or

- benefits due before January 1984.

Beneficiaries can change their minds and file a new Form W-4V to start, stop or change the withholding.

351. If a recipient of Social Security benefits elects Medical Insurance (Part B) under Medicare and the premiums are deducted from the individual's benefits, is the whole benefit, before the deduction, a Social Security benefit?

Yes, the individual is treated as if he received the whole benefit and later paid separately for the Medical Insurance (Part B) coverage. Both the Commissioner of Social Security and the Railroad Retirement Board will include the entire amount as paid to the individual in the statements they furnish.

SOCIAL SECURITY TAXES

352. What are the Social Security and Medicare tax rates for employers and employees?

The tax rate is the same for both the employer and the employee. Every employer who employs one or more persons and every employee in covered employment is subject to the tax imposed under the Federal Insurance Contributions Act (FICA).[1]

The tax consists of two taxes: the OASDI tax (the tax for old-age, survivors, and disability insurance) and the Hospital Insurance (HI) tax (for Medicare Part A).

For 2019, the maximum earnings base (the maximum amount of annual earnings subject to the tax) for the OASDI tax is $132,900. There is no maximum earnings base for the HI tax. All wages and self-employment income are subject to the HI tax.

For employees and employers, the rate of the OASDI tax is 6.20 percent, and the rate of the HI tax is 1.45 percent. Thus, the maximum OASDI tax for an employee in 2019 (with maximum earnings of $132,900) is $8,239.80. The maximum HI tax is unlimited because all wages are subject to the tax.

OASDI TAX ON EMPLOYEES AND EMPLOYERS

Year	% Rate (OASDI)	Max. Wage Base	Max. Tax (each)	Max. Tax (both)
1986	5.7	$42,000	$2,394.00	$4,788.00
1987	5.7	43,800	2,496.60	4,993.20
1988	6.06	45,000	2,727.00	5,454.00
1989	6.06	48,000	2,908.80	5,817.60
1990	6.2	51,300	3,180.60	6,361.20
1991	6.2	53,400	3,310.80	6,621.60
1992	6.2	55,500	3,441.00	6,882.00
1993	6.2	57,600	3,571.20	7,142.40
1994	6.2	60,600	3,757.20	7,514.40
1995	6.2	61,200	3,794.40	7,588.80
1996	6.2	62,700	3,887.40	7,774.80
1997	6.2	65,400	4,054.80	8,109.60
1998	6.2	68,400	4,240.80	8,481.60
1999	6.2	72,600	4,501.20	9,002.40
2000	6.2	76,200	4,724.40	9,448.80
2001	6.2	80,400	4,984.80	9,969.60
2002	6.2	84,900	5,263.80	10,527.60

---

1. IRC Secs. 3101, 3111.

Year	% Rate (OASDI)	Max. Wage Base	Max. Tax (each)	Max. Tax (both)
2003	6.2	87,000	5,394.00	10,788.00
2004	6.2	87,900	5,449.80	10,899.60
2005	6.2	90,000	5,580.00	11,160.00
2006	6.2	94,200	5,840.40	11,680.80
2007	6.2	97,500	6,045.00	12,090.00
2008	6.2	102,000	6,324.00	12,648.00
2009-2011	6.2	106,800	6,621.60	13,243.20
2012	6.2	110,100	6,826.20	13,652.40
2013	6.2	113,700	7,049.40	14,098.80
2014	6.2	117,000	7,254.00	14,508.00
2015-2016	6.2	118,500	7,347.00	14,694.00
2017	6.2	127,200	7,886.40	15,772.80
2018	6.2	128,700	7,979.40	15,958.80
2019	6.2	132,900	8,239.80	16,479.60

Note: The 1.45 percent Medicare tax applies to all wages.

The OASDI maximum earnings base and maximum tax are subject to automatic adjustment in 2018, and after based on changes in wage levels.

Under the Patient Protection and Affordable Care Act of 2010, new Medicare taxes were imposed starting in 2013. Under the provisions of the new law most taxpayers will continue to pay the 1.45 percent Medicare tax, but single people earning more than $200,000 and married couples earning more than $250,000 will be taxed at an additional 0.9 percent (2.35 percent in total) on the excess over those base amounts. Self-employed persons pay 3.8 percent on earnings over those thresholds.

Employers will collect the extra 0.9 percent on wages exceeding $200,000 just as they would withhold Medicare taxes and remit them to the IRS. However, companies won't be responsible for determining whether a worker's combined income with his or her spouse made them subject to the tax.

Instead, some employees will have to remit additional Medicare taxes when they file income tax returns, and some will get a tax credit for amounts overpaid. Married couples with combined incomes approaching $250,000 will have to keep tabs on both spouses' pay to avoid an unexpected tax bill.

Beginning in 2013, Medicare tax was, for the first time, applied to investment income. A tax of 3.8 percent is imposed on net investment income of single taxpayers with Adjusted Gross Income (AGI) above $200,000 and joint filers with AGI over $250,000.

Net investment income is interest, dividends, royalties, rents, gross income from a trade or business involving passive activities, and net gain from disposition of property (other than property held in a trade or business). Net investment income is reduced by the deductions that are allocable to that income. However, the tax doesn't apply to income in tax-deferred retirement accounts such as 401(k) plans.

Not all earnings are subject to Social Security taxes. A person can be an employee but be exempt from the Social Security tax. An example is an individual hired by a federal agency on a temporary basis as an emergency firefighter to help fight forest fires. The individual performed the service for three months, twelve hours a day, and the federal agency supplied the necessary equipment and gave him directions on a daily basis. The Internal Revenue Service ruled that, although the individual was an employee under common-law rules, he was exempt from Social Security taxes, as the Internal Revenue Code exempts from the definition of employment those services performed for the United States by an individual serving on a temporary basis in case of fire or other emergencies.

353. If an employee works for two employers during the year and more than the maximum tax is paid on his or her wages, will the overpayment be refunded to the employee and his or her employers?

Each employer is required to withhold the employee's tax, and to pay the employer's tax, on wages up to the maximum earnings base for the year. Consequently, if an employee works for more than one employer during the year, the taxes paid may exceed the maximum payable for the year. In this case, the employee is entitled to a refund of his or her overpayment, or the overpayment will be credited to his or her income tax for the year. His or her employers, however, are not entitled to any refund or credit. Each employer is liable for tax on his or her wages, up to the maximum earnings base.

However, a group of corporations concurrently employing an individual will be considered a single employer if one of the group serves as a common paymaster for the entire group. This will result in such corporations having to pay no more in Social Security taxes than a single employer pays.

354. Does an employer receive an income tax deduction for Social Security tax payments?

Yes, the employer's Social Security tax is deductible as a business expense, but only if wages upon which taxes are paid are also deductible.[1]

355. Must Social Security taxes be paid on cash tips?

Yes, an employee must pay Social Security taxes on cash tips of twenty dollars or more a month from one employer. These tips are treated as wages for Social Security and income tax withholding purposes and must be reported. Cash tips of less than twenty dollars a month are not reported.

The employee is required to report tips to an employer within ten days following the month in which the tips equal or exceed twenty dollars.

---

1. See IRC Sec. 162.

The employer must pay the usual employer tax on tips.

The employer must withhold income tax and deduct the employee Social Security and Hospital Insurance (HI) tax on tips reported to him. The withholding is to be made from any wages (other than tips) that are under the employer's control. Employers may deduct the tax due on tips during a calendar quarter on an estimated basis, and adjust the amount deducted from wages paid to the employee either during the calendar quarter or within thirty days thereafter. If these wages are not sufficient to cover the employee tax due, the employee may (but is not required to) furnish the employer with additional funds to cover the tax.

The employee is directly responsible for paying any portion of the employee tax that the employer cannot collect from wages or from funds furnished by the employee. The employer is required to give statements to both the employee and the Internal Revenue Service, showing the difference between the amount of the employee tax due and the amount collected by the employer.

Food or beverage establishments are provided with a business tax credit, equal to the amount of the employer's Social Security tax obligation (7.65 percent) attributable to reported tips in excess of those treated as wages for purposes of satisfying the minimum wage provisions of the Fair Labor Standards Act (FLSA). An employer must pay a Social Security tax on the tip income of employees, and tips can be counted as satisfying one-half of the minimum wage requirement.

The credit also applies to tips received from customers in connection with the delivery or serving of food or beverages, regardless of whether the food or beverages are for consumption on an establishment's premises. The credit is available, even if the employee failed to report the tips.[1]

356. How are uncollected Social Security and other taxes collected?

A person must report on their tax return any Social Security and Medicare taxes, or railroad retirement taxes that remained uncollected at the end of 2017. These uncollected taxes will be shown on Form W-2.

Reporting social security, Medicare, Additional Medicare, or railroad retirement taxes on tips not reported to an employer:

- If a person received $20 or more in cash and charge tips in a month from any one job and did not report all of those tips to the employer, they must report the Social Security, Medicare, and Additional Medicare taxes on the unreported tips as additional tax on their return. The individual must use Form 4137, Social Security and Medicare Tax on Unreported Tip Income, to figure Social Security and Medicare taxes and/or Form 8959, Additional Medicare Tax, to figure Additional Medicare Tax.

---

1. For further information regarding income and employment taxes on tips, see *IRS Publication 531 (Reporting Tip Income)*. https://www.irs.gov/uac/about-publication-531?_ga=1.112418689.485733028.1477248207. Current through August 29, 2018. (Last accessed October 8, 2018).

Reporting uncollected Social Security, Medicare, Additional Medicare, or railroad retirement taxes on tips reported to an employer:

- A person may have uncollected taxes if their regular pay was not enough for the employer to withhold all the taxes owed and the employee did not give the employer enough money to pay the rest of the taxes.

- If the employer could not collect all of the Social Security and Medicare, and Additional Medicare taxes, or railroad retirement taxes owed on tips reported, the uncollected taxes will be shown in box 12 of Form W-2 (codes A and B). These must be reported as additional tax on the return. Unlike the uncollected portion of the regular (1.45 percent) Medicare tax, uncollected Additional Medicare Tax is not reported on Form W-2.

357. How does an individual report Social Security taxes for domestic help?

The threshold amount for Social Security coverage of a domestic worker is $2,100 in 2019, unchanged from the $2,100 it was in 2018 and was $2,000 in 2017 and 2016.[1] This threshold amount is indexed in future years for increases in average wages in the economy. Indexing occurs in $100 increments, rounded down to the nearest $100.

Calculation details

Amounts in formula	1995 threshold	$1,000
	1993 average wage index	23,132.67
	2016 average wage index (latest reported)	48,664.73
Computation	$1,000 times 48,664.73 divided by 23,132.67 equals $2,103.72, which rounds down to $2,100	

Exempt from Social Security taxes are any wages paid to a worker for domestic services performed in any year during which the worker is under age eighteen, except for workers under age eighteen whose principal occupation is household employment. Being a student is considered to be an occupation for purposes of this test. Thus, for example, the wages of a student who is sixteen years old and also babysits will be exempt from the reporting and payment requirements, regardless of whether the amount of wages paid is above or below the threshold. On the other hand, the wages of a seventeen-year-old single mother, who leaves school and goes to work as a domestic to support her family, will be subject to the reporting and payment requirements.

Employers may satisfy their tax obligations through regular estimated tax payments or increased tax withholding from their own wages. Estimated tax penalties will apply in appropriate circumstances.

---

1. See IRC Sec. 3121(x) and https://www.ssa.gov/oact/cola/CovThresh.html (Last accessed October 26, 2017).

Example 1. Assume an employer pays a domestic employee $1,000 in wages for calendar year 2016. Because the amount of these taxes is below the $2,100 threshold, the employer is not subject to reporting.

Example 2. Assume an employer pays a domestic employee $2,500 in wages for calendar year 2017. Because the amount of these wages is above the $2,100 threshold, the employer is subject to reporting.

In addition, wages paid to Election Workers are also reported but at the $1,800 level for 2019 which is unchanged from 2017 and 2018.

COVERAGE THRESHOLDS FOR DOMESTIC EMPLOYEES[a] AND ELECTION OFFICIALS/WORKERS[b]

Year	Domestic Employees	Election Workers	Year	Domestic Employees	Election workers
1994	$1,000	$100	2007	$1,500	$1,300
1995	1,000	1,000	2008	1,600	1,400
1996	1,000	1,000	2009	1,700	1,500
1997	1,000	1,000	2010	1,700	1,500
1998	1,100	1,000	2011	1,700	1,500
1999	1,100	1,000	2012	1,800	1,500
2000	1,200	1,100	2013	1,800	1,600
2001	1,300	1,200	2014	1,900	1,600
2002	1,300	1,100	2015	1,900	1,600
2003	1,400	1,200	2016	2,000	1,700
2004	1,400	1,200	2017	2,000	1,800
2005	1,400	1,200	2018	2,100	1,800
2006	1,500	1,300	2019	2,100	1,800

a. Prior to 1994, the threshold wage amount was $50 per calendar quarter for domestic employee. For 1994 and later, the threshold applies to calendar year wages.

b. The thresholds for election officials & workers apply to calendar year earnings.

358. What is the rate of Social Security and Medicare tax for a self-employed person?

The tax on self-employed persons is imposed under the Self-Employment Contributions Act.[1]

The self-employment tax consists of two taxes: the OASDI tax (the tax for old-age, survivors, and disability insurance) and the Hospital Insurance (HI) tax (for Medicare Part A).

For 2019 the maximum earnings base (the maximum amount of net earnings subject to the tax) for the OASDI tax is $132,900. There is no maximum earnings base for the HI tax. In other words, all earnings from self-employment are subject to the HI tax.

---

1. IRC Sec. 1401.

The rate of the OASDI tax is 12.40 percent, and the rate of the HI tax is 2.90 percent. Thus, the maximum OASDI tax for a self-employed person in 2017 (with maximum earnings of $132,900) is $16,479.60. The maximum HI tax for a self-employed person is unlimited, because all self-employment earnings are subject to the tax.

For self-employed taxpayers with income above $200,000 ($250,000 for married filing jointly) the HI tax will be 3.8 percent in tax years 2013 and after.

There is a special federal (and generally following through to state) income tax deduction of 50 percent of the Social Security and Medicare self-employment tax.[1] This income tax deduction is designed to treat the self-employed in much the same manner as employees and employers are treated for Social Security, Medicare, and income tax purposes under present law.

OASDI TAX ON SELF-EMPLOYED PERSONS*

Year	% Rates (OASDI)	Max. Earnings Base	Max. Tax
1986	11.4	$42,000	$4,788.00
1987	11.4	43,800	4,993.20
1988	12.12	45,000	5,454.00
1989	12.12	48,000	5,817.60
1990	12.4	51,300	6,361.20
1991	12.4	53,400	6,621.60
1992	12.4	55,500	6,882.00
1993	12.4	57,600	7,142.40
1994	12.4	60,600	7,514.40
1995	12.4	61,200	7,588.80
1996	12.4	62,700	7,774.80
1997	12.4	65,400	8,109.60
1998	12.4	68,400	8,481.60
1999	12.4	72,600	9,002.40
2000	12.4	76,200	9,448.80
2001	12.4	80,400	9,969.60
2002	12.4	84,900	10,527.60
2003	12.4	87,000	10,788.00
2004	12.4	87,900	10,899.60
2005	12.4	90,000	11,160.00
2006	12.4	94,200	11,680.80
2007	12.4	97,500	12,090.00
2008	12.4	102,000	12,648.00

---

1. IRC Sec. 164.

Year	% Rates (OASDI)	Max. Earnings Base	Max. Tax
2009-2011	12.4	106,800	13,243.20
2012	12.4	110,100	13,652.40
2013	12.4	113,700	14,098.80
2014	12.4	117,000	14,508.00
2015-2016	12.4	118,500	14,694.00
2017	12.4	127,200	15,772.80
2018	12.4	128,700	15,958.80
2019	12.4	132,900	16,479.60

*There is a special income tax deduction of 50 percent of the self-employment tax.

Note: The 2.90 percent Medicare tax applies to all self-employment earnings.

The OASDI maximum earnings base and maximum tax are subject to automatic adjustment in 2019, and after based on changes in wage levels.

If a self-employed person reports earnings on a fiscal-year basis, the tax rate to be used is the one that applies to the calendar year in which the fiscal year began.

359. If a self-employed person also receives wages as an employee, what portion of income is subject to tax as self-employment income?

Only the difference between the maximum earnings base for the year and the wages received as an employee is subject to tax as self-employment income.[1]

> *Example 1*. Mr. Smith, an attorney, is employed as a part-time instructor for a law school, and his salary is $30,000 a year. During 2018, Mr. Smith earned an additional $100,000 from his private practice, which counts as $92,350 for Social Security purposes (i.e., 92.35 percent of $100,000). Only $88,500 of his net earnings from self-employment is subject to the OASDI self-employment tax ($118,500 − $30,000). Note, however, that all of Mr. Smith's wages and $92,350 of his self-employment income are subject to the HI self-employment tax, because all wages and self-employment income are subject to the HI tax.

No self-employment tax is due unless net earnings from self-employment are at least $434 for the taxable year ($400/92.35 percent). Nevertheless, in some cases, the amount of income subject to OASDI self-employment tax may be less than $400.

> *Example 2*. Assume the same facts as in Example 1, except that Mr. Smith's salary as a law instructor is $127,400. Mr. Smith's net earnings from self-employment after application of the 92.35 percent factor ($92,350) exceed $400, and therefore must be reported. However, only $200 is subject to the OASDI self-employment tax ($127,400 − $127,200), but the entire $127,400 is subject to the HI tax.

360. Must a Social Security beneficiary who works pay Social Security and Medicare taxes?

Yes, even though receiving Social Security benefits, the beneficiary must pay taxes at the same rate as other individuals. Social Security and Medicare taxes must be paid even if the earnings are too small to increase the Social Security benefits the beneficiary will receive in the future.

---

1. IRC Sec. 1402(b)(2).

Example. Ms. Anderson, age seventy-three, receives $800 a month in Social Security retirement benefits. She also works part-time and earns $4,000 for the year. Ms. Anderson must pay $306 in Social Security and Medicare HI taxes.

361. How does a life insurance agent pay Social Security taxes on first-year and renewal commissions?

If the agent is an *employee* when the policy is sold, both first-year and renewal commissions are *wages* at the time they are paid. Consequently, they are subject to the employer-employee tax in the year they are received by him. It does not matter whether, at the time of payment, the agent is an employee or a self-employed person. If the agent is a self-employed individual when the policy is sold, first-year and renewal commissions are treated as net earnings from self-employment in the year they are received.[1] (See Social Security Taxes, Q 352 to Q 363).

Renewal commissions paid to the estate (or other beneficiary) of a deceased life insurance agent in a year after death are not subject to the employer-employee tax. Renewal commissions paid to a disabled life insurance agent are not subject to the Social Security tax, if he or she became entitled to disability insurance benefits before the year in which the renewal commission is paid and did not work for the employer during the period for which the payment is made. The renewal commissions of a self-employed agent do not constitute net earnings from self-employment to a widow(er) (they were not derived from a trade or business carried on by the widow(er)).

362. Must the self-employment tax be included in a person's estimated tax return?

Yes. Failure to pay self-employment taxes can result in penalty.

363. What is the federal income tax deduction for medical expense insurance premiums?

No premiums other than those for medical expense insurance will qualify for the deduction. If the taxpayer itemizes deductions, he or she may deduct the full amount of the medical expense insurance premiums subject to the 10 percent (7.5 percent prior to January 1, 2017 for those taxpayers that were over age sixty-five) Adjusted Gross Income (AGI) floor. A self-employed individual may be able to deduct up to 100 percent of medical expense insurance premiums.[2] The monthly premium for Medicare Part B is treated as a medical expense insurance premium for this purpose.

---

1. 20 CFR Part 404, Subpart K.
2. IRC Sec. 162(l).

WAGES AND SELF-EMPLOYMENT INCOME

364. What earnings are subject to Social Security tax and are counted in computing Social Security benefits?

Earnings that are the *wages* of an employee or the *self-employment income* of a self-employed person. However, earnings are counted as "wages" or as "self-employment income" only if they are earned in employment or self-employment covered by the Social Security Act.

365. For Social Security purposes, what is meant by the term "wages"?

"Wages" mean pay received by an employee for employment covered by the Social Security Act. The maximum amount of wages subject to the Old-Age, Survivors and Disability Insurance tax (OASDI) and credited to a worker's Social Security record for any calendar year cannot exceed:

$4,800 paid in any of the years	1959-1965
$6,600 paid in any of the years	1966-1967
$7,800 paid in any of the years	1968-1971
$9,000 paid in the year	1972
$10,800 paid in the year	1973
$13,200 paid in the year	1974
$14,100 paid in the year	1975
$15,300 paid in the year	1976
$16,500 paid in the year	1977
$17,700 paid in the year	1978
$22,900 paid in the year	1979
$25,900 paid in the year	1980
$29,700 paid in the year	1981
$32,400 paid in the year	1982
$35,700 paid in the year	1983
$37,800 paid in the year	1984
$39,600 paid in the year	1985
$42,000 paid in the year	1986
$43,800 paid in the year	1987
$45,000 paid in the year	1988
$48,000 paid in the year	1989
$51,300 paid in the year	1990
$53,400 paid in the year	1991
$55,500 paid in the year	1992

$57,600 paid in the year.	1993
$60,600 paid in the year.	1994
$61,200 paid in the year.	1995
$62,700 paid in the year.	1996
$65,400 paid in the year.	1997
$68,400 paid in the year.	1998
$72,600 paid in the year.	1999
$76,200 paid in the year.	2000
$80,400 paid in the year.	2001
$84,900 paid in the year.	2002
$87,000 paid in the year.	2003
$87,900 paid in the year.	2004
$90,000 paid in the year.	2005
$94,200 paid in the year.	2006
$97,500 paid in the year.	2007
$102,000 paid in the year.	2008
$106,800 paid in any of the years	2009-2011
$110,100 paid in the year.	2012
$113,700 paid in the year.	2013
$117,000 paid in the year.	2014
$118,500 paid in the year.	2015-2016
$127,200 paid in the year.	2017
$128,400 paid in the year.	2018
$132,900 paid in the year.	2019

Employees pay the tax on wages up to the base amount from each employer, but receive a refund on their income tax returns for the excess of total taxes paid over the tax on the base amount. Each employer pays the tax on wages up to the base amount for all of its employees. In addition to the regular Social Security tax on wages, all wages are subject to the Part A Medicare Hospital Insurance tax (HI).

The maximum earnings base is automatically adjusted each year by the Social Security Administration, if average nationwide (covered and noncovered) total wages have increased.

Note that the maximum amount of wages subject to the OASDI tax is also the maximum amount credited to a worker's record. For example, if an employee is paid $132,900 or less in 2019, the full amount of wages will be subject to OASDI tax and will be credited to the Social Security record for benefit purposes. But if an employee is paid $140,000 in 2019, only $132,900 will be subject to OASDI tax and credited to the Social Security record (but HI taxes will be paid on the entire $140,000). In other words, earnings in excess of the maximum amount for a particular calendar year are not considered wages for Social Security coverage purposes.

A stabilizer provision protects the system from trust-fund depletions that could occur when price increases outpace wage gains. This stabilizer provision goes into effect if reserves in the trust funds providing retirement, disability, and survivor benefits fall below 20 percent of what is needed to meet outgo for a year. When the stabilizer takes effect, automatic cost-of-living benefit increases will be based on the lower of the annual percentage increase in the Consumer Price Index or the annual percentage rise in the nation's average wage.[1]

Later, if the fund reserves exceed 32 percent of what is estimated to be needed for a year, recipients will be entitled to extra cost-of-living increases, to compensate for losses in inflation protection resulting from having benefit increases tied to wage levels.[2]

366. Are only payments in cash counted as wages?

No, amounts paid by check, promissory note, or in other media (such as goods, clothing, board or lodging) usually count as wages. In a few cases, however, only cash pay is counted (see Q 382; Domestic and Household Workers, Q 357).

Any fringe benefit that is not specifically excluded from Social Security taxes is wages for Social Security purposes. The amount of wages is the difference between the discount price paid by the employee for the benefit and its fair market value.

The following five categories of fringe benefits are *not* wages:

(1)   "De minimis" fringe (a property or service furnished by the employer that is so small in value that accounting for it would be administratively impractical)

(2)   Gyms and other athletic facilities (the value of an employer-provided on-premises athletic facility)

(3)   No-additional-cost service (any service provided by an employer to the employee for the employee's use)

(4)   Qualified employee discount (employee discount with respect to property or services)

(5)   Working-condition fringe (any employer-provided service or property to the employee, such as a parking space)

Ordinarily, only pay actually received by the employee in a calendar year is counted as wages for that year. However, pay that is "constructively received" during the year is also counted. Wages are constructively received when they have been credited or set apart for the employee without any substantial limitation or restriction on the time or manner of payment and are available to him so that he can get them at any time. A special provision applies to pay under a nonqualified deferred compensation plan that is generally based on payments made after 1983.

---

1. 42 USC 415(i)(1)(C).
2. 42 USC 415(i)(5)(A).

367. Are employer payments for group life insurance covered wages?

The cost of group-term life insurance that is includable in the gross income of the employee is considered "wages" subject to Social Security tax.[1] This provision does not apply to coverage of former employees who separated from service before January 1, 1989, to the extent the cost is not for any period the employee was employed by the employer after separation.

The general rule is that the employee may exclude the cost of the first $50,000 of employer-provided group-term life insurance from income. Therefore, generally, only the cost of coverage in excess of $50,000 will be subject to the Social Security tax.[2]

The employer is required to report amounts includable in the wages of current employees for purposes of the Social Security tax on the employees' W-2. Generally, the employer may treat the wages as though paid on any basis, so long as they are treated as paid at least once each year.

The Social Security tax must be paid by the employee if the payment for the group-term life insurance is considered wages and is for periods during which there is no longer an employment relationship between the employer and the employee. The employer is required to state the portion of an employee's wages that consist of payments for group-term life insurance and the amount of the Social Security tax separately.

368. Are vacation pay and severance pay wages?

Yes, but the Internal Revenue Service ruled in 1996 that contributions of an employee's forfeitable vacation pay benefit, to a qualified stock purchase plan with a cash or deferred arrangement, are excludable from gross wages for Social Security purposes.

The company involved in the ruling had established a qualified stock-purchase plan with profit-sharing features and cash or deferred arrangements. Company employees were entitled to annual leave based on years of service, and had to use it during the same year or forfeit it. Employees who did not use all of their paid vacation in excess of two weeks could elect to have the equivalent in pay contributed to the qualified plan. The employees could take the vacation time, forfeit the time, or contribute its value to the plan. They did not have the option to receive cash or any other taxable benefit in lieu of the contribution to the plan. Thus, the Internal Revenue Service considered the contribution of vacation pay to be a nonelective employer contribution and excluded from wages for Social Security purposes under IRC Sec. 3121(a)(5)(A).[3]

369. Are payments on account of sickness or accident disability counted as wages for Social Security purposes?

Yes, generally payments made to, or on behalf of, an employee or an employee's dependents for sickness or disability are considered wages. The following payments, however, are specifically excluded from the definition of wages:

(1)   Any payment that an employer makes to an employee, or on the employee's behalf, on account of the employee's sickness or accident disability, or related medical or

---

1. IRC Sec. 3121(a)(2).
2. IRC Sec. 79.
3. Technical Advice Memoranda 9635002. (November 9, 1995).

hospitalization expenses, if the payment is made more than six consecutive months following the last calendar month in which the employee worked for the employer. Payments made during the six consecutive months are included as wages.

(2)   The exclusion listed in (1) above also applies to any payment made by a third party (such as an insurance company). In addition, if the employee contributed to the employer's sick pay plan that portion of the third-party payments attributable to the employee's contribution is not wages.

(3)   Payments of medical or hospitalization expenses connected with sickness or accident disability are excluded from wages beginning with the first payment, only if made under a plan or system of the employer for medical or hospitalization expenses connected with sickness or accident disability.

(4)   Payments under workers' compensation law are not wages.

For payments to be excluded under a plan or system, the plan must provide for all employees generally or for a class or classes of employees. Some or all of the following features may also be a part of the plan:

- set a definite basis for determining who is eligible, such as length of service, or occupation, or salary classification;

- set definite standards for determining the minimum duration of payments; and

- provide a formula for determining the minimum amount to be paid an eligible employee.

Sick pay that is not paid under a plan or system by the employer is counted as wages for Social Security purposes, if paid before the end of six calendar months after the last month in which the employee worked.

370. Are payments made under a deferred compensation plan counted as wages?

Yes, generally, under a special timing rule, the "amount deferred" by an employee under a traditional nonqualified deferred compensation plan – whether a salary reduction or supplemental plan, whether a funded or unfunded plan, or whether a private or (eligible or ineligible) Section 457 plan – of an employer covered by the Social Security tax is considered "wages" for Social Security tax purposes at the *later of*:

(1)   when the services are performed; or

(2)   when the employee's rights to such amount are no longer subject to a substantial risk of forfeiture.[1] Once an amount is treated as wages, it (and any income attributable to it) will not be treated as wages for Social Security tax purposes in any later year.[2]

---

1. IRC Sec. 3121(v)(2)(A).
2. IRC Sec. 3121(v)(2)(B).

In general, many employees would prefer to have amounts deferred treated as wages for Social Security purposes at the time the services are performed. At such time, their salaries, in all likelihood, already exceed the Social Security taxable wage base (in 2019, $132,900 for OASDI), and the amounts deferred would thus escape Social Security taxes. (Remember, however, that the HI tax applies to all wages.)

Regulations expressly identify certain plans and benefits that do not provide for the deferral of compensation for Social Security tax purposes: stock options, stock appreciation rights, and other stock value rights; some restricted property received in connection with the performance of services; compensatory time, disability pay, severance pay, and death benefits; certain benefits provided in connection with impending termination (including window benefits); excess (golden) parachute payments; benefits established twelve months before an employee's termination, if indication that benefits were provided in contemplation of termination; benefits established after termination of employment; and compensation paid for current services.[1]

Under the regulations, the manner in which the amount deferred for a period is determined depends upon whether the nonqualified deferred compensation plan is an *account balance plan* or a *nonaccount balance plan*. If the plan is an *account balance plan*, the amount deferred for a period equals the principal amount credited to the employee's account for the period, increased or decreased by any income or loss attributable to the principal amount through the date the principal amount is required to be taken into account as wages for Social Security tax purposes. A plan is an *account balance plan* only if, under the terms of the plan, a principal amount is credited to an individual account for an employee, the income attributable to each principal account is credited or debited to the individual account, and the benefits payable to the employee are based solely on the balance credited to the individual account.[2]

If the plan is a *nonaccount balance plan*, the amount deferred for a period equals the present value of the additional future payment or payments to which the employee has obtained a legally binding right under the plan during that period.

371. Are payments made to or from a qualified pension or annuity plan counted as wages?

No, neither the employer's contribution to the plan nor payments to the employee from the plan are treated as wages. They are not subject to Social Security tax and are not creditable for benefit purposes.

The following payments made to or under a deferred compensation plan are *excludable* from the definition of wages:

(1)   Payments made from or to qualified pension, profit-sharing, or stock bonus plans if, at the time of payment, the trust is exempt from tax under IRC Sec. 501(a),

---

1. Treas. Regs. §§31.3121(v)(2)-1(b)(4), 31.3306(r)(2)-1(a).
2. Treas. Regs. §§31.3121(v)(2)-1(c)(1), 31.3306(r)(2)-1(a); see also IRS PLR 9417013 (amounts deferred in defined-contribution-type plan with delayed vesting are amounts attributable to employer contributions when such amounts vest).

unless the payment is made to an employee of the trust as remuneration for services rendered as an employee and not as a beneficiary of the trust.[1]

(2) Payments made under or to an IRC Sec. 403(a) annuity plan.[2]

(3) Payments made under a Simplified Employee Pension (SEP), other than any contributions made pursuant to a salary reduction agreement described in IRC Sec. 408(k)(6).[3]

(4) Payments under an annuity contract described in IRC Sec. 403(b), other than a payment for the purchase of the contract that is made by reason of a salary reduction agreement (whether evidenced by a written instrument or otherwise).[4]

(5) Payments under or to an exempt governmental deferred compensation plan.[5]

(6) Payments to supplement pension benefits under a plan or trust described above to take into account some or all of the increase in the cost of living since retirement.[6]

(7) Payments under a cafeteria plan (IRC Sec. 125), if the payment is not treated as wages without regard to the plan and it is reasonable to believe that IRC Sec. 125 would not treat any wages as constructively received.[7]

(8) Payments under a SIMPLE IRA plan arrangement, other than elective contributions under IRC Sec. 408(p)(2)(A)(i).[8]

(9) Amounts exempted from Section 457 requirements under Section 457(e)(11)(A)(ii) (plans paying solely length of service awards to bona fide volunteers (or their beneficiaries) on account of qualified services performed by such volunteers) and maintained by an eligible employer.[9]

However, the definition of wages *does* include certain employer contributions under qualified cash or deferred arrangements that are not included in gross income.[10]

372. If a teacher takes a reduction in salary to provide funds for a tax-sheltered annuity, how are his or her wages computed for Social Security purposes?

The salary before the reduction will be treated as wages.[11] In other words, the amount of reduction, although paid to the insurer by the employer, is nevertheless not considered an

---

1. IRC Sec. 3121(a)(5)(A).
2. IRC Sec. 3121(a)(5)(B).
3. IRC Sec. 3121(a)(5)(C).
4. IRC Sec. 3121(a)(5)(D).
5. IRC Sec. 3121(a)(5)(E).
6. IRC Sec. 3121(a)(5)(F).
7. IRC Sec. 3121(a)(5)(G).
8. IRC Sec. 3121(a)(5)(H).
9. IRC Sec. 3121(a)(5)(I).
10. IRC Sec. 3121(v)(1)(A).
11. See IRC Sec. 3121(a)(5)(D); Rev. Rul. 65-208, 1965-2 CB 383.

employer contribution to a retirement fund. For example, suppose that a teacher, whose salary is $75,000, takes a $2,000 salary cut for 2019 so that this amount can be used to purchase a tax-sheltered annuity for his or her benefit. Social Security taxes will still be payable on the full $75,000, and this is the amount that will be credited to the teacher's Social Security account for benefit purposes.

Employer payments from employer funds into such plans are excluded from wages.

373. Are cash tips considered wages?

Tips received by an employee in the course of employment by any one employer are wages for Social Security purposes, if the tips total or exceed twenty dollars in a calendar month. This includes all tips received directly from customers, tips from charge customers that are paid by the employer to the employee, and any tips received under a tip-splitting arrangement. Noncash tips, such as passes, tickets, or services, are not counted as wages. Tips are considered received when the employee reports the tips to the employer. If the employee fails to report the tips to the employer, the tips are treated as received when the employee actually received them.

For each calendar month during which an employee receives twenty dollars or more in tips, the employee must give the employer a written statement of cash and charge tips by the tenth day of the month after the month in which the tips are received. IRS Form 4070 (Employee's Report of Tips to Employer),[1] which is in IRS Publication 1244 (Employee's Daily Record of Tips and Report to Employer),[2] is available for this purpose.

A club, hotel, or restaurant may require customers to pay a service charge, which is given to the employees. These service charges added to a bill or fixed by the employer that the customer must pay, when paid to an employee, don't constitute a tip but rather constitute non-tip wages. These non-tip wages are subject to social security tax, Medicare tax and federal income tax withholding. In addition, the employer can't use these non-tip wages when computing the credit available to employers under section 45B of the Internal Revenue Code, because these amounts are not considered to be tips.

Common service charges or "auto-gratuities" in service industries include:

- Large party charge (restaurant),
- Bottle service charge (restaurant and night-club),
- Room service charge (hotel and resort),
- Contracted luggage assistance charge (hotel and resort), and
- Mandated delivery charge (pizza or other retail deliveries).

(For method of reporting tips, see SOCIAL SECURITY TAXES, Q 352 to Q 363.)

---

1. *See* https://www.irs.gov/pub/irs-pdf/p1244.pdf. IRS Form 4070 (Employee's Report of Tips to Employer) (Last accessed October 8, 2018).
2. https://www.irs.gov/pub/irs-pdf/p1244.pdf. IRS Publication 1244 (Employee's Daily Record of Tips and Report to Employer) (Last accessed October 8, 2018).

374. Are noncash tips considered wages?

Noncash tips such as tickets, services, passes, do not count as wages.

NOTE: Establishments that require customers to pay a service charge for use of banquet facilities or dining rooms where the money is given to the employees is NOT considered a cash tip, but part of wages. Some of these include: large party charges, bottle service charges, contracted luggage assistance charges, mandated delivery charges.

375. Do prizes and awards from someone not an employer count as wages?

No. Prizes from someone other than the beneficiary's employer do not count as wages.

376. Do taxes withheld from pay count as a beneficiary's wage?

Yes. However, Social Security taxes paid by the employer from the employer's funds for agricultural work or domestic service performed in a private home DO NOT count as wages.

377. Do expense reimbursements and travel expenses count as wages?

No, not generally. However, they CAN count as wages if:

(a)   the employer does not require verification of expenses OR

(b)   the employer can keep any amount in excess of the verifiable expenses.

Expenditures must be in advancement of the employer's business – expenses for items of personal use are not business expenses.

378. Are payments made to a disabled former employee counted as wages?

No. If the person is a disabled beneficiary, any payments received from the employer after 1972 does count as wages as long as:

(a)   the beneficiary was entitled to disability insurance benefits before the year of which payment was made; AND

(b)   the beneficiary did not work for the employer during the pay period in which the payment was made.

379. Do wages include the portion of an employee's Social Security taxes paid by an employer?

Yes, except for domestic service in the private home of the employer and agricultural labor. However, payments by a state or local employer are wages for Social Security tax purposes, only if the payment is pursuant to a salary reduction agreement (whether evidenced by a written instrument or otherwise). The term "salary reduction agreement" includes any salary reduction arrangement, regardless of whether there is approval or choice of participation by individual employees or whether such approval or choice is mandated by state statute.

380. Are a salesperson's commissions considered to be wages?

Yes, they are wages if the salesperson is an employee. (See Social Security Taxes, Q 352 to Q 363.) When the commissions are the sole pay and no advances are given, the commissions are wages in the calendar year in which they are paid. However, when advances are made against future commissions, the year in which the advances are paid is the year to which the amount advanced is credited.

381. Under what circumstances are the first-year and renewal commissions of a life insurance agent treated as wages?

If the agent is an *employee* when the policy is sold, both first-year and renewal commissions are treated as wages when they are *paid* to him. Thus, the commissions are subject to the employer-employee tax in each year as he receives them (see SOCIAL SECURITY TAXES, Q 352 to Q 363. For retirement-test purposes, however, if the agent is an employee when the policy is sold, both first-year and renewal commissions are treated as "earned" in the month and year in which the policy was sold (see LOSS OF BENEFITS BECAUSE OF "EXCESS" EARNINGS, Q 318 to Q 336).

382. Is the value of meals and lodging furnished by an employer to an employee considered wages for Social Security taxation purposes?

The Supreme Court has held that the value of meals and lodging furnished to an employee for the convenience of the employer is not wages for Social Security coverage and tax purposes.[1]

Such meals must be provided at the employer's place of business. The employee must accept lodging at the employer's place of business in order for the value of the lodging to be excluded from wages.

The Social Security Amendments of 1983 state, however, that the exclusion of income from income tax withholding by the employer does not necessarily affect the treatment of the income for Social Security coverage and taxation purposes in other cases.

Self-Employment Income

383. What is taxable and creditable self-employment income?

It is that part of an individual's net earnings from self-employment that is subject to Social Security tax and counted for Social Security benefits. In determining what part of a person's net earnings from self-employment is creditable for Social Security purposes, the following rules apply:

- 92.35 percent of all net earnings from self-employment is taxable and creditable self-employment income unless the trade, business, or profession is not covered by the Social Security Act. The 92.35 percent factor has been used only in 1990 and after (when the self-employed first began paying the full employer-employee tax rate).

---

1. *Rowan Companies, Inc. v. U.S.*, 452 U.S. 247 (1981).

- If such amount for the taxable year is less than $400, the net earnings are not treated as self-employment income. That is, no Social Security tax is paid on the net earnings, and they are not credited to the person's Social Security account.

- The maximum amount of self-employment income for a taxable year that is subject to the Old-Age, Survivors, and Disability Insurance tax (OASDI) and used to determine benefits cannot exceed:

Amount	Year
$132,900	2019
$128,400	2018
$127,200	2017
$118,500	2015-2016
$117,000	2014
$113,700	2013
$110,100	2012
$106,800	2009-2011
$102,000	2008
$97,500	2007
$94,200	2006
$90,000	2005
$87,900	2004
$87,000	2003
$84,900	2002
$80,400	2001
$76,200	2000
$72,600	1999
$68,400	1998
$65,400	1997
$62,700	1996
$61,200	1995
$60,600	1994
$57,600	1993
$55,500	1992
$53,400	1991
$51,300	1990
$48,000	1989
$45,000	1988
$43,800	1987
$42,000	1986

$39,600.	1985
$37,800.	1984
$35,700.	1983
$32,400.	1982
$29,700.	1981
$25,900.	1980
$22,900.	1979
$17,700.	1978
$16,500.	1977
$15,300.	1976
$14,100.	1975
$13,200.	1974
$10,800.	1973
$9,000.	1972
$7,800.	1968-1971
$6,600.	1966-1967
$4,800.	1959-1965

There is no limit to the amount of self-employment income subject to the (Part A) Medicare Hospital Insurance tax (HI). The HI tax applies to all self-employment income.

Net earnings in excess of the maximum amount for a particular taxable year are not considered self-employment income for Social Security purposes.

384. How is the amount of self-employment income figured if a person has both wages and net earnings from self-employment in the same year?

If a person has both wages (as an employee) and net earnings from self-employment in a taxable year, *self-employment income* is the difference, if any, between wages and the maximum Social Security earnings base for that year (see Q 383).

> *Example.* Mr. Smith, an attorney, is also employed part-time as an instructor in a law school. In 2018, he draws a salary of $30,000 from the school and also earns $100,000 in private practice, which counts as $92,350 for Social Security purposes (i.e., 92.35 percent of $100,000). His self-employment income for OASDI purposes for 2019 is $102,900 ($132,900 maximum less $30,000 wages). Only $102,900 is subject to self-employment Social Security tax. $30,000 is subject to the employer-employee tax. Note, however, that $92,350 of the $100,000 earned in private practice is subject to the Part A Medicare Hospital Insurance tax for self-employed individuals. In addition, Mr. Smith must pay the Medicare Hospital Insurance tax for employees on the $30,000 he earned as a law school instructor.

385. In general, what constitutes net earnings from self-employment?

Net earnings from self-employment may be the net income from a trade, business, or profession carried on by the individual alone, or it may be his or her distributive share of the ordinary net income of a partnership. In computing net earnings from self-employment, gross income and deductions are, for the most part, the same as for income tax purposes. However, the following differences must be taken into account:

- Rentals from real estate are excluded in determining net earnings from self-employment unless:

    (1) the rentals are received in the course of a trade or business by a real estate dealer; or

    (2) services are rendered primarily for the convenience of the occupants of the premises, as in the case of hotels, motels, etc. (but income from renting property for business or commercial use (such as a store, factory, office space, etc.) is excluded, regardless of the amount of services rendered to the tenant); or

    (3) in the case of farm rentals, the farm landlord materially participates in the management or in the production of farm commodities on land rented to someone else.

- Dividends on stock and interest on bonds do not count for Social Security, unless they are received in the course of business by a dealer in stocks or securities. The term "bond" includes debentures, notes, certificates, and other evidence of indebtedness issued with interest coupons or in registered form by a corporation. Bonds also include government bonds. Other interest received in the course of a trade or business *does* count for Social Security. For example, interest received by a merchant on accounts or notes receivable are included in computing net earnings from self-employment.

- Partnerships are treated as individuals when it comes to the dividend and interest exclusion. Dividends and interest on securities held for investment are excluded from net earnings of the partners. However, if a partnership is in business as a securities dealer, income on the securities held for resale by the partnership is included as net earnings of the partners.

- Capital gains and losses, and gains and losses from the sale or exchange of property which is not inventory or stock in trade, are excluded in computing net earnings from self-employment.

- Retirement payments received by a retired partner from a partnership, of which the individual is a member or a former member, are excluded from net earnings from self-employment if the following conditions are met:

    (1) The payments are made under a written plan of the partnership that provides for periodic payments because of retirement, to partners generally or to a class or classes of partners, to continue at least until the partner's death

    (2) The partner rendered no services in any business conducted by the partnership (or its successors) during the taxable year of the partnership ending within or with the taxable year in which such payments were received

(3) At the end of the partnership's taxable year, there is no obligation from the other partners to the retired partner other than for the retirement payments under the plan

(4) The partner's share in the capital of the partnership has been paid in full by the end of the partnership's taxable year

- No deductions for net operating losses of other years are permitted in determining net earnings from self-employment.

- The following retirement benefits for ministers are not considered earnings from self-employment:

    (1) Retirement benefits received from a church plan after retirement

    (2) The rental value or allowance of a parsonage, including utilities, furnished to the minister after retirement

- Income taxable as "dividends" to shareholders of a Subchapter S corporation (a corporation electing not to be taxed as a corporation) is not considered "net earnings from self-employment."

386. When did Social Security coverage begin for self-employed individuals?

Most became covered beginning in 1951.

EXCEPTIONS:

- Farmers, ministers and some others were not covered until 1955

- Additional groups of professionals were covered after 1955

- Self-employed Medical Doctors (physicians) were covered for taxable years ending on or after December 31, 1965

387. How is self-employment income calculated?

Self-employment income is calculated from "net earnings from self-employment" which is derived from a "trade or business" covered by the law.

An individual is self-employed in the eyes of Social Security if

- a sole proprietor (including an independent contractor)

    - The term sole proprietor also includes the member of a single member LLC that's disregarded for federal income tax purposes and a member of a qualified joint venture.

- a partner in a partnership (including a member of a multi-member limited liability company (LLC) that has elected to be treated as a partnership for federal tax purposes)

- or are otherwise in business for oneself.

Self-employment tax must usually be paid upon net earnings from self-employment of $400 or more. Generally, the amount subject to self-employment tax is 92.35 percent of net earnings from self-employment. Net earnings are calculated by subtracting ordinary and necessary trade or business expenses from the gross income derived from the trade or business. One can be liable for paying self-employment tax even if currently receiving Social Security benefits. The law sets a maximum amount of net earnings subject to the Social Security tax. For 2019 this amount is $132,900 – up from $128,400 from 2018. All net earnings are subject to the Medicare tax.

Optional Methods

For those with a loss or small amount of income from self-employment, it may be of benefit to use one of the two optional methods to compute net earnings from self-employment. Refer to Form 1040, Schedule SE for the "Farm Optional Method" and the "Non-Farm Optional Method" [1] to review the optional method. An optional method may give credit toward social security coverage or increase the earned income credit or the child and dependent care credit.

Church Employee

An employee of a church or qualified church-controlled organization who elected exemption from social security and Medicare taxes must pay self-employment tax if the church or qualified church-controlled organization paid more than $108.28 to the employee, unless they are personally exempt from self-employment tax. For more information on church-related income and self-employment taxes, refer to Publication 517. [2]

Self-Employment Tax Rate

The law sets the self-employment tax rate as a percentage of net earnings from self-employment. This rate consists of 12.4 percent for social security and 2.9 percent for Medicare taxes.

Additional Medicare Tax

Additional Medicare Tax applies to self-employment income above a threshold. The threshold amounts are $250,000 for a married individual filing a joint return, $125,000 for a married individual filing a separate return, and $200,000 for all others.

Reporting Self-Employment Tax

Compute self-employment tax on Schedule SE. When figuring adjusted gross income on Form 1040, one-half of the self-employment tax can be deducted.

---

1. Form 1040 Schedule SE https://www.irs.gov/pub/irs-pdf/i1040sse.pdf (Last accessed October 8, 2018).
2. *Social Security and Other Information for Members of the Clergy and Religious Workers.* https://www.irs.gov/pub/irs-pdf/p517.pdf (Last accessed October 8, 2018).

388. Can an illegal activity or a hobby be a trade or business?

Illegal activity: Simply because an activity is illegal does not prevent it from being considered a trade or business. For example, professional gamblers or drug smugglers would be considered self-employed and required to report income and pay self-employment taxes. Of course, the act of reporting may bring the attention of law enforcement to the illegal activities.

Hobbies: Hobbies are generally not considered to be trades or businesses. If the activity is intended to further the hobby rather than make a profit, the activity is not a trade or business.

389. What exclusions apply to trades and business for Social Security?

The term "trade or business" does not include the following for Social Security purposes:

- Work as an employee, except newspaper vendors who are age eighteen or older.

- Work by U.S. citizens performing services in the U.S. as employees of a foreign government and, in some circumstances, as employees of an instrumentality wholly owned by a foreign government, or an international organization.

- Employees of a State or political subdivision thereof who are paid solely on a fee basis and whose services are not otherwise covered as employment under a Federal-State coverage agreement.

- Work as an employee or employee representative covered by the Railroad Retirement system.

- Work as a public official (except public officials of a State or political subdivision who are paid solely on a fee basis and whose services are not covered under a Federal-State coverage agreement).

- Self-employment by members of certain religious sects exempt from self-employment taxes.

- Services performed by ordained, commissioned or licensed ministers if they elected to be exempted from coverage under the Internal Revenue Code, and by members of religious orders who have not taken a vow of poverty.

- Services performed by Christian Science practitioners, if they have elected to be exempted from coverage under the Internal Revenue Code.

- Deemed self-employment income of employees of church or church-controlled organizations that have elected to be exempt from payment of Social Security taxes for its employees.

- Services by a member of a religious order who has taken a vow of poverty when these services are performed in the exercise of the duties required by the order. However, effective October 30, 1972, these services may be covered as employment for the order if the order irrevocably elects coverage for its entire active membership and its lay employees.

390. Can you get an extension for filing an Annual Report of Earnings?

Yes. An extension if possible for a valid reason. A written request must be made before the annual report is due. Valid reasons include:

- illness or disability;

- absence or travel from home for a great distance that causes the individual not to have access to records needed;

- inability to get evidence from another source;

- inability of an accountant to compile data required;

- any other situation that has a direct bearing on the obligation to complete the report.

391. Does farm rental income count as net earnings?

Yes, IF the property owner or landlord, as part of the rental agreement, materially participates in the production of the crop or livestock. If the property owner or landlord does not materially participate, then the farm rental income is not income for Social Security considerations.

392. How does a self-employed life insurance agent report first-year and renewal commissions?

If the agent is self-employed *when the policy is sold*, commissions are treated as earnings from self-employment in the year they are paid to the agent. It is immaterial whether the agent is an employee or self-employed when the commissions are received. For retirement-test purposes, renewal commissions paid to a self-employed agent after retirement are not included as earnings after the initial month of retirement if they were the result of services rendered prior to retirement (See Social Security Taxes, Q 352 to Q 363). (For treatment of commissions as "earnings" for "retirement test" purposes, see LOSS OF BENEFITS BECAUSE OF "EXCESS" EARNINGS, Q 318 to Q 336.)

RAILROAD RETIREMENT

Employee and Spousal Annuities

393. Who is eligible for an employee annuity?

The Railroad Retirement Act[1] provides annuities for employees who have reached a specific age and have been credited with a specified number of years of service. The Act also provides annuities for employees who become disabled. The basic requirement for a regular employee retirement annuity is 120 months (ten years) of creditable railroad service (or five years, if the five years are performed after 1995). Service months need not be consecutive, and, in some cases, military service may be counted as railroad service.

Benefits are based on months of service and earnings credits. Earnings are creditable up to certain annual maximums on the amount of compensation subject to railroad retirement taxes.

(1) *Annuities based on ten years of service (or five years in certain cases).* An employee with ten years of railroad service (or five years, if the five years were performed after 1995), but less than thirty years of service, is eligible for an annuity if he: (a) has attained retirement age, or (b) has attained age sixty-two (the annuity cannot begin prior to the first full month during which the employee is age sixty-two) but is less than retirement age. Early retirement annuity reductions are applied to annuities awarded before retirement age.

(2) *Annuities based on thirty years of service.* An employee who has been credited with thirty years of railroad service is eligible for a regular annuity based on age and service the first full month he or she is age sixty. Early retirement reductions are applied to annuities awarded before age sixty-two.

Starting in the year 2000, the age at which full benefits are payable increases in gradual steps until it reaches age sixty-seven. This affects people born in 1938 and later. Reduced annuities will still be payable at age sixty-two, but the maximum reduction will be 30 percent, rather than 20 percent, by the year 2022. Part of an annuity is not reduced beyond 20 percent if the employee had any creditable railroad service before August 12, 1983. These reductions do not affect those who retire at age sixty-two with thirty years of service.

There are two types of disability annuities for employees who have been credited with at least ten years of railroad service. An employee may receive an *occupational disability* at age sixty, if he or she has at least ten years of railroad service, or at any age, if the employee has at least twenty years (240 months) of service, when the employee is permanently disabled for his or her *regular railroad occupation*. An employee who cannot be considered for a disability annuity based on ability to work in his or her regular railroad occupation may receive a *total disability* annuity at any age, if he or she is permanently disabled for *all regular work* and has at least ten years (120 months) of creditable railroad service.

---

1. 45 U.S.C. 231 et. seq.

A five-month waiting period beginning with the month after the month of the onset of disability is required before disability annuity payments can begin.

While an annuity based on disability is not paid until the employee has stopped working for a railroad, employment rights need not be relinquished until the employee attains age sixty-five.

394. Who is entitled to a supplemental annuity?

An employee with a current connection with the railroad industry at the time of retirement may qualify for a supplemental annuity, in addition to the regular employee annuity. Supplemental annuities are paid from a separate account funded by employer taxes in addition to those assessed for regular annuities. The supplemental annuity is reduced if the employee receives a private pension based on contributions from a railroad employer.

An employee is entitled to a supplemental annuity if he or she:

(1)   has been credited with railroad service in at least one month before October 1981;

(2)   is entitled to the payment of an employee annuity awarded after June 30, 1966;

(3)   has a current connection with the railroad industry when the employee annuity begins;

(4)   has given up the right to return to work, and either;

(5)   is age sixty-five or older and has completed twenty-five years of service; or

(6)   is age sixty or older and under age sixty-five, has completed thirty years of service, and is awarded an annuity on or after July 1, 1974.

A supplemental annuity that begins after December 21, 1974 does not affect the payment of the regular employee annuity. The payment of a supplemental annuity does not affect the amount of a spouse or survivor annuity.

395. What is a "current connection" with the railroad industry?

An employee who worked for a railroad in at least twelve of the thirty consecutive months immediately preceding the month his annuity begins will meet the current-connection requirement. If the employee has twelve months' service in an earlier thirty-consecutive-month period, he may still meet the current-connection requirement. This alternative generally applies if the employee did not have any regular employment outside the railroad industry after the end of the thirty-consecutive-month period that included twelve months of railroad service.

If an employee died before retirement, railroad service in at least twelve of the thirty consecutive months before death will meet the current-connection requirement for the purpose of paying survivor benefits.

However, if an employee does not qualify on this basis, but has twelve months of service in an earlier thirty-month period, he or she may still meet the current connection requirement. This alternative generally applies if the employee did not have any regular employment outside the railroad industry after the end of the last thirty-month period which included twelve months of railroad service, and before the month the annuity begins or the date of death.

Once a current connection is established at the time the railroad retirement annuity begins, an employee never loses it, no matter what kind of work is performed thereafter.

396. Can nonrailroad work before retirement break a former railroad employee's current connection?

Full or part-time work for a nonrailroad employer in the interval between the end of the last thirty-month period including twelve months of railroad service and the month an employee's annuity begins, or the month of death if earlier, CAN break a current connection.

Self-employment in an *unincorporated business* WILL NOT break a current connection. However, if the business is incorporated, self-employment may break a current connection.

Federal employment with the Department of Transportation, National Transportation Safety Board, Surface Transportation Board, National Mediation Board, Railroad Retirement Board, or Transportation Security Administration will not break a current connection. State employment with the Alaska Railroad, as long as that railroad remains an entity of the State of Alaska, will not break a current connection. Also, railroad service in Canada for a Canadian railroad will neither break nor preserve a current connection.

397. What are the exceptions to the normal methods of determining a current connection?

A current connection can also be maintained, for purposes of supplemental and survivor annuities, but **not** for an occupational disability annuity, if

- the employee completed twenty-five years of railroad service

- was involuntarily terminated without fault from his or her last job in the railroad industry, and

- did not thereafter decline an offer to return to work in the same class or craft as his or her most recent railroad service, regardless of the distance to the new position.

Provided that all of these requirements are met, an employee's current connection may not be broken, even if the employee works in regular nonrailroad employment after the thirty-month period and before retirement or death.

This exception to the normal current connection requirement became effective October 1, 1981, but only for employees still living on that date who left the rail industry on or after October 1, 1975, or who were on leave of absence, on furlough, or absent due to injury on October 1, 1975.

398. What are the effects of a buy out on the existence of a current connection?

In cases where an employee has no option to remain in the service of his or her railroad employer, the termination of the employment is considered involuntary, regardless of whether the employee does or does not receive a buy-out.

However, if an employee has the choice of either accepting a position in the same class or craft in the railroad industry or termination with a buy-out, accepting the buy-out is a part of his or her voluntary termination, and the employee would not maintain a current connection under the exception provision.

399. How are annuities for spouses of railroad retirees computed?

Regular railroad retirement annuities are computed under a two-tier formula. The spouse annuity formula is based on certain percentages of the employee's Tier I and Tier II amounts.

The Tier I portion of an employee's annuity is based on both railroad retirement credits and any Social Security credits that the employee also earned. Computed using Social Security benefit formulas, an employee's Tier I benefit approximates the Social Security benefit that would be payable if all the employee's work were performed under the Social Security Act.

The Tier II portion of the employee's annuity is based on railroad retirement credits only, and may be compared to the retirement benefits paid over and above Social Security benefits to workers in other industries.

The first tier of a spouse annuity, before any applicable reductions, is 50 percent of the railroad employee's unreduced Tier I amount.

The second-tier amount, before any reductions, is 45 percent of the employee's unreduced Tier II amount.

400. How does spousal railroad retirement annuity compare to a Social Security benefit?

The average railroad annuity awarded to spouses during 2017, excluding divorced spouses, was $1,091 a month, while the average monthly Social Security spouse benefit was about $719.

Annuities awarded during 2016 to the spouses of employees who were at or over Full Retirement Age (FRA) and who retired directly from the rail industry with at least twenty-five years of service averaged $1,333 a month; and the average award to the spouses of employees retiring at age sixty or over with at least thirty years of service was $1,489 a month.

401. When is a spouse eligible for an annuity if caring for a child of the retired employee?

A spouse of an employee receiving an age and service annuity (or a spouse of a disability annuitant who is otherwise eligible for an age and service annuity) is eligible for a spouse annuity at any age if caring for the employee's unmarried child, and the child is under age eighteen or a disabled child of any age who became disabled before age twenty-two.

402. Can a spouse of a railroad employee in a same-sex marriage file for a railroad retirement spouse annuity?

Yes. On June 26, 2013, the Supreme Court found Section 3 of the Defense of Marriage Act (DOMA), which prevented the Federal government from recognizing marriages of same-sex couples, to be unconstitutional. As a result, the Railroad Retirement Board began accepting applications for benefits from those eligible spouses in same-sex marriages who were validly licensed under State law. On June 26, 2015, the Supreme Court further found that the Constitution required all States to license same-sex marriages, and to recognize lawfully licensed same-sex marriages performed in other States.

403. If a divorced spouse becomes entitled to an annuity will the affect the monthly rated paid to the retired employee or current spouse?

No. If a divorced spouse becomes entitled to an annuity based on the employee's railroad service, the award of the divorced spouse's benefit would not affect the amount of the employee's annuity, nor would it affect the amount of the railroad retirement annuity that may be payable to the current spouse.

404. What is the effect if the employee and the spouse or divorced spouse are both railroad employees?

If both started railroad employment after 1974, the amount of any spouse or divorced spouse annuity is reduced by the amount of the employee annuity to which the spouse is also entitled. If both the employee and spouse are qualified railroad employees and either had some railroad service before 1975, both can receive separate railroad retirement employee and spouse annuities, without a full dual benefit reduction

Railroad Retirement Benefits

405. Can the collection of Social Security benefits result in an overpayment of a railroad retirement annuity account?

Yes, in the case of the Tier I portion.

The Tier I portion of a railroad retirement annuity is based on both the railroad retirement and Social Security credits acquired by an employee and figured under Social Security formulas. It approximates what Social Security would pay if railroad work were covered by Social Security. Tier I benefits are, therefore, reduced by the amount of any actual Social Security benefit paid based on nonrailroad employment, to prevent a duplication of benefits based on the same earnings.

The Tier I dual benefit reduction also applies to the annuity of an employee qualified for Social Security benefits on the earnings record of another person, such as a spouse. And, the Tier I portion of a spouse or survivor annuity is reduced for any Social Security entitlement, even if the Social Security benefit is based on the spouse's or survivor's own earnings. These reductions follow principles of Social Security law which limit payment to the higher of any two or more benefits that are payable to an individual at one time.

If a railroad retirement annuitant is also awarded a Social Security benefit, in most cases a combined monthly dual benefit payment will be issued by the Railroad Retirement Board (RRB). The Social Security Administration determines the amount of the Social Security benefit due, and the RRB determines the amount of the railroad retirement annuity due. The Tier I portion of a railroad retirement annuity is reduced by the amount of the Social Security benefit due.

A person should notify the RRB when he or she files for Social Security benefits. If the Social Security Administration begins paying benefits directly to a railroad retirement annuitant without the RRB's knowledge, a Tier I overpayment will occur. This frequently happens when a railroad employee's spouse or widow(er) is awarded Social Security benefits not based on the employee's earnings.

Also, annuitants who are receiving their Social Security benefits directly from the Social Security Administration must notify the RRB if their Social Security benefits are subsequently increased for any reason other than annual cost-of-living increases, such as a recomputation to reflect post-retirement earnings. As such recomputations are usually retroactive, they can result in substantial Tier I overpayments.

While Social Security benefit information is provided to the RRB because of routine information exchanges between the RRB and the Social Security Administration, it will generally not be provided in time to avoid such a benefit overpayment.

406. Why is a railroad retirement annuity reduced when a Social Security benefit is also payable?

The Tier I portion of a railroad retirement annuity is based on both the railroad retirement and Social Security credits acquired by an employee and computed under Social Security formulas. It approximates what Social Security would pay if railroad work were covered by Social Security. Tier I benefits are, therefore, reduced by the amount of any actual Social Security benefit paid on the basis of nonrailroad employment, in order to prevent a duplication of benefits based on Social Security-covered earnings.

The tenets of Social Security law payment to the higher of any two or more benefits payable to an individual at one time, the Tier I dual benefit reduction applies to an annuity even if the Social Security benefit is based on the earnings record of someone other than the railroad employee, such as a spouse or former spouse. An annuitant is required to advise the RRB if any benefits are received directly from the Social Security Administration or if those benefits increase (other than for a cost-of living increase).

The Tier II portion of a railroad retirement annuity is based on the railroad employee's railroad service and earnings alone and is computed under a separate formula. It is not reduced for entitlement to a Social Security benefit.

407. Are there any exceptions to the railroad annuity reduction for Social Security benefits?

No. There are no exceptions to the railroad retirement annuity reduction for social security benefits.

408. What is the effect of workers' compensation or disability benefits on railroad retirement?

If an employee is receiving a railroad retirement disability annuity, Tier I benefits for the employee and spouse may, under certain circumstances, be reduced for receipt of workers' compensation or public disability benefits.

409. How do dual benefit restrictions apply when both spouses are railroad employees?

If both parties began working for the railroad after 1974, the amount of any spouse or divorced spouse annuity is reduced by the amount of the employee annuity to which the spouse or divorced spouse is also entitled.

If either party had some railroad service before 1975, the spouse/divorced spouse Tier I amount is reduced by the amount of the railroad employee Tier I to which the spouse/divorced spouse is entitled. The spouse/divorced spouse Tier I amount cannot be reduced below zero. The initial reduction is restored in the spouse Tier II amount. Divorced spouses are not entitled to a Tier II component and are not eligible to have the reduction restored.

In survivor cases, if the widow or widower is entitled to a railroad retirement employee annuity and neither the widow or widower nor the deceased employee had any railroad service before 1975, the survivor annuity (Tier I and Tier II) payable to the widow or widower is reduced by the total amount of the widow or widower's own employee annuity.

If a widow or dependent widower is also a railroad employee annuitant, and either the widow or widower or the deceased employee had 120 months of railroad service before 1975, the Tier I reduction may be partially restored in the survivor Tier II amount.

If either the deceased employee or the widow or widower had some railroad service before 1975 but less than 120 months of service, the widow or widower's own employee annuity and the Tier II portion of the survivor annuity would be payable to the widow or widower. The Tier I portion of the survivor annuity would be payable only to the extent that it exceeds the Tier I portion of the widow or widower's own employee annuity.

410. How does the Tier I pension reduction affect spousal or widow/widower benefits?

The Tier I portion of a spouse's or widow or widower's annuity may be reduced for receipt of any Federal, State, or local government pension separately payable to the spouse or widow or widower based on her or his own earnings. The reduction generally does not apply if the employment on which the public service pension is based was covered under the Social Security Act throughout the last sixty months of public employment. Most military service pensions and payments from the Department of Veterans Affairs will not cause a reduction. Pensions paid by a foreign government or interstate instrumentality will also not cause a reduction. For spouses and widow or widowers subject to a public service pension reduction, the Tier I reduction is equal to two-thirds of the amount of the public service pension.

411. Can pensions from federal, state, or local government also result in dual benefit reductions?

Yes. Tier I benefits for employees first eligible for a railroad retirement annuity **and** a Federal, State, or local government pension after 1985 may be reduced for receipt of a public pension based, in part or in whole, on employment not covered by social security or railroad retirement after 1956. This may also apply to certain other payments not covered by railroad retirement or social security, such as from a non-profit organization or from a foreign government or a foreign employer. Usually, an employee's tier I benefit will not be reduced by more than half of his or her pension from noncovered employment. However, if the employee is under age sixty-five and receiving a disability annuity, the tier I benefit may be reduced by an added amount if the pension from noncovered employment is a public disability benefit.

Military service pensions, payments by the Department of Veterans Affairs, or certain benefits payable by a foreign government as a result of a totalization agreement between that government and the United States will not cause a reduction.

412. Are there benefits other than Social Security that will require dual benefit reductions?

For employees first eligible for a railroad retirement annuity and a Federal, State, or local government pension after 1985, there may be a reduction in Tier I for receipt of a public pension based, in part or in whole, on employment not covered by Social Security or railroad retirement after 1956. This may also apply to certain other payments not covered by Social Security, such as payments from a non-profit organization or from a foreign government or a foreign employer. However, it does not include military service pensions, payments by the Department of Veterans Affairs, or certain benefits payable by a foreign government because of a totalization agreement between that government and the United States.

The Tier I portion of a spouse or widow or widower's annuity may also be reduced for receipt of any Federal, State, or local government pension separately payable to the spouse or widow or widower based on her or his own earnings. The reduction generally does not apply if the employment on which the public pension is based was covered under the Social Security Act throughout the last sixty months of public employment. In addition, most military service pensions and payments from the Department of Veterans Affairs will not cause a reduction. Pensions paid by a foreign government or interstate instrumentality will also not cause a reduction.

If an employee is receiving a disability annuity, Tier I benefits for the employee and spouse may, under certain circumstances, be reduced for receipt of workers' compensation or public disability benefits.

If annuitants become entitled to any of the above payments, they should promptly notify the RRB. If there is any question as to whether a payment requires a reduction in an annuity, an RRB field office should be contacted.

413. Can additional earning result in railroad retirement overpayments?

Unreported post-retirement work and earnings in nonrailroad employment (including self-employment) are a major cause of overpayments in railroad retirement annuities. Like Social Security benefits, railroad retirement Tier I benefits and vested dual benefits paid to employees and spouses, plus Tier I, Tier II, and vested dual benefits paid to survivors, are subject to deductions if post-retirement earnings exceed certain exempt amounts, which increase annually.

These earnings deductions do not apply to those who have attained full Social Security retirement age. Full retirement age for employees and spouses ranges from age sixty-five for those born before 1938 to age sixty-seven for those born in 1960 or later. Full retirement age for survivor annuitants ranges from age sixty-five for those born before 1940 to age sixty-seven for those born in 1962 or later.

For those under full retirement age throughout 2019, the exempt earnings amount is $17,640. For beneficiaries attaining full retirement age in 2019, the exempt earnings amount is $46,920 for the months before the month full retirement age is attained. Prior to the calendar year in which full retirement age is attained, the earnings deduction is $1 in benefits for every $2 of earnings over the exempt amount. For those attaining full retirement age during a calendar year, the deduction is $1 for every $3 of earnings over the exempt amount in the months before the month full retirement age is attained.

Annuitants who work after retirement and expect that their earnings for a year will be more than the annual exempt amount must promptly notify the nearest RRB field office and furnish an estimate of their expected earnings. This way their annuities can be adjusted to take the excess earnings into consideration and prevent an overpayment. Annuitants whose original estimate changes significantly during the year, either upwards or downwards, should also notify the RRB.

Retired employees and spouses, regardless of age, who work for their last pre-retirement nonrailroad employer are also subject to an earnings deduction in their Tier II and railroad retirement supplemental annuity benefits, if applicable, of $1 for every $2 in earnings up to a maximum reduction of 50 percent. This earnings restriction does not change from year to year and does not allow for an exempt amount. Retired employees and spouses should therefore promptly notify the RRB if they return to employment for their last pre-retirement nonrailroad employer, or if the amount of their earnings from such employment changes.

A spousal benefit is subject to reductions not only for the spouse's earnings, but also for the earnings of the employee, regardless of whether the earnings are from service for the last pre-retirement nonrailroad employer or any other post-retirement employment. (An annuity paid to a divorced spouse may continue despite the employee's work activity.)

414. How do earnings after retiring affect disability annuities?

Special restrictions limiting earnings to $950 per month during 2019, exclusive of disability-related work expenses, apply to disabled railroad retirement employee annuitants. In addition, any work performed by a disabled annuitant may be considered an indication of an individual's recovery from disability, regardless of the amount of earnings. Therefore, any earnings by a dis-ability annuitant must be reported promptly to avoid potential overpayments.

These disability work restrictions apply until the disabled employee annuitant attains full retirement age. This transition is effective no earlier than full retirement age even if the annui-tant had thirty years of service. Also, a disabled employee annuitant who works for his or her last pre-retirement nonrailroad employer would be subject to the additional earnings deduction that applies in these cases.

415. What effect does railroad work have on the annuity?

No railroad retirement annuity is payable for any month in which an employee, spouse or survivor annuitant performs compensated service for a railroad or railroad union. This includes local lodge compensation for $25.00 or more in a calendar month, and work by a local lodge or division secretary collecting insurance premiums, regardless of the amount of salary.

416. How does railroad retirement benefits compare to Social Security benefits?

The average age annuity being paid by the Railroad Retirement Board (RRB) at the end of fiscal year 2017 to career rail employees was $3,415 a month, and for all retired rail employees the average was $2,730. The average age retirement benefit being paid under Social Security was over $1,370 a month. Spouse benefits averaged $1,010 a month under railroad retirement compared to $695 under Social Security.

The Railroad Retirement Act also provides supplemental railroad retirement annuities of between $23 and $43 a month, which are payable to employees who retire directly from the rail industry with twenty-five or more years of service.

417. Are benefits for recent retirees on the average larger than in prior years?

Yes, because recent awards are based on higher average earnings. Age annuities awarded to career railroad employees retiring at the end of fiscal year 2016 averaged about $4,030 a month while monthly benefits awarded to workers retiring at full retirement age under Social Security averaged $1,855. If spouse benefits are added, the combined benefits for the employee and spouse would total $5,560 under railroad retirement coverage, compared to $2,780 under Social Security. Adding a supplemental annuity to the railroad family's benefit increases average total benefits for current career rail retirees to over $5,590 a month.

418. Must retiring railroad employees give up their rights to railroad jobs?

Depends.

AGE-BASED RETIREMENT: An employee annuity based on age cannot be paid until the employee stops railroad employment and gives up any rights to return to work for a railroad employer.

DISABILITY-BASED RETIREMENT: While an annuity based on disability is not paid until an employee has stopped working for a railroad, employment rights need not be relinquished until the employee attains full retirement age. For a supplemental annuity to be paid by the RRB, or for an eligible spouse to begin receiving annuity payments, a disabled annuitant under full retirement age must relinquish employment rights.

Regardless of age and/or earnings, no railroad retirement annuity is payable for any month in which a retired or disabled employee annuitant, a spouse annuitant or a survivor annuitant works for an employer covered under the Railroad Retirement Act, including labor organizations. Such work includes service for $25 or more in a calendar month to a local lodge or division of a railway labor organization. Also, work by a local lodge or division secretary collecting insurance premiums, regardless of the amount of salary, is railroad work which must be stopped.

Railroad retirement annuitants may work in nonrailroad employment, but benefits may be reduced if a beneficiary under full retirement age works after retirement and earnings exceed annual exempt amounts. Additional earnings deductions are assessed if a retired or disabled employee annuitant, or a spouse annuitant, works for his or her last pre-retirement nonrailroad employer, regardless of age or the level of earnings.

Other restrictions may also apply to any earnings by disabled employees.

419. Can railroad retirement annuities be garnished or subject to division in property settlements?

Partially.

Garnishment

Certain percentages of railroad retirement annuity, be it for an employee, a spouse, a divorced spouse, or survivor annuity may be subject to garnishment or other legal action to enforce obligations such as child support or alimony payments.

Also, a court-ordered partition payment may be paid even if the employee is not entitled to an annuity provided that the employee has ten years of railroad service or five years after 1995 and both the employee and former spouse are sixty-two.

Property Settlements/DIVISIONS

Employee Tier II benefits, vested dual benefits, and supplemental annuities ARE subject to court-ordered property settlements in proceedings related to divorce, annulment or legal separation.

Tier I benefits are not subject to property settlements.

Applying for Railroad Benefits

420. How does one apply for railroad annuities?

Applications are filed through the RRB's field offices. Applicants may file in person or by telephone and mail. Those filing in person may do so at any RRB office or at one of the office's customer outreach program service locations. Applicants filing by telephone receive the same information and instructions that are provided to those filing in person; forms requiring signatures and other documents are then handled by mail. A toll-free number is available for questions at 1-877-772-5772.

421. Can an application be filed prior to a person's actual retirement?

Yes. The RRB accepts annuity applications up to three months in advance of an annuity beginning date, which allows the RRB to complete the processing of most new claims by a person's retirement date. An employee can be in compensated service while filing a disability application provided that the compensated service is not active service and terminates within ninety days from the date of filing. When an employee files a disability application while still in compensated service, it will be necessary to provide a specific ending date of the compensation. Compensated service includes not only compensation with respect to active service performed by an employee for an employer, but also includes pay for time lost, wage continuation payments, certain employee protection payments, and any other payment for which the employee will receive additional creditable service.

Applicants can contact their local RRB field office to schedule a pre-retirement consultation (by phone or in person) and to confirm their eligibility and learn procedures and documentation required. Railroad employees can also get estimates of their future annuities over the Internet by visiting the RRB's website. To do so, employees must first establish an RRB online account at www.rrb.gov.

422. What documentation is required for apply for an annuity?

- Proof of age.

- Notice of any Social Security benefit award or other Social Security claim determination.

- Information regarding any other Federal, State, or local government pension for which he or she also qualifies, as well as certain other payments not covered by railroad retirement or Social Security, such as from a non-profit organization or from a foreign government or a foreign employer.

- An employee or survivor filing for a disability annuity is required to submit supporting medical information from his or her treating physician, as well as any reports or records from recent hospitalizations.

  - Specialized medical examinations given by a doctor named by the RRB may be required.

- Proof of any military service claimed.

- A spouse, divorced spouse, or widow(er) applying for a railroad retirement annuity must furnish proof of marriage to the employee.

- A divorced spouse must furnish proof of a final divorce from the employee, as well as proof that any subsequent marriages have terminated.

- A spouse, divorced spouse, or survivor also qualified to receive a pension from a Federal, State, or local government must submit information regarding that pension.

423. When is a spouse eligible for spouse annuities?

The Railroad Retirement Act provides annuities for the spouse (and divorced spouse) of an employee who is entitled to an employee annuity. A spouse may receive an annuity based on age, or on having a child of the employee in his or her care. A divorced spouse may only receive an annuity based on age. No spouse or divorced spouse annuity may be paid based upon disability.

To be eligible for an annuity, a spouse must:

(1)   be the husband or wife of an employee who is entitled to an annuity; and

(2)   stop working for any railroad employer.

Where the employee has completed ten years but less than thirty years of railroad service, and has attained age sixty-two, the spouse must be:

(1)   retirement age or older;

(2)   less than retirement age and have in his or her care a disabled child or a minor child (a child under eighteen years old if the spouse claimant is a wife or under sixteen years old if the spouse claimant is a husband) of the employee; or

(3)   age sixty-two or older but under retirement age. (In such case, all annuity components are reduced for each month the spouse is under retirement age at the time the annuity begins.)

Where the employee has completed thirty years of railroad service and is age sixty or older, the spouse must be:

(1)   age sixty or older;

(2)   less than age sixty and have in his or her care a disabled or minor child of the employee; or

(3)   age sixty but less than retirement age.

To be eligible for a *divorced spouse annuity*, the employee annuitant must be at least age sixty-two, must have been married for at least ten years, and the divorced spouse must:

(1)   be the divorced wife or husband of an employee;

(2)   stop working for a railroad employer;

(3)   not be entitled to a retirement or disability benefit under the Social Security Act, based on a Primary Insurance Amount (PIA) that is equal to or greater than one-half of the employee's Tier I PIA; and either

(4)   have attained retirement age; or

(5)   have attained age sixty-two but be under retirement age. (The annuity is reduced for each month the spouse is under retirement age at the time the annuity begins.)

The amount of the divorced spouse's annuity is, in effect, equal to what Social Security would pay in the same situation, and therefore less than the amount of the spouse annuity otherwise payable.

424. Can railroad retirees receive benefits at earlier ages than Social Security workers?

Yes. Railroad employees with thirty or more years of creditable service are eligible for regular annuities based on age and service the first full month they are age sixty, and railroad employees with less than thirty years of creditable service are eligible for regular annuities based on age and service the first full month they are age sixty-two.

No early retirement reduction applies if a rail employee retires at age sixty or older with thirty years of service and his or her retirement is after 2001, or if the employee retired before 2002 at age sixty-two or older with thirty years of service.

Early retirement reductions are otherwise applied to annuities awarded before full retirement age, the age at which an employee can receive full benefits with no reduction for early retirement. This ranges from age sixty-five for those born before 1938 to age sixty-seven for those born in 1960 or later, the same as under Social Security.

Under Social Security, a worker cannot begin receiving retirement benefits based on age until age sixty-two, regardless of how long he or she worked, and Social Security retirement benefits are reduced for retirement prior to full retirement age regardless of years of coverage.

425. How does early retirement reduce the annuity amount versus Full Retirement Age?

The early retirement annuity reductions applied to annuities awarded before full retirement age are increasing. For employees retiring between age sixty-two and full retirement age with less than thirty years of service, the maximum reduction will be 30 percent by the year 2022. Prior to 2000, the maximum reduction was 20 percent.

Age reductions are applied separately to the Tier I and Tier II components of an annuity. The Tier I reduction is 1/180 for each of the first thirty-six months the employee is under full retirement age when his or her annuity begins and 1/240 for each additional month (if any). This will result in a gradual increase in the reduction at age sixty-two to 30 percent for an employee once the age sixty-seven retirement age is in effect.

These same reductions apply to the Tier II component of the annuity. However, if an employee had any creditable railroad service before August 12, 1983, the retirement age for Tier II purposes will remain sixty-five, and the Tier II benefit will not be reduced beyond 20 percent.

The following chart shows how the gradual increase in full retirement age will affect employees.

Employee Retires with Less than 30 Years of Service

Year of Birth*	Full Retirement Age**	Annuity Reduction at Age 62
1937 or earlier	65	20.00%
1938	65 and 2 months	20.833%
1939	65 and 4 months	21.667%
1940	65 and 6 months	22.50%
1941	65 and 8 months	23.333%
1942	65 and 10 months	24.167%
1943 through 1954	66	25.00%
1955	66 and 2 months	25.833%
1956	66 and 4 months	26.667%
1957	66 and 6 months	27.50%
1958	66 and 8 months	28.333%
1959	66 and 10 months	29.167%
1960 or later	67	30.00%

*A person attains a given age the day before his or her birthday. Consequently, someone born on January 1 is considered to have attained his or her given age on December 31 of the previous year.

**If an employee has less than ten years of railroad service and is already entitled to an age-reduced social security benefit, the Tier I reduction is based on the reduction applicable on the beginning date of the social security benefit, even if the employee is already of full retirement age on the beginning date of the railroad retirement annuity.

426. Are disability annuities subject to reduction due to age?

Employee annuities based on disability are not subject to age reductions **except** for employees with less than ten years of service, but who have five years of service after 1995. Such employees may qualify for a Tier I benefit before retirement age based on total disability, but only if they have a disability insured status (disability freeze) under Social Security rules, counting both railroad retirement and social security-covered earnings. Unlike with a ten-year employee, a Tier II benefit is not payable in these disability cases until the employee attains age sixty-two. The employee's Tier II benefit will be reduced for early retirement in the same manner as the Tier II benefit of an employee who retired at age sixty-two with less than thirty years of service.

427. Can the spouse of a railroad employee receive benefits at earlier ages than Social Security workers?

If a retired railroad employee with thirty or more years of service is age sixty, the employee's spouse is also eligible for an annuity the first full month the spouse is age sixty.

Certain early retirement reductions are applied if the employee first became eligible for a sixty/thirty annuity July 1, 1984, or later, and retired at ages sixty or sixty-one before 2002. If the employee was awarded a disability annuity, has attained age sixty and has thirty years of service, the spouse can receive an unreduced annuity the first full month she or he is age sixty, regardless of whether the employee annuity began before or after 2002, as long as the spouse's annuity beginning date is after 2001.

To qualify for a spouse's benefit under Social Security, an applicant must be at least age sixty-two, or any age if caring for a child who is entitled to receive benefits based on the applicant's spouse's record.

428. What benefits does Social Security offer that are not available under railroad retirement?

Social Security does pay certain types of benefits that are not available under railroad retirement. For example, Social Security provides children's benefits when an employee is disabled, retired or deceased. Under current law, the Railroad Retirement Act only provides children's benefits if the employee is deceased.

However, the Railroad Retirement Act includes a special minimum guaranty provision which ensures that railroad families will not receive less in monthly benefits than they would have if railroad earnings were covered by Social Security rather than railroad retirement laws. This guaranty is intended to cover situations in which one or more members of a family would otherwise be eligible for a type of Social Security benefit that is not provided under the Railroad Retirement Act. Therefore, if a retired rail employee has children who would otherwise be eligible for a benefit under Social Security, the employee's annuity can be increased to reflect what Social Security would pay the family.

429. How do railroad retirement and Social Security lump-sum benefits differ?

Both the railroad retirement and Social Security systems provide a lump-sum death benefit. The railroad retirement lump-sum benefit is generally payable only if survivor annuities are not immediately due upon an employee's death. The Social Security lump-sum benefit may be payable regardless of whether monthly benefits are also due. Both railroad retirement and Social Security provide a lump-sum benefit of $255. However, if a railroad employee completed ten years of creditable railroad service before 1975, the average railroad retirement lump-sum benefit payable is $1,015. Also, if an employee had less than ten years of service, but had at least five years of such service after 1995, he or she would have to have had an insured status under Social Security law (counting both railroad retirement and Social Security credits) in order for the $255 lump-sum benefit to be payable.

The Social Security lump sum is generally only payable to the widow(er) living with the employee at the time of death. Under railroad retirement, if the employee had ten years of service before 1975, and was not survived by a living-with widow(er), the lump sum may be paid to the funeral home or the payer of the funeral expenses.

Survivor Benefits

430. What survivor benefits are payable under the Railroad Retirement Act?

The Railroad Retirement Act provides annuities for the widow(er), surviving divorced spouse, or remarried widow(er) of an employee. The deceased employee must have completed ten years of railroad service (or five years of service after 1995) and have had a current connection with the railroad industry at the time of his or her death. A widow(er), surviving divorced spouse, or remarried widow(er) may receive an annuity based on age, on disability, or on having a child of the employee in his or her care.

A *widow(er)* of an employee who has completed ten years of railroad service (or five years of service after 1995) and had a current connection with the railroad industry at death is eligible for an annuity if he or she has not remarried, and:

(1)   has attained retirement age;

(2)   is at least fifty but less than sixty years of age and becomes disabled (this results in a reduced annuity);

(3)   is less than retirement age but has in his or her care a child who either is under age eighteen (sixteen with respect to the Tier I component) or is disabled and who is entitled to a child's annuity; or

(4)   is at least sixty years of age but has not attained retirement age. If eligibility is based on (4), all components of the annuity are reduced for each month the widow(er) is age sixty-two or over but under retirement age when the annuity begins. For each month, the widow(er) is at least sixty but under age sixty-two, all components of the annuity are reduced as if the widow(er) were age sixty-two.

A *surviving divorced spouse* of an employee who completed ten years of railroad service (or five years of service after 1995) and had a current connection with the railroad industry at death is eligible for an annuity, if he or she:

(1)   is unmarried;

(2)   was married to the employee for at least ten years; and

(3)   is not entitled to a Social Security retirement benefit that is equal to or higher than the surviving divorced spouse's annuity before any reduction for age.

In addition, the divorced spouse must meet one of the following requirements:

(1)   have attained retirement age;

(2)   be at least fifty years old but less than retirement age and disabled (this results in a reduced annuity);

(3)   be less than retirement age but have in his or her care a child who either is under age sixteen or is disabled and who is entitled to a child's benefit; or

(4)   is at least sixty years of age but has not attained retirement age. In this case, the annuity is reduced for each month the surviving spouse is under retirement age when the annuity begins.

If a surviving divorced spouse marries after attaining age sixty (or age fifty if he or she is a disabled surviving divorced spouse), the marriage is deemed not to have occurred.

A widow(er) of an employee who completed ten years of railroad service (or five years of service after 1995) and had a current connection with the railroad industry at death is eligible for an annuity as a *remarried widow(er)*, if he or she:

(1)   remarried either after having attained age sixty (after age fifty if disabled) or before age sixty but the marriage terminated; and

(2)   is not entitled to a Social Security retirement benefit that is equal to or higher than the full amount of the remarried widow(er) annuity before any reduction for age.

In addition, the remarried widow(er) must meet one of the following requirements:

(1)   have attained retirement age;

(2)   be at least fifty but less than sixty years of age and disabled (this results in a reduced annuity);

(3)   have not attained retirement age but have in his or her care a child who either is under age sixteen or is disabled, and who is entitled to a child's annuity; or

(4)   be at least age sixty but have not attained retirement age. (In this case, the annuity is reduced for each month the remarried widow(er) is under retirement age when the annuity begins.)

If an employee does not qualify on the above basis but has twelve months of service in an earlier thirty-month period, he or she may still meet the current connection requirement. This alternative generally applies if the employee did not have any regular employment outside the railroad industry after the end of the last thirty-month period, which included twelve months of railroad service, and before the month the annuity begins or the date of death.

Full or part-time work for a nonrailroad employer in the interval between the end of the last thirty-month period, including twelve months of railroad service, and the beginning date of an employee's annuity, or the month of death if earlier, can break a current connection.

Self-employment in an unincorporated business will not break a current connection; however, self-employment can break a current connection if the business is incorporated.

Working for certain U.S. Government agencies – Department of Transportation, National Transportation Safety Board, Surface Transportation Board, Transportation Security

Administration, National Mediation Board, Railroad Retirement Board — will not break a current connection. State employment with the Alaska Railroad, so long as that railroad remains an entity of the State of Alaska, will not break a current connection. Also, railroad service in Canada for a Canadian railroad will neither break nor preserve a current connection.

A current connection can also be maintained, for purposes of supplemental and survivor annuities, if the employee completed twenty-five years of railroad service, was involuntarily terminated without fault from his or her last job in the rail industry, and did not thereafter decline an offer of employment in the same class or craft in the rail industry, regardless of the distance to the new position. Once a current connection is established at the time the railroad retirement annuity begins, an employee never loses it no matter what kind of work is performed thereafter.

431. What if service requirements are not met for disability?

If a deceased employee did not have an insured status, jurisdiction of any survivor benefits payable is transferred to the Social Security Administration and survivor benefits are paid by that agency instead of the RRB. Regardless of which agency has jurisdiction, the deceased employee's railroad retirement and Social Security credits will be combined for benefit computation purposes.

432. Are children and other dependents eligible for survivor benefits?

Other survivor annuities are payable to:

- A child under age eighteen.

- A child age eighteen in full-time attendance at an elementary or secondary school, until the student attains age nineteen or the end of the school term after the student attains age nineteen.

- A disabled child over age eighteen, if the child became totally and permanently disabled before age twenty-two.

- A dependent grandchild meeting any of the requirements described previously for a child, if both the grandchild's parents are deceased or disabled.

- A parent at age sixty who was dependent on the employee for at least half of the parent's support. If the employee was also survived by a widow(er) or child who can qualify for an annuity, the parent's annuity is limited to the amount that Social Security would pay.

In order to be eligible for a child's annuity, the child must be:

(1)   a child of an employee who has completed ten years of railroad service (or five years of service after 1995) and had a current connection with the railroad industry when he died;

(2)   unmarried at the time the application was filed; and

(3)   dependent upon the employee.

433. What happens to survivors with dual benefits?

Survivor annuities, like retirement annuities, consist of Tier I and Tier II components. Tier I is based on the deceased employee's combined railroad retirement and Social Security credits, and is generally equivalent to the amount that would have been payable under Social Security. Tier II amounts are percentages of the deceased employee's Tier I amount.

The Tier I portion is reduced by the amount of any Social Security benefits received by a survivor annuitant, even if the Social Security benefits are based on the survivor's own earnings. This reduction follows the principles of Social Security law under which only the higher of a retirement or survivor benefit is, in effect, payable to a beneficiary. When both railroad retirement annuities and Social Security benefits are payable, the payments are generally combined into a single payment, issued through the Railroad Retirement Board.

The Tier I annuity portion of a widow's or widower's annuity may be reduced for receipt of any federal, state, or local government pension based on the widow(er)'s own earnings. The reduction does not apply if the employment on which the public pension is based was covered under Social Security as of the last day of the individual's employment.

Military service pensions based entirely on active duty before 1957 will cause a reduction. However, payments from the Department of Veterans Affairs will not cause a reduction. For those subject to the government-pension reduction, the Tier I reduction is equal to two-thirds of the amount of the government pension.

If a widow or widower is qualified for a railroad retirement employee annuity as well as a survivor annuity, a special guarantee applies in some cases. If both the widow (or widower) and the deceased employee started railroad employment after 1974, only the railroad retirement employee annuity or the survivor annuity chosen by the annuitant is payable. If either the deceased employee or the survivor annuitant had some service before 1975 but had not completed 120 months of railroad service before 1975, the employee annuity and the Tier II portion of the survivor annuity would be payable to the widow or widower. The Tier I portion of the survivor annuity would be payable, only to the extent that it exceeds the Tier I portion of the employee annuity. If either the deceased employee or the survivor annuitant completed 120 months of railroad service before 1975, the widow or dependent widower would receive both an employee annuity and a survivor annuity, without a full dual-benefit reduction.

434. Are there work and earnings limitations for those receiving survivor annuities?

A survivor annuity is not payable for any month in which the survivor works for a railroad or railroad union.

Survivors who are receiving Social Security benefits have their railroad retirement annuity and Social Security benefit combined for earnings-limitation purposes. The combined annuity and benefits are reduced by one dollar for every two dollars of earnings over $17,640 (in 2019) if the survivor is under the full retirement age. Benefits are reduced by one dollar for every three dollars of earnings over $46,920 for 2019, in the year an annuitant reaches full retirement age; however, only earnings earned prior to the month the full retirement age is reached count toward the $46,920 limit. The earnings limitation does not apply to annuitants who are older than the full retirement age, starting with the month they reach full retirement age. See Q 253 for a discussion of the full retirement age.

If the annuitant is under the full retirement age in the first year, benefits are payable, if the individual earns more than the annual exempt amount, work deductions apply only if monthly earnings are greater than one-twelfth of the annual exempt amount ($1,470 in 2019).

These earnings restrictions do not apply to disabled widows or widowers under age sixty or to disabled children. However, any work or earnings by a disability annuitant is reviewed to determine whether it indicates recovery from the disability.

435. Can survivors' annuities be offset by receipt of other benefits?

Under the Railroad Retirement Act, the Tier I portion of a survivor annuity is subject to reduction if any Social Security benefits are also payable, even if the Social Security benefit is based on the survivor's own earnings. This reduction follows the principles of Social Security law which, in effect, limit payment to the highest of any two or more benefits payable to an individual at one time.

The Tier I portion of a widow(er)'s annuity may also be reduced for the receipt of any Federal, State, or local government pension based on the widow(er)'s own earnings. The reduction generally does not apply if the employment on which the public pension is based was covered under the Social Security Act throughout the last sixty months of public employment. However, most military service pensions and payments from the Department of Veterans Affairs will not cause a reduction. For those subject to the public pension reduction, the Tier I reduction is equal to 2/3 of the amount of the public pension.

436. When do survivor benefits end?

Payment stops upon death, and no annuity is payable for the month of death.

A *widow or widower's annuity* or *surviving divorced spouse's* benefit stops if:

(1)   the annuity was based on caring for a child under age eighteen (sixteen, for a surviving divorced spouse) or a disabled child and the child is no longer under age eighteen (sixteen, for a surviving divorced spouse) or disabled; or

(2)   the annuity was based on disability and the beneficiary recovers from the disability before age sixty.

A disability annuity can be reinstated if the disability recurs within seven years. Remarriage will reduce a widow or widower's annuity rate, and, in some cases, prevent payment.

A *child's* or *grandchild's annuity* will stop if the child:

(1)   marries;

(2)   reaches age eighteen; or

(3)   recovers from the disability on which the annuity was based.

If the child is eighteen and a full-time elementary or high school student, the annuity stops upon graduation from high school, attainment of age nineteen, or the end of the first school term after attainment of age nineteen.

A *parent's survivor annuity* may stop upon remarriage; in certain cases, a remarried parent is entitled to a Tier I benefit.

437. What lump-sum death benefits are payable?

A lump-sum death benefit is payable to certain survivors of an employee with ten or more years of railroad service, or less than ten years if at least five years were after 1995, and a current connection with the railroad industry if there is no survivor immediately eligible for a monthly annuity upon the employee's death.

If the employee did not have ten years of service before 1975, the lump sum is limited to $255 and is payable only to the widow(er) living in the same household as the employee at the time of the employee's death.

If the employee had less than ten years of service but had five years after 1995, he or she must have met Social Security's insured status requirements for the lump sum to be payable.

If the employee had ten years of service before 1975, the lump sum is payable to the living-with widow(er). If there is no such widow(er), the lump sum may be paid to the funeral home or the payer of the funeral expenses. These lump sums averaged $1,015 in fiscal year 2017.

If a widow(er) is eligible for monthly benefits at the time of the employee's death, but the widow(er) had excess earnings deductions which prevented annuity payments or for any other reason did not receive monthly benefits in the twelve-month period beginning with the month of the employee's death totaling at least as much as the lump sum, the difference between the lump-sum benefit and monthly benefits actually paid, if any, is payable in the form of a deferred lump-sum benefit. The average for all types of lump sums was $921 in fiscal year 2016.

The railroad retirement system also provides, under certain conditions, a residual lump-sum death benefit which ensures that a railroad family receives at least as much in benefits as the employee paid in railroad retirement taxes before 1975. This benefit is, in effect, a refund of an employee's pre-1975 railroad retirement taxes, after subtraction of any benefits previously paid on the basis of the employee's service. This benefit is seldom payable.

Railroad Retirement Taxes

438. What are the railroad retirement tax rates for employees and employers?

Railroad retirement Tier I taxes are coordinated with Social Security taxes and increase automatically when Social Security taxes rise. Employees and employers pay Tier I taxes that are the same as Social Security taxes. In addition, both employees and employers pay Tier II taxes, to finance railroad retirement benefit payments over and above Social Security levels.

Tier I is the first level of the regular annuity for employees. It is calculated in generally the same way as a Social Security benefit.

Tier II is the second tier of a regular annuity and is computed under a separate formula. Tier II is based on railroad service alone. Tier II benefits are equal to 7/10 of 1 percent of the employee's average monthly earnings, using the Tier II tax base in the sixty months of highest earnings multiplied by the employee's years of service in the rail industry.

The Tier I tax rate for employees and employers is 7.65 percent. In 2019, the Tier II tax rate for employers is 13.1 percent and the Tier II tax rate for employees is 4.9 percent. Tier II taxes are imposed on a maximum of $95,400 of earnings (in 2018). The Tier II tax rates are adjusted each year based on the amount of assets and expenses of the railroad retirement system.

Tax Rate for Employees and Employers

Employers and Employees each		Tier II tax rate	
Hospital insurance (HI) tax rate	Tier I tax rate including HI tax	Employers	Employees
1.45%	7.65%	13.1% (2019)	4.9% (2019)

* Medicare Hospital Insurance (HI) tax applies to all annual earnings.

Regular Railroad Retirement Taxes

Tier I	Tax rate	Taxable earnings
Employees	7.65%	$132,900* (2019)
Employers	7.65%	$132,900* (2019)
Tier II		
Employees	4.9% (2019)	$95,400 (2019)
Employers	13.1% (2019)	$95,400 (2019)

Taxes on Someone Earning $132,900 (2019)

	Tier I	Tier II	Total
Employees	$10,166.85	$4,674.60	$14,841.45
Employers	$10,166.85	$12,497.40	$22,664.25

* Medicare Hospital Insurance (HI) tax applies to all annual earnings.

Railroad employees who also worked for a Social Security-covered employer in the same year may, under certain circumstances, receive a tax credit or refund equivalent to any excess Social Security taxes withheld.

Employees who worked for two or more railroads in a year, or who had Tier I taxes withheld from their Railroad Retirement Board sickness insurance benefits in addition to their railroad earnings, may be eligible for a tax credit or refund of any excess Tier I or Tier II railroad retirement taxes withheld. Such tax credits or refunds may be claimed on an employee's federal income tax return.

439. How do railroad retirement and Social Security payroll taxes compare?

Railroad retirement payroll taxes, like railroad retirement benefits, are calculated on a two-tier basis. Rail employees and employers pay Tier I taxes at the same rate as Social Security taxes, 7.65 percent, consisting of 6.2 percent for retirement on earnings up to $132,900 in 2019, and 1.45 percent for Medicare hospital insurance on all earnings. An additional 0.9 percent in Medicare taxes (2.35 percent in total) will be withheld from employees on earnings above $200,000.

In addition, rail employees and employers both pay Tier II taxes which are used to finance railroad retirement benefit payments over and above Social Security levels.

In 2019, the Tier II tax rate on earnings up to $94,500 is 4.9 percent for employees and 13.1 percent for employers.

BENEFITS FOR SERVICE MEMBERS AND VETERANS

Military Retirement – Generally

440. In general, who is entitled to military retirement benefits?

Members of the armed forces may retire after a certain amount of active service. Monthly retirement pay, up until December 31, 2017, is based on a percentage of base pay of the highest rank held, as well as number of years of service. After 2017, a new plan called Blended Retirement has been introduced.

Service members who become disabled while in service may be placed on either temporary or permanent disability retirement, depending on the degree and length of disability, and also on whether they satisfy certain other conditions of eligibility.

Reservists are entitled to receive retirement benefits if they meet certain eligibility requirements.

Members of the uniformed services may also participate in the federal Thrift Savings Plan (see Q 479, Q 551).

441. Who is considered a member of a uniformed service?

A member of a uniformed service consists of any of the following:

- An appointed, enlisted, inducted, or retired member of:

    - one of the armed services without a specified component; or

    - a component of the Army, Navy, Air Force, Marine Corps, or Coast Guard, including any of the following Reserve components: Army, Navy, Marine Corps, Air Force, or Coast Guard Reserve, the Reserve Corps of the Public Health Service, the U.S. National Guard, the Air National Guard of the U.S., and, under limited circumstances, the National Guard or Air National Guard of the States or the District of Columbia. (NOTE: A temporary member of the Coast Guard Reserve is not considered a member of a uniformed service.)

- A commissioned officer (including a retired commissioned officer) of the National Oceanic and Atmospheric Administration or the Regular or Reserve Corps of the Public Health Service.

- A member of the Fleet Reserve or Fleet Marine Corps Reserve.

- A midshipman at the U.S. Naval Academy, and a cadet at the U.S. Military, Coast Guard, or Air Force Academy.

- A member of the Reserve Officers' Training Corps and the Naval or Air Force Reserve Officers' Training Corps, when ordered to annual training duty for fourteen days or more, and while performing authorized travel to and from that duty.

- In route to or from a place of final acceptance for entry upon active military or naval service, provided that they were:

  ○ ordered or directed to proceed to such place; and

  ○ have been provisionally accepted for duty, or have been selected for active military, or naval service under the Universal Military Training and Service Act.

442. What does "active duty" and "active duty for training" mean?

The term "active duty" means:

- full-time duty (other than active duty for training) performed by a member of the uniformed services;

- full-time duty (other than for training purposes) as a commissioned officer of the National Oceanic and Atmospheric Administration or its predecessor organization the Coast and Geodetic Survey, or in the Regular or Reserve Corps of the Public Health Service;

- service as a cadet at the United States Military, Air Force, or Coast Guard Academy, or as a midshipman at the United States Naval Academy; and

- authorized travel to or from the duties described above.

The term "active duty for training" means:

- full-time duty performed by a member of a Reserve component of a uniformed service in the active military or naval service of the U.S. for training purposes;

- full-time duty as a commissioned officer of the Reserve Corps of the Public Health Service for training purposes;

- full-time duty as a member of the Army National Guard or Air National Guard of any State;

- annual training duty performed for a period of fourteen days or more as a member of the Reserve Officers' Training Corps, the Naval Reserve Officers' Training Corps, or the Air Force Reserve Officers' Training Corps; and

- authorized travel to and from any duty or service described above.

443. What effect does a dishonorable discharge have on noncontributory military service wage credits?

A discharge under dishonorable conditions prohibits the granting of noncontributory military service wage credits for any period of active service to which the discharge applies. The following types of separations are issued under dishonorable conditions:

- A dishonorable discharge

- A bad conduct discharge issued as a result of a sentence by a general court martial

- A discharge for desertion

- In the case of an officer, a resignation accepted "for the good of the service"

- A discharge on the grounds that the person was a conscientious objector who refused to do military duty, to wear the uniform, or otherwise to comply with lawful orders of competent military authority

- A discharge by reason of conviction by a civil court for treason, sabotage, espionage, murder, rape, arson, burglary, robbery, kidnapping, assault with intent to kill, assault with a dangerous weapon, or an attempt to commit any of these crimes

Military Retirement Plans – High-3 and Blended Retirement

444. What retirement benefits are available for those who first became members before August 1, 1986?

An immediate annuity is available to a service member who completes twenty years of service. Until January 1, 2018, no benefits were available to a servicemember who did not complete twenty years of service. However, effective January 1, 2018, a new retirement plan has been introduced called the Blended Retirement System (BRS). The current retirement system is being retained as a legacy system.

The retirement annuity is based in part on the servicemember's retirement "pay base," as well as the date on which the individual became a member of the uniformed service.

For those becoming members of a uniformed service for the first time *on or before September 7, 1980*, the retired pay base equals the servicemember's final monthly basic pay to which he was entitled the day before retirement.

For persons becoming members of a uniformed service for the first time *after September 7, 1980*, the monthly retired pay base is one thirty-sixth of the total amount of the monthly basic pay that the servicemember received for the highest thirty-six months (whether or not consecutive) of active duty.

In order to compute the monthly retirement benefit, the monthly retired pay base is multiplied by an amount equaling 2.5 percent for each year of service, up to a maximum of thirty years. The benefits range from 50 percent at twenty years of service to 75 percent at thirty or more years of service.

Retired pay is adjusted annually by the increase in the cost of living, as measured by the Consumer Price Index for All Urban Wage Earners and Clerical Workers (CPI).

The uniformed services retirement system is noncontributory. However, the servicemember contributes, while on active duty, to the Social Security system and, thereby, earns eligibility for a Social Security retirement benefit. Members may also contribute to the federal Thrift Savings Plan (see Q 479).

445. What is the retirement system for those who became members between August 1, 1986 and December 31, 2017?

Under the Military Retirement Reform Act of 1986, anyone who becomes a member of a uniformed service on or after August 1, 1986 through December 31, 2017, is subject to a new retirement system.

The average monthly basic pay for the highest three years of pay during service becomes the pay base for servicemembers. This is known as "high-3." (or high-thirty-six for the average of highest thirty-six months of pay). The multiplier, or percentage, for each year of service that is multiplied by the pay base remains unchanged at 2.5 percent for each year of service. The maximum number of years creditable toward retirement is thirty – or 75 percent of pay base.

Under this system, where the servicemember has retired and has completed fewer than thirty years of service, the percent reached above is reduced by one percentage point for each year between thirty years and the number of years completed.

This means that a twenty-year retiree will receive 40 percent of the pay base (as opposed to 50 percent under the system for those who became servicemembers before August 1, 1986). A thirty-year retiree, however, will receive the full 75 percent of the pay base, the same as under the old system.

	Multiplier	
Years of Service	Before 62	After 62
20	40.0	50.0
21	43.5	52.5
22	47.0	55.0
23	50.5	57.5
24	54.0	60.0
25	57.5	62.5
26	61.0	65.0
27	64.5	67.5
28	68.0	70.0
29	71.5	72.5
30	75.0	75.0

Cost-of-living adjustments to retirement benefits are guaranteed in years of inflation. Annual benefit increases will equal the increase in the Consumer Price Index (CPI), less one percentage point. This formula is known as "CPI Minus 1."

There is a one-time recomputation of retirement pay at age sixty-two, in recognition of the fact that at about age sixty-two military retirement pay becomes the primary source of retirement income for career military personnel. At the point when a retiree reaches age sixty-two, retirement pay is recomputed as if the one percentage point penalty for retirement at less than thirty years of service had not been applied. Additionally, at the same time, the retirement pay is increased to the level it would have reached if cost-of-living adjustments had been made under the full CPI rather than the "CPI Minus 1" formula.

In short, at age sixty-two, the level of military retirement pay is restored to the level at which it would have been under the law for military members who entered the service prior to August 1, 1986. Note, however, that all cost-of-living adjustments after age sixty-two are under the "CPI Minus 1" formula. Thus, military retirees will lose 1 percent to inflation each year after age sixty-two.

A servicemember retiring after thirty years of service will receive 75 percent of basic pay both before and after age sixty-two. His retirement pay will be affected only by the change in the cost-of-living adjustment formula.

446. May service members contribute to the Thrift Savings Plan?

Yes. All active duty and Ready Reserve members of the uniformed services can participate in the Thrift Savings Plan (TSP) (see Q 551). The uniformed services include the Army, Navy, Air Force, Marine Corps, Coast Guard, Public Health Service, and the National Oceanic and Atmospheric Administration.

Uniformed service members can contribute up to 100 percent of their base pay. If a member contributes from base pay, he or she can elect to contribute up to 100 percent of any incentive pay, special pay, or bonus pay. Deferred contributions to the TSP generally cannot exceed $18,500 (in 2018). Catch-up contributions of up to $6,000 for members over age fifty are also available (see Q 551). The maximum annual addition limit is $55,000. The "catch-up" contribution is separate from the elective deferred and annual addition limits.

The individual service secretaries may designate certain critical specialties as eligible for matching contributions in the same way that contributions are matched for FERS participants. There is no automatic 1 percent contribution for uniformed service members.

447. How has the military retirement system changed?

Significantly. The National Defense Authorization Act (NDAA) for Fiscal Year 2016, created a new military retirement system that went into effect in January 2018. The BRS blends a defined benefit annuity with a defined contribution plan, through the Thrift Savings Plan (TSP). Service members who joined after 2006 but before January 1, 2018 will have the option of remaining with the existing system or opting into the BRS. The primary difference between BRS and the legacy "High-3" system is that BRS adjusts the years of service multiplier from 2.5 percent to 2.0 percent for calculating monthly retirement pay. In addition, the BRS includes automatic government contributions of 1 percent of basic pay and government matching contributions of up to an additional 4 percent of basic pay to a service member's TSP account. The law also included a continuation pay provision, which is a direct cash payout (like a bonus), in return for additional obligated service.

448. Why was the Blended Retirement System created?

Prior to the creation of the BRS, 81 percent of service members did not receive a government pension after leaving the service. Under BRS about 85 percent of service members will receive a government retirement benefit if they serve at least two years, even if they do not qualify for a full retirement. This expansion of government retirement benefits ensures a greater number of service members receive government-provided retirement benefits, which had been previously only available to the 19 percent of active duty individuals and 14 percent of National Guard and Reservists who had served twenty or more years.

449. Who is affected by the implementation of the BRS?

The BRS went into effect on January 1, 2018. New service members, who join the uniformed services for the first time on or after January 1, 2018, will be enrolled automatically in BRS. All members who were serving as of December 31, 2017 are grandfathered under the legacy retirement system. No member who was serving on, or prior to, December 31, 2017, will be automatically switched to the BRS. Active duty service members who had fewer than twelve years of service as of December 31, 2017, and National Guard and Reserve service members in a paid status, who had accrued fewer than 4,320 retirement points as of December 31, 2017, may choose to opt into the BRS. The opt-in window for BRS is from January 1, 2018, to December 31, 2018.

450. How are those that remain in the "High-3" legacy retirement plan affected?

Nothing changes for those who choose to remain in the legacy retirement system.

451. Are members of the United States Public Health Service Commissioned Corps (USPHS) or the National Oceanic and Atmospheric Administration Commissioned (NOAA) Officer Corps affected by the implementation of the BRS?

Yes, the Uniformed Services Blended Retirement System impacts all seven of the uniformed services of the United States.

452. Which is the better plan for individuals to select?

Everyone should carefully consider the decision. For those members who do not intend to serve a full twenty-year career, or think they are unlikely to serve a full twenty-year career, BRS is probably the better choice because it ensures they will receive government contributions toward their retirement. Those who do plan to serve a full twenty years will want to compare their lifetime benefits under both the BRS and the legacy retirement systems to see which is more beneficial.

453. Does prior military service under the 2.5 percent legacy system remain as the calculator if someone opts for the BRS system?

No, opting into the BRS is a complete move into the new retirement system. For example, if you had eight years under the legacy retirement system and twelve years under BRS, at retirement all twenty years are calculated under the BRS multiplier of 2.0 percent.

454. Does the BRS change the ability to participate in the Survivor Benefit Plan?

No, all service members will still have the option of participating in the Survivor Benefit Plan.

455. Does the BRS affect Veteran Affairs disability compensation?

No, for most members retiring under BRS, there will be no impact to their eligibility to receive VA disability compensation, Combat-Related Special Compensation (CRSC), or Concurrent Retirement and Disability Pay (CRDP). However, if a service member covered by BRS elects the lump-sum option, there may be an impact to his or her ability to receive some or all of his or her VA disability compensation due to the law requiring an offset of the retired pay that has already been received via the lump sum. Regardless, however, those with CRSC-qualifying disabilities will still be able to receive CRSC even if they elect a lump sum. Those qualified for CRDP will be able to receive VA disability compensation and military retired pay without offset.

456. Is CSB/REDUX still available to service members?

No, authority to elect the Career Status Bonus (CSB)/REDUX ended on December 31, 2017. No CSB will be offered after this date.

457. When do service members need to make a choice about BRS?

Service members who are eligible to opt into BRS will have all of calendar year 2018 to make their opt-in decision. The enrollment period goes from January 1, 2018 through December 31, 2018. Members of the Army, Navy, or Air Force who wish to remain in the legacy system do not have to do anything,. However, Marines will have to affirmatively decline enrollment in the BRS via the Marine Online portal.

458. Is there any difference if someone opts into BRS at the start of 2018 or at the end?

Eligible service members may opt into BRS anytime between January 1, 2018, and December 31, 2018. However, those opting into the new retirement system will begin receiving automatic and applicable matching government contributions effective the first pay period that begins on or after the day the member opts into the BRS. Therefore, if waiting until the end of 2018, the contributions will be smaller for the year.

459. What is the process for opting in to BRS?

The individual will need to complete the **mandatory** BRS Opt-In Course on Joint Knowledge Online or their services' Learning Management System (if available) and physically opt into

BRS anytime from January 1, 2018 to December 31, 2018. Members of the Army, Navy, and Air Force will utilize myPay; Coast Guard and members of the Commissioned Officer Corps of the National Oceanic and Atmospheric Administration (NOAA) will opt-in via Direct Access; and Marines will make their decision via Marine Online (MOL).

- When opting in via myPay, a service member must first click a link that says, "Blended Retirement System Opt-In".

- The service member must acknowledge no less than three times that he or she is aware and fully understands the decision to opt-in is irrevocable and that he or she is opting into the BRS.

- Service members joining on or after January 1, 2018 (meaning those who have a Date of Initial Entry into Military Service (DIEMS)) on or after January 1, 2018) will be automatically enrolled in the BRS.

460. If an individual mistakenly opted into the Blended Retirement System, can they change their choice?

The decision to opt-in is irrevocable. Following mandatory training, the opt-in process is a multi-step layered process that requires the Service member to consciously opt-in with intent. A member must acknowledge no less than three times that he or she is aware and fully understands the decision to opt-in is irrevocable. The only option is to apply with the Board for Correction of Military/Naval Records for relief for any matter related to pay and benefits and prove a specific error or injustice.

461. Does the service members spouse need to concur with the member's decision to opt into the BRS?

No, although DoD encourages service members to make their opt-in decision in consultation with their spouse, significant other, financial advisor, or other trusted advisor prior to making an opt-in election, the law does not require spousal concurrence with the decision.

462. Does participation in the BRS affect a service member's ability to participate in the Survivor benefit plan?

No, service members will still have the option of participating in the Survivor Benefit Plan.

463. Can a new service member get a waiver to join the High-3 legacy retirement system?

No. This option was only available to members who entered the service on, or prior to, December 31, 2017.

464. If an individual has a break in service, can they still opt into the Blended Retirement System?

If someone left the military prior to January 1, 2018 and rejoined the service after the opt-in decision year on January 1, 2019 or later, they will be offered thirty days to decide whether to stay in the legacy retirement system or elect the new BRS. They will need to have had fewer than twelve years of service as of December 31, 2017, or, for reservists or National Guard, fewer than 4,320 retirement points as of December 31, 2017. For those reentering the service during 2018, they will have the remaining time in calendar year 2018 or thirty days, whichever is longer, to decide to opt into BRS.

465. What is the Thrift Saving Plan (TSP) and what is the Federal Retirement Thrift Board (FRTIB)?

The TSP is a defined contribution retirement savings and investment plan that offers the same types of savings and tax benefits many private corporations offer their employees under 401(k) or similar plans. The FRTIB is an independent government agency required by law to manage the TSP.

466. How does the Thrift Saving Plan figure into the BRS?

The BRS includes a defined contribution component through TSP. Uniformed service members who are covered by the BRS are eligible to receive government automatic and matching contributions to their TSP accounts. These government contributions to TSP are portable retirement savings that begin early in a member's career.

467. If a service member is part of the BRS and retires after twenty years, will they still get an annuity?

Yes, for those service members who retire after at least twenty years of service (twenty qualifying years for the National Guard and Reserve), their retirement remains a defined benefit in which the service member will get monthly retirement pay. Under BRS, the service member's monthly retired pay will be calculated with a 2.0 percent multiplier (in lieu of the 2.5 percent under the legacy High-3 system), times the average of the service member's highest thirty-six months of basic pay.

468. What are the ramifications for the service members remaining in the legacy (High-3) retirement system?

For those remaining in the legacy retirement system, nothing about the current retirement plan changes. The individual will still need to complete twenty years of service (or twenty qualifying years of service if you are in the National Guard or Reserve) to receive a military retirement pension.

469. Are the retirement proceeds under the BRS subject to division of assets in a divorce?

Yes, they can be. A member's pension under the BRS is similarly subject to a divorce decree as it is under the legacy retirement plan and subject to state court decisions.

470. When does an individual begin collecting retirement pay?

BRS does not change any of the existing rules about when the military retired pay defined benefit begins. If the individual served at least twenty years on active duty, retired pay will begin on the first day of the first month following retirement. If the individual served at least twenty qualifying years of service in the National Guard or Reserve, eligibility to receive retired pay begins at age sixty. This age of eligibility for retired pay may be reduced for members of the National Guard and Reserve who have certain qualifying active duty service performed after 2008.

471. Does the BRS plan offer a lump sum option as the High-3 plan?

The lump sum provision of BRS gives service members choices at retirement. A service member may choose to receive either 25 percent or 50 percent of the discounted present value of a portion of their future retirement pay, in exchange for reduced monthly retirement pay. Monthly retirement pay returns to the full amount when the service member reaches full Social Security retirement age, which for most is age sixty-seven. No such lump sum option exists under the legacy, High-3, military retirement system.

472. What is continuation pay?

BRS includes a continuation pay provision as a method to encourage service members to continue serving in the uniformed services. Continuation pay is a direct cash payout, much like a bonus. It is payable between the completion of eight years of service, but before completion of twelve years of service, as determined and announced by the particular branch. Members receive continuation pay in return for additional obligated service. Active component service members (including Active Guard Reserve (AGR) and Full Time Support (FTS)) enrolled in the BRS will be eligible for a cash incentive of two and one-half to thirteen times their regular monthly basic pay. Reserve Component members will be eligible for one-half to six times their monthly basic pay (as if serving on active duty). Each service will publish guidance related to Continuation Pay rates. The rates for each calendar year will be determined by the retention needs of the Military Services and published.

473. How are the eight to twelve years of service calculated for continuation pay?

Active duty service members and National Guard and Reserve service members in a pay status are eligible for continuation pay when they complete between their eighth to twelfth year of service, which is calculated from that service member's Pay Entry Base Date (PEBD). Continuation pay may be paid at any time during this period, as determined by the Service.

474. Will a service member be eligible for other bonuses, such as a reenlistment bonus, if they receive continuation pay?

Yes. Continuation pay can be received in conjunction with other bonus if not otherwise prohibited by law.

475. Can continuation pay be collected more than one time?

No. Continuation pay is a one-time payout to a service member, regardless of whether they change service, component, or career specialty.

476. Can the service obligation for continuation pay and other bonuses, such as a reenlistment bonus, be served concurrently?

Yes. The service obligation, because of continuation pay, can be served concurrently.

477. Can someone receive continuation pay while in active duty and then complete their obligation in another service or component?

This depends. Continuation pay is designed to retain you in your current occupation, service, and component.

478. Is continuation pay part of the service member's retirement package?

Continuation pay is not part of a service member's retirement benefit, but it is part of the Department of Defense strategy to maintain existing rates of retention of experienced personnel for the All-Volunteer Force. Department of Defense analysis suggests that the reduction in the monthly retired pay may result in fewer members staying for a full career. Providing continuation pay as a retention tool will help encourage these members to stay.

Survivor Annuity

479. What is the Survivor Benefit Plan?

The Survivor Benefit Plan provides survivor monthly benefits for eligible widows, widowers, and dependent children of eligible military personnel. Benefits are essentially the same as those provided federal government employees.

Those eligible to participate in the Survivor Benefit Plan (SBP) must be:

(1)   entitled to retired or retainer pay; or

(2)   eligible for retired pay but for the fact that they are under sixty years of age.

The standard annuity is paid to those entitled to retired or retainer pay. The reserve-component annuity is paid to those who are eligible but under age sixty. If a person entitled to retired or retainer pay is married or has a dependent child, he is automatically covered by the SBP *with maximum coverage*, unless he elects lesser coverage or declines participation before the first day he becomes eligible for the retired or retainer pay. Unmarried service personnel who have no dependent children can elect a survivor annuity in favor of someone who has an insurable interest in their life. Retired pay is, of course, reduced for Plan participants.

A retiree who has a spouse and a child (or children) at retirement can elect survivor benefits for the *spouse only* or for the *child (or children) only*. Absent some election, coverage for both the spouse and child (or children) is automatic. The spouse must concur in:

(1)   an election not to participate in the plan;

(2)   an election to provide the spouse with an annuity at less than the maximum level; and

(3)   an election to provide an annuity for a dependent child but not the spouse.

An election not to participate in the Plan by a person eligible for retired pay is irrevocable unless revoked before the date on which the person first becomes entitled to that pay. An election by a person under age sixty not to participate in the Plan becomes irrevocable if not revoked by the end of the ninety-day period beginning on the date he receives notification that he has completed the required years of service.

480. Who is eligible to receive Survivor Benefit Plan benefits?

The Survivor Benefit Plan provides a monthly annuity payment effective the first day after the death of the retiree. The annuity is paid to one of the following:

- The eligible surviving widow or widower

- The surviving dependent children in equal shares, if the eligible widow or widower or eligible former spouse is dead, dies, or otherwise becomes ineligible

- The dependent children in equal shares, if the retiree elected to provide an annuity for dependent children but not for the spouse or former spouse

- The former spouse under certain conditions

The following criteria apply for the purposes of determining eligible beneficiaries:

- A *widow* is the surviving wife of a person who, if not married to the retiree at the time he became eligible for retired pay, was married to him for at least one year immediately before his death or is the mother of issue by that marriage.

- A *widower* is the surviving husband of a retiree who, if not married to the person at the time she became eligible for retired pay, was married to her for at least one year immediately before her death or is the father of issue by that marriage.

- A *former spouse* is the surviving former husband or wife of a person who is eligible to participate in the Plan.

- A *dependent child* is a person who is:

  ○ unmarried,

  ○ under eighteen years of age; or at least eighteen, but under twenty-two years of age, and pursuing a full-time course of study or training in a high school, vocational school or college; or incapable of self-support because of a mental or physical incapability existing before age eighteen or incurred on or after that birthday, but before age twenty-two, while pursuing such a full-time course of study or training,

  ○ the child of a retiring participant, including an adopted child, a stepchild, foster child, or recognized natural child who lived with the retiree in a regular parent-child relationship.

- A *person with an insurable interest* is any person who has a bona fide financial interest in the continued life of the retiree. The relationship of the person to the retiree normally does not extend beyond the mother, father, brother, sister, or single child of the retiree.

The annuity payable to a surviving spouse of the retiree is paid for life, except that if the annuitant remarries before age fifty-five, the remarriage terminates the annuity. If the remarriage is terminated by death, annulment, or divorce, payment of the annuity is resumed upon the termination of the remarriage. Survivor Benefits are subject to Cost-Of-Living Adjustments (COLA).

481. What is the amount of the Survivor Benefit Plan annuity?

The amount of a Survivor Benefit Plan annuity payable to a widow, widower, former eligible spouse, or dependent children is based on a figure known as the *base amount*. The base amount is:

(1)   the amount of monthly retired pay to which a retiree became entitled when first eligible, or later became entitled to by being advanced on the retired list, performing active duty, or being transferred from the temporary disability retired list to the permanent disability retired list; or

(2)   any lesser amount designated by the retiree on or before the first day of eligibility for retired pay, but not less than $300. This is unchanged for 2019.

A retiree who wants maximum survivor benefits for a spouse and children (at the cost of maximum reduction in retirement pay), will designate as the base amount on which survivor benefits are figured the full amount of retired pay. For a lower level of survivor benefits (in exchange for a smaller reduction in retirement pay), a base amount less than full retirement pay will be designated.

The following are categories of dependents and the rules for determining the amount of annuity payable:

(1)   In the case of a standard annuity for a widow, widower or child, the monthly annuity is an amount equal to 55 percent of the base amount, if the beneficiary is under sixty-two years of age or is a dependent child when becoming entitled to the annuity. If the beneficiary (other than a dependent child) is sixty-two years of age or older when becoming entitled to the annuity, the monthly annuity is an amount equal to 35 percent of the base amount.

(2)   In the case of a standard annuity for an ex-spouse or person with an insurable interest in the annuitant (other than a widow, widower, or dependent child), the monthly annuity payable to the beneficiary is an amount equal to 55 percent of the retired pay of the person who elected to provide the annuity.

(3)   An annuity is also payable to a surviving spouse of a member who dies on active duty after: (a) becoming eligible to receive retired pay, (b) qualifying for

retired pay, except that he or she has not applied for or been granted that pay, or (c) completing twenty years of active service but before he or she is eligible to retire as a commissioned officer because he or she has not completed ten years of active commissioned service. An annuity is payable to the dependent child of the servicemember if there is no surviving spouse or if the servicemember's surviving spouse subsequently dies.

If a person receiving an annuity in item (3) in preceding list is under sixty-two or is a dependent child when the servicemember or former servicemember dies, the monthly annuity is an amount equal to 55 percent of the retired pay to which the servicemember or former servicemember would have been entitled if the servicemember or former servicemember had been entitled to that pay based upon his or her years of active service when he or she died.

If a person receiving an annuity in item (3) in the preceding list (other than a dependent child) is sixty-two or older when the servicemember or former servicemember dies, the monthly annuity is an amount equal to 35 percent of the retired pay to which the service-member or former servicemember would have been entitled if the servicemember or former servicemember had been entitled to that pay based upon his or her years of active service when he or she died.

482. Are Survivor Benefit Plan annuities subject to cost-of-living increases?

Yes, whenever retirees receive a cost-of-living increase in their retired pay, Survivor Benefit Plan annuities are increased at the same time by the same total percent. The percent-age is applied to the monthly annuity payable before any reduction is made, in consideration of the annuitant's eligibility for Dependency and Indemnity Compensation or Social Security survivor benefits.

483. How does the Survivor Benefit Plan reduce the regular retirement annuity?

The Survivor Benefit Plan reduces the regular retirement annuity according to the follow-ing formulas.

Where the individual first becomes a member of the uniformed service before March 1, 1990, the reduction is the lesser of:

(1)   an amount equal to 2.5 percent of the first $364 of the base amount of the annuity subject to the survivor benefit, plus 10 percent of the remainder; or

(2)   an amount equal to 6.5 percent of the base amount of the annuity subject to the survivor benefit.

Where the individual first becomes a member of the uniformed service on or after March 1, 1990, the reduction for the Survivor Benefit Plan is a flat 6.5 percent of the base amount of the annuity.

"Base amount" does not include cost-of-living increases.

Disability Retirement

484. When is a servicemember entitled to retire on permanent disability?

When he has been called or ordered to active duty for a period of more than thirty days (excluding Ready Reserve training duty), and:

(1)   he is unfit to perform his duties because he has incurred a physical disability while entitled to basic pay;

(2)   the disability is of a permanent and stable nature based on commonly accepted medical principles;

(3)   the disability is not due to intentional or willful neglect, and not incurred during a period of unauthorized absence; and

(4)   one of the following applies: (a) the disability is rated at least 30 percent under the Department of Veterans Affairs disability rating schedule, or (b) the service member has completed at least twenty years of service.

Where the service member has not completed twenty years of service but has a disability of at least 30 percent, as explained in (a) in preceding list, one of the following tests must additionally be satisfied:

(1)   The disability must be incurred in the line of duty.

(2)   The disability must be the proximate result of performing active duty.

(3)   The servicemember must have completed at least eight years of service.

Where the active-duty or inactive training period is thirty days or less, a regular servicemember or reservist is entitled to permanent disability based on *injury* where the following conditions are met:

(1)   He is unfit to perform his duties because he has incurred a physical disability while entitled to basic pay.

(2)   The disability is of a permanent and stable nature based on commonly accepted medical principles.

(3)   The disability is the proximate result of performing active duty or inactive training.

(4)   The disability is not due to intentional misconduct or willful neglect, and not incurred during a period of unauthorized absence.

(5)   One of the following applies:

    (a) the disability is rated at least 30 percent under the Department of Veterans Affairs disability rating schedule, or

    (b) the servicemember has completed at least twenty years of service.

485. How is disability retirement pay determined?

Disability retirement pay is figured by either of two methods, at the retiree's option, up to a maximum of 75 percent of basic pay:

(1)   2.5 percent of monthly basic pay multiplied by the number of years of active service; or

(2)   the percentage rating of disability.

A servicemember who meets the requirements of temporary disability may be placed on temporary disability retirement for up to five years. Retired pay for temporary disability is no less than 50 percent of basic pay. A servicemember will be permanently retired for physical disability if still disabled after five years.

486. What is Combat-Related Special Compensation (CRSC)?

Combat-Related Special Compensation (CRSC) is a program created by Congress to allow eligible military retirees to receive monthly VA disability compensation in addition to retired pay.

CRSC is a special compensation for combat-related disabilities. It is non-taxable, and retirees must apply to their branch of service to receive it.

What are the qualifications to be eligible for Combat-Related Special Compensation (CRSC)?

Eligibility includes the following:

- You are entitled to receive military retired pay (regardless of time served on active duty).

- You are rated at least 10 percent by the VA.

- You have service-connected disabilities that were incurred as a direct result of war or instrumentality of war.

Disabilities include combat-related include injuries incurred as a direct result of:

- armed conflict,

- hazardous duty,

- an instrumentality of war,

- simulated war (war games or maneuvers).

487. What is Concurrent Retirement and Disability Pay (CRDP)?

Concurrent Retirement and Disability Pay (CRDP) is a program created by Congress to allow eligible military retirees to receive monthly VA disability compensation in addition to retired pay.

CRDP is a restoration of retired pay for retirees with service-connected disabilities that was lost due to the VA compensation offset prior to January 1, 2004. Through this law an eligible retiree's retired pay was fully restored. CRDP is taxed in the same manner as retirement pay and is taxable income. No application is required. Eligible retirees receive CRDP automatically.

What are the qualifications to be eligible for Concurrent Retirement and Disability Pay (CRDP)?

Eligibility includes:

- a regular retiree with twenty or more years of active service who has a VA disability rating of 50 percent or greater,

- a reserve retiree with twenty qualifying years of service who has a VA disability rating of 50 percent or greater and who has reached retirement age, or

- retired under Temporary Early Retirement Act (TERA) and have a VA disability rating of 50 percent or greater.

Reservists' and National Guard Retirement Pay

488. Are Reservists and National Guard members entitled to retirement pay?

To qualify for retirement pay in the Reserves, a person must complete at least twenty years of "satisfactory Federal service" as a member of the armed forces. He meets this requirement for a year by earning at least fifty points each year. Points are earned for both inactive duty and active duty. The branch of service will advise the reservist of point totals and the number of years of satisfactory federal service he has completed. The last eight qualifying years must have been spent in a Reserve unit. Entitlement to Reserve retirement pay begins at age sixty.

The Reserve point system is an element used in computing retirement pay. In totaling points, there is no limit to the number of active points that may be earned in a year, but no more than sixty inactive-duty points may be counted for any one year.

Military Retirement – National Guard and Reservists

489. How is the Retirement System changes for the National Guard and Reservists?

The new military retirement system blends elements of the legacy retirement system with government automatic and matching contributions to a member's Thrift Savings Plan (TSP)—a more modern, 401(k)-style portable defined contribution plan that many civilian government employees enjoy today. Many of the elements of the legacy retirement system remain and both National Guard and Reserve service members should have a familiarity with how it works. The Blended Retirement System does not change when a National Guard or Reserve member is eligible to retire, and National Guard and Reserve service members covered by the Blended Retirement System are still eligible for reduced age retirement if they perform qualifying active service.

490. How is eligibility for the BRS different for National Guard members and Reservists?

Eligibility to opt-in is much broader for the National Guard and Reserve than the active component. Eligibility to opt into BRS is based on retirement points. National Guard and Reserve members who had fewer than 4,320 retirement points as of December 31, 2017, and who are in a pay status, will be eligible to opt into BRS, regardless of how many service or qualifying years they have accumulated.

491. Why does the Department of Defense use a retirement point system for National Guard and Reservists?

The different eligibility criteria for National Guard and Reserve members is based on language in the National Defense Authorization Act of 2016 that mandated use of 10 U.S.C. §12733 to compute eligibility for Reserve component members.

492. Why are 4,320 retirement points required?

For retirement, National Guard and Reserve service is converted to equivalent active service by dividing accumulated retirement points by 360. The military considers a month to constitute thirty days for pay purposes, therefore each day is calculated as 1/30th of a month and twelve months would then equal 360 days. Using this formula, National Guardsmen or Reservists with 4,320 retirement points would have twelve equivalent years of active service.

493. Does the BRS change how National Guard members and Reservist acquire retirement points?

No. The Blended Retirement System does not change how retirement points are calculated for members of the National Guard and Reserve. Points are still earned by participating in drill, attending annual training, and completing active duty, among other eligible categories. BRS does not affect when a member of the National Guard or Reserve is eligible to retire. Retirement eligibility and timing remains the same as it is under the legacy retirement system. National Guard or Reserve members with twenty or more qualifying years are eligible to receive their monthly retired pay starting at age sixty or earlier based on qualifying active service.

494. Are members of the Individual Ready Reserve (IRR) or Standby Reserve eligible to participate in the BRS?

Members of the IRR and Standby Reserve are eligible to participate in the BRS. However, they must be receiving pay to enroll in BRS. Therefore, members of the IRR and Standby Reserve who are eligible to enroll in the new system (because they were in the IRR or Standby Reserve as of December 31, 2017), but who do not drill in a paid status or are not on orders during calendar year 2018, will be allowed a one-time extension of the enrollment window beyond 2018 if and when they enter a paid status.

495. How long does a member of the Individual Ready Reserve or the Standby Reserve have to opt-in once they are in paid status?

If a member of the IRR and Standby Reserve returns to a pay status in 2018, they will have the remainder of 2018 to make an opt-in decision. After 2018, all BRS-eligible members of the IRR and Standby Reserve will have thirty days to opt into the Blended Retirement System upon the first time he or she returns to a pay status.

496. How will the process work when a National Guard or Reservist retires under the Blended Retirement System?

The Blended Retirement System does not affect when a member (either active duty, National Guard, or Reserve) is eligible to retire. It remains the same; qualified National Guard and Reserve service members are eligible to receive their retirement pay starting at age sixty or earlier based on qualifying active service.

497. How is Reserve retired pay computed?

Generally, reserve retired pay is computed by:

(1)   dividing the reservist's cumulative active- and inactive-point total by 360, to convert the points into years of service;

(2)   taking the monthly basic pay rate for the member's grade and length of service at the time he or she becomes entitled to retired pay at age sixty;

(3)   multiplying that rate by 2.5 percent multiplied by the years of service that are credited to him or her through the point conversion process (but not in excess of thirty years).

Where the reservist first became a member after September 7, 1980, instead of using his or her actual pay rate as described in (2) above, he or she uses an average of the basic monthly pay to which he or she would have been entitled had he or she been on active duty for the three years in which he or she was a member of an armed force.

498. How does the Survivor Benefit Plan work for Reservists?

Generally, the Survivor Benefit Plan for Reservists follows the rules for the regular service member's Survivor Benefit Plan. With respect to the amount of reduction in retired pay of the reserve component annuity, the reduction is the lesser of:

(1)   an amount equal to 2.5 percent of the first $364 of the base amount of the annuity subject to the survivor benefit, plus 10 percent of the remainder; or

(2)   an amount equal to 6.5 percent of the base amount of the annuity subject to the survivor benefit.

Veterans
Dependency and Indemnity Compensation
499. What is Dependency and Indemnity Compensation?

Dependency and Indemnity Compensation (DIC) is the benefit program providing monthly payments to a surviving spouse, child, or parent of the veteran due to a *service-connected* (line-of duty or service-related injury or illness) death that occurs after 1956. (Where the death occurred prior to 1957, certain survivors could have elected to take benefits under DIC.)

Generally, DIC is payable to survivors of service members or reservists who died from:

(1)   disease or injury incurred or aggravated in the line of duty while on active or inactive duty training; or

(2)   disability compensable under laws administered by the Department of Veterans Affairs.

Veterans and dependents may obtain information on benefits by calling the toll-free number 1-800-827-1000. Callers are automatically connected to the Department of Veterans Affairs regional office serving the area from which their call originates. In addition, Veterans and dependents can contact the Department of Veterans Affairs online at https://www.ebenefits.va.gov/ebenefits/contact or 1-800-983-0987.

500. Who is eligible for DIC benefits?

Dependency and Indemnity Compensation (DIC) benefits are payable to an eligible *surviving spouse*, regardless of the survivor's income or employment status. The survivor's death or remarriage terminates the benefit. Benefit eligibility is not reestablished if the survivor's remarriage is terminated by death or divorce. A surviving spouse may receive DIC payments, as well as Social Security survivor benefits.

The surviving spouse must have been married:

(1)   before expiration of fifteen years after the end of the period of active duty, active duty for training, or inactive training duty, in which the injury or disease causing death was incurred or aggravated;

(2)   for one or more years; or

(3)   for any period of time if a child was born of or before the marriage.

The surviving spouse's benefit is increased when the spouse has children under age eighteen. Where there is no surviving spouse eligible to receive DIC, children under eighteen are eligible to receive DIC benefits.

The definition of "*child*" includes the veteran's legitimate child, legally adopted child, step-child who is a member of the veteran's household or was a member at the time of the veteran's death, and illegitimate child (provided a number of requirements are met).

DIC payments are made to children who are unmarried and who:

(1)   are under age eighteen; or

(2)   before attaining age eighteen, become permanently incapable of self-support; or

(3)   after attaining age eighteen and until completion of education or training (but not after attaining age twenty-three), are pursuing a course of instruction at an approved educational institution.

Eligibility of *parents* to receive DIC is measured by an annual income test, rather than by dependency. A remarriage of a parent does not terminate the benefits. Parent's DIC benefits continue until death.

501. How is the amount of the DIC benefit determined?

DIC payments to surviving spouses of veterans whose service-connected deaths occur on or after January 1, 1993, are standardized; there had been a schedule of benefits based on the military rank of the deceased veteran. In 2018, a monthly base rate of $1,283.11 is payable to the surviving spouses of all such veterans. That rate is increased by $272.46 a month, if the veteran was totally disabled due to service-connected disabilities continuously for at least eight years prior to death. Note that 2019 numbers were not available as this 2019 edition went to press but it is expected that the base rate will be increased but please confirm with the U.S. Department of Veterans Affairs at benefits.va.gov.

If there is a surviving spouse with one or more children below the age of eighteen of a deceased veteran, the DIC paid monthly to the surviving spouse is increased by $317.87 for each child.

In addition to an annual limitation, the amount of DIC payable monthly to a *parent* depends upon whether there is only one parent, whether two surviving parents are or are not living together, and whether a parent has remarried and is living with a spouse.

The maximum monthly benefit payable to *one parent only* is $622. No DIC is payable if the parent's annual income exceeds $14,974. *Two parents not living together* are entitled to a maximum monthly benefit of $450 each. Again, no DIC is paid to a parent whose annual income exceeds $14,974. *Two parents living together* (or remarried parents living with spouses, when both parents are alive) are entitled to a maximum monthly benefit of $423 each. No DIC is paid to a parent if total combined annual income exceeds $20,128.

The monthly rate of DIC payable to a parent is increased by $343 if such parent is:

(1)   a patient in a nursing home; or

(2)   helpless or blind, or so nearly helpless and blind as to need or require the regular aid and attendance of another person.

Death Prior to January 1, 1993

For surviving spouses of veterans who died prior to January 1, 1993, monthly payments are made according to the veteran's pay grade at the time of death or under the new formula, whichever provides the highest benefit. (See Appendix C, Table 4, Servicemembers and Veterans Tables, for benefits based on pay grade.)

If the veteran did not die in active service, the pay grade will be determined as of:

(1)   the time of last discharge or release from active duty; or

(2)   the time of discharge or release from any period of active duty for training or inactive duty training, if death results from service-connected disability incurred during such period. The discharge must have been other than dishonorable.

The monthly rate of DIC is increased by $343 if the surviving spouse is:

(1)   a patient in a nursing home; or

(2)   helpless and blind, or so nearly helpless and blind as to need the regular aid and attendance of another person.

The monthly rate of DIC will be increased by $152.06, if the surviving spouse is permanently housebound by reason of disability and does not qualify for the aid and attendance allowance described above.

DIC Benefits for Children

If a *child* is under age eighteen, and there is no surviving spouse entitled to DIC, DIC is paid in equal shares to the children of the deceased veteran at the following monthly rates:

- one child, $541.76;

- two children, $779.37;

- three children, $1,016.99;

- four children, $1,210.26;

- five children, $1,403.53;

- six children, $1,596.80;

- seven children, $1,790.07;

- eight children, $1,983.34;

- nine children, $2,76.61;

- more than nine children, $2,176.61 plus $189.48 for each child in excess of three.

If a child is eighteen or over, and the child became permanently incapable of self-support while under eighteen and eligible for DIC, the child's DIC is continued past age eighteen and increased by $317.87 per month. If DIC is payable to a surviving spouse with a child, age eighteen or older, who became permanently incapable of support while under eighteen, the Department of Veterans Affairs will pay an additional sum of $541.76 for such child.

If DIC is payable to a spouse with a child, age eighteen or over and under age twenty-three, who is attending an approved educational institution, DIC is paid to the child, concurrently with the payment of DIC to the spouse, in the amount of $317.87 per month if in school or $541.76 per month if considered to be helpless.

Disability Benefits – Service-Connected

502. What benefits are available for service-connected disability?

There are three kinds of benefits for a service-connected disability:

(1)   compensation paid by Department of Veterans Affairs;

(2)   severance pay; and

(3)   disability retirement pay.

Disability retirement is discussed in BENEFITS FOR FEDERAL GOVERNMENT EMPLOYEES, Q 532 to Q 583.

Monthly compensation is paid by the Department of Veterans Affairs without regard to other income, on the basis of average impairments of earning capacity in civilian employment. A person eligible for both disability retirement pay and this compensation may elect which to receive, but cannot receive full benefits from both sources.

The veteran must be disabled by injury or disease incurred in, or aggravated by, active service in the line of duty. Discharge or separation must be other than dishonorable, and the injury cannot have resulted from willful misconduct. Reservists disabled while on active training duty may qualify for compensation.

The monthly compensation amount depends on the veteran's degree of disability. The rates in the subsequent table are for 2018. Note that 2019 numbers were not available as this 2019 edition went to press. However, it is expected that the Cost of Living Increase for military benefits will be 2 percent, the largest increase in years. The tables will likely be out in December 2018 or January 2019.

VA Disability Rating: 10% – 20% (No Dependents)

Percentage	Rate
10%	$136.24
20%	$269.30

VA Disability Rating: 30% – 60% Without Children

Dependent Status	30%	40%	50%	60%
Veteran Alone	$417.15	$600.90	$855.41	$1,083.52
Veteran with Spouse Only	$466.15	$666.90	$937.41	$1,182.52
Veteran with Spouse & One Parent	$505.15	$719.90	$1,003.41	$1,261.52
Veteran with Spouse and Two Parents	$544.15	$772.90	$1,069.41	$1,340.52
Veteran with One Parent	$456.15	$653.90	$921.41	$1,162.52
Veteran with Two Parents	$495.15	$706.90	$987.41	$1,241.52
Additional for A/A spouse	$46.00	$61.00*	$76.00	$91.00

VA Disability Rating: 30% – 60% With Children

Dependent Status	30%	40%	50%	60%
Veteran with Spouse & Child	$503.15	$714.90	$998.41	$1,255.52
Veteran with Child Only	$450.15	$644.90	$910.41	$1,149.52
Veteran with Spouse, One Parent and Child	$542.15	$767.90	$1,064.41	$1,334.52
Veteran with Spouse, Two Parents and Child	$581.15	$820.90	$1,130.41	$1,413.52
Veteran with One Parent and Child	$489.15	$697.90	$976.41	$1,228.52
Veteran with Two Parents and Child	$528.15	$750.90	$1,042.41	$1,307.52
Add for Each Additional Child Under Age 18	$24.00	$32.00	$41.00	$49.00
Each Additional Schoolchild Over Age 18	$79.00	$106.00	$133.00	$159.00
Additional for A/A spouse	$46.00	$61.00	$76.00	$91.00

VA Disability Rating: 70% – 100% Without Children

Dependent Status	70%	80%	90%	100%
Veteran Alone	$1,365.48	$1,587.25	$1,783.68	$2,973.86
Veteran with Spouse Only	$1,481.48	$1,719.25	$1,932.68	$3,139.67
Veteran with Spouse & One Parent	$1,574.48	$1,825.25	$2,051.68	$3,272.73
Veteran with Spouse and Two Parents	$1,667.48	$1,931.25	$2,170.68	$3,405.79
Veteran with One Parent	$1,458.48	$1,693.25	$1,902.68	$3,106.92
Veteran with Two Parents	$1,551.48	$1,799.25	$2,021.68	$3,239.98
Additional for A/A spouse	$106.00	$122.00	$137.00	$152.06

VA Disability Rating: 70% – 100% With Children

Dependent Status	70%	80%	90%	100%
Veteran with Spouse & Child	$1,566.48	$1,816.25	$2041.68	$3,261.10
Veteran with Child Only	$1,442.48	$1,675.25	$1,882.68	$3,084.75
Veteran with Spouse, One Parent and Child	$1,659.48	$1,922.25	$2,160.68	$3,394.16

Dependent Status	70%	80%	90%	100%
Veteran with Spouse, Two Parents and Child	$1,752.48	$2,028.25	$2,279.68	$3,527.22
Veteran with One Parent and Child	$1,535.48	$1,781.25	$2,001.68	$3,217.81
Veteran with Two Parents and Child	$1,628.48	$1,887.25	$2,120.68	$3,350.87
Add for Each Additional Child Under Age 18	$57.00	$65.00	$74.00	$82.38
Each Additional Schoolchild Over Age 18	$186.00	$212.00	$239.00	$266.13
Additional for A/A spouse	$106.00	$122.00	$137.00	$152.06

Rates for each school child are shown separately. They are not included with any other compensation rates. All other entries on this chart reflecting a rate for children show the rate payable for children under 18 or helpless. To find the amount payable to a 70 percent disabled Veteran with a spouse and four children, one of whom is over eighteen and attending school, take the 70 percent rate for a veteran with a spouse and 2 children, $1,659.48, and add the rate for two school children, $186.00 × 2= $372. The total amount payable is $2,031.48.

Where the veteran has a spouse who is determined to require A/A, add the figure shown as "additional for A/A spouse" to the amount shown for the proper dependency code. For example, veteran has A/A spouse and 2 minor children and is 70 percent disabled. Add $106.00, additional for A/A spouse, to the rate for a 70 percent veteran with dependency code 12, $1,628.48. The total amount payable is $1,734.48.

A service-connected disability rating may be increased or decreased in accordance with medical findings of changes in the affected condition. However, once a condition has been rated at or above a particular evaluation for twenty continuous years, the rating is protected by law and may not be changed (unless the rating was established by fraud).

Any veteran entitled to monthly compensation whose disability is rated not less than 30 percent is entitled to additional compensation for dependents. The current rates listed below are based upon 100 percent disability. If the disability rating is at least 30 percent, but less than 100 percent, the amount of dependent benefits will be approximately the same percent of these rates as the percent-of-disability rating.

A child's benefit usually ends at age eighteen. However, each dependent child between ages eighteen and twenty-three who is attending an approved school is eligible for $260 monthly if the veteran is totally disabled, and a proportionate amount if the veteran is partially disabled.

The spouse of a totally disabled veteran is entitled to $317 a month if: (1) a patient in a nursing home; or (2) helpless and blind, or so nearly helpless and blind as to need or require the regular aid and attendance of another person. The spouse of a veteran who is not totally disabled, but at least 30 percent disabled, is entitled to a proportionate monthly benefit.

These dependency allowances are not payable if the service member receives any other allowance for dependents under any other law (with the exception of Social Security benefits). The higher of the two amounts may be elected, but not both. Social Security benefits for total and permanent disability will not be reduced by the amount of any service-connected disability compensation received from the Department of Veterans Affairs.

Service personnel are entitled to *disability severance pay* when separated from service for physical disability, but are not eligible for disability retirement pay where:

(1)   the rated disability is less than 30 percent; or

(2)   length-of-service credits are insufficient.

Disability severance pay is a lump sum equal to twice the monthly base and longevity pay multiplied by years of service, but not exceeding the amount of two years' basic pay, and is payable by the member's branch of service.

Veterans with a 10 percent disability rating may be entitled to a program of vocational rehabilitation, if the Department of Veterans Affairs finds that the veteran has a "serious employment handicap" and needs rehabilitative services to prepare for, obtain, or retain suitable employment.

Any veteran receiving a pension awarded between January 30, 1985, and December 31, 1995 can apply for a vocational rehabilitation evaluation. If an evaluation shows the veteran can achieve a vocational goal if provided the appropriate rehabilitative services, the Department of Veterans Affairs will help develop a plan of services which can lead to employment. There is no requirement that a pensioner participate in an evaluation or training and, if the veteran elects to enter a rehabilitative program, the pension benefit is protected until the veteran is employed.

The Department of Veterans Affairs makes disability payments based on a presumption that veterans who served in Vietnam were exposed to Agent Orange and other herbicides. The conditions the Department of Veterans Affairs recognizes on this basis are soft-tissue sarcoma, non-Hodgkin's lymphoma, chloracne, Hodgkin's disease, Porphyria Cutanea Tarda (PCT), multiple myeloma (a cancer involving the bone marrow), and respiratory cancers (lung, bronchus, larynx, and trachea). All Department of Veterans Affairs medical centers provide a special examination to assist Vietnam veterans who were exposed to Agent Orange in determining their current health status.

Death Benefits – Service-Connected

503. What other service-connected death benefits are available?

BURIAL EXPENSE REIMBURSEMENT

For veterans who died after September 1, 2001, the Department of Veterans Affairs reimburses survivors up to $2,000 (or more, in the case of a federal employee who dies in the performance of duty) for the burial expenses of a veteran who dies as a result of service-connected disability or disabilities. For deaths before September 11, 2001, the reimbursement is up to $1,500.

For nonservice connected deaths, if the veteran died on or after October 1, 2018, the VA will pay a $300 burial allowance and $780 for a plot. If hospitalized by the VA at the time of death, the VA will pay a $780 burial allowance and $780 for a plot.

DISPOSITION OF REMAINS AND BURIAL

When a member of the armed forces dies while on active duty, active or inactive training duty, or while receiving hospital treatment for a service-connected ailment, his or her branch of service will provide for the disposition of his or her remains. Additional costs of transportation of the remains of the deceased may be allowed if the veteran died while hospitalized or residing in a Department of Veterans Affairs facility, or while in transit, at Department of Veterans Affairs' expense, to or from a hospital, domiciliary, or a Department of Veterans Affairs regional office.

Other allowances include burial in a national cemetery, American flag, and transportation from place of death to place of burial. The next of kin is also entitled to a headstone, or a headstone monetary allowance (in the event the veteran purchased a headstone prior to death).

DEATH GRATUITY

A lump sum of $100,000 is paid to the survivors of a servicemember who dies on active duty or active or inactive training duty. A non-taxable amount of $12,420 is paid to a former servicemember who dies within 120 days after separation from active duty. This death gratuity is paid by the branch of service of the deceased to the spouse, if living; otherwise to any children in equal shares; otherwise to parents, brothers or sisters, as designated by the deceased.

GOVERNMENT HOUSING

Dependents of a servicemember may remain in government housing for ninety days without charge after the servicemember's death.

EDUCATIONAL ASSISTANCE PROGRAM

Survivors and dependents may also be eligible for the survivors' and dependents' educational assistance program. The purpose of this program is:

(1)   to enable children to obtain an education they might not otherwise have had an opportunity to obtain; and

(2)   to enable surviving spouses to prepare to support themselves and their families at a standard of living that the veteran, but for death or disability, could have expected to provide.

Pension, Disability, and Death Benefits Not Service-Connected

504. When is a veteran eligible for nonservice-connected pension, disability, and death benefits?

Veterans with limited income who are discharged under conditions other than dishonorable may be eligible for: (1) an Improved Pension, (2) Section 306 pension, or (3) old law pension. The old law pension is for veterans who died before July 1, 1960.

The pension-eligible veteran must have:

(1)   had ninety days active service during the Mexican border period, World War I, World War II, the Korean Conflict, or Vietnam Era;

(2)   been discharged because of service-connected disability; or

(3)   at the time of death been receiving (or entitled to receive) compensation or retirement pay based on a service-connected disability incurred during wartime.

505. When is a surviving spouse and dependents eligible for nonservice-connected pension, disability, and death benefits?

A surviving spouse must have lived continuously with the veteran from the time of marriage until the veteran's death, except where there was a separation due to the misconduct of, or caused by, the veteran, without fault on the surviving spouse's part. The surviving spouse's valid remarriage or death permanently terminates the benefit. However, if the remarriage is annulled, or is terminated by death or divorce (unless the divorce was secured by fraud or collusion), the surviving spouse is not barred from receiving benefits.

The surviving spouse must have been married to the veteran:

(1)   for at least one year; or

(2)   for any period, if a child was born either before or after the marriage.

For Vietnam Era veterans, the marriage must have taken place before May 8, 1985.

506. Are children entitled to benefits?

Unmarried children and surviving spouses under eighteen of a deceased veteran may be eligible for a pension. The pension is based on need. Regardless of the income limit, however, benefits will be denied a child or surviving spouse who owns capital which, in the Department of Veterans Affairs' judgment, should be consumed for his or her support.

Unmarried children and surviving spouses over eighteen may qualify for pensions in their own right, if they are:

(1)   permanently incapable of self-support since prior to age eighteen, or

(2)   under twenty-three and attending a Department of Veterans Affairs approved educational institution.

507. What is the amount of the Improved Pension?

Under the "Improved Pension Program," which went into effect on January 1, 1979, the 2018 maximum annual rates payable (effective December 1, 2017) are presented in the subsequent tables. Note that 2019 figures were not available as this 2019 edition went to press.

Veterans and Dependents

Veteran without dependent spouse or child.	$13,166
Veteran with one dependent (spouse or child).	$17,241
Veteran in need of regular aid and attendance without dependents	$21,962
Veteran in need of regular aid and attendance with one dependent	$26,036
Veteran permanently housebound without dependents	$16,089
Veteran permanently housebound with one dependent	$20,166
Two veterans married to each other.	$17,241
Mexican border period and World War I veteran	add $2,991 to the applicable annual rate
Increase for each additional dependent child	$2,250

Spouse and Dependents

Surviving spouse without dependent children	$8,830
Surviving spouse with one dependent child.	$11,557
Surviving spouse in need of regular aid and attendance without dependent child . . .	$14,113
Surviving spouse in need of regular aid and attendance with one dependent child. . .	$16,837
Surviving spouse permanently housebound without dependent child	$10,792
Surviving spouse permanently housebound with one dependent child	$14,113
Increase for each additional dependent child	$2,250
Child not in custody of veteran's surviving spouse, or child if no living surviving spouse of the veteran.	$2,250

Benefits are generally paid monthly and are reduced by the annual countable income of the claimant and any dependent of the claimant. Generally, all nonpension income is included for this purpose, but income paid for certain educational or medical expenses are excluded from the computation.

In addition, the pension may be denied or discontinued if the claimant's net worth is such that it is reasonable that some portion of the estate be used for his support. Additional pension for a child may be denied if the child's net worth is excessive.

Pensioners must provide income and net worth reports to the Department of Veterans Affairs on an annual basis.

508. What is the Section 306 Pension?

The veteran, surviving spouse, and children who came on the pension rolls on or after July 1, 1960 but prior to January 1, 1979 may continue to receive a pension at the monthly rate in effect as of December 31, 1978. The pension will be paid so long as the veteran remains permanently and totally disabled, there is no charge in dependency, and income does not exceed the adjusted income limitation. The income limitation is Consumer Price Index (CPI)-sensitive. There was a 2.0 percent Cost of Living Adjustment effective December 1, 2017.

Pensions range from $5 to $197 monthly for veterans with no dependents, and up to $222 per month for veterans with dependents. If the annual income of a veteran with no children exceeds $14,974, no pension is paid. Where there is one child and annual income exceeds $20,128, no pension is paid.

A surviving spouse with no minor children may receive up to $139 a month but, if annual income exceeds $14,974, no pension is paid. Where there is one child and annual income exceeds $20,128, no pension is paid.

Where there is no eligible surviving spouse, a child may receive sixty-one dollars a month with twenty-six dollars added for each additional child and the total divided among them. A child is not entitled if the income, not counting his or her own earnings, exceeds $12,244.

509. What is the Old Law Pension?

Eligible veterans, their surviving spouses and children of certain deceased veterans who died before July 1, 1960, may be entitled to an Old Law pension or death benefit. Where the veteran's surviving spouse or children are claiming Old Law death benefits, it must be shown that the veteran died of causes not due to service. The veteran must have served during World War I, World War II or the Korean conflict.

These pensions are not payable to a veteran or surviving spouse without children, or to an entitled child, if the claimant receives other income over $13,112 annually, or to a veteran or surviving spouse with child if his or her other income is in excess of $18,899.

Government Life Insurance

Servicemembers' Group Life Insurance

510. Who is eligible to be insured automatically under Servicemembers' Group Life Insurance (SGLI)?

Any member of the uniformed services (Army, Navy, Air Force, Marine Corps, Coast Guard, Commissioned Corps of the United States Public Health Service, and the National Oceanic and Atmospheric Administration) on active duty, active duty for training, or inactive duty training in a commissioned, warrant, or enlisted rank or grade, or as a cadet or midshipman of one of the service academies. Also, any member of the Ready Reserve in a unit or position that may require active duty or active duty for training, and each year performs at least twelve periods of inactive-duty training that is creditable for retirement purposes.

511. What is the SGLI Online Enrollment System?

SOES is the Servicemembers' Group Life Insurance (SGLI) On-Line Enrollment System. It replaces the paper-based SGLI/Family SGLI (FSGLI) enrollment, maintains elections and beneficiary information, and provides 24/7 self-service access to SGLI information. SGLI provides insurance coverage to eligible members of the active and reserve components. SOES centralizes

SGLI/FSGLI data into one authoritative system capable of providing consistent SGLI/FSGLI information to members and their leadership.

Beginning October 1, 2017, Army members can manage their Servicemembers' Group Life Insurance (SGLI) coverage using the SGLI Online Enrollment System (SOES). Army members join the Navy and Air Force in using the new system. Navy began using SOES on April 5, 2017 and Air Force on August 2, 2017. Air Force, Navy, and Army members should look for information from their service about when they should access SOES to confirm and certify their SGLI elections.

SOES access for other branches of service is planned for release on the following schedule:

1. Marine Corps – December 2017

2. Coast Guard, National Oceanic and Atmospheric Administration – Implementation began October 1, 2018

512. What can Service members do in SOES?

Servicemembers may:

- Increase, reduce or cancel SGLI and FSGLI coverage

- Add a beneficiary or edit SGLI beneficiary information

- View, save, print or email a SGLI Coverage Certificate

If they don't have access to a computer, Members can complete paper elections using the SGLV 8286 and provide it to their Personnel Office to ensure their wishes are known. When computer access is obtained, go into SOES and make the appropriate elections/updates. They will only be able to submit changes via paper if a computer is not readily available, or if the member is only eligible for part-time coverage, such as Guard or reserve members who are not assigned to a unit, or not scheduled to drill at least twelve times per year.

It should be noted that beneficiaries will need to contact the Casualty Office to make a claim.

513. Can reservists and National Guard members with part-time SGLI also access their coverage online?

No, online access is only available to those with full-time SGLI coverage. This includes:

- Active duty members

- Reserve and Guard members assigned to a unit and scheduled to drill twelve times or more per year

SGLI members with part-time coverage will continue to use the paper SGLV 8286 to make coverage and beneficiary changes.

514. Can service members automatically enroll in Veteran's Group Life Insurance through SOES?

No, SOES is only for SGLI coverage for eligible active-duty and reserve components. Service-members may apply for VGLI using the SGLV 8714 or online at www.benefits.va.gov/insurance/vgli.asp upon separation. VGLI is lifetime renewable group term insurance for Servicemembers who had SGLI at separation or for up to two years following separation due to total disability. Generally, Servicemembers must apply for VGLI within one year and 120 days of separation. Applications received within 240 days of separation do not require a health questionnaire.

NOTE: Servicemembers who are totally disabled at separation may qualify for the SGLI Disability Extension, free coverage for up to two years from separation, before conversion to VGLI. Servicemembers cannot use SOES to apply for this coverage. Instead, Servicemembers who believe they may be eligible should use the SGLV 8715.

515. What is the amount and nature of the coverage?

The maximum amount of SGLI is $400,000. Members on active duty in the Uniformed Services of the Army, Navy, Air Force, Marine Corps, Coast Guard, Commissioned Corps of the United States Public Health Service, and the National Oceanic and Atmospheric Administration are automatically insured for $400,000.

Automatic insurance coverage is $400,000, unless the member elects in writing:

(1)   not to be insured; or

(2)   to be insured for less than $400,000.

Members may elect coverage in increments of $50,000, between $50,000 and $400,000. Any person who elects not to be insured or to be insured in an amount less than $400,000 may thereafter be insured for $400,000 upon written application, proof of good health, and compliance with such other terms and conditions as may be prescribed by the Administrator.

The coverage under SGLI is group-term life insurance evidenced by a certificate issued to the insured and is entirely separate from and in addition to any other government life insurance the insured may have or later acquire. The insurance is underwritten by a pool of commercial insurers, with one acting as the primary insurer and the others participating as reinsurers.

The program is administered by the Office of Servicemembers' Group Life Insurance, 290 West Mt. Pleasant Ave., Livingston, New Jersey, 07039, and is supervised by the Department of Veterans Affairs. Contact information is listed below:

Toll-free telephone: 1-800-419-1473

Toll-free fax numbers:
Death and accelerated benefits claims only: 1-877-832-4943
All other fax inquiries: 1-800-236-6142

E-mail:

Death and accelerated benefits claims only: osgli.claims@prudential.com

All other inquiries: osgli.osgli@prudential.com

General Correspondence:

Office of Servicemembers' Group Life Insurance

PO Box 41618

Philadelphia, PA 19176-9913

New VGLI Applications and VGLI Reinstatements:

OSGLI

PO Box 41618

Philadelphia, PA 19176-9913

516. When is coverage terminated and can the policy be converted?

A servicemember may convert SGLI coverage to Veterans' Group Life Insurance (VGLI) within one year and 120 days from discharge. A servicemember has 120 days following separation to apply for VGLI. The member will be sent a computer printout application, usually within forty-five to sixty days following release from duty. The completed application and the first premium must be sent within 120 days after separation from service. If an application for VGLI is filed after this 120-day period, proof of insurability must be provided, and the application must be submitted within one year after the SGLI terminates. A servicemember is not eligible to apply for VGLI more than one year and 120 days after separation from service.

SGLI may be converted to an individual policy of life insurance with a commercial company that participates in SGLI within 120 days following release from active duty. The policies are issued at a standard premium rate regardless of health. A policy cannot be issued for an amount greater than the prior SGLI coverage.

517. Who pays the cost of SGLI?

The government pays, from a revolving fund in the U.S. Treasury, the administrative expenses of the SGLI program and costs traceable to the extra hazard of duty in the uniformed services. The balance is paid by the insured members. As of 2018, a serviceman pays, by deduction, 7¢ a month per $1,000, or $28 a month for $400,000 of insurance. A Ready Reservist (one who is assigned to a unit or position that requires at least twelve periods of inactive-duty training that is creditable for retirement purposes) pays the same rates as those servicemen on active duty. Reservists with part-time coverage pay a premium at an annual rate of $28 a year for $400,000 of coverage. There is an additional $1.00 per month charge for TSGLI (Traumatic Injury Protection Insurance), which increases the cost of coverage for $400,000 to $29.00 per month.[1]

---

1. Servicemembers and Veterans Group Life Insurance Handbook https://www.benefits.va.gov/INSURANCE/docs/SGLI_VGLI_handbookv1_8.pdf (April 2017) Last accessed October 25, 2018.

518. How does a person designate a beneficiary?

Death proceeds are paid to the beneficiary or beneficiaries designated by the insured in writing or in SOES. If no named beneficiary survives, payment is made in the following order of preference:

(1)   Surviving spouse

(2)   Child or children of the insured and descendants of deceased children by representation

(3)   Insured parents or their survivors

(4)   Executor or administrator of insured's estate

(5)   Insured's other next of kin entitled under laws of the insured's domicile at time of his or her death

An adopted child may qualify for SGLI based on the death of both of his or her natural and adopted parents. But no person who consents to the adoption of a child may be recognized as a parent for SGLI purposes. A child, in other words, cannot claim from more than one father or one mother in an adoption case. An illegitimate child is considered the child of his or her natural mother.

If a person otherwise entitled to payment does not make claim within one year after the insured's death, or if payment to that person is prohibited by federal law, payment may be made in the order of precedence as if the person had not survived the insured, and any such payment is a bar to recovery by any other person.

If a person entitled to benefits does not file a claim for benefits within two years after the insured's death and there is no notice that a claim will be made, the Department of Veterans Affairs may pay the benefit to someone it deems is appropriate. Such payment is a bar to recovery by any other person.

The insured may elect settlement of the proceeds either in a lump sum or in thirty-six equal monthly installments. If no election is made by the insured, the payment will be made in a lump sum.

519. Does payment TSGLI reduce the amount of SGLI payable at the time of the service member's death?

No. Payment of TSGLI has no impact on the amount of SGLI payable. As an example, if a service member is insured with $400,000 of SGLI coverage and had received a TSGLI payment of $50,000 due to a traumatic injury that member remains insured for the full $400,000 of SGLI coverage, which will be paid upon the service member's death.

520. Will SGLI pay if the service member is killed wearing privately purchased body armor or helmets?

Yes. SGLI claims are paid regardless of body armor or helmet type. Wearing body armor or a helmet is not a requirement for a SGLI claim to be paid.

521. Will SGLI pay if the service member is in a motor vehicle accident, an airline accident or a motorcycle accident and is not wearing seat belts or helmets?

SGLI or VGLI claims are paid regardless of whether the service member was or was not wearing a seatbelt. In the case of motorcycle crashes, SGLI or VGLI proceeds will be paid to the beneficiary or beneficiaries, regardless of whether a helmet was worn.

522. Does SGLI cover Reservists and National Guard members?

Yes, in addition to coverage while at drill, Reservists and National Guard members that have been assigned to a unit in which they are scheduled to perform at least twelve periods of inactive duty that is creditable for retirement purposes, full-time SGLI coverage is in effect 365 days of the year. They are also covered for 120 days following separation or release from duty.

523. Does SGLI cover deaths as of the result of a terrorist attack?

Yes, SGLI or VGLI proceeds will be paid if a service member dies in a terrorist attack. There are no exclusions that apply to SGLI or VGLI coverage including the location of the death (which includes "black-zoned" or "no-go" areas.

Veterans' Group Life Insurance

524. Who is eligible for Veterans' Group Life Insurance (VGLI)?

Servicemembers leaving active duty can convert their SGLI to Veterans' Group Life Insurance (VGLI) without medical examination. The day after SGLI coverage ceases for any member on active duty for training, or inactive duty training, the policy is automatically converted to VGLI, subject to timely payment of the initial premium. Reservists performing active duty or inactive duty for training under a call or orders specifying a period of less than thirty-one days, who are injured or disabled, and become uninsurable at standard rates, are eligible for VGLI. Also, members of the Individual Ready Reserve and Inactive National Guard are eligible for SGLI. An application for coverage must be filed by a member of these groups.

All Retired Reserve SGLI policyholders will have their policies automatically exchanged for policies under the VGLI program. Retired reservists may retain lifetime coverage under VGLI, instead of being cut off from coverage at age sixty-one or when receiving retired pay (as is the case with Retired Reserve SGLI).

In addition, VGLI is extended generally to reservists and National Guard members who decide to separate prior to reaching twenty-year retirement.

Veterans, who were granted a service-connected disability but are otherwise in good health, may apply to the Department of Veterans Affairs for up to $10,000 life insurance coverage at standard insurance rates, within two years from the date the Department of Veterans Affairs notifies the veteran that the disability has been rated as service-connected. This applies even if the disability rating is zero percent.

525. What is the amount of Veterans' Group Life Insurance and the enrollment and eligibility periods?

The maximum amount of VGLI is $400,000. No one may carry a combined amount of SGLI and VGLI more than $400,000 at any one time. Also, the amount is limited to an amount equal to or less than the amount of the veteran's terminating SGLI. VGLI is available only in increments of $10,000.

VGLI is *renewable* five-year term insurance. It has no cash, loan, paid-up, or extended values, and lapses for nonpayment of premiums (except in the case of a mental incompetent who dies within one year after becoming insured).

ENROLLMENT:

An individual has one year and 120 days from date of separation to apply for VGLI. If the applicant applies for coverage within 240 days of date of separation, they will not need to answer health questions.

ELIGIBILITY:

An individual is eligible to apply for VGLI, if they had SGLI, and are within one year and 120 days of the following events:

- Release from active duty or active duty for training under a call or order to duty that does not specify a period of less than thirty-one days

- Separation, retirement, or release from assignment from the Ready Reserves/ National Guard

- Assignment to the Individual Ready Reserves (IRR) of a branch of service or to the Inactive National Guard (ING). This includes members of the United States Public Health Service Inactive Reserve Corps (IRC)

- Placement on the Temporary Disability Retirement List (TDRL)

They are also eligible to apply for VGLI, if they had part-time SGLI and while performing duty, suffered an injury or disability that rendered them uninsurable at standard premium rates. This includes travel directly to and from duty.

VGLI has a reinstatement period of five years after a policy has lapsed.

526. How is the beneficiary designated under Veterans' Group Life Insurance?

VGLI proceeds are paid to the designated beneficiary or beneficiaries when a valid claim is established. If no beneficiary survives, or the insured fails to designate a beneficiary, payment is made in the following order of preference:

(1)   Surviving spouse

(2)   Child or children of the insured and descendants of deceased children by representation

(3)   Insured's parents or survivor of them

(4)   Executor or administrator of insured's estate

(5)   Insured's other next of kin entitled under laws of the insured's domicile at the time of death

There are no restrictions on beneficiary designations, and the insured may change the designation without the knowledge or consent of the beneficiary. This right cannot be waived or restricted. The Department of Veterans Affairs does not recognize state court divorce decrees that require veterans to keep their ex-spouses as beneficiaries on their Department of Veterans Affairs life insurance policies. The forms required for a change of beneficiary may be obtained from the Office of Servicemembers' Group Life Insurance, any Department of Veterans Affairs office, or by calling the Department of Veterans Affairs Insurance Center at 1-800-419-1473.

Any designation of beneficiary or beneficiaries for SGLI filed with a uniformed service is considered a designation for VGLI, but only for sixty days after the VGLI becomes effective. Where the insured is incompetent at the end of the sixty-day period, the designation made for SGLI may continue in force until the disability is removed, but not for more than five years after the effective date of the insured's VGLI.

The designation of beneficiary or beneficiaries, except for a designation by an incompetent, must be in writing signed by the insured and received by the administrative office to be effective.

No claim for VGLI will be denied because of a failure to file a claim within four years of the insured's death.

If the insured, in the application for VGLI, does not limit the beneficiary's payments, the beneficiary can elect to receive the insurance in a single payment or in thirty-six equal monthly installments.

Payment of benefits under VGLI, made to or on account of a beneficiary, are exempt from taxation and the claims of creditors. The benefits are not liable to attachment, levy, or seizure by or under any legal or equitable process.

527. What are the premium rates for Veterans' Group Life Insurance?

Premium rates depend on age. Premium payment options include the use of automatic payments by deductions from Department of Veterans Affairs benefits or retirement checks, and an option to take a one-month discount for annual payments. These rates were established on July 1, 2014 and remain in effect at the time of printing of this 2019 edition.[1]

---

1. VLGI Premium Rates https://www.benefits.va.gov/insurance/vgli_rates_new.asp.

VETERANS' GROUP LIFE INSURANCE

Monthly Premium Rates

Up to age 54

Amount of Insurance	Age 29 or less	Age 30-34	Age 35-39	Age 40-44	Age 45-49	Age 50-54
$400,000	$32.00	$40.00	$52.00	$68.00	$88.00	$144.00
390,000	$31.20	$39.00	$50.70	$66.30	$85.80	$140.40
380,000	$30.40	$38.00	$49.40	$64.60	$83.60	$136.80
370,000	$29.60	$37.00	$48.10	$62.90	$81.40	$133.20
360,000	$28.80	$36.00	$46.80	$61.20	$79.20	$129.60
350,000	$28.00	$35.00	$45.50	$59.50	$77.00	$126.00
340,000	$27.20	$34.00	$44.20	$57.80	$74.80	$122.40
330,000	$26.40	$33.00	$42.90	$56.10	$72.60	$118.80
320,000	$25.60	$32.00	$41.60	$54.40	$70.40	$115.20
310,000	$24.80	$31.00	$40.30	$52.70	$68.20	$111.60
300,000	$24.00	$30.00	$39.00	$51.00	$66.00	$108.00
290,000	$23.20	$29.00	$37.70	$49.30	$63.80	$104.40
280,000	$22.40	$28.00	$36.40	$47.60	$61.60	$100.80
270,000	$21.60	$27.00	$35.10	$45.90	$59.40	$97.20
260,000	$20.80	$26.00	$33.80	$44.20	$57.20	$93.60
250,000	$20.00	$25.00	$32.50	$42.50	$55.00	$90.00
240,000	$19.20	$24.00	$31.20	$40.80	$52.80	$86.40
230,000	$18.40	$23.00	$29.90	$39.10	$50.60	$82.80
220,000	$17.60	$22.00	$28.60	$37.40	$48.40	$79.20
210,000	$16.80	$21.00	$27.30	$35.70	$46.20	$75.60
200,000	$16.00	$20.00	$26.00	$34.00	$44.00	$72.00
190,000	$15.20	$19.00	$24.70	$32.30	$41.80	$68.40
180,000	$14.40	$18.00	$23.40	$30.60	$39.60	$64.80
170,000	$13.60	$17.00	$22.10	$28.90	$37.40	$61.20
160,000	$12.80	$16.00	$20.80	$27.20	$35.20	$57.60
150,000	$12.00	$15.00	$19.50	$25.50	$33.00	$54.00
140,000	$11.20	$14.00	$18.20	$23.80	$30.80	$50.40
130,000	$10.40	$13.00	$16.90	$22.10	$28.60	$46.80
120,000	$9.60	$12.00	$15.60	$20.40	$26.40	$43.20
110,000	$8.80	$11.00	$14.30	$18.70	$24.20	$39.60
100,000	$8.00	$10.00	$13.00	$17.00	$22.00	$36.00
90,000	$7.20	$9.00	$11.70	$15.30	$19.80	$32.40

VETERANS' GROUP LIFE INSURANCE

Monthly Premium Rates
Up to age 54

Amount of Insurance	Age 29 or less	Age 30-34	Age 35-39	Age 40-44	Age 45-49	Age 50-54
80,000	$6.40	$8.00	$10.40	$13.60	$17.60	$28.80
70,000	$5.60	$7.00	$9.10	$11.90	$15.40	$25.20
60,000	$4.80	$6.00	$7.80	$10.20	$13.20	$21.60
50,000	$4.00	$5.00	$6.50	$8.50	$11.00	$18.00
40,000	$3.20	$4.00	$5.20	$6.80	$8.80	$14.40
30,000	$2.40	$3.00	$3.90	$5.10	$6.60	$10.80
20,000	$1.60	$2.00	$2.60	$3.40	$4.40	$7.20
10,000	$0.80	$1.00	$1.30	$1.70	$2.20	$3.60

VETERANS' GROUP LIFE INSURANCE

Monthly Premium Rates
Ages 55 and up

Amount of Insurance	Age 55-59	Age 60-64	Age 65-69	Age 70-74	Age 75 and up
$400,000	$268.00	$432.00	$600.00	$920.00	$1,840.00
390,000	$261.30	$421.20	$585.00	$897.00	$1,794.00
380,000	$254.60	$410.40	$570.00	$874.00	$1,748.00
370,000	$247.90	$399.60	$555.00	$851.00	$1,702.00
360,000	$241.20	$388.80	$540.00	$828.00	$1,656.00
350,000	$234.50	$378.00	$525.00	$805.00	$1,610.00
340,000	$227.80	$367.20	$510.00	$782.00	$1,564.00
330,000	$221.10	$356.40	$495.00	$759.00	$1,518.00
320,000	$214.40	$345.60	$480.00	$736.00	$1,472.00
310,000	$207.70	$334.80	$465.00	$713.00	$1,426.00
300,000	$201.00	$324.00	$450.00	$690.00	$1,380.00
290,000	$194.30	$313.20	$435.00	$667.00	$1,334.00
280,000	$187.60	$302.40	$420.00	$644.00	$1,288.00
270,000	$180.90	$291.60	$405.00	$621.00	$1,242.00
260,000	$174.20	$280.80	$390.00	$598.00	$1,196.00
250,000	$167.50	$270.00	$375.00	$575.00	$1,150.00
240,000	$160.80	$259.20	$360.00	$552.00	$1,104.00
230,000	$154.10	$248.40	$345.00	$529.00	$1,058.00

VETERANS' GROUP LIFE INSURANCE

Monthly Premium Rates
Ages 55 and up

Amount of Insurance	Age 55-59	Age 60-64	Age 65-69	Age 70-74	Age 75 and up
220,000	$147.40	$237.60	$330.00	$506.00	$1,012.00
210,000	$140.70	$226.80	$315.00	$483.00	$966.00
200,000	$134.00	$216.00	$300.00	$460.00	$920.00
190,000	$127.30	$205.20	$285.00	$437.00	$874.00
180,000	$120.60	$194.40	$270.00	$414.00	$828.00
170,000	$113.90	$183.60	$255.00	$391.00	$782.00
160,000	$107.20	$172.80	$240.00	$368.00	$736.00
150,000	$100.50	$162.00	$225.00	$345.00	$690.00
140,000	$93.80	$151.20	$210.00	$322.00	$644.00
130,000	$87.10	$140.40	$195.00	$299.00	$598.00
120,000	$80.40	$129.60	$180.00	$276.00	$552.00
110,000	$73.70	$118.80	$165.00	$253.00	$506.00
100,000	$67.00	$108.00	$150.00	$230.00	$460.00
90,000	$60.30	$97.20	$135.00	$207.00	$414.00
80,000	$53.60	$86.40	$120.00	$184.00	$368.00
70,000	$46.90	$75.60	$105.00	$161.00	$322.00
60,000	$40.20	$64.80	$90.00	$138.00	$276.00
50,000	$33.50	$54.00	$75.00	$115.00	$230.00
40,000	$26.80	$43.20	$60.00	$92.00	$184.00
30,000	$20.10	$32.40	$45.00	$69.00	$138.00
20,000	$13.40	$21.60	$30.00	$46.00	$92.00
10,000	$6.70	$10.80	$15.00	$23.00	$46.00

These premium rates (listed on the previous three pages) are subject to change, depending on emerging experience.

528. How is Veterans' Group Life Insurance converted to an individual policy?

VGLI may be converted to an individual policy at any time, upon written application for conversion to the participating company selected and payment of the required premiums. The individual policy will be issued without medical examination on a plan currently written by the company.

The process is as follows - the policyholder must:

- Select a company from the listing of participating companies,[1]

- Apply to a local sales office of the company selected,

- Obtain a letter from OSGLI verifying coverage (VGLI Conversion Notice),

- Give a copy of that notice to the agent who takes the application.

Policyholders may convert their coverage to a commercial policy at standard premium rates, without having to provide proof of good health. The conversion policy must be a permanent policy, such as a whole life policy.

Other types of policies, such as Term, Variable Life, or Universal Life Insurance are not allowed as conversion policies. In addition, supplementary policy benefits such as Accidental Death and Dismemberment or Waiver of Premium for Disability are not considered part of the conversion policy.

On request, the administrative office will furnish a list of life insurance companies participating in the program and companies (not participating in the program) that meet qualifying criteria, terms, and conditions established by the administrator, and that agree to sell insurance to former members in accordance with the rules described.

529. Will SGLI pay benefits if an insured dies while wearing privately-owned body armor or helmet?

SGLI claims are paid regardless of body armor or helmet type. Wearing body armor or a helmet is not a requirement for a SGLI claim to be paid.

530. Will SGLI or VGLI pay deny benefits if an insured is not complying with seatbelt or helmet laws and dies in a traffic accident?

SGLI or VGLI claims are paid regardless of whether the member was or was not wearing a seatbelt or in the case of a motorcycle accident, whether or not a helmet was being worn.

531. Are there limitations of effectiveness of coverage for National Guard or Reservists?

In the case of Reservists or a National Guard member assigned to a unit and scheduled to perform at least twelve periods of inactive duty that is creditable for retirement purposes, full-time SGLI coverage is in effect 365 days of the year. Coverage also extends for 120 days following separation or release from duty.

---

1. List of participating companies https://www.benefits.va.gov/INSURANCE/resources-forms.asp (Last accessed October 12, 2018).

BENEFITS FOR FEDERAL GOVERNMENT EMPLOYEES

Introduction

532. What are the two retirement systems for federal employees?

There are two retirement systems for federal employees: The **Civil Service Retirement System (CSRS)** and the **Federal Employees' Retirement System (FERS)**.

The CSRS, created on August 1, 1920, was the only retirement system for federal employees until the FERS became public law in 1986. The Civil Service Retirement System (CSRS) is a defined benefit, contributory retirement system. Employees share in the expense of the annuities to which they become entitled. CSRS covered employees contribute 7.0, 7.5, or 8.0 percent of pay to CSRS and, while they generally pay no Social Security retirement, survivor, and disability (OASDI) tax, they must pay the Medicare tax (currently 1.45 percent of pay). The employing agency matches the employee's CSRS contributions. CSRS employees may increase their earned annuity by contributing up to 10 percent of the basic pay for their creditable service to a voluntary contribution account. Employees may also pay into the Thrift Savings Plan, a plan which offers tax-deferred contributions.

FERS created a new federal retirement program coordinated with Social Security retirement benefits for federal employees hired after 1983. While federal employees who remain in CSRS are exempt from Social Security taxes, FERS employees are covered under Social Security. FERS also provides a guaranteed basic annuity and a tax-deferred savings plan similar to a Section 401(k) retirement plan.

FERS is a retirement plan that provides three different sources of benefits:

- a Basic Benefit Plan,
- Social Security, and
- the Thrift Savings Plan (TSP).

Two of the three parts of FERS (Social Security and the TSP) are transferrable from federal service to the private sector. The Basic Benefit and Social Security parts of FERS require paying a contribution each pay period. The federal agency withholds the cost of the Basic Benefit and Social Security from pay as payroll deductions as well as contributing the governmental share. Upon retirement, the retiree receives annuity payments each month until death.

The TSP part of FERS is an account that that is automatically established. Each pay period there is a deposit made by the federal agency equal to 1 percent of the basic pay for the pay period into the TSP account. Employees can also make their own contributions to the TSP account which are matched by the agency. Contributions are tax-deferred.

The Thrift Savings Plan is administered by the Federal Retirement Thrift Investment Board.

Federal Employees' Retirement System

533. Who is covered under the Federal Employees' Retirement System?

The Federal Employees' Retirement System (FERS) is a three-tier retirement system for federal workers who began work with the government after 1983. In addition, a number of federal employees hired before 1984 elected to transfer from the Civil Service Retirement System (CSRS) to FERS during a 1987 transfer period.

The following are excluded from FERS coverage:

- A person not covered by Social Security, including a person covered by full CSRS.

- A person who has served without a break in service of more than 365 days since December 31, 1983, in the position of:

    o Vice President of the United States

    o member of Congress (U.S. House of Representatives and the U.S. Senate)

    o a senior executive Service or Senior Foreign Service non-career appointee; or

    o persons appointed by the President or Vice President to positions where the maximum rate of basic pay is at or above the rate for Level V of the Executive Schedule.

- An employee who is rehired after December 31, 1986, who has had a break in service and who, at the time of the last separation from the service, had at least five years of civilian service creditable under CSRS rules, any part of which was covered by CSRS or the Foreign Service Retirement system.

- An employee who has not had a break in service of more than three days ending after December 31, 1986, and who, as of December 31, 1986, had at least five years of creditable civilian service under CSRS rules (even if none of this service was covered by CSRS).

534. What is creditable service under FERS?

Creditable service under FERS usually includes:

- Federal covered service, that is, service in which the individual's pay is subject to FERS retirement deductions, such as service under a career or career conditional appointment,

- Unused Sick Leave under FERS can be used to increase an individual's total creditable service for annuity computation purposes only;

- Federal service performed before 1989, where an employee's pay is not subject to retirement deductions, such as, service under a temporary appointment, as long as a deposit is paid. The following are exceptions to the rule that the service must have been performed before 1989.

- Part-time, Intermittent, Temporary "PIT" service performed abroad after December 31, 1988, and before May 24, 1998, under a temporary part-time or intermittent appointment pursuant to sections 309 and 311 of the Foreign Service Act of 1980.

- Service performed under the Foreign Service Pension System

- Service as a Senate Employee Child Care Center worker

- Service as a volunteer or volunteer leader in the Peace Corps

- Service as a VISTA volunteer

- Service before 12/31/1990 with either the Democratic or Republican Senatorial Campaign or National Congressional Committees

- Service before 12/21/2000 with the Library of Congress Child Development Center

- Service as a Senior Official

- Congressional Employees that do no elect program coverage and are subject to the Social Security Amendments of 1983

- Service performed under a Federal Reserve Bank Plan

- Non-appropriated fund instrumentality (NAF) service under P.L. 107-107 that can be used for title to an annuity under the FERS, but not in the computation

- CSRS refund service that flips to FERS

535. Who is eligible for FERS benefits?

Unreduced retirement benefits are provided at age sixty with twenty or more years of service, at age sixty-two with five or more years of service, and at "minimum retirement age" with thirty years of service. The Minimum Retirement Age (MRA) is currently fifty-seven. FERS uses "the Rule of 80", meaning to be eligible for retirement, the employee must reach eighty years when combining chronological years and years of service.

Eligibility is determined by age and number of years of creditable service. In some cases, the individual must reach Minimum Retirement Age (MRA).

Eligibility information:

If born	Minimum Retirement Age is
Before 1948	55 years
In 1948	55 years and 2 months
In 1949	55 years and 4 months
In 1950	55 years and 6 months
In 1951	55 years and 8 months
In 1952	55 and 10 months
In 1953-1964	56 years
In 1965	56 years and 2 months
In 1966	56 years and 4 months
In 1967	56 years and 6 months
In 1968	56 years and 8 months
In 1969	56 years and 10 months
In 1970 and after	57 years

Beginning in the year 2021, the minimum retirement age again increases by two-month increments until the year 2027. The minimum retirement age for employees with thirty or more years of service is fifty-seven in the year 2027 and after. The minimum retirement age for reduced benefits is also being gradually increased from fifty-five to fifty-seven. An employee must have at least ten years of service to be eligible for reduced retirement benefits. For an employee retiring with less than thirty years of service, a reduction of 5 percent per year for each year under age sixty-two is imposed. Thus, benefits for an employee retiring at age fifty-five are reduced 35 percent.

An employee can leave government employment prior to the date that he is eligible for a retirement benefit and still be eligible for a Basic Annuity at a later date. If the employee has five years of creditable service and does not withdraw contributions when he terminates government service, he may receive a deferred, unreduced annuity when he attains age sixty-two with at least five years of civil service employment; age sixty with at least twenty years of service; or at minimum retirement age (currently age fifty-five) with at least thirty years of service.

An employee is entitled to a Basic Annuity at age fifty with twenty years of service, or at any age after completing twenty-five years of service, if:

(1)   his retirement is involuntary (except by removal by cause for misconduct or delinquency) and he did not decline a reasonable offer for a position which is not lower than two grades below his present position; or

(2)   his retirement is voluntary because his agency is undergoing a major reduction in employees, reorganization, or a transfer of function in which a number of employees are separated or downgraded.

536. What is Early Retirement under FERS?

The early retirement benefit is available in certain involuntary separation cases and in cases of voluntary separations during a major reorganization or reduction in force. To be eligible, an individual must either have twenty years of service and be age fifty or older; or have twenty-five years of service at any age.

The term "involuntary separation" means any separation against the will and without the consent of the employee, other than "for cause" for misconduct or delinquency. The most common cause of an involuntary separation is a reduction in force. Another frequent cause for an involuntary separation is when the location of an office or unit is moved to an area outside the commuting area of the old worksite. Employees who decline reasonable offers of other positions are not eligible for discontinued service annuities. An exception exists if a position was accepted under a "general mobility" agreement where the individual agreed to be subject to geographic reassignment. In this instance, the individual would not be eligible for discontinued service annuity rights if the position was moved outside the commuting area.

A separation would not qualify for discontinued service if an agency

- makes an individual a reasonable offer and they choose to decline the offer and resign, they will not qualify for discontinued service retirement, or

- separates the individual by adverse action procedures for not complying with a directed reassignment to a position that is a "reasonable offer".

A reasonable offer is defined as:

- a written offer of another position in the same agency and commuting area for which the individual is qualified, and

- which is no more than two grades or pay levels below the current grade or pay level.

The commuting area is defined as the geographic area that usually constitutes one area for employment purposes. It includes any population center (or two or more neighboring ones) and the surrounding localities in which people live and reasonably can be expected to travel back and forth daily in their usual employment.

537. What is Deferred Retirement under FERS?

This refers to delayed payment of benefits until the age and service requirements are met for the immediate retirement benefit. Eligibility is based on at least five years of creditable civilian services with benefits being available as follows:

- Aged sixty-two with five years of service

- Minimum Retirement Age and thirty years of service

- Minimum Retirement Age with ten years of service

- Note that retiring at MRA with at least ten years of service but less than thirty years of service will cause the benefit to be reduced by 5 percent a year for each year until the beneficiary is age sixty-two, unless the individual has twenty years of service and the benefit starts at age sixty or later.

538. Can military retirement pay be credited under FERS?

Depends. A person cannot receive credit for any military service in a FERS retirement computation, if receiving military retirement pay, unless they were awarded the retirement pay:

- due to a service-connected disability either incurred in combat with an enemy of the United States or caused by an instrumentality of war and incurred in the line of duty during a period of war, or

- under the provisions of Chapter 1223, Title 10, U.S.C. (pertaining to retirement from a reserve component of the Armed Forces).

However, a person can elect to waive the retirement pay and have the military service added to their civilian service in computing the FERS annuity. In addition to waiving the military retirement pay, they MUST pay a deposit for their post 1956 military deposit prior to separating from the agency in order for it to be creditable in the FERS retirement.

Basic Annuity
539. What is the Basic Annuity?

The Basic Annuity is the **second tier** of benefits under FERS.

The FERS annuity is based on a percentage multiplied by

- length of Federal service eligible for FERS retirement
  - this is "creditable Federal service", and
  - An employee must have five years minimum creditable service
- the "High-3" period rate of pay
  - the average annual rate of basic pay of the employee's highest-paid consecutive three years of service.
  - the "high-3" period does not have to be the last three years of service – but generally is those years

The FERS annuity begins after one full calendar month after the employee's retirement. Under this system it is best to retire on the last day of the month.

Social Security is the first tier of benefits.

Social Security includes retirement, disability, and survivor benefits, and health insurance benefits under Medicare. The Basic Annuity provides retirement, disability, and survivor benefits in addition to those provided by Social Security. The Basic Annuity guarantees a specific monthly retirement payment, based on the employee's age, length of creditable service, and "high-3" years' average salary.

540. How much must an employee contribute to the Basic Annuity?

From the time of the creation of FERS and 2012, ALL employees contributed 0.8 percent of his or her basic pay to the Basic Annuity. New Federal workers starting in 2013 contributed 3.1 percent while those hired before 2013 continue to contribute 0.8 percent. The Bipartisan Budget Act of 2013 increased the contribution for those hired after December 31, 2013 to 4.4 percent. There are currently proposals before Congress to increase the percentage where FERS employee deduction rates will increase by 1 percent per year until they reach 7.25 percent of basic pay.

Certain FERS members pay an additional 0.5 percent to the Basic Annuity. These members include firefighters, law enforcement personnel, air traffic controllers, members of Congress, and Congressional employees. Basic pay does not include bonuses, overtime pay, military pay, holiday pay, cash awards, or special allowances given in addition to basic pay. The federal government makes a contribution to the Basic Annuity plan pursuant to a formula.

541. What annuities are available to a retiring employee?

The following annuities are available to a retiring federal employee:

- An annuity, with no survivor benefit;

- A lump-sum credit of the employee's contributions (excluding interest), with a reduced annuity

- An annuity to the employee for life, with a survivor annuity payable for the life of the surviving spouse

- A lump-sum credit of the employee's contributions (excluding interest), with a reduced annuity that is further reduced to provide a survivor benefit

- A reduced annuity with a survivor benefit to a person with an insurable interest, provided the employee is in good health

Note, however, that an employee cannot elect against providing survivor benefits to his spouse, unless his spouse consents to the election in writing.

542. What is the amount of the Basic Annuity?

The amount of the Basic Annuity depends on the employee's years of service and highest three-year (high-3) average salary. It also depends on whether an annuity supplement is added into the Basic Annuity formula.

For employees *under age sixty-two (or age sixty-two or older with less than twenty years of FERS service)*, the formula, not including the supplement where applicable, is:

- 1.0 percent × high-3 average salary × length of service.

For employees *age sixty-two or older with at least twenty years of FERS service*, the formula is:

- 1.1 percent × high-3 average salary × length of service.

(No annuity supplement is payable if the employee is age sixty-two or older.)

For certain employees, including law enforcement officers, firefighters, air traffic control-lers, and employees of Congress, the formula is:

(1)   1.7 percent × high-3 average salary × years of service up to twenty years; plus

(2)   1.0 percent × high-3 average salary × years of service over twenty years; plus

(3)   the annuity supplement, where applicable.

All periods of creditable service are totaled to determine length of service. Years and months of creditable service (extra days are dropped) are then used in the annuity computa-tion formula.

High-3 average salary is the highest pay obtainable by averaging an employee's rates of basic pay in effect over any three consecutive years of service. The three years need not be continuous, but they must consist of consecutive periods of service. In other words, two or more separate periods of employment that follow each other can be joined to make up the three consecutive years.

> *Example*. Steve James retires at age 65 after 30 years of civil service employment. His high-3 aver-age salary is $61,000 ($60,000 + $61,000 + $62,000 ÷ 3 = $61,000). His FERS benefit is computed as follows:
>
> (1)   1.1 percent × $61,000 = $671
>
> (2) $671 × 30 years of service = $20,130 Basic Annuity.

543. How is the Basic Annuity adjusted for cost-of-living increases?

The Basic Annuity for employees age sixty-two or older is adjusted for cost-of-living increases pursuant to the following schedule:

(1)   Where the change in the Consumer Price Index for All Urban Wage Earners and Clerical Workers (CPI) for the year is less than 2.0 percent, the annuity is increased by the full amount of the CPI increase.

(2)   Where the change in the CPI for the year is at least 2.0 percent, but is not more than 3.0 percent, the annuity is increased by 2.0 percent.

(3)   Where the change in the CPI for the year is more than 3.0 percent, the annuity is increased by the CPI less 1 percent. For example, if the CPI increases 4.5 percent, the Basic Annuity will increase 3.5 percent.

The cost-of-living increase for 2019 is 2.0 percent for FERS and 2.8 percent for CSRS. This is the largest percentage increase in seven years. The cost-of-living adjustment for 2017 was 0.3 percent. There was NO cost-of-living (COLA) increase for 2016.

The following chart provides a historical perspective of cost-of-living increases

RETIREE COLAs

Year	CSRS Rate	FERS Rate
2019	2.8	2.0
2018	2.0	2.0
2017	0.3	0.3
2016	0	0
2015	1.7	1.7
2014	1.5	1.5
2013	1.7	1.7
2012	3.6	2.6
2011	0	0
2010	0	0
2009	5.8	4.8
2008	2.3	2.0
2007	3.3	2.3
2006	4.1	3.1
2005	2.7	2.0
2004	2.1	2.0
2003	1.4	1.4
2002	2.6	2.0
2001	3.5	2.5
2000	2.4	2.0
1999	1.3	1.3

544. What is the Annuity Supplement?

An Annuity Supplement is added to the Basic Annuity as a substitute for Social Security, when the employee is receiving the Basic Annuity and is under age sixty-two. It is equal to the estimated amount of Social Security benefits that the employee would be eligible to receive at age sixty-two based on civil service employment earnings. The supplement ends when the employee first becomes eligible for a Social Security retirement benefit (age sixty-two).

The supplement is payable to:

(1)   employees who retire after the minimum retirement age (currently between ages fifty-six and fifty-seven) with thirty years of service;

(2)   employees who retire at age sixty with twenty years of service; and

(3)   employees who retire involuntarily and have reached minimum retirement age (currently age fifty-six).

The supplement is not subject to cost-of-living increases and is reduced for excess earnings after retirement in much the same way that Social Security benefits are reduced for excess earnings. In 2019, the supplement is reduced by one dollar for every two dollars that the beneficiary earns over $17,640.

Survivor Benefits

545. What survivor benefits are payable under FERS?

Survivor benefits are paid upon the death of an employee or retired civil service employee. Benefits are paid on a monthly basis or in a lump sum to eligible survivors. The spouse, former spouse, and dependent children of a deceased employee may be entitled to a survivor annuity.

A spouse may be entitled to a "post-retirement survivor benefit." The annuity of a married employee who retires is generally reduced by 10 percent to provide a survivor annuity for the spouse, unless the employee and his or her spouse both waive the survivor annuity. A surviving spouse is entitled to 50 percent of the employee's unreduced annuity increased by cost-of-living benefit adjustments. There is also a 5 percent reduction in the annuity of a married employee who retires and selects a 25 percent survivor annuity.

There is a permanent actuarial reduction in the retiree's annuity in the case of a retiree who marries after retirement and elects a survivor benefit. The reduction may not be more than 25 percent of the retiree's annuity. The reduction is permanent and unaffected by any future termination of the marriage.

The surviving spouse must have been married to the employee for at least nine months or must be the parent of a child of the marriage at the time of death, or the death of the retired employee must have been accidental.

If the survivor is under age sixty and Social Security survivor benefits are *not* payable, benefits are the lesser of:

(1)   current CSRS survivor benefits; or

(2)   50 percent (25 percent if elected) of accrued annuity plus a Social Security "equivalent." When Social Security survivor benefits are payable, FERS pays 50 percent (25 percent if elected) of the deceased retiree's annuity.

If the employee was unmarried at the time of retirement and then married after retirement, he or she may elect a reduced annuity with a survivor benefit for his or her spouse. Such an election must take place within two years after the marriage.

If the spouse dies before the retired employee, and the retired employee remarries, the new spouse is eligible to receive the same survivor benefits as the former spouse. The retired employee must elect to take a reduced annuity with a survivor benefit for his or her new spouse.

A retired employee and spouse who have elected against a survivor benefit can change their election within eighteen months. The retired employee must pay the full cost of providing the survivor annuity if an election is made during this second election period.

There is also a survivor benefit for the spouse of an employee who dies prior to retirement. The surviving spouse is entitled to the basic employee death benefit, which is a guaranteed amount of around $33,000 for 2018, plus 50 percent of the employee's final salary or, if higher, his or her "high-3" average. In addition, if the deceased employee completed ten or more years of service, the surviving spouse is entitled to an annuity equal to 50 percent of the unreduced annuity the employee would have been entitled to had he or she reached retirement age. Survivor benefits are subject to cost-of-living adjustments. Cost of living increases for 2019 are 2.0 percent.

The $33,000 payment, which is indexed to the Consumer Price Index, can be paid in a lump sum or in monthly installments over a three-year period.

The surviving spouse must have been married to the employee for at least nine months or must be the parent of a child of the marriage, or the death of the employee must have been accidental. The deceased employee must also have at least eighteen months of creditable service while subject to FERS.

546. Is the former spouse of a deceased employee entitled to a survivor benefit?

Yes, the former spouse of a deceased employee may be entitled to a survivor benefit if he or she:

(1)   was married to the deceased employee for at least nine months;

(2)   has not remarried prior to age fifty-five; and

(3)   a court order or court-approved property settlement agreement provides for payment of a survivor annuity to the former spouse.

The survivor annuity is payable to a former spouse when:

(1)   the deceased employee has at least eighteen months of creditable service under FERS; or

(2)   the deceased former employee has title to a deferred annuity and has ten years of service.

A former spouse who does not meet the requirements listed above may still be entitled to an annuity if the retiree, at the time of retirement, elected to provide the former spouse with a survivor annuity.

The amount of the survivor annuity for a former spouse is the same as that for a spouse, except that the Guaranteed Amount of about $33,000 for 2018, (see Q 545) is not payable unless payment is required under a court order or agreement. Cost of living increases for 2019 are 2.0 percent.

547. Is there a survivor benefit for the children of a deceased employee?

If a retiree or an employee has eighteen months of creditable service under FERS before he or she dies, his or her dependent children are entitled to monthly annuities reduced by the amount of any Social Security survivor benefits they receive.

The annuity begins on the day after the death, and ends on the last day of the month before the one in which the child:

(1) dies;

(2) marries;

(3) reaches age eighteen; or

(4) if over eighteen, becomes capable of self-support.

The annuity of a child who is a student ends on the last day of the month before the child:

(1) marries;

(2) dies;

(3) ceases to be a student; or

(4) attains the age of twenty-two. If a student drops out of school or his annuity is terminated, it can be restored if he later returns to school and is still under age twenty-two and unmarried.

Annuity payments restart again if the child's marriage has ended and he or she is still eligible for benefits because of disability or enrollment as a full-time student while under age twenty-two. If a child's marriage ends because of divorce or death, the child's annuity and health benefits coverage is restored, beginning the first day of the month in which dissolution of the marriage occurs.

The amount of the benefit depends on whether the child is eligible to receive Social Security benefits and whether the deceased worker's spouse is still living.

If the retiree or employee is survived by a spouse or the child has a living parent, each eligible child is entitled to receive an annuity in 2018 equal to the lesser of:

(1) $1,537 per month, divided by the number of qualified children; or

(2) $512 per month.

Note that 2019 numbers were not available as this 2019 edition went to press. These figures should be available on the OPM website during March 2019.

If the retiree or employee is *not* survived by a spouse or the child has *no* living parent, each eligible child is entitled to receive an annuity in 2018 equal to the lesser of:

(1) $1,844 per month, divided by the number of qualified children; or

(2) $614 per month.

548. Is a person with an insurable interest in a retiree or employee eligible for a survivor benefit?

A retiree or employee can designate that a survivor annuity be paid to a person with an insurable interest in the life of the retiree or employee. The benefit is equal to 50 percent of the retiree's benefit, but is reduced, depending on the difference in the age of the person with the insurable interest and the age of the retiring employee.

If the age difference is thirty years or more, the annuity is reduced 40 percent; if the age difference is twenty-five to twenty-nine years, the reduction is 35 percent; if the age difference is twenty to twenty-four years, the reduction is 30 percent; if the age difference is fifteen to nineteen years, the reduction is 25 percent; if the age difference is ten to fourteen years, the reduction is 20 percent; if the age difference is five to nine years, the reduction is 15 percent; if the age difference is less than five years, the reduction is 10 percent.

549. When is a lump-sum survivor benefit paid?

A lump-sum survivor benefit is payable immediately after the death of an employee if the employee:

(1)   has *less* than eighteen months of creditable service; or

(2)   leaves *no* widow, widower, former spouse, or children who are eligible for a survivor annuity.

The lump-sum survivor benefit is the amount paid into the Civil Service Retirement and Disability Fund by the employee. It also includes accrued interest.

The employee, former employee, or annuitant has the right to name the lump-sum survivor benefit beneficiary. If no beneficiary is named, the lump sum is payable to the widow or widower; if there is no widow or widower, it is paid to his living children in equal shares; if no children, it is paid to his parents; if no parents, it is paid to the executor or administrator of his estate; if none of the above, it is paid to the next of kin under the laws of the state where the deceased was domiciled.

Disability Benefits

550. What disability benefits are paid under FERS?

Disability benefits are payable to an employee with eighteen months of creditable service who, because of injury or disease, can no longer perform his job in a useful and efficient manner.

The beneficiary is entitled to a benefit equal to 60 percent of his high-3 average pay during the first year of disability, reduced dollar for dollar by any Social Security disability benefit. After the first year, the beneficiary is entitled to 40 percent of his high-3 average pay, reduced by 60 percent of the Social Security disability benefit.

The benefit is further adjusted at age sixty-two to equal the *lesser* of:

(1)   a retirement benefit computed as if he had worked during his years of disability; or

(2)   the disability benefits he would receive after the benefit is offset by any Social Security disability benefit.

Disability benefits are adjusted after the first year of disability by the increase in the Consumer Price Index for All Urban Wage Earners and Clerical Workers (CPI). Where the change in the CPI for the year is less than 2.0 percent, the benefit is increased by the full amount of the CPI increase. Where the change in the CPI for the year is at least 2.0 percent but is not more than 3.0 percent, the benefit is increased by 2 percent. Where the change in the CPI for the year is more than 3.0 percent, the benefit is increased by the CPI less 1 percent. Periodic medical examinations are required until the beneficiary reaches age sixty.

Thrift Savings Plan

551. What is the Thrift Savings Plan for FERS employees?

The Thrift Savings Plan (TSP) is a tax-deferred retirement savings and investment plan that offers Federal employees and members of the uniformed services, including the Ready Reserve, the same type of savings and tax benefits that many private corporations offer their employees under 401(k) plans. By participating in the TSP, Federal employees have the opportunity to save part of their income for retirement, receive matching agency contributions, and reduce their current taxes. It was established by Congress in the Federal Employees' Retirement System Act of 1986.

The Thrift Plan creates a third tier of benefits under FERS. A thrift plan account is set up automatically for every employee covered under FERS. Members of the uniformed services may also participate in the Plan (see Q 479).

The government contributes 1 percent of pay to an account for each employee, even if the employee declines to contribute to the plan. In addition, the government matches employee contributions as follows:

(1)   Contributions up to the first 3 percent of pay, dollar for dollar

(2)   Contributions that are more than 3 percent but not more than 5 percent of pay, fifty cents per dollar

A FERS employee may contribute up to 100 percent of his or her salary towards the Thrift Plan. However, the maximum amount that a FERS employee can contribute is $18,500 in 2018, up from 18,000 in 2017. Federal employees who are fifty or older are allowed to make additional "catch-up" contributions of $6,000 in 2018, unchanged from 2017. Contribution levels for 2019 were not available at time of printing of this 2019 edition.

Contributions, and earnings on contributions, are not subject to federal income taxation until distributed to the employee at retirement. In addition, contributions reduce the employee's gross income for federal income tax purposes. (Contributions are subject to Social Security taxes, however.)

Contributions can be directed by employees to five investment funds:

(1)   Government Securities Investment (G) Fund

(2)   Fixed Income Index Investment (F) Fund

(3)   Common Stock Index Investment (C) Fund

(4)   Small Capitalization Stock Index Investment (S) Fund

(5)   International Stock Index Investment (I) Fund

FERS employees may elect to invest any portion of their current account balances and/or future contributions in the G Fund, F Fund, C Fund, S Fund, or I Fund.

The Thrift Savings Plan also allows participants to invest in five Lifecycle funds. These Lifecycle funds are L 2050, L 2040, L 2030, L 2020, and L Income. These L funds invest their assets in the G, F, C, S, and I funds in different proportions. It is recommended that, if a participant chooses a lifecycle fund, that he or she choose the one closest to when the money will be needed.

Thrift Plan payments may be made in the following manner:

(1)   At retirement or disability, if eligible for a Basic Annuity, the payment may be made as an immediate or deferred annuity, a lump-sum payment, a fixed-term payment, or by transfer to an IRA or other qualified pension plan

(2)   At death, funds in the Thrift Plan are paid to eligible survivors or to beneficiaries as specified by FERS

(3)   At termination of employment, if eligible for a deferred Basic Annuity, the payment may be made as an immediate or deferred annuity, a transfer to an IRA or other qualified pension plan, or over a fixed term after the employee retires with a Basic Annuity

(4)   At termination of employment, if not eligible for a deferred Basic Annuity, the payment must be transferred to an IRA or qualified pension plan

(5)   At age fifty-nine-and-a-half or during a period of financial hardship (See next.)

A participant must withdraw his or her account balance in a single payment or begin receiving his or her Thrift Savings Plan account balance in monthly payments (or in the form of a Thrift Savings Plan annuity) by April 1 of the later of:

(1)   the year following the year in which the participant reaches age seventy-and-a-half; or

(2)   the year following the year in which the participant separates from federal service. If the participant does not make an election so that payment can be made by this deadline, the Federal Retirement Thrift Investment Board must use the Thrift Savings Plan to purchase an annuity for the participant.

A participant who has turned age fifty-nine-and-a-half can withdraw an amount up to his or her vested Thrift Savings Plan account balance before separating from government employment. A participant is allowed only one withdrawal under this provision. In addition, a participant can obtain a withdrawal before separating from government employment on the basis of financial hardship. A financial hardship withdrawal is limited to the amount the participant contributed to the Thrift Savings Plan (plus the earnings attributed to those contributions). There is no limit on the number of such withdrawals. The participant may ask the Thrift Savings Plan to transfer all or a portion of the withdrawal to an IRA or other eligible retirement plan.

A participant can continue to contribute to the Thrift Savings Plan after obtaining an aged-based withdrawal but is not eligible to contribute to the Thrift Savings Plan for a period of six months after obtaining a financial hardship withdrawal. After six months of ineligibility to contribute, the participant can resume Thrift Savings Plan contributions only by making a new Thrift Savings Plan election on Form TSP-1.

The spouse of a FERS participant must consent to an in-service withdrawal and the spouse of a CSRS participant is entitled to notice when the participant applies for an in-service withdrawal.

Federal employees who separate or enter leave-without-pay status to serve in the military may make up contributions to the Thrift Plan missed because of military service. A federal employee would be permitted to contribute an amount equal to what an employee would have been eligible to contribute. The federal government must give such an employee two to four times the length of his military service to make up the Thrift Plan contributions. The government would match employee contributions in the same manner as regular matching contributions under the Thrift Plan.

552. Can members of the Civil Service Retirement System take advantage of the Thrift Plan?

Yes, but the government does not contribute to the employee's plan, no matter how much the employee contributes. The Federal employee may contribute up to 100 percent of annual pay, but the contribution is limited to $18,500 in 2018. This is up from $18,000 for 2017. Additional catch-up contributions of $6,000 are allowed for those who are age fifty or older in 2018. Contribution figures were not available for 2019 at the time of printing.

Civil Service Retirement System

553. Which federal employees are covered under the Civil Service Retirement System?

The Civil Service Retirement System (CSRS) covers employees of the U.S. government and the District of Columbia who were hired before January 1, 1984, unless coverage is specifically excluded by law. Among the exclusions from CSRS coverage are employees who are subject to another federal retirement system. Employees subject to the Federal Employees' Retirement System (FERS) are excluded from participation in CSRS.

CSRS coverage for pre-1984 employees is automatic for all federal employees except those who are employed by Congress. Congressional employees had to elect coverage.

554. Who is eligible for a CSRS retirement annuity?

An employee must meet two requirements in order to be eligible for a CSRS retirement annuity. First, the employee must complete at least five years of civilian service with the government. Second, the employee, unless retiring on account of total disability, must have been employed under the CSRS for at least one year out of the last two years before separation from service.

The total service of an employee or member of Congress is measured in full years and months. Anything less than a full month is not counted. An employee's service is credited from the date of original employment to the date of separation. No credit is allowed for a period of separation from service in excess of three calendar days.

An employee is allowed credit for periods of military service, if performed prior to the date of separation from a civilian position.

555. Who is eligible for a CSRS retirement annuity?

There are five categories of benefits under the Civil Service Retirement System (CSRS). Eligibility is based on age and the number of years of creditable service and any other specific requirements. In addition, the individual must have served in a position subject to CSRS coverage for one of the last two years before retirement. If meeting one of the following sets of requirements, an individual may be eligible for an immediate retirement benefit. An immediate annuity is one that begins within thirty days after your separation.

Optional: If you leave Federal service before you meet the age and service requirements for an immediate retirement benefit, you may be eligible for deferred retirement benefits. To be eligible, you must have at least five years of creditable civilian service and be age sixty-two or be sixty years of age and have twenty years of service or be fifty-five years of age and have thirty years of service.

Special/Early Optional: An agency must be undergoing a major reorganization, reduction-in-force, or transfer of function determined by the Office of Personnel Management. An annuity is reduced if the individual is under age fifty-five. To be eligible, the person must be fifty years of age with twenty years of service or of any age with twenty-five years of service.

Special Provision Retirement: The individual can retire under special provisions for air traffic controllers or law enforcement and firefighter personnel, nuclear materials courier, Supreme Court Police and Capitol Police. To be eligible, the person must be fifty years of age with twenty years of service or if an air traffic controller, the person can retire at any age with twenty-five years of service.

Discontinued Service: To be eligible, the person must be fifty years of age with twenty years of service or if an air traffic controller, can retire at any age with twenty-five years of service. The separation must be involuntary and not a removal for misconduct or delinquency.

Special Requirements: The person must be disabled for useful and efficient service in their current position and any other vacant position at the same grade or pay level within their commuting area and current agency for which they are qualified. They must have been disabled prior to retirement and the disability should be expected to last for more than one year. They must have five years of creditable service.

556. How are CSRS benefits paid for?

CSRS benefits are funded by deductions from the basic pay of covered employees, matching contributions from their employing agencies, and by payments from the General Treasury for the balance of the cost of the system. Under the current law, the employee and the employing agency *each* contribute:

- 8.0 percent of basic pay for Members of Congress

- 7.5 percent of basic pay for Congressional employees, law enforcement officers, and firefighters

- 7.0 percent of basic pay for other employees

The portion of compensation withheld and contributed to the retirement and disability fund is includable in the employee's gross income, in the same taxable year in which it would have been included if it had been paid to the employee directly. No refund is allowed for taxes attributable to mandatory contributions from the employee's salary to the Civil Service Retirement Fund.

557. Who is entitled to an immediate annuity?

An immediate annuity begins no later than one month after separation from service. This includes an annuity for an employee who retires optionally – for age, for disability, or due to involuntary separation from service. It does not include an annuity for a separated employee who is entitled to a deferred retirement annuity at a future date.

An employee who is separated from service is entitled to an annuity:

(1)   at age fifty-five with thirty years of service;

(2)   at age sixty with twenty years of service;

(3)   at age sixty-two with five years of service; or

(4)   at age fifty with twenty years of service as a law enforcement officer or firefighter, or a combination of such service totaling at least twenty years.

An employee whose separation is involuntary, except for removal for cause on charges of misconduct or delinquency, is entitled to a reduced annuity after twenty-five years of service or after age fifty and twenty years of service. However, no annuity is payable if the employee has declined a reasonable offer of another position in the employee's agency for which the employee is qualified, which is not lower than two grades (pay levels) below the employee's grade and which is within the employee's commuting area.

Also entitled to this reduced annuity is an employee who, while serving in a geographic area designated by the Office of Personnel Management, is voluntarily separated during a period in which:

(1)   the agency in which the employee is serving is undergoing a major reorganization, a major reduction in force, or a major transfer of function; and

(2)   a significant percentage of employees serving in this agency will be separated or subject to an immediate reduction in the rate of basic pay.

Such early retirements must be approved by the Office of Personnel Management. The annuities are reduced by 2 percent for each year the employee is under age fifty-five.

558. Are there alternative forms of CSRS retirement annuities?

Yes, an employee may, at the time of retirement, elect the following alternative forms of annuities:

(1)   Payment of an annuity to the employee for life

(2)   Payment of an annuity to the employee for life, with a survivor annuity payable for the life of a surviving spouse

(3)   Payment of an annuity to the employee for life, with benefit to a named person having an insurable interest

(4)   Election of lump-sum credit option and reduced monthly annuity

559. What is an annuity for life?

The annuitant has a right to receive monthly payments during his or her lifetime unless she is convicted of certain offenses against the United States.

Upon the annuitant's death, any accrued annuity that remains unpaid will be paid to:

(1)   the deceased annuitant's executor or administrator; or

(2)   if there is no executor or administrator, to the decedent's next of kin under state law, after thirty days have passed from the date of death.

560. What are the features of an annuity with a survivor benefit?

An annuity with survivor benefit entitles the survivor to an annuity equal to 55 percent of the annuity amount prior to reduction for the election of the survivor benefit. An annuity for a married employee will automatically include an annuity for a surviving spouse, unless the employee and spouse waive the spouse's annuity in writing. The written-waiver requirement can be overcome only in instances where the employee's spouse cannot be located or where other exceptional circumstances are present.

Generally, the survivor benefit is paid until the survivor dies or remarries. However, remarriage of a widow or widower who is at least age fifty-five does not terminate the survivor annuity. Where the survivor annuity is terminated because the survivor had remarried prior to reaching age fifty-five, the annuity may be restored if the remarriage is dissolved by death, annulment, or divorce.

Where the spouse properly consents, an employee may elect to reduce that portion of the annuity that is to be treated as a survivor annuity.

The portion of the employee's annuity treated as a survivor annuity will be reduced according to a formula. The reduction is 2.5 percent of the first $3,600 chosen as a base, plus 10 percent of any amount over $3,600. For example, if the employee chooses $4,800 as a base, the reduction in the annual annuity would be 2.5 percent of the first $3,600 ($90 a year), plus 10 percent of the $1,200 balance ($120 a year), making a total reduction of $210 ($90 + $120) a year.

If marriage is terminated after retirement by the divorce, annulment, or death of the spouse named as beneficiary, the retiree may elect to have the annuity recomputed, and payment at the single-life unreduced rate will be made for each full month the employee is not married. Should the employee remarry, he has two years from the date of remarriage to notify the Office of Personnel Management in writing that he wants the annuity reduced again to provide a survivor annuity for the new spouse.

If a retired employee dies, absent a waiver of benefits by the survivor, the surviving spouse will receive 55 percent of the yearly annuity that the deceased employee had earned at the time of death. This earned annuity is computed in the same manner as if the deceased employee had retired, but with no reduction for being under age fifty-five, and no increase for voluntary contributions.

The surviving spouse's annuity begins on the day after the employee's death and terminates on the last day of the month before the surviving spouse dies or remarries before age fifty-five.

561. How does an annuity with benefit to a named person having an insurable interest work?

If the employee is in good health at retirement, he or she may elect an Annuity with Benefit to Named Person Having an Insurable Interest. A disabled dependent relative or former spouse is considered as having an insurable interest. An employee electing this annuity will have their annuity reduced by a percentage amount as follows:

Age of Named Person In Relation to Retiring Employee's Age	Reduction in Annuity of Retiring Employee
Older, same age, or less than 5 years younger	10%
5 but less than 10 years younger	15%
10 but less than 15 years younger	20%
15 but less than 20 years younger	25%
20 but less than 25 years younger	30%
25 but less than 30 years younger	35%
30 or more years younger	40%

Upon the employee's death after retirement, the named beneficiary will receive an annuity equal to 55 percent of the employee's reduced annuity rate. The survivor's annuity begins on the day after the retired employee's death and terminates on the last day of the month before the survivor dies. However, if the person named as having an insurable interest dies before the employee, the employee's annuity will be restored to life rate upon written request.

562. Is there a lump-sum credit option upon retirement under CSRS?

Employees are allowed to receive a payment equal to the value of the contributions they made to the retirement program over their working years. The lump-sum payments option is paid in one payment at first and then in two installments of equal amounts. Workers eligible to voluntarily retire who have a critical or life-threatening illness can receive the lump sum in one payment.

563. How is the reduced annuity computed?

First, determine the amount of the member's contributions into the plan. The member's regular annuity is then calculated. To determine the amount of monthly reduction of the annuity, the computation is as follows:

- LS/PV = monthly reduction in annuity, where LS equals the lump-sum credit and PV equals the present value factor of the annuity

The present value factors of CSRS and FERS appear in the Reduced Annuity Tables, below.

To obtain the amount of the reduced monthly annuity, subtract the monthly reduction figure obtained above from the amount of the regular (unreduced) monthly annuity.

Example. Mr. Edwards, a member of the CSRS, is sixty-four at the time he retires from government service. His contributions to CSRS total $25,000. His present value factor (from the table) is 168.2. Using the formula above, $25,000 ÷ 168.2 = $148.63. Mr. Edwards' monthly annuity would therefore be reduced by $148.63.

Reduced Annuity Tables

CSRS

Present Value Factors

Age at Retirement	Factor	Age at Retirement	Factor
40	277.6	66	157.9
41	274.7	67	153.1
42	272.1	68	148.0
43	269.1	69	142.8
44	265.0	70	138.0
45	260.0	71	133.1
46	255.1	72	128.0
47	250.8	73	123.1
48	245.9	74	118.4
49	240.3	75	113.5
50	234.8	76	108.2
51	230.2	77	103.2
52	225.9	78	98.2
53	221.4	79	93.1
54	216.8	80	88.4
55	211.9	81	83.6
56	207.2	82	78.4
57	202.3	83	73.7
58	197.6	84	69.5
59	193.1	85	65.8
60	188.7	86	62.0
61	183.7	87	57.9
62	178.3	88	54.0
63	173.2	89	50.7
64	168.2	90	47.2
65	163.0		

FERS

Present Value Factors for Most Employees

Age at Retirement	Factor	Age at Retirement	Factor
40	185.6	66	149.4
41	185.3	67	145.1
42	185.2	68	140.5

FERS

Present Value Factors for Most Employees

Age at Retirement	Factor	Age at Retirement	Factor
43	184.9	69	135.9
44	184.1	70	131.5
45	182.8	71	127.0
46	181.6	72	122.4
47	180.7	73	118.0
48	179.5	74	113.6
49	177.9	75	109.0
50	176.4	76	104.1
51	175.4	77	99.5
52	174.7	78	94.9
53	174.1	79	90.1
54	173.3	80	85.7
55	172.5	81	81.1
56	171.8	82	76.2
57	171.2	83	71.8
58	170.7	84	67.8
59	170.5	85	64.2
60	170.5	86	60.6
61	170.1	87	56.7
62	167.5	88	52.9
63	163.0	89	49.7
64	158.5	90	46.4
65	154.0		

Computing the CSRS Annuity

564. How is the amount of the CSRS annuity determined?

The amount of an annuity depends primarily on the employee's length of service and high-3 average pay. These two factors are used in a formula to determine the basic annuity, which may then be reduced or increased for various reasons.

The high-3 average pay is the highest pay obtainable by averaging the rates of basic pay in effect during any three consecutive years of service, with each rate weighted by the time it was in effect. The three years need not be continuous, but they must consist of consecutive periods of service. Thus, two or more separate periods of employment that follow each other may be joined to make up the three consecutive years of service on which the high-3 average pay is based. The pay rates for each period of employment are weighted on an annual basis.

Example. Mr. Smith's final three years of government service included pay rates of:

6 months at $14,500	—	½ year	×	$14,500	=	$7,250
18 months at $15,000	—	1½ years	×	$15,000	=	22,500
12 months at $15,000	—	1 year	×	$15,000	=	15,000
						$44,750

Mr. Smith's average pay is computed as:

$$\frac{\$44,750}{3} = \$14,917$$

A three-step formula is used to determine the basic annuity.

- *Step I.* 1.5 percent × Average Pay × number of years of service up to five years, plus

- *Step II.* 1.75 percent × Average Pay × number of years of service over five and up to ten years, plus

- *Step III.* 2 percent × Average Pay × number of years of service over ten.

Note that for employees with over ten years of service, all three steps apply. For those with fewer than ten years of service, only steps I and II apply. For those with fewer than five years of service, only Step I applies.

Example. Mr. Martin retires from civil service employment with thirty years of service. The three consecutive years of service with the highest rates of basic pay were his last three years before retirement.

Rate of pay during 28th year of service	$14,500
Rate of pay during 29th year of service	15,000
Rate of pay during 30th year of service	15,500
	$45,000 (total)

$$\frac{\$45,000}{3} = \$15,000$$

The general formula, using Mr. Martin's $15,000 average pay and thirty years of service, is applied as follows:

1.	1.5%	×	$15,000	×	5 years	=	$1,125.00
2.	1.75%	×	$15,000	×	5 years	=	1,312.50
3.	2%	×	$15,000	×	20 years	=	6,000.00
					Basic Annuity	=	$8,437.50

The employee's basic annuity may not exceed 80 percent of his average pay. If the formula produces an amount exceeding the 80 percent maximum, it must be reduced to an amount that equals 80 percent of the average pay.

565. What is the special computation for Law Enforcement, Firefighters, and Nuclear Materials Couriers?

If retired under special provisions for firefighters, law enforcement, nuclear material couriers, Supreme Court Police, or Capitol Police:

- First twenty years of CSRS law enforcement officer, firefighter and/or nuclear material courier service – retiree receives 2.5 percent of high-3 average salary for each year

- Plus all remaining CSRS service receives 2 percent of high-3 average salary for each year

566. What is the substitute computation method?

A substitute computation method is provided as an alternative for employees with a high-3 of under $5,000. Instead of taking the 1.5 percent, 1.75 percent, and 2 percent of the high-3 average pay, the employee may substitute 1 percent of the high-3 average pay plus $25 for all parts of the general formula. If the high-3 average pay is between $2,500 and $3,333, substitute the 1 percent plus $25 for the 1.5 percent and 1.75 percent in the first and second parts of the general formula. If the high-3 average pay is between $3,334 and $4,999, substitute the 1 percent plus $25 for the 1.5 percent in the first part of the general formula.

567. How is the benefit determined for disability retirement?

An employee under age sixty who retires on account of total disability will receive no less than the guaranteed minimum annuity, which is the *lesser* of:

(1)   40 percent of the employee's high-3 average pay; or

(2)   the amount obtained under the general formula, after adding to years of actual service the number of years the employee is under age sixty on the date of separation.

An employee must have completed at least five years of government service in order to be eligible for disability benefits. The provision for a minimum disability annuity does not apply to employees over age sixty. The disability annuity rate for an employee over age sixty is always computed by using actual service in the general formula.

568. Can an employee obtain a larger retirement annuity by making voluntary contributions?

Yes, an employee can obtain a larger retirement annuity by making voluntary contributions, in multiples of twenty-five dollars, to purchase an additional annuity. Total voluntary contributions may not exceed 10 percent of the employee's total basic pay.

Voluntary contributions are interest-bearing. The interest rate is determined at the end of each year by the Treasury Department. Each $100 in the account provides an additional annuity in the amount of seven dollars, plus twenty cents for each full year the employee is over age fifty-five at retirement.

Death Benefits
569. Is there a death benefit under the CSRS?

Death benefits are of two kinds: survivor annuities and lump-sum payments.

Survivor annuities are payable to an employee's surviving spouse and children upon the death of the employee.

A **lump-sum benefit** is payable upon the death of the employee if there is no spouse or dependent children entitled to an annuity, or, if one is payable, after the right of the last person entitled thereto has been terminated.

While not formally called a "death benefit," where the employee has retired, annuities are payable to the surviving spouse (unless the spouse had waived survivor benefit entitlement) and, where applicable, payable to a named person with an insurable interest.

Annuity Eligibility Requirements
570. Who is eligible for a survivor annuity?

Employee's Spouse. In order for the surviving spouse to qualify for a survivor annuity:

(1)   the spouse must have been married to the employee for at least nine months before death; or

(2)   the spouse must be the parent of the deceased's child born of the marriage.

These requirements are waived where:

(1)   the employee dies as a result of an accident; or

(2)   the employee had previously married and subsequently divorced the surviving spouse, and the aggregate time married is at least nine months.

Employee's Child. Generally, for a deceased employee's child to qualify for the survivor annuity, the child must be unmarried, under eighteen years of age, and a dependent of the employee. The following rules also apply:

(1)   An adopted child is considered to be the employee's child.

(2)   A stepchild is considered to be the employee's child, even if the child did not live with the deceased employee. An illegitimate child, however, must prove he or she was dependent upon the deceased employee.

(3)   An illegitimate child is considered to be the employee's child, even if the child did not live with the deceased employee. An illegitimate child, however, must prove he or she was dependent upon the deceased employee.

(4)   A child who lived with the employee and for whom the employee had filed an adoption petition is considered to be the employee's child, but only where the surviving spouse did in fact adopt the child following the employee's death.

Notwithstanding the age requirement above, each of the following persons is considered to be a child for purposes of the survivorship annuity:

(1)   An unmarried dependent child, regardless of age, who is incapable of self-support because of a mental or physical disability incurred before age eighteen

(2)   An unmarried dependent child between eighteen and twenty-two, who is a student (pursuing a full-time course of study or training in residence in a high school, trade school, college, university, or comparable recognized educational institution)

Benefits for a child end upon marriage. However, annuity payments restart again if the child's marriage has ended and he or she is still eligible for benefits because of disability or enrollment as a full-time student while under age twenty-two. If a child's marriage ends because of divorce or death, the child's annuity and health benefits coverage is restored beginning the first day of the month in which dissolution of the marriage occurs.

Computing the Survivor Annuity

571. How is the survivor annuity computed?

If an employee dies after completing at least eighteen months of civilian service, there is a guaranteed minimum survivor annuity based upon the employee's average pay over the total civilian service.

The annuity, however, is at least 55 percent of the smaller of:

(1)   40 percent of the deceased employee's high-3 average pay; or

(2)   the regular computation obtained after increasing service by the period of time between the date of death and the date the employee would have become age sixty.

This guaranteed minimum does not apply if 55 percent of the employee's earned annuity produces a higher benefit than the guaranteed minimum. Also, since active service cannot be projected beyond age sixty in any case, the guaranteed minimum does not apply where the employee dies after reaching age sixty.

For 2018, where an employee is survived by a spouse and is survived by children who qualify for survivor benefits, each surviving child is entitled to a benefit equal to whichever of the following amounts is the least:

(1)   60 percent of the employee's high-3 average pay, divided by the number of qualified children;

(2) $1,537 per month, divided by the number of qualified children; or

(3) $512 per month. When an employee leaves no surviving spouse but leaves children who qualify for survivor benefits, each child will be paid the least of:

  (a) 75 percent of the employee's high-3 average pay, divided by the number of qualified children;

  (b) $1,844 per month, divided by the number of qualified children; or

  (c) $614 per month.

Note that 2019 figures were not available at the time on the printing of this 2019 edition.

A child's annuity begins on the day after the employee or annuitant dies and continues until the last day of the month before the child marries, dies, or reaches age eighteen, except in the following cases:

(1)   For a child age eighteen or over who is incapable of self-support because of a disability that began before age eighteen, payments stop at the end of the month before the child becomes capable of self-support, marries, or dies.

(2)   The annuity of a student age eighteen or over stops at the end of the month before the child ceases to be a student, reaches age twenty-two, marries, or dies, whichever occurs first.

Lump-Sum Death Benefit
572. When does the lump-sum death benefit become payable?

The lump-sum death benefit becomes payable to the estate of the proper party where the employee dies:

(1)   without a survivor; or

(2)   with a survivor, but the survivor's right to an annuity terminates before a claim for a survivor annuity has been filed.

The lump-sum benefit consists of the amount paid into the Civil Service Retirement and Disability Fund by the employee, plus any accrued interest.

If all rights to a CSRS annuity cease before the total annuity paid equals the lump-sum credit, the difference between the lump-sum credit and the total annuity paid becomes payable to the estate of the proper party. Thus, if an employee leaves a spouse or children who are eligible for a survivor annuity, a lump-sum death benefit may be payable after all survivors' annuities have been paid. The lump-sum benefit would consist of that portion of the employee's lump-sum credit that has not been exhausted by the annuity payments to survivors.

Annuity Payments

573. How are annuity payments made?

Annuities are paid by monthly check. The Office of Personnel Management authorizes the payment, and the Treasury Department issues the check. After the initial check, each regular check is dated the first workday of the month after the month for which the annuity is due. For example, the annuity payment for the month of April will be made by a check dated May 1.

An employee annuity begins on the first day of the month after:

(1)   separation from service; or

(2)   pay ceases and the service and age requirements for entitlement to an annuity are met.

Any other annuity payable begins on the first day of the month after the occurrence of the event on which payment is based.

Disability Retirement

574. When is an annuity payable for disability retirement?

An immediate annuity is payable to an employee for disability retirement when each of the following conditions is met:

(1)   The employee has completed five years of civilian service.

(2)   The employee has become totally disabled for useful and efficient service in the position occupied, or the duties of a similar position at the same grade or level.

A claim for disability retirement must be filed with the Office of Personnel Management before separation from service or within one year thereafter. The one-year requirement may be waived in cases of incompetency.

The annuity payable will be the earned annuity based on the high-3 average salary, the years of actual service, and the three-part formula (see Q 564), but not less than:

(1)   40 percent of the high-3 average salary; or

(2)   the amount computed under the general formula after adding to years of actual service the number of years he is under age sixty on the date of separation.

Unless the disability is permanent in nature, an employee receiving a disability retirement annuity must be medically examined annually until age sixty. The Government pays for the examination.

Upon recovery before reaching age sixty, the annuity is continued temporarily (not to exceed one year) to give the individual an opportunity to find a position. If re-employed in Government service within the year, the annuity stops on re-employment. If the individual is not re-employed, the annuity stops at the expiration of the 180-day period.

Cost-of-Living Adjustments

575. Is there a cost-of-living adjustment to CSRS annuities?

Annuities for retirees and survivors are subject to a cost-of-living adjustment in December of each year. The increases are reflected in the annuity payment received the following month. The percentage of the cost-of-living increase each year is determined by the average price index for the third quarter of each year over the third quarter average of the Consumer Price Index for Urban Wage Earners and Clerical Workers of the previous year.

The cost-of-living increase for 2019 is 2.8 percent, the 2018 was 2.0 percent, the 2017 COLA was 0.3 percent, but there was NO cost-of-living (COLA) increase for annuitants in 2016.

Refund of Contributions

576. Is there a refund of contributions if an employee leaves government service?

Yes, an employee who leaves government service or transfers to government work under another retirement system may withdraw his retirement lump-sum credit (contributions plus any interest payable), so long as the employee:

(1)   is separated from the job for at least thirty-one consecutive days;

(2)   is transferred to a position that is not subject to CSRS or FERS and remains in that position for at least thirty-one consecutive days;

(3)   files an application for a refund of retirement deductions;

(4)   is not reemployed in a position subject to CSRS or FERS at the time the application is filed; and

(5)   will not become eligible to receive an annuity within thirty-one days after filing the application.

Life Insurance Benefits

577. In general, what life insurance benefits are available to federal civil service employees?

The Federal Government established the Federal Employees' Group Life Insurance (FEGLI) Program on August 29, 1954. It is the largest group life insurance program in the world, covering over 4 million Federal employees and retirees, as well as many of their family members.

All federal civil service employees – whether CSRS or FERS members – and employees of the District of Columbia are automatically insured under the provisions of a group policy purchased by the U.S. Office of Personnel Management. Most employees are eligible for FEGLI coverage.

FEGLI provides group term life insurance. As such, it does not build up any cash value or paid-up value. It consists of Basic life insurance coverage and three options. In most cases, new Federal employees are automatically covered by Basic life insurance and payroll deduct premiums from the paycheck unless coverage is waived. In addition to the Basic, there are three forms of Optional insurance that can be elected. An individual must have Basic insurance in order to elect any of the options. Unlike Basic, enrollment in Optional insurance is not automatic – the individual must take action to elect the options.

Basic insurance coverage may be declined by written notice only. If coverage has been declined, the employee cannot obtain coverage for at least one year and, then, only if the applicant is in good health. Special rules apply if the employee has experienced a break in service of at least 180 days. Under this exception, all previous waivers of life insurance coverage are canceled, but any of the optional coverages must be affirmatively elected within thirty-one days after the employee's return. Each insured receives a certificate setting forth the group insurance benefits, to whom benefits are payable, to whom claims are submitted, and summarizing the provisions of the policy. The group insurance is underwritten by a large number of private insurance companies and claims are settled by the Office of Federal Employees' Group Life Insurance, P.O. Box 6080, Scranton, PA 18505-6080.

Group insurance includes:

(1)   group-term life coverage without a medical examination; and

(2)   accidental death and dismemberment insurance protection.

The amount of each type of insurance is based on the employee's "basic insurance amount," which is determined by rounding the employee's annual salary to the next higher multiple of $1,000, and adding $2,000. However, in no case may the basic insurance amount be less than $10,000.

The group accidental death and dismemberment insurance provides payment for:

(1)   loss of life or loss of two or more members; and

(2)   loss of one hand or one foot, or for permanent and total loss of sight in one eye.

The accidental death benefit equals the employee's basic insurance amount and is paid in addition to the group life insurance.

An insured individual who is certified by a doctor as terminally ill may elect to receive a lump-sum payment of Basic Insurance. Optional insurance is not available for payment as a Living Benefit. The effective date of a Living Benefit election is the date on which the Living Benefit payment is cashed or deposited. Once an election becomes effective, it cannot be revoked. No further election of Living Benefits can be made. If the insured individual has assigned his or her insurance, he or she cannot elect a Living Benefit; nor can an assignee elect a Living Benefit on behalf of an insured individual. If an individual has elected a Living Benefit, he or she may assign his or her remaining insurance. An individual may elect to receive either a full Living Benefit (all of the Basic Insurance) or a partial Living Benefit (a portion of the Basic Insurance, in a multiple of $1,000). The amount of Basic Insurance elected as a Living Benefit will be reduced by an actuarial amount representing the amount of interest lost to the fund because of the early payment of benefits.

An individual may assign ownership of all life insurance, except Option C (which covers family members). If an individual wishing to make an assignment owns more than one type of coverage, he or she must assign all the insurance; an individual cannot assign only a portion of the coverage. Option C cannot be assigned. If the insurance is assigned to two or more individuals, corporations, or trustees, the insured individual must specify percentage shares (rather than dollar amounts or types of insurance) to go to each assignee.

578. How does an employee designate the beneficiary or beneficiaries?

An employee's designation of beneficiary or beneficiaries is made in a signed and witnessed writing that is received before the employee's death by his employing office. The Designation of Beneficiary (Form SF 2823) needs to be completed.[1] If no beneficiary is designated when the employee dies, payment is made in the following order: to the employee's widow or widower; or, if none, to the child or children of the employee in equal shares and descendants of deceased children by representation; or, if none, to the parents of the employee in equal shares or the entire amount to the surviving parent; or, if none, to the duly appointed executor or administrator of the employee; or, if none, to the next of kin of the employee, under the law of the employee's domicile at the time of death. All forms are available on the website.[2]

Beneficiaries receiving insurance proceeds in excess of $7,500 receive a money market account instead of a check from the government. Beneficiaries entitled to less than $7,500 receive a single check from the government for the full amount of insurance coverage. Insurance proceeds earn interest in the money market account. Beneficiaries receive special checkbooks and can write checks on the money market account for $250, up to the full amount of the insurance payment.

579. When does insurance coverage cease?

Subject to the exceptions below, an employee's group insurance coverage ceases on the earliest of:

(1)   the date of separation from the service;

(2)   the date on which a period of twelve months of continuous nonpay status ends; or

---

1. Form SF 2823 https://www.opm.gov/forms/pdf_fill/sf2823.pdf. – Form revised 2014 (Last accessed October 15, 2018).
2. https://www.opm.gov/healthcare-insurance (Last accessed October 15, 2018).

(3)   the date of any other change in employment that results in the employee's ineligibility for insurance coverage.

In addition, coverage may be terminated at the end of the pay period in which it is determined that periodic pay, after all other deductions, is insufficient to cover the required withholdings (such as court-ordered child support) to a point at which deductions for federal employee group life insurance cannot be made.

An exception to the termination rule occurs where:

(1)   the employee retires on an immediate annuity; or

(2)   the employee becomes entitled to workers' compensation.

An employee who does not want insurance may waive group insurance coverage. In such a case, coverage ceases on the last day of the pay period in which the agency receives the employee's waiver of coverage.

580. Can an employee convert to an individual policy?

Yes, if coverage ceases as a result of one of the occurrences described in Q 579 above, the employee may apply for an individual life insurance policy. The employee's coverage cannot exceed the amount for which he was insured at the time of the terminating event. The conversion excludes the Option C coverage. (See Q 582.) The insured may convert all or any part of the Basic and Optional coverage. No medical examination is required, although a few questions about health may be asked to see if the insured might qualify for a lower premium. These questions are not mandatory but if unanswered, the insured may pay a higher premium than necessary.

The employee's request for conversion information must be submitted to the Office of Federal Employee's Group Life Insurance and postmarked within thirty-one days following the date of the terminating event, or within thirty-one days of the date the employee received notice of loss of the group coverage and right to convert, whichever is later. Detailed information concerning how to apply for the policy may be obtained from the Office of Federal Employees' Group Life Insurance, P.O. Box 6080, Scranton, PA 18505-6080.

581. What is the cost of basic insurance?

The employee pays two-thirds, by means of salary withholding, of the cost of that amount of group-term life and accidental death and dismemberment that equals his or her basic insurance amount. The cost of the additional group-term life (i.e., that amount in excess of his or her basic insurance amount) is paid entirely by the government. The amount withheld from the bi-weekly pay of an employee is fifteen cents for each $1,000 of his or her basic insurance amount; the amount withheld from the monthly pay of an employee is 32.5 cents for each $1,000 of coverage. The following table shows the amount withheld from pay to meet the employee's share of the cost. The figures reported here were current as published on the opm.gov website as of October 15, 2018 at https://www.opm.gov/retirement-services/publications-forms/benefits-administration-letters/2015/15-203a1.pdf.

INSURANCE WITHHOLDINGS
Amount of Withholdings Per Pay Period

Basic Insurance Amount	Biweekly	Monthly	Basic Insurance Amount	Biweekly	Monthly
$18,000	$2.70	$5.85	$80,000	$12.00	$26.00
19,000	2.85	6.18	81,000	12.15	26.33
20,000	3.00	6.50	82,000	12.30	26.65
21,000	3.15	6.83	83,000	12.45	26.98
22,000	3.30	7.15	84,000	12.60	27.30
23,000	3.45	7.48	85,000	12.75	27.63
24,000	3.60	7.80	86,000	12.90	27.95
25,000	3.75	8.13	87,000	13.05	28.28
26,000	3.90	8.45	88,000	13.20	28.60
27,000	4.05	8.78	89,000	13.35	28.93
28,000	4.20	9.10	90,000	13.50	29.25
29,000	4.35	9.43	91,000	13.65	29.58
30,000	4.50	9.75	92,000	13.80	29.90
31,000	4.65	10.08	93,000	13.95	30.23
32,000	4.80	10.40	94,000	14.10	30.55
33,000	4.95	10.73	95,000	14.25	30.88
34,000	5.10	11.05	96,000	14.40	31.20
35,000	5.25	11.38	97,000	14.55	31.53
36,000	5.40	11.70	98,000	14.70	31.85
37,000	5.55	12.03	99,000	14.85	32.18
38,000	5.70	12.35	100,000	15.00	32.50
39,000	5.85	12.68	101,000	15.15	32.83
40,000	6.00	13.00	102,000	15.30	33.15
41,000	6.15	13.33	103,000	15.45	33.48
42,000	6.30	13.65	104,000	15.60	33.80
43,000	6.45	13.98	105,000	15.75	34.13
44,000	6.60	14.30	106,000	15.90	34.45
45,000	6.75	14.63	107,000	16.05	34.78
46,000	6.90	14.95	108,000	16.20	35.10
47,000	7.05	15.28	109,000	16.35	35.43
48,000	7.20	15.60	110,000	16.50	35.75
49,000	7.35	15.93	111,000	16.65	36.08
50,000	7.50	16.25	112,000	16.80	36.40
51,000	7.65	16.58	113,000	16.95	36.73

INSURANCE WITHHOLDINGS
Amount of Withholdings Per Pay Period

Basic Insurance Amount	Biweekly	Monthly	Basic Insurance Amount	Biweekly	Monthly
52,000	7.80	16.90	114,000	17.10	37.05
53,000	7.95	17.23	115,000	17.25	37.38
54,000	8.10	17.55	116,000	17.40	37.70
55,000	8.25	17.88	117,000	17.55	38.03
56,000	8.40	18.20	118,000	17.70	38.35
57,000	8.55	18.53	119,000	17.85	38.68
58,000	8.70	18.85	120,000	18.00	39.00
59,000	8.85	19.18	121,000	18.15	39.33
60,000	9.00	19.50	122,000	18.30	39.65
61,000	9.15	19.83	123,000	18.45	39.98
62,000	9.30	20.15	124,000	18.60	40.30
63,000	9.45	20.48	125,000	18.75	40.63
64,000	9.60	20.80	126,000	18.90	40.95
65,000	9.75	21.13	127,000	19.05	41.28
66,000	9.90	21.45	128,000	19.20	41.60
67,000	10.05	21.78	129,000	19.35	41.93
68,000	10.20	22.10	130,000	19.50	42.25
69,000	10.35	22.43	131,000	19.65	42.58
70,000	10.50	22.75	132,000	19.80	42.90
71,000	10.65	23.08	133,000	19.95	43.23
72,000	10.80	23.40	134,000	20.10	43.55
73,000	10.95	23.73	135,000	20.25	43.88
74,000	11.10	24.05	136,000	20.40	44.20
75,000	11.25	24.38	137,000	20.55	44.53
76,000	11.40	24.70	138,000	20.70	44.85
77,000	11.55	25.03	139,000	20.85	45.18
78,000	11.70	25.35	140,000	21.00	45.50
79,000	11.85	25.68			

582. What optional insurance coverages are available to the civil service employee?

Optional insurance coverages currently available include:

(1) optional life insurance (termed Option A – Standard Insurance);

(2) additional optional life insurance (Option B – Additional Insurance); and

(3)   optional life insurance on family members (Option C – Family Coverage).

Beneficiary provisions for optional insurances on the life of the employee are the same as for basic (regular) insurance.[1]

Option A – Standard Insurance

Employees covered under the basic life insurance program can purchase $10,000 of optional group-term life insurance. This coverage includes accidental death and dismemberment.

The premium is paid entirely by the employee through withholding, and the cost is as follows:

Withholding for $10,000 Insurance

Age Group	Biweekly	Monthly
Under age 35	$0.20	$0.43
35 through 39	0.30	0.65
40 through 44	0.40	0.87
45 through 49	0.70	1.52
50 through 54	1.10	2.38
55 through 59	2.00	4.33
60 and over	6.00	13.00

Where Option A insurance has been declined, the employee is eligible to enroll for this coverage only by meeting the two requirements for canceling a waiver of basic life insurance. Neither a retiree nor an employee receiving basic life insurance while receiving workers' compensation can cancel a previous declination of Option A – Standard.

Option B – Additional Optional Insurance

An employee with basic life insurance can purchase Option B – additional optional life insurance on himself – without regard to whether he has purchased Option A insurance. Option B coverage comes in one, two, three, four, or five multiples of an employee's annual pay (after the pay has been rounded to the next higher thousand).

The cost of Option B insurance, like Option A, is paid entirely by the employee through withholdings. The rates per $1,000 of coverage are as follows:

Withholding for $1,000 Insurance

Age Group	Biweekly	Monthly
Under age 35	$0.02	$0.043
35 through 39	0.03	0.065
40 through 44	0.04	0.087
45 through 49	0.07	0.152

---

1. Rates are found at https://www.opm.gov/retirement-services/publications-forms/benefits-administration-letters/2015/15-203a1.pdf. (Last accessed October 15, 2018).

	Withholding for $1,000 Insurance	
Age Group	Biweekly	Monthly
50 through 54	0.11	0.238
55 through 59	0.20	0.433
60 through 64	0.44	0.953
65 through 69	0.54	1.170
70 through 74	0.96	2.080
75 through 79	1.80	3.900
80 and over	2.64	5.720

Retiring employees or compensationers can elect to continue Option B coverage on an unreduced basis by continuing to pay premiums after age sixty-five. Annuitants and compensationers who elect unreduced Option B can later cancel that election and have the full reduction.

Option C – Family Coverage

Option C – life insurance coverage on the life of spouse and dependents – is available in either one, two, three, four, or five multiples of coverage. One multiple is equal to $5,000 for a spouse and $2,500 for each dependent child. The cost of this insurance is paid entirely by the employee through withholding. The rates for coverage of the spouse and child (or children) are as follows:

	Withholding per Multiple	
Age of Person	Biweekly	Monthly
Under age 35	$0.22	$0.48
35 through 39	0.27	0.59
40 through 44	0.41	0.89
45 through 49	0.59	1.28
50 through 54	0.92	1.99
55 through 59	1.48	3.21
60 through 64	2.70	5.85
65 through 69	3.14	6.80
70 through 74	3.83	8.30
75 through 79	5.26	11.40
80 and over	7.20	15.60

Retiring employees can choose to elect unreduced Option C coverage by continuing to pay premiums after age sixty-five. Annuitants and compensationers who elect unreduced Option C can later cancel that election and have the full reduction.

Foster children are covered under Option C. Dependency of the foster child must be established before the child is approved for coverage under Option C. These figures are current

as of October 15, 2018 as reported at https://www.opm.gov/retirement-services/calcula
tors/fegli-calculator/option-c-family-insurance/.

An easy-to-use calculator is available on the OPM website,[1]

583. May a retiring employee continue life insurance coverage?

With respect to basic (regular) life insurance, an employee who retires on an immediate
annuity can continue his basic life insurance (excluding accidental death and dismemberment),
so long as he satisfies the "five or less than five" rule. This requires that the retiree be insured
either: (1) through the five years of service immediately preceding his retirement; or (2) if less
than five years, then throughout the period or periods of service during which he was entitled to
coverage. An additional requirement for continuing basic insurance is that the employee cannot
have converted the policy to an individual life policy.

The retiring employee's basic life options are as follows:

Election	Monthly Cost Before 65	Monthly Cost After 65
1. 75% REDUCTION — Amount of insurance reduces 2% per month after age 65 to a minimum of 25% of Basic Insurance Amount at retirement.	$.325 per $1,000*	No Cost
2. 50% REDUCTION — Amount of insurance reduces 1% per month after age 65 to a minimum of 50% of Basic Insurance Amount at retirement.	$.965 per $1,000*	$.64 per $1,000*
3. NO REDUCTION — 100% of Basic Insurance Amount at retirement is retained after age 65.	$2.265 per $1,000*	$1.94 per $1,000*

*of Basic Insurance Amount at retirement

Where the employee chooses the 75 percent Reduction and retired before December 31, 1989, there is no cost to the individual after retirement, regardless of age. If the
employee retires after December 31, 1989 and elects the 75 percent Reduction, the life
insurance withholdings will be at the same rate to age sixty-five as for active employees, and
withholdings will be deducted from his annuity. After the individual reaches age sixty-five,
withholding will stop.

Where the employee chooses the 50 percent Reduction or No Reduction, the full cost of
the additional protection is deducted from the retiree's monthly annuity payment. The withholdings begin at retirement and continue for life or until the election is canceled or coverage
is otherwise discontinued.

---

1. https://www.opm.gov/retirement-services/calculators/fegli-calculator/ (Last acccessed October 25, 2018)..

Where the employee elected Option A – Standard Insurance, the retiree may continue the insurance so long as it was in force during the "five or less than five" period explained earlier. The cost of the Option A life insurance will be withheld from the annuity until the end of the calendar month in which he attains age sixty-five. After that time, the Option A life insurance will be continued without cost to the retiree.

Option A life insurance, in all cases, is subject to a reduction of 2 percent at the end of each full calendar month following the date on which the employee attains age sixty-five or retires, whichever occurs later. These reductions continue until a minimum (but in no event, less than 25 percent of the amount of Option A life in force before the first reduction) is reached.

An employee who retires on an immediate annuity can continue the amount of Option B – Additional Life Insurance so long as it was in force for the required "five or less than five" period explained above. The full cost of the Option B life that is continued will be withheld from the retiree's annuity until the calendar month in which the retiree attains age sixty-five. Beginning with the end of that calendar month, Option B life insurance will be continued without cost to the retiree. The amount of Option B life insurance is subject to a reduction of 2 percent each month beginning with the second calendar month after the date on which the employee attains age sixty-five or retires, whichever occurs later. These reductions continue for fifty months, at which time the Option B life coverage ends.

Retiring employees or compensationers can elect to continue Option B coverage on an unreduced basis by continuing to pay premiums after age sixty-five. Annuitants and compensationers who elect unreduced Option B can later cancel that election and have the full reduction. Annuitants and compensationers who have Option B coverage on a reduction schedule will be offered the opportunity to elect an unreduced schedule on a prospective basis.

An employee who retires on an immediate annuity may continue his Option C – Family Coverage that was in force during the "five or less than five" period. The full cost of the optional family coverage that is continued will be withheld from the retiree's annuity until the calendar month in which the retiree attains age sixty-five. Beginning with the end of that calendar month, the optional family life coverage will be continued without cost to the retiree. Optional family life coverage that is continued after retirement is subject to the same method of reduction as is the additional optional life insurance (see previous). Thus, coverage of optional family life will end following the expiration of the same fifty months.

Retiring employees can choose to elect unreduced Option C coverage by continuing to pay premiums after age sixty-five. Annuitants and compensationers who elect unreduced Option C can later cancel that election and have the full reduction.

A recipient of federal workers' compensation avoids a termination of federal employee group life insurance so long as he has met the "five or less than five" rule. This rule applies to basic life insurance, as well as any of the optional coverages. No accidental death and dismemberment insurance is available to the workers' compensation recipient.

584. How are State and Local Government employees covered under Social Security and Medicare?

State and local government employees are covered through Social Security and Medicare in one of the following ways:

- The coverage is mandated by law.

- There is a Section 218 agreement between the state and the Social Security Administration (SSA).

585. What is a Section 218 Agreement?

A Section 218 agreement (referring to section 218 of the Social Security Act) is an agreement entered into voluntarily between the state government and the Social Security Administration to provide Social Security coverage, Medicare Hospital Insurance (HI) coverage or both to local and state government employees. Under the agreement, the state decides whether to cover retirement system groups, non-retirement system groups or both. Section 218 agreements are irrevocable.

All States, including the fifty states, Puerto Rico, the Virgin Islands, and approximately sixty interstate instrumentalities, have a Section 218 Agreement with SSA. These agreements allow the States, if they desire, to provide Social Security and Medicare Hospital Insurance (HI) or Medicare HI-only coverage for public employees.

Section 218 agreements cover positions, not individuals. If the position is covered for Social Security and Medicare under a Section 218 agreement, then any employee filling that position is subject to Social Security and Medicare taxes. Employees covered under a Section 218 agreement have the same coverage and benefit rights as employees in the private sector.

Public employees are brought under a Section 218 agreement in groups known as coverage groups. There are two basic coverage groups: absolute coverage groups and retirement system coverage groups. An absolute coverage group is composed of employees whose positions are not covered under a public retirement system. A retirement system coverage group is composed of employees whose positions are covered under a public retirement system.

A public retirement system may be covered under a Section 218 agreement only after a referendum is held. All States are authorized to use the majority vote referendum process. If a majority of all the eligible members vote in favor of coverage, all current and future employees in positions under the retirement system will be covered.

In addition to the majority vote referendum procedure, certain States and all interstate instrumentalities are authorized to divide a retirement system based on whether the employees in positions under the retirement system want coverage. Under the divided vote referendum, only those employees who vote "yes" and all future employees who become members of the retirement system will be covered. Members who vote "no" are not covered as long as they maintain continuous employment in a position within the same public retirement system coverage group.

586. What types of coverage are provided under a Section 218 agreement?

A Section 218 provides Old-Age, Survivors, Disability and Hospital Insurance (OASDHI) coverage and protection. Employees have the same Social Security and Medicare Hospital Insurance (HI) coverage and rights that employees in the private sector who are covered for Social Security and Medicare on a mandatory basis.

587. Is Social Security and Medicare Hospital Insurance coverage mandatory or voluntary?

Social Security and Medicare Hospital Insurance became mandatory for state and local government employees after July 2, 1991 – if they meet the following criteria:

- They are not covered under a public retirement system; AND

- They are not covered under a Section 218 agreement unless specifically excluded by law

Exclusions from Mandatory Social Security and Medicare Coverage

The following situations exclude a person from being covered by mandatory Social Security and Medicare:

- Hiring took place to relieve the individual from unemployment

- Employment consists of services as either a patient or an inmate in a hospital, home or other institution

- Temporary services performed during an emergency such as a fire, storm, earthquake, snowstorm/blizzard, flood or other emergency

- Performance of services as an elected official or election worker and pay is less that the threshold amount mandated by Federal law

    o 1968 through 1977: Less than $50

    o 1978 through 1994: Less than $100

    o 1995 through 1999: Less than $1,000

    o 2000 and 2001: Less than $1,100

    o 2002 through 2005: Less than $1,200

    o 2006 and 2007: Less than $1,300

    o 2008: Less than $1,400

    o 2009 through 2012: Less than $1,500

- ○ 2013 through 2015: Less than $1,600

- ○ 2016: Less than $1,700

- ○ 2017: Less than $1,800

- ○ 2018: Less than $1,800

- ○ 2019: Less than $1,800

Note that in some states, poll workers are covered under a Section 218 agreement making the dollar amounts different.

- Performance of services which are compensated solely on a fee basis

- Performance of services at a school where enrolled and regularly attending classes (although some states cover this under a Section 218 agreement)

- Performance of services as a non-resident alien with the below-listed conditions being met:

  - ○ Temporary United States resident

  - ○ Possession of a F1, J1, M1 or Q1 visa

  - ○ Performance of the type of work for which admitted to the United States

588. What are the employment coverage thresholds for domestic employees for Social Security and Medicare Hospital Insurance?

For 2019, the domestic employee coverage threshold amount is $2,100. The list below shows the coverage thresholds for domestic employees beginning with 1994.

- 1994 through 1997: Less than $1,000

- 1998 and 1999: Less than $1,100

- 2000: Less than $1,200

- 2001 and 2002: Less than $1,300

- 2003 through 2005: Less than $1,400

- 2006 and 2007: Less than $1,500

- 2008: Less than $1,600

- 2009 through 2011: Less than $1,700

- 2012 and 2013: Less than $1,800

- 2014 and 2015: Less than $1,900

- 2016 and 2017: Less than $2,000

- 2018 and 2019: Less than $2,100

589. What are the definition of terms used in Section 218 Agreements?

Several terms are used when referencing Section 218 Agreements – these include:

- State: For a Section 218 agreement, the term "state" includes all 50 United States, Puerto Rico, the U.S. Virgin Islands, and interstate instrumentalities. It DOES NOT include the District of Columbia, Guam, American Samoa, and the Commonwealth of the Northern Mariana Islands.

- Political Subdivision: For a Section 218 agreement, the term "political subdivision" means the separate legal entity of a state that has governmental powers and functions. This can include cities, counties, towns, townships, villages, school districts, utility service districts, etc.

- Interstate Instrumentality: For a Section 218 agreement, the term "interstate instrumentality" is an independent legal entity, created by two or more states, to carry out some function of government, such as a regional transportation commission or a bridge commission.

- Employee: For a Section 218 agreement, the term "employee" means the definition of employee in Section 210 of the Social Security Act. It can include appointed or elected officials.

590. What are coverage groups and retirement systems?

Several terms are used when referencing Section 218 Agreements – these include:

- Coverage Groups: A coverage group is a group of state and local governmental employees brought under a Section 218 agreement. The state decides, as defined by state and federal law, which groups to cover and when Social Security coverage begins. There are two kinds of coverage groups – absolute coverage groups and retirement system coverage groups.

  Absolute coverage groups contain employees in positions not covered by a state or local retirement system. Coverage is provided for all of these employees unless specifically excluded. Some employees can be ineligible for inclusion in the retirement system because of numerous factors, including age, service length, date of hire, etc.

- Retirement Systems: A retirement system is any pension, annuity, retirement fund or similar vehicle or system maintained by a state or local government or instrumentality with the purpose of providing retirement benefits to participating employees. The IRS determines whether retirement systems not covered by Section 219 are exempt from mandatory Social Security and Medicare coverage.

591. Can states divide retirement systems?

Yes, twenty-three states are authorized to divide retirement systems based on the whether employees in positions in that retirement system WANT Social Security coverage. Under the divided vote referendum, only those employees that vote "YES" and all future employees who become members of the retirement system will be covered. Members who vote "NO" are not covered as long as they maintain continuous employment in a position within the same public retirement system coverage group.

These states authorized to divide coverage include:

Alaska	New Jersey
California	New Mexico
Connecticut	New York
Florida	North Dakota
Georgia	Pennsylvania
Hawaii	Rhode Island
Illinois	Tennessee
Kentucky	Texas
Louisiana	Vermont
Massachusetts	Wisconsin
Minnesota	Washington
Nevada	

CASE STUDIES USED IN PLANNING FOR SOCIAL SECURITY MAXIMIZATION

As people approach retirement age, a common concern which arises is that they will not have enough money to maintain the lifestyle to which they became accustomed to during their working years. Interest in understanding how Social Security benefits are calculated and established—and how to MAXIMIZE those benefits—is becoming more of an interest to individuals now that postretirement income has been shifted from the employer to the individual. The traditional "Defined Benefit" pension plan established by the employer as a fringe benefit has shifted to the "Defined Contribution" plan, such as 401(k) plans, managed by the individual.

Even with concerns regarding the future of the program, Social Security represents a source of retirement income that most individuals consider a critical and expected component of their retirement plan. Social Security provides workers (who have reached the defined eligibility)—as well as spouses, widows/widowers, and dependent children with an identified and steady monthly income that will increase over time—and in many cases, continue for as long as the individual lives. Although it does not fully replace an individual's earnings, in many cases it serves as a significant portion (or all) of the income of retirees. It is obvious that it is important to think about and analyze when advising an individual on when they should claim benefits under Social Security.

There is a myriad of strategies that can help maximize Social Security benefits for an individual or a couple. These strategies will vary based on the individual situation, the individuals involved, and the goals and desires of the parties. There is no "cookie-cutter" or "one-size-fits-all" situation; for each individual or couple involved, there can be a dozen or more strategies that can be formulated. Which strategy is "best" or correct will vary. One party may wish to maximize monthly income, while another may wish to establish a program to maximize lifetime benefits (the total amount collected from start of benefits to end-of-life).

Many factors will affect strategies:

- Income level over last thirty-five years (determination of Primary Insurance Amount [PIA])

- Income levels of spouse and eligibility for benefits

- Income needs during retirement

- Desire to maximize monthly income versus total benefits collected

- Life expectancy

- Age and Life expectancy of spouse

- Widow/Widower benefits

- Other sources of income: pensions, 401(k), investments

- Application of Earnings Test

- Marital status (Single, Married, Divorced)

- Filing date including:

  - Reduction Factor for early filing

  - Use of Delayed Retirement Credit by waiting to file after Full Retirement Age (FRA)

  - Use of "File and Suspend", Spousal Benefit, "Restricted Application" strategies

- Effect of other provisions such as Public Employee Pensions, Windfall Elimination Provision (WEP) and Government Pension Offset (GPO)

The Case Studies included in this section, developed by Premier Social Security Consulting, LLC and their principals, Marc Kiner and Jim Blair are not designed to be all-inclusive. As stated above, each situation is unique and will require both investigation and analysis. These Case Studies are designed to show you selected situations and some of the various outcomes that will result based on the different choices made. As you will see, the outcomes will vary based on the variance of the various factors detailed above. Please keep in mind that the figures used in the Case Studies are based upon cash flow not Present Value. Often different choices will cause one spouse's benefits to increase while the other spouse's is lessened—but coordination of choices can lead to a higher combined benefit. Depending upon the choices made, the dollar amounts of the money collected over the life of the beneficiary can vary greatly—literally by hundreds of thousands of dollars and often 15, 20 or even close to 30 percent. Winding the confusing and complicated road of Social Security benefits requires both skill and focus. It is necessary to consider all factors—to review all options—to ensure the most favorable and lucrative outcome. For more information on how Premier Social Security Consultants can help you or your clients maximize the amount of Social Security benefits, please see the information in the front of this book.

CASE STUDIES

CASE STUDY #1 Amanda: Divorced woman with two deceased ex-husbands, eligible for Surviving Divorced benefit

CASE STUDY #2 Bob and Lisa: Married couple close in age, one is a high earner and the other has above average earnings

CASE STUDY #3 Brenda: Divorced woman with deceased ex-husband, eligible for Surviving Divorced benefit

CASE STUDY #4 Bruce and Debbie: Married couple with one high earner and other spouse with insufficient credits, approximately same age

CASE STUDY #5 Carl: Widower

CASE STUDY #6 George and Joan: Married couple approximately four years apart in age, husband had significantly more earnings

CASE STUDY #7 Greg and Alice: Married couple, approximately seven years apart in age, one is a high earner and other is a middle-income earner

CASE STUDY #8 Jeff and Gary: Married same-sex couple, three years apart in age, one spouse with significantly more earnings than the other

CASE STUDY #9 Jose and Kathy: Divorced couple, both now unmarried and past Full Retirement Age

CASE STUDY #10 Larry and Judy: Married couple, one is a high earner with a spouse subject to Windfall Elimination Provision/Government Pension Offset

CASE STUDY #11 Mike and Rita: Married couple, approximately a year apart in age, husband made moderately more than wife

CASE STUDY #12 Roger and Susan: Husband already at FRA with significantly younger spouse with children

CASE STUDY #13 Sandy: Widow approaching FRA

CASE STUDY #14 Virginia: Single woman

CASE STUDY #15 Shaun and JoAnn: Married couple, roughly the same age, one spouse is a high earner, the other spouse subject to the Government Pension Offset

CASE STUDY #16 Rick and Julie: Married couple two years apart in age—one is a higher earner, the other had a middle-income level

CASE STUDY #17 Paul and Kirsten: Married couple four years apart in age, with husband having significantly higher earnings

CASE STUDY #18 Mark and Cindy: Married couple roughly the same age, with husband having significantly higher earnings than wife

CASE STUDY #19 Justin and Georgia: Married couple three years apart in age, both spouses are high earners

CASE STUDY #20 Don and Mary Ann: Married couple three years apart in age, husband is high earner and wife is middle income earner

CASE STUDY #21 Mike and Leslie: Married couple approximately eleven years apart in age, husband made slightly less than wife

CASE STUDY #22 Harold and Belinda: Married couple approximately four years apart in age, wife expected to die first, husband made moderately more than wife

CASE STUDY #23 Gordon and Cynthia: Married couple three years apart in age, husband is sole breadwinner

CASE STUDY #24 Tony & Jesse: Married couple approximately five years apart in age, husband has reached Full Retirement Age, wife expected to survive husband by seven years

CASE STUDY #25 Andrew and Leanne: Married couple approximately two years apart in age, husband has reached Full Retirement Age but has filed and suspended

CASE STUDY #1
Amanda

Overview: Amanda was married to both of her ex-husbands for more than ten years. Both have passed away and she is now eligible for Surviving Divorced Spouse benefits from either divorced spouse's record or her own retirement benefits. She can file for the survivor benefits at age sixty or later and she can apply on her own work record at any time starting with age sixty-two, one month. Her Full Retirement Age is sixty-six, eight months but her full benefit age for surviving divorced spousal benefits is age sixty-six, four months. She is currently single. She has options such as filing for either ex-spousal benefit at age sixty or her own after attainment of age sixty-two, one month. She can take the higher benefit in the beginning or a lower amount before full retirement (or benefit) age and the higher benefit at a later age. Even though she is eligible on her own work record, she will end up taking only surviving divorced spousal benefits as both are higher than her own. Her own benefit increased for full delayed retirement credits (26.67 percent) is not higher than either of the divorced spousal benefit.

Amanda	DOB: November 25, 1958 Full Retirement Age Benefit: **$1,548** at **66** years and **8** months Expected Death Age: **87.04**
Surviving Divorced Spouse #1	Full Retirement Age Benefit: **$2,186** at **66** years and **4** months
Surviving Divorced Spouse #2	Full Retirement Age Benefit: **$2,457** at **66** years and **4** months

	Strategy	**Amanda**
1	November 2018 Amanda files for 71.5% of Surviving Divorced Spouse #1 Benefit ($1,562) at age 60. March 2025 Amanda files for 100% of Surviving Divorced Spouse #2 ($2,457) at age 66, 4 months.	$737,876
2	November 2018 Amanda files for 71.5% of Surviving Divorced Spouse #2 Benefit ($1,756) at age 60. March 2025 Amanda files for 100% of Surviving Divorced Spouse #1 ($2,186) at age 66, 4 months.	$684,328
3	March 2025 Amanda files for 100% of Surviving Divorced Spouse #2 ($2,457) at age 66, 4 months.	$619,164

CASE STUDY #2
Bob and Lisa

Overview: Bob and Lisa are a married couple who have no ex-spouses or children eligible for benefits on their earnings record. Bob is a high wage earner and Lisa is an above average wage earner. They are close in age; however, Bob's Full Retirement Age is sixty-six and Lisa's Full Retirement Age is sixty-six, two months. They have nine reasonable options. The determination of the best option, however, belongs to Bob and Lisa. Factors to take into consideration are dependent on when they want benefits to begin.

Benefits before Full Retirement Age lowers the monthly benefit amount and this reduction is permanent. Earnings from employment or the net profit from self-employment will may influence benefits paid. The importance of survivor benefits (widow or widower benefits) will determine if benefits are taken at age sixty-two, age seventy or somewhere in between.

Bob and Lisa want to make sure they maximize benefits. To maximize benefits, one of them (normally the higher earner) will wait until age seventy to take benefits. This directly effects and maximizes the survivor benefit. Keeping in mind with all options they will want to coordinate spousal benefits to reduce the breakeven point for waiting until age seventy.

Bob	DOB: August 16, 1954 Full Retirement Age Benefit: **$2,540** at **66** years and **0** months Expected Death Age: **84.06**
Lisa	DOB: January 9, 1955 Full Retirement Age Benefit: **$1,777** at **66** years and **2** months Expected Death Age: **87**

	Strategy	**Bob**	**Lisa**	**Total**
1	August 2024 Bob files for worker benefits ($3,352) at age 70 for 132.00% of PIA (48 Months Delayed Retirement Credit). January 2025 Lisa files for worker benefits ($2,322) at age 70 for 130.67% of PIA (46 Months Delayed Retirement Credit). Widows benefit $3,352	$586,600	$512,060	$1,098,660
2	March 2021 Lisa files for worker benefits ($1,777) at age 66, 2 months for 100.00% of PIA. August 2024 Bob files for worker benefits ($3,352) at age 70 for 132.00% of PIA (48 Months Delayed Retirement Credit). Widows benefit $3,352	$586,600	$501,152	$1,087,752

	Strategy	Bob	Lisa	Total
3	January 2018 Lisa files for worker benefits ($1,406) at age 63 for 79.167% of PIA (38 Months Reduction). August 2024 Bob files for worker benefits ($3,352) at age 70 for 132.00% of PIA (48 Months Delayed Retirement Credit). Widows benefit $3,352	$583,248	$473,038	$1,056,286
4	August 2020 Bob files for worker benefits ($2,540) at age 66 for 100.00% of PIA. January 2025 Lisa files for worker benefits ($2,322) at age 70 for 130.67% of PIA (46 Months Delayed Retirement Credit). Widows benefit $2,540	$566,420	$483,640	$1,050,060
5	August 2020 Bob files for worker benefits ($2,540) at age 66 for 100.00% of PIA. March 2021 Lisa files for worker benefits ($1,777) at age 66, 2 months for 100.00% of PIA. Widows benefit $2,540	$566,420	$472,732	$1,039,152
6	January 2018 Lisa files for worker benefits ($1,406) at age 63 for 79.167% of PIA (38 Months Reduction). August 2020 Bob files for worker benefits ($2,540) at age 66 for 100.00% of PIA. Widows benefit $2,540	$563,880	$444,618	$1,008,498
7	January 2018 Bob files for worker benefits ($2,102) at age 63, 5 months for 82.778% of PIA (31 Months Reduction). January 2025 Lisa files for worker benefits ($2,322) at age 70 for 130.67% of PIA (46 Months Delayed Retirement Credit).	$531,806	$473,688	$1,005,494
8	January 2018 Bob files for worker benefits ($2,102) at age 63, 5 months for 82.778% of PIA (31 Months Reduction). March 2021 Lisa files for worker benefits ($1,777) at age 66, 2 months for 100.00% of PIA. Widows benefit $1,957	$531,806	$455,625	$987,431
9	January 2018 Bob files for worker benefits ($2,102) at age 63, 5 months for 82.778% of PIA (31 Months Reduction). January 2018 Lisa files for worker benefits ($1,406) at age 63 for 79.167% of PIA (38 Months Reduction). Widows benefit $2,102	$531,806	$429,288	$961,094

CASE STUDY #3
Brenda

Overview: Brenda was married to her ex-husband for more than ten years. Her ex-spouse has passed away and she is now eligible for Surviving Divorced Spouse benefits or her own retirement benefits. She can file for the survivor benefit at any time now since she is past age sixty. She is currently single although since she is past age sixty, even if she remarries she is still entitled to Surviving Divorced Spouse benefits. She has options such as filing for the ex-spousal benefit and taking her own at age seventy, filing on her own before her Full Retirement Age and staying on those benefits, etc.

Brenda	DOB: May 3, 1953 Full Retirement Age Benefit: **$2,630** at **66** years and **0** months Expected Death Age: **86.09**
Surviving Divorced Spouse	Full Benefit Age Benefit: **$1,888** at **66** years and **0** months

	Strategy	Brenda
1	January 2018 Brenda files for 93.67% (16 Months Reduction) of survivor benefits ($1,769) at age 64, 8 months. May 2023 Brenda files for worker benefits ($3,471) at age 70 for 132.00% of PIA (48 Months Delayed Retirement Credit).	$810,887
2	May 2019 Brenda files for 100.00% of Survivor Benefit ($1,888) at age 66. May 2023 Brenda files for worker benefits ($3,471) at age 70 for 132.00% of PIA (48 Months Delayed Retirement Credit).	$788,295
3	May 2019 Brenda files for worker benefits ($2,630) at age 66 for 100.00% of PIA	$654,870
4	January 2018 Brenda files for worker benefits ($2,396) at age 64, 8 months for 91.11% of PIA (16 Months Reduction).	$634,940

CASE STUDY #4
Bruce and Debbie

<u>*Overview*</u>: Bruce and Debbie are a married couple who have no ex-spouses they are eligible to draw benefits from since they are currently married. They have no children who are eligible for benefits on their earnings record. Bruce is a high earner and Debbie did not earn enough credits to be eligible for Social Security benefits from her own work record. Both have a Full Retirement Age of sixty-six, four months. Factors to take into consideration are dependent on when they want benefits to begin. Debbie cannot begin benefits until Bruce files an application for benefits. Neither can take advantage of the restricted application strategy.

If Bruce takes benefits before his Full Retirement Age, he will not only reduce his own benefit but also the widows benefit payable to Debbie if she survives him. The importance of that benefit will have a lot to do with the decision Bruce makes when determining his filing date for Social Security.

Bruce	DOB: November 3, 1956 Full Retirement Age Benefit: **$2,302** at **66** years and **4 months** Expected Death Age: **84.09**
Debbie	DOB: January 10, 1956 Full Retirement Age Benefit: **$0** at **66** years and **4 months** Expected Death Age: **87.01**

	Strategy	Bruce	Debbie	Total
1	March 2023 Bruce files for worker benefits ($2,302) at age 66, 4 months for 100.00% of PIA. March 2023 Debbie files for 100.00% of spousal benefits ($1,151) at age 67, 2 months. Widows benefit $2,302	$508,742	$295,807	$804,549
2	November 2026 Bruce files for worker benefits ($2,977) at age 70 for 129.33% of PIA (44 Months Delayed Retirement Credit). November 2026 Debbie files for 100.00% of spousal benefits ($1,151) at age 70, 10 months. Widows benefit $2,977	$526,929	$257,313	$784,242
3	December 2018 Bruce files for worker benefits ($1,697) at age 62, 1 month for 73.75% of PIA (51 Months Reduction). May 2022 Debbie files for 100.00% of spousal benefits ($1,151) at age 66, 4. Widows benefit $1,697	$461,584	$296,427	$758,011

	Strategy	Bruce	Debbie	Total
4	December 2018 Bruce files for worker benefits ($1,697) at age 62, 1 month for 73.75% of PIA (51 Months Reduction).	$461,584	$258,754	$720,338
	December 2018 Debbie files for 72.92% (41 Months Reduction) of spousal benefits ($839) at age 62, 11 months.			
	Widows benefit $1,697			

CASE STUDY #5
Carl

Overview: Carl's spouse died leaving him eligible for widower benefits. Carl has the option to file for benefits as a widower and switch to his own work record later (no later than age seventy) or file on his own work record before his Full Retirement Age and take the survivor benefit at his Full Retirement Age.

Carl	DOB: June 3, 1954 Full Retirement Age Benefit: **$2,244** at **66** years and **0** months Expected Death Age: **84.07**
Widower	Survivor Benefit: **$1,886**

	Strategy	Carl
1	January 2018 Carl files for 88.52% (29 Months Reduction) of survivor benefits ($1,669) at age 63, 7 months. June 2024 Carl files for worker benefits ($2,962) at age 70 for 132.00% of PIA (48 Months Delayed Retirement Credit).	$646,863
2	June 2020 Carl files for 100.00% of Survivor Benefit ($1,886) at age 66. June 2024 Carl files for worker benefits ($2,962) at age 70 for 132.00% of PIA (48 Months Delayed Retirement Credit).	$608,878
3	January 2018 Carl files for 88.52% (29 Months Reduction) of survivor benefits ($1,669) at age 63, 7 months. June 2020 Carl files for 100% of worker benefits ($2,244) at age 66.	$548,813
4	June 2020 Carl files for 100% of worker benefits ($2,244) at age 66.	$500,412
5	January 2018 Carl files for worker benefits ($1,882) at age 63, 7 months for 83.89% of PIA (29 Months Reduction). June 2020 Carl files for 100% of survivor benefits ($1,886) at age 66.	$475,156

CASE STUDY #6
George and Joan

Overview: George and Joan, a married couple four years apart in age. George will reach Full Retirement Age (FRA) at age sixty-six and Joan at age sixty-six and four months. The husband, George, had significantly more income than the wife, Joan. Joan is expected to survive George by approximately six and a half years.

George	DOB: November 14, 1952 Full Retirement Age Benefit: **$2,647** at **66** years and **0** months Expected Death Age: **84.05**
Joan	DOB: September 7, 1956 Full Retirement Age Benefit: **$724** at **66** years and **4** months Expected Death Age: **87.02**

	Strategy	George	Joan	Total
1	October 2018 Joan files for worker benefits ($533) at age 62, 1 month for 73.75% of PIA (51 Months Reduction). November 2018 George files a 'restricted application' at age 66 for 100% of spousal benefit ($362). November 2022 George files for worker benefits ($3,494) at age 70 for 132.00% of PIA (48 Months Delayed Retirement Credit). November 2022 Joan files for 98.611% (2 months reduction) of spousal benefits ($591) at age 66, 2 months. Survivor benefit $3,494	$621,838	$496,595	$1,118,433
2	January 2023 Joan files for worker benefits ($724) at age 66, 4 months for 100.00% of PIA. November 2022 George files for worker benefits ($3,494) at age 70 for 132.00% of PIA (48 Months Delayed Retirement Credit). January 2023 Joan files for 100.00% of spousal benefits ($599) at age 66, 4 months. Survivor benefit $3,494	$604,462	$502,259	$1,106,721

	Strategy	George	Joan	Total
3	November 2018 George files for worker benefits ($2,647) at age 66 for 100.00% of PIA.	$584,987	$435,346	$1,020,333
	January 2023 Joan files for worker benefits ($724) at age 66, 4 months for 100.00% of PIA.			
	January 2023 Joan files for 100.00% of spousal benefits ($599) at age 66, 4 months.			
	Survivor benefit $2,647			
4	January 2018 George files for worker benefits ($2,499) at age 65, 2 months for 94.444% of PIA (10 Months Reduction).	$577,269	$423,654	$1,000,923
	January 2023 Joan files for worker benefits ($724) at age 66, 4 months for 100.00% of PIA.			
	January 2023 Joan files for 100.00% of spousal benefits ($599) at age 66, 4 months.			
	Survivor benefit $2,499			
5	October 2018 Joan files for worker benefits ($533) at age 62, 1 month for 73.75% of PIA (51 Months Reduction).	$584,987	$418,933	$1,003,920
	November 2018 George files for worker benefits ($2,647) at age 66 for 100.00% of PIA.			
	November 2018 Joan files for 69.167% (50 Months Reduction) of spousal benefits ($414) at age 62, 2 months.			
	Survivor benefit $2,647			
6	January 2018 George files for worker benefits ($2,499) at age 65, 2 months for 94.444% of PIA (10 Months Reduction).	$577,269	$406,989	$984,258
	October 2018 Joan files for worker benefits ($533) at age 62, 1 month for 73.75% of PIA (51 Months Reduction).			
	October 2018 Joan files for 68.75% (51 Months Reduction) of spousal benefits ($411) at age 62, 1 month.			
	Survivor benefit $2,499			

CASE STUDY #7
Greg and Alice

Overview: Greg and Alice are a married couple. Greg is a high earner and Alice is a middle-income earner. There is over seven year's difference in their ages. He should consider waiting beyond his Full Retirement Age to take his benefit to increase the survivor benefit to Alice. Based on normal life expectancies, Alice will receive widow's benefits sooner and longer than a surviving spouse who was similar in age to their spouse. Alice will, however, have various filing options available to her. She should keep in mind that if she survives Greg before filing for any benefits she will need to reconsider her options to include widow's benefits.

Greg	DOB: August 29, 1955 Full Retirement Age Benefit: **$2,153** at **66** years and **2** months Expected Death Age: **84.08**
Alice	DOB: January 11, 1963 Full Retirement Age Benefit: **$1,449** at **67** years and **0** months Expected Death Age: **87.07**

	Strategy	Greg	Alice	Total
1	February 2025 Alice files for worker benefits ($1,020) at age 62, 1 month for 70.42% of PIA (59 Months Reduction). August 2025 Greg files for worker benefits ($2,813) at age 70 for 130.67% of PIA (46 Months Delayed Retirement Credit). Survivor benefit $2,813	$495,088	$534,452	$1,029,540
2	August 2025 Greg files for worker benefits ($2,813) at age 70 for 130.67% of PIA (46 Months Delayed Retirement Credit). January 2030 Alice files for worker benefits ($1,449) at age 67 for 100.00% of PIA. Survivor benefit $2,813	$495,088	$527,039	$1,022,127
3	August 2025 Greg files for worker benefits ($2,813) at age 70 for 130.67% of PIA (46 Months Delayed Retirement Credit). January 2033 Alice files for worker benefits ($1,796) at age 70 for 124.00% of PIA (36 Months Delayed Retirement Credit). Survivor benefit $2,813	$495,088	$505,064	$1,000,152

	Strategy	Greg	Alice	Total
4	October 2021 Greg files for worker benefits ($2,153) at age 66, 2 months for 100.00% of PIA. February 2025 Alice files for worker benefits ($1,020) at age 62, 1 month for 70.42% of PIA (59 Months Reduction). Survivor benefit $2,153	$477,966	$452,612	$930,578
5	October 2021 Greg files for worker benefits ($2,153) at age 66, 2 months for 100.00% of PIA. January 2030 Alice files for worker benefits ($1,449) at age 67 for 100.00% of PIA. Survivor benefit $2,153	$477,966	$445,199	$923,165
6	October 2021 Greg files for worker benefits ($2,153) at age 66, 2 months for 100.00% of PIA. January 2033 Alice files for worker benefits ($1,796) at age 70 for 124.00% of PIA (36 Months Delayed Retirement Credit). Survivor benefit $2,153	$477,966	$423,224	$901,190
7	January 2018 Greg files for worker benefits ($1,641) at age 62, 5 months for 76.25% of PIA (45 Months Reduction). February 2025 Alice files for worker benefits ($1,020) at age 62, 1 month for 70.42% of PIA (59 Months Reduction). Survivor benefit $1,641	$438,147	$389,124	$827,271
8	January 2018 Greg files for worker benefits ($1,641) at age 62, 5 months for 76.25% of PIA (45 Months Reduction). January 2033 Alice files for worker benefits ($1,796) at age 70 for 124.00% of PIA (36 Months Delayed Retirement Credit). Survivor benefit $1,796	$438,147	$378,956	$817,103
9	January 2018 Greg files for worker benefits ($1,641) at age 62, 5 months for 76.25% of PIA (45 Months Reduction). January 2030 Alice files for worker benefits ($1,449) at age 67 for 100.00% of PIA. Survivor benefit $1,641	$438,147	$381,711	$819,858

CASE STUDY #8
Jeff and Gary (Same-Sex Couple)

Overview: Jeff and Gary are a married couple. With the ruling on same sex marriages by the Supreme Court, Jeff and Gary were married and eligible for the same benefits as any other married couple. All of the same requirements must be met for eligibility before benefits can be paid. Restricted Application strategies are available for Jeff. Both have their own earnings and can file independently of each other; however, they can also coordinate spousal benefits to maximize the benefits paid to them over their lifetimes. To maximize benefits, Jeff will wait until age seventy to file for benefits which will increase his monthly benefit payment and maximize the surviving spousal benefit payable to Gary should he survive Jeff.

Jeff	DOB: February 9, 1952 Full Retirement Age Benefit: **$2,568** at **66** years and **0** months Expected Death Age: **84.05**
Gary	DOB: August 25, 1954 Full Retirement Age Benefit: **$1,146** at **66** years and **0** months Expected Death Age: **84.06**

	Strategy	**Jeff**	**Gary**	**Total**
1	January 2018 Gary (Spouse) files for worker benefits ($948) at age 63, 5 months for 82.78% of PIA (31 Months Reduction). February 2018 Gary files a 'restricted application' at age 66 for 100% of spousal benefit ($573) February 2022 Jeff (Primary) files for worker benefits ($3,389) at age 70 for 132.00% of PIA (48 Months Delayed Retirement Credit). February 2022 Gary (Spouse) files for 100.00% of spousal benefits ($138) at age 67, 6 months. Survivor benefit $3,389	$613,801	$339,389	$953,190
2	August 2020 Gary (Spouse) files for worker benefits ($1,146) at age 66 for 100.00% of PIA. August 2020 Jeff files a 'restricted application at age 68, 6 months for 100% of spousal benefit ($573). February 2022 Jeff (Primary) files for worker benefits ($3,389) at age 70 for 132.00% of PIA (48 Months Delayed Retirement Credit). February 2022 Gary (Spouse) files for 100.00% of spousal benefits ($138) at age 67, 6 months. Survivor benefit $3,389	$596,611	$347,819	$944,430

	Strategy	Jeff	Gary	Total
3	February 2022 Jeff (Primary) files for worker benefits ($3,389) at age 70 for 132.00% of PIA (48 Months Delayed Retirement Credit). August 2024 Gary (Spouse) files for worker benefits ($1,512) at age 70 for 132.00% of PIA (48 Months Delayed Retirement Credit). Survivor benefit $3,389	$586,297	$321,275	$907,572
4	February 2018 Jeff (Primary) files for worker benefits ($2,568) at age 66 for 100.00% of PIA. August 2020 Gary (Spouse) files for worker benefits ($1,146) at age 66 for 100.00% of PIA. August 2020 Gary (Spouse) files for 100.00% of spousal benefits ($138) at age 66. Survivor benefit $2,568	$567,528	$324,852	$892,380
5	January 2018 Jeff (Primary) files for worker benefits ($2,553) at age 65, 11 months for 99.44% of PIA (1 Months Reduction). August 2020 Gary (Spouse) files for worker benefits ($1,146) at age 66 for 100.00% of PIA. August 2020 Gary (Spouse) files for 100.00% of spousal benefits ($138) at age 66. Survivor benefit $2,553	$566,766	$324,387	$891,153
6	February 2018 Jeff (Primary) files for worker benefits ($2,568) at age 66 for 100.00% of PIA. August 2024 Gary (Spouse) files for worker benefits ($1,512) at age 70 for 132.00% of PIA (48 Months Delayed Retirement Credit). Survivor benefit $2,568	$567,528	$295,824	$863,352
7	January 2018 Jeff (Primary) files for worker benefits ($2,553) at age 65, 11 months for 99.44% of PIA (1 Months Reduction). August 2024 Gary (Spouse) files for worker benefits ($1,512) at age 70 for 132.00% of PIA (48 Months Delayed Retirement Credit). Survivor benefit $2,553	$566,766	$295,359	$862,125

	Strategy	Jeff	Gary	Total
8	January 2018 Gary (Spouse) files for worker benefits ($948) at age 63, 5 months for 82.78% of PIA (31 Months Reduction). February 2018 Jeff (Primary) files for worker benefits ($2,568) at age 66 for 100.00% of PIA. February 2018 Gary (Spouse) files for 79.17% (30 Months Reduction) of spousal benefits ($109) at age 63, 6 months. Survivor benefit $2,568	$567,528	$314,153	$881,681
9	January 2018 Jeff (Primary) files for worker benefits ($2,553) at age 65, 11 months for 99.44% of PIA (1 Months Reduction). January 2018 Gary (Spouse) files for worker benefits ($948) at age 63, 5 months for 82.78% of PIA (31 Months Reduction). January 2018 Gary (Spouse) files for 78.47% (31 Months Reduction) of spousal benefits ($108) at age 63, 5 months. Survivor benefit $2,553	$566,766	$313,575	$880,341

CASE STUDY #9
Jose and Kathy

Overview: Jose and Kathy are a divorced couple. They were married for over ten years and have been divorced for over two years. They are both are single. They each have their own earnings and are eligible for a benefit from their own work record. Both are past their Full Retirement Age and have filing options independent of the other. They can elect benefits six months retroactive from when they determined their options. Kathy is eligible for benefits from Jose's record as a divorced spouse regardless of the filing status of Jose.

Kathy	DOB: July 16, 1951 Full Retirement Age Benefit: **$1,002** at **66** years and **0** months Expected Death Age: **86.08**
Jose	DOB: April 11, 1951 Full Retirement Age Benefit: **$2,270** at **66** years and **0** months Expected Death Age: **84.05**

	Strategy	<u>Kathy</u>
1	July 2017 Kathy files a 'restricted application' for 100.00% of ex-spousal benefits ($1,135) at age 66. July 2021 Kathy files for worker benefits ($1,322) at age 70 for 132.00% of PIA (48 Months Delayed Retirement Credit). Widows benefit $2,270	$347,320
2	July 2017 Kathy files for worker benefits ($1,002) at age 66 for 100.00% of PIA. July 2021 Kathy files for 100.00% of ex-spousal benefits ($133) at age 66. Widows benefit $2,270	$315,530
3	July 2021 Kathy files for worker benefits ($1,322) at age 70 for 132.00% of PIA (48 Months Delayed Retirement Credit). Widows benefit $2,270	$292,840

CASE STUDY #10
Larry and Judy

Overview: Larry is a high earner. Judy worked most of her career in employment that was not covered by Social Security and is eligible for a pension from that work. She also has some work under Social Security covered employment and has earned her 40 credits. Judy's own benefit based from her own Social Security covered work will be reduced due to the Windfall Elimination Provision (WEP). Before the WEP offset, Judy's Social Security benefit would be $571 per month at her Full Retirement Age. WEP reduces this benefit to $254. Her non-covered pension also affects her spousal and potential survivor benefit. These benefits are reduced due to the Government Pension Offset (GPO) by 2/3rds of the amount of her non-covered pension. Her non-covered pension is $1,476 and therefore her spousal and potential survivor benefits are reduced $984.

Larry	DOB: December 23, 1952 Full Retirement Age Benefit: **$2,589** at **66** years and **0** months Expected Death Age: **84.05**
Judy	DOB: February 25, 1955 Full Retirement Age Benefit: **$254** at **66** years and **2** months Expected Death Age: **87**

	Strategy	Larry	Judy	Total
1	January 2018 Judy (Spouse) files for worker benefits ($200) at age 62, 11 months for 78.75% of PIA (39 Months Reduction). January 2019 Larry files a 'restricted application' at age 66 for 100% of spousal benefit ($127). December 2022 Larry (Primary) files for worker benefits ($3,417) at age 70 for 132.00% of PIA (48 Months Delayed Retirement Credit). December 2022 Judy (Spouse) files for 100.00% of spousal benefits ($56) at age 67, 10 months. Widows benefit $2,433	$597,237	$194,769	$792,006
2	April 2021 Judy (Spouse) files for worker benefits ($254) at age 66, 2 months for 100.00% of PIA. February 2021 Larry files a 'restricted application' at age 68, 4 months for 100% of spousal benefit ($127). December 2022 Larry (Primary) files for worker benefits ($3,417) at age 70 for 132.00% of PIA (48 Months Delayed Retirement Credit). December 2022 Judy (Spouse) files for 100.00% of spousal benefits ($56) at age 67, 10 months. Widows benefit $2,433	$593,681	$197,391	$791,072

	Strategy	Larry	Judy	Total
3	December 2018 Larry (Primary) files for worker benefits ($2,589) at age 66 for 100.00% of PIA. April 2021 Judy (Spouse) files for worker benefits ($254) at age 66, 2 months for 100.00% of PIA. April 2021 Judy (Spouse) files for 100.00% of spousal benefits ($56) at age 66, 2 months. Widows benefit $1,605	$572,169	$151,315	$723,484
4	January 2018 Larry (Primary) files for worker benefits ($2,430) at age 65, 1 months for 93.89% of PIA (11 Months Reduction). April 2021 Judy (Spouse) files for worker benefits ($254) at age 66, 2 months for 100.00% of PIA. April 2021 Judy (Spouse) files for 100.00% of spousal benefits ($56) at age 66, 2 months. Widows benefit $1,446	$563,760	$142,252	$706,012
5	January 2018 Judy (Spouse) files for worker benefits ($200) at age 62, 11 months for 78.75% of PIA (39 Months Reduction). December 2018 Larry (Primary) files for worker benefits ($2,589) at age 66 for 100.00% of PIA. Widows benefit $1,605	$572,169	$137,885	$710,054
6	January 2018 Larry (Primary) files for worker benefits ($2,430) at age 65, 1 months for 93.89% of PIA (11 Months Reduction). January 2018 Judy (Spouse) files for worker benefits ($202) at age 62, 11 months for 78.75% of PIA (39 Months Reduction). Widows benefit $1,446	$563,760	$129,286	$693,046

CASE STUDY #11
Mike and Rita

Overview: Mike and Rita, a married couple where the wife is a little more than one year older than the husband. Both Mike and Rita reach Full Retirement Age (FRA) at sixty-six years of age. The husband, Mike, had moderately more income than the wife, Rita. Despite being a few years older, Rita is expected to survive Mike by approximately one year.

Mike	DOB: March 10, 1954 Full Retirement Age Benefit: **$2,482** at **66** years and **0** months Expected Death Age: **84.06**
Rita	DOB: December 25, 1952 Full Retirement Age Benefit: **$1,788** at **66** years and **0** months Expected Death Age: **86.09**

	Strategy	**Mike**	**Rita**	**Total**
1	March 2020 Mike files for worker benefits ($2,482) at age 66 for 100.00% of PIA. March 2020 Rita files a 'restricted application at age 67, 3 months for 100% of spousal benefit ($1,241). December 2022 Rita files for worker benefits ($2,360) at age 70 for 132.00% of PIA (48 Months Delayed Retirement Credit). Survivor benefit $2,482	$551,004	$516,777	$1,067,781
2	January 2018 Mike files for worker benefits ($2,123) at age 63, 10 months for 85.56% of PIA (26 Months Reduction). December 2018 Rita files a 'restricted application at age 66 for 100% of spousal benefit ($1,241). December 2022 Rita files for worker benefits ($2,360) at age 70 for 132.00% of PIA (48 Months Delayed Retirement Credit). Survivor benefit $2,360	$526,504	$533,928	$1,060,432
3	December 2022 Rita files for worker benefits ($2,360) at age 70 for 132.00% of PIA (48 Months Delayed Retirement Credit). March 2024 Mike files for worker benefits ($3,276) at age 70 for 132.00% of PIA (48 Months Delayed Retirement Credit). Survivor benefit $3,276	$570,024	$485,352	$1,055,376

	Strategy	Mike	Rita	Total
4	December 2018 Rita files for worker benefits ($1,788) at age 66 for 100.00% of PIA. March 2024 Mike files for worker benefits ($3,276) at age 70 for 132.00% of PIA (48 Months Delayed Retirement Credit). Survivor benefit $3,276	$570,024	$463,068	$1,033,092
5	January 2018 Rita files for worker benefits ($1,678) at age 65, 1 month for 93.889% of PIA (11 Months Reduction). March 2023 Mike files for worker benefits ($3,276) at age 70 for 132.00% of PIA (48 Months Delayed Retirement Credit). Survivor benefit $3,276	$570,024	$455,456	$1,025,480
6	December 2018 Rita files for worker benefits ($1,788) at age 66 for 100.00% of PIA. March 2020 Mike files for worker benefits ($2,482) at age 66 for 100.00% of PIA. Survivor benefit $2,482	$551,004	$453,540	$1,004,544
7	January 2018 Rita files for worker benefits ($1,678) at age 65, 1 month for 93.889% of PIA (11 Months Reduction). March 2020 Mike files for worker benefits ($2,482) at age 66 for 100.00% of PIA. Survivor benefit $2,482	$551,004	$445,928	$996,932
8	January 2018 Mike files for worker benefits ($2,123) at age 63, 10 months for 85.56% of PIA (26 Months Reduction). December 2018 Rita files for worker benefits ($1,788) at age 66 for 100.00% of PIA. Survivor benefit $2,123	$526,504	$449,232	$975,736
9	January 2018 Mike files for worker benefits ($2,123) at age 63, 10 months for 85.56% of PIA (26 Months Reduction). January 2018 Rita files for worker benefits ($1,678) at age 65, 1 months for 93.89% of PIA (11 Months Reduction).	$526,504	$441,620	$968,124

CASE STUDY #12
Roger and Susan

Overview: Roger is Full Retirement Age. Susan is younger and will not reach age sixty-two until 2023. Roger and Susan have two children. One is almost age eighteen and the other is age sixteen. Roger needs to file for retirement benefits, so the children can receive benefits until they reach age eighteen or if still in high school, until age nineteen or they graduate whichever comes first. If Roger does nothing, the children lose all benefits and those benefits are never recovered.

Roger	DOB: August 28, 1952 Full Retirement Age Benefit: **$2,278** at **66** years and **0** months Expected Death Age: **84.05**
Susan	DOB: June 21, 1961 Full Retirement Age Benefit: **$1,209** at **67** years and **0** months Expected Death Age: **87.06**

	Strategy	Roger	Susan	Sophia Allison	Total
1	August 2022 Roger files for worker benefits ($3,006) at age 70 for 132.00% of PIA (48 Months Delayed Retirement Credit). July 2023 Susan files for worker benefits ($851) at age 62, 1 month for 70.417% of PIA. Widows benefit $3,006	$390,780	$612,632	$0 $0	$1,003,412
2	August 2022 Roger files for worker benefits ($3,006) at age 70 for 132.00% of PIA (48 Months Delayed Retirement Credit). June 2028 Susan files for worker benefits ($1,209) at age 67 for 100.00% of PIA. Widows benefit $3,006	$390,780	$597,513	$0 $0	$988,293
3	August 2022 Roger files for worker benefits ($3,006) at age 70 for 132.00% of PIA (48 Months Delayed Retirement Credit). June 2031 Susan files for worker benefits ($1,499) at age 70 for 124.00% of PIA. Widows benefit $3,006	$390,780	$566,459	$0 $0	$957,239

	Strategy	Roger	Susan	Sophia Allison	Total
4	August 2018 Roger files for worker benefits ($2,278) at age 66 for 100.00% of PIA.	296,140	$491,056	$29,048 $1,712	$817,956
	August 2018 Allison files for child's benefits ($856). Benefits end October 2018 at age 18.				
	August 2017 Sophia files for child's benefits ($856). Benefits increase ($1,139) October 2018. Benefits end July 2020 at age 18.				
	July 2023 Susan files for worker benefits ($851) at age 62, 1 month for 70.42% of PIA (59 Months Reduction).				
	Widows benefit $2,278				
5	August 2018 Roger files for worker benefits ($2,278) at age 66 for 100.00% of PIA.	$296,140	$475,937	$29,048 $1,712	$802,837
	August 2018 Allison files for child's benefits ($854). Benefits end October 2018 at age 18.				
	August 2018 Sophia files for child's benefits ($854). Benefits increase ($1,139) October 2018. Benefits end July 2020 at age 18.				
	June 2028 Susan files for worker benefits ($1,209) at age 67 for 100.00% of PIA.				
	Widows benefit $2,278				
6	August 2018 Roger files for worker benefits ($2,278) at age 66 for 100.00% of PIA.	$296,140	$444,883	$29,048 $1,712	$771,783
	August 2018 Allison files for child's benefits ($854). Benefits end October 2018 at age 18.				
	August 2018 Sophia files for child's benefits ($854). Benefits increase ($1,139) October 2018. Benefits end July 2020 at age 18.				
	June 2031 Susan files for worker benefits ($1,499) at age 70 for 124.00% of PIA.				
	Widows benefit $2,278				

CASE STUDY #13
Sandy (Widow)

Overview: Sandy is a widow approaching Full Retirement Age and must decide if she will take benefits from her own work record prior to Full Retirement Age and widows at Full Retirement Age or take widows benefits prior to Full Retirement Age. Benefits on her own work record will not exceed the widow's benefit even if she waits until age seventy.

Sandy	DOB: December 31, 1952 Full Retirement Age Benefit: $1,425 at 66 years and 0 months Expected Death Age: 86.09
	SS Survivor Benefit in 2018: $2,599 at 66 years and 0 Months

	Strategy	Lifetime Benefit
1	January 2018 Sandy files for worker benefits ($1,337) at age 65, 1 month for 93.889% of PIA (11 Months Reduction). December 2018 Sandy files for 100.00% of Survivor Benefit at age 66 ($2,599).	$661,858
2	December 2018 Sandy files for 100% of survivor benefits ($2,599) at age 66.	$647,151
3	January 2018 Sandy files for 95.6% (11 Months Reduction) of survivor benefits ($2,484) at age 65, 1 month.	$645,840

CASE STUDY #14

Virginia (Single Woman)

Overview: Virginia is a single individual. She is not eligible for benefits from any other individual's work record. Her options are limited to filing for benefits on her own work record at some point between ages sixty-two, one month and seventy. If she delays benefits past her Full Retirement Age she should claim and suspend to protect her right to go back and request those benefits should she determine she needs or wants the benefits.

Virginia	DOB: September 28, 1956 Full Retirement Age Benefit: **$2,024** at **66** years and **4** months Expected Death Age: **87.02**

	Strategy	<u>Virginia</u>
1	September 2026 Virginia files for worker benefits ($2,617) at age 70 for 129.33% of PIA (44 Months Delayed Retirement Credit).	$539,102
2	January 2023 Virginia files for worker benefits ($2,024) at age 66, 4 months for 100.00% of PIA.	$506,000
3	October 2018 Virginia files for worker benefits ($1,492) at age 62, 1 months for 73.75% of PIA (51 Months Reduction).	$449,092

CASE STUDY #15
Shaun and JoAnn

Overview: Married couple about four months apart in age. Shaun is a high earner. JoAnn has work under both Social Security covered earnings and as a public employee covered under the Public Employees Retirement System. This pension from work not covered by Social Security will not only reduce her own Social Security benefit but also any spousal or survivor benefit she may be entitled to receive. Since her non-covered pension is low, the effect is lessened. The restricted application strategy is still available for each.

Shaun	DOB: April 8, 1954 Full Retirement Age Benefit: **$2,510** at **66** years and **0** months Expected Death Age: **84.06**
JoAnn	DOB: December 30, 1953 Full Retirement Age Benefit: **$790** at **66** years and **0** months Expected Death Age: **86.09**

	Strategy	Shaun	JoAnn	Total
1	December 2019 JoAnn files for worker benefits ($790) at age 66 for 100.00% of PIA. April 2020 Shaun files a 'restricted application' at age 66 for 100% of spousal benefit ($395). April 2024 Shaun files for worker benefits ($3,313) at age 70 for 132.00% of PIA (48 Months Delayed Retirement Credit). April 2024 JoAnn files for 100.00% of spousal benefits ($172) at age 70, 4 months. Survivor benefit $3,020	$595,422	$247,928	$873,350
2	January 2018 JoAnn files for worker benefits ($689) at age 64, 1 month for 87.222% of PIA (23 Months Reduction). April 2020 Shaun files a 'restricted application' at age 66 for 100% of spousal benefit ($395). April 2024 Shaun files for worker benefits ($3,313) at age 70 for 132.00% of PIA (48 Months Delayed Retirement Credit). April 2024 JoAnn files for 100.00% of spousal benefits ($172) at age 70, 4 months. Survivor benefit $3,020	$595,422	$241,021	$836,443

	Strategy	Shaun	JoAnn	Total
3	April 2020 Shaun files for worker benefits ($2,510) at age 66 for 100.00% of PIA. April 2020 JoAnn files a 'restricted application' at age 66, 4 months for 100% of spousal benefit ($962). December 2023 JoAnn files for worker benefits ($1,042) at age 70 for 132.00% of PIA (48 Months Delayed Retirement Credit). Survivor benefit $2,217	$557,220	$278,795	$836,015
4	December 2023 JoAnn files for worker benefits ($1,042) at age 70 for 132.00% of PIA (48 Months Delayed Retirement Credit). December 2023 Shaun files a 'restricted application' at age 69, 8 months for 100% of spousal benefit ($395). April 2024 Shaun files for worker benefits ($3,313) at age 70 for 132.00% of PIA (48 Months Delayed Retirement Credit). Survivor benefit $3,020	$578,042	$254,936	$832,978
5	December 2019 JoAnn files for worker benefits ($790) at age 66 for 100.00% of PIA. April 2020 Shaun files for worker benefits ($2,510) at age 66 for 100.00% of PIA. April 2020 JoAnn files for 100.00% of spousal benefits ($172) at age 66, 4 months. Survivor benefit $2,217	$557,220	$267,715	$824,935
6	January 2018 JoAnn files for worker benefits ($689) at age 64, 1 month for 87.222% of PIA (23 Months Reduction). April 2020 Shaun files for worker benefits ($2,510) at age 66 for 100.00% of PIA. April 2020 JoAnn files for 100.00% of spousal benefits ($172) at age 66, 4 months. Survivor benefit $2,217	$557,220	$260,736	$817,956
7	January 2018 Shaun files for worker benefits ($2,133) at age 63, 9 months for 85.00% of PIA (27 Months Reduction). December 2019 JoAnn files a 'restricted application' at age 66 for 100% of spousal benefit ($962). December 2023 JoAnn files for worker benefits ($1,042) at age 70 for 132.00% of PIA (48 Months Delayed Retirement Credit). Survivor benefit $1,840	$531,117	$304,588	$835,705

	Strategy	Shaun	JoAnn	Total
8	January 2018 Shaun files for worker benefits ($2,133) at age 63, 9 months for 85.00% of PIA (27 Months Reduction). December 2019 JoAnn files for worker benefits ($790) at age 66 for 100.00% of PIA. December 2019 JoAnn files for 100.00% of spousal benefits ($172) at age 66. Survivor benefit $1,840	$531,117	$259,732	$790,849
9	January 2018 Shaun files for worker benefits ($2,133) at age 63, 9 months for 85.00% of PIA (27 Months Reduction). January 2018 JoAnn files for worker benefits ($689) at age 64, 1 month for 87.222% of PIA (23 Months Reduction). January 2018 JoAnn files for 84.03% (23 Months Reduction) of spousal benefits ($97) at age 64, 1 months. Survivor benefit $1,840	$531,117	$238,034	$769,151

CASE STUDY #16
Rick and Julie

Overview: Rick and Julie, married couple two years apart in age. Both will reach Full Retirement Age at age sixty-six. The husband, Rick was a higher earner. The wife, Julie was a middle-income earner. Both are eligible for the restricted application to maximize their monthly benefit. Julie is expected to survive Rick by five years.

Rick	DOB: December 28, 1951 Full Retirement Age Benefit: **$2,331** at **66** years and **0** months Expected Death Age: **84.04**
Julie	DOB: September 26, 1953 Full Retirement Age Benefit: **$1,098** at **66** years and **0** months Expected Death Age: **86.09**

	Strategy	Rick	Julie	Total
1	January 2018 Julie files for worker benefits ($969) at age 64, 4 months for 88.89% of PIA (20 Months Reduction). January 2018 Rick files a 'restricted application' at age 66, 1 month for 100% of spousal benefit ($549). December 2021 Rick files for worker benefits ($3,076) at age 70 for 132.00% of PIA (48 Months Delayed Retirement Credit). December 2021 Julie files for 100.00% of spousal benefits ($67) at age 68, 3 months. Survivor benefit $3,076	$554,875	$379,068	$933,943
2	September 2019 Julie files for worker benefits ($1,098) at age 66 for 100.00% of PIA. September 2019 Rick files a 'restricted application' at age 67, 9 months for 100% of spousal benefit ($549). December 2021 Rick files for worker benefits ($3,076) at age 70 for 132.00% of PIA (48 Months Delayed Retirement Credit). December 2021 Julie files for 100.00% of spousal benefits ($67) at age 68, 3 months. Survivor benefit $3,076	$543,895	$383,826	$927,721

	Strategy	Rick	Julie	Total
3	December 2017 Rick files for worker benefits ($2,331) at age 66 for 100.00% of PIA. September 2019 Julie files a 'restricted application' at age 66 for 100% of spousal benefit ($1,165). September 2023 Julie files for worker benefits ($1,449) at age 70 for 132.00% of PIA (48 Months Delayed Retirement Credit). Survivor benefit $2,331	$512,820	$401,386	$914,206
4	December 2021 Rick files for worker benefits ($3,076) at age 70 for 132.00% of PIA (48 Months Delayed Retirement Credit). September 2023 Julie files for worker benefits ($1,449) at age 70 for 132.00% of PIA (48 Months Delayed Retirement Credit). Survivor benefit $3,076	$529,072	$372,599	$901,671
5	December 2017 Rick files for worker benefits ($2,331) at age 66 for 100.00% of PIA. September 2019 Julie files for worker benefits ($1,098) at age 66 for 100.00% of PIA. September 2019 Julie files for 100.00% of spousal benefits ($67) at age 66. Survivor benefit $2,331	$512,820	$348,385	$861,205
6	December 2017 Rick files for worker benefits ($2,331) at age 66 for 100.00% of PIA. January 2018 Julie files for worker benefits ($976) at age 64, 4 months for 88.89% of PIA (20 Months Reduction). January 2018 Julie files for 86.11% (20 Months Reduction) of spousal benefits ($57) at age 64, 4 months. Survivor benefit $2,331	$512,820	$342,777	$855,597

CASE STUDY #17
Paul and Kirsten

Overview: Paul and Kirsten, a married couple four years apart in age. Paul will reach Full Retirement Age at age sixty-six and Kirsten will reach Full Retirement Age at age sixty-six and two months. The husband, Paul, had significantly more income than the wife, Kirsten. Kirsten is expected to survive Paul by approximately six plus years.

Paul	DOB: December 4, 1952 Full Retirement Age Benefit: **$2,418** at **66** years and **0** months Expected Death Age: **84.05**
Kirsten	DOB: October 9, 1956 Full Retirement Age Benefit: **$1,482** at **66** years and **4** months Expected Death Age: **87.02**

	Strategy	**Paul**	**Kirsten**	**Total**
1	November 2018 Kirsten files for worker benefits ($1,092) at age 62, 1 months for 73.75% of PIA (51 Months Reduction). December 2018 Paul files a 'restricted application' at age 66 for 100% of spousal benefit ($741). December 2022 Paul files for worker benefits ($3,191) at age 70 for 132.00% of PIA (48 Months Delayed Retirement Credit). Survivor benefit $3,191	$587,611	$494,513	$1,082,124
2	December 2022 Paul files for worker benefits ($3,191) at age 70 for 132.00% of PIA (48 Months Delayed Retirement Credit). February 2023 Kirsten files for worker benefits ($1,482) at age 66, 4 months for 100.00% of PIA. Survivor benefit $3,191	$552,043	$505,511	$1,057,554
3	December 2022 Paul files for worker benefits ($3,191) at age 70 for 132.00% of PIA (48 Months Delayed Retirement Credit). October 2026 Kirsten files for worker benefits ($1,916) at age 70 for 129.33% of PIA (44 Months Delayed Retirement Credit). Survivor benefit $3,191	$552,043	$495,421	$1,047,464

	Strategy	Paul	Kirsten	Total
4	January 2018 Paul files for worker benefits ($2,270) at age 65, 1 months for 93.89% of PIA (11 Months Reduction). February 2023 Kirsten files for worker benefits ($1,482) at age 66, 4 months for 100.00% of PIA. Survivor benefit $2,270	$526,640	$432,752	$959,392
5	January 2018 Paul files for worker benefits ($2,270) at age 65, 1 months for 93.89% of PIA (11 Months Reduction). October 2026 Kirsten files for worker benefits ($1,916) at age 70 for 129.33% of PIA (44 Months Delayed Retirement Credit). Survivor benefit $2,270	$526,640	$422,662	$949,302
6	January 2018 Paul files for worker benefits ($2,270) at age 65, 1 months for 93.89% of PIA (11 Months Reduction). November 2018 Kirsten files for worker benefits ($1,092) at age 62, 1 months for 73.75% of PIA (51 Months Reduction). Survivor benefit $2,270	$526,640	$421,754	$948,394

CASE STUDY #18
Mark and Cindy

Overview: Mark and Cindy, a married couple less than a year apart in age. The couple both born at the latter end of the Baby Boom, will reach Full Retirement Age (FRA) later than those born a decade earlier. Mark will achieve FRA at age sixty-six and eight months, while Cindy will reach FRA at sixty-six and ten months. The husband, Mark, had significantly more income than the wife, Cindy. Cindy is expected to survive Mark by approximately three years.

Mark	DOB: September 4, 1958 Full Retirement Age Benefit: **$2,543** at **66** years and **8** months Expected Death Age: **85.01**
Cindy	DOB: July 18, 1959 Full Retirement Age Benefit: **$1,292** at **66** years and **10** months Expected Death Age: **87.05**

	Strategy	Mark	Cindy	Total
1	September 2028 Mark files for worker benefits ($3,221) at age 70 for 126.67% of PIA (40 Months Delayed Retirement Credit). July 2029 Cindy files for worker benefits ($1,619) at age 70 for 125.33% of PIA (38 Months Delayed Retirement Credit). Survivor benefit $3,221	$583,001	$399,247	$982,248
2	September 2028 Mark files for worker benefits ($3,221) at age 70 for 126.67% of PIA (40 Months Delayed Retirement Credit). July 2029 Cindy files for worker benefits ($1,619) at age 70 for 125.33% of PIA (38 Months Delayed Retirement Credit). Survivor benefit $3,221	$583,001	$392,426	$975,427
3	August 2021 Cindy files for worker benefits ($920) at age 62, 1 month for 71.25% of PIA (57 Months Reduction). September 2028 Mark files for worker benefits ($3,221) at age 70 for 126.67% of PIA (40 Months Delayed Retirement Credit). Survivor benefit $3,221	$583,001	$367,118	$950,119

	Strategy	Mark	Cindy	Total
4	May 2025 Mark files for worker benefits ($2,543) at age 66, 8 months for 100.00% of PIA.	$562,003	$373,483	$935,486
	July 2029 Cindy files for worker benefits ($1,619) at age 70 for 125.33% of PIA (38 Months Delayed Retirement Credit).			
	Survivor benefit $2,543			
5	May 2025 Mark files for worker benefits ($2,543) at age 66, 8 months for 100.00% of PIA.	$562,003	$366,662	$928,665
	May 2026 Cindy files for worker benefits ($1,292) at age 66, 10 months for 100.00% of PIA.			
	Survivor benefit $2,543			
6	August 2021 Cindy files for worker benefits ($920) at age 62, 1 month for 71.25% of PIA (57 Months Reduction).	$562,003	$341,354	$903,357
	May 2025 Mark files for worker benefits ($2,543) at age 66, 8 months for 100.00% of PIA.			
	Survivor benefit $2,543			
7	October 2020 Mark files for worker benefits ($1,832) at age 62, 1 month for 72.08% of PIA (55 Months Reduction).	$505,632	$346,465	$852,097
	July 2029 Cindy files for worker benefits ($1,619) at age 70 for 125.33% of PIA (38 Months Delayed Retirement Credit).			
	Survivor benefit $1,832			
8	October 2020 Mark files for worker benefits ($1,832) at age 62, 1 month for 72.08% of PIA (55 Months Reduction).	$505,632	$339,644	$845,276
	May 2026 Cindy files for worker benefits ($1,292) at age 66, 10 months for 100.00% of PIA.			
	Survivor benefit $1,832			
9	October 2020 Mark files for worker benefits ($1,832) at age 62, 1 month for 72.08% of PIA (55 Months Reduction).	$505,632	$314,336	$819,968
	August 2021 Cindy files for worker benefits ($920) at age 62, 1 month for 71.25% of PIA (57 Months Reduction).			
	Survivor benefit $1,832			

CASE STUDY #19
Justin and Georgia

Overview: Justin and Georgia, a married couple three years apart in age. Justin will reach Full Retirement Age at age sixty-six and Georgia at age sixty-six and two months. The husband, Justin was a high earner. The wife, Georgia, was also a high earner. Justin can take advantage of the restricted application at his Full Retirement Age. Georgia does not have the restricted application strategy available. Georgia is expected to survive Justin by six years.

Justin	DOB: November 1, 1952 Full Retirement Age Benefit: **$2,625** at **66** years and **0** months Expected Death Age: **84.05**
Georgia	DOB: December 9, 1955 Full Retirement Age Benefit: **$2,688** at **66** years and **2** months Expected Death Age: **87.01**

	Strategy	Justin	Georgia	Total
1	January 2018 Georgia files for worker benefits ($2,004) at age 62, 1 months for 74.583% of PIA (49 Months Reduction). October 2018 Justin files a 'restricted application' at age 66 for 100% of spousal benefit ($1,344) October 2022 Justin files for worker benefits ($3,465) at age 70 months for 132.00% of PIA (48 Months Delayed Retirement Credit). Survivor benefit $3,465	$666,078	$702,009	$1,368,087
2	February 2022 Georgia files for worker benefits ($2,688) at age 66, 2 months for 100.00% of PIA. February 2022 Justin files a 'restricted application' at age 69, 4 months for 100% of spousal benefit ($1,344) October 2022 Justin files for worker benefits ($3,465) at age 70 months for 132.00% of PIA (48 Months Delayed Retirement Credit). Survivor benefit $3,465	$613,662	$728,301	$1,341,963
3	February 2022 Georgia files for worker benefits ($2,688) at age 66, 2 months for 100.00% of PIA. October 2021 Justin files for worker benefits ($3,465) at age 70 for 132.00% of PIA (48 Months Delayed Retirement Credit). Survivor benefit $3,465	$602,910	$728,301	$1,331,211

	Strategy	Justin	Georgia	Total
4	October 2021 Justin files for worker benefits ($3,465) at age 70 for 132.00% of PIA (48 Months Delayed Retirement Credit). December 2025 Georgia files for worker benefits ($3,512) at age 70 for 130.67% of PIA (46 Months Delayed Retirement Credit). Survivor benefit $3,512	$602,910	$719,960	$1,322,870
5	October 2018 Justin files for worker benefits ($2,625) at age 66 for 100.00% of PIA. December 2025 Georgia files for worker benefits ($3,512) at age 70 for 130.67% of PIA (46 Months Delayed Retirement Credit). Survivor benefit $3,512	$582,750	$719,960	$1,302,710
6	January 2018 Justin files for worker benefits ($2,493) at age 65, 3 months for 95.00% of PIA (9 Months Reduction). December 2025 Georgia files for worker benefits ($3,512) at age 70 for 130.67% of PIA (46 Months Delayed Retirement Credit). Survivor benefit $3,512	$575,883	$719,960	$1,295,843
7	October 2018 Justin files for worker benefits ($2,625) at age 66 for 100.00% of PIA. February 2022 Georgia files for worker benefits ($2,688) at age 66, 2 months for 100.00% of PIA. Survivor benefit $2,688	$582,750	$674,688	$1,257,438
8	January 2018 Justin files for worker benefits ($2,493) at age 65, 3 months for 95.00% of PIA (9 Months Reduction). February 2022 Georgia files for worker benefits ($2,688) at age 66, 2 months for 100.00% of PIA. Survivor benefit $2,688	$575,883	$674,688	$1,250,571
9	January 2018 Georgia files for worker benefits ($2,004) at age 62, 1 months for 74.583% of PIA (49 Months Reduction). October 2018 Justin files for worker benefits ($2,625) at age 66 for 100.00% of PIA. Survivor benefit $2,625	$582,750	$644,049	$1,226,799

	Strategy	Justin	Georgia	Total
10	January 2018 Justin files for worker benefits ($2,493) at age 65, 3 months for 95.00% of PIA (9 Months Reduction). January 2018 Georgia files for worker benefits ($2,004) at age 62, 1 months for 74.583% of PIA (49 Months Reduction). Survivor benefit $2,493	$575,883	$634,941	$1,210,824

CASE STUDY #20
Don and MaryAnn

Overview: Don and MaryAnn, are a married couple two years apart in age. Don will reach Full Retirement Age (FRA) at age sixty-six. MaryAnn will reach FRA at age sixty-six, two months. The husband, Don, was a high wage earner. The wife, MaryAnn was a middle-income earner. MaryAnn is expected to survive Don by five years.

Don	DOB: March 21, 1953 Full Retirement Age Benefit: **$2,647** at **66** years and **0** months Expected Death Age: **84.06**
MaryAnn	DOB: January 15, 1955 Full Retirement Age Benefit: **$1,076** at **66** years and **2** months Expected Death Age: **87.01**

	Strategy	Don	MaryAnn	Total
1	January 2018 Mary Ann files for worker benefits ($851) at age 63 for 79.17% of PIA (38 Months Reduction). March 2019 Don files a 'restricted application' at age 66 for 100% of spousal benefit ($538). March 2023 Don files for worker benefits ($3,494) at age 70 for 132.00% of PIA (48 Months Delayed Retirement Credit). March 2023 Mary Ann files for 100.00% of spousal benefits ($247) at age 68, 2 months. Survivor benefit $3,494	$542,936	$389,966	$932,902
2	March 2021 Mary Ann files for worker benefits ($1,076) at age 66, 2 months for 100.00% of PIA. March 2021 Don files a 'restricted application' at age 68 for 100% of spousal benefit ($538) March 2023 Don files for worker benefits ($3,494) at age 70 for 132.00% of PIA (48 Months Delayed Retirement Credit). March 2023 Mary Ann files for 100.00% of spousal benefits ($247) at age 68, 2 months. Survivor benefit $3,494	$530,024	$396,328	$926,352

	Strategy	Don	MaryAnn	Total
3	March 2019 Don files for worker benefits ($2,647) at age 66 for 100.00% of PIA. March 2021 Mary Ann files for worker benefits ($1,076) at age 66, 2 months for 100.00% of PIA. March 2021 Mary Ann files for 100.00% of spousal benefits ($247) at age 66, 2 months. Survivor benefit $2,647	$518,812	$359,906	$878,718
4	January 2018 Mary Ann files for worker benefits ($851) at age 63 for 79.17% of PIA (38 Months Reduction). March 2019 Don files for worker benefits ($2,647) at age 66 for 100.00% of PIA. March 2019 Mary Ann files for 83.33% (24 Months Reduction) of spousal benefits ($205) at age 64, 2 months. Survivor benefit $2,647	$518,812	$351,240	$870,052
5	March 2023 Don files for worker benefits ($3,494) at age 70 for 132.00% of PIA (48 Months Delayed Retirement Credit). January 2025 Mary Ann files for worker benefits ($1,406) at age 70 for 130.67% of PIA (46 Months Delayed Retirement Credit). Survivor benefit $3,494	$517,112	$351,856	$868,968
6	January 2018 Don files for worker benefits ($2,441) at age 64, 10 months for 92.22% of PIA (14 Months Reduction). March 2021 Mary Ann files for worker benefits ($1,076) at age 66, 2 months for 100.00% of PIA. March 2021 Mary Ann files for 100.00% of spousal benefits ($247) at age 66, 2 months. Survivor benefit $2,441	$512,610	$349,606	$862,216
7	January 2018 Don files for worker benefits ($2,441) at age 64, 10 months for 92.22% of PIA (14 Months Reduction). January 2018 Mary Ann files for worker benefits ($851) at age 63 for 79.17% of PIA (38 Months Reduction). January 2018 Mary Ann files for 74.17% (38 Months Reduction) of spousal benefits ($183) at age 63. Survivor benefit $2,441	$512,610	$339,190	$851,800

	Strategy	Don	MaryAnn	Total
8	March 2019 Don files for worker benefits ($2,647) at age 66 for 100.00% of PIA. January 2025 Mary Ann files for worker benefits ($1,406) at age 70 for 130.67% of PIA (46 Months Delayed Retirement Credit). Survivor benefit $2,647	$518,812	$309,506	$828,318
9	January 2018 Don files for worker benefits ($2,441) at age 64, 10 months for 92.22% of PIA (14 Months Reduction). January 2025 Mary Ann files for worker benefits ($1,406) at age 70 for 130.67% of PIA (46 Months Delayed Retirement Credit). Survivor benefit $2,441	$512,610	$299,206	$811,816

CASE STUDY #21
Mike and Leslie

Overview: Mike and Leslie are a married couple almost eleven years apart in age. The age difference results in their Full Retirement Age (FRA) being a year apart. Mike reaches Full Retirement Age (FRA) at age sixty-six and Leslie reaches FRA at age sixty-seven. The husband, Mike, made slightly less than his wife, Leslie. Leslie is expected to survive Mike by approximately twelve years.

Mike	DOB: March 16, 1951 Full Retirement Age Benefit: **$2,023** at **66** years and **0** months Expected Death Age: **84.05**
Leslie	DOB: November 12, 1961 Full Retirement Age Benefit: **$2,198** at **67** years and **0** months Expected Death Age: **87.06**

	Strategy	Mike	Leslie	Total
1	March 2021 Mike files for worker benefits ($2,670) at age 70 for 132.00% of PIA (48 Months Delayed Retirement Credit). December 2023 Leslie files for worker benefits ($1,547) at age 62, 1 month for 70.42% of PIA (59 Months Reduction). Survivor benefit $2,670	$657,130	$461,910	$1,119,040
2	March 2021 Mike files for worker benefits ($2,670) at age 70 for 132.00% of PIA (48 Months Delayed Retirement Credit). November 2028 Leslie files for worker benefits ($2,198) at age 67 for 100.00% of PIA. Survivor benefit $2,670	$618,588	$461,910	$1,080,498
3	March 2021 Mike files for worker benefits ($2,670) at age 70 for 132.00% of PIA (48 Months Delayed Retirement Credit). November 2031 Leslie files for worker benefits ($2,725) at age 70 for 124.00% of PIA (36 Months Delayed Retirement Credit). Survivor benefit $2,725	$572,250	$461,910	$1,034,160
4	March 2017 Mike files for worker benefits ($2,023) at age 66 for 100.00% of PIA. November 2031 Leslie files for worker benefits ($2,725) at age 70 for 124.00% of PIA (36 Months Delayed Retirement Credit). Survivor benefit $2,725	$572,250	$447,083	$1,019,333

	Strategy	Mike	Leslie	Total
5	March 2017 Mike files for worker benefits ($2,023) at age 66 for 100.00% of PIA. December 2023 Leslie files for worker benefits ($1,547) at age 62, 1 month for 70.42% of PIA (59 Months Reduction). Survivor benefit $2,023	$550,375	$447,083	$997,458
6	March 2017 Mike files for worker benefits ($2,023) at age 66 for 100.00% of PIA. November 2028 Leslie files for worker benefits ($2,198) at age 67 for 100.00% of PIA. Survivor benefit $2,198	$540,708	$447,083	$987,791

CASE STUDY #22
Harold and Belinda

Overview: Harold and Belinda, a married couple four years apart in age. Harold will reach Full Retirement Age (FRA) at age sixty-six and two months. Belinda will reach FRA at age sixty-six. The husband, Harold, made moderately more than his wife, Belinda. Although Belinda is expected to live to age eighty-six and eight months she is expected to die approximately two years before Harold.

Harold	DOB: June 10, 1956 Full Retirement Age Benefit: **$2,331** at **66** years and **4** months Expected Death Age: **84.08**
Belinda	DOB: April 3, 1952 Full Retirement Age Benefit: **$1,738** at **66** years and **0** months Expected Death Age: **86.08**

	Strategy	Harold	Belinda	Total
1	July 2018 Harold files for worker benefits ($1,719) at age 62, 1 month for 73.75% of PIA (51 Months Reduction). July 2018 Belinda files a 'restricted application' at age 66, 3 months for 100% of spousal benefit ($1,165). April 2022 Belinda files for worker benefits ($2,294) at age 70 for 132.00% of PIA (48 Months Delayed Retirement Credit). Survivor benefit $2,294	$480,799	$511,225	$992,024
2	April 2022 Belinda files for worker benefits ($2,294) at age 70 for 132.00% of PIA (48 Months Delayed Retirement Credit). June 2026 Harold files for worker benefits ($3,014) at age 70 for 129.33% of PIA (44 Months Delayed Retirement Credit). Survivor benefit $3,014	$530,464	$458,800	$989,264
3	April 2022 Belinda files for worker benefits ($2,294) at age 70 for 132.00% of PIA (48 Months Delayed Retirement Credit). October 2022 Harold files for worker benefits ($2,331) at age 66, 4 months for 100.00% of PIA. Survivor benefit $2,331	$512,820	$458,800	$971,620

	Strategy	Harold	Belinda	Total
4	April 2018 Belinda files for worker benefits ($1,738) at age 66 for 100.00% of PIA. June 2026 Harold files for worker benefits ($3,014) at age 70 for 129.33% of PIA (44 Months Delayed Retirement Credit). Survivor benefit $3,014	$530,464	$431,024	$961,488
5	January 2018 Belinda files for worker benefits ($1,708) at age 65, 9 months for 98.33% of PIA (3 Months Reduction). June 2026 Harold files for worker benefits ($3,014) at age 70 for 129.33% of PIA (44 Months Delayed Retirement Credit). Survivor benefit $3,014	$530,464	$428,708	$959,172
6	April 2018 Belinda files for worker benefits ($1,738) at age 66 for 100.00% of PIA. October 2022 Harold files for worker benefits ($2,331) at age 66, 4 months for 100.00% of PIA. Survivor benefit $2,331	$512,820	$431,024	$943,844
7	January 2018 Belinda files for worker benefits ($1,708) at age 65, 9 months for 98.33% of PIA (3 Months Reduction). October 2022 Harold files for worker benefits ($2,331) at age 66, 4 months for 100.00% of PIA. Survivor benefit $2,331	$512,820	$428,708	$941,528
8	April 2018 Belinda files for worker benefits ($1,738) at age 66 for 100.00% of PIA. July 2018 Harold files for worker benefits ($1,719) at age 62, 1 month for 73.75% of PIA (51 Months Reduction). Survivor benefit $1,738	$466,343	$431,024	$897,367
9	January 2018 Belinda files for worker benefits ($1,708) at age 65, 9 months for 98.33% of PIA (3 Months Reduction). July 2018 Harold files for worker benefits ($1,719) at age 62, 1 month for 73.75% of PIA (51 Months Reduction). Survivor benefit $1,719	$465,849	$428,708	$894,557

CASE STUDY #23
Gordon and Cynthia

Overview: Gordon and Cynthia, a married couple three years apart in age. The husband, Gordon, was the sole breadwinner. Cynthia has no retirement benefit of her own. Gordon will reach Full Retirement Age (FRA) at age sixty-six and two months, while Cynthia's FRA is sixty-six and six months. Gordon does not have the claim and suspend strategy available. If he waits to file beyond his FRA Cynthia must also wait to file. Cynthia is expected to survive Gordon by approximately six years.

Gordon	DOB: January 13, 1955 Full Retirement Age Benefit: **$2,338** at **66** years and **2** months Expected Death Age: **84.08**
Cynthia	DOB: December 5, 1957 Full Retirement Age Benefit: **$0** at **66** years and **6** months Expected Death Age: **87.03**

	Strategy	Gordon	Cynthia	Total
1	January 2025 Gordon files for worker benefits ($3,055) at age 70 for 130.67% of PIA (46 Months Delayed Retirement Credit). January 2025 Cynthia files for 100.00% of spousal benefits ($1,169) at age 67, 1 month. Survivor benefit $3,055	$537,680	$407,374	$945,054
2	March 2021 Gordon files for worker benefits ($2,338) at age 66, 2 months for 100.00% of PIA. June 2024 Cynthia files for 100.00% of spousal benefits ($1,169) at age 66, 6 months. Survivor benefit $2,338	$519,036	$368,235	$887,271
3	March 2021 Gordon files for worker benefits ($2,338) at age 66, 2 months for 100.00% of PIA. March 2021 Cynthia files for 73.75% (39 Months Reduction) of spousal benefits ($862) at age 63, 3 months. Survivor benefit $2,338	$519,036	$345,672	$864,708
4	January 2018 Gordon files for worker benefits ($1,850) at age 63 for 79.167% of PIA (38 Months Reduction). June 2024 Cynthia files for 100.00% of spousal benefits ($1,169) at age 66, 6 months. Survivor benefit $1,850	$481,000	$336,027	$817,027

	Strategy	Gordon	Cynthia	Total
5	January 2018 Gordon files for worker benefits ($1,850) at age 63 for 79.167% of PIA (38 Months Reduction). January 2020 Cynthia files for 67.92% (53 Months Reduction) of spousal benefits ($793) at age 62, 1 month Survivor benefit $1,850	$481,000	$309,248	$790,248

CASE STUDY #24
Tony & Jesse

Overview: Tony and Jessie, a married couple five years apart in age. Tony reached his Full Retirement Age (FRA) at age sixty-six and has decided not to begin benefits until at least age sixty-six and eleven months or January of the following year. Jessie will reach her FRA at age sixty-six and two months. Jessie is expected to survive Tony by approximately seven years.

Tony	DOB: February 14, 1951 Full Retirement Age Benefit: **$2,592** at **66** years and **0** months Expected Death Age: **84.06**
Jessie	DOB: February 2, 1956 Full Retirement Age Benefit: **$1,578** at **66** years and **4** months Expected Death Age: **87.01**

	Strategy	Tony	Jessie	Total
1	February 2018 Jessie files for worker benefits ($1,157) at age 62 for 73.33% of PIA (52 Months Reduction). February 2018 Tony files a 'restricted application' at age 67 for 100% of spousal benefit ($789). February 2021 Tony files for worker benefits ($3,421) at age 70 for 132.00% of PIA (48 Months Delayed Retirement Credit). Survivor benefit $3,421	$623,658	$554,281	$1,177,939
2	February 2021 Tony files for worker benefits ($3,421) at age 70 for 132.00% of PIA (48 Months Delayed Retirement Credit). June 2022 Jessie files for worker benefits ($1,578) at age 66, 4 months for 100.00% of PIA. Survivor benefit $3,421	$595,254	$560,635	$1,155,889
3	February 2021 Tony files for worker benefits ($3,421) at age 70 for 132.00% of PIA (48 Months Delayed Retirement Credit). February 2026 Jessie files for worker benefits ($2,040) at age 70 for 129.33% of PIA (44 Months Delayed Retirement Credit). Survivor benefit $3,421	$595,254	$543,871	$1,139,125

	Strategy	Tony	Jessie	Total
4	January 2018 Tony files for worker benefits ($2,781) at age 66, 11 months for 107.33% of PIA (11 Months Delayed Retirement Credit). June 2022 Jessie files for worker benefits ($1,578) at age 66, 4 months for 100.00% of PIA. Survivor benefit $2,781	$586,791	$502,395	$1,089,186
5	January 2018 Tony files for worker benefits ($2,781) at age 66, 11 months for 107.33% of PIA (11 Months Delayed Retirement Credit). February 2018 Jessie files for worker benefits ($1,157) at age 62 for 73.33% of PIA (52 Months Reduction). Survivor benefit $2,781	$586,791	$496,041	$1,082,832
6	January 2018 Tony files for worker benefits ($2,781) at age 66, 11 months for 107.33% of PIA (11 Months Delayed Retirement Credit). February 2026 Jessie files for worker benefits ($2,040) at age 70 for 129.33% of PIA (44 Months Delayed Retirement Credit). Survivor benefit $2,781	$586,791	$485,631	$1,072,422

CASE STUDY #25
Andrew and Leanne

Overview: Andrew and Leanne, a married couple about two years apart in age. Andrew reached his Full Retirement Age (FRA) at age sixty-six and has decided not to begin benefits but filed and suspended before the change in the law. Leanne will reach her FRA at age sixty-six. Leanne can take advantage of the restricted application strategy. Leanne is expected to survive Tony by approximately four years.

Andrew	DOB: January 24, 1950 Full Retirement Age Benefit: **$2,442** at **66** years and **0** months Expected Death Age: **84.06**
Leanne	DOB: October 10, 1952 Full Retirement Age Benefit: **$1,163** at **66** years and **0** months Expected Death Age: **86.08**

	Strategy	Andrew	Leanne	Total
1	January 2016 Andrew filed and suspended worker benefit. October 2018 Leanne files a 'restricted application' at age 66 for 100% of spousal benefit ($1,221). January 2020 Andrew files for worker benefits ($3,223) at age 70 for 132.00% of PIA (48 Months Delayed Retirement Credit). October 2022 Leanne files for worker benefits ($1,535) at age 70 for 132.00% of PIA (48 Months Delayed Retirement Credit). Survivor benefit $3,223	$560,802	$426,524	$987,326
2	January 2016 Andrew filed and suspended worker benefit. January 2020 Andrew files for worker benefits ($3,223) at age 70 for 132.00% of PIA (48 Months Delayed Retirement Credit). October 2018 Leanne files for worker benefits ($1,163) at age 66 for 100.00% of PIA. October 2018 Leanne files for 100.00% of spousal benefits ($58) at age 66. Survivor benefit $3,223	$560,802	$381,380	$942,182

	Strategy	Andrew	Leanne	Total
3	January 2016 Andrew filed and suspended worker benefit.	$560,802	$380,765	$941,567
	January 2018 Leanne files for worker benefits ($1,104) at age 65, 3 months for 95.00% of PIA (9 Months Reduction).			
	January 2018 Leanne files for 93.75% of spousal benefits ($54) at age 65, 3 months.			
	January 2020 Andrew files for worker benefits ($3,223) at age 70 for 132.00% of PIA (48 Months Delayed Retirement Credit).			
	Survivor benefit $3,223			
4	January 2016 Andrew elected worker benefits ($2,442) for 100.00% of PIA.	$542,124	$405,844	$947,968
	October 2018 Leanne files a 'restricted application' at age 66 for 100% of spousal benefit ($1,221).			
	October 2021 Leanne files for worker benefits ($1,535) at age 70 for 132.00% of PIA (48 Months Delayed Retirement Credit).			
	Survivor benefit $2,442			
5	January 2016 Andrew elected worker benefits ($2,442) for 100.00% of PIA.	$542,124	$361,570	$903,694
	October 2018 Leanne files for worker benefits ($1,163) at age 66 for 100.00% of PIA.			
	October 2018 Leanne files for 100.00% of spousal benefits ($58) at age 66.			
	Survivor benefit $2,442			
6	January 2016 Andrew elected worker benefits ($2,442) for 100.00% of PIA.	$542,124	$360,085	$902,209
	January 2018 Leanne files for worker benefits ($1,104) at age 65, 3 months for 95.00% of PIA (9 Months Reduction).			
	January 2018 Leanne files for 93.75% of spousal benefits ($54) at age 65, 3 months.			
	Survivor benefit $2,442			

PART II
MEDICARE

INTRODUCTION

1001. What is Medicare?

Medicare is a federal health insurance program for persons aged sixty-five or older and for certain younger persons who either have End-Stage Renal Failure (ESRD) (permanent kidney failure requiring either dialysis or a transplant) or are disabled.

Medicare is administered by the Centers for Medicare & Medicaid Services (CMS), a federal agency within the Department of Health and Human Services, although it originally began under the Social Security Administration in 1966. The Social Security Administration processes applications for Medicare and provides general information about the program. Although Medicare is a federal government program, much of the program is handled through the private sector. For example, various private insurance companies – called Medicare Administrative Contractors (MACs) – process and pay Medicare claims under contracts with CMS. Medicare beneficiaries receive health care through private service providers, including: hospitals and outpatient centers, nursing homes, and home health agencies; physicians; suppliers of medical equipment; and clinical laboratories. CMS also contracts with groups of doctors and other health care professionals to monitor the quality of care delivered to Medicare beneficiaries. CMS is located at 7500 Security Boulevard, Baltimore, Maryland 21244. The website for CMS is cms.hhs.gov.

Medicare consists of:

- Part A (Hospital Insurance);

- Part B (Medical Insurance);

- Part C (Medicare Advantage, formerly known as Medicare+Choice); and

- Part D (Prescription Drug Insurance).

Medicare Parts A and B are often referred to collectively as "original" or "traditional" or "fee-for-service" Medicare.

Medicare Part A – Hospital Insurance

Part A (Hospital Insurance) provides insurance for institutional care, primarily inpatient hospital care, as well as skilled nursing home care, posthospital home health care, and hospice care. Part A is financed for the most part by Social Security payroll tax deductions, which are deposited in the Federal Hospital Insurance Trust Fund. Medicare beneficiaries share some Part A costs through payment of deductibles and coinsurance and, occasionally, premiums.

Medicare Part B – Medical Insurance

Part B (Medical Insurance) provides insurance for physician's services, outpatient hospital care, physical therapy, ambulance trips, durable medical equipment, and a number of other services not covered under Part A. Part B is financed through monthly premiums and coinsurance paid by those who enroll and contributions from the federal government, both of which are deposited into the Federal Supplementary Medical Insurance Trust Fund. The government's share of the cost of Medicare Part B usually is about 75 percent of program costs.

In Parts A and B, as of July 2018, approximately 59.1 million people were enrolled. Of those, 50.3 million were over the age of sixty-five and 8.8 million are enrolled under a disability qualification.

Medicare Part C – Medicare Advantage

Part C (Medicare Advantage) provides insurance through contracts between CMS and a variety of different private managed care and fee-for-service organizations. Most Medicare beneficiaries can choose to receive benefits through the original Medicare fee-for-service program (Parts A and B) or through a Medicare Advantage plan. Medicare beneficiaries who enroll in a Medicare Advantage plan pay both the Part B premium and any additional premium and cost-sharing required by the plan itself. Types of Medicare Advantage plans include the following:

- Coordinated care plans, including Health Maintenance Organizations (HMOs) and Preferred Provider Organizations (PPOs). In an HMO, a Medicare beneficiary must obtain health care through affiliated health care providers except in an emergency. In a PPO, a Medicare beneficiary may obtain health care through providers outside the PPO's network, but may be charged more for using such providers.

- Private Fee-For-Service (PFFS) plans that reimburse providers on a fee-for-service basis. Private plans establish their own rate schedules for payments to providers and for charges to Medicare beneficiaries. Although Medicare limits how much may be charged to beneficiaries, the payment schedules may be different than what traditional Medicare pays.

- As of July 2018, there were 20.1 million people enrolled in Medicare Advantage.

Medicare Part D – Prescription Drug Coverage

Part D (Prescription Drug Insurance) provides insurance for outpatient prescription drugs through private insurance companies which have been approved by Medicare. In exchange for a monthly premium, Medicare Part D participants receive limited coverage for prescription drug benefits up to a catastrophic coverage threshold, above which Part D will cover roughly 95 percent of prescription drug costs. Approximately 43.8 million have enrolled in Part D during 2018.

1002. What federal agency administers Medicare?

The Centers for Medicare & Medicaid Services (CMS), whose central office is in Woodlawn, Maryland (near Baltimore), directs the Medicare program as well as the federal portion of the Medicaid program, the State Children's Health Insurance Program (SCHIP), and the new Health Insurance Marketplace under the Patient Protection and Affordable Care Act (PPACA). Before 2001 CMS was called the Health Care Financing Administration (HCFA). The Social Security Administration processes Medicare applications and claims, but it does not set Medicare policy. CMS sets the standards that health care providers such as hospitals, skilled nursing facilities, home health agencies, and hospices must meet in order to be certified as qualified providers of services. It also establishes the reimbursement rates for all Medicare-covered services.

1003. Are same-sex couples eligible to receive spousal Medicare benefits?

Yes. The Social Security Administration now recognizes same-sex marriages in all states and some marital legal relationships such as civil unions and domestic partnerships for the purposes of determining entitlement to Social Security, Medicare and Supplemental Security Income. The SSA is also recognizing same-sex marriages and some nonmartial legal relationships entered into in foreign jurisdictions as well.[1] Social Security is now processing some retirement, surviving spouse and lump-sum death payment claims for same-sex couples in nonmarital legal relationships and paying benefits where they are due. In addition, the Social Security Administration considers same-sex marriage when determining SSI eligibility and benefit amounts.

On June 26, 2015, the United States Supreme Court issued a decision in *Obergefell v. Hodges*,[2] holding that same-sex couples have a constitutional right to marry in all states. This decision enables same-sex couples to be married in one state and have their marriage recognized by all other states. As a direct result of this decision, more same-sex couples will be recognized as being married for the purposes of determining their entitlement to Social Security benefits and as well as Supplemental Security Income (SSI) payments. The Social Security Administration recommends that someone who is the spouse, divorced spouse, or surviving spouse or a same-sex marriage or other legal same-sex relationship to immediately apply for benefits. Immediate applying will preserve the filing date, which can affect benefits.

This has been a changing area of law. In June 2013, the Supreme Court ruling in *United States v. Windsor*,[3] had established that same sex couples who were married in a jurisdiction where same-sex marriages are recognized were eligible for spousal benefits, such as the spousal survivor benefit, the spousal retirement benefit, and the lump sum death benefit. At that time, the Social Security Administration reviewed its own policies regarding same-sex marriage after the Supreme Court decision, and concluded that same-sex couples who are legally married in one state remain married for federal tax purposes even if they reside in a state that does not recognize their marriage.[4]

1004. Who can provide services or supplies under Medicare?

A wide array of health care organizations and medical professionals can offer services or supplies to Medicare beneficiaries. All such providers must meet any licensing requirements applicable under state or local law. Certain types of institutional providers must meet additional Medicare certification requirements and sign participation agreements with CMS before payments will be made for their services. Such providers include:

- hospitals;

- Skilled Nursing Facilities (SNFs);

1. SSA Publication No. 05-10014, January 2017, What Same-Sex Couples Need to Know, https://www.ssa.gov/pubs/EN-05-10014.pdf (Last accessed October 15, 2018).
2. 576 U.S. ___, 135 S.Ct. 2587, 192 L.Ed.2d 609 (2015).
3. 570 U.S. ___, 133 S.Ct. 2675, 186 L.Ed. 808 (2013).
4. Rev. Rul. 2013-17.

- home health agencies;

- hospice programs;

- certain outpatient rehabilitation facilities;

- certain diagnostic laboratories;

- certain organizations providing outpatient physical therapy and speech pathology services;

- certain facilities providing kidney dialysis or transplant services;

- rural health clinics.

Medicare provider participation agreements include numerous rules that participating providers must agree to follow, many of which relate to how much such providers can charge Medicare beneficiaries. Other rules, however, mandate cooperation with quality improvement organizations and state health agency and accrediting organizations. Different rules apply to different types of Medicare providers. For example, hospitals are subject to additional requirements, such as compliance with the Emergency Medical Treatment and Active Labor Act (EMTALA), which prohibits refusing to treat certain indigent patients who need emergency care. Despite these rules, a nonparticipating hospital may still be paid by Medicare in case of emergency treatment provided to a Medicare beneficiary, assuming the nonparticipating hospital is the closest one available to handle the emergency.

In addition to the specified types of providers who must satisfy certification requirements and sign participation agreements to receive payment, other types of providers – such as physicians and certain suppliers – are encouraged to sign participation agreements primarily governing how they are paid. For physicians and suppliers, whether they are participating or nonparticipating does not affect their eligibility to be paid by Medicare; only the mechanisms for payment vary.

1005. In general, what benefits are provided under the Part A (Hospital Insurance) program?

The program, which automatically covers eligible persons, generally provides the following benefits:

- The cost of Inpatient Hospital Care for up to ninety days in each benefit period (also known as a "spell of illness")

  - for 2018, the patient paid a deductible amount of $1,340 for the first sixty days plus $335 a day for each day). There are also sixty nonrenewable lifetime reserve days (days ninety-one to one hundred fifty) with coinsurance of $670 in 2018.

  - for 2019, the patient will pay a deductible amount of $1,364 for the first sixty days plus $341 a day for each day). There are also sixty nonrenewable lifetime

> reserve days (days ninety-one to one hundred fifty) with coinsurance of $682 in 2018.

- The cost of Post-Hospital Skilled Nursing Facility Care for up to one-hundred days in each benefit period

  o for 2018, patient paid $167.50 per day after the first twenty days

  o for 2019, the patient will pay $170.50 after the first twenty days.

  o Note that the first twenty days following a three-day inpatient hospital stay have a $0 (zero) deductible.

- The cost of Home Health Service Visits (subject to a limit of one-hundred post-institutional home health service visits in a spell of illness for Medicare beneficiaries enrolled in Parts A and B) made under a plan of treatment established by a physician. Additional coverage for home health care services that do not meet the Part A coverage criteria may be available under Part B (Medical Insurance). (See Q 1009.)

- The cost of Hospice Care for terminally ill patients.

For a detailed explanation of these benefits, see Q 1018 through Q 1061.

1006. In general, what benefits are provided under Part B (Medical Insurance)?

Part B (Hospital Insurance), which is a voluntary program that must be elected by an eligible Medicare beneficiary, generally provides coverage of the following benefit costs (subject in most cases to a 20 percent copayment requirement in addition to an annual deductible):

- Physicians' services, whether furnished in a hospital, clinic, office, home, or elsewhere.

- A one-time initial wellness physical ("Welcome to Medicare Visit") within twelve months of enrolling in Part B (Medical Insurance), plus a yearly wellness visit to develop or update a personalized plan based on individual health profile.

- Various screening tests (including tests for breast cancer, cardiovascular disease, colorectal cancer, diabetes, glaucoma, HIV, obesity, prostate cancer, and sexually transmitted infections, as well as annual pap smears and pelvic exams), plus in some cases self-management training, counseling, and supplies. Most screening tests do not require cost-sharing.

- Certain preventive measures (including annual flu shot, pneumococcal vaccine, and Hepatitis B vaccine for certain beneficiaries; generally no cost-sharing).

- Pulmonary rehabilitation services for individuals with certain levels of chronic obstructive pulmonary disease.

- Home health care visits, if not covered under Part A (Hospital Insurance) (subject to special rules, including in most cases no cost-sharing other than for durable medical equipment).

- Outpatient medical and surgical services, supplies, and outpatient hospital services for the diagnosis or treatment of an illness or injury.

- Laboratory services (generally no cost-sharing), and X-rays, MRIs, CT scans, EKGs and certain other diagnostic tests.

- Outpatient physical therapy, speech language pathology, and occupational therapy services (subject to specific rules and limits; some services to inpatients may be covered depending on the circumstances).

- Rural health clinic services and federally qualified health center services.

- Prosthetic and orthotic devices (subject to various limits), including replacement of such devices; and surgical dressings and casts.

- Home dialysis supplies and equipment, self-care home dialysis support services, institutional dialysis and supplies, and kidney disease education services (subject to various limits).

- Certain chiropractic and podiatric services (subject to various restrictions).

- Rental or purchase of durable medical equipment, such as walkers.

- Ambulance services, under certain circumstances.

- Eyeglasses (or contact lenses) following cataract surgery (subject to various limits).

- Lung, heart, kidney, pancreas, intestine, and liver transplants, under certain circumstances, and immunosuppressive drugs after a transplant.

- Outpatient mental health services (subject in some cases to additional copayment requirements).

For a detailed explanation of these benefits, see Q 1067 through Q 1133.

1007. In general, what benefits are provided under Part C (Medicare Advantage)?

Part C (Medicare Advantage), is a voluntary program that must be elected by an eligible Medicare beneficiary. A Medicare Advantage Plan is offered by a private company that contracts with Medicare to provide a person with all his Part A and Part B benefits. Medicare Advantage Plans include Health Maintenance Organizations (HMOs), Preferred Provider Organizations (PPOs), Private Fee-for-Service Plans (PFFS), Special Needs Plans

(SNPs), and Medicare Medical Savings Account Plans (MSAs). Most Medicare Advantage Plans offer prescription drug coverage. An individual with ESRD (End Stage Renal Disease) generally cannot join Part C.

Part C (Medicare Advantage), generally provides coverage of the following benefit costs:

- Choice of primary care physician based on the type of plan selected. For example, In HMO Plans, a primary care physician, hospital choice, and services generally must be chosen from those in the plan's network (except emergency care, out-of-area urgent care, or out-of-area dialysis).

- Prescription drug costs are covered in most plans. For some PFFS plans, a person may need to join a Medicare Prescription Drug Plan to get coverage.

- In order to see a specialist, a person with a Medicare Advantage HMO or SNP plan will generally need to get a referral. Those who have Part C PPO or PFFS plans will generally not need a referral in order to see a specialist.

- Pulmonary rehabilitation services for individuals with certain levels of chronic obstructive pulmonary disease.

- Often coverages such as vision, dental, and hearing are provided

Out of pocket costs in a Medicare Advantage Plan (Part C) depend on:

- Whether the plan charges a monthly premium.

- Whether the plan pays any of the monthly Medicare Part B (Medical Insurance) premium (which must be paid for).

- Whether the plan has a yearly deductible or any additional deductibles.

- How much must be paid for each visit or service (copayment or coinsurance). Example: the plan may charge a copayment, such $10 or $20 for each occurrence of a doctor visit. These amounts can be different than those under Original Medicare.

- The type of health care services needed and how often used.

- Whether the doctor or supplier visited accepts assignment (if in a PPO, PFFS, or MSA plan and coverage is obtained out-of-network).

- Whether plan rules such as using network providers is followed.

- Whether extra benefits needed are charged for.

- The plan's yearly limit on out-of-pocket costs for all medical services.

- Whether Medicaid or state help is part of the coverage.

For a detailed explanation of these benefits, see Q 1148 through Q 1166.

1008. In general, what benefits are provided under Part D (Prescription Drug Insurance)?

Prescription drug coverage is available to everyone covered by Medicare. A person must join a plan, run by an insurance company or other private company approved by Medicare, in order to receive Medicare drug coverage. Each plan can vary in cost and in the drugs that may be covered.

- Part D (Prescription Drug Plan) plans are sometimes called PDPs and add drug coverage to Original Medicare, some Medicare Cost Plans, some Medicare Private Fee-for-Service (PFFS) Plans, and Medicare Medical Savings Account (MSA) Plans.

  - Each Medicare Prescription Drug Plan has its own list of covered drugs (called a formulary). Many Medicare drug plans place drugs into different "tiers" on their formularies. Drugs in each tier have a different cost.

- There are rules to understand in enrolling in a specific Part D (Prescription Drug Plan), as enrolling in this type of plan may preclude the use of Part C (Medicare Advantage) prescription drug coverage.

For a detailed explanation of these rules and benefits, see Q 1168 through Q 1174.

1009. What is the difference between home health care coverage under Part A (Hospital Insurance) and Part B (Medical Insurance)?

Medicare coverage of home health services unassociated with a hospital or skilled nursing facility stay has been gradually transferred from Part A to Part B. For most beneficiaries, Medicare Part A continues to cover the first one-hundred visits in a spell of illness following a three-day (seventy-two continuous hours) hospital stay or a Skilled Nursing Facility (SNF) stay. For persons with Part A coverage only, the post institutional and 100-visit limitations do not apply.

Under Part B (Medical Insurance), home health care coverage does not require a preceding institutional stay, nor does it have a one-hundred-visit limit, but coverage is nonetheless subject to various restrictions. If a patient exhausts Part A coverage for home health care, Medicare benefits may still be available for the care under Part B. Other than the Part B coinsurance required for durable medical equipment, if applicable, there is no copayment requirement for home health care coverage.

1010. Is there any overall limit to the benefits a person can receive under Medicare?

While Medicare contains many limits on individual benefits, including financial cost-sharing obligations for beneficiaries, and provides no coverage in certain circumstances, the program imposes no single overall limit on the amount of benefits any individual person may receive.

Under Part A (Hospital Insurance), benefits begin anew in each benefit period (although lifetime reserve days for inpatient hospital care are limited to sixty total), but inpatient care in a psychiatric hospital is subject to a lifetime limit of 190 days. Part B (Medical Insurance) generally does not impose dollar limits. In addition, there are limits on Skilled Nursing Facility (SNF) benefits as well as therapy services.

Medicare may limit benefit payments for services for which other third-party insurance programs (e.g., workers' compensation, automobile or liability insurance, and employer health plans) may ultimately be liable. Such limits arise under Medicare's Coordination of Benefits and Secondary Payer programs.

1011. When do Medicare benefits become available?

Medicare benefits generally become available at the beginning of the month in which an individual reaches age sixty-five. An individual whose birthday falls on the first day of a month is treated as having reached age sixty-five on the last day of the month immediately preceding his or her birthday. Assuming an individual is otherwise eligible for Medicare, benefits become available at age sixty-five even if the individual is still working. Individuals who qualify for Medicare on the basis of disability – other than those who are disabled due to Lou Gehrig's disease (Amyotrophic Lateral Sclerosis) – must be continuously disabled for twenty-four months before they will be able to receive Medicare benefits. There is no waiting period for Medicare benefits when eligibility is based on disability due to Lou Gehrig's disease or on end-stage renal disease.

1012. What is a Medicare card?

A Medicare card is issued after a person becomes eligible for Medicare benefits. The card shows the person's coverage (Part A – Hospital Insurance, Part B – Medical Insurance, or both) and the effective date of each type of coverage. The card also shows the person's Medicare claim number. The claim number usually has nine digits (similar to a Social Security number, but not the same number) and one or two letters. On some cards, there will be another number after the letter. When a husband and wife both have Medicare, each receives a separate card and claim number. Each spouse must use the exact name and claim number shown on his or her card.

Important points to remember include:

- A covered person should always show his Medicare card when receiving services that Medicare covers in whole or in part.

- A covered person should always write his entire Medicare claim number (including any letters) on all checks for Medicare premium payments, all claims, and any correspondence about Medicare. Also, the covered person should have his Medicare card available when making a telephone inquiry relating to Medicare.

- A covered person should carry his Medicare card whenever away from home.

- If a Medicare card is lost, a replacement card should be requested immediately through the Medicare Replacement Card section of the Social Security Administration's website (mymedicare.gov). A replacement card may also be requested by going to a Social Security office or calling Social Security at 1-800-772-1213. Social Security can provide temporary proof of Medicare coverage until a replacement card arrives (in approximately four weeks from the date of a request).

- A covered person should use his Medicare card only after the effective date(s) shown on the card.

- Medicare cards made of metal or plastic, which are sold by some manufacturers, are not a substitute for the officially issued Medicare card.

- No one should ever permit another individual to use his Medicare card.

1013. What care is not covered under Part A (Hospital Insurance) and Part B (Medical Insurance)?

Medicare Parts A (Hospital Insurance) and Part B (Medical Insurance) contain a number of specific exclusions. These include the following:

Services "Not Reasonable and Necessary"

Medicare does not pay for services that are not reasonable and necessary for the diagnosis or treatment of an illness or injury. These services include:

- drugs or devices that have not been approved by the Food and Drug Administration (FDA);

- medical procedures and services performed using drugs or devices not approved by FDA;

- services, including drugs or devices, not considered safe and effective because they are experimental or investigational.

If a doctor places an individual in a hospital or skilled nursing facility when the kind of care the individual needs could be provided elsewhere, the individual's stay will not be considered reasonable and necessary, and Medicare will not pay for it. If an individual stays in a hospital or skilled nursing facility longer than necessary, Medicare payments will end when inpatient care is no longer reasonable or necessary.

If a doctor (or other practitioner) comes to treat a person or that person visits the doctor for treatment more often than is medically necessary, Medicare will not pay for the "extra" visits.

Exclusions

In addition, Medicare does not pay for:

- most outpatient prescription drugs (except under Medicare Part D);

- routine or annual physical exams (other than the Welcome to Medicare initial visit and annual wellness visits introduced by the Patient Protection and Affordable Care Act (PPACA);

- most dental care and dentures;

- routine foot care;

- routine eye care;

- hearing aids;

- personal comfort items;

- cosmetic surgery.

Custodial Care

Medicare also does not cover custodial care when that is the only kind of care the patient needs. Care is considered custodial when it is primarily for the purpose of helping with daily living or meeting personal needs and could be provided safely and reasonably by persons without professional skills or training. Much of the care provided in nursing homes to people with chronic long-term illnesses or disabilities is considered custodial care.

> *Example*: Custodial care includes help in walking, getting in and out of bed, bathing, dressing, eating, and taking medicine. Even if an individual is in a participating hospital or skilled nursing facility or the individual is receiving care from a participating home health agency, Medicare does not cover the stay if the patient needs only custodial care.

There are exceptions to the custodial care restrictions in the case of hospice care.

Service Providers Who Are Not Covered

Medicare will not pay for services performed by immediate relatives or members of a patient's household. Nor will Medicare pay for services paid for by another government program. Medicare will not pay for any item or service with regard to which there is no legal obligation to pay (for the beneficiary or anyone else), such as free health-related services (e.g., vaccinations) provided at community events. In certain cases, such as health care covered by workers' compensation or an employer-based health plan for an active employee, Medicare acts as the secondary payer, paying to the extent of Medicare's coverage limits but only after another source of insurance pays and then only to the extent the primary payer did not cover the item or service.

Health Care Outside of the United States

Medicare generally does not pay for any health services provided outside the United States, but there are exceptions for emergencies and for inpatient hospital care where the foreign hospital is closer to an individual's residence than a comparable U.S. hospital and is equipped to handle the needed care.

Waiver of Liability

Under Medicare law, a person will not be held responsible for payment of the cost of certain health care services for which the person was denied Medicare payment if the person did not know or could not reasonably be expected to know that the services were not covered by Medicare. This provision is often referred to as a "Waiver of Liability." The waiver provision applies only when the care was denied because it was one of the following:

(1)   custodial care;

(2)   not reasonable or necessary under Medicare program standards for diagnosis or treatment;

(3)   for home health services, the patient was not homebound or not receiving skilled nursing care on an intermittent basis; or

(4)   the only reason for the denial is that, in error, the patient was placed in a skilled nursing facility bed that was not approved by Medicare.

The limitation of liability provision also does not apply to Part B (Medical Insurance) services provided by a nonparticipating physician or supplier who did not accept assignment of the claim. However, in certain situations Medicare will protect the patient from paying for services provided by a nonparticipating physician on a nonassigned basis that are denied as "not reasonable and necessary." If a physician knows or should know that Medicare will not pay for a particular service as "not reasonable and necessary," the physician must give the patient written notice – before performing the service – of the reasons why the physician believes Medicare will not pay. The physician must get the patient's written agreement to pay for the services. If the patient does not receive this notice, the patient is not required to pay for the service. If the patient pays for the service, but did not receive a notice, the patient may be entitled to a refund.

1014. What are the rules regarding self-referrals?

Doctors cannot make self-referrals for certain designated health services. Designated health services include:

(1)   clinical laboratory services;

(2)   physical therapy services;

(3)   occupational therapy services;

(4)   radiology services, including MRI, CAT scans, and ultrasound services;

(5)   radiation therapy services and supplies;

(6)   durable medical equipment and supplies;

(7)   parenteral and enteral nutrients, equipment, and supplies;

(8)   prosthetics, orthotics, and prosthetic devices and supplies;

(9)   home health services;

(10)   outpatient prescription drugs; and

(11)   inpatient and outpatient hospital services.

The law prohibits a doctor who has a financial relationship with an entity from referring Medicare patients to that entity to receive a designated health service. The prohibition also applies if a doctor's immediate family member has a financial relationship with the entity. A financial relationship can exist as an ownership or investment interest in *or* a compensation arrangement with an entity. The law is triggered by the mere fact that a financial relationship exists; it does not matter what the doctor intends when making a referral.

An entity cannot bill Medicare, Medicaid, the beneficiary, or anyone else for a designated health service furnished to a Medicare patient under a prohibited referral. If a person collects any amount for services billed in violation of the law, a refund must be made.

A person can be subject to a civil money penalty or exclusion from Medicare if that person:

(1)   presents or causes to be presented a claim to Medicare or bill to any individual, third-party payer, or other entity for any designated health service the person knows or should know was furnished as the result of a prohibited referral; or

(2)   fails to make a timely refund.

1015. What are Quality Improvement Organizations?

The QIO Program is one the largest federal programs dedicated to improving health quality for Medicare beneficiaries. The QIO program is part HHS Services' National Quality Strategy which is intended to provide better care and better health at lower cost. By law, the mission of the QIO Program is to improve the effectiveness, efficiency, economy, and quality of services delivered to Medicare beneficiaries. Based on this statutory charge, and CMS's program experience, CMS identifies the core functions of the QIO Program as:

- Improving quality of care for beneficiaries and families

- Maximizing learning and collaboration for improving care

- Supporting the spread of and sustaining of new practices and models of care

- Protecting the integrity of the Medicare Trust Fund by ensuring that Medicare pays only for services and goods that are reasonable and necessary and that are provided in the most appropriate setting; and

- Protecting beneficiaries by expeditiously addressing individual complaints, such as beneficiary complaints; provider-based notice appeals; violations of the Emergency Medical Treatment and Labor Act (EMTALA); and other related responsibilities as articulated in QIO-related law.

Quality Improvement Organizations (QIOs), previously known as Peer Review Organizations, are groups of practicing doctors, health quality experts, clinicians, consumers and other health care professionals who are paid by the federal government to review and improve the care given to Medicare patients. Generally, QIOs are private, not-for-profit organizations.

In August 2014, CMS reorganized the structure of the QIO program. The reorganization separated review of Medicare Beneficiary Quality of Care and appeals from Quality Improvement work carried out in provider and community settings.

There are two types of QIOs that work under the direction of the Centers for Medicare & Medicaid Services in support of the QIO Program:

Beneficiary and Family Centered Care (BFCC)-QIOs

Two Beneficiary and Family Centered Qualify Improvement Organizations (BFCC-QIOs) address quality of care concerns and appeals – cover all fifty states and three territories.

- BFCC-QIOs help Medicare beneficiaries exercise their right to high-quality health care. They manage all beneficiary complaints and quality of care reviews to ensure consistency in the review process while taking into consideration local factors important to beneficiaries and their families. They also handle cases in which beneficiaries want to appeal a healthcare provider's decision to discharge them from the hospital or discontinue other types of services. While BFCC-QIOs are the primary point of contact for Medicare beneficiaries and their families, quality of care complaints can also be made by calling 1-800-MEDICARE. The two designated BFCC-QIOs – Livanta and KEPRO, serve all fifty states and three territories, which are grouped into five regions.

Quality Innovation Network (QIN)-QIOs

Fourteen Quality Innovation Network – Quality Improvement Organizations (QIN-QIOs) work with providers, stakeholders, and Medicare beneficiaries to improve health care quality for selected health conditions.

- QIN-QIOS serve regions of two to six states each.

- From 2014 through 2019, QIN-QIOs will focus on four major goals:

    o Promoting effective prevention and treatment of chronic disease by promoting safe care that is patient and family-centered reliable and accessible

    o Making care safer and reducing harm caused in the delivery of care

    o Promoting effective communication and coordination of care

    o Making care more affordable

QIOs also decide whether care meets the standards of quality generally accepted by the medical profession. QIOs have the authority to deny payments if care is not medically necessary or not delivered in the most appropriate setting.

QIOs investigate individual patient complaints about the quality of care and respond to:

(1) requests for review of notices of noncoverage issued by hospitals to beneficiaries; and

(2) requests for reconsideration of QIO decisions by beneficiaries, physicians, and hospitals.

The QIO will tell the patient in writing if the service received was not covered by Medicare.

If a patient is admitted to a Medicare-participating hospital, the patient will receive *An Important Message from Medicare About Your Rights*,[1] which explains the patient's rights as a hospital patient and provides the name, address and phone number of the QIO in the patient's state.

If a patient believes he has been improperly refused admission to a hospital, forced to leave a hospital too soon, or denied coverage of a medical procedure or treatment, the patient should ask for a written explanation of the decision. This written notice must fully explain how the patient can appeal the decision, and it must give the patient the name, address and phone number of the QIO where an appeal or request for review can be submitted.

If a patient disagrees with the decision of a QIO, the patient can appeal by requesting reconsideration. Then, if the patient disagrees with the QIO's reconsideration decision and the amount in question is $200 or more, the patient can request a hearing by an Administrative Law Judge. Cases involving $2,000 or more can eventually be appealed to a federal court. QIOs also provide alternate dispute resolution options.

Different appeal procedures apply to issues involving other types of Part A (Hospital Insurance) coverage such as skilled nursing facility, home health, or hospice care.

For a detailed explanation of the appeals process, see Q 1175 through Q 1190.

QIO Program Transformation

CMS redesigned its QIO Program to further enhance the quality of services for Medicare beneficiaries. The new program structure maximizes learning and collaboration in improving care, enhances flexibility, supports the spread of effective new practices and models of care, helps achieve the priorities of the National Quality Strategy and the goals of the CMS Quality Strategy, and delivers program value to beneficiaries, patients, and taxpayers.

The QIO Program changes include separating case review from quality improvement, extending the contract period of performance from three (3) to five (5) years, removing requirements to restrict QIO activity to a single entity in each state/territory, and opening contractor consideration to a broad range of entities to perform the work.

Now, one group of QIOs (BFCC-QIOs) addresses quality of care concerns and appeals, while another group (QIN-QIOs) works with providers, stakeholders, and Medicare beneficiaries to improve the quality of health care for targeted health conditions. QIOs will have new skills for transforming practices, employing lean methodologies, assisting Medicare providers with their transition to the Quality Payment Program, and developing innovative approaches to quality improvement.

---

1. https://www.cms.gov/medicare/medicare-general-information/bni/downloads/revisedimportantmessagefrommedicare05_2007.pdf (Last Accessed November 1, 2018).

1016. When should a person use the Medicare fraud and abuse hotline?

If a person has reason to believe that a doctor, hospital, or other provider of health care services is performing unnecessary or inappropriate services, or is billing Medicare for services not received, the person should report this information to Medicare at 1-800-MEDICARE (1-800-633-4227). The person reporting alleged fraud and abuse should be prepared to communicate details of the transactions raising questions, including:

(1)   the exact nature of the suspected wrongdoing including the service or item being questioned and the reason Medicare shouldn't have paid;

(2)   the date it occurred;

(3)   the name and address of the party involved;

(4)   the payment amount approved and paid by Medicare;

(5)   the date on the MSN;

(6)   name and Medicare number of the person reporting; and

(7)   any other information that is helpful.

If an individual reports information that serves as the basis for the collection of $100 or more, CMS may pay a portion of the amount collected to the individual (up to a maximum of $1,000). Specific requirements include:

(1)   The allegation must be specific – not general.

(2)   The suspected fraud must be confirmed as potential fraud by the Program Safeguard Contractor, the Zone Program Integrity Contractor, or the Medicare Drug Integrity Contractor and formally referred as part of a case to the Office of the Inspector General.

(3)   The individual reporting cannot be an "excluded individual" (such as being a participant in the fraud or part of another reward program).

(4)   The individual or organization isn't already under investigation by law enforcement.

(5)   The report leads to the recovery of at least $100 in Medicare money.

The incentive reward can't exceed 10% of the overpayments recovered in the case or $1,000, whichever is less. If multiple individuals qualify for a reward, the reward is shared among them.

A person can also report the fraud to the Office of the Inspector General of the Department of Health and Human Services at https://forms.oig.hhs.gov/hotlineoperations/report-fraud-form.aspx?AspxAutoDetectCookieSupport=1.

1017. Should a person receive Medicare benefits through the original fee-for-service Medicare Parts A and B (Hospital Insurance and Medical Insurance) or through a Medicare Advantage plan?

A person living in an area serviced by a Medicare Advantage plan has a choice between traditional Medicare Parts A and B or a Medicare Advantage plan. If a person chooses Parts A and B, that beneficiary can go to almost any doctor, hospital, or other health care provider the beneficiary prefers. Generally, a fee is charged each time a service is used, Medicare pays its share of the bill, and the patient is responsible for paying the balance. Beneficiaries may purchase a private Medicare Supplemental Insurance (Medigap) policy to cover or help defray the patient's share of charges not covered by Medicare. See Q 1175 through Q 1190 on Medigap insurance.

Medicare Advantage plans in general cover the same core benefits as original Medicare Parts A and B, but may also include other coverage, including prescription drug coverage. Because Medicare Advantage plans are structured to be more inclusive, beneficiaries covered by Medicare Advantage do not need to purchase a separate Medigap plan (and are usually prohibited from doing so). Medicare Advantage plans are provided through private insurers, and the exact terms of the plans – including beneficiary cost-sharing obligations – are established by the private insurers, subject to approval by CMS. Medicare Advantage plans may also charge additional premiums (in addition to the Medicare Part B premium) to reflect the additional benefits offered. Most types of Medicare Advantage plans contain managed care features that attempt to control costs by limiting the providers to which a beneficiary may go for care (or imposing higher cost-sharing requirements if a beneficiary obtains services from an out-of-network provider).

An individual who elects a Medicare Advantage plan one year can always return to traditional Medicare Parts A and B (Hospital and Medical Insurance) in a different year. Also, regardless of whether a person chooses Parts A and B (Hospital and Medical Insurance) Medicare or a Medicare Advantage plan, the individual retains all Medicare protections and appeal rights. See Q 1124 through Q 1156 for a detailed description of Medicare Advantage.

PART A: HOSPITAL INSURANCE

Eligibility

1018. Who is eligible for benefits under Part A (Hospital Insurance)?

All persons age sixty-five and over who are entitled to monthly Social Security cash benefits (or would be entitled except that an application for cash benefits has not been filed), or monthly cash benefits under Railroad Retirement programs (whether retired or not), are eligible for Medicare Part A benefits. An individual may be eligible for Social Security or Railroad Retirement program benefits based on the individual's own work record or as the current or surviving spouse of someone eligible for such benefits. Such individuals are eligible for Part A (Hospital Insurance) benefits if they are at least sixty-five years old. For example, a woman age sixty-five or over who is entitled to a spouse's or widow's Social Security benefit is eligible for benefits under Part A.

Persons age sixty-five and over can receive Medicare benefits even if they continue to work. Enrollment in the program while working will not affect the amount of future Social Security benefits.

Certain Social Security or Railroad Retirement disability beneficiaries are eligible for Medicare Parts A and B after entitlement to disability benefits for twenty-four months or more. Eligible categories of disability beneficiaries include disabled workers at any age, disabled widows and widowers at least age fifty but not yet age sixty-five, beneficiaries age eighteen or older who receive benefits because of disability beginning before age twenty-two, and disabled qualified Railroad Retirement annuitants. Medicare coverage is automatic. No application is required.

A person who becomes re-entitled to disability benefits within five years after the end of a previous period of entitlement (within seven years in the case of disabled widows or widowers and disabled children) is automatically eligible for Medicare coverage without the need to wait another twenty-four months. In addition, in most cases, an individual covered by Medicare on the basis of disability, but who loses disability benefits for some reason, will again be eligible for Medicare coverage without needing to meet the twenty-four-month waiting period requirement, if the current impairment is the same as (or directly related to) that in the previous period of disability.

Medicare coverage will continue if the individual returns to work during a nine-month trial period and for up to fifteen additional months (a total of twenty-four months).

Individuals with ALS (Amyotrophic Lateral Sclerosis, also known as Lou Gehrig's disease) are eligible for Medicare Part A (Hospital Insurance) the first month they are eligible for Social Security or Railroad Retirement disability benefits. The normal twenty-four month waiting period does not apply.

Medicare Part A also covers individuals with End-Stage Renal Disease (ESRD) who are not yet age sixty-five but who are either currently or fully insured for, or are entitled to, Social

Security or Railroad Retirement benefits. Spouses or dependent children of eligible individuals may also be covered if the spouse or dependent child has ESRD.

1019. What are the special eligibility rules for persons with End-Stage Renal Disease (ESRD)?

End-Stage Renal Disease (ESRD) is a situation where a person's kidneys are ceasing to function on a permanent basis leading to the necessity of long-term dialysis or a kidney transplant to maintain life. Individuals in this situation may become entitled to Medicare based on the ESRD diagnosis. Benefits because of ESRD are for all covered services, not only those related to the kidney failure condition. Insured workers (and their spouses and dependents) with ESRD who require renal dialysis, or a kidney transplant are deemed disabled for Medicare coverage purposes even if they are working.

Coverage can begin with the first day of the third month after the month dialysis treatments begin. This three-month waiting period is waived if the individual participates in a self-care dialysis training course during the waiting period.

Medicare coverage for an ESRD patient who is a candidate for a kidney transplant begins with the month in which the patient is hospitalized for the transplant, if the transplant occurs during the three-month period beginning with that month. If a transplant is delayed more than two months following the initial month of hospitalization for a transplant, coverage is effective on the first day of the second month before the month of transplant.

Coverage is also provided under Medicare for the self-administration of erythropoietin for home renal dialysis patients.

For some individuals who have Medicare solely on the basis of their end-stage renal disease, Medicare is the secondary payer if the person with ESRD has Group Health Plan (GHP) coverage either directly or through a family member for a coordination period of thirty months regardless of the number of employees and regardless of whether coverage is based on current employment status. During this period, if an employer plan pays less than the provider's charges, Medicare may supplement the plan's payments. (See Q 1021.) Medicare is secondary to GHP coverage provided through the Consolidated Omnibus Budget Reconciliation Act (COBRA), or a retirement plan. Medicare is secondary during the coordination period even if the employer policy or plan contains a provision stating that its benefits are secondary to Medicare. The GHP may not differentiate in the benefits it provides to individuals who have ESRD. Specifically, GHPs are prohibited from terminating coverage, imposing benefit limitations, or charging higher premiums on the basis of the existence of the individual's ESRD.

START OF COVERAGE:

When the beneficiary first enrolls in Medicare based on ESRD, Medicare coverage can start at different times based on the situation:

1.   FOURTH MONTH OF DIALYSIS: On the fourth month of dialysis when the beneficiary participates in dialysis treatment in a dialysis facility.

2.   FIRST MONTH OF DIALYSIS: Medicare coverage can start as early as the first month of dialysis if:

- The beneficiary takes part in a home dialysis training program in a Medicare-approved training facility to learn how to do self-dialysis treatment at home;

- The beneficiary begins home dialysis training before the third month of dialysis; and

- The beneficiary expects to finish home dialysis training and give self-dialysis treatments.

3.   ADMISSION FOR KIDNEY TRANSPLANT: Medicare coverage can start the month the beneficiary is admitted to a Medicare-approved hospital for kidney transplant or for health care services that are needed before the transplant if the transplant takes place in the same month or within the two following months.

4.   DELAY IN KIDNEY TRANSPLANT: Medicare coverage can start two months before the month of the transplant if the transplant is delayed more than two months after the beneficiary is admitted to the hospital for that transplant or for health care services that are needed before the transplant.

END OF COVERAGE

1.   If the beneficiary has Medicare only because of ESRD, Medicare coverage will end when one of the following conditions is met:

- twelve months after the month the beneficiary stops dialysis treatments, or

- thirty-six months after the month the beneficiary had a kidney transplant.

There is a separate thirty-month coordination period each time the beneficiary enrolls in Medicare based on kidney failure. For example, if the beneficiary gets a kidney transplant that continues to work for thirty-six months, Medicare coverage will end. If after thirty-six months the beneficiary enrolls in Medicare again because they start dialysis or get another transplant, the Medicare coverage will start right away. There will be no three-month waiting period before Medicare begins to pay.

1020. What are the special eligibility rules for government employees?

In general, federal employees began paying the Hospital Insurance (HI) portion of Social Security taxes in 1983 and thus became eligible for Medicare. A transitional provision provides credit for retroactive hospital quarters of coverage for federal employees who were employed before 1983 and also on January 1, 1983. Certain categories of federal employees are not covered, however, including inmates in federal penal institutions, certain interns, and certain temporary employees.

State and local government employees hired after March 31, 1986, generally also pay HI taxes and are covered under Medicare. A person who was performing substantial and regular service for a state or local government before April 1, 1986, is not covered, provided he was a bona fide employee on March 31, 1986, and the employment relationship was not entered into in order to meet the requirements for exemptions from coverage.

State or local government employees who were employed before April 1, 1986, but whose employment terminated after March 31, 1986, are covered under Medicare if they are later rehired. Certain individuals are not automatically covered under Medicare even if employed by a state or local government, including those employed:

(1)   to relieve them of unemployment;

(2)   in a hospital, home, or institution where they are inmates or patients;

(3)   on a temporary basis because of an emergency such as a storm, earthquake, flood, fire or snow;

(4)   as interns, student nurses or other student employees of District of Columbia government hospitals, unless the individuals are medical or dental interns or medical or dental residents in training.

State governments may voluntarily enter into agreements to extend Medicare coverage to employees not covered under the rules above.

1021. When is Medicare considered a secondary payer?

There are limitations on Medicare payments for services covered under group health plans. Medicare is secondary payer, under specified conditions, for services covered under any of the following:

• Group health plans of employers that employ at least twenty employees and that cover Medicare beneficiaries age sixty-five or older who are covered under the plan by virtue of an individual's current employment status with an employer or the current employment status of a spouse of any age.

• Group health plans (without regard to the number of individuals employed and irrespective of current employment status) that cover individuals who have end-stage renal disease. Generally, group health plans are always primary payers throughout the first thirty months of end-stage renal disease based on Medicare eligibility or entitlement.

• Large group health plans (that is, plans of employers that employ at least 100 employees) that cover Medicare beneficiaries who are under age sixty-five, entitled to Medicare based on disability, and covered under the employer plan by virtue of the individual's or a family member's current employment status with an employer.

A "group health plan" means any arrangement made by one or more employers or employee organizations to provide health care directly or through other methods such as insurance or reimbursement, to current or former employees, the employer, others associated or formerly associated with the employer in a business relationship, or their families, that:

(1)   is of, or contributed to by, one or more employers or employee organizations;

(2)   involves more than one employer or employee organization and provides for common administration; and

(3)   provides substantially the same benefits or the same benefit options to all those enrolled under the arrangement.

Group health plans include self-insured plans, plans of governmental entities (federal, state, and local), and employee organization plans (union plans, employee health and welfare funds, or other employee organization plans). Group health plans also include employee-pay-all plans, which are plans under the auspices of one or more employers or employee organizations, but which receive no financial contributions from them. Not included in the definition of group health plans are plans that are unavailable to employees, for example, a plan only for self-employed persons.

A large group health plan means a group health plan that covers employees of either:

- a single employer or employee organization that employed at least 100 full-time or part-time employees on 50 percent or more of its regular business days during the previous calendar year; or

- two or more employers, or employee organizations, at least one of which employed at least 100 full-time or part-time employees on 50 percent or more of its regular business days during the previous calendar year.

An employer or insurer is prohibited from offering Medicare beneficiaries financial or other benefits as incentives not to enroll in, or to terminate enrollment in, a group health plan that is, or would be, primary to Medicare. The prohibition precludes offering to Medicare beneficiaries an alternative to the employer primary plan (for example, coverage of prescription drugs) unless the beneficiary has primary coverage other than Medicare. An example would be primary coverage through an employee's own or a spouse's employer.

Other prohibited actions by group health plans or large group health plans include, but are not limited to, the following:

- Failure to pay primary benefits as required

- Offering coverage that is secondary to Medicare to individuals entitled to Medicare

- Terminating coverage because the individual has become entitled to Medicare, except as permitted under certain COBRA continuation coverage provisions

- In the case of a large group health plan, denying or terminating coverage because an individual is entitled to Medicare based on disability without denying or terminating coverage for similarly situated individuals who are not entitled to Medicare based on disability

- Imposing limitations on benefits for a Medicare-entitled individual that do not apply to others enrolled in the plan, such as providing less comprehensive health care coverage, excluding benefits, reducing benefits, charging higher deductibles or coinsurance, providing for lower annual or lifetime benefit limits, or more restrictive pre-existing illness limitations

- Charging a Medicare-entitled individual higher premiums

- Requiring a Medicare-entitled individual to wait longer for coverage to begin

- Paying providers and suppliers no more than the Medicare payment rate for services furnished to a Medicare beneficiary but making payments at a higher rate for the same services to an enrollee who is not entitled to Medicare

- Providing misleading or incomplete information that would have the effect of inducing a Medicare entitled individual to reject the employer plan, thereby making Medicare the primary payer. An example of this would be informing the beneficiary of the right to accept or reject the employer plan but failing to inform the individual that, if he rejects the plan, the plan will not be permitted to provide or pay for secondary benefits

- Including in its health insurance cards, claims forms, or brochures distributed to beneficiaries, providers, and suppliers, instructions to bill Medicare first for services furnished to Medicare beneficiaries without stipulating that such action may be taken only when Medicare is the primary payer

- Refusing to enroll an individual for whom Medicare would be secondary payer, when enrollment is available to similarly situated individuals for whom Medicare would not be secondary payer

If a group health plan or large group health plan makes benefit distinctions among various categories of individuals (distinctions unrelated to the fact that the individual is disabled), the group health plan or large group health plan may make the same distinctions among the same categories of individuals entitled to Medicare whose plan coverage is based on current employment status. For example, if a group health plan or large group health plan does not offer coverage to employees who have worked less than one year and who are *not* entitled to Medicare based on disability or age, the group health plan or large group health plan is not required to offer coverage to employees who have worked less than one year and who *are* entitled to Medicare based on disability or age.

A group health plan or large group health plan may pay benefits secondary to Medicare for an aged or disabled beneficiary who has current employment status if the plan coverage is COBRA continuation coverage because of reduced hours of work. Medicare is primary payer for this beneficiary because, although he has current employment status, the group health plan coverage is by virtue of the COBRA law rather than by virtue of the current employment status.

Aged Beneficiaries and Spouses

Medicare benefits are secondary to benefits payable by a group health plan for services furnished during any month in which the individual is age sixty-five or older, eligible for Medicare Part A, and meets one of the following conditions:

(1)   The individual is covered under a group health plan of an employer that has at least twenty employees (including a multiemployer plan in which at least one of the participating employers meets that condition), and coverage under the plan is by virtue of the individual's current employment status.

(2)   The individual is the aged spouse (including a divorced or common-law spouse) of an individual (of any age) who is covered under a group health plan by virtue of the individual's current employment status.

Disabled Beneficiaries

Medicare benefits are secondary to benefits payable by a large group health plan for services furnished during any month in which the individual:

(1)   is entitled to Medicare Part A benefits based on disability;

(2)   is covered under a large group health plan; and

(3)   has large group health plan coverage by virtue of her own or a family member's current employment status.

Medicare becomes primary if the services are:

(1)   furnished to Medicare beneficiaries who have declined to enroll in the group health plan;

(2)   not covered under the plan for the disabled individual or similarly situated individuals;

(3)   covered under the plan but not available to particular disabled individuals because they have exhausted their benefits under the plan;

(4)   furnished to individuals whose COBRA continuation coverage has been terminated because of the individual's Medicare entitlement; or

(5)   covered under COBRA continuation coverage notwithstanding the individual's Medicare entitlement.

End-Stage Renal Disease

A group health plan may not consider that an individual is eligible for or entitled to Medicare benefits based on end-stage renal disease. An individual who has end-stage renal disease but who has not filed an application for entitlement to Medicare on that basis is eligible for Medicare based on end-stage renal disease. A group health plan may not differentiate in the benefits it provides between individuals who have end-stage renal disease and others enrolled in the plan, based on the existence of end-stage renal disease, or in any other manner.

Generally, Medicare is secondary payer during the first thirty months of end-stage renal disease-based eligibility or entitlement. Medicare becomes primary after the thirtieth month of end-stage renal disease-based eligibility or entitlement.

Examples of group health plan actions that constitute differentiation in plan benefits (and that may constitute "taking into account" Medicare eligibility or entitlement) include:

- terminating coverage of the individuals with end-stage renal disease, when there is no basis for such termination unrelated to end-stage renal disease that would result in termination for individuals who do not have end-stage renal disease;

- imposing on persons who have end-stage renal disease, but not on others enrolled in the plan, benefit limitations such as less comprehensive health plan coverage, reductions in benefits, exclusions of benefits, a higher deductible or coinsurance, a longer waiting period, a lower annual or lifetime benefit limit, or more restrictive pre-existing illness limitations;

- charging individuals with end-stage renal disease higher premiums;

- paying providers and suppliers less for services furnished to individuals who have end-stage renal disease, such as paying 80 percent of the Medicare rate for renal dialysis;

- failure to cover routine maintenance dialysis or kidney transplants, when a plan covers other dialysis services or other organ transplants.

Other Secondary Payer Rules

An employee may reject the employer's plan and retain Medicare as the primary payer, but regulations prevent employers from offering a health plan or option designed to induce the employee to reject the employer's plan and retain Medicare as primary payer.

For persons who are not eligible for Social Security or Railroad Retirement benefits, see Q 1022.

Medicare is also the secondary payer:

(1)   when medical care can be paid for under no-fault insurance or liability insurance (including automobile insurance);

(2)   if the individual is entitled to veterans' benefits;

(3)   if the individual is entitled to black lung benefits; or

(4)   if the individual is covered by workers' compensation.

Although Medicare is sometimes the secondary payer when liability insurance is available, Medicare may make a conditional payment if it receives a claim for services covered by liability insurance. In these cases, Medicare recovers its conditional payment from the settlement amount when the liability settlement is reached.

A third-party payer must give notice to Medicare if it learns that Medicare has made a primary payment in a situation where the third-party payer made or should have made the primary payment. A third-party payer is considered to learn that Medicare has made a primary payment when the third-party payer receives information that Medicare had made a primary payment, or when it receives information sufficient to draw the conclusion that Medicare has made a primary payment.

> *Example 1.* The third-party payer has received a copy of an Explanation of Medicare Benefits form, and the form shows that Medicare has made a primary payment for services for which the third party has made, or ought to have made, primary payment.

> *Example 2.* A beneficiary for whom Medicare should be secondary payer states in correspondence provided to the third-party payer that Medicare has made primary payment for a given item or service for which the beneficiary has primary coverage under the third-party payer's plan.

> *Example 3.* A beneficiary who is eligible for Medicare files a claim for primary payment with a third-party payer, the claim is denied, the beneficiary appeals, and the denial is reversed. (The third-party payer should assume that Medicare made a conditional primary payment in the interim.)

The Centers for Medicare & Medicaid Services must mail questionnaires to individuals, before they become entitled to benefits under Part A (Hospital Insurance) or enroll in Part B (Medical Insurance), to determine whether they are covered under a primary plan. Payments will not be denied for covered services solely on the grounds that a beneficiary's questionnaire fails to note the existence of other health plan coverage.

Providers and suppliers are required to complete information on claim forms regarding potential coverage under other plans. Civil monetary penalties are established for an entity that knowingly, willfully, and repeatedly fails to complete a claim form with accurate information.

Contractors are required to submit annually a report to the Centers for Medicare & Medicaid Services regarding steps taken to recover mistaken payments.

1022. Can a person age sixty-five or over qualify for Part A (Hospital Insurance) benefits without qualifying for Social Security or Railroad Retirement benefits?

Certain individuals age sixty-five or over and otherwise ineligible for Part A (Hospital Insurance) may enroll voluntarily and pay a monthly premium if they also enroll in Part B (Medical Insurance). (See Q 1062.) Any such person must also be a resident of the United States and also either a U.S. citizen or an alien lawfully admitted for permanent residence status (who has continuously resided in the United States for at least five years immediately before applying for Medicare benefits). Generally, people don't pay a monthly premium for Part A, but if actually purchasing it, it can cost up to $437.00 per month in 2019 ($422.00 in 2018).

1023. Is there any way that an individual not automatically eligible for Part A (Hospital Insurance) can be enrolled?

Yes, provided the individual:

(1)   has attained age sixty-five;

(2)   is enrolled in Part B (Medical Insurance) (see Q 1062 through Q 1133);

(3)   is a resident of the United States and is either:

(a) a citizen; or

(b) an alien lawfully admitted for permanent residence who has resided in the United States continuously during the five years immediately preceding the month in which he applies for enrollment; and

(4)   is not otherwise entitled to Part A (Hospital Insurance) benefits.

Certain disabled individuals under age sixty-five may also be able to obtain Part A (Hospital Insurance) coverage by paying monthly premiums. This category of eligibility applies to someone who previously qualified for Medicare coverage on the basis of disability and continues to be disabled, but whose income exceeds the level allowed under Social Security for payment of disability income benefits to disabled persons and thus loses eligibility for Medicare benefits under the normal disability provisions.

Certain government employees who otherwise do not qualify for automatic Part A (Hospital Insurance) may also be able to enroll for Part A coverage by paying a premium.

For individuals who voluntarily enroll in Part A (Hospital Insurance) by paying a premium, the premium was $437 a month in 2019, an increase of $15.00 from 2018 (but see paragraph below for premium reduction exception). This premium amount increases by up to 10 percent for those who must pay a premium surcharge for late enrollment. (See Q 1063 and Q 1064.)

The Part A (Hospital Insurance) premium is reduced – by about 45 percent (to $240 a month in 2019) – for individuals with credits for thirty or more quarters paid into the Social Security system (and certain current, surviving and divorced spouses of such individuals). Those with fewer than thirty credits will be charged the full monthly rate of $437 for 2019. The reduced premium amount increases by up to 10 percent for those who must pay a premium surcharge for late enrollment. (See Q 1063 and Q 1064.)

An individual who qualifies for the reduction is an individual who:

(1)   has thirty or more quarters of coverage;

(2)   has been married for at least the previous one-year period to a worker who has thirty or more quarters of coverage;

(3)   had been married to a worker who had thirty or more quarters of coverage for a period of at least one year before the death of the worker;

(4)   is divorced from, after at least ten years of marriage to, a worker who had thirty or more quarters of coverage at the time the divorce became final; or

(5)   is divorced from, after at least ten years of marriage to, a worker who subsequently died and who had thirty or more quarters of coverage at the time the divorce became final.

Administration

1024. How do the Centers for Medicare & Medicaid Services (CMS) administer Part A (Hospital Insurance)?

The Centers for Medicare & Medicaid Services (CMS) enters into agreements with state agencies and with private insurance companies (such as Blue Cross and other health insurance organizations) to administer Part A (Hospital Insurance). A Medicare Administrative Contractor (MAS) is a private health care insurer that has been awarded a geographic jurisdiction to process Medicare Part A and Part B medical claims or Durable Medical Equipment (DME) claims for Medicare Fee-For-Service (FFS) beneficiaries.

State agencies survey institutions to determine whether they meet the conditions for participation as a hospital, skilled nursing facility, home health agency, or hospice. They also help the institutions meet the conditions for participation.

Private insurance organizations contracting with CMS determine the amount of Part A (Hospital Insurance) benefits payable to hospitals, skilled nursing facilities, hospices, and home health agencies; pay Part A benefits to such providers out of funds advanced by the federal government; help the providers establish and maintain necessary financial records; serve as a channel of communication of information relating to Part A (Hospital Insurance); and audit records of hospitals, skilled nursing facilities, hospices, and home health agencies, as necessary, to insure that payment of Part A benefits is proper.

The private insurance organizations that contract with CMS to administer Part A are now called Medicare Administrative Contractors (MACs), but previously were referred to as fiscal intermediaries. Each provider of services can nominate a MAC to work with or can deal directly with the CMS. MACs are reimbursed for their reasonable costs of administration.

Most skilled nursing facilities and home health agencies must submit cost reports to MACs in a standardized electronic format. Hospitals have been required to submit cost reports in electronic format for a number of years. No payments are made to a provider unless it has furnished the information needed to determine the amount of payments due the provider. In general, providers submit this information through cost reports that cover a twelve-month period. A provider may request a delay or waiver of the electronic submission requirement by submitting a written request with supporting documentation to its MAC no later than thirty days after the end of its cost reporting period.

MACs perform many activities including:

- processing Medicare FFS claims;

- making and accounting for Medicare FFS payments;

- enrolling providers in the Medicare FFS program;

- handling provider reimbursement services and audit institutional provider cost reports;

- handling redetermination requests (1st stage appeals process);

- responding to provider inquiries;

- educating providers about Medicare FFS billing requirements;

- establishing Local Coverage Determinations (LCD's);

- reviewing medical records for selected claims;

- coordinating with CMS and other FFS contractors.

1025. What is the Prospective Payment System?

Section 1886(d) of the Social Security Act established a system of payment for the operating costs of acute care hospital inpatient stays under Medicare Part A based on prospectively set rates. Medicare pays for most inpatient hospital care under this Prospective Payment System (PPS), called more precisely the Inpatient Prospective Payment System (IPPS). Under Medicare's PPS, hospitals are paid a predetermined rate/fixed amount per discharge for inpatient services furnished to Medicare beneficiaries.

Under the IPPS, each case is categorized into predetermined rates based on payment categories called Diagnosis-Related Groups (DRGs). Each DRG has a payment weight assigned to it, based on the average resources used to treat Medicare patients in that DRG. In some cases, Medicare payment will be more than the hospital's cost; in other cases, the payment will be less than the hospital's costs. In special cases, where costs for necessary care are unusually high or the length of stay is unusually long, the hospital receives additional payment.

The base payment rate is divided into a labor-related and nonlabor share. The labor-related share is adjusted by the wage index applicable to the area where the hospital is located, and if the hospital is in Alaska or Hawaii, the nonlabor share is adjusted by a cost of living adjustment factor. This base payment rate is multiplied by the DRG relative weight assigned to it.

If a hospital treats a high-percentage of low-income patients, it receives a percentage add-on payment applied to the DRG-adjusted base payment rate. This add-on, known as the Disproportionate Share Hospital (DSH) adjustment, provides for a percentage increase in Medicare payment for hospitals that qualify under either of two statutory formulas designed to identify hospitals that serve a disproportionate share of low-income patients. For qualifying hospitals, the amount of this adjustment may vary based on the outcome of the statutory calculation.

Also, if the hospital is an approved teaching hospital it receives a percentage add-on payment for each case paid through IPPS. This add-on known as the Indirect Medical Education (IME) adjustment, varies depending on the ratio of residents-to-beds under the IPPS for operating costs, and according to the ratio of residents-to-average daily census under the IPPS for capital costs.

Finally, for particular cases that are unusually costly, known as outlier cases, the IPPS payment is increased. This additional payment is designed to protect the hospital from large financial losses due to unusually expensive cases. Any outlier payment due is added to the DRG-adjusted base payment rate, plus any DSH or IME adjustments.

Reimbursement for inpatient hospital services is based on uniform sums for hundreds of DRGs (varying between rural and urban facilities). All other services are reimbursed on a reasonable cost basis.

Health Maintenance Organizations (HMOs) are covered by special reimbursement provisions to reward them financially because of what is believed to be their more favorable operating experience.

The PPS does not change the coverage available to a beneficiary under Part A (Hospital Insurance). For example, the PPS does not determine the length of a stay in the hospital or the extent of care a patient should receive, but is likely a factor that providers consider when providing covered care. The law requires participating hospitals to accept Medicare payments as payment in full, and those hospitals are prohibited from billing a Medicare patient for anything other than the applicable deductible and coinsurance amounts, plus any amounts due for noncovered items or services such as television, telephone or private duty nurses. Providers are limited by these Medicare payment rules even when the cost of a patient's care greatly exceeds the payment the hospital will receive from Medicare.

Despite the requirement to provide care for as long as it is medically necessary, the PPS provides hospitals with a possible incentive to refuse to admit patients for medical procedures that might not be reimbursed by Medicare. Hospitals also have an incentive to treat and discharge patients within or in less than the time frame established by the reimbursement rate for a particular DRG.

The CMS contracts with Quality Improvement Organizations (QIOs) in each state to conduct preadmission, continued stay, and retrospective reviews of the services delivered by a hospital. The reviews determine whether such services are reasonable and necessary. The QIO is also responsible for ensuring that the cost control incentives of the PPS do not adversely affect patients' access to hospitals or the quality of hospital care.

If the hospital, without consulting the QIO, recommends against admitting a patient, review of this decision may be obtained by the patient by writing the QIO in the patient's state. If the QIO participated in the preadmission denial of the patient, then a reconsideration of that denial may be requested by the patient.

For a detailed explanation of the appeal process, see Q 1175 through Q 1190.

1026. What are some examples of Prospective Payment Systems in use?

The following are summaries of Medicare Part A prospective payment systems for six provider settings:

Provider Setting	Classification System	Summary Description
Inpatient acute care hospital	Diagnosis-Related Groups (DRGs)	Primary diagnosis determines assignment to one of 535 DRGs
		The DRG payment rate is adjusted based on age, sex, secondary diagnosis and major procedures performed. DRG payment is per stay.
		Additional payment (outlier) made only if length of stay far exceeds the norm
Inpatient rehabilitation hospital or distinct unit	Case-Mix Groups (CMGs)	Patient Assessment Instrument (PAI) determines assignment of patient to one of 95 Case-Mix Groups (CMGs). CMG determines payment rate per stay
		Rehabilitation Impairment Categories (RICs) are based on diagnosis; CMGs are based on RIC, patient's motor and cognition scores and age. Discharge assessment incorporates comorbidities
		PAI includes comprehension, expression, and swallowing
Skilled Nursing Facility	Resource Utilization Groups, Third Version (RUG-III)	Fifty-eight groups
		Each beneficiary assigned a per diem payment based on Minimum Data Set (MDS) comprehensive assessment
		A specified minimum number of minutes per week is established for each rehabilitation RUG based on MDS score and rehabilitation team estimates
Home Health Agency	Home Health Resource Groups (HHRGs)	Eighty HHRGs
		The Outcome & Assessment Information Set (OASIS) determines the HHRG and is completed for each 60-period
		A predetermined base payment for each 60-day episode of care is adjusted according to patient's HHRG
		No limit to number of 60-day episodes

Provider Setting	Classification System	Summary Description
		Payment is adjusted if patient's condition significantly changes
Hospice	Each day of care is classified into one of four levels of care	Per diem rate for each of four levels of care:
		Routine home care
		Continuous home care
		Inpatient respite care
		General inpatient care
		Geographic wage adjustments determine the only variation in payment rates within each level

1027. Is Part A (Hospital Insurance) a compulsory program?

Yes, in the sense that every person who works in employment or self-employment covered by the Social Security Act, or in employment covered by the Railroad Retirement Act, must pay the Part A (Hospital Insurance) tax, the system is compulsory. An employee working in covered employment does not have the ability to choose not to pay the Hospital Insurance (HI) tax that funds Part A. Coverage under Part A (Hospital Insurance) for eligible individuals is automatic, but an individual could choose to pay his medical expenses out-of-pocket and not take advantage of the benefits available under Part A. See Q 1018 for eligibility.

Financing Part A (Hospital Insurance)

1028. How is Part A (Hospital Insurance) financed?

Medicare Part A (Hospital Insurance) is financed by a separate Hospital Insurance (HI) tax imposed upon employers, employees, and the self-employed.[1] The tax must be paid by every individual, regardless of age, who is subject to the regular Social Security tax or to the Railroad Retirement tax.

It must also be paid by all federal employees and by all state and local government employees:

(1)   hired after March 1986; or

(2)   not covered by a state retirement system in conjunction with their employment (beginning July 2, 1991).

Unlike the Social Security tax which applies to earnings up to $132,900, the Hospital Insurance (HI) tax applies to ALL earnings. The rates of the HI tax are 1.45 percent each for employees and employers, and 2.90 percent for self-employed persons. There is an additional Hospital Insurance tax of 0.9 percent on earned income exceeding $200,000 for individuals

---

1. See 26 U.S.C. 1401(b), 3101(b) and 26 U.S. C. 310(b).

and $250,000 for married couples filing jointly. In addition, there is a Medicare tax applied to investment income. This 3.8 percent tax is imposed on Net Investment Income of single taxpayers with adjusted gross income above $200,000 and joint filers with AGI over $250,000.[1]

There is a special federal (and generally following through to state) income tax deduction of 50 percent of the OASDI/Hospital Insurance self-employment tax. This income tax deduction, which is available regardless of whether or not the taxpayer itemizes deductions, is designed to treat the self-employed in much the same manner as employees and employers are treated for Social Security and income tax purposes.

Net Investment Income

The following are strategies to reduce the tax on net investment income:

- Sell securities in a loss position that are held in a taxable account to offset earlier gains from such accounts.

- Instead of giving cash, give appreciated securities to charity. That way, the gains will not be included on the tax return, but the client still has a charitable deduction.

- If possible, have the client become more active in business activities in which they have invested, such as those conducted through partnerships and S corporations. Try to convert them from passive status to nonpassive status, because income and gains from nonpassive business activities do not count as investment income and are therefore exempt from the 3.8 percent tax. The surest way to make an activity nonpassive is to spend over 500 hours a year in it. In some cases, however, it can take only 100 hours or even less.

- If possible, defer gains subject to the 3.8 percent tax by spreading them out with an installment sale (the sales proceeds are received over several years) or a Section 1031 like-kind exchanges. Investment real estate is the best candidate for these strategies.

- The purchase of permanent life insurance can also help manage net investment income. Withdrawals up to an owner's investment in the contract, as well as policy loans, are not included in income.

Benefits

1029. In general, what benefits are provided under Part A (Hospital Insurance)?

Part A (Hospital Insurance) provides the following main types of benefits:

(1)   *Inpatient hospital care* for up to ninety days in each "benefit period" (also known as a "spell of illness"). The patient paid a deductible of $1,364 in 2019 for the first

---

1. 26 U.S.C. 1411.

sixty days and coinsurance of $341 a day for each additional day up to a maximum of thirty days. In addition, each person has a nonrenewable lifetime "reserve" of sixty additional hospital days with coinsurance of $682 a day.

(2)   *Posthospital extended care in a skilled nursing facility* for up to 100 days in each "benefit period." The patient pays nothing for the first twenty days in 2019. After twenty days the patient pays coinsurance of $170.50 a day in 2019 for each additional day up to the maximum of 100 days (including the twenty days at no charge).

(3)   The first 100 *posthospital home health service* visits following a hospital or skilled nursing facility stay. The services must be made under a plan of treatment established by a physician. There is no charge for home health care visits under Part A, except that there is 20 percent cost-sharing payable by the patient for durable medical equipment (other than the purchase of certain used items). The 100-visit and post-institutional care limits apply only to Medicare beneficiaries enrolled in both Parts A and B.

(4)   *Hospice care* for terminally ill patients.

Qualified Medicare Beneficiaries

1030. When will a state pay Medicare costs for a person who is elderly or disabled with low income?

Federal law requires state Medicaid programs to pay Medicare costs for certain elderly and disabled persons with low incomes and very limited resources.

There are two programs to help people pay their Medicare expenses.

QUALIFIED MEDICARE BENEFICIARY (QMB) PROGRAM

The QMB program is for persons with limited resources (assets) whose incomes are at or below the national poverty level. If an individual is a QMB, the program covers the cost of Medicare premiums, coinsurance, and deductibles that Medicare beneficiaries normally pay out of their own pockets. QMBs do not pay:

- Medicare's Part A hospital deductible;

- the Part A daily coinsurance charges for extended hospital and skilled nursing facility stays;

- the Part B (Medical Insurance) premium, which was $134 for new enrollees for 2018, was increased to $135.50 for 2019. Existing beneficiaries of Part B will be protected by the "hold harmless" clause and pay $109.00, up slightly from the $104.90 of the past four years. (see Q 1067);

- the annual Part B deductible of $185 for 2019

- the 20 percent coinsurance for services covered by Medicare Part B, depending on which doctor the patient goes to.

QMBs remain responsible for paying for medical supplies and services not covered by Medicare, such as routine physicals, dental care, hearing aids, and eyeglasses.

SPECIFIED LOW-INCOME MEDICARE BENEFICIARY (SLMB) PROGRAM

While the QMB programs helps people whose income is at or below the national poverty level, the SLMB program is for persons whose incomes are slightly higher than the poverty level, but not more than 20 percent higher (in other words, up to 120 percent of the federal poverty level). Individuals attempting to qualify for assistance under the SLMB program must satisfy the same asset limits as under the QMB program. SLMBs do not pay the monthly Part B premium, but otherwise remain responsible for Medicare's deductibles and coinsurance, as well as for charges for health care services and medical supplies not covered by Medicare.

QUALIFYING INDIVIDUAL (QI) PROGRAM

Application must be made every year for QI benefits which are granted on a first-come, first-served basis, with priority given to people who received QI benefits the previous year. QI benefits are not granted to those that qualify for Medicaid). This program helps pay for Medicare Part B only.

QUALIFIED DISABLED AND WORKING INDIVIDUALS (QDWI) PROGRAM

This program helps pay for Medicare Part A. Any individual can qualify if meeting any of the following criteria:

- Working but disabled and under age sixty-five

- Lost premium-free Part A when returned to work

- Not getting medical assistance from the state

- Meet income and resource requirements from the state

If an individual meets QMB, SLMB or QI requirements, they automatically qualify for Extra Help to pay for Medicare prescription drug coverage.

1031. How does a person qualify for assistance under the QMB program?

The rules vary from state to state but generally, to qualify for assistance under the QMB program, a person must meet the following requirements:

(1)   The person must be entitled to Part A (Hospital Insurance). If the person does not have Part A or does not know whether he or she is entitled to Part A, the individual should check with any Social Security Administration office or call 1-800-772-1213.

(2)   The person's financial resources, such as bank accounts, stocks, and bonds, cannot exceed specified limits ($7,560 for an individual; $11,340 for a married couple through 2018). Some things – the home you live in, one automobile, burial plots, home furnishings, personal jewelry, and life insurance – usually do not count as resources.

(3)   The person's income must be at or below specified monthly limits ($1,032 per month for an individual, $1,392 per month for a couple, through 2018). The income limits are higher in Alaska and Hawaii. Income includes, but is not limited to, Social Security benefits, pensions, and wages. Interest payments and dividends can also count as income.

(4)   Specified Low-Income Medicare Beneficiary (SLMB) who are limited to Part B premiums have income limits of $1,234 per month for an individual or $1,666 for a couple. Qualifying Individuals (QI) have income limits of $1,386 per month for an individual or $1,872 for a couple. Qualified Disabled and Working Individuals (QDWI) have income limits of $4,132 per month for an individual or $5,572 for a couple.

Qualified Medicare Beneficiary (QMB) Program: If a person qualifies for the QMB Program, they are assisted in paying Part A and Part B premiums, deductibles, coinsurance, and copayments. To qualify for QMB they must be eligible for Medicare Part A, and have an income not exceeding 100 percent of the federal poverty level (FPL) + $20 (amount of the monthly SSI income disregard). This will be effective the first month following the month QMB eligibility is approved. Eligibility can't be retroactive.

Specified Low-Income Medicare Beneficiary (SLMB) Program: To qualify for the SLMB Program, a person must be eligible for Medicare Part A and have an income that is at least 100 percent, but doesn't exceed 120 percent of the FPL + $20 (amount of the monthly SSI income disregard). If qualifying for SLMB, they get help paying for your Part B premium.

Qualified Individual (QI) Program: To qualify for the QI Program, they must be eligible for Medicare Part A, and have an income not exceeding 135 percent of the FPL + $20 (amount of the monthly SSI income disregard).

Qualified Disabled and Working Individual (QDWI) Program: To qualify for QDWI, a person must be entitled to Medicare Part A because of a loss of disability-based Part A due to earnings exceeding Substantial Gainful Activity; have an income not higher than 200 percent of the FPL, and resources not exceeding twice the maximum for SSI ($4,000 for an individual, and $6,000 for married couple in 2018); and not be otherwise eligible for Medicaid. If qualified they get help paying the Part A premium. If their income is between 150 percent and 200 percent of the FPL, the state can ask the individual to pay a part of your Medicare Part A premium.

1032. What if a person's income is slightly higher than the poverty level?

If a person does not qualify for QMB assistance because his income is too high, he may be able to get help under the Specified Low-Income Beneficiary (SLMB) program. To qualify for SLMB assistance, a person must meet the following requirements:

(1)   The person must be entitled to Hospital Insurance (Part A). If the person does not have Part A or does not know whether he is entitled to Part A, check with any Social Security Administration office or call 1-800-772-1213.

(2)   A person's financial resources, such as bank accounts, stocks, and bonds, cannot exceed $7,560 for one person or $11,340 for a couple through 2018. The following usually do not count as resources: the home you live in, one automobile, burial plots, home furnishings, personal jewelry, and life insurance.

(3)   A person's income cannot exceed the national poverty level by more than 20 percent (in other words, up to 120 percent of the federal poverty level). This means the SLMB income limits through 2018 are $1,214 monthly for an individual and $1,646 monthly for a couple.

1033. How does a person apply for QMB or SLMB assistance?

A person with Part A (Hospital Insurance) must file an application for Medicare assistance programs at a state, county, or local Medicaid office. The following criteria will need to be met:

- Eligible for, or signed up for Medicare Part A.

- Income for 2019 at, or below, 120 percent of Federal Poverty Level.

- Limited financial resources as defined by law.

Inpatient Hospital Services

1034. Specifically, what inpatient hospital services are paid for under Part A (Hospital Insurance)?

Subject to a deductible and coinsurance, Medicare Part A (Hospital Insurance) pays for inpatient hospital service for up to ninety days in each "benefit period" (also called a "spell of illness"). Medicare will also pay (except for a coinsurance amount) for sixty additional hospital days over each person's lifetime (called the "lifetime reserve" days).

Medicare pays for hospital care if the patient meets the following four conditions:

(1)   a physician prescribes inpatient hospital care for treatment of an illness or injury;

(2)   the patient requires the kind of care that can be provided only as an inpatient in a hospital;

(3)   the hospital is participating in Medicare (except in certain emergency situations); and

(4)   the utilization review committee of the hospital, a Quality Improvement Organization (QIO), or the applicable Medicare Administrative Contractor (MAC) does not disapprove of the stay.

The patient must pay a deductible of $1,364 in 2019 for the first sixty days in each benefit period. If the stay is longer than sixty days during a benefit period, coinsurance of $341 a day must be paid for each additional day up to a maximum of thirty days.

Thus, a ninety-day stay in 2019 would cost the patient $11,594. After ninety days, the patient pays the full bill unless the lifetime reserve of sixty days is drawn upon. The patient must pay coinsurance of $682 a day in 2019 for each of the sixty additional lifetime reserve days.

The coinsurance amounts are based on those in effect when services are furnished, rather than on those in effect at the beginning of the beneficiary's benefit period.

A "benefit period" is a way of measuring the patient's use of services under Part A (Hospital Insurance). A new ninety-day benefit period starts with each new spell of illness, beginning with the day a patient begins receiving inpatient hospital care. A benefit period ends when the patient has been out of a hospital or other facility primarily providing skilled nursing or rehabilitative services for sixty days in a row (including the day of discharge). After one benefit period has ended, another one will start whenever the patient again receives inpatient hospital care.

There is no limit to the number of ninety-day benefit periods a person can have in a lifetime (except in the case of hospitalization in a psychiatric hospital for mental illness), but the lifetime reserve of sixty days is not renewable. Also, special limited benefit periods apply to hospice care. (See Q 1043.)

> *Example 1.* Mr. Smith enters the hospital on February 5. He is discharged on February 15. He has used ten days of his first benefit period. Mr. Smith is not hospitalized again until August 20. Since more than sixty days have elapsed between his hospital stays, he begins a new benefit period in August. Part A (Hospital Insurance) will again pay for up to sixty days of inpatient hospital coverage, subject to Mr. Smith's payment of the deductible, and another thirty days subject to Mr. Smith's payment of coinsurance.

> *Example 2.* Mr. Jones enters the hospital on September 14. He is discharged on September 24. He also has used ten days of his first benefit period. He is then readmitted to the hospital on October 20. Because fewer than sixty days have elapsed between hospital stays, Mr. Jones remains in the same benefit period and will not be required to pay another hospital deductible when he re-enters the hospital on October 20. This means that the first day of his second admission is counted as the eleventh day of hospital care in that benefit period. Mr. Jones will not begin a new benefit period until he has been out of the hospital (and has not received any skilled care in a skilled nursing facility) for sixty consecutive days.

"Lifetime reserve" days include an extra sixty hospital days a patient can use if the patient has a lengthy illness and needs to stay in the hospital for more than ninety days. A patient has only sixty reserve days in a lifetime. For example, if a patient uses eight reserve days in that individual's first hospital stay covered under Medicare Part A, he or she will have only fifty-two reserve days left to use during subsequent hospital stays, whether or not such stays fall within new benefit periods. A patient can decide when and whether to use lifetime reserve days.

If a patient does not want to use lifetime reserve days, the patient must tell the hospital in writing, either at the time of admission or at any time up to ninety days after discharge. If a patient uses reserve days and then decides that he or she did not want to use them, the patient must request approval from the hospital to have the lifetime reserve days restored. A patient must pay the full hospital costs for any day after the first ninety days in a benefit period if the patient is not using lifetime reserve days to offset the costs after the ninety days. During 2019, Part A (Hospital Insurance) paid for all covered services except $682 a day for each reserve day the patient uses.

Medicare beneficiaries have the right to receive all the hospital care that is necessary for the proper diagnosis and treatment of their illness or injury. Under federal law, a beneficiary's discharge date must be determined solely by medical needs, not by the Diagnosis-Related Group (DRG) or Medicare payments. Beneficiaries have the right to be fully informed about decisions affecting their Medicare coverage and payment for their hospital stay and for any posthospital services. They also have the right to request a review by a Quality Improvement Organization (QIO) of any written notice of noncoverage they receive from the hospital stating that Medicare will no longer pay for their hospital care. QIOs are usually groups of physicians who are paid by the federal government to review medical necessity, appropriateness and quality of hospital treatment furnished to Medicare patients. (See Q 1025.)

The following inpatient services are covered by Part A (Hospital Insurance):

- *Bed and board in a semiprivate room* (two to four beds) or a ward (five or more beds). Part A (Hospital Insurance) will pay the cost of a private room only if it is required for medical reasons (e.g., the patient needs isolation for medical reasons or needs immediate hospitalization and no other accommodations are available). If the patient requests a private room, Part A will pay the cost of semiprivate accommodations; the patient must pay the extra charge for the private room. The patient or family must be told the amount of this extra charge when a private room is requested. Normally, Medicare patients are assigned to semiprivate rooms. Ward assignments are made only under extraordinary circumstances.

- *All meals*, including special diets.

- *Nursing services* provided by or under the supervision of licensed nursing personnel (other than the services of a private duty nurse or attendant).

- Services of the hospital's *medical social workers*.

- Use of regular hospital *equipment, supplies, and appliances*, such as oxygen tents, wheel chairs, crutches, casts, surgical dressings, splints, and hospital "admission packs" (toilet articles) when routinely furnished by the hospital to all patients. Certain equipment, supplies and appliances used by the patient in the hospital continue to be covered after the patient has been discharged. Examples include a cardiac pacemaker and an artificial limb.

- *Drugs and biologicals* ordinarily furnished by the hospital. A limited supply of drugs needed for use outside the hospital is also covered, but only if medically necessary in order to facilitate the patient's departure from the hospital and the supply is necessary until the patient can obtain a continuing supply. Drugs and biologicals that the hospital obtains for the patient from a private source (community pharmacy) are covered when the hospital is responsible for making payment to the supplier.

- *Diagnostic or therapeutic items and services* ordinarily furnished by the hospital or by others (including clinical psychologists, as defined by the Centers for Medicare & Medicaid Services), under arrangements made with the hospital.

- *Operating and recovery room costs*, including hospital costs for anesthesia services.

- Services of *interns and residents in training* under an approved teaching program.

- *Blood transfusions*, after the first three pints. Part A (Hospital Insurance) helps pay for blood (whole blood or units of packed red blood cells), blood components, and the cost of blood processing and administration. If the patient receives blood as an inpatient of a hospital or skilled nursing facility, Part A will pay for these blood costs, except for any nonreplacement fees charged for the first three pints of whole blood or units of packed red cells per calendar year. The nonreplacement fee is the amount that some hospitals and skilled nursing facilities charge for blood that is not replaced. The patient is responsible for the nonreplacement fees for the first three pints or units of blood furnished by a hospital or skilled nursing facility. If the patient is charged nonreplacement fees, the patient has the option of either paying the fees or having the blood replaced. If the patient chooses to have the blood replaced, the patient can either replace the blood personally or arrange to have another person or an organization replace it. A hospital or skilled nursing facility cannot charge a patient for any of the first three pints of blood that the patient replaces or arranges to replace. If the patient has already paid for or replaced blood under Part B (Medical Insurance) of Medicare during the calendar year, the patient does not have to meet those costs again under Part A.

- *X-rays* and other radiology services, including radiation therapy, billed by the hospital.

- *Lab tests*.

- *Respiratory or inhalation therapy*.

- *Independent clinical laboratory services* under arrangement with the hospital.

- *Alcohol detoxification and rehabilitation services* when furnished as inpatient hospital services. Alcohol detoxification and rehabilitation services may also be covered under Part B (Medical Insurance) when furnished as physician services.

- *Dental services* when the patient requires hospitalization because of the severity of the dental procedure or because of the patient's underlying medical condition and clinical status.

- Cost of *special care units*, such as an intensive care unit, coronary care unit, etc.

- *Rehabilitation services*, such as physical therapy, occupational therapy, and speech pathology services.

- *Appliances* (such as pacemakers, colostomy fittings, and artificial limbs) that are permanently installed while the patient is in the hospital.

- *Lung and heart-lung transplants*. (See Q 1124 for additional information on this coverage and what benefits are covered Part A and Part B.)

Part A (Hospital Insurance) does not pay for:

- Services of physicians and surgeons, including the services of pathologists, radiologists, anesthesiologists, and physiatrists. (Part A [Hospital Insurance] also does not pay for the services of a resident physician or intern other than those provided by an intern or resident in training under an approved teaching program.)

- Services of a private duty nurse or attendant, unless the patient's condition requires such services and the nurse or attendant is a bona fide employee of the hospital.

- Personal convenience (comfort) items supplied at the patient's request, such as television rental, radio rental, or telephone.

- The first three pints of whole blood (or packed red blood cells) received in a calendar year.

- Supplies, appliances, and equipment for use outside the hospital, unless continued use is required (e.g., a pacemaker).

1035. Are inpatient hospital benefits provided for care in a psychiatric hospital?

Yes, but benefits for psychiatric hospital care are subject to a lifetime limit of 190 days. Furthermore, if the patient is already in a mental hospital when he becomes eligible for Medicare, the time spent there in the 150-day period before becoming eligible will be counted against the maximum of 150 days available in such cases (including any later period of such hospitalization when he has not been out of a mental hospital for at least sixty consecutive days between hospitalizations). This latter limitation does not apply to inpatient service in a general hospital for care other than psychiatric care.

1036. What special provisions apply to care in Religious Nonmedical Health Care Institutions (RNHCI)?

A Religious Nonmedical Health Care Institution (RNHCI) is an institution that provides nonmedical nursing items and services to Medicare beneficiaries who choose to rely solely upon a religious method of healing and who feel that acceptance of medical services would be inconsistent with their religious beliefs. In general, these institutions can participate in Medicare as hospitals, and the regular coverages and exclusions relating to inpatient hospital care will apply. Thus, the patient paid a $1,364 deductible in 2019 for the first sixty days, and coinsurance of $341 a day in 2019 for the next thirty days (plus $682 per day in 2019 for the sixty lifetime reserve days). A RNHCI may also be paid as a skilled nursing facility, but extended care benefits will be paid for only thirty days in a calendar year (instead of the usual 100 days), and the patient must pay the coinsurance amount ($170.50 per day in 2019) for each day of service (instead of only for each day after the twentieth day).

A federal district court ruled in 1996 that certain Christian Science facilities were not eligible for Medicare and Medicaid payments. In response to the ruling, Congress deleted any references to Christian Science sanatoriums in the Social Security Act and replaced them with the term "religious nonmedical health care institutions." RNHCI are subject to detailed eligibility criteria to protect the health and safety of patients and to special limits on the total amount of reimbursement available through Medicare.

1037. Can patients choose their own hospitals?

Except for certain emergency cases, Medicare will make payments only to "qualified" hospitals, skilled nursing facilities, home health agencies, and hospices.

Medicare generally does not pay for hospital or medical services outside the United States. (Puerto Rico, the U.S. Virgin Islands, Guam, American Samoa, and the Northern Mariana Islands are considered part of the United States.)

Medicare will pay for both emergency and nonemergency inpatient hospital care in a foreign hospital if the foreign hospital is closer to, or substantially more accessible than the nearest U.S. hospital (that is adequately equipped and available to handle the patient's care) to the patient's U.S. residence. Medicare also authorizes payment for emergency care in a Canadian hospital when the emergency occurred in transit between Alaska and another U.S. state without unreasonable delay and by the most direct route. Necessary physicians' services in connection with Mexican or Canadian hospitalization that qualifies for Medicare coverage are also authorized under Medicare. If a person receives emergency treatment in a Canadian or Mexican hospital or lives near a Canadian or Mexican hospital, he should have the hospital help him contact a Medicare administrative contractor.

1038. How is it certified that hospitalization is required?

CMS requires that all inpatient hospital admissions have an initial "certification" that states, among other details, that the hospitalization is reasonable and necessary and expected to last at least two "midnights." CMS provided a transition period for compliance through 2013.

1039. What must a hospital do to qualify for Medicare payments?

Generally, a hospital must meet certain standards and enter into a Medicare participation agreement in order to be paid by Medicare. However, Medicare may pay nonparticipating hospitals in certain emergency cases.

Hospice Care

1040. What is hospice care?

Hospice care is an approach to treatment that recognizes that the impending death of an individual warrants a change in focus from curative care to palliative care (relief of pain and other uncomfortable symptoms). The goal of hospice care is to help terminally ill individuals continue life with minimal disruption to normal activities. A hospice uses an interdisciplinary approach to deliver medical, social, psychological, emotional, and spiritual services through the use of a broad spectrum of professional and other caregivers, with the goal of making the individual as physically and emotionally comfortable as possible. Counseling and respite services are available to the family of the hospice patient. Hospice programs consider both the patient and the family as a unit of care.

Medicare Part A (Hospital Insurance) provides coverage for hospice care for terminally ill Medicare beneficiaries who elect to receive care from a participating hospice.

A hospice is an organization that is primarily engaged in providing pain relief, symptom management, and supportive services to terminally ill people.

1041. How is hospice care covered under Part A (Hospital Insurance)?

Under the Part A (Hospital Insurance) hospice benefit, Medicare pays for hospice services every day and also permits a hospice to provide appropriate custodial care, including homemaker services and counseling. Hospice care under Medicare includes both home care and inpatient care, when needed, and a variety of services not otherwise covered under Medicare (such as custodial care).

Medicare payments to a hospice are based on one of four prospectively determined rates for each day in which a qualified Medicare beneficiary is under the care of the hospice. The four rate categories are *routine home care*, *continuous home care*, *inpatient respite care*, and *general inpatient care*. Payment rates are adjusted to reflect local differences in area wage levels.

Hospice care is covered under Part A (Hospital Insurance) when the beneficiary:

(1)   is eligible for Part A benefits;

(2)   is certified by a physician as terminally ill (i.e., have a life expectancy of six months or less); and

(3)   files a statement electing to waive all other Medicare coverage for hospice care from hospice programs other than the one chosen, and elects not to receive other services related to treatment of the terminal condition. (The beneficiary can later revoke the election.)

The following are covered hospice services:

- Doctor care

- Nursing care provided by or under the supervision of a registered professional nurse.

- Medical social services provided by a social worker under a physician's direction.

- Counseling (including dietary counseling) with respect to care of the terminally ill patient and adjustment to the patient's approaching death.

- Short-term inpatient care (including both respite care and procedures necessary for pain control and acute and chronic symptom management) provided in a participating hospice, hospital, or skilled nursing facility. The respite care may be provided only on an intermittent, nonroutine, and occasional basis and may not be provided consecutively over longer than five days.

- Medical equipment, appliances and supplies.

- Services of a home health aide and homemaker services.

- Prescription drugs, including outpatient drugs for pain relief and symptom management.

- Physical therapy, occupational therapy, and speech-language pathology services to control symptoms or to enable the patient to maintain activities of daily living and basic functional skills.

- Dietary counseling

- Grief and loss counseling

- Short-term respite care

Services of a home health aide, homemaker services, and nursing care provided by or under the supervision of a registered professional nurse, may be provided on a twenty-four-hour, continuous basis only during periods of crisis and only as necessary to maintain the terminally ill patient at home.

The definition of hospice care also includes any other item or service which is specified in the patient's plan of care and for which Medicare may pay.

A "hospice program" for Medicare purposes is a public agency or private organization that is primarily engaged in providing the care and services listed above and makes the services available (as needed) on a twenty-four-hour basis. A hospice program also provides bereavement counseling for the immediate family of the terminally ill patient. The care and services must be provided in the patient's home, on an outpatient basis, and on a short-term inpatient basis. The nursing, physician, counseling, and medical social service benefits must be provided directly on a routine basis. The remaining hospice benefits may be provided through arrangements with other hospice programs (provided the agency or organization maintains professional management responsibility for all services).

The Centers for Medicare & Medicaid Services (CMS) may waive certain service requirements for hospices not located in urbanized areas that can demonstrate that they have been unable, despite diligent efforts, to recruit appropriate personnel. For these hospices, CMS may waive the provision requiring physical or occupational therapy or speech-language pathology services and dietary counseling.

A hospice program must have an interdisciplinary group of personnel (at least one physician, one registered nurse, one social worker, and one pastoral or other counselor) to establish the policies of the program and provide the required care and services. The group must maintain central clinical records on all patients, utilize volunteers, and is required to continue hospice care for any patient who is unable to pay for such care.

1042. What is not covered under Part A (Hospital Insurance) in regard to hospice?

Medicare won't cover any of these procedures once the hospice benefit starts:

- Treatment intended to cure a terminal illness and/or related conditions. A hospice patient always has the right to stop hospice coverage to pursue a cure.

- Prescription drugs to address the illness rather than for symptom control or pain relief.

- Care from any hospice provider that wasn't set up by the hospice medical team. All care for the terminal illness must be given by or arranged by the hospice team. A patient CAN still see their regular doctor or nurse practitioner if they have chosen him or her to be the attending medical professional who helps supervise the hospice care.

- Room and board. Medicare doesn't cover room and board if you get hospice care in your home or if living in a nursing home or a hospice inpatient facility. If the hospice team determines that short-term inpatient or respite care services is needed, Medicare will cover the stay in the facility although there may be a small copayment for the respite stay.

- Hospital outpatient care, Hospital inpatient care, or ambulance transportation, unless arranged by the hospice team or unrelated to the terminal illness and related conditions.

1043. What is the hospice benefit period?

The benefit period consists of:

- two ninety-day periods followed by

- an unlimited number of sixty-day periods.

At the beginning of the first ninety-day hospice benefit period, both the beneficiary's attending physician (if any) and the medical director or physician member of the hospice interdisciplinary team must certify in writing that the beneficiary is terminally ill. Terminally ill is defined as having a life expectancy of six months or less. The medical director or physician member of the hospice interdisciplinary team must recertify that the beneficiary is terminally ill at the beginning of all successive benefit periods. An individual can change their hospice provider once during each benefit period. If health improves, or the illness goes into remission, hospice care can end.

1044. What does the patient pay for hospice care?

There are no deductibles under the hospice benefit. The beneficiary does not pay for Medicare-covered services for the terminal illness, except for small coinsurance amounts for outpatient drugs and inpatient respite care. For outpatient prescription drugs, the patient is responsible for about 5 percent of the cost of drugs or five dollars, whichever is less. For inpatient respite care, the patient pays 5 percent of the amount paid by Medicare for a respite care day, but the total of all coinsurance for respite care may not exceed the Medicare Part A inpatient hospital deductible for the year in which the hospice period began.

1045. How is respite care covered?

Respite care as an inpatient in a hospice (to give a period of relief to the family providing home care for the patient) is limited to no more than five days in a row. Respite care requires coinsurance in the amount of 5 percent of the amount that Medicare pays for the respite care. The total respite care coinsurance amount may not exceed the inpatient hospital deductible for the year in which the hospice period began.

Skilled Nursing Facility Care

1046. What is a qualified skilled nursing facility?

For purposes of Medicare Part A (Hospital Insurance), a skilled nursing facility is a specially qualified facility that specializes in skilled care. It has the staff and equipment to provide skilled nursing care or skilled rehabilitative services and other related health services.

A skilled nursing facility may be a skilled nursing home, or a distinct part of an institution, such as a ward or wing of a hospital, or a section of a facility another part of which is an old-age home. Not all nursing homes will qualify; those which offer only custodial care are excluded. The facility must be primarily engaged in providing skilled nursing care or rehabilitation services for injured, disabled or sick persons. Skilled nursing care means care that can be performed only by, or under the supervision of, licensed nursing personnel. Skilled rehabilitation services may include such services as physical therapy performed by, or under the supervision of, a professional therapist. Skilled nursing care and skilled rehabilitation services must be needed and received on a daily basis (at least five days a week) or the patient is not eligible for Medicare coverage.

At least one registered nurse must be employed full-time, and adequate nursing service (which may include services by practical nurses) must be provided at all times. Every patient must be under the supervision of a physician, and a physician must always be available for emergency care. Generally, the facility must be certified by the state and meet all state licensing requirements. The facility also must have a written agreement with a hospital that is participating in the Medicare program for the transfer of patients.

Medicare also requires that qualified skilled nursing facilities provide patients with the following rights:

(1)   equal access and admission;

(2)   notice of rights and services;

(3)   transfer and discharge rights;

(4)   the right to pretransfer and predischarge notice;

(5)   access and visitation rights;

(6)   rights relating to the protection of resident funds; and

(7)   certain other specified rights.

An institution which is primarily for the care and treatment of mental diseases or tuberculosis is not a skilled nursing facility.

Many nursing homes in the United States do not qualify as "skilled nursing facilities" for purposes of Medicare and are not certified to provide services reimbursed by Medicare. In some facilities, only certain portions participate in Medicare.

1047. Does Part A (Hospital Insurance) pay for custodial care in a skilled nursing facility?

No. Medicare does not pay for custodial care when that is the ONLY kind of care needed.

Care is considered custodial when it is primarily for the purpose of helping the patient with Activities of Daily Living (ADL) or meeting personal needs and could be provided safely and reasonably by people without professional skills or training.

For example, custodial care includes help in walking, getting in and out of bed, bathing, dressing, eating, and taking medicine.

1048. Do most nursing home residents qualify for Part A (Hospital Insurance) coverage?

No. Most residents of nursing homes will not qualify for Medicare coverage, because Medicare coverage is restricted to patients in need of skilled nursing and rehabilitative services on a daily basis. Many nursing home residents are in need primarily of custodial care, which is not covered by Medicare.

The initial determination of Medicare coverage is made by the nursing home, but the nursing home cannot charge the patient for care provided before it notifies the patient in writing that it believes Medicare will not pay for the care. The patient may not challenge the nursing home's noncoverage determination until a claim has been submitted to and denied by the Medicare intermediary. The patient does have the right to require a nursing home to submit its claim to the Medicare intermediary so that the intermediary can determine if the nursing home was correct in denying coverage.

1049. Under what circumstances does a patient qualify for skilled nursing facility benefits under Part A (Hospital Insurance)?

In order to qualify for skilled nursing facility benefits under Part A (Hospital Insurance), the patient generally must meet all of these five conditions:

(1)   The patient's condition requires daily skilled nursing or skilled rehabilitative services which, as a practical matter, can only be provided in a skilled nursing facility.

(2)   The patient has been in a hospital at least three days in a row (not counting the day of discharge) before being admitted to a participating skilled nursing facility.

(3)   The patient is admitted to the skilled nursing facility within a short time (generally within thirty days) after leaving the hospital.

(4)   The patient's care in the skilled nursing facility is for a condition that was treated in the hospital, or for a condition that arose while receiving care in the skilled nursing facility for a condition which was treated in the hospital.

(5)   A medical professional certifies that the patient needs, and receives, skilled nursing or skilled rehabilitation services (posthospital extended care) on a daily basis.

If a patient leaves a skilled nursing facility and is readmitted within thirty days, the patient does not need to have a new three-day stay in a hospital for care to be covered.

Except for a coinsurance amount payable by the patient after the first twenty days, Part A (Hospital Insurance) will pay the reasonable cost of post-hospital care in a skilled nursing facility for up to 100 days in a benefit period.

1050. What items and services generally are (and are not) covered under Part A (Hospital Insurance) when provided in a participating skilled nursing facility?

The following items and services are covered when provided in a participating skilled nursing facility:

- Bed and board in a semiprivate room (two to four beds in a room), unless the patient's condition requires isolation or no semiprivate rooms are available.

- Nursing care provided by, or under the supervision of, a registered nurse (but not private-duty nursing).

- Drugs, biologicals, supplies (such as splints and casts), appliances (such as wheelchairs) and equipment for use in the facility.

- Medical social services, including the assessment of the patient's medical and nursing requirements, the patient's financial resources, home situation, and the community services available to him. Such services may also include the assessment of the social and emotional factors related to the patient's illness, and the patient's need for care, response to treatment, and adjustment to care in the skilled nursing facility. Appropriate action to obtain case work services to assist in resolving problems in these areas is covered by Medicare.

- Medical services of interns and residents in training under an approved teaching program of a hospital.

- Other diagnostic or therapeutic services provided by a hospital with which the facility has a transfer agreement.

- Rehabilitation services, such as physical, occupational, and speech therapy, furnished by the skilled nursing facility, or by others under arrangements made by the skilled nursing facility.

- All meals, including special diets furnished by the facility.

- Blood transfusions, other than the first three pints of blood.

- Such other health services as are generally provided by a skilled nursing facility.

The following services are not covered even if provided by the skilled nursing facility:

- Personal convenience (comfort) items that the patient requests, such as a television, radio, or telephone

- Private duty nurses or attendants

- Any extra charges for a private room, unless it is determined to be medically necessary

- Custodial care, including assistance with the Activities of Daily Living (i.e., walking, getting in and out of bed, bathing, dressing, and feeding), special diets, and supervision of medication that can usually be self-administered, when that is the only care required by the patient

- Physician's services provided to a patient while the patient is in a skilled nursing facility are covered by Part B (Medical Insurance), not Part A (Hospital Insurance)

1051. What provisions are made under Part A (Hospital Insurance) for care in a skilled nursing facility?

Federal regulations include the following services for skilled rehabilitation and nursing care:

(1) Insertion and sterile irrigation and replacement of catheters;

(2) Application of dressing involving prescription medications and aseptic techniques;

(3) Treatment of extensive bed sores or other widespread skin disorders;

(4) Therapeutic exercises or activities supervised or performed by a qualified occupational or physical therapist;

(5) Training to restore a patient's ability to walk; and

(6) Range of motion exercises that are part of a physical therapist's active treatment to restore a patient's mobility.

A number of services involving the development, management and evaluation of a patient care plan may qualify as skilled services. These services are "skilled" if the patient's condition requires the services to be provided or supervised by a professional to meet the patient's needs, promote recovery, and ensure the patient's medical safety. For example, a patient with a history of diabetes and heart problems, who is recovering from a broken arm, may require skin care, medication, a special diet, an exercise program to preserve muscle tone, and observation to detect signs of deterioration or complications. Although none of these required services necessarily falls within the definition of "skilled" on its own, the combination, provided by a professional, may be considered "skilled."

To qualify for skilled nursing facility reimbursement, skilled physical therapy must be:

(1) specifically related to a physician's active treatment plan;

(2) of a complexity, or involving a condition, that requires a physical therapist;

(3) necessary to establish a safe maintenance program or provided where the patient's condition will improve within a predictable time; and

(4) of the necessary frequency and duration.

1052. How much does the patient pay for skilled nursing facility care?

The patient pays nothing for the first twenty days of covered services in each spell of illness; after twenty days, coinsurance is payable for each additional day, up to a maximum of eighty days for days twenty-one through 100. For a patient in a skilled nursing facility in 2019, the coinsurance is $170.50 per day.

Thus, a 100-day stay in a skilled nursing facility during 2019 will cost the patient $13,640 (up $480 from the 2018 cost of $13,160).

There is no lifetime limit on the amount of skilled nursing facility care provided under Part A (Hospital Insurance). Except for the coinsurance (which must be paid after the first twenty days in each spell of illness), Medicare will cover the cost of 100 days' post-hospital care in each benefit period, regardless of how many benefit periods the person may have. After 100 days of coverage, the patient must pay the full cost of skilled nursing facility care.

Skilled nursing facilities cannot require a patient to pay a deposit or other payment as a condition of admission to the facility unless it is clear that services are not covered under Medicare.

1053. When can payment be made for skilled nursing care under Part A (Hospital Insurance)?

Subject to the patient's coinsurance obligation after the first twenty days, Medicare Part A (Hospital Insurance) will be made for skilled nursing care only if the following conditions are met:

(1) The beneficiary files a written request for payment (another person may sign the request if it is impracticable for the patient to sign).

(2) A physician certifies that the patient needs skilled nursing care on an inpatient basis. Recertification is required for extended stays. Part A (Hospital Insurance) will not pay for a person's stay if the individual needs skilled nursing or rehabilitation services only occasionally, such as once or twice a week, or if a person does not need to be in a skilled nursing facility to obtain skilled rehabilitation services. Part A (Hospital Insurance) also generally will not pay for a person's continued stay in a skilled nursing facility if the rehabilitation services are no longer improving his or her condition and could be carried out by someone other than a physical therapist or physical therapist assistant.

(3) The facility is "participating" under Medicare law.

See Q 1049 for more information on skilled nursing care.

Home Health Care

1054. When are post-institutional home health services covered under Part A (Hospital Insurance)?

If a person needs post-institutional skilled health care in his or her home for the treatment of an illness or injury, Medicare pays for covered home health services furnished by a participating home health agency. In general, Part A (Hospital Insurance) covers the cost of 100 home health visits made on an "intermittent" basis during a home health spell of illness under a plan of treatment established by a physician. However, patients may be eligible for additional home health benefits under Part B (see Q 1095).

A "home health agency" is a public agency or private organization that:

(1)   is primarily engaged in providing skilled nursing services and other therapeutic services;

(2)   has policies, established by a group of professional personnel, including one or more physicians and one or more registered professional nurses, to govern the services which it provides, and provides for supervision of its services by a physician or registered professional nurse;

(3)   maintains clinical records on all patients;

(4)   is licensed pursuant to applicable state and local law;

(5)   has in effect an overall plan and budget;

(6)   meets additional requirements and conditions of participation as the Centers for Medicare & Medicaid Services (CMS) finds necessary in the interest of the health and safety of individuals who are furnished services by the home health agency;

(7)   meets additional requirements as specified by CMS for the effective and efficient operation of the program.

A "home health agency" does not include any agency or organization that is primarily for the care and treatment of mental diseases.

A number of rules and procedures have been established to stop fraud and abuse, including regulations requiring all home health agencies serving Medicare to obtain surety bonds. Agencies must be bonded and must provide quality care to at least ten patients before applying to provide care to Medicare patients. At least seven of the ten patients must be receiving active care at the time the agency applies to participate in Medicare.

1055. What conditions must be met for Part A (Hospital Insurance) to cover home health visits?

In general, Part A (Hospital Insurance) pays for the first 100 home health visits in a "home health spell of illness" only if all six of the following conditions are met:

(1)   The care is post-institutional home health services

(2)   The care includes intermittent skilled nursing care, physical therapy, or speech therapy

(3)   The person is confined at home and a doctor must certify that you're homebound

(4)   The person is under the care of a physician who determines the need for home health care and sets up a home health plan for the person

(5)   The home health agency providing services participates in Medicare

(6)   The services are provided on a visiting basis in the person's home or, if it is necessary to use equipment that cannot be readily made available in the home, on an outpatient basis in a hospital, skilled nursing facility, or licensed rehabilitation center

The term "post-institutional home health services" means home health services furnished to an individual:

(1)   After discharge from a hospital or rural primary care hospital in which the individual was an inpatient for at least three consecutive days before discharge. Home health services must be initiated within fourteen days after the date of discharge.

(2)   After discharge from a skilled nursing facility in which the individual was provided posthospital extended care services covered by Medicare. Home health services must be initiated within fourteen days after the date of discharge.

The term "home health spell of illness" means a period of consecutive days

(1)   beginning with the first day a person is furnished post-institutional home health services (in a month in which the person is entitled to benefits under Part A) and

(2)   ending with the close of the first period of sixty consecutive days thereafter for which the person is neither an inpatient in a hospital or skilled nursing facility nor provided home health services.

"Part-time or intermittent services" is defined as skilled nursing and home health services (combined) furnished any number of days per week, for less than eight hours per day and twenty-eight or fewer hours per week (or, subject to review on a case-by-case basis as to the need for care, less than eight hours each day and thirty-five or fewer hours per week). Home benefit doesn't apply if more than part-time or intermittent skilled nursing is required – although home health care is allowed if the patient is getting adult day care.

"Intermittent" is defined as skilled nursing care provided on fewer than seven days each week, or less than eight hours each day (combined) for twenty-one days or less (with extensions in exceptional circumstances when the need for additional care is finite and predictable).

A physician must certify that the patient is under a physician's care, under a plan of care established and periodically reviewed no less frequently than every two months by a doctor, confined to the home, and in need of skilled nursing care on an intermittent basis or physical or speech therapy, or has a continued need for occupational therapy when eligibility for home health services has been established (because of a prior need for intermittent skilled nursing care, speech therapy, or physical therapy in the current or prior certification period).

Home health aides, whether employed directly by a home health agency or made available through contract with another entity, must successfully complete a training and competency evaluation program or competency evaluation program approved by CMS.

Generally, a physician may not set up a home health care plan for a patient with any agency in which the physician has a significant ownership interest or a significant financial or contractual relationship. However, a physician who has a financial interest in an agency which is a sole community health agency may carry out certification and plan of care functions for patients served by that agency.

1056. What post-institutional home health services are covered under Part A (Hospital Insurance)?

In general, the following post-institutional home health services are covered under Part A (Hospital Insurance):

- Part-time or intermittent skilled nursing care (See Q 1055)

- Physical therapy

- Speech therapy

- Continuing occupational services

If a person needs part-time or intermittent skilled nursing care, physical therapy, or speech therapy, Medicare also pays for:

- Part-time or intermittent services of home health aides. Covered services include, but are not limited to —

  - personal care;

  - simple dressing changes that do not require the skills of a licensed nurse;

  - assistance with medications that are ordinarily self-administered and that do not require a licensed nurse;

  - assistance with activities supportive of skilled therapy services; and

  - routine care of prosthetic devices.

- Medical social services.

- Medical supplies, including catheters, catheter supplies, ostomy bags, and ostomy care supplies.

- Durable medical equipment, including iron lungs, oxygen tents, hospital beds, and wheelchairs (subject to a 20 percent coinsurance as described below).

- Occupational therapy.

The patient generally pays nothing under Part A (Hospital Insurance) for the first 100 home health visits; Medicare pays the full approved cost of all covered home health visits. The patient may be charged, however, for any services or costs that Medicare does not cover. Also, if a patient needs durable medical equipment, the patient is responsible for a 20 percent coinsurance payment for the equipment. The home health agency will submit claims for payment. The patient does not submit bills to Medicare.

Both Part A (Hospital Insurance) and Part B (Medical Insurance) cover home health visits, but for beneficiaries covered by both Parts A and B, Part A pays for the first 100 visits following a hospital or skilled nursing facility stay while Part B pays for home health services without regard to a preceding hospital or skilled nursing facility stay.

Medicare does not cover home care services furnished primarily to assist people in meeting personal, family, and domestic needs. These noncovered services include general household services such as laundry, meal preparation, shopping, or assisting in bathing, dressing, or other personal needs.

Home health services generally not covered by Medicare also include:

- twenty-four-hour-a-day nursing care at home;

- drugs and biologicals;

- blood transfusions;

- meals delivered to the home;

- homemaker services; and

- venipuncture (drawing of blood for the purpose of obtaining a blood sample), if venipuncture is the only skilled service needed by the beneficiary.

Although a patient in general must be "confined" to home to be eligible for home health care benefits, payment will be made for services furnished at a hospital, skilled nursing facility, or rehabilitation center, if the patient's condition requires the use of equipment that ordinarily cannot be taken to the patient's home. Medicare usually will not pay the patient's transportation costs.

A patient is considered "confined to the home" if he or she has a condition, due to illness or injury, that restricts the ability to leave home except with the assistance of another person or the aid of a supportive device (such as crutches, a cane, a wheelchair, or a walker), or if the patient has a condition such that leaving home is medically unsafe. Although a patient does not have to be bedridden to be considered "confined to the home," the condition should be such that there exists a normal inability to leave home, that leaving home requires a considerable and taxing effort, and that absences from home are infrequent or of relatively short duration, or are attributable to the need to receive medical treatment.

For these purposes "infrequent" means an average of five or fewer absences per calendar month, excluding absences to receive medical treatment that cannot be furnished in the home. "Short duration" means an average of three or fewer hours per absence from the home within a calendar month, excluding absences to receive medical treatment that cannot be furnished in the home.

Absences for medical treatment must be:

(1)   based on and in conformance with a physician's order;

(2)   by or under the supervision of a licensed health professional; and

(3)   for the purpose of diagnosis or treatment of an illness or injury.

Examples of patients qualifying as homebound include:

(1)   a person paralyzed from a stroke who is confined to a wheelchair and who requires crutches in order to walk;

(2)   a person who is blind or senile and requires the assistance of another person in leaving his or her residence;

(3)   a person who has lost the use of upper extremities and is unable to open doors, use stairways, etc., and, therefore, requires the assistance of another person to leave his or her residence; and

(4)   a person with a psychiatric problem if the person's illness is manifested in part by a refusal to leave his or her home environment or is of such a nature that it would not be considered safe for the patient to leave home unattended, even if the patient has no physical limitations.

1057. How does Medicare pay the costs of home health services?

The Centers for Medicare & Medicaid Services (CMS) have established a prospective payment system for all costs of home health services. In defining a payment amount under a prospective payment system, CMS considers an appropriate unit of service and the number, type, and duration of visits provided within that unit of service. CMS also considers potential changes in the mix of services provided within a unit and their cost. The general design of a unit of service is to provide for continued access to quality services. All bills for service must be submitted by the home health agency for payment and not by any other person or entity.

Prospective payment amounts are intended to be standardized in a manner that eliminates the effect of variations in relative case mix and wage levels among different home health agencies in a budget-neutral manner. Under the system, CMS may recognize regional differences or differences based upon whether the services or agencies are in an urbanized area. The standard prospective payment amount (or amounts) is adjusted for each fiscal year.

General Information

1058. Does Part A (Hospital Insurance) pay the cost of outpatient hospital services?

No. Outpatient diagnostic and treatment services are covered under Part B (Medical Insurance), not Part A (Hospital Insurance). (See Q 1062 through Q 1133.)

1059. Does a person need to be in financial need to receive Part A (Hospital Insurance) benefits?

No. Medicare benefits are not subject to any means testing and there is no specific dollar limit on coverage.

1060. Will the deductible and coinsurance amounts paid by patients for Part A (Hospital Insurance) remain the same in future years?

No. The $1,364 initial deductible for Part A inpatient hospital care for 2019 is based on the 1966-68 figure of forty dollars and on increases in average per diem inpatient hospital cost since 1966 (with some legislative adjustments). Further adjustments have been made since 1987 based on increases in average national hospital costs. The daily coinsurance amounts for inpatient hospital care are based on a percentage of the deductible. Thus, the daily coinsurance for inpatient hospital care for the sixty-first through ninetieth days in a benefit period is one-fourth of the initial deductible ($341 in 2019). The coinsurance for each lifetime reserve day (a total of sixty in a lifetime), used after the ninetieth inpatient hospital stay day is half of the inpatient care deductible ($682 in 2019). The daily coinsurance for posthospital extended care in a skilled nursing facility after the first twenty days of such care (up to the maximum of 100 days, including the first twenty) is one-eighth of the inpatient hospital stay deductible (thus, $170.50 in 2019).

1061. What is Medicare's position regarding treatment of a patient with a living will or durable power of attorney for health care?

Medicare requires that all hospitals, skilled nursing facilities, nursing facilities, providers of home health care or personal care services, hospices, and prepaid health plans to provide a Medicare patient with written information concerning rights under state law to make decisions concerning medical care, including the right to accept or refuse medical or surgical treatment and the right to formulate – at the patient's option – advance directives. The regulations do not apply to providers of outpatient hospital services.

The term "advance directive" is defined as a written instrument, such as a living will or durable power of attorney for health care, recognized under state law, relating to the provision of health care when the individual is incapacitated. No individual is required to execute an advance directive. A health care proxy (durable power of attorney) is a document that names someone you trust to make health decisions if you can't. A living will is a document which identifies which treatment you want if your life is threatened, including decisions such as dialysis and ventilators, DNR (Do Not Resuscitate orders, feeding tubes, and organ donation.

The provider must:

(1)   inform the individual, in writing, of state laws regarding advance directives;

(2)   inform the individual, in writing, of the policies of the provider regarding the implementation of advance directives, including (if permitted under state law) a clear and precise explanation of any objection a provider may have, on the basis of conscience, to honoring an individual's directive;

(3)   document in the individual's medical record whether or not the individual has executed an advance directive;

(4)   educate staff on issues concerning advance directives; and

(5)   provide for community education on issues concerning advance directives.

Written information on advance directives must be provided to an individual upon each admission to a medical facility and each time an individual comes under the care of a home health agency, personal care provider, or hospice. For example: if a person is admitted as an inpatient to a hospital and then to a nursing home, both the hospital and the nursing home are required to provide information on advance directives to the individual. If the patient is incapacitated at the time of admission and is unable to receive information or articulate whether or not an advance directive has been executed, the facility may give advance directive information to the patient's family or surrogate.

All patients are generally entitled to the medically necessary care ordered by a physician and that a provider, under normal procedures, would be required to furnish; providers cannot delay or withhold such care because the individual has not executed an advance directive or the provider is waiting for an advance directive to be executed. However, once a provider receives documentation that an advance directive has been executed, the directive takes precedence over the facility's normal procedures, to the extent required by state law.

A health care provider is not required to implement an advance directive if, as a matter of conscience, the provider cannot implement an advance directive and state law allows any health care provider to conscientiously object. The provider must inform individuals that complaints concerning noncompliance with the advance directive requirements may be filed with the state survey and certification agency.

PART B: MEDICAL INSURANCE

Eligibility

1062. Who is eligible for Part B (Medical Insurance) benefits?

Anyone who is eligible for Part A (Hospital Insurance), whether automatically or through payment of Part A premiums (including disabled individuals who lose entitlement to automatic Part A benefits but may still enroll by paying premiums), may enroll in Part B (Medical Insurance).

Even if a person does not qualify for Part A benefits, that person may enroll in Part B (Medical Insurance) as long as he is at least age sixty-five, a U.S. resident and either

(1) a U.S. citizen or

(2) an alien lawfully admitted for permanent residence who has resided in the United States continuously during the five years immediately prior to the month in which he applies for enrollment in Part B.

See Q 1018 for eligibility rules for Part A (Hospital Insurance).

1063. How does a person enroll in Part B (Medical Insurance)?

Individuals who are receiving Social Security and Railroad Retirement benefits are enrolled automatically in Part B (Medical Insurance) when they become entitled to Part A (Hospital Insurance). They may, however, elect not to be covered by Part B (Medical Insurance) by signing a form sent to them by the Social Security Administration. Others may enroll online through the Social Security Administration's website (www.ssa.gov) or at the nearest Social Security office. An individual who already has Part A coverage and wants to add Part B coverage may also call 1-800-772-1213.

The initial enrollment period for Part B (Medical Insurance) is a period of seven full calendar months, the beginning and end of which is determined for each person by the day on which he is first eligible to enroll. The initial enrollment period begins on the first day of the third month before the month a person first becomes eligible to enroll and ends with the close of the last day of the third month following the month a person first becomes eligible to enroll. For example, if the person's sixty-fifth birthday is April 10, 2019, that person's initial enrollment period begins January 1, 2019 and ends July 31, 2019.

If a person decides not to enroll during the initial enrollment period, that individual may enroll later during a general enrollment period. There is a general enrollment period from January 1 through March 31 of each year, with such enrollment effective the following July 1. Under certain circumstances, a person who does not enroll during his initial enrollment period may be able to enroll during a special enrollment period. (See Q 1064.) The special enrollment period is a period provided by statute to enable certain individuals to enroll in Medicare without waiting for the general enrollment period.

In order to obtain coverage at the earliest possible date, a person must enroll before the beginning of the month in which he reaches age sixty-five. For a person who enrolls during the initial enrollment period, the effective date of coverage is as follows:

(1)   If the person enrolls before the month in which age sixty-five is reached, coverage will commence the first day of the month in which age sixty-five is reached.

(2)   If the person enrolls during the month in which age sixty-five is reached, coverage will commence the first day of the following month.

(3)   If the person enrolls in the month after the month in which age sixty-five is reached, coverage will commence the first day of the second month after the month of enrollment.

(4)   If the person enrolls more than one month (but at least within three months) after the month in which age sixty-five is reached, coverage will commence the first day of the third month following the month of enrollment.

An eight-month special enrollment period is provided if Medicare has been the secondary payer of benefits for individuals age sixty-five and older who are covered under an employer group health plan because of current employment. The special enrollment period generally begins with the month after the month in which coverage under the private plan ends. Coverage under Part B (Medical Insurance) will begin with the first day of the month after the month in which coverage under the private plan ends if the individual enrolls in that month or with the first day of the month after the month of enrollment if the individual enrolls during the balance of the special enrollment period. (See Q 1064.)

1064. What if a person declines to enroll during the Part B (Medical Insurance) initial enrollment period?

Anyone who is eligible but fails to enroll in Part B (Medical Insurance) during the initial enrollment period may enroll during a general enrollment period. There are general enrollment periods each year from January 1st through March 31st. Coverage begins the following July 1st.

The Part B premium will be higher for a person who fails to enroll within twelve months, or who drops out of the plan and later re-enrolls. The monthly premium will be increased by 10 percent for each full twelve months during which such an individual could have been, but was not, enrolled.

If a person declines to enroll (or terminates enrollment) at a time when Medicare is secondary payer to an employer group health plan covering that person, the months in which the individual is covered under the employer group health plan (based on current employment) will not be counted as months during which the individual could have been but was not enrolled in Part B (Medical Insurance) for the purpose of determining if the premium amount should be increased above the basic rate. Individuals to whom this applies may later enroll during a "special enrollment period." The special enrollment period lasts for eight months after the earlier of the termination of the individual's group health plan coverage or termination of employment.

In general, individuals must meet the following conditions to enroll during a special enrollment period:

(1)   They must be eligible for Part B (Medical Insurance) on the basis of age or disability, but not on the basis of end-stage renal disease.

(2)   When first eligible for Part B (Medical Insurance coverage), they must be covered under a group health plan on the basis of current employment status of the individual or the individual's spouse.

(3)   For all months thereafter, they must maintain coverage under a group health plan. (Generally, if an individual fails to enroll in Part B (Medical Insurance) during any available special enrollment period, that individual is not entitled to any additional special enrollment periods. But if an individual fails to enroll during a special enrollment period because coverage under the same or a different group health plan was restored before the end of that particular special enrollment period, that failure to enroll does not preclude additional special enrollment periods.)

1065. Is there a special enrollment period for disabled workers who lose benefits under a group health plan?

Yes. Certain disabled beneficiaries are eligible for a special enrollment period and waiver of the Part B premium surcharge.

These individuals are disabled beneficiaries:

(1)   who were enrolled in an employment-based group health plan (by reason of current or former employment or the current or former employment of a family member) at the time of initially becoming eligible for Medicare;

(2)   who elected not to enroll in Part B during their initial enrollment period; and

(3)   whose continuous enrollment under the group health plan is involuntarily terminated at a time when the enrollment is by reason of the individual's former employment (or the former employment of a family member).

The special enrollment period begins on the first day of the month that includes the date of the involuntary termination and continues for six months.

1066. How does a person terminate or cancel coverage under Part B (Medical Insurance)?

A person's Part B (Medical Insurance) coverage continues until the individual's enrollment is terminated. A beneficiary may terminate coverage by filing a notice that he no longer wishes to participate in the program or by not paying the monthly premium.

The termination of coverage takes effect at the close of the month following the month in which a notice is filed. A grace period, however, is provided before coverage is terminated for not paying premiums. The grace period in which overdue premiums can be paid and coverage continued generally runs for three months from the month for which the unpaid premium was due, but may be extended an additional three months in certain cases where the Centers for Medicare & Medicaid Services (CMS) determines that there was good cause for failure to pay the overdue premiums within the initial three-month grace period).

A termination notice filed by a person enrolled in Part B (Medical Insurance) before the first day of the month in which Part B coverage is scheduled to begin will terminate coverage on the first day of the month in which coverage would otherwise have been effective. If a termination notice is filed in or after the month in which Part B coverage is effective, the coverage is terminated at the close of the month following the month in which the notice is filed.

In the case of a person entitled to Part A (Hospital Insurance) based on twenty-four or more months of disability, rather than on having attained age sixty-five, Part B (Medical Insurance) generally ends at the close of the last month for which the individual is entitled to Part A benefits.

Financing Part B (Medical Insurance)

1067. How is Part B (Medical Insurance) financed?

Medical Insurance is voluntary and is financed through premiums paid by people who enroll and through funds from the federal government. Monthly premiums are in addition to the deductible and coinsurance amounts that must be paid by beneficiaries.

Most persons enrolled in 2019 pay a standard monthly premium of $135.50 per month. The basic Part B (Medical Insurance) premium is set to cover approximately 25 percent of program costs each year. The federal government pays the remaining cost from general revenues. In September-October of each year, the CMS announce the premium rate for the twelve-month period starting the following January.

Single persons with annual incomes over $85,000 (as indexed in 2017) and married couples with incomes over $170,000 (as indexed in 2017) pay a higher percentage of the cost of Part B (Medical Insurance).

These higher income beneficiaries will pay monthly premiums as follows during 2019:

1.   Beneficiaries who file an individual tax return with 2017 income levels:

   –   Greater than $85,000 and less than or equal to $107,000: $189.60

   –   Greater than $107,000 and less than or equal to $133,500: $270.90

   –   Greater than $133,500 and less than or equal to $160,000: $352.20

   –   Greater than $160,000 and less than or equal to $500,000: $433.40

   –   Greater than $500,000: $460.50

2.   Beneficiaries who file a joint tax return with 2017 income levels:

  –   Greater than $170,000 and less than or equal to $214,000: $189.60

  –   Greater than $214,000 and less than or equal to $267,000: $270.90

  –   Greater than $267,000 and less than or equal to $320,000: $352.20

  –   Greater than $320,000 and less than or equal to $750,000: $433.40

  –   Greater than $750,000: $460.50

3.   Beneficiaries who are married and lived with their spouse at any time during the year, but file a separate tax return from their spouse in 2017:

  –   Less than/equal to $85,000: $135.50

  –   Greater than $85,000 and less than or equal to $415,000: $433.40

  –   Greater than $415,000: $460.50

The premium rate for a person who enrolls after his initial enrollment period (when he is first eligible for Part B coverage), or who re-enrolls after terminating Part B coverage, will be increased by up to 10 percent for each full twelve months the person stayed out of the program. Special enrollment periods apply to certain individuals with employer group health plan coverage, and they are not subject to the late enrollment penalty as long as they enroll during such a special enrollment period. See Q 1064 for more detail on the special enrollment period.

Basic Monthly Premium Part B (Medical Insurance)

Year	Monthly Premium
1994	41.10
1995	46.10
1996	42.50
1997	43.80
1998	43.80
1999	45.50
2000	45.50
2001	50.00
2002	54.00
2003	58.70
2004	66.60
2005	78.20
2006	88.50
2007	93.50

Basic Monthly Premium Part B (Medical Insurance)

Year	Monthly Premium
2008	96.40
2009	96.40
2010	110.50
2011	115.40
2012	99.90
2013-2015	104.90
2016	121.80 or 104.90
2017	134.00 or 109.00
2018	134.00 or 109.00
2019	135.50[1]

Income-Adjusted Monthly Premium
Part B (Medical Insurance in 2019)

Single Taxpayer	Married Taxpayers Filing Jointly	Total Premium
Not greater than $85,000	Not greater than $170,000	$135.50
$85,000 - $107,000	$170,000 - $214,000	189.60
$107,000 - $133,500	$214,000 - $267,000	270.90
$133,500 - $160,000	$267,000 - $320,000	352.20
$160,000 - $500,000	$320,000 - $750,000	433.40
More than $500,000	More than $750,000	460.50
	Married Taxpayers Separately	**Total Premium**
	Not greater than $85,000	$135.50
	$85,000 - $415,000	433.40
	$415,000 and up	460.50

1068. How is Income determined for purposes of setting a person's Part B (Hospital Insurance) Premium?

If the person's Modified Adjusted Gross Income (MAGI) is above the thresholds discussed in Q 1067, then additional Part B premiums are required. Modified Adjusted Gross Income is Adjusted Gross Income (AGI) plus tax exempt interest income.

To determine the 2019 income-related monthly adjustment amounts, Medicare uses the most recent Federal tax return that the IRS provides. This information is from a tax return filed in 2018 for tax year 2017. Sometimes, the IRS only provides information from a return filed in 2017 for tax year 2016. If Medicare uses the 2016 tax year data and the taxpayer filed a return for tax year 2017 or did not need to file a tax return for tax year 2017, the taxpayer can contact Medicare and records will be updated.

---

1. Some subject to the "hold harmless" provision may pay slightly less.

If a person's income has gone down due to any of the following situations and the change makes a difference in the income level Medicare considers, the taxpayer should contact Medicare to explain the latest information and Medicare may need a new decision about your income-related monthly adjustment amount:

- The taxpayer married, divorced, or became widowed

- The taxpayer or spouse stopped working or reduced work hours

- The taxpayer or spouse lost income-producing property due to a disaster or other event beyond the taxpayer's control

- The taxpayer or spouse experienced a scheduled cessation, termination, or reorganization of an employer's pension plan

- The taxpayer or spouse received a settlement from an employer or former employer because of the employer's closure, bankruptcy, or reorganization

If any of these apply, Medicare needs to see documentation verifying the event and the reduction in income. The documentation provided should relate to the event and may include a death certificate, a letter from an employer about retirement, or something similar. If a taxpayer filed a Federal income tax return for the year in question, a signed copy needs to be shown to Medicare.

If the taxpayer disagrees with the decision regarding the income-related monthly adjustment amounts, there is a right to appeal. The taxpayer may request an appeal in writing by completing a *Request for Reconsideration* (Form SSA-561-U2)[1] or by contacting the local Social Security office. Appeal forms can be found on the Social Security website (www.socialsecurity.gov/online). Forms can also be requested by calling 1-800-772-1213. Taxpayers do not need to file an appeal if they are requesting a new decision because one of the events listed took place which caused income to decrease or if it can be shown that information used was wrong.

Avoiding Higher Part B Premiums

An individual can reduce their Part B premium in a few ways:

- **Understand the timing**. There is a two-year lag for the extra premiums: This year's income will appear on a client's 2019 tax return, which will be filed in 2020. Medicare uses those numbers to set Part B premiums for 2020.

- **Take Action**. Continually take losses in taxable accounts. Each year, an individual can deduct $3,000 of net capital losses. Any excess losses can be carried over to future years. There is no time limit for using them.

---

1. https://www.ssa.gov/forms/ssa-561.pdf Request for Reconsideration (Form SSA-561-U2) (Last accessed October 16, 2018).

Another idea is to convert a traditional IRA to a Roth IRA. An individual can start a conversion at any age. This increases income in the current tax year but lowers it in future years as withdrawals from Roth IRAs are tax-free in most cases.

After a conversion, a person can recharacterize (reverse) some or all of the conversion back to a traditional IRA, until October 15 of the following year. By then, a calculation can be made to determine how much can be converted without moving into a higher tax bracket. And after age sixty-three, recharacterizations can involve fine-tuning to keep an individual below the Part B premium thresholds.

Also, the purchase of permanent life insurance can also help manage Part B premiums. Distributions from permanent life insurance are received income-tax free up to an individual's basis in the contract. After that, policy loans, which are not taxable, can be taken from the policy.

If a person's situation changes, he or she might be able to reduce the Part B premium. Certain situations provide grounds to appeal, including getting married, divorced, or being widowed. If a person or their spouse stops working or cuts work hours, an appeal can be made for the excess Part B premium.

1069. What assistance is available for those who cannot afford Medicare costs?

An elderly or disabled person with a low income who is eligible for Medicare may be able to have some or all Medicare expenses paid by their state. Federal law requires state Medicaid programs to pay Medicare costs for certain elderly and disabled persons with low incomes and very limited assets.

There are four programs to help people pay their Medicare expenses:

(1)   the Qualified Medicare Beneficiary (QMB) program;

(2)   the Specified Low-Income Medicare Beneficiary (SLMB) program; and

(3)   the Qualifying Individual (QI) program.

(4)   the Qualified Disabled and Working Individuals (QDWI) program.

QMB PROGRAM:

The QMB program is for a person with limited resources whose income is at or below the national poverty level. It covers the cost of Medicare Part A (Hospital Insurance) premiums, coinsurance, and deductibles that a Medicare beneficiary normally pays out of his own pocket. The QMB program also pays the basic Part B (Medical Insurance) premium, which is $135.50 in 2019 for most individuals (see Q 1067).

SLMB PROGRAM:

While the QMB program helps those whose income is at or below the national poverty level, the SLMB program is for a person whose income is slightly higher than the poverty level, but not more than 20 percent higher. The program pays the Part B (Medical Insurance) premiums $135.50 in 2019 see Q 1067) for a person qualifying under the SLMB program, but not any of the Part A or Part B deductibles and coinsurance. SLMBs also remain responsible for charges for health care services and medical supplies not covered by Medicare.

QI PROGRAM:

The QI program assists individuals and married couples whose income is more than 20 percent greater than the Federal poverty level, but not more than 38 percent greater, by paying the full monthly Part B (Medical Insurance) premium each month. As with SLMBs, persons covered under the QI program remain responsible for Medicare's deductibles and coinsurance and for charges for health care services and medical supplies not covered by Medicare.

QDWI PROGRAM:

The QDWI program assists individuals with the cost of the Part A premium. An individual can qualify by meeting any of the following criteria:

- a working disabled person under 65

- lost their premium-free Part A upon return to work

- not getting medical assistance from the state

- meeting the income and resource limits required by your state

See Q 1031 and Q 1032 for more details on eligibility for the QMB and SLMB programs.

1070. What are the Income and Resource limits for the Qualified Medicare Beneficiary (QMB) program?

For 2018, the income and resource limitations are:

- Individual monthly income limit: $1,032

- Married couple monthly income limit: $1,392

- Individual resource limit: $7,560

- Married couple resource limit: $11,340

Those that qualify for this program automatically qualify for extra assistance for Medicare Prescription Drug coverage (Part D).

1071. What are the Income and Resource limits for the Specified Low-Income Medicare Beneficiary (SLMB) program?

For 2018, the income and resource limitations are:

- Individual monthly income limit: $1,234

- Married couple monthly income limit: $1,666

- Individual resource limit: $7,560

- Married couple resource limit: $11,340

Those that qualify for this program automatically qualify for extra assistance for Medicare Prescription Drug coverage (Part D).

1072. What are the Income and Resource limits for the Qualifying Individual (QI) program?

For 2018, the income and resource limitations are:

- Individual monthly income limit: $1,386

- Married couple monthly income limit: $5,572

- Individual resource limit: $7,560

- Married couple resource limit: $11,340

Note: Individuals must apply every year for the QI program and assistance is granted on a first-come, first-serve basis. Priority is given to QI recipients of the prior year. QI is not available for those that qualify for Medicaid.

Those that qualify for this program automatically qualify for extra assistance for Medicare Prescription Drug coverage (Part D).

1073. What are the Income and Resource limits for the Qualifying Disabled and Working Individuals (QDWI) program?

For 2018, the income and resource limitations are:

- Individual monthly income limit: $4,132

- Married couple monthly income limit: $1,872

- Individual resource limit: $7,560

- Married couple resource limit: $11,340

1074. How are premiums paid under Part B (Medical Insurance)?

Most persons covered by Part B (Medical Insurance) have the premiums deducted from their Social Security, Railroad Retirement, or federal civil service retirement benefit payments. Persons who are not receiving any of these government benefits pay the premiums directly to the government.

Direct payment of premiums is usually made on a quarterly basis with a grace period, determined by the Centers for Medicare & Medicaid Services (CMS), of up to ninety days.

Public assistance agencies may enroll, and pay premiums for, certain public assistance recipients (usually recipients of public assistance under the Supplemental Security Income program). States must pay premiums for specified low-income persons. (See Q 1069.)

If a person's Social Security or Railroad Retirement benefits are suspended because of excess earnings, and benefits will not be resumed until the next taxable year, the person will be billed directly for overdue Medicare premiums. If Social Security or Railroad Retirement benefits will be resumed before the close of the taxable year, overdue premiums are deducted from the Social Security or Railroad Retirement cash benefits when they resume.

Premiums must be paid for the entire month of death even though coverage ends on the day of death.

1075. How are "approved charges" for covered medical services determined under Part B (Medical Insurance)?

There are three major elements that determine how much Medicare Part B pays for physician services:

(1) A fee schedule for the payment of physician services

(2) A method to control the rates of increase in Medicare expenditures for physicians' services

(3) Limits on the amounts that nonparticipating physicians can charge beneficiaries

Payments under the fee schedule must be based on national uniform Relative Value Units (RVUs) based on the resources used in furnishing a service. National RVUs must be established for physician work, practice expense, and malpractice expense.

Prior to the creation of RVUs, Medicare paid for services using "UCR – Usual, Customary and Reasonable rates. The Medicare fee schedule was created in 1989 and about 7,000 distinct services listed in what is called the Current Procedural Terminology owned by the AMA. Each service in the fee schedule is scored under the (RBRVS) (Resource Based Relative Value Scale) to set the payment amount.

The formula consists of three RVUs – **physician work** (51 percent), **practice expense** (45 percent) and **malpractice expense** (4 percent). These RVUs are multiplied by "geographic practice cost indices" (GCPI) and adjusted to account for different regional wages and costs. These percentages are revisited and adjusted on a yearly basis. Annual updates to the physician work, practice expense and professional liability insurance relative values are based on recommendations from the AMA/Specialty Society Relative Value Scale Update Committee (RUC), which was formed in 1991 to make recommendations to CMS on the relative values to be assigned to new or revised codes in the Current Procedural Terminology (CPT®) code book. The relative values in the RBRVS were originally developed to correspond to the approximately 10,000 CPT procedure codes. The RBRVS is updated annually to reflect new and revised CPT codes.

Physician Work: The factors used to determine this component includes the time it takes to perform the services, the technical skill and physical effort required, the required mental effort and judgment and stress due to the potential risk to the patient. The physician work relative values are updated each year to account for changes in medical practice and CMS reviews the entire scale at least every five years.

Practice Expense: These values are based on a formula using average Medicare-approved charges from 1991 (the year before the RBRVS was implemented) and the proportion of each specialty's revenues attributable to practice expenses. In January 1999, CMS began a transition to resource-based practice expense relative values for each CPT code, which differ based on the site of service.

Professional Liability Insurance/Malpractice: On January 1, 2000, CMS implemented the PLI relative value units. With this implementation and the final transition of the resource-based practice expense relative units on January 1, 2002, all components of the RBRVS became resource-based.

Adjustments in RVUs because of changes resulting from a review of those RVUs may not cause total physician fee schedule payments to differ by more than $20 million from what they would have been had the adjustments not been made. If this amount is exceeded, the Centers for Medicare & Medicaid Services (CMS) must make an adjustment to the conversion factor to preserve budget neutrality. Congress also has the power to override the statutory formula and often does so.

CMS is required to review and, if necessary, adjust the Geographic Practice Cost Indices (GPCIs) at least every three years. CMS also must phase in the adjustment over two years and implement only one-half of any adjustment if more than one year has elapsed since the last GPCI revision.

1076. How are Part B (Medical Insurance) payments made?

Part B (Medical Insurance) payments are made in two ways. Payment can be made directly to the doctor, supplier, or other health care provider. This is the *assignment method* of payment. Payment can also be made directly to the patient, who then pays the provider.

Under the assignment method, the health care provider agrees to accept the amount approved by the Medicare Administrative Contractor (MAC) as total payment for Medicare-covered services.

The assignment method can save the patient time and money. The health care provider sends the claim to Medicare. Medicare pays the health care provider 80 percent of the Medicare-approved charge, after subtracting any part of the annual deductible the patient has not paid. The health care provider can charge the patient *only* for the part of the annual deductible the patient has not met and for the Part B coinsurance, which is generally the remaining 20 percent of the approved amount. Of course, a provider also can charge the patient for any services that Medicare does not cover.

If a health care provider does not accept assignment, the provider is considered "*nonparticipating*," and Medicare pays the patient 80 percent of the approved charge, after subtracting any part of the annual deductible the patient has not paid. The health care provider can bill the patient for the provider's actual charge, even if it is more than the charge approved by the MAC.

Doctors, suppliers, and other providers of Part B (Medical Insurance) services are in most cases required to submit Medicare claims for a patient, even if the providers do not take assignment. Claims are submitted on a form called a CMS-1500,[1] requesting that Part B (Medical Insurance) payment be made for a patient's covered services. The provider completes the form and the patient signs it before it is sent to the proper MAC. Generally, the provider must submit a claim within one year of providing the service or may be subject to certain penalties. A patient should notify the MAC in the patient's area if a Medicare provider refuses to submit a claim to Medicare and the patient believes the services may be covered by Medicare.

If a patient is enrolled in a health care organization such as an HMO, a claim will seldom need to be submitted. Medicare generally pays an HMO a set amount, and the HMO provides medical care for its members. Doctors, suppliers, and other providers of Part B (Medical Insurance) services bill the HMO directly for reimbursement at contractually-agreed rates.

Utilizing a doctor who accepts assignment under Medicare may make a substantial difference in a patient's out-of-pocket costs.

> *Example.* Jane Smith has surgery after meeting the annual deductible for 2019 Part B (Medical Insurance). Dr. Ralph Jones, who is not a participating physician and does not limit his charges to the Medicare fee schedule, bills Ms. Smith $1,200 for the surgery. The Medicare fee schedule sets the charge for this surgery at $1,100. Medicare will pay $880 (80 percent of the Medicare fee), and Ms. Smith must pay the remaining $320 of the $1,200 fee.
>
> If Dr. Jones had been a participating physician under Medicare, Ms. Smith would have had to pay only $220 (20 percent of the approved charge of $1,100 that Medicare does not pay).

If a physician does not accept the assignment method, the physician must refund all amounts collected from Medicare beneficiaries on claims for services that are deemed not medically necessary. The MAC will send a notice to the beneficiary and physician advising them of the basis for denial, the right of appeal, and the requirement of a refund.

Even though a doctor does not accept assignment, for most covered services there are limits on the amount a nonparticipating provider can actually charge a Medicare beneficiary. In general, the most a doctor can charge is 115 percent of what Medicare approves. The 115 percent limit also applies to fees for physical and occupational therapy services, suppliers, injections, and other services billable under the physician fee schedule.

Physicians must give written notice prior to elective surgery for which the fee is $500 or more. The notice must state the physician's estimated actual charge, the estimated Medicare-approved charge, the excess of the actual charge over the approved charge, and the applicable coinsurance amount. This requirement applies to nonemergency surgical procedures only. (Emergency surgery is surgery performed under conditions and circumstances which afford no alternatives to the physician or the patient and, if delayed, could result in death or permanent

---

1. https://www.cms.gov/Medicare/CMS-Forms/CMS-Forms/downloads/cms1500805.pdf, Form CMS-1500 (Last accessed October 16, 2018).

impairment of health.) If the physician fails to make this fee disclosure, and the surgery was nonemergency surgery, the physician must refund amounts collected in excess of the Medicare-approved Part B (Medical Insurance) charge. The physician is subject to sanctions if the physician knowingly and willfully fails to comply with this refund requirement.

1077. How can a person find out if a doctor accepts assignment of all Medicare claims?

Doctors and suppliers sign agreements in advance to accept assignment on all Medicare claims. They are given the opportunity to sign participation agreements each year.

Medicare beneficiaries may use the Physician Compare tool available on the CMS website[1] to find participating physicians. A listing of all Medicare approved suppliers can also be found on the CMS website.[2] The names and addresses of Medicare-participating doctors and suppliers are also listed by geographic area in the *Medicare-Participating Physician Directory*[3] and the *Medicare-Participating Supplier Directory*.[4] Both directories are available in Social Security offices, from Medicare Administrative Contractors, in state and area offices of the Administration on Aging, at most hospitals, and at www.medicare.gov. Medicare beneficiaries may also call 1-800-MEDICARE (1-800-633-4227) to locate physicians and suppliers.

Medicare-participating doctors and suppliers may display emblems or certificates that show they accept assignment on all Medicare claims.

1078. What are Medicare providers and Medicare suppliers?

The term "provider" generally means a hospital, a rural primary care hospital, a skilled nursing facility, a comprehensive outpatient rehabilitative facility, a home health agency, or a hospice that has in effect an agreement to participate in Medicare. A clinic, rehabilitation agency, or a public health agency that has a similar agreement to furnish outpatient physical therapy or speech pathology services, or a community mental health center with a similar agreement to furnish partial hospitalization services, is also considered a provider.[5]

In general, "suppliers" are individuals or entities – other than doctors or health care facilities – that furnish equipment or services covered by Part B (Medical Insurance). For example, ambulance firms, independent laboratories, and entities that rent or sell medical equipment are considered suppliers.

There are different definitions of the term supplier and specific regulations governing different types of suppliers. Durable Medical Equipment, Prosthetics, Orthotics, and Supplies (DMEPOS) encompass the types of items included in the definition of "medical equipment and supplies." A "DMEPOS supplier" refers to all individuals or organizations that furnish these items. This can include a physician or Medicare Part A (Hospital Insurance) provider. A DMEPOS supplier must

---

1. https://www.medicare.gov/physiciancompare/search.html (Last accessed October 16, 2018).

2. https://www.medicare.gov/supplierdirectory/search.html (Last accessed October 16, 2018).

3. https://www.medicare.gov/forms-help-and-resources/find-doctors-hospitals-and-facilities/quality-care-finder.html (Last accessed October 16, 2018).

4. https://www.medicare.gov/supplierdirectory/search.html Medicare-Participating Supplier Directory (Last accessed October 16, 2018).

5. https://www.cms.gov/Medicare/Provider-Enrollment-and-Certification/MedicareProviderSupEnroll/index.html?redirect=/MedicareProviderSupEnroll. (Last accessed October 16, 2018).

meet Medicare DMEPOS standards in order to obtain a supplier number. Those individuals or entities that do not furnish DMEPOS items but only furnish other types of health care services, such as physician's services or nurse practitioner services, are not subject to these standards. A supplier number is also not necessary before Medicare payment can be made with respect to medical equipment and supplies furnished incident to a physician's service.

For Medicare purposes, DMEPOS suppliers either accept or do not accept assignment. If a DMEPOS supplier accepts assignment, it agrees to accept the Medicare-approved amount as payment in full for the covered item. Such suppliers are referred to as "participating suppliers." Participating DMEPOS suppliers are listed in directories available to Medicare beneficiaries and receive Medicare Part B payment directly from the Medicare program. Nonparticipating DMEPOS suppliers may accept assignment on a case-by-case basis; for claims on which they accept assignment, they receive payment directly from Medicare. If a beneficiary receives a service from a nonparticipating DMEPOS supplier on a nonassigned basis, however, payment is made to the beneficiary (who in turn pays the DMEPOS supplier).

Medicare suppliers are required to meet a number of standards, including the following:

(1)   Complying with all applicable state and federal license and regulatory requirements

(2)   Maintaining a physical facility on an appropriate site

(3)   Having proof of appropriate liability insurance

(4)   Delivering Medicare-covered items to Medicare beneficiaries

(5)   Honoring all warranties

(6)   Maintaining and repairing items rented to beneficiaries

(7)   Accepting returns of substandard or unsuitable items from beneficiaries

1079. What portion of the cost must be borne by the patient?

The patient pays an annual deductible each year under Part B (Medical Insurance). For 2019, the deductible is $185, which means that the patient pays for the first $185 of covered expenses incurred during the calendar year. After the deductible is met, the patient pays 20 percent of approved charges, and Medicare pays 80 percent. There is no cost-sharing for certain Part B services and supplies, including most home health services, pneumococcal vaccine, flu shots, the costs of second opinions for certain surgical procedures when Medicare requires these opinions, and certain outpatient clinical diagnostic laboratory tests.

1080. How does a patient find out how much Medicare will pay on a claim?

After the doctor, provider, or supplier sends in a Part B (Medical Insurance) claim, Medicare sends the patient a notice called *Explanation of Your Medicare Part B Benefits*[1] to explain the decision on the claim.

---

1. Your Medicare Benefits https://www.medicare.gov/Pubs/pdf/10116-Your-Medicare-Benefits.pdf (Last accessed October 16, 2018).

This notice shows what charges were made and what Medicare approved. It shows what the coinsurance is and what Medicare is paying. If the annual deductible has not been met, that is also shown. The notice also gives the address and telephone number of the Medicare Administrative Contractor.

Benefits

1081. What doctors' services are covered under Part B (Medical Insurance)?

Under Part B (Medical Insurance), Medicare usually pays 80 percent of the approved charges for doctors' services and other services that are covered under Part B after the patient pays an annual deductible. Part B helps pay for covered services received from the doctor in the doctor's office, in a hospital, in a skilled nursing facility, in the patient's home, or any other location. Doctors' fees and services covered by Part B include:

- *Doctors' services* are covered wherever furnished in the United States. This includes the cost of house calls, office visits, and doctors' services in a hospital or other institution. Such services include the fees of physicians, surgeons, pathologists, radiologists, anesthesiologists, physiatrists, and osteopaths.

- Services from certain *specially qualified practitioners* who are not physicians but are approved by Medicare, including certified registered nurse anesthetists, certified nurse midwifes, clinical psychologists, clinical social workers (other than in a hospital), physician assistants, and nurse practitioners and clinical nurse specialists in collaboration with a physician.

- Services of *clinical psychologists* are covered if they would otherwise be covered when furnished by a physician (or as an incident to a physician's services).

- Services by *licensed chiropractors* for manual manipulation of the spine to correct a subluxation. Part B does not otherwise pay for any other diagnostic or therapeutic services, including X-rays, furnished by a chiropractor. Medicare pays for manual manipulation of the spine to correct a subluxation without requiring an X-ray (which previously was required) to prove that the subluxation exists.

- Fees of *podiatrists* are covered, including fees for the treatment of plantar warts, but not for routine foot care. Examples of common problems covered by Part B include ingrown toenails, hammer toe deformities, bunion deformities, and heel spurs. Routine foot care not covered by Part B includes cutting or removal of corns and calluses, trimming of nails, and other hygienic care. Part B does help pay for some routine foot care if the patient is being treated by a medical doctor for a medical condition affecting the patient's legs or feet (such as diabetes or peripheral vascular disease) which requires that a podiatrist or doctor of medicine or osteopathy perform the routine care.

  Medicare helps pay for therapeutic shoes and shoe inserts for people who have severe diabetic foot disease. The doctor who treats the diabetes must certify the patient's need for therapeutic shoes. The shoes and inserts must be prescribed by a podiatrist and furnished by a podiatrist, orthotist, prosthetist, or pedorthist. Medicare helps pay for one pair of therapeutic shoes per calendar year and for inserts. Shoe modifications may be substituted for inserts. The fitting of shoes or inserts is included in the Medicare payment for the shoes.

- The cost of diagnosis and treatment of *eye and ear ailments* is covered. Also covered is an *optometrist's treatment of aphakia*.

- *Plastic surgery* for purely cosmetic reasons is excluded; but plastic surgery for repair of an accidental injury, an impaired limb or a malformed part of the body is covered.

- *Radiological or pathological services* furnished by a physician to a hospital inpatient are covered.

Part B also covers:

(1)   medical and surgical services, including anesthesia;

(2)   diagnostic tests and procedures that are part of the patient's treatment;

(3)   radiology and pathology services by doctors while the patient is a hospital inpatient or outpatient;

(4)   treatment of mental illness, (Medicare payments are limited);

(5)   X-rays;

(6)   services of the doctor's office nurse;

(7)   drugs and biologicals that cannot be self-administered;

(8)   transfusions of blood and blood components;

(9)   medical supplies; and

(10) physical/occupational therapy and speech-language pathology services.

(11) clinical research studies

Part B does *not* cover:

(1)   most routine physical examinations (the "Welcome to Medicare" initial screening and subsequent annual updates are generally not considered the same as a routine physical), and tests directly related to such examinations (except some Pap smears and mammograms);

(2)   most routine foot care and dental care;

(3)   examinations for prescribing or fitting eyeglasses or hearing aids and most eyeglasses and hearing aids;

(4)   immunizations (except annual flu shots, pneumococcal pneumonia vaccinations or immunizations required because of an injury or immediate risk of infection, and hepatitis B for certain persons at risk);

(5)   cosmetic surgery, unless it is needed because of accidental injury or to improve the function of a malformed part of the body;

(6)   most prescription drugs;

(7)   custodial care at home or in a nursing home; and

(8)   orthopedic shoes.

Charges imposed by an immediate relative (e.g., a doctor who is the son/daughter or brother/sister of the patient) are *not* covered.

Doctors cannot make self-referrals for certain designated health services.

Designated health services include any of the following items or services:

(1)   Clinical laboratory services

(2)   Physical therapy services

(3)   Occupational therapy services

(4)   Radiology services, including MRI, CAT scans, and ultrasound services

(5)   Radiation therapy services and supplies

(6)   Durable medical equipment and supplies

(7)   Parenteral and enteral nutrients, equipment, and supplies

(8)   Prosthetics, orthotics, and prosthetic devices and supplies

(9)   Home health services

(10)   Outpatient prescription drugs

(11)   Inpatient and outpatient hospital services

The law prohibits a doctor who has a financial relationship with an entity from referring Medicare patients to that entity to receive a designated health service. The prohibition also applies if a doctor's immediate family member has a financial relationship with an entity. A financial relationship can exist as an ownership or investment interest in, or a compensation arrangement with, an entity. The law is triggered by the mere fact that a financial relationship exists; it does not matter what the doctor intends when making a referral. An entity cannot bill Medicare, Medicaid, the beneficiary, or anyone else for a designated health service furnished to a Medicare patient under a prohibited referral.

The law prohibits Medicare payments for designated health services in violation of the law. If a person collects any amount for services billed in violation of the law, a refund must be made. A person can be subject to a civil money penalty or exclusion from Medicare if that person:

(1)   presents or causes to be presented a claim to Medicare or bill to any individual, third-party payer, or other entity for any designated health service the person knows or should know was furnished as a result of a prohibited referral; or

(2)   fails to make a timely refund.

1082. What outpatient hospital services are covered under Part B (Medical Insurance)?

Part B (Medical Insurance) helps pay for covered services a patient receives as an outpatient from a participating hospital for diagnosis or treatment of an illness or injury. Under certain conditions, Part B helps pay for emergency outpatient care the patient receives from a nonparticipating hospital. The patient must meet the annual Part B (Medical Insurance) deductible before Medicare will begin paying for outpatient hospital charges and then pay a 20 percent copayment.

Major outpatient hospital services covered by Part B include:

(1)   services in an emergency room or outpatient clinic, including same-day surgery;

(2)   laboratory tests billed by the hospital;

(3)   mental health care in a partial hospitalization psychiatric program, if a physician certifies that inpatient treatment would be required without it;

(4)   X-rays and other radiology services billed by the hospital;

(5)   medical supplies such as splints and casts;

(6)   drugs and biologicals that cannot be self-administered; and

(7)   blood transfusions furnished to the patient as an outpatient (after the first three pints).

Outpatient hospital services not covered by Part B (Medical Insurance) include:

(1)   most routine physical examinations and tests that are directly related to the examinations;

(2)   eye or ear examinations to prescribe or fit eyeglasses or hearing aids;

(3)   most immunizations;

(4)   most prescription drugs;

(5)   most routine foot care; and

(6)   most dental care.

1083. When are outpatient physical therapy and speech-language pathology services covered under Part B (Medical Insurance)?

Outpatient physical therapy and speech-language pathology services are covered if received as part of a patient's treatment in a doctor's office or as an outpatient of a participating hospital, skilled nursing facility, or home health agency; or approved clinic, rehabilitative agency, or public health agency. Services must be furnished under a plan established by a physician or therapist providing the services. A physician is required to review periodically all plans of care.

A podiatrist (when acting within the scope of his or her practice) is a physician for purposes of establishing a plan for outpatient physical therapy. Dentists and podiatrists are also within the definition of physicians for the purpose of outpatient ambulatory surgery in a physician's office.

1084. Are partial hospitalization services connected to mental health services covered?

Yes. Partial hospitalization services (sometimes called day treatments) related to treatment of mental illness are items and services prescribed by a physician and provided in a program under the supervision of a physician pursuant to an individualized written plan of treatment.

The program must be furnished by a hospital to its outpatients or by a community mental health center and must be in a distinct and organized intensive ambulatory treatment service offering less than twenty-four-hour daily care.

Covered items and services include the following:

- individual and group therapy with physicians or psychologists (or other mental health professionals to the extent authorized by state law);

- occupational therapy requiring the skills of a qualified occupational therapist;

- services of social workers, trained psychiatric nurses, and other staff trained to work with psychiatric patients;

- drugs and biologicals furnished for therapeutic purposes (which cannot be self-administered);

- individualized activity therapies that are not primarily recreational or diversionary;

- family counseling, the primary purpose of which is treatment of the individual's condition;

- patient training and education, to the extent the training and educational activities are closely and clearly related to the individual's care and treatment;

- diagnostic services; and

- other necessary items and services (but not including meals and transportation).

Medicare doesn't cover:

- meals;

- transportation to or from mental health care services;

- support groups that bring people together to talk and socialize (this is different from group psychotherapy, which is covered); or

- testing or training for job skills that isn't part of your mental health treatment.

1085. Are certified nurse-midwife services covered under Part B (Medical Insurance)?

Yes. A certified nurse-midwife is a registered professional nurse who meets the following requirements:

(1) Is currently licensed to practice in the state as a nurse-midwife in the state where services are performed (assuming the state requires such licensure)

(2) Has completed a program of study and clinical experience for nurse-midwives that is accredited by an accrediting body approved by the U.S. Department of Education

(3) Is certified as a nurse-midwife by the American College of Nurse-Midwives or the American College of Nurse-Midwives Certification Council

CNMs in most states are required to

- possess a minimum of a graduate degree, such as a M.S. in Nursing or a Doctorate of Nursing Practice.

- pass the NCLEX examination to become a registered nurse.

- pass the American Midwifery Certification Board exams.

- hold an active RN license in the state in which they practice.

- keep up to date on latest medical knowledge as pertains to their field.

Certified nurse-midwife services are services furnished by a certified nurse-midwife and such services and supplies as are incident to nurse-midwife service. The service must be authorized under state law.

The definition of nurse-midwife services includes coverage of services outside the maternity cycle.

The amount paid by Part B (Medical Insurance) for such services is based upon a fee schedule and generally is covered to the same extent such services would be covered if performed by a physician. (Medicare will pay 80 percent of the lesser of the actual charge or 100 percent of the physician fee schedule charge for the service.) Payment is made by assignment only, however.

1086. Is dental work covered under Part B (Medical Insurance)?

Part B (Medical Insurance) helps pay for services of a dentist in certain cases when the medical problem is more extensive than the teeth or structures directly supporting the teeth. Dental work for jaw or facial bone surgery, whether required because of accident or disease, is covered. If a patient needs to be hospitalized because of the severity of a dental procedure, Part A (Hospital Insurance) may pay for the patient's inpatient hospital stay even if the dental care itself is not covered by Medicare.

Part B (Medical Insurance) generally does not pay for routine dental care, such as the treatment, cleaning, procedures, filling, removal, or replacement of teeth or other dental devices; root canal therapy; surgery for impacted teeth; or other surgical procedures involving the teeth or structures directly supporting the teeth.

1087. What medical equipment is covered under Part B (Medical Insurance)?

Part B (Medical Insurance) covers a wide array of medical equipment, including: surgical dressings, splints, casts, and other devices for reduction of fractures and dislocations; rental or purchase of durable medical equipment, such as iron lungs, oxygen tents, hospital beds, and wheelchairs, for use in the patient's home; prosthetic devices, such as artificial heart valves or synthetic arteries, designed to replace part or all of an internal organ (but not false teeth, hearing aids, or eyeglasses); colostomy or ileostomy bags and certain related supplies; breast prostheses (including a surgical brassiere) after a mastectomy; braces for arm, leg, back, or neck; and artificial limbs and eyes. Orthopedic shoes are not covered unless they are part of leg braces and the cost is included in the orthopedist's charge. Adhesive tape, antiseptics, and other common first-aid supplies are also not included.

Durable medical equipment is equipment that can be used again by other patients, must primarily serve a medical purpose, must not be useful to people who are not sick or injured, and must be appropriate for use in the patient's home. Part B (Medical Insurance) pays for different kinds of durable medical equipment in different ways: some equipment must be rented, other equipment must be purchased, and for some equipment the patient may choose rental or purchase. A doctor should prescribe medical equipment for the patient.

Medicare covers medically necessary Durable Medical Equipment (DME) that your doctor prescribes for use in your home. Only your doctor can prescribe medical equipment. Depending on the equipment, the patient may need to rent the equipment, buy the equipment or have a choice whether to rent or buy. DME meets these criteria:

- Durable (can withstand repeated use);

- Used for a medical reason;

- Not usually useful to someone who isn't sick or injured;

- Used in the patient's home;

- Has an expected lifetime of at least three years.

Suppliers of medical equipment and supplies (durable medical equipment, prosthetic devices, orthotics and prosthetics, surgical dressings, home dialysis supplies and equipment, immuno-suppressive drugs, therapeutic shoes for diabetics, oral cancer drugs, and self-administered erythropoietin) are not reimbursed by Medicare for these items unless they have a Medicare supplier number. A supplier cannot obtain a supplier number unless the supplier meets uniform national standards.

The standards require suppliers to:

(1)   comply with all applicable state and federal licensure and regulatory requirements;

(2)   maintain a physical facility;

(3)   have proof of appropriate liability insurance; and

(4)   meet other requirements established by the Centers for Medicare & Medicaid Services.

The requirement for suppliers to obtain a supplier number does not apply to medical equipment and supplies furnished as incident to a physician's service.

1088. Is ambulance service covered by Part B (Medical Insurance)?

Yes. Part B (Medical Insurance) helps pay for the "reasonable costs" of medically necessary ambulance transportation, including air ambulances, but only if the patient's condition does not permit the use of other methods of transportation and the ambulance, equipment and personnel meet Medicare requirements. Part B (Medical Insurance) can help pay for ambulance transportation from the scene of an accident to a hospital, from a patient's home to a hospital or skilled nursing facility, between hospitals and skilled nursing facilities, or from a hospital or skilled nursing facility to the patient's home. Also, if the patient is an inpatient in a hospital or skilled nursing facility that cannot provide a medically necessary service, Part B can help pay for round-trip ambulance transportation to the nearest appropriate facility. Medicare does not pay for ambulance use from a patient's home to a doctor's office.

Some individuals may be affected by a Medicare demonstration program if:

- They have scheduled, non-emergency ambulance transportation for three or more round trips in a ten-day period or at least once a week for three weeks or more

- The transportation is from an ambulance company based in one of these states:

    - New Jersey

    - Pennsylvania

    - South Carolina

    - Maryland

- Delaware

- District of Columbia

- North Carolina

- Virginia

- West Virginia

Under this demonstration, the ambulance company may send a request for prior authorization to Medicare before the fourth round trip in a thirty-day period. They'll do this so everyone will know earlier in the process if Medicare is likely to cover the services.

If prior authorization request isn't approved and the person continues getting these services, Medicare will deny the claim and the ambulance company may bill the patient for all charges. Either the patient or the ambulance service can request prior authorization. If prior authorization request isn't approved and services continue, Medicare will deny the claim and the ambulance company may bill the patient for all charges.

In some cases, Medicare may cover ambulance transportation when these apply:

- End-Stage Renal Disease (ESRD)

- Need for dialysis

- Need ambulance transportation to or from a dialysis facility

Part B (Medical Insurance) usually helps pay for ambulance transportation only in the patient's local area. However, if there are no local facilities equipped to provide the care the patient needs, Part B will help pay for necessary ambulance transportation to the closest facility outside the patient's local area that can provide the necessary care. If the patient chooses to go to another institution that is farther away, Medicare payment will be based on the reasonable charge for transportation to the closest facility.

Necessary ambulance services in connection with a covered inpatient stay in a Canadian or Mexican hospital may also be covered by Part B.

Medicare pays for use of an air ambulance only in extremely urgent emergency situations. If a patient could have been moved by land ambulance without serious danger to life or health, Medicare pays only the land ambulance rate. The patient is responsible for the difference between the air ambulance rate and the land ambulance rate. Medicare MAY pay for emergency ambulance transportation in an airplane or helicopter if the health condition requires immediate and rapid ambulance transportation that ground transportation can't provide, and one of these applies:

- The pickup location can't be easily reached by ground transportation.

- Long distances or other obstacles, like heavy traffic, could stop from getting to care quickly if traveled by ground ambulance.

1089. How much will Medicare Part B (Medical Insurance) pay for outpatient treatment of mental illness?

Part B (Medical Insurance) helps pay the cost of outpatient mental health services a patient receives from physicians, clinical psychologists, clinical social workers and other nonphysician practitioners. Prior to 2014, when treatment was furnished on an outpatient basis, mental health treatment services were subject to a payment limitation called the "outpatient mental health limitation." Under this limitation, Part B paid a lower percentage for mental health services than for other services. Beginning in 2014, however, Part B (Medical Insurance) began to pay 80 percent of approved charges for outpatient mental health services just as for most other Part B services.

Partial hospitalization (sometimes called day treatment) is a program of outpatient mental health care. Partial hospitalization services mean a distinct and organized intensive ambulatory treatment program that offers less than twenty-four hour daily care and furnishes mental health care services. Under certain conditions, Part B (Medical Insurance) helps pay for these programs when provided by hospital outpatient departments or by community mental health centers.

The Centers for Medicare & Medicaid Services (CMS) define community mental health centers as any entity that:

(1)   provides outpatient services, including specialized outpatient services for children, the elderly, individuals who are chronically mentally ill, and residents of its mental health service area who have been discharged from inpatient treatment at a mental health facility;

(2)   provides twenty-four-hour-a-day emergency care services;

(3)   provides day treatment or other partial hospitalization services, or psychosocial rehabilitation services;

(4)   provides screening for patients being considered for admission to state mental health facilities;

(5)   provides consultation and education services; and

(6)   meets applicable licensing or certification requirements for community mental health centers in the state in which it is located.

1090. What mental health services does Medicare Part B cover?

Medicare Part B (Medical Insurance) covers mental health services and visits with these types of health professionals: Psychiatrist or other doctors, Clinical psychologists, Clinical social workers, Clinical nurse specialist, Nurse practitioners, and Physician assistants. Medicare only covers these visits, often called counseling or therapy, when they're provided by a health care provider who accepts assignment.

Part B covers outpatient mental health services, including services that are usually provided outside a hospital, like in these settings: A doctor's or other health care provider's office, a hospital outpatient department, a community mental health center.

Part B also covers outpatient mental health services for treatment of inappropriate alcohol and drug use.

Part B helps pay for these covered outpatient services:

- One depression screening per year which must be done in a primary care doctor's office or primary care clinic that can provide follow-up treatment and referrals.

- Individual and group psychotherapy with doctors or certain other licensed professionals

- Family counseling – if intended to help the Medicare patient.

- Testing to find out if you're getting the services you need and if your current treatment is helping you.

- Psychiatric evaluation.

- Medication management.

- Certain prescription drugs that aren't usually "self-administered".

- Diagnostic tests.

- Partial hospitalization

- A one-time "Welcome to Medicare" visit. This visit includes a review of your potential risk factors for depression.

- A yearly "wellness" visit.

1091. When is the cost of vaccines covered?

The cost of pneumococcal pneumonia vaccine is covered, and the cost of hepatitis B vaccine for high and intermediate risk individuals is covered when it is administered in a hospital or renal dialysis facility. Also covered is the cost of flu vaccine and its administration. Neither the annual deductible nor the Part B (Medical Insurance) 20 percent coinsurance applies to flu and pneumonia vaccines. If the provider giving the patient the shot accepts assignment (i.e., accepts the Medicare payment as payment in full), there will be no cost to the patient. If the provider does not accept assignment, the patient may have to pay charges in addition to the Medicare-approved amount. Any health care professional complying with the Medicare rules can give a patient a flu shot or the pneumonia vaccine.

1092. Is the cost of antigens covered under Part B (Medical Insurance)?

Under certain circumstances, Part B (Medical Insurance) helps pay for antigens prepared for a patient by a physician, but only if the physician preparing the antigens also has examined the patient and developed the plan of treatment and dosage.

1093. When are organ transplants covered under Part B (Medical Insurance)?

Part B (Medical Insurance) provides coverage for liver transplants for adult Medicare beneficiaries depending on the medical reason for the transplant. Generally, Part B covers transplants for end-stage liver disease unrelated to malignancies. Effective in 2012, Medicare Administrative Contractors also became authorized to cover liver transplants in cases involving specified types of malignancies.

In addition, Part A covers the transplant of the following organs at Medicare-certified facilities: Heart, lung, kidney (in-patient services, kidney registry fee, related lab tests, cost of finding the kidney, costs of care for the donor, blood), pancreas (coupled with ESRD and kidney transplant), intestine, liver.

Part A also covers some stem cell transplants under certain conditions. Part B covers corneal transplants, under some conditions. Stem cell and corneal transplants are not limited to Medicare-approved transplant centers.

1094. Can Part B (Medical Insurance) help pay for outpatient services at a comprehensive outpatient rehabilitation facility?

Under certain circumstances, Part B (Medical Insurance) helps pay for outpatient services received from a Medicare-participating Comprehensive Outpatient Rehabilitation Facility (CORF).

Outpatient services must be performed by a doctor or other qualified professional. Covered services include physicians' services; physical, speech, occupation, and respiratory therapies; counseling; and other related services. A CORF patient must be referred by a physician who certifies that there is a need for skilled rehabilitation services and creates (and periodically reviews) a plan of treatment for the patient.

Until 2019, CORF services are generally subject to a special prospective payment system and to an annual limit applicable to all kinds of outpatient rehabilitation services (often referred to as the "therapy cap"). However, on February 9, 2018, President Trump signed into law the Bipartisan Budget Act of 2018 (BBA of 2018) (Public Law 115-123). This new law includes two provisions related to Medicare payment for outpatient therapy services including physical therapy (PT), speech-language pathology (SLP), and occupational therapy (OT) services:

- Section 50202 of the BBA of 2018 repeals application of the Medicare outpatient therapy caps and its exceptions process while adding limitations to ensure appropriate therapy.

- Section 53107 of the BBA of 2018 relates to the payment of OT and PT services furnished by an assistant.

The new law, through section 50202 of the BBA of 2018, preserves the former therapy cap amounts as thresholds above which claims must include confirmation that services are medically necessary as justified by appropriate documentation in the medical record. Just as with the incurred expenses for the therapy cap amounts, there is one amount for PT and SLP services combined and a separate amount for OT services. For 2018 the cap is:

- $2,010 for PT and SLP services combined, and

- $2,010 for OT services.

The new law also retains the targeted medical review (MR) process but at a lower threshold amount of $3,000. For CY 2018 (and each calendar year until 2028 at which time it is indexed annually by the MEI), the MR threshold is $3,000 for PT and SLP services and $3,000 for OT services. The targeted MR process means that not all claims exceeding the MR threshold amount are subject to review as they once were.

1095. Are home health services covered under Part B (Medical Insurance)?

For Medicare beneficiaries who have both Part A (Hospital Insurance) and Part B (Medical Insurance) coverage, home health services not directly related to hospital or skilled nursing facility stays are now covered and paid for by Part B (Medical Insurance).

Part A (Hospital Insurance) covers up to 100 post institutional home health care visits for beneficiaries with both Parts A and B. Home health services covered by Part B (Medical Insurance) tend to be for chronic conditions, and are different from home care services needed for convalescence and rehabilitation following a hospital stay. If a Medicare beneficiary continues to need home health care following exhaustion of Part A coverage, however, Part B also covers such care. Medicare pays for the costs of part-time skilled care with no coinsurance requirement and for 80 percent of the cost of durable medical equipment when supplied by a certified home health agency.

1096. Are independent clinical laboratory services covered under Part B (Medical Insurance)?

Part B (Medical Insurance) pays the full approved fee for covered clinical diagnostic tests provided by certain independent laboratories (or laboratories in physicians' offices) that are participating in Medicare. Such laboratories must be licensed in accordance with applicable state and local law (or otherwise approved for such licensure) and must also meet certain requirements specified in the Clinical Laboratory Improvement Amendments of 1988. In order to be paid by Medicare for approved charges, such laboratories must accept assignment for the tests and not bill the patient for the tests.

1097. Are screening pap smears and pelvic exams covered by Part B (Medical Insurance)?

Generally, a screening pap smear and pelvic exam (including a clinical breast exam) are covered every twenty-four months for all women for cervical and vaginal cancer screenings.

Annual coverage is provided for women:

(1)   at high risk for cervical or vaginal cancer; or

(2)   of childbearing age who have had a pap smear during the preceding three years indicating the presence of cervical or vaginal cancer or other abnormality.

The Part B deductible is waived for screening pap smears and pelvic exams. Pelvic exams are paid under the physician fee schedule as are Pap test specimen collection, and breast exams.

1098. Are breast cancer screening and diagnostic mammography covered by Part B (Medical Insurance)?

Screening and diagnostic mammography are covered.

"Screening mammography" is defined as a radiologic procedure furnished to a woman without signs or symptoms of breast disease, for the purpose of early detection of breast cancer, and includes a physician's interpretation of the results of the procedure.

"Diagnostic mammography" means a radiologic procedure furnished to a man or woman with signs or symptoms of breast disease, or a personal history of breast cancer or a personal history of biopsy-proven benign breast disease, and includes a physician's interpretation of the results of the procedure.

Medicare covers an annual screening (eleven full months must have passed since the last screening) mammogram for all women age forty and over. Women with Part B between ages thirty-five and thirty-nine can get one baseline mammogram.

Diagnostic mammogram is available whenever medically necessary. The Part B deductible for screening mammography is waived.

1099. Are prostate screening tests covered under Part B (Medical Insurance)?

Annual prostate cancer screening for men aged fifty and older is covered.

Covered procedures include (once every twelve months):

    (1)   digital rectal exam; and

    (2)   Prostate-Specific Antigen (PSA) blood test.

No Part B deductible or coinsurance is required for the screening PSA blood test, but Part B deductible and coinsurance is required with regard to the rectal exam. Payment to providers for the PSA blood test will be made under the clinical laboratory fee schedule, and other services will be paid under the physician fee schedule.

1100. How is colorectal screening covered under Part B (Medical Insurance)?

Covered colorectal screening procedures include several types of colorectal cancer screening tests to help find precancerous growths or find cancer early. The following tests are included:

(1) Screening Fecal Occult Blood Test: A fecal occult blood test every twelve months for persons age fifty and over.

(2) Screening Flexible Sigmoidoscopy: Flexible sigmoidoscopy for persons age fifty and over, to be done once every four years.

(3) Screening Colonoscopy: A screening colonoscopy for persons at high risk for colorectal cancer, to be done once every twenty-four months (every ten years for all others – or forty-eight months after a previous flexible sigmoidoscopy).

(4) Screening Barium Enema: A screening barium enema for persons aged fifty and over, to be done every forty-eight months for those deemed not at high risk and every twenty-four months for others. The Part B deductible is waived for these exams, but Part B coinsurance is increased to 25 percent for a patient for both flexible sigmoidoscopies and colonoscopies. Payment for screening colonoscopies is made only when the procedures are performed in a hospital.

(5) Multitarget stool DNA Test (Cologuard) – Medicare covers this test once every thirty-six months for people that meet ALL of the below conditions:

- Aged fifty to eighty-five

- Show no signs or symptoms of colorectal disease including, but not limited to:

  - lower gastrointestinal pain

  - blood in stool

  - positive guaiac fecal occult blood test or fecal immunochemical test

  - average risk for developing colorectal cancer, meaning

- no personal history of adenomatous polyps, colorectal cancer, inflammatory bowel disease, including Crohn's Disease and ulcerative colitis

- no family history of colorectal cancers or adenomatous polyps, familial adenomatous polyposis, or hereditary nonpolyposis colorectal cancer.

Costs in Original Medicare

- For barium enemas, cost is twenty percent of the Medicare-approved amount for the doctor's services. In a hospital outpatient setting, a copayment is incurred.

- In 2019, there is no charge for a multi-target stool DNA test (like Cologuard).

- If a screening colonoscopy or screening flexible sigmoidoscopy results in the biopsy or removal of a lesion or growth during the same visit, the procedure is considered diagnostic and coinsurance and/or a copayment charges will incur, but the Part B deductible doesn't apply.

- There is no charge for the screening fecal occult blood test. This screening test is covered if you get a referral from your doctor, physician assistant, nurse practitioner, or clinical nurse specialist.

- There is no charge for the screening colonoscopy or screening flexible sigmoidoscopy, if your doctor accepts assignment.

1101. Are diabetes self-management services covered under Part B (Medical Insurance)?

Services furnished in nonhospital-based programs for diabetes outpatient self-management training are covered under Part B (Medical Insurance). Medicare will cover up to ten hours of initial diabetes self-management training. This includes tips for eating healthy, being active, monitoring blood sugar, taking medication, and reducing risks. Services must be provided by a certified provider, and the physician (or other qualified health care professional) managing the patient's condition must certify that the services are needed under a comprehensive plan of care. Certified providers for these services include physicians as well as hospital outpatient facilities and dialysis facilities.

This may also include up to two hours of follow-up training each year. Generally, follow up has to be in a group setting of two to twenty people, lasting for at least thirty minutes, occur in the calendar year after the initial training, and be ordered by a doctor as part of the plan of care.

Coverage includes certain types of home blood glucose monitors, testing strips, lancets, and self-management training. Medicare also covers certain medical nutrition therapy (nutritional assessment, one-on-one counseling, and therapy services) services for individuals with diabetes or renal disease, but only if they have not separately received diabetes outpatient self-management training within a specified period and are not receiving maintenance dialysis.

1102. Are diabetes screenings covered under Part B (Medical Insurance)?

Part B covers lab tests in the event that the following risk factors exist:

- High blood pressure (hypertension)

- History of abnormal cholesterol and triglyceride levels (dyslipidemia)

- Obesity

- History of high blood sugar (glucose)

Part B also covers these tests if two or more of these apply:

- Age sixty-five or older

- Overweight

- Family history of diabetes (parents, brothers, sisters)

- History of gestational diabetes (diabetes during pregnancy), or delivery of a baby weighing more than nine pounds

1103. Are glaucoma tests covered under Part B (Medical Insurance)?

Medicare Part B covers a glaucoma test once every twelve months for people at high risk for glaucoma. The screening must be done or supervised by an eye doctor who's legally allowed to do this test.

Anyone with Part B who is at high risk for glaucoma is covered. High risk includes:

- diabetes;

- family history of glaucoma;

- African-American aged fifty or older; and

- Hispanic-American aged sixty-five or older.

1104. Is screening for depression covered under Part B (Medical Insurance)?

Yes, Medicare Part B covers one depression screening per year. It must be done in a primary care setting (like a doctor's office) that can provide follow-up treatment and/or referrals, if needed.

1105. Is screening for Hepatitis C covered under Part B (Medical Insurance)?

Medicare Part B covers one Hepatitis C screening test. Medicare also covers yearly repeat screening for certain people at high risk.

People with Medicare who meet one of these conditions are eligible:

- Those at high risk because they have a current or past history of illicit injection drug use

- Those who had a blood transfusion before 1992

- Those born between 1945 and 1965

1106. Is screening for HIV covered under Part B (Medical Insurance)?

Medicare Part B covers HIV (Human Immunodeficiency Virus) screenings. HIV is the virus that can lead to AIDS (Acquired Immunodeficiency Syndrome). Medicare covers this test once every twelve months for people who meet the guidelines below. Medicare also covers this screening up to three times during a pregnancy.

People with Part B are covered if they are:

- younger than fifteen and older than sixty-five, and are at increased risk for the virus;

- between fifteen and sixty-five, and ask for the test; and

- pregnant.

1107. Is obesity screening and counseling covered under Medicare Part B (Medical Insurance)?

Medicare covers fifteen-minute face-to-face individual behavioral therapy sessions and thirty-minute face-to-face group behavioral counseling sessions to help in weight loss. This counseling may be covered if provided in a primary care setting (like a doctor's office), where it can be coordinated with other care and a personalized prevention plan. Persons with a Body Mass Index (BMI) of thirty or greater are covered.

1108. Is tobacco (smoking) cessation and counseling covered under Medicare Part B (Medical Insurance)?

Medicare Part B covers up to eight face-to-face visits in a twelve-month period. These visits must be provided by a qualified doctor or other Medicare-recognized practitioner.

1109. Is alcohol misuse screening and counseling covered under Medicare Part B (Medical Insurance)?

Medicare Part B covers this screening once per year. Eligible persons include:

- Adults with Part B (including pregnant women) who use alcohol, but don't meet the medical criteria for alcohol dependency.

- If the primary care doctor determines misuse of alcohol, four brief face-to-face counseling sessions per year are available (if you're competent and alert during counseling). A qualified primary care doctor or other primary care practitioner must provide the counseling in a primary care setting (like a doctor's office).

1110. Is aortic aneurysm screening covered under Medicare Part B (Medical Insurance)?

Medicare Part B covers a one-time abdominal aortic aneurysm ultrasound. You must get a referral for it from your doctor. Eligible parties include those considered at risk if:

- you have a family history of abdominal aortic aneurysms;

- you're a man aged sixty-five to seventy-five and have smoked at least one-hundred cigarettes in your lifetime.

1111. Is Sexually Transmitted Infections (STI) screening and counseling covered under Medicare Part B (Medical Insurance)?

Medicare Part B covers Sexually Transmitted Infection (STI) screenings for chlamydia, gonorrhea, syphilis and/or Hepatitis B once every twelve months or at certain times during pregnancy. Medicare also covers up to two individual twenty to thirty minute, face-to-face, high-intensity behavioral counseling sessions each year for sexually active adults at increased risk for STIs.

Eligible individuals include:

- people with Part B who are pregnant and certain people who are at increased risk for an STI when the tests are ordered by a primary care doctor or other primary care practitioner;

- sexually active adults who are at an increased risk for STIs are also eligible for behavioral counseling sessions.

1112. When does Medicare Part B (Medical Insurance) cover bone mass measurements (bone density)?

Part B (Medical Insurance) covers procedures to identify bone mass, detect bone loss, or determine bone quality, including a physician's interpretation of the results.

Persons qualifying for these procedures include:

- estrogen-deficient women at risk for osteoporosis;

- individuals with vertebral abnormalities, osteopenia, or possible osteoporosis;

- individuals diagnosed with primary hyperparathyroidism;

- persons receiving long-term glucocorticoid steroid therapy; and

- individuals being monitored to assess the response to, or efficacy of, an approved osteoporosis drug.

The Part B deductible is waived for these tests. Medicare covers this test once every twenty-four months, or more often if medically necessary. It is only covered when ordered by a doctor or other qualified medical provider.

1113. Does Medicare Part B (Medical Insurance) cover cardiovascular disease risk reduction and behavior therapy?

Yes. A cardiovascular disease risk reduction visit is covered that includes:

- Encouraging aspirin use when benefits outweigh risks

- Screening for high blood pressure

- Counseling to promote a healthy diet

Medicare also covers cardiovascular disease screenings that check cholesterol and other blood fat (lipid) levels. High levels of cholesterol can increase for heart disease and stroke. These screenings will identify high cholesterol.

1114. Does Medicare Part B (Medical Insurance) cover lung cancer screening?

Medicare covers lung cancer screening with Low Dose Computed Tomography (LDCT) for people with Medicare who meet these criteria:

- Are age fifty-five though age seventy-seven

- Are either a current smoker or have quit smoking within the last fifteen years

- Have a tobacco smoking history of at least thirty "pack years" (an average of one pack a day for thirty years)

- Have a written order from their physician or qualified non-physician practitioner.

- Before the first lung cancer screening, the patient needs schedule an appointment with their doctor to discuss the benefits and risks of lung cancer screening and decide if the test is right.

- The service is furnished by an appropriate radiology imaging center and a reading radiologist that meet Medicare standards.

1115. Does Medicare Part B (Medical Insurance) cover medical nutrition therapy?

Medicare may cover medical nutrition therapy for those that have diabetes or kidney disease, and the doctor refers this service.

These services can be given by a registered dietitian or Medicare-approved nutrition professional, and include a nutritional assessment and counseling to help manage diabetes or kidney disease.

Individuals covered included those who have ANY of these issues:

- Diabetes

- Renal disease (people who have kidney disease, but aren't on dialysis)

- Have had a kidney transplant within the last three years and doctor refer the patient for this service.

Medicare covers three hours of one-on-one counseling services the first year, and two hours each year after that. If conditions, treatment, or diagnosis changes, a doctor's referral can enable more hours of treatment.

A doctor must prescribe these services and renew the referral yearly if continuing treatment is needed into another calendar year.

1116. Are flu shots covered under Medicare Plan B?

Yes, Medicare Part B (Medical Insurance) covers one flu shot per flu season at no cost.

1117. Are cervical and vaginal screenings covered under Medicare Plan B?

Medicare Part B (Medical Insurance) covers Pap tests and pelvic exams to check for cervical and vaginal cancer. As part of the exam, Part B also covers a clinical breast exam to check for breast cancer. Part B covers these screening tests:

- Once every twenty-four months for all women

- Once every twelve months if one of these apply:

  - You're at high risk for cervical or vaginal cancer.

  - You're of childbearing age and have had an abnormal Pap test in the past thirty-six months.

Part B also covers Human Papillomavirus (HPV) tests (when received with a Pap test) once every five years if you're age thirty to sixty-five without HPV symptoms.

1118. What is the "Welcome to Medicare" visit and the annual yearly screenings?

A **"Welcome to Medicare" preventive visit:** A person can get this visit only within the first twelve months having Part B. This visit includes a review of medical and social history related to health and education and counseling about preventive services, including these:

- Certain screenings, flu and pneumococcal shots, and referrals for other care, if needed

- Height, weight, and blood pressure measurements

- A calculation of body mass index

- A simple vision test

- A review of potential risk for depression and level of safety

- An offer to talk about creating advance directives

- A written plan as to which screenings, shots, and other preventive services are needed

This visit is covered one time. You don't need to have this visit to be covered for yearly "Wellness" visits.

Yearly "Wellness" visits: This visit is to develop or update a personalized prevention help plan. This plan is designed to help prevent disease and disability based on current health and risk factors. A questionnaire, called a "Health Risk Assessment," is completed as part of this visit. It can also include:

- A review of medical and family history

- Developing or updating a list of current providers and prescriptions.

- Height, weight, blood pressure, and other routine measurements.

- Detection of any cognitive impairment.

- Personalized health advice.

- A list of risk factors and treatment options.

- A screening schedule (like a checklist) for appropriate preventive services.

1119. Does Medicare Part B covers Hepatitis B shots?

Yes. People with Part B at medium or high risk for Hepatitis B are covered. The risk for Hepatitis B increases if one of these applies:

- hemophilia

- end-stage renal disease (ESRD)

- diabetes

- living with someone who has Hepatitis B

- employed as a health care worker and have frequent contact with blood or bodily fluids

Other factors may also increase risk for Hepatitis B.

1120. Does Medicare Part B covers pneumococcal shots?

Yes. Medicare Part B covers pneumococcal shots to help prevent pneumococcal infections (like certain types of pneumonia). The two shots protect against different strains of the bacteria. Medicare covers the first shot at any time, and also covers a different second shot if it's given one year (or later) after the first shot. Talk with your doctor or other health care provider to see if you need one or both of the pneumococcal shots.

1121. Under what conditions is an injectable drug for postmenopausal osteoporosis covered by Part B (Medical Insurance)?

The cost of an injectable drug provided by a home health agency to a patient for the treatment of a bone fracture related to postmenopausal osteoporosis is covered under the following conditions:

(1)   the patient's attending physician certifies that the patient has suffered a bone fracture related to postmenopausal osteoporosis and is unable to learn the skills needed to

self-administer (or is physically or mentally incapable of administering) the drug; and

(2)   the patient is confined to the patient's home (in such a way as meets the requirements for Medicare coverage of home health services).

1122. When are eyeglasses covered under Part B (Medical Insurance)?

Generally, Medicare Part B does not pay for eyeglasses or contact lenses.

Part B (Medical Insurance) will pay for one pair of conventional eyeglasses or conventional contact lenses if necessary after cataract surgery with insertion of an intraocular lens.

Part B (Medical Insurance) will also pay for cataract spectacles, cataract contact lenses, or intraocular lenses that replace the natural lens of the eye after cataract surgery.

Medicare Part B does not pay for routine eye exams or eyeglasses. The beneficiary pays 20 percent of the Medicare-approved amount for one pair of eyeglasses or one set of contact lenses after each cataract surgery with an intraocular lens. Medicare will only pay for contact lenses or eyeglasses from a supplier enrolled in Medicare, no matter who submits the claim. The beneficiary must pay additional costs of upgraded frames and also 100 percent of non-covered services. The Part B deductible applies.

1123. Under what circumstances are the services of nurse practitioners and clinical nurse specialists covered under Part B (Medical Insurance)?

The services of nurse practitioners and clinical nurse specialists are covered when the services performed are those authorized under state law and regulations, provided there is no facility or other provider charges paid in connection with the service. Also, a clinical nurse specialist must be a registered nurse licensed to practice in the state who holds a master's degree in a defined clinical area of nursing and from an accredited educational institution.

1124. When are lung and heart-lung transplants covered under Part B (Medical Insurance)?

Medicare covers lung transplants for beneficiaries with progressive end-stage pulmonary disease when performed by facilities that:

(1)   make an application to the Centers for Medicare & Medicaid Services (CMS) for approval as a lung transplant facility;

(2)   supply documentation showing their satisfaction of compliance with federal regulations on lung transplants; and

(3)   are approved by CMS under criteria based on federal regulations.

Medicare also covers lung transplantation for end-stage cardiopulmonary disease when it is expected that transplant of the lung will result in improved cardiac function.

In addition, Medicare covers heart-lung transplants for beneficiaries with progressive end-stage cardiopulmonary disease when such transplants are performed in a facility that has been approved by Medicare for both heart and lung transplantation.

Facilities must meet specific criteria in areas such as patient selection, patient management, commitment, plans, experience and survival rates, maintenance of data, organ procurement, laboratory services, and billing. Facilities must have patient selection criteria for determining suitable candidates for lung transplants.

For facilities that are approved to perform lung transplants, Medicare Part A (Hospital Insurance) covers all medically reasonable and necessary inpatient services. (See Q 1018 through Q 1061 for discussion of Hospital Insurance.) Physician services, as well as other nonhospital services related to the transplant, and pre- and posttransplant care, may be covered under Part B (Medical Insurance) and paid under the physician fee schedule or on a reasonable cost basis or other applicable basis. Under certain circumstances, kidney and liver transplants also may be covered.

1125. Are prescription drugs used in immunosuppressive therapy covered under Part B (Medical Insurance)?

Payment may be made for prescription drugs used in immunosuppressive therapy that have been approved for marketing by the Food and Drug Administration and that meet one of the following conditions:

(1) The approved labeling includes the indication for preventing or treating the rejection of a transplanted organ or tissue.

(2) The approved labeling includes the indication for use in conjunction with immunosuppressive drugs to prevent or treat rejection of a transplanted organ or tissue.

(3) The drugs have been determined by a Medicare Administrative Contractor to be reasonable and necessary for the specific purpose of preventing or treating the rejection of a patient's transplanted organ or tissue, or for use in conjunction with immunosuppressive drugs for the purpose of preventing or treating the rejection of a patient's transplanted organ or tissue.

Coverage under Part B (Medical Insurance) is generally available only for prescription drugs used in immunosuppressive therapy, furnished to an individual who receives an organ or tissue transplant for which Medicare payment is made, for up to thirty-six months after the date of discharge from the hospital during which the covered transplant was performed.

Such drugs are covered regardless of whether they can be self-administered.

1126. Are ambulatory surgical services covered under Part B (Medical Insurance)?

An ambulatory surgical center is a facility that provides surgical services that do not require a hospital stay. Part B (Medical Insurance) will pay for the use of an ambulatory surgical center for certain approved surgical procedures, generally those that do not pose a significant risk to the patient's health if performed in an outpatient setting (and that do not typically require an overnight hospital stay). The center must have an agreement to participate in the Medicare program. Medicare also helps pay for physician and anesthesia services that are provided in connection with the procedure.

1127. When are rural health clinic services covered by Part B (Medical Insurance)?

Part B (Medical Insurance) helps pay for services of physicians, nurse practitioners, physician assistants, nurse midwives, visiting nurses (under certain circumstances), clinical psychologists, and clinical social workers furnished by a rural health clinic. Part B (Medical Insurance) also helps pay for certain laboratory tests in these clinics. The patient is responsible for the annual Part B (Medical Insurance) deductible plus 20 percent of the Medicare-approved charge for the clinic services.

Rural health clinics must meet requirements concerning where they are located. They must be in areas where there are insufficient numbers of needed health care practitioners (not just primary care physicians). Clinics that no longer meet the shortage area requirements will be permitted to retain their designation only if the Centers for Medicare & Medicaid Services (CMS) determines that such clinics are essential to the delivery of primary care services that would otherwise be unavailable in the area.

1128. Does Medicare Part B (Medical Insurance) reimburse for telehealth services in rural areas?

Part B (Medical Insurance) payments are made for professional consultation via telecommunications systems with a health care provider furnishing a service for which Medicare payment would be made for a beneficiary residing in a rural county that was designated as a health professional shortage area (and in certain other nonurban areas).

Payments for telehealth services are generally equal to what Medicare would have paid for the services if delivered other than through telecommunications.

Part B covers certain services, like office visits and consultations that are provided:

- Using an interactive two-way telecommunications system (with real-time audio and video)

- By a doctor or certain other health care provider who isn't at your location.

In some rural areas, these services are covered under certain conditions and only if you're located at one of these places:

- A doctor's office

- A hospital

- A critical access hospital

- A rural health clinic

- A federally qualified health center

- A hospital-based or critical access hospital-based dialysis facility

- A skilled nursing facility

- A community mental health center

1129. Does Part B (Medical Insurance) help pay for federally qualified health center services?

Federally qualified health centers are located in both rural and urban areas, and any Medicare beneficiary may seek services at them. As part of the "federally qualified health center benefit," Part B (Medical Insurance) helps pay for the following outpatient services:

(1)   Physician services

(2)   Services and supplies furnished as incident to a physician's professional services

(3)   Nurse practitioner or physician assistant services

(4)   Services and supplies furnished as incident to a nurse practitioner or physician assistant services

(5)   Clinical psychologist and clinical social worker services

(6)   Services and supplies furnished as incident to a clinical psychologist or clinical social worker services

(7)   Visiting nurse services

(8)   Nurse-midwife services

(9)   Preventive primary services

Preventive primary services include medical social services, nutritional assessment and referral, preventive health education, children's eye and ear examinations, prenatal and postpartum screening, immunizations, voluntary family planning services, and other services outlined in the recommendations of the U.S. Preventive Services Task Force for patients age sixty-five and older. Preventive services do not include eyeglasses, hearing aids, group or mass information programs or health education classes, or preventive dental services. Preventive services covered under special provisions of Medicare, such as screening mammographies, may be provided by a federally qualified health center only if the center meets the special provisions that govern those benefits.

A Medicare beneficiary does not have to pay the Part B (Medical Insurance) annual deductible for services provided under the federally qualified health center benefit. A beneficiary remains responsible for 20 percent of the Medicare-approved charge for the clinic. Federally qualified health centers often provide services in addition to those specified under the Medicare federally qualified health center benefit. Examples of these services are X-rays and equipment like crutches and canes. As long as the center meets Medicare requirements to provide these services, Part B (Medical Insurance) can help pay for them. The patient is responsible for any unmet part of the patient's annual Part B (Medical Insurance) deductible plus 20 percent of the Medicare-approved charge for the service.

1130. What other benefits are provided under Part B (Medical Insurance)?

Additional benefits include the following:

- The cost of *blood clotting factors and supplies* related to their administration for hemophilia patients who are able to use them to control bleeding without medical or other supervision. The number of clotting factors necessary to have on hand for a specific period is determined for each patient individually.

- *Outpatient radiation therapy* given under the supervision of a doctor.

- *Oral anti-nausea drugs used as part of an anticancer chemotherapeutic regimen.* The drug must be administered by a physician (or prescribed by a physician) for use immediately before, at, or within forty-eight hours after, the time of administration of the chemotherapeutic agent and used as a full replacement for the antiemetic therapy which would otherwise be administered intravenously.

- *Portable diagnostic X-ray services* received by a patient at home or at other locations if they are ordered by a doctor and if they are provided by a Medicare-approved supplier.

- Under certain circumstances, *liver, and kidney transplants* in a Medicare-approved facility.

- *Prosthetic devices* needed to replace an internal body organ. These include Medicare-approved corrective lenses needed after a cataract operation, ostomy bags and certain related supplies, and breast prostheses (including a surgical brassiere) after a mastectomy. Part B (Medical Insurance) also helps pay for artificial limbs and eyes, and for arm, leg, back, and neck braces. Part B does not pay for orthopedic shoes unless they are an integral part of leg braces and the cost is included in the charge for the braces. Part B also does not pay for dental plates or other dental devices.

- The drug *Epoetin alfa* when used to treat Medicare beneficiaries with anemia related to chronic kidney failure or related to use of AZT in HIV-positive beneficiaries or for other uses that a Medicare Administrative Contractor finds medically appropriate. The Epoetin alfa must be administered incident to the services of a doctor in the office or in a hospital outpatient department. Part B (Medical Insurance) also helps pay for Epoetin alfa that is self-administered by home dialysis patients or administered by their caregivers.

- *Oral cancer drugs* if they are the same chemical entity as those administered intravenously and covered prior to 1994. In addition, off-label anticancer drugs are covered in some cases.

- *Cardiac rehabilitation* is covered if it is a comprehensive program that includes exercise, education, and counseling. Patients must meet certain conditions and have a doctor's referral. Also covered are intensive cardiac rehabilitation programs that are typically more rigorous or more intense than cardiac rehabilitation programs.

- A comprehensive program of pulmonary rehabilitation is covered if the patient has moderate to very severe Chronic Obstructive Pulmonary Disease (COPD) and has a referral for pulmonary rehabilitation from the doctor treating the chronic respiratory disease.

1131. What services are covered under Part B (Medical Insurance) with no cost-sharing obligation?

The number of services covered by Part B (Medical Insurance) without any cost-sharing obligations for patients – in other words, subject to neither the Part B deductible nor coinsurance – has expanded in recent years.

Such services include:

(1)   the cost of second opinions for certain surgical procedures when Medicare requires a second opinion,

(2)   the cost of home health services (but a 20 percent coinsurance charge applies for durable medical equipment, except for the purchase of certain used items),

(3)   the cost of a flu shot and pneumococcal vaccine,

(4)   certain outpatient clinical diagnostic laboratory tests, and

(5)   a screening PSA test for prostate cancer.

Medicare Coverage of Blood

1132. Does Medicare help pay for blood?

Both Part A (Hospital Insurance) and Part B (Medical Insurance) can help pay for blood (whole blood or units of packed red blood cells), blood components, and the cost of blood processing and administration.

If a patient receives blood as an inpatient of a hospital or skilled nursing facility, Part A (Hospital Insurance) will pay all of the blood costs, except for a deductible charged for the first three pints of whole blood or units of packed red cells in each benefit period. The deductible is the charge that some hospitals and skilled nursing facilities make for blood which is not replaced.

The patient is responsible for the deductible for the first three pints or units of blood furnished by a hospital or skilled nursing facility in a calendar year. If the patient is charged a deductible, the patient has the option of either paying the deductible or having the blood replaced. A hospital or skilled nursing facility cannot charge a patient for any of the first three pints of blood the patient replaces. Any blood deductible satisfied under Part B (Medical Insurance) will reduce the blood deductible requirements under Part A (Hospital Insurance).

Part B (Medical Insurance) can help pay for blood and blood components received as an outpatient or as part of other covered services, except for a deductible charged for the first three pints or units received in each calendar year. After the patient has met the annual deductible, Part B (Medical Insurance) pays 80 percent of the approved charge for blood starting with the fourth pint in a calendar year.

Private Contracts

1133. Can physicians enter into private contracts with Medicare beneficiaries?

Yes, physicians or practitioners can sign private contracts with Medicare beneficiaries for whom no claim is to be submitted to Medicare and for which the physician or practitioner receives no reimbursement from Medicare, on a per person basis, or from an organization that receives reimbursement under Medicare for the item or service. Services provided under private contracts are not covered under Medicare.

A private contract is not valid unless it:

(1)   is written and signed by the beneficiary before any item or service is provided pursuant to the contract;

(2)   is entered into when the beneficiary is not facing an emergency or urgent health care situation; and

(3)   contains specific items listed below.

Among other provisions, the contract must clearly indicate to the beneficiary that by signing the contract the beneficiary:

(1)   agrees not to submit a claim to Medicare even if the items or services would otherwise by covered;

(2)   agrees to be responsible, through insurance or otherwise, for payment of the items and services and understands that no reimbursement will be provided under Medicare;

(3)   acknowledges that no limits will apply to amounts that could be charged for the items and services;

(4)   acknowledges that Medigap plans do not make payments for these items and services because Medicare does not make payment; and

(5)   acknowledges that the beneficiary has a right to have the items and services provided by other physicians or practitioners for whom payment would be made under Medicare.

Private contracts are not valid unless the physician files an affidavit with the Medicare Administrative Contractor (MAC) for the area in which the physician practices not later than ten days after the first contract to which the affidavit applies is entered into. The affidavit must identify the physician or practitioner, be signed by the physician or practitioner, and provide that – except for emergency services – the physician or practitioner will not submit any claim to Medicare for any item or service provided to any beneficiary for two years beginning on the date the affidavit is signed.

If the physician or practitioner knowingly and willfully submits a claim to Medicare for any item or service furnished to a beneficiary (except emergency services) during the two-year period:

(1)   the physician or practitioner will no longer be allowed to furnish services under private contracts for the remainder of the two-year period; and

(2)   no Medicare payment will be made for any item or service furnished by the physician or practitioner during the remainder of the two-year period.

PART C: MEDICARE ADVANTAGE

Definition

1134. What is Medicare Advantage?

Medicare Advantage is a type of Medicare health plan offered by private companies that contract with Medicare to provide the Part A and Part B benefits. If enrolled in a Medicare Advantage Plan, most Medicare services are covered through the plan and aren't paid for under Original Medicare. Most Medicare Advantage Plans offer prescription drug coverage. Medicare Advantage was formerly known as Medicare+Choice permits contracts between the Centers for Medicare & Medicaid Services (CMS) and a variety of different private managed care and fee-for-service entities. Most Medicare beneficiaries may choose to receive benefits either through the original Medicare Fee-for-Service program [Medicare Part A (Hospital Insurance) and Medicare Part B (Medical Insurance)]. Medicare Advantage Plans cover all Medicare services and may even offer extra coverage. Each plan can charge different out-of-pocket costs and have different rules of getting service.

Main types of Medicare Advantage plans include:

- coordinated care plans, including

    - Health Maintenance Organizations (HMOs),

    - Preferred Provider Organizations (PPOs),

    - Provider-Sponsored Organizations (PSOs),

    - HMO Point of Service (HMOPOS), and

    - Medical Savings Account.

- Private Fee-for-Service plans which reimburse providers on a fee-for-service basis.

Out of pocket costs can vary and depend on:

- whether the plan charges a monthly premium;

- whether the plan pays any or all of the monthly Part B premium;

- whether the plan has a yearly deductible or any additional deductibles;

- how much you pay for each visit or service (copay or coinsurance) – which CAN be different than under original Medicare;

- the type of health care services used;

- whether you go to a doctor who accepts assignment and follow the plans rules such as using network providers;

- any charges for extra benefits;

- the plan's yearly limit on your out-of-pocket costs for all medical services;

- whether Medicaid is part of the coverage.

1135. Who can join a Medicare Advantage plan?

You can generally join a Medicare HMO, PPO, PFFS or MSA type plan as long as the following conditions are met:

- You live in the service area of the plan you want to join. The plan can give you more information about its service area. If you live in another state for part of the year, check to see if the plan will cover you there.

- You have Medicare Part A and Part B.

- You **do not** have End-Stage Renal Disease (ESRD).

1136. What happens if plans leave Medicare and Medicare Advantage?

At the end of the year, plans can decide to leave the Medicare Program, although in recent years, very few plans have left.

Generally, a person will be automatically returned to original Medicare if they don't choose to join another Medicare Advantage Plan. Subscribers will also have the right to buy a Medigap policy. No matter what choice is made, the individual is still in the Medicare Program and will get all Medicare-covered services. If returning to original Medicare and prescription drug coverage is desired, Part D will have to be purchased.

1137. How much do Medicare Advantage (Part C) plans cost?

The out of pocket charges for a Medicare Advantage plan depend on several factors:

- Whether the plan charges a monthly premium.

- Whether the plan pays any of the monthly Part B premium.

- Whether the plan has a yearly deductible or any additional deductibles.

- How much the copay is for each visit or service?

- The type of health care services needed and how often they are used.

- Whether the doctor or supplied who accepts assignment.

- Whether the subscriber follows the plan's rules or decides to use out of network health providers

- Extra benefits and the plan charges for those benefits.

- The plan's yearly limit on out-of-pocket costs for all medical services.

- Whether you have Medicaid or get help from your state.

1138. What is a Health Maintenance Organization (HMO)?

A Medicare HMO is a type of managed care plan that provides to its enrolled Medicare beneficiary members, either directly or through arrangement with others, at least all the Medicare-covered services that are available to Medicare beneficiaries who are not enrolled in the HMO and who reside in the geographic area serviced by the HMO. Some HMOs also provide services not covered by Medicare, either free to the Medicare enrollee (that is, funded out of the payment Medicare makes to the HMO) or for an additional charge to the enrollee. HMOs typically charge a set monthly premium and nominal copayments for services instead of Medicare's coinsurance and deductibles.

Each HMO has its own network of hospitals, skilled nursing facilities, home health agencies, doctors, and other professionals. Depending on how the plan is organized, services are usually provided either at one or more centrally located health facilities or in the private practice offices of the doctors and other health care professionals who are part of the HMO. A beneficiary generally must receive all covered care through the HMO or from health care professionals referred to by the plan. In most cases, prescription drugs are covered in the HMO.

Most HMOs allow an enrollee to select a primary care doctor from those who are part of the HMO. If the beneficiary does not make a selection, a primary care physician will be assigned. If your primary doctor leaves the plan, the beneficiary will need to select another physician from within the plan. The primary care doctor is responsible for managing the beneficiary's medical care, including admitting the beneficiary to a hospital or referring the beneficiary to specialists. The beneficiary is allowed to change his or her primary care doctor as long as another primary care doctor affiliated with the HMO is selected. In most cases, the referral from the primary care doctor to the specialist is required, although certain services, such as mammograms don't require a referral.

Before enrolling in an HMO, the beneficiary should find out whether the plan has a "risk" or a "cost" contract with Medicare. There is an important difference:

- **Risk Plans**. These plans have "lock-in" requirements. This means that the beneficiary generally is locked into receiving all covered care through the HMO or through referrals by the plan. In most cases, if the beneficiary receives services that are not authorized by the HMO, neither the plan nor Medicare will pay. The only exceptions recognized by all Medicare-contracting plans are for emergency services, which the beneficiary may receive anywhere in the United States, and for services the beneficiary urgently needs when temporarily out of the HMO's service area.

- **Cost Plans**. These plans do not have lock-in requirements. If a beneficiary enrolls in a cost plan, the beneficiary can either go to health care providers affiliated with the HMO or go outside the plan. If a beneficiary goes outside the plan, the plan probably will not pay, but Medicare will. Medicare will pay its share of charges it approves.

The beneficiary will be responsible for Medicare's coinsurance, deductibles, and other charges, just as if receiving care under the regular Medicare program.

1139. What is a Medicare Advantage Private Fee-For-Service (PFFS) plan?

A Medicare PFFS plan is a type of Medicare Advantage Plan (Part C) offered by a private insurance company. PFFS plans aren't the same as Original Medicare or Medigap. The plan determines how much it will pay doctors, other health care providers, and hospitals, and how much you must pay when you get care. A Medicare Advantage Private Fee-For-Service (PFFS) plan is defined as a plan offered by a private insurance company that reimburses doctors, hospitals, and other providers on a fee-for-service basis, does not place them at risk, does not vary payment rates based on utilization, and does not restrict which doctor or hospital the member can use. In this type of plan, it is not necessary for the member to select a primary care physician or to get referrals to see specialists.

Subject to some limits and review by the Centers for Medicare & Medicaid Services (CMS), the private insurance company, not CMS, decides how much to reimburse for services received by the beneficiary. The beneficiary pays the Part B premium ($135.50 for new beneficiaries in 2019), any additional monthly premium the private fee-for-service plan charges, and any deductible or coinsurance required by the plan, including any copayment required per visit or service.

1140. What is a Medicare Advantage Provider-Sponsored Organization (PSO)?

For purposes of Medicare Advantage, PSOs are a type of managed care. They are public or private entities established by or organized by a health care provider (such as a hospital) or a group or network of affiliated health care providers (such as a geriatric unit of a hospital) that provide a substantial proportion of health care items and services directly through that provider or group. Affiliated providers share, directly or indirectly, substantial financial risk and have at least a majority financial interest in the PSO.

1141. What is a Preferred Provider Organization (PPO) Plan?

A Medicare PPO Plan is a type of Medicare Advantage Plan offered by a private insurance company. In a PPO Plan, the member pays less when using doctors, hospitals, and other health care providers that belong to the plan's network. In the alternative, the member pays more if they use doctors, hospitals, and providers outside of the network.

In most cases, the member can get health care from any doctor, health care provider or hospital with the PPO plan. In addition, members can usually go to health care providers outside of the plan at an additional cost. Generally a person doesn't need to choose a primary care physician nor do they generally need to obtain referrals for specialists

1142. What is a Medicare Advantage Religious Fraternal Benefit (RFB) plan?

A Religious Fraternal Benefit (RFB) plan may restrict enrollment to members of the church, convention, or group with which the society is affiliated. These plans must meet Medicare financial solvency requirements, and Medicare may adjust payment amounts to these plans to take into account the actuarial characteristics and experience of plan enrollees. In addition to meeting Medicare requirements, any RFB plan must also satisfy certain provisions of the Internal Revenue Code and qualify as a tax-exempt organization in accordance with the Code.

1143. What is a Medicare Special Needs (SNP) plan?

Medicare Special Needs Plans (SNPs) are a type of Medicare Advantage Plan (like an HMO or PPO). Membership is limited to individuals with specific diseases or characteristics, and customize their benefits, choice of providers, and drug formularies to best meet the specific needs of the groups they serve. Medicare SNPs typically have specialists in the diseases or conditions that affect their members.

A plan must limit membership to these groups:

(1)   people who live in certain institutions (like a nursing home) or who require nursing care at home, or

(2)   people who are eligible for both Medicare and Medicaid, or

(3)   people who have specific chronic or disabling conditions (like diabetes, End-Stage Renal Disease (ESRD), HIV/AIDS, chronic heart failure, or dementia).

Plans may further limit membership. You can join a SNP at any time.

Generally, a member of an SNP must get care and services from doctors or hospitals in the Medicare SNP network (except emergency or urgent care, such as care for a sudden illness or injury that needs immediate medical care, or if you have End-Stage Renal Disease (ESRD) and need out-of-area dialysis).

All SNPs MUST provide Medicare prescription drug coverage. Medicare SNPs often coverage extra services tailed to the special group served, such as extra hospital days, etc. Medicare SNPs may not be available in all parts of the country.

In most cases, SNPs will require a member to have a primary care doctor, or the plan may require the individual to have a care coordinator to help with health care. Generally, a referral to see a specialist in a SNP is required. Certain services, such as yearly screening for mammograms, pap smears and pelvic exams don't require a referral.

1144. Who can join a Medicare Special Needs (SNP) plan?

Membership in a SNP is limited by the very nature of the plan. A plan must limit membership to:

(1)   persons who live in certain institutions (such as a nursing home) or who require nursing care at home; or

(2)   persons who are eligible for both Medicare and Medicaid; or

(3)   persons who have specific chronic or disabling conditions (like diabetes, End-Stage Renal Disease (ESRD), HIV/AIDS, chronic heart failure, or dementia).

In order to join, one must have Medicare Part A and Part B, live in the plan's service area, and meet the eligibility requirements (see next question).

1145. What kinds of Medicare Special Needs (SNP) plans and eligibility requirements are there?

Membership in a SNP is limited by the very nature of the plan. A plan must limit membership to:

(1)   Institutional SNP (I-SNP) – people who live in certain institutions (such as a nursing home) or who require nursing care at home.

(2)   Dual-Eligible SNP (D-SNP) – people who are eligible for both Medicare and Medicaid.

(3)   Chronic Condition SNP (C-SNP) – people who have specific chronic or disabling conditions (like diabetes, End-Stage Renal Disease (ESRD), HIV/AIDS, chronic heart failure, or dementia). One or more of the following chronic conditions must exist:

- Chronic alcohol and other drug dependence

- Autoimmune disorders

- Cancer (excluding pre-cancer conditions)

- Cardiovascular disorders

- Chronic heart failure

- Dementia

- Diabetes mellitus

- End-stage liver disease

- End-Stage Renal Disease (ESRD) requiring dialysis (any mode of dialysis)

- Severe hematologic disorders

- HIV/AIDS

- Chronic lung disorders

- Chronic and disabling mental health conditions

- Neurologic disorders

- Stroke

1146. What is a Medicare MSA Plan?

There are consumer-directed Medicare Advantage Plans, called a Medicare MSA Plans. These plans are similar to Health Savings Account Plans available outside of Medicare. You can choose your health care services and providers.

Medicare MSA Plans combine a high-deductible insurance plan with a medical savings account that you can use to pay for your health care costs. These plans have two parts:

1. **High-deductible health plan:** The first part is a special type of high-deductible Medicare Advantage Plan (Part C). The plan will only begin to cover your costs once you meet a high yearly deductible, which varies by plan.

2. **Medical Savings Account (MSA):** The second part is a special type of savings account. The Medicare MSA Plan deposits money into your account. You can use money from this savings account to pay your health care costs before you meet the deductible.

1147. How does a Medicare MSA Plan work?

- Select and join a high-deductible Medicare MSA Plan.

- Set up an MSA with a bank the plan selects.

- Medicare gives the plan an amount of money each year for health care coverage.

- The plan deposits some money into the account.

- The insured can use the money in your account to pay health care costs, including health care costs that aren't covered by Medicare. When using account money for Medicare-covered Part A and Part B services, it counts towards the plan's Deductible.

- If a person uses all of the money in the account and has additional health care costs, they will have to pay for Medicare-covered services out-of-pocket until reaching the plan's deductible.

- During the time the person is paying out-of-pocket for services before the deductible is met, doctors and other providers can't charge more than the Medicare-approved amount.

- After reaching the deductible, the plan will cover Medicare-covered services.

- Money remaining in the account at the end of the year stays in the account, and may be used for health care costs in future years.

Eligibility, Election, and Enrollment

1148. What is the enrollment/disenrollment process for Medicare Advantage?

Beneficiaries entitled to Part A (Hospital Insurance) and enrolled in Part B (Medical Insurance) are eligible to enroll in any Medicare Advantage plan that serves the geographic area in which they reside, except beneficiaries with end-stage renal disease (although beneficiaries who develop end-stage renal disease may remain in the plan if already enrolled) and beneficiaries receiving inpatient hospice care. Part B only enrollees are ineligible.

The Centers for Medicare & Medicaid Services (CMS) have established procedures for enrollment and disenrollment in Medicare Advantage options. Newly eligible enrollees who do not choose a Medicare Advantage plan are deemed to have chosen the original Medicare fee-for-service option (in other words, Medicare Parts A and B). Individuals generally remain enrolled in the Medicare option of their choice unless and until they choose another plan. CMS retains the power to implement "passive enrollment" in cases where a Medicare Advantage plan terminates, or CMS determines that remaining in the Medicare Advantage plan poses a risk to the members. Under passive enrollment, CMS treats beneficiaries as enrolled in whatever plan CMS chooses unless the beneficiaries affirmatively elect otherwise.

1149. Can someone with End Stage Renal Disease opt for Medicare Advantage?

If a person has ESRD, they will normally get health care through Original Medicare. They can only join a Medicare Advantage Plan (Part C) in certain situations, like these:

- They are already in a Medicare Advantage Plan when they developed ESRD. They may be able to stay in their plan or join another plan offered by the same company.

- They are already getting health benefits (for example, through an employer health plan) through the same organization that offers the Medicare Advantage Plan.

- They had ESRD, but have had a successful kidney transplant and still qualify for Medicare benefits (based on age or a disability). A person can stay in Original Medicare or join a Medicare Advantage Plan.

- They may be eligible to join a Medicare Special Needs Plan (SNP) for people with ESRD if one is available in the area.

A person has a one-time right to join another plan if both of these are true:

- They have ESRD and are in a Medicare Advantage Plan.

- The plan leaves Medicare or no longer provides coverage in the area.

A person doesn't have to use their one-time right to join a new plan immediately. If they go directly to Original Medicare after the plan leaves or stops providing coverage, they'll still have a one-time right to join a Medicare Advantage Plan later.

1150. What are the enrollment periods for Medicare Advantage plans?

Beneficiaries can choose a Medicare Advantage plan at initial Medicare eligibility or during one of the enrollment periods described in the subsequent list:

- The annual coordinated enrollment period runs from October 15 through December 7 of each year. Enrollments at this time are effective the following January 1. Beneficiaries may switch from one Medicare Advantage plan to another during this period.

- The Medicare Advantage Disenrollment Period (January 1 – February 14 in prior years) is being replaced with a different arrangement. In 2019, a new Medicare Advantage Open Enrollment Period will run from January 1 – March 31 each year. If you're enrolled in a Medicare Advantage plan, you'll have a one-time opportunity to:

  - Switch to a different Medicare Advantage plan.

  - Drop your Medicare Advantage plan and return to Original Medicare, Part A and Part B.

  - Sign up for a stand-alone Medicare Part D Prescription Drug Plan (if you return to Original Medicare). Most Medicare Advantage plans include prescription drug coverage already. Usually you can't enroll in a stand-alone Medicare Prescription Drug plan if you already have a Medicare Advantage plan, but there are some situations where you can. Call your Medicare Advantage plan if you have questions.

  - Drop your stand-alone Medicare Part D Prescription Drug Plan.

- Special election periods are available in which a beneficiary can disenroll if the Medicare Advantage plan in which that beneficiary was enrolled terminates, the beneficiary moves out of the plan's service area, the beneficiary demonstrates that the plan has violated its contract or misrepresented the plan in marketing, or any other conditions specified by the Centers for Medicare & Medicaid Services (CMS).

- Newly eligible beneficiaries who elect a Medicare Advantage option may also disenroll into original Medicare fee-for-service program [Part A (Hospital Insurance) and Part B (Medical Insurance)] any time during the first twelve months of their enrollment.

Medicare Advantage plans must accept all beneficiaries on a first-come, first-served basis, subject to capacity limits.

Plans may disenroll beneficiaries only for cause (i.e., failure to pay premiums or disruptive behavior) or plan termination in a beneficiary's geographic area. Beneficiaries terminated for cause are enrolled in the original Medicare fee-for-service program. Others may have a special election period.

1151. How is enrollment information provided to Medicare beneficiaries?

At least fifteen days before the required November coordinated election period (see Q 1160), the Centers for Medicare & Medicaid Services (CMS) must mail to each beneficiary general information on Medicare and comparative information on Medicare Advantage plans available in their area. A new development for 2019 is that Medicare Advantage insurance companies can send beneficiaries certain documents electronically, instead of by mail. For example, plans must send you an Evidence of Coverage document every year. Now the plan can email it to you instead of mailing it.

General information includes information on covered benefits, cost sharing, and balance billing liability under the original fee-for-service program [Medicare Part A (Hospital Insurance) and Part B (Medical Insurance)]; election procedures; grievance and appeals rights; and information on Medigap insurance and Medicare SELECT.

Comparative information includes extensive information on benefits and beneficiary liability, premiums, service areas, quality and performance, and supplemental benefits. A sophisticated search engine is available at www.medicare.gov to assist beneficiaries in deciding between Medicare Advantage and traditional Medicare Parts A and Parts B and in locating a Medicare Advantage plan in a beneficiary's area. Beneficiaries may also call CMS at 1-800-772-1213.

Benefits and Beneficiary Protections

1152. What basic benefits are provided by Medicare Advantage plans?

All Medicare Advantage plans are required to provide at least the same benefits available under traditional Medicare Part A (Hospital Insurance) and Part B (Medical Insurance), with the exception of the Part A hospice benefit. If a beneficiary requires hospice services, those benefits are provided through Part A (Hospital Insurance).

Medicare Advantage plans may also offer mandatory and optional supplemental benefits, subject to approval by the Centers for Medicare & Medicaid Services (CMS). Mandatory supplemental benefits must be approved unless CMS determines that offering such benefits would substantially discourage enrollment in the Medicare Advantage plan. Medicare Advantage plans may also offer optional supplemental benefits. Optional supplemental benefits are benefits – such as vision, dental and wellness care – that a beneficiary chooses to add to his or her Medicare Advantage plan coverage. Beneficiaries who enroll in Medicare Advantage plans offering either mandatory or optional supplemental benefits (or both) pay the cost of such benefits through additional premiums or cost-sharing obligations such as copayments or coinsurance.

1153. What standards must Medicare Advantage plans meet for protection of beneficiaries?

In general, Medicare Advantage plans must offer similar protections to Medicare beneficiaries enrolled in traditional Medicare Part A (Hospital Insurance) and Part B (Medical Insurance), including disclosure, access, quality of care, grievance and appeals procedures, confidentiality, and information on advance directives.

1154. What are the rules regarding nondiscrimination for Medicare Advantage plans?

Medicare Advantage plans cannot screen potential enrollees based on their health status, nor can a Medicare Advantage plan discriminate with respect to participation, payment, or indemnification against any provider acting within the scope of the provider's license or certification. Medicare Advantage plans may, however, selectively contract with providers based on a provider's willingness to accept the provisions of the Medicare Advantage plan's contract.

1155. What are the rules regarding disclosure to enrollees?

A Medicare Advantage plan must provide in a clear, accurate, and standardized form, certain plan information to each enrollee, including the following information about the plan:

- service area;

- benefits;

- number;

- mix and distribution of providers;

- out-of-area coverage;

- emergency coverage;

- supplemental benefits;

- prior authorization rules;

- appeals and grievance procedures;

- quality assurance program; and

- disenrollment procedures.

Upon request, enrollees must be provided comparative information, information on the plan's utilization control mechanisms, information on the number of grievances and appeals, and compensation arrangements.

1156. What are the access-to-services requirements for Medicare Advantage plans?

Medicare Advantage plans are permitted to select the providers who may furnish benefits to enrollees, as long as benefits are available and accessible to all enrollees with reasonable promptness and assured continuity, twenty-four hours a day, seven days a week.

The plan must also cover services provided other than through the organization for:

    (1)   nonemergency services needed immediately because of an unforeseen illness or injury, if it was not reasonable to obtain the services through the plan;

(2)   renal dialysis services for enrollees who are temporarily out of the plan's service area; and

(3)   maintenance or post stabilization care after an emergency condition has been stabilized, subject to guidelines established by the Centers for Medicare & Medicaid Services (CMS).

Medicare Advantage plans are required to pay for emergency services without regard to prior authorization or whether the provider has a contractual relationship with the plan. An emergency medical condition is defined using a "prudent layperson" standard (including conditions that may be manifested by "severe pain").

Private fee-for-service plans must demonstrate that the plan includes a sufficient number and range of providers willing to furnish services. This requirement is presumed to have been met if the plan has established payment rates that are not less than payment rates under Medicare, and/or has contracts or agreements with a sufficient number and range of providers.

1157. Is there a quality assurance program for Medicare Advantage plans?

Medicare Advantage plans must have an internal quality assurance program. There are numerous requirements for internal quality assurance programs, including that such programs include chronic care improvement plans, conduct certain types of quality improvement projects, and encourage contracted providers to participate in various government quality improvement initiatives.

Medicare Advantage plans are deemed to have satisfied certain of the Medicare quality assurance requirements by receiving accreditation (and having periodic review and re-accreditation) from a private organization approved by the Centers for Medicare & Medicaid Services (CMS). CMS may also deem Medicare Advantage plans – generally, organizations with good track records – to have satisfied certain of the quality assurance program requirements. A change for 2019 is that CMS longer mandates that Medicare Advantage plans complete Quality Improvement Project (QIP) requirements. CMS found that Quality Improvement (QI) requirements already include the QIP activities.

1158. How are grievances handled by Medicare Advantage plans?

Medicare Advantage plans must maintain meaningful procedures for hearing and resolving grievances. Medicare Advantage plans also must have a procedure for making determinations regarding whether an enrollee is entitled to receive services and the amount the individual is required to pay for such services. Determinations must be made on a timely basis. The explanation of a plan's determination must be in writing and must explain the reasons for the denial in understandable language and describe the reconsideration and appeals processes. The time period for reconsiderations will be specified by the Centers for Medicare & Medicaid Services (CMS) but must not be greater than sixty days after the request by the enrollee. Reconsiderations of coverage determinations to deny coverage based on lack of medical necessity must be made by a physician with expertise in the field of medicine that relates to the condition necessitating treatment.

Plans are required to have an expedited review process in cases where the normal time frame for making a determination or reconsideration could seriously jeopardize the life or health of the enrollee or the enrollee's ability to regain maximum function. Either the beneficiary or the physician can request an expedited review. Requests for expedited reviews made by physicians (even those not affiliated with the organization) must be granted by the plan. Expedited determinations and reconsiderations must be made within time periods specified by CMS, but not later than seventy-two hours after the request for expedited review, or such longer period as CMS may permit in specified cases.

CMS is required to contract with an independent, outside entity to review and resolve plan reconsiderations not favorable to the beneficiary. If the independent review is unfavorable to the beneficiary, the beneficiary has the right to the same appeals process (e.g., Administrative Law Judge, judicial review) as under existing HMO procedures.

1159. Are there special rules covering provider participation?

Yes, a Medicare Advantage plan must establish procedures relating to participation of physicians in the plan, such as notice of rules of participation, written notice of adverse participation decisions, and an appeals process. Medicare Advantage plans must consult with participating physicians regarding medical policy, quality, and medical management procedures.

Plans are prohibited from restricting health care professionals from advising their patients about the patient's health status or treatment options.

A provider, health professional, or other entity is treated as having a contract with a private fee-for-service plan if the provider, health professional, or other entity provides services that are covered under a private fee-for-service plan, and before providing those services, was informed of the individual's enrollment, and either was informed of the terms and conditions of payment for the services under the private fee-for-service plan or was given a reasonable opportunity to obtain information concerning the terms and conditions. A major change for 2019 is that certain providers will no longer be required to meet enrollment requirements.

In addition CMS, in 2019, is lifting certain restrictions on the types of Medicare Advantage plans that insurance companies can offer. Under these restrictions, a company couldn't offer multiple plans within the same county if the plans appeared too similar to one another.

1160. Are there billing limits under Medicare Advantage?

Noncontracting physicians and other entities must accept as payment in full the amount that would have been paid under Medicare Advantage or a Medicare fee-for-service plan. Noncontracting providers must also accept, as payment in full, the amount that would have been paid under traditional Medicare.

Contracting physicians, providers, and other entities of private fee-for-service plans must accept as payment in full an amount not to exceed (including any deductibles, coinsurance, copayments or balance billing permitted under the plan) an amount equal to 115 percent (the "limiting charge") of the plan's payment rate. Plans must establish procedures to carry out this requirement. If a plan does not establish and enforce its procedures, the plan is subject to sanctions.

Private fee-for-service plans must provide enrollees with an explanation of benefits that includes a clear statement regarding enrollee liability, including any balance billing. The plan must also provide that the hospital give enrollees prior notice before they receive inpatient services and certain other services, when the amount of balance billing could be substantial. The notice must include a good faith estimate of the likely amount of balance billing based upon the presenting conditions of the enrollee.

Premiums

1161. How do Medicare Advantage plans submit proposed premiums?

All Medicare Advantage plans must submit to the Centers for Medicare & Medicaid Services (CMS) information on enrollment capacity.

- *Managed care plans* must submit Adjusted Community Rate (ACR) proposals for basic and supplemental benefits, the plan's premium for the basic and supplemental benefits, a description of the plan's proposed cost-sharing requirements, the actuarial value of cost sharing for basic and supplemental benefits, and a description of any additional benefits and the value of these benefits.

- *Private fee-for-service plans* must submit ACRs for basic and additional benefits, the premium for the basic and additional benefits, a description of the plan's proposed cost-sharing requirements and the actuarial value of the cost sharing, a description of additional benefits and the actuarial value of these benefits, and the supplemental premium.

In general, the CMS must review ACRs, premiums, and the actuarial values and approve or disapprove these rates, amounts, and values. CMS does not review premiums of private fee-for-service plans.

Organizations cannot contract to enroll Medicare beneficiaries under the Medicare Advantage program until they have met standards published by the CMS.

1162. What other Medicare Advantage premium rules should a beneficiary know about?

- A Medicare Advantage plan can terminate an enrollee for failure to pay premiums, but only under specified conditions.

- A Medicare Advantage organization cannot offer cash or other monetary rebates as an inducement for enrollment or otherwise.

- Premiums cannot vary among plan enrollees in the same Medicare Advantage plan.

- No state can impose a premium tax or similar tax on premiums of Medicare Advantage plans or the offering of these plans.

- For 2019, CMS is allowing certain Medicare Advantage plans to charge different annual deductibles for beneficiaries that meet certain medical criteria.

- Also CMS Is allowing Medicare Advantage plans to seamlessly renew coverage for beneficiaries automatically year by year.

Contracts with Medicare Advantage Organizations

1163. How does a plan become part of the Medicare Advantage program?

A Medicare Advantage plan must generally be organized and licensed under state law as a risk-bearing entity to offer health insurance or health benefits coverage.

New regional Preferred Provider Organizations (PPOs) are also eligible for temporary waiver-of-state-licensure requirements. This is intended to facilitate the introduction of these multistate plans. The Centers for Medicare & Medicaid Services (CMS) has indicated that it will grant these waivers only in cases where the organization is licensed in one state and has submitted applications in the other states. The length of the waiver will typically be for less than one year, but will depend on how long states take to process applications.

A plan cannot receive payment from Medicare unless it has a contract with CMS. The contract period is for one year and may be automatically renewed in the absence of notice by either party of intention to terminate.

CMS can terminate a contract under the following circumstances:

(1)   the organization has failed to substantially carry out the contract;

(2)   the organization was carrying out the contract in a manner substantially inconsistent with the efficient and effective administration of the Medicare Advantage program; or

(3)   the organization no longer substantially meets Medicare Advantage conditions. CMS generally may not contract with a plan that has been terminated within the last five years.

Medicare Advantage plans must meet minimum enrollment requirements: 5,000 subscribers or plans in urban areas, 1,500 subscribers for plans in rural areas. These requirements can be waived in the first three contract years. Beginning in 2019, in some instances, CMS is not requiring certain providers to meet enrollment requirements.

Medicare Advantage plans must provide prompt payment to noncontracting providers and to enrollees in the case of private fee-for-service plans. If CMS determines (after notice of an opportunity for a hearing) that a plan has failed to pay providers or enrollees promptly, CMS can provide for direct payment. In these cases, CMS will reduce Medicare Advantage payments accordingly.

CMS may impose sanctions under the following circumstances if a plan:

(1) fails to provide medically necessary services required under law or the contract, and the failure adversely affects or has the substantial likelihood of adversely affecting the enrollee;

(2) imposes premiums in excess of the premium permitted;

(3) acts to expel or refuses to reenroll an individual in violation of the Medicare Advantage requirements;

(4) engages in practices that effectively deny or discourage enrollment;

(5) misrepresents or falsifies information to CMS or to others;

(6) violates rules regarding physician participation;

(7) employs or contracts with individuals who are excluded from participation in Medicare; or

(8) performs any other actions that are grounds for termination and, in the case of private fee-for-service plans, does not enforce balance billing limits. The remedies may include civil money penalties, suspension of enrollment, or suspension of payment.

Medicare Advantage plans must assume full financial risk for the provision of Medicare services, except that plans can:

(1) obtain insurance or make other arrangements for costs in excess of amounts periodically determined by CMS;

(2) obtain insurance or make arrangements for services needing to be provided other than through the plan;

(3) obtain insurance or make other arrangements for not more than 90 percent of the amount by which its fiscal year costs exceeded 115 percent of its income for the year; or

(4) make arrangements with providers or health institutions to assume all or part of the risk on a prospective basis for the provision of basic services.

Medigap Insurance Program

1164. What rules apply regarding Medigap insurance and Medicare Advantage plans?

As a general matter, a Medigap insurance policy cannot be sold or issued to a Medicare beneficiary or an individual with the knowledge that the policy duplicates health benefits to which the individual is already entitled under Medicare, including under a Medicare Advantage plan.

A Medicare Advantage plan is not considered a Medigap insurance policy. Medigap insurance policies supplement original fee-for-service Medicare coverage (Medicare Part A (Hospital Insurance) and Part B (Medical Insurance)). As an alternative to original Medicare Parts A and B, Medicare Advantage plans offer at a minimum the same basic coverage as traditional fee-for-service Medicare. Medicare Advantage plans may also offer additional benefits, subject to payment of additional premiums by enrollees (if the Medicare Advantage plan so requires). The additional benefits often duplicate what would otherwise be available through a private Medigap policy. See Q 1175 through Q 1190 for more information on Medigap insurance.

1165. What are the special rules regarding Medigap protections under the Medicare Advantage program?

If an individual described below seeks to enroll in a Medigap policy within sixty-three days of the events described next, the issuer may not:

(1) deny or condition the issuance of a Medigap policy that is offered or available;

(2) discriminate in the pricing of a policy because of health status, claims experience, receipt of health care, or medical condition; and

(3) impose a preexisting condition exclusion.

See Q 1175 through Q 1190 for more information about Medigap insurance.

There is guaranteed issuance of Medigap Plans A, B, C, F, K or L for:

(1) Individuals enrolled under an employee welfare benefit plan that provides benefits supplementing Medicare if the plan terminates or ceases to provide all benefits.

(2) Persons enrolled with a Medicare Advantage organization who discontinue under circumstances permitting disenrollment other than during an annual election period. These include:

(a) the termination of the entity's certification,

(b) the individual moves outside the entity's service area, or

(c) the individual elects to terminate due to cause.

(3) Persons enrolled with a risk or cost contract HMO, a similar organization operating under a demonstration project authority, a health care prepayment plan, or a Medicare SELECT policy, if enrollment ceases under the same circumstances that permit discontinuance of a Medicare Advantage election. In the case of a SELECT policy, there must also be no applicable provision in state law for continuation of the coverage.

(4) Individuals enrolled under a Medigap policy, if enrollment ceases because of the bankruptcy or insolvency of the issuer, or because of other involuntary termination

of coverage (and there is no provision under applicable state law for the continuation of coverage), or the issuer violated or misrepresented a provision of the policy.

There is guaranteed issuance of Medigap Plans A, B, C, F, K, L, or the Medigap insurance policy that the individual most recently previously enrolled in, if the individual:

(1)   was enrolled under a Medigap policy;

(2)   subsequently terminates enrollment and enrolls with a Medicare Advantage organization, a risk or cost contract HMO, a similar organization operating under a demonstration project authority or a Medicare SELECT policy; and

(3)   terminates the Medicare Advantage enrollment within twelve months, but only if the individual was never previously enrolled with a Medicare Advantage organization.

There is guaranteed issuance of *any* Medigap plan to an individual who, upon first becoming eligible for Medicare at age sixty-five, enrolled in a Medicare Advantage plan and disenrolled from the plan within twelve months of the effective date of enrollment.

Medicare Advantage Marketing Rules

1166. What are the rules about the marketing of Medicare Advantage plans?

Significant restrictions apply to marketing of Medicare Advantage plans to Medicare beneficiaries. These restrictions include:

- Prohibiting "cold calls" and other unsolicited contact. This prohibition includes door-to-door sales and unsolicited telephone calls. The rules do not prohibit plan mailings, but the final regulations prohibit calling to confirm that the beneficiary received the mailing. Agents may call in response to specific requests by beneficiaries to be contacted.

- Prohibiting sales activities at educational events. Events designed to provide the public with objective information about Medicare must be free of any marketing materials or enrollment information for a specific plan or organization. Plans and agents may hold sales events that are clearly labeled as such, but they may not be disguised as educational events.

- Prohibiting plans and agents from providing meals at Medicare sales meetings. Light refreshments and "snacks" are permissible.

- Prohibiting sales activities in settings where individuals receive health care services. This rule permits marketing in common areas such as waiting rooms but prohibits marketing in treatment rooms. Plans may arrange meetings with residents in long-term care facilities as with any other private residence.

- Prohibiting the marketing of any nonhealth insurance product (such as life insurance or annuities) during a Medicare marketing or sales meeting.

Agents are also required to document that, prior to making an appointment, beneficiaries agree to the scope of products to be discussed at the meeting. Appointments made in person require written documentation; appointments made over the phone require recorded documentation. At a meeting in an agent's office or on the phone, additional products may not be discussed unless the beneficiary requests the information. In a meeting at a beneficiary's home, an agent may not discuss any product not within the originally-identified scope of the meeting. They must schedule a separate appointment at least forty-eight hours later.

Marketing materials must include:

All Medicare Advantage plans must give a complete description of plan rules to potential members in an enrollment kit that includes:

- Any network requirements

- Specifics on the plan's coverage and costs

- Eligibility requirements

- Instructions on how to file an appeal or grievance

- Written notice advising potential enrollees that costs can change year to year

- Instructions and forms on how to enroll

- Cover letter with the plan's customer service phone number along with the number to contact Medicare

- Information on how to apply for Extra Help

- Plan ratings information

- Translated marketing materials in any non-English language that is the primary language of at least 5 percent of the individuals in a plan's benefit package (PBP) service area, available on their websites and in hard-copy upon request

- Upon enrollment, a pharmacy and provider directory

If an individual decides to enroll in a Medicare Advantage plan, the plan must provide a Summary of Benefits, which details coverage and costs under the plan. The plan must also provide the member with a handbook and Evidence of Coverage (EOC), which explains the plan's coverage. Plans must send this EOC to new members no later than January of that plan year. They must also provide a pharmacy and provider directory upon enrollment, and every three years thereafter.

1167. What are the pros and cons of Medicare Advantage plans?

Upsides:

- Some insurance companies offer zero dollar premium for the Medicare Advantage plan.

- Medicare Advantage plan availability can depend on the county and state

- Medicare Advantage might cover benefits beyond the coverage of Part A and Part B

  - Vision or dental coverage might be offered.

- Each plan has a maximum out-of-pocket limit on health care costs for the year.

  - Once limit is met – no cost forcovered services.

- Can be convenient to have all coverage in one plan

- Most – although not all – Medicare Advantage plans offer prescription coverage which is only available in Medicare through Part D

Downsides:

- Since Medicare Advantage plans are run through private insurance companies, there are often differences in rules from company to company

  - Specifics of each plan depend on decisions of the insurance company.

  - Some may require higher out-of-pocket costs than with Original Medicare.

  - Plan premiums, benefits, and copayments may change each year.

  - The insurance company may mandate strict rules for coverage for certain services or health products, such as referrals to see specialists.

  - Subscribers may have to change doctors or hospitals to one within the Medicare Advantage plan's network for coverage or pay a higher cost.

- Medicare Advantage plans have annual contracts with Medicare and can choose not to renew their contract for the following year.

- Each Medicare Advantage plan can have a different out of pocket limit, and that amount may change each year.

- Most require copays/coinsurance

- Certain drugs may not be covered – formulary can change at any time.

- Preferred health providers may not be in network.

- Difficult to compare plans

- Often no nationwide coverage

PART D: PRESCRIPTION DRUG INSURANCE

1168. What is Medicare Part D?

Medicare Part D is the prescription drug insurance program added to Medicare by the Medicare Prescription Drug, Improvement, and Modernization Act of 2003 (MMA).

Part D is a voluntary program of health insurance that covers a portion of outpatient prescription drug costs not generally covered by other Medicare programs, especially traditional Medicare Part A (Hospital Insurance) and Part B (Medical Insurance). Part D prescription drug plans are offered only through private insurance companies. Medicare beneficiaries wishing to enroll in a Part D plan may stay with original Medicare Parts A and B and enroll in a stand-alone Part D prescription drug insurance plan, or they may choose a Medicare Advantage plan that includes Part D prescription drug benefits as part of the Medicare Advantage plan's comprehensive benefit package. Part D prescription drug insurance is partially financed through premiums paid by participants, whether for stand-alone Part D plans or as part of a Medicare Advantage plan.

1169. When did Medicare Part D become effective?

Medicare Part D (Prescription Drug Insurance) became effective January 1, 2006, with initial enrollment for the first year beginning November 15, 2005, and running for six months.

1170. Who is eligible for Medicare Part D?

Any Medicare beneficiary who is entitled to Medicare Part A or enrolled in Part B is eligible to participate in Part D (Prescription Drug Insurance).

1171. What does the Part D (Prescription Drug Insurance) cost?

Generally, Part D (Prescription Drug Insurance) plans require beneficiaries to pay monthly premiums, meet an annual deductible, and pay coinsurance. Because Part D plans are offered only through private insurance plans, the premiums, deductibles and coinsurance vary from plan to plan. Premiums may be paid separately for a stand-alone Part D plan or as part of the monthly premium for a comprehensive Medicare Advantage plan.

Beneficiaries who choose not to enroll in Part D during their initial enrollment period may face a late enrollment penalty if they later choose to enroll in a Part D plan. The late enrollment penalty is the greater of "an amount that [the CMS] determines is actuarially sound for each uncovered month" or "1 percent of the base beneficiary premium" (the national average premium for the year of late enrollment) per month. The late enrollment penalty is calculated by multiplying 1 percent of the "national base beneficiary premium" ($32.42 in 2014, $33.13 in 2015, $34.10 in 2016, $35.63 in 2017, $35.02 in 2018 and $33.19 in 2019) times the number of full, uncovered months you were eligible but didn't join a Medicare Prescription Drug Plan and went without other creditable prescription drug coverage. The final amount is rounded to the nearest ten cents and added to your monthly premium. For example, for a beneficiary enrolling late in 2017, the penalty is approximately thirty-five cents per full month in which the beneficiary was eligible to enroll in a Part D plan but failed to do so.

Beneficiaries who have other sources of prescription drug coverage (such as through a former employer) may be able to maintain that coverage and delay enrollment in a Part D plan without incurring a penalty in the future. As long as a beneficiary maintains coverage that qualifies as "creditable coverage" (meaning generally that the coverage is at least as valuable – at least actuarially equivalent – as the standard Part D prescription drug package specified by Medicare), the beneficiary will not be subject to late enrollment penalties if he later enrolls in a Part D plan. Failure to maintain creditable prescription drug coverage for a period of sixty-three days or longer may subject an individual to a late enrollment penalty.

Entities (such as a former employer) offering prescription drug coverage to Part D eligible individuals must disclose to those individuals whether the coverage they provide is creditable coverage as defined by CMS. These entities must also inform CMS of the status of this coverage. See Q 1189.

1172. What benefits does Part D (Prescription Drug Insurance) provide?

Medicare establishes a standard prescription drug benefit under Part D (Prescription Drug Insurance). Participants with incomes below 135 percent, and between 135 percent and 150 percent, of the federal poverty guidelines will have lower cost-sharing requirements than under the standard benefit.

The Part D standard drug benefit in 2019 was:

Prescription Drug Expenses	Beneficiary Costs	Medicare Pays
First $415	100% (up to $400)	Nothing
$415 to $3,820	25% (up to $955)	75% (up to $2,865)
$3,820 to $7,653.75	100% (up to $3,820)	Nothing
Above $7,653.75	Up to 5% (based on income)	95% or more

In the "Coverage Gap" ($3,820 to $7,653.25), a Medicare beneficiary may have to pay for 30 percent of brand name drugs or 37 percent of generic drugs. Once a Medicare beneficiary has paid $4,700 out-of-pocket, the beneficiary is out of the Coverage Gap.

Beneficiaries with incomes below 135 percent of the federal poverty guidelines have no cost-sharing obligation for prescription drug expenses above $7,653.25. Beneficiaries with incomes between 135 percent and 150 percent of the federal poverty guidelines have $2.95 and $7.40 co-pays for generic and name-brand prescriptions. Those with incomes above 150 percent of the federal poverty level have 5 percent copays.

For 2019, 135 percent of the federal poverty guidelines is $16,389 for a single person and $22,221 for a married couple; 150 percent of the federal poverty guidelines is $18,210for a single person and $24,690 for a married couple.

Part D plans are available only through private insurance companies. Those insurers may offer prescription drug plans that vary from the Part D standard benefit as long as the plans:

(1)   provide coverage, the actuarial value of which is at least equal to the actuarial value of the standard prescription drug coverage;

(2)   offer access to negotiated prices; and

(3)   are approved by the CMS.

Part D plans may also provide supplemental prescription drug coverage that offers cost-sharing reductions and optional drugs. A plan may charge a supplemental premium for the supplemental coverage. However, insurers offering Part D plans with supplemental coverage in an area must also offer a prescription drug plan in the area that provides only basic coverage for no additional supplemental premium. Basic coverage is either the statutorily defined standard benefit or the actuarial equivalent of such standard benefit without any supplemental benefits.

The monthly Medicare Part D base premium is set to pay 25.5 percent of the cost of standard coverage, based on bids submitted annually by Part D plans. The CMS releases the Medicare Part D base premium in early August each year. Actual premiums are based on this set premium, but can vary greatly by plans and regions. Beneficiaries with higher incomes must pay a premium adjustment based on their income. This premium adjustment is called the Income-Related Monthly Adjustment Amount (IRMAA), and is automatically deducted from the Social Security benefit.

COSTS FOR 2019

Beneficiaries who file individual tax returns with income that is:	Beneficiaries who file joint tax returns with income that is:	Medicare Part D Income Related Monthly Adjustment Amount*
		2019
Less than or equal to $85,000	Less than or equal to $170,000	$0.00
Greater than $85,000 and less than or equal to $107,000	Greater than 170,000 than or equal to $214,000	$12.40
Greater than $107,000 and less than or equal to $133,500	Greater than $214,000 and less than or equal to $267,000	$31.90
Greater than $133,500 and less than or equal to $160,000	Greater than $267,000 and less than or equal to $320,000	$51.40
Greater than $160,000 and less than or equal to $500,000	9 $320,000 and less than or equal to $750,000	$70.90
Greater than $500,000	Greater than $750,000	$77.40

COSTS FOR 2018

Beneficiaries who file individual tax returns with income that is:	Beneficiaries who file joint tax returns with income that is:	Medicare Part D Income Related Monthly Adjustment Amount*
		2018
Less than or equal to $85,000	Less than or equal to $170,000	$0.00
Greater than $85,000 and less than or equal to $107,000	Greater than 170,000 than or equal to $214,000	$13.00

Beneficiaries who file individual tax returns with income that is:	Beneficiaries who file joint tax returns with income that is:	Medicare Part D Income Related Monthly Adjustment Amount*
Greater than $107,000 and less than or equal to $133,500	Greater than $214,000 and less than or equal to $267,000	$33.60
Greater than $133,500 and less than or equal to $160,000	Greater than $267,000 and less than or equal to $320,000	$54.20
Greater than $160,000	Greater than $320,000	$74.80

COSTS FOR 2014 THROUGH 2017

Beneficiaries who file individual tax returns with income that is:	Beneficiaries who file joint tax returns with income that is:	Medicare Part D Income Related Monthly Adjustment Amount*			
		2017	2016	2015	2014
Less than or equal to $85,000	Less than or equal to $170,000	$0.00	$0.00	$0.00	$0.00
Greater than $85,000 and less than or equal to $107,000	Greater than $170,000 and less than or equal to $214,000	$13.30	$12.70	$12.30	$12.10
Greater than $107,000 and less than or equal to $160,000	Greater than $214,000 and less than or equal to $320,000	$34.20	$32.80	$31.80	$31.10
Greater than $160,000 and less than or equal to $214,000	Greater than $320,000 and less than or equal to $428,000	$55.20	$52.80	$51.30	$50.20
Greater than $214,000	Greater than $428,000	$76.20	$72.90	$70.80	$69.30

The Patient Protection and Affordable Care Act (PPACA) includes benefits to make Medicare prescription drug coverage (Part D) more affordable for beneficiaries. This is done through providing coverage through a coverage gap (also called the "donut hole") in Medicare prescription drug coverage.

The PPACA coverage provides the following:

- A discount on covered brand-name drugs when a person buys the drug at a pharmacy or orders the drugs through the mail

- Some coverage for generic and brand-name drugs

- Additional savings on brand-name and generic drugs during the coverage gap over the next several years until it is closed in 2020

- The coverage gap closes by maintaining the 50 percent discount the manufacturers offer and increasing what Medicare drug plans cover

1173. What notice must an employer who maintains a prescription drug plan provide to Medicare-eligible individuals?

Employers and plan sponsors who offer prescription drug coverage to individuals eligible for Medicare Part D (Prescription Drug Insurance) must advise those individuals whether the offered coverage is "creditable." Eligible individuals who do not enroll in Part D when first available, but who enroll later, have to pay higher premiums permanently, unless they have creditable prescription drug coverage. (See Q 1189.)

To determine that coverage is creditable, a sponsor need only determine that total expected paid claims for Medicare beneficiaries under the sponsor's plan will be at least equal to the total expected paid claims for the same beneficiaries under the defined standard prescription drug coverage under Part D. The determination of creditable-coverage status for disclosure purposes does not require attestation by a qualified actuary (unless the employer or union is applying for the retiree drug subsidy available under the MMA).

To assist sponsors in making the determination that coverage is creditable, the Centers for Medicare & Medicaid Studies (CMS) issued guidance with example "safe harbor" benefit designs. A plan design will automatically be deemed creditable if it includes:

1. coverage for brand and generic prescriptions;

2. reasonable access to retail providers and, optionally, for mail order coverage;

3. benefits payments designed to pay on average at least 60 percent of participants' prescription drug expenses; and

4. at least one of the following:

    a. an annual prescription drug benefit maximum of at least $25,000;

    b. an actuarial expectation that the plan will pay benefits of at least $2,000 per Medicare-eligible individual; or

    c. for plans that cover both medical expenses and prescription drugs, an annual deductible of no more than $250, an annual benefit maximum of at least $25,000, and a lifetime maximum of at least $1,000,000.

Under the CMS guidance, once a sponsor determines whether coverage is creditable, the sponsor must provide notice to all Part D-eligible individuals covered by or applying for the plan, including Part D-eligible dependents. In lieu of determining who is Part D-eligible, an employer sponsor may provide notice to all active employees, along with an explanation of why the notice is being provided.

The required notice to beneficiaries must, at a minimum:

1. contain a statement that the employer has determined that the coverage is creditable (or not creditable);

2.   explain the meaning of creditable coverage;

3.   explain why creditable coverage is important, and caution that higher Part D premiums could result if there is a break in creditable coverage of sixty-three days or more before enrolling in a Part D plan; and

4.   if coverage is not creditable, explain that an individual may generally enroll in Part D only from November 15 through December 31 of each year.

CMS recommends that sponsors also provide the following clarifications in their notices:

- An explanation of a beneficiary's rights to a notice, i.e., the times when a beneficiary can expect to receive a notice and the times that a beneficiary can request a copy of the notice.

- An explanation of the plan provisions that affect beneficiaries when they (or their dependents) are Medicare Part D-eligible. These options may include, for example:

  - that they can retain their existing coverage and choose not to enroll in a Part D plan; or

  - that they can enroll in a Part D plan as a supplement to, or in lieu of, the other coverage;

  - if their existing prescription drug coverage is under a Medigap policy, that they cannot have both their existing prescription drug coverage and Part D coverage and that, if they enroll in Part D coverage, they should inform their Medigap insurer of that fact and the Medigap insurer must remove the prescription drug coverage from the Medigap policy and adjust the premium, as of the date the Part D coverage starts.

- Whether the covered individuals and/or their covered dependents will still be eligible to receive all of their current health coverage if they or their dependents enroll in a Medicare Part D prescription drug plan.

- A clarification of the circumstances (if any) under which the individual could re-enroll in employment-based prescription drug coverage if the individual drops the current coverage and enrolls in Medicare prescription drug coverage. (For Medigap insurers, this would be a clarification that the individual cannot get his prescription drug coverage back under such circumstances).

- Information on how to get extra help paying for a Medicare prescription drug plan including the contact information for the Social Security Administration (SSA).

Sponsors must also disclose to CMS whether the coverage is creditable. The disclosure must be made to CMS on an annual basis, and upon any change that affects whether the coverage is creditable. CMS has posted guidance on the timing and format of the required disclosure and a model Disclosure to CMS form on the CMS website at www.cms.hhs.gov/creditablecoverage.

Prescription Drug Marketing Rules

1174. What are the rules about the marketing of Medicare Part D (Prescription Drug Insurance) plans?

There are significant restrictions regarding the marketing of Medicare Part D plans:

- The rules broadly prohibit "cold calls" and other unsolicited contact. This prohibition includes door-to-door sales and unsolicited telephone calls. The rules do not prohibit plan mailings, but the final regulations prohibit calling to confirm that the beneficiary received the mailing. Agents may call in response to specific requests by beneficiaries to be contacted.

- The rules prohibit sales activities at educational events. Events designed to provide the public with objective information about Medicare must be free of any marketing materials or enrollment information for a specific plan or organization. Plans and agents may hold sales events that are clearly labeled as such, but they may not be disguised as educational events.

- The rules prohibit plans and agents from providing meals at Medicare sales meetings. The Centers for Medicare & Medicaid Services (CMS) has not yet defined the terms, but light refreshments and "snacks" are permissible.

- The rules prohibit sales activities in settings where individuals receive healthcare services. This rule permits marketing in common areas such as waiting rooms, but prohibits marketing in treatment rooms. Plans may arrange meetings with residents in long-term care facilities as with any other private residence.

- The rules prohibit marketing any nonhealth insurance product (such as life insurance or annuities) during a Medicare marketing or sales meeting.

The rules also require agents to document that, prior to making an appointment, beneficiaries agree to the scope of products to be discussed at the meeting. Appointments made in person require written documentation; appointments made over the phone require recorded documentation. At a meeting in an agent's office or on the phone, additional products may not be discussed unless the beneficiary requests the information. In a meeting at a beneficiary's home, an agent may not discuss any product not within the originally-identified scope of the meeting. They must schedule a separate appointment at least forty-eight hours later.

The same marketing restrictions apply to both Medicare Advantage and Medicare Part D prescription drug plans.

MEDIGAP INSURANCE

1175. What is Medigap Insurance?

"Medigap" insurance is a term referring to Medicare Supplement Insurance policies. Medicare provides basic protection against the cost of health care, but it does not pay all medical expenses. For this reason, many private insurance companies sell these supplemental insurance policies known as "Medigap" policies. The federal government does not sell or service insurance, but regulates the coverage offered by Medigap insurance. Many Medicare beneficiaries enrolled in Part A (Hospital Insurance) and Part B (Medical Insurance) also maintain Medigap policies to cover costs not paid for by Parts A and B.

Medigap insurance is a private insurance policy designed to help pay deductibles and/or coinsurance incurred by beneficiaries who are enrolled in original Medicare Part A (Hospital Insurance) and Part B (Medical Insurance). A Medigap policy may also pay for certain items or services generally not covered by Medicare at all, such as medical expenses incurred during foreign travel. Medigap policies coordinate only with original Medicare Parts A and B, not with Medicare Advantage plans. By law, a Medicare beneficiary cannot be sold a Medigap plan that duplicates benefits otherwise available to that beneficiary under Medicare, including through a Medicare Advantage plan.

1176. Is there an open enrollment period for Medigap policies?

Yes, an open enrollment period for selecting Medigap policies guarantees that, for six months immediately following the effective date of enrolling in Medicare Part B (Medical Insurance), a person age sixty-five or older cannot be denied Medigap insurance or charged higher premiums because of health problems.

GUARANTEED COVERAGE:

No matter how a person enrolls in Part B (Medical Insurance) – whether by automatic notification or through an initial, special or general enrollment period – a person is covered by the guarantees if both of the following are true:

- The person is age sixty-five or older and is enrolled in Medicare for the first time, based on age rather than disability

- The person applies for Medigap insurance within six months of enrollment in Part B (Medical Insurance)

PRE-EXISTING CONDITIONS:

In some cases, however, even when a person buys a Medigap policy during his open enrollment period, the policy may still exclude coverage for "pre-existing conditions" during the first six months the policy is in effect. Pre-existing conditions are conditions that were either diagnosed or treated during the six-month period immediately before the Medigap policy became effective. (See Q 1192 for exceptions to this rule.)

Once the Medigap open enrollment period ends, a person may not be able to buy the policy of his or her choice. He or she may have to accept whatever Medigap policy an insurance company is willing to sell him or her.

In the case of individuals enrolled in Medicare Part B prior to age sixty-five, Medigap insurers are required to offer coverage, regardless of medical history, for a six-month period when the individual reaches age sixty-five. Insurers are prohibited from discriminating in the price of policies for an individual based on that person's medical or health status.

Also, although Medigap policies are standardized, premiums can vary widely. Insurers can reject an applicant who applies for a Medigap policy after the open enrollment period.

Once issued, all Medigap polices are guaranteed renewable. This means that they continue in force as long as the premium is paid.

1177. Does a Medicaid recipient need Medigap insurance?

Low-income people who are eligible for Medicaid usually do NOT need additional insurance. Medicaid generally covers almost all the health care needs of a beneficiary that are not paid for by Medicare, in addition to covering long-term nursing home care. If a person purchases Medigap insurance and later becomes eligible for Medicaid, that individual may ask that Medigap insurance benefits and premiums be suspended for up to two years while the individual is covered by Medicaid. If the person becomes ineligible for Medicaid benefits during the two years, the Medigap policy is automatically reinstated as of the date of Medicaid termination and on terms at least as favorable as those in effect at the time of initial suspension, provided the person gives proper notice and begins paying premiums again.

1178. Are there Federal standards for Medigap policies?

Yes, Congress established federal standards for Medigap policies in 1990 and again in 2010. Most states have adopted regulations limiting the sale of Medigap insurance to no more than ten standard policies. One of the ten is a basic policy offering a "core package" of benefits.

These standardized plans are identified as follows: A, B, C, D, F, G, K, L, M, and N. (Plans E, H, I, and J have not been sold since June 1, 2010, although beneficiaries who had purchased such policies before that date are able to maintain their coverage. Plans M and N became available June 1, 2010.) Plan A is the core package. Plans B, C, D, F, G, M, and N each have a different combination of benefits, but they all include the core package. Plans K and L do not include the core benefit package; they instead offer catastrophic coverage. The basic Plan A policy, offering the core package of benefits, is available in all states. The availability of other plans varies from state to state.

The core package of benefits which all policies (except Plans K and L) must contain includes:

- Part A (Hospital Insurance) coinsurance for the sixty-first through ninetieth day of inpatient hospitalization in any Medicare benefit period;

- Part A (Hospital Insurance) coinsurance for the sixty lifetime reserve days that can be used for an inpatient hospitalization that lasts more than ninety days;

- Part A (Hospital Insurance) expenses for an extra 365 days in the hospital;

- Part A (Hospital Insurance) and Part B (Medical Insurance) deductible for the cost of the first three pints of blood;

- Part B (Medical Insurance) coinsurance (20 percent of allowable charges in most cases); and

- Part A (Hospital Insurance) hospice coinsurance, if any.

1179. What else should be known about Medigap policies?

When dealing with Medigap coverage, there are some other rules that apply that should be known including:

- **Requirement of Medicare coverage**: Medicare Part A and Part B are required to have a Medigap policy.

- **Medicare Advantage**: A subscriber to a Medicare Advantage Plan can apply for a Medigap policy but must leave the Medicare Advantage Plan before the Medigap policy begins.

- **Separate premiums**: Premiums paid to the private insurance company for the Medigap policy is in addition to the monthly Part B premium paid to Medicare.

- **One policy per person**: A Medigap policies covers one person. Spousal coverage in Medigap coverage requires a separate policy.

- **Insurance providers**: Many insurance companies are licensed in each state to sell Medigap coverage.

- **Guaranteed renewability**: All standardized Medigap policies guaranteed renewable regardless of health and cannot be cancelled as long as the premiums are paid.

- **Prescription drug coverage**: Medigap policies sold after January 1, 2006 cannot include prescription drug coverage. Prescription drug coverage is available under Medicare Part D.

- **Not Compatible with MSAs**: It's illegal for anyone to sell you a Medigap policy if you have a Medicare Medical Savings Account (MSA) plan.

- **Other Exclusions**: Medigap plans do not cover long-term care, vision and eyeglass expenses, dental care, hearing aids or private nursing.

The following insurance plans should not be confused with Medigap coverage as they are different types of insurance:

- Medicare Advantage Plans (like an HMO, PPO, or Private Fee-for-Service Plan)

- Medicare Prescription Drug Plans

- Medicaid

- Employer or union plans, including the Federal Employees Health Benefits Program (FEHBP)

- TRICARE

- Veterans' benefits

- Long-term care insurance policies

- Indian Health Service, Tribal, and Urban Indian Health plans

1180. Do Medigap policies cover medical expenses outside of the United States?

Yes, some Medigap policies offer additional coverage for expenses for health care services or supplies that are incurred outside the United States. Specifically, standard Medigap Plans C, D, E, F, G, H, I, J, M, and N provide foreign travel emergency health care coverage traveling outside the United States. (Plans E, H, I, and J are no longer sold, but if purchased before June 1, 2010 they were able to be retained.

Medigap Plans C, D, E, F, G, H, I, J, M, and N each pay 80 percent of the billed charges for certain medically necessary emergency care charges outside the United States after meeting a $250 deductible for the year. These policies cover foreign travel emergency care if it begins during the first sixty days of a trip, and if Medicare doesn't otherwise cover the care. Foreign travel emergency coverage with Medigap policies has a lifetime limit of $50,000.

1181. What additional benefits can be offered in the standard Medigap plans?

The following additional benefits above the basic core benefits can be covered:

- The entire Part A (Hospital Insurance) deductible payable for each new spell of illness requiring inpatient hospitalization

- The Part A (Hospital Insurance) coinsurance for days twenty-one-one-hundred of skilled nursing home care

- The annual Part B (Medical Insurance) deductible

- 80 percent of the "balance billing" paid by Part B (Medical Insurance) beneficiaries whose doctors do not accept assignment; 100 percent of other Part B (Medical Insurance) excess charges billed to beneficiaries

- 80 percent of the Medicare-eligible costs of medically necessary emergency care when the insured is traveling outside the United States

- "Innovative benefits" that are appropriate, cost-effective, and consistent with the goal of simplifying Medigap insurance – with prior approval by the state insurance commissioner

Certain policies sold before 2006 also offered limited coverage of outpatient prescription drug costs. Beneficiaries who purchased those policies before implementation of the Part D (Prescription Drug Insurance) benefit could maintain the policies, but no new policies with such benefits have been allowed after the introduction of Part D. Part D coverage in general is more generous than that available through old Medigap policies.

1182. What benefits are provided in each of the standard Medigap policies and the high deductible Medigap policies?

The Medigap policies offer the following benefits.

Basic Medigap Policy

Policy A is the basic core benefit package which includes:

(1)   Medicare Part A coinsurance and hospital costs up to an additional 365 days after Medicare benefits are exhausted

(2)   Medicare Part B coinsurance or copayment

(3)   First three pints of blood

(4)   Medicare Part A hospice coinsurance or copayment

Policies with Additional Coverages

Policy B includes:

(1)   the basic core benefit package; and

(2)   payment of the Part A (Hospital Insurance) deductible payable for each new benefit period.

Policy C includes:

(1)   the basic core benefit package;

(2)   the Part A (Hospital Insurance) deductible;

(3)   the Part A coinsurance for care in a skilled nursing home (days twenty-one-100);

(4)   the Part B (Medical Insurance) deductible; and

(5)   coverage of foreign travel emergencies up to 80 percent

Policy D includes:

(1)   the basic core benefit package;

(2)   the Part A (Hospital Insurance) deductible;

(3)   the Part A coinsurance for care in a skilled nursing home (days twenty-one-100); and

(4)   coverage of foreign travel emergencies up to 80 percent.

Policy F includes:

(1)   the basic core benefit package;

(2)   the Part A (Hospital Insurance) deductible;

(3)   the Part A coinsurance for care in a skilled nursing home (days twenty-one-100);

(4)   the Part B (Medical Insurance) deductible;

(5)   coverage of foreign travel emergencies up to 80 percent; and

(6)   100 percent coverage of excess provider charges under Part B (Medical Insurance).

In addition, there is a policy that is the same as Policy F (called the Plan High F) but with a $2,300 deductible in 2019. This deductible is increased $60 from $2018. The deductible for 2018 was not yet published at time of printing. This high-deductible policy covers 100 percent of covered out-of-pocket expenses once the deductible has been satisfied in a year. It requires the beneficiary of the policy to pay annual out-of-pocket expenses (other than premiums) in the amount of $2,300 before the policy begins payment of benefits. The deductible increases by the percentage increase in the Consumer Price Index for all urban consumers for the twelve-month period ending with August of the preceding year.

Policy G includes:

(1)   the basic core benefit package;

(2)   the Part A (Hospital Insurance) deductible;

(3)   the Part A coinsurance for care in a skilled nursing home (days twenty-one-100);

(4)   coverage of foreign travel emergencies up to 80 percent; and

(5)   100 percent coverage of excess provider charges under Part B (Medical Insurance).

Policies without Core Benefits – Catastrophic Plans

Beginning in 2006, two more standard plans became available. These two plans do not include the entire core benefit package.

Policy K includes:

(1)   Medicare Part A coinsurance and hospital costs up to an additional 365 days after Medicare benefits are exhausted

(2)   coverage of 50 percent of Part B coinsurance, blood costs under Parts A and B, Part A hospice coinsurance, and Part A skilled nursing facility coinsurance;

(3)   coverage of 100 percent of Part A hospital inpatient coinsurance and 365 extra lifetime days of coverage of inpatient hospital services;

(4)   50 percent of the Part A deductible; and

(5)   a limit on annual out-of-pocket spending under Part A and Part B to $5,240 in 2018

Policy L includes:

(1)   Medicare Part A coinsurance and hospital costs up to an additional 365 days after Medicare benefits are exhausted

(2)   coverage of 75 percent the Part B coinsurance, blood costs under Parts A and B, Part A hospice coinsurance, and Part A skilled nursing facility coinsurance;

(3)   coverage of 100 percent of the Part A hospital inpatient coinsurance and 365 extra lifetime days of coverage of inpatient hospital services;

(4)   75 percent of the Part A deductible; and

(5)   a limit on annual out-of-pocket spending under Part A and Part B to $2,620 in 2018.

Policies Added In 2010

Effective June 1, 2010, two new plans became available (both of which include the basic core benefit package):

- **Policy M** is a duplicate of Policy D, but with 50 percent coinsurance on the Part A deductible.

- **Policy N** is a duplicate Policy D with the Part B coinsurance being paid at 100 per-cent, *minus* a $20 copayment per physician visit and a $50 copayment per emergency room visit (unless the beneficiary was admitted to the hospital).

Policies Discontinued for Sale after June 1, 2010 But Still In Effect

The following plans are no longer available for purchase effective June 1, 2010 (but if an individual already had or bought one of these plans before June 1, 2010, that individual could keep that plan).

Policy E includes:

(1)   the basic core benefit package;

(2)   the Part A (Hospital Insurance) deductible;

(3)   the Part A coinsurance for care in a skilled nursing home (days twenty-one-one-hundred);

(4)   coverage of foreign travel emergencies; and

(5)   coverage of preventive screening and care.

Policy H includes:

(1)   the basic core benefit package;

(2)   the Part A (Hospital Insurance) deductible;

(3)   the Part A coinsurance for care in a skilled nursing home (days twenty-one-one-hundred);

(4)   coverage of foreign travel emergencies; and

(5)   coverage of 50 percent of the cost of outpatient prescription drugs after payment of a $250 deductible, up to a maximum benefit of $1,250. (See the paragraph below regarding prescription drug coverage.)

Policy I includes:

(1)   the basic core benefit package;

(2)   the Part A (Hospital Insurance) deductible;

(3)   the Part A coinsurance for care in a skilled nursing home (days twenty-one-one-hundred);

(4)   coverage of foreign travel emergencies;

(5)   at-home recovery assistance;

(6)   100 percent of excess charges under Part B (Medical Insurance); and

(7)   50 percent of the cost of outpatient prescription drugs after payment of a $250 deductible, up to a maximum benefit of $1,250. (See the paragraph below regarding prescription drug coverage.)

Policy J includes:

(1)   the basic core benefit package;

(2)   the Part A (Hospital Insurance) deductible;

(3)   the Part A coinsurance for care in a skilled nursing home (days twenty-one-one-hundred);

(4)   the Part B (Medical Insurance) annual deductible;

(5)   coverage of foreign travel emergencies;

(6)   at-home recovery assistance;

(7)   100 percent of excess charges under Part B;

(8)   preventive screening and care; and

(9)   50 percent of the cost of outpatient prescription drugs after payment of a $250 deductible, up to a maximum benefit of $3,000. (See the paragraph below regarding prescription drug coverage.)

There is also a policy that is the same as Policy J but with a $2,300 deductible. This high-deductible policy covers 100 percent of covered out-of-pocket expenses (in 2019) once the deductible has been satisfied in a year. This deductible increased $60 from 2018. It requires the beneficiary of the policy to pay annual out-of-pocket expenses (other than premiums) in the amount of $2,300 before the policy begins payment of benefits.

As of January 1, 2006, beneficiaries who held standard policies H, I, or J could choose between enrolling in Part D or maintaining their prescription drug coverage under their Medigap policies. Beneficiaries who chose to enroll in Part D could keep their existing plan H, I, or J, minus the prescription drug benefit, or could purchase a new Medigap policy. As of January 1, 2006, plans H, I, and J could be sold, but without the prescription drug benefit.

Medigap Coverage in Massachusetts, Minnesota and Wisconsin

Medigap plan choices in Massachusetts, Minnesota, and Wisconsin are different because these states already required standardized Medigap policies prior to 1992.

Medigap Benefits	Comparison of Coverage of Medigap Plans									
	A	B	C	D	F n1	G	K	L	M	N
Part A coinsurance and hospital costs up to an additional 365 days after Medicare benefits are used up	Yes	Yes	Yes	Yes	Yes	Yes	Yes	Yes	Yes	Yes
Part B coinsurance or copayment	Yes	Yes	Yes	Yes	Yes	Yes	50%	75%	Yes	Yes n3
Blood (first 3 pints)	Yes	Yes	Yes	Yes	Yes	Yes	50%	75%	Yes	Yes
Part A hospice care coinsurance or copayment	Yes	Yes	Yes	Yes	Yes	Yes	50%	75%	Yes	Yes
Skilled nursing facility care coinsurance	No	No	Yes	Yes	Yes	Yes	50%	75%	Yes	Yes
Part A deductible	No	Yes	Yes	Yes	Yes	Yes	50%	75%	50%	Yes
Part B deductible	No	No	Yes	No	Yes	No	No	No	No	No
Part B excess charge	No	No	No	No	Yes	Yes	No	No	No	No
Foreign travel exchange (up to plan limits)	No	No	80%	80%	80%	80%	No	No	80%	80%
Out of Pocket Limit n2	NA	NA	NA	NA	NA	NA	$5,120	$2,560	NA	NA

Note 1: Plan F also offers a high-deductible plan. If you choose this option, this means you must pay for Medicare-covered costs up to the deductible amount of $2,300 in 2019 before your Medigap plan pays anything.

Note 2: After you meet your out-of-pocket yearly limit and your yearly Part B deductible, the Medigap plan pays 100 percent of covered services for the rest of the calendar year.

Note 3: Plan N pays 100 percent of the Part B coinsurance, except for a copayment of up to $20 for some office visits and up to a $50 copayment for emergency room visits that don't result in inpatient admission.

1183. What are the most popular Medigap policies?

Ranked by sales, clearly Policy Plan F is the most popular, followed by Plans C, N and G, according to America's Health Insurance Plans in 2015.[1]

Rank	Plan	Share of total*
1	F	57%[2]
2	C	8%
3	N	8%
4	G	8%
5	B	3%
6	D	2%
7	A	1%
8	K	1%
9	E	1%
10	L	<0.5%
11	M	<0.5%

1184. Is Medicare Supplement Plan F being eliminated?

The Medicare Access and CHIP Reauthorization Act of 2015 (MACRA) passed by Congress and signed into law on April 16, 2015 changed the law on various aspects of health care, including some Medicare Supplement plans. The new law states that on or after January 1, 2020, a Medicare Supplement policy that provides coverage of the Part B deductible may not be sold or issued to a newly eligible Medicare beneficiary. Anyone whose birthday is December 31, 1954 (turning 65 on December 31, 2019) may be the last group able to enroll in Medicare Supplement Plan F. After January 1, 2020, individuals will not be able to enroll in Medicare Supplement Plan C, one of the closest alternatives to Plan F, either, since it also covers the Part B deductible. Those who already have Plan F, can keep it. The law only affects new enrollees.

1185. What effect does MACRA have on Medigap plans?

Section 401 of the Medicare Access and CHIP Reauthorization Act (MACRA)[3] mandates that effective on January 1, 2020, all newly eligible Medicare beneficiaries cannot sign up for

---

1. https://www.ahip.org/trends-in-medigap-enrollment-2015/ (Last accessed November 1, 2018).
2. No new enrollees after December 31, 2018.
3. https://www.gpo.gov/fdsys/pkg/BILLS-114hr2enr/pdf/BILLS-114hr2enr.pdf (Last accessed October 17, 2018).

a Medigap plan that covers the Medicare Part B deductible, currently $185 in 2019. Medicare beneficiaries that have those plans already will be exempted and can keep the plans.

Effectively, the new law is eliminating two of the ten plans – Plan C and Plan F, the two most popular Medigap policies. These policies provide first-dollar coverage for EVERY doctor and hospital visit. As of 2015, more than two-thirds (7.5 million) of the 11.8 million Medigap customers had either Plan C or Plan F. It should be noted that there was a 28 percent increase in signups for Plan G, which increased from 697,000 to 895,000 in one year. Those in favor of the elimination of the first-dollar coverage argue that beneficiaries have no incentive to question their care, since they have no additional cost and that health care providers are not incented to manage the amount of care provided. Others argue that it could cause seniors to limit seeing care due to unaffordable costs.

MACRA could lead to more seniors purchasing Medicare Advantage when becoming eligible. Those that choose Medicare Advantage and later decide to switch to original Medicare and want to purchase a Medigap policy may find themselves locked out – Medigap insurers can deny policies based on underwriting health status as they only have to sell the Medigap plans when seniors enroll in Medicare at age sixty-five or within a year of using a Medicare Advantage plan.

1186. What are Medicare SELECT policies?

The difference between Medicare SELECT and regular Medigap insurance is that a Medicare SELECT policy may (except in emergencies) limit Medigap benefits to items and services provided by certain selected health care providers (including hospitals) or may pay only partial benefits when a patient gets health care from other health care providers.

Insurers, including some HMOs, offer Medicare SELECT in the same way they offer standard Medigap insurance. The policies are required to meet certain federal standards and are regulated by the states in which they are approved. A person is able to choose from among the available Medigap policies in the state, but the premiums charged for Medicare SELECT policies are generally lower than premiums for comparable Medigap policies that do not have Medicare SELECT's managed care feature.

State insurance departments have information about Medicare SELECT policies that have been approved for sale in their states.

1187. Should a person purchase the most comprehensive Medigap policy if he can afford the premiums?

Not necessarily. A person must determine which benefits he is likely to need before purchasing a Medigap policy. Often, a person does not need the most comprehensive policy.

For example, Policy A is the least expensive policy and offers the basic core package of benefits. Policies F and G might be considered if a person uses nonparticipating doctors – those who charge more than the amount approved by Medicare; however, excess charges are limited to 115 percent of what Medicare pays (see Q 1076). If the doctors charge no more than the amount approved by Medicare, less expensive policies such as Policy C or Policy D may be appropriate. Policy D also includes important benefits not covered by Policy A, such as coverage of custodial care at home following an illness or injury and the cost of coinsurance for skilled nursing home care.

1188. What Medigap insurance protections are there for those enrolled in the Medicare Advantage program?

Medicare Advantage expands the types of health plans that can contract with Medicare to enroll beneficiaries.

A person who currently has a Medigap policy may enroll in a Medicare Advantage plan and can keep the Medigap policy after enrollment. Keeping the Medigap policy may give a person time to determine whether to stay in the Medicare Advantage plan or return to the original Medicare plan with Medigap insurance. However, expenses paid for by the Medicare Advantage plan will not be reimbursed by the Medigap insurer. Eventually the person should drop Medigap coverage if satisfied with the Medicare Advantage plan.

A person already enrolled in a Medicare Advantage plan cannot buy Medigap insurance but may have the right to purchase a Medigap policy by returning to the original fee-for-service Medicare program (Parts A and B). To be guaranteed the right to buy Medigap insurance, the person must have enrolled in the Medicare Advantage plan at age sixty-five, must terminate enrollment in the Medicare Advantage plan within twelve months of entry into that plan, and must not have had any previous enrollment in a Medicare managed care plan.

If a Medicare Advantage plan terminates coverage because it leaves the Medicare program, plan enrollees have certain rights to new coverage, but these are time-limited. The Medicare Advantage plan is required to provide information to assist making a decision about enrolling in another Medicare Advantage plan or switching to original Medicare Parts A and B with a Medigap policy to supplement the coverage. In general, most individuals with Medicare have the right to guaranteed issue of any Medigap policies designated A, B, C, or F that are offered to new enrollees by issuers in the state.

This right applies to individuals by virtue of the involuntary termination of their coverage. However, certain Medicare beneficiaries in terminating Medicare Advantage plans may have another basis for entitlement to guaranteed issue of a Medigap policy. If a person had been enrolled in the Medicare Advantage plan for fewer than twelve months, was never enrolled in any other Medicare HMO, and had a previous Medigap policy, that person may return to the former Medigap policy if the previous Medigap insurance company still sells the policy in the state.

If that coverage is not available under the previous Medigap policy, the individual may purchase Medigap polices A, B, C, or F from any insurer that sells these policies in the state.

The insurance company selling the policy may not:

(1)   deny or condition the sale of the policy;

(2)   discriminate in the pricing of the policy because of health status, prior history of claims experience, receipt of health care for a medical condition; or

(3)   impose an exclusion for any pre-existing condition.

But the individual has only sixty-three days after coverage ends to select a Medigap insurer. Also, if the individual moves outside the Medicare Advantage plan's service area, that person has sixty-three days to select a Medigap insurer.

An individual is guaranteed issuance of *any* Medigap policy if:

(1)   at least sixty-five years old;

(2)   eligible for Medicare;

(3)   enrolled in a Medicare Advantage plan; and

(4)   disenrolled from that plan within twelve months of the effective date of enrollment.

See Q 1134 through Q 1166 for a complete description of Medicare Advantage (Part C).

1189. Are there rules for selling Medigap insurance?

Yes, both state and federal laws govern sales of Medigap insurance. Companies or agents selling Medigap insurance must avoid certain illegal practices.

It is unlawful to sell or issue to an individual entitled to benefits under Part A (Hospital Insurance) or enrolled under Part B (Medical Insurance):

(1)   a health insurance policy with knowledge that the policy duplicates health benefits the individual is otherwise entitled to under Medicare or Medicaid;

(2)   a Medigap policy with knowledge that the individual is entitled to benefits under another Medigap policy; or

(3)   a health insurance policy, other than a Medigap policy, with knowledge that the policy duplicates health benefits to which the individual is otherwise entitled.

Penalties do not apply, however, to the sale or issuance of a policy or plan that duplicates health benefits to which the individual is otherwise entitled if, under the policy or plan, all benefits are fully payable directly to or on behalf of the individual without regard to other health benefit coverage of the individual. In addition, for the penalty to be waived in the case of the sale or issuance of a policy or plan that duplicates benefits under Medicare or Medicaid, the application for the policy must include a statement, prominently displayed, disclosing the extent to which benefits payable under the policy or plan duplicate Medicare benefits.

The National Association of Insurance Commissioners (NAIC) has identified ten separate types of health insurance policies that must provide an individualized statement of the extent to which the policy duplicates Medicare. These policies include the following:

- Policies that provide benefits for expenses incurred for an accidental injury only

- Policies that provide benefits for specified limited services

- Policies that reimburse expenses incurred for specified disease or other specific impairments (including cancer policies, specified disease policies, and other policies that limit reimbursement to named medical conditions)

- Policies that pay fixed dollar amounts for specified disease or other specified impairments (including cancer, specified disease policies, and other policies that pay a scheduled benefit or specified payment based on diagnosis of the conditions named in the policy)

- Indemnity policies and other policies that pay a fixed dollar amount per day, excluding long-term care policies

- Policies that provide benefits for both expenses incurred and fixed indemnity

- Long-term care policies providing both nursing home and noninstitutional coverage

- Long-term care policies primarily providing nursing home benefits only

- Home care policies

- Other health insurance policies not specifically identified above

Certain policies are *not* required to carry a disclosure statement:

(1) Policies that do not duplicate Medicare benefits, even incidentally

(2) Life insurance policies that contain long-term care riders or accelerated death benefits

(3) Disability insurance policies

(4) Property and casualty policies

(5) Employer and union group health plans

(6) Managed-care organizations with Medicare contracts

(7) Health Care Prepayment Plans (HCPPs) that provide some or all Medicare Part B benefits under an agreement with the Centers for Medicare & Medicaid Services

Policies offering only long-term care nursing home care, home health care, or community-based care, or any combination of the three, are allowed to coordinate benefits with Medicare and are not considered duplicative, provided the coordination is disclosed.

An insurer is subject to civil money and criminal penalties for failing to provide the appropriate disclosure statement. Federal criminal and civil penalties (fines) may also be imposed against any insurance company or agent that knowingly:

- sells a health insurance policy that duplicates a person's Medicare or Medicaid coverage, or any private health insurance coverage the person may have;

- tells a person that they are employees or agents of the Medicare program or of any government agency;

- makes a false statement that a policy meets legal standards for certification when it does not;

- sells a person a Medigap policy that is not one of the ten approved standard policies (after the new standards have been put in place in the person's state);

- denies a person that individual's Medigap open enrollment period by refusing to issue the person a policy, placing conditions on the policy, or discriminating in the price of a policy because of the person's health status, claims experience, receipt of health care, or the person's medical condition; or

- uses the United States mail in a state for advertising or delivering health insurance policies to supplement Medicare if the policies have not been approved for sale in that state.

The sale of a Medigap policy to a Medicaid beneficiary generally is prohibited, but there is no prohibition on sale of policies to low-income Medicare beneficiaries for whom Medicaid pays only the Part B (Medical Insurance) premiums.

1190. What should a consumer be aware of when shopping for Medigap insurance?

The Centers for Medicare & Medicaid Services (CMS) offers the following suggestions when shopping for Medigap insurance:

(1) *Review the plans.* The benefits in each of the standardized Medigap policies are the same no matter which insurance company sells it. Review the plans and choose the benefits that you need most.

(2) *Shop carefully before purchasing.* Although each of the standardized Medigap policies is the same no matter which insurance company sells it, the costs may be very different. Companies use different ways to price Medigap policies. Companies also differ in customer service. Call different insurance companies and compare cost and service before purchasing.

(3) *Don't buy more than one Medigap policy at a time.* It is illegal for an insurance company to sell a person a second Medigap policy unless they are told in writing that first Medigap policy will be cancelled when the second Medigap policy goes into effect. Anyone who tries to sell a Medigap policy when a person already has one should be reported.

(4) *Check for pre-existing conditions exclusions.* Before purchasing a Medigap policy, a consumer should find out whether it has a waiting period before it fully covers any pre-existing conditions. If the person has a health problem that was diagnosed or treated during the six months immediately before the Medigap policy starts, the policy might not cover the costs right away for care related to that health problem. Medigap policies must cover pre-existing conditions after the policy has been in effect for six months. Some insurance companies may have shorter waiting periods

before covering a pre-existing condition. Other insurance companies may not have any waiting period. If a policy is purchased during the Medigap open-enrollment period, the insurance company must shorten the waiting period for pre-existing conditions by the amount of previous health coverage.

(5)   ***Be careful of switching from one Medigap policy to another*. A consumer should only switch policies to get different benefits, better service, or a better** price. However, a policy that does not meet the person's needs should not be kept simply because the person has had it for a long time. If deciding to buy a new Medigap policy, the company must count the time the person had the same benefits under the first policy towards the pre-existing conditions waiting period. However, a waiting period may be necessary for pre-existing conditions for new benefits that covered under the first policy. A statement must be signed that says that the first policy will be canceled. The first policy should not be canceled until the consumer is sure that he wants to keep the new policy. A person has thirty days to decide if he wants to keep the new policy. This is called the free-look period.

(6)   ***Make sure to get a policy within thirty days*.** A consumer should get his policy within thirty days. If the person does not, he should call the company and ask them to put in writing why the policy was delayed. If sixty days go by without an answer, he should call his State Insurance Department.

(7)   ***Watch out for illegal marketing practices*.** It is illegal for an insurance company or agent to pressure a person into buying a Medigap policy, or lie or mislead a person to get him to switch from one company or policy to another. False advertising is also illegal. Another type of illegal advertising involves mailing cards to people who may want to buy insurance. If a person fills out and returns the card enclosed in the mailing, the card may be sold to an insurance agent who will try to sell him a policy.

(8)   ***Neither the state nor federal government sells or services Medigap policies*.** State Insurance Departments approve Medigap policies sold by private insurance companies. This means that the company and Medigap policy meet requirements of state law. Do not believe statements that Medigap insurance is a government-sponsored program. It is illegal for anyone to tell a person that they are from the government and try to sell him a Medigap policy. If this happens, that person should be reported to their State Insurance Department. It is also illegal for a company or agent to claim that a Medigap policy has been approved for sale in any state in which it has not been.

(9)   ***Find out if the insurance company is licensed*.** An insurance company must meet certain standards in order to sell policies in a state. A person should check with his State Insurance Department to make sure that the insurance company with whom he is doing business is licensed in his state. This is for the consumer's protection. Insurance agents must also be licensed by the state and the state may require them to carry proof that they are licensed. The proof will show their name and the name of the companies they represent. Do not buy a policy from any insurance agent that cannot prove that he is licensed. A business card is not a license.

(10) ***Start looking early so as not to be rushed.*** Do not be pressured into buying a Medigap policy. Good sales people will not rush a person. Keep in mind, that if a consumer is within his six-month Medigap open enrollment period or in a situation where he has a guaranteed right to buy a Medigap policy, there are time limits to follow. Buying the Medigap policy of choice may be harder after the Medigap open-enrollment or special-protection period ends. This will be especially true if a pre-existing health condition exists. If a consumer is not sure whether a Medigap policy is what is needed, the salesperson should be asked to explain it to him with a friend or family member present.

(11) ***Keep agents' and/or companies' names, addresses, and telephone numbers.*** Write down the agents' and/or companies' names, addresses, and telephone numbers, or ask for a business card with this information.

(12) ***If deciding to buy, fill out the application carefully.*** Do not believe an insurance agent who says that medical history on an application is not important. Some companies ask for detailed medical information. Consumers must answer the medical questions even if they are applying during a Medigap open-enrollment period or are in a situation where they have the right to buy a Medigap policy. During these two times, the company cannot use answers to turn consumers down or use this information to decide how much to charge for a Medigap policy. However, if a consumer leaves out any of the medical information they ask for, the company could refuse coverage for a period of time for any medical condition that was not reported. The company also could deny a claim or cancel a Medigap policy if a consumer sends in a bill for care of a health problem that was not reported.

(13) ***Beware of nonstandardized plans.*** It is illegal for anyone to sell a policy and call it a Medigap policy if it does not match the standardized Medigap policies sold in that state. A doctor may offer a "retainer agreement" that says he can provide certain non-Medicare-covered services and not charge the Medicare coinsurance and deductible amounts. This type of agreement may be illegal. If a doctor refuses to see a person as a Medicare patient unless that person pays him a yearly fee and signs a "retainer agreement," the person should call 1-800-MEDICARE.

(14) ***Look for an outline of coverage.*** A clearly worded summary of a Medigap policy must be given to each consumer. Read it carefully.

(15) ***Do not pay cash.*** Pay by check, money order, or bank draft payable to the insurance company, not to the agent or anyone else. Get a receipt with the insurance company's name, address, and telephone number for records.

CMS publishes a consumer-directed manual called "Choosing a Medigap Policy: A Guide to Health Insurance for People with Medicare". The guide is updated annually and is available on the CMS website at www.medicare.gov.

HOW TO SUBMIT CLAIMS AND APPEALS

Claims Procedure

1191. How does Medicare pay for Part A (Hospital Insurance) services?

Part A (Hospital Insurance) helps pay for covered services received in a hospital or skilled nursing facility or from a home health agency or hospice program. Hospitals, skilled nursing facilities, home health agencies, and hospices are called "providers" under Part A. Providers submit their claims directly to Medicare. The patient cannot submit claims for services. The provider will charge the patient for any part of the Part A (Hospital Insurance) deductible he has not met and any coinsurance he owes. Providers cannot require the patient to make a deposit before being admitted for inpatient care that is or may be covered under Part A.

Intermediaries process claims submitted on the patient's behalf by hospitals, skilled nursing facilities, home health agencies, hospices, and certain other providers of services. When the Medicare intermediary pays a claim, the patient gets a *Notice of Medicare Benefit*. This notice is not a bill.

1192. How does a person submit Part B (Medical Insurance) claims?

Doctors, suppliers, and other providers of Part B (Medical Insurance) services are in most cases required to submit Medicare claims for the patient even if they do not take assignment. They must submit the claims by December 31 of the following year for services furnished during the first nine months of the year. Claims must be submitted by December 31 of the second following year for services furnished during the last three months of the year. A patient should notify the Medicare Administrative Contractor (MAC) for their area if the doctor or supplier refuses to submit a Part B (Medical Insurance) claim and the patient believes the services may be covered by Medicare.

The doctor or supplier must submit a form, called a CMS-1500,[1] requesting that a Part B (Medical Insurance) payment be made for the patient's covered services, whether or not assignment is taken. The doctor or supplier completes form CMS-1500. The patient must sign the form before the doctor or supplier sends it to the proper Medicare carrier. If a patient's claim is for the rental or purchase of durable medical equipment, a doctor's prescription or certificate of medical necessity must be included with the claim.

In general, if the patient is enrolled in a coordinated care plan (such as an HMO), a claim will seldom need to be submitted on the patient's behalf. Medicare pays the HMO a set amount and the HMO provides the patient's medical care. Physicians, suppliers, and other providers of Part B (Medical Insurance) services bill the HMO to receive payment for their services at a contractually-agreed rate.

---

1. CMS-1500 https://www.cms.gov/Medicare/CMS-Forms/CMS-Forms/CMS-Forms-Items/CMS1188854.html (Last accessed October 17, 2018).

After the doctor, provider, or supplier sends in a Part B claim, Medicare will send the patient a notice called *Explanation of Your Medicare Part B Benefits*[1] to tell the patient the decision on the claim. The notice gives the address and toll-free number for contacting the MAC if needed.

Payment can be made directly to the doctor or supplier. This is the *assignment method*. The doctor or supplier is prohibited from charging the patient anything above the 20 percent coinsurance amount and the amount of the patient's deductible, if the deductible has not been paid. Medicare pays the doctor or supplier 80 percent of the approved charge. If a provider does not accept assignment, the MAC still pays 80 percent of the approved charge, but directly to the patient who then pays the provider. The MAC will withhold from the payment any amount of the deductible not yet paid.

1193. What must an itemized bill contain?

The itemized bill must show:

(1)   the date the patient received the services;

(2)   the place where the patient received the services;

(3)   a description of the services;

(4)   the charge for each service;

(5)   the doctor or supplier who provided the services; and

(6)   the patient's name and health insurance claim number, including the letter at the end of the number.

If the bill does not contain all of this information, payment may be delayed. It is also helpful if the nature of the patient's illness (diagnosis) is shown on the bill.

A doctor or supplier submitting a claim for the rental or purchase of durable medical equipment should include the bill from the prescription. The prescription must show the equipment needed, the medical reason for the need, and estimate how long the equipment will be medically necessary.

Before Medicare pays any charge for Part B (Medical Insurance) services or supplies, a beneficiary's record must show that the individual has satisfied the applicable Part B deductible for that year. Once a beneficiary has satisfied the deductible, physicians, other health care professionals, or supplies should send in future bills for covered services as soon as possible so that Medicare payment can be made promptly. If all medical bills for the year amount to less than the deductible, Part B (Medical Insurance) cannot pay any part of a person's bills for the year.

---

1. Explanation of Benefits https://www.medicare.gov/forms-help-resources/mail-you-get-about-medicare/explanation-of-benefits-eob (Last accessed October 17, 2018).

1194. What happens if the patient dies and payments are due?

Part A (Hospital Insurance) payments due from Medicare will be paid directly to the hospital, skilled nursing facility, home health agency, or hospice that provided covered services.

Special rules apply for services covered under Part B (Medical Insurance). If a bill was paid by the patient or with funds from the patient's estate, payment will be made either to the estate representative or to a surviving member of the patient's immediate family. If someone other than the patient paid the bill, payment may be made to that person. If the bill has not been paid and the doctor or supplier does not accept assignment, Part B (Medical Insurance) payment can be made to the person who has a legal obligation to pay the bill for the deceased patient. This person can claim Part B (Medical Insurance) payment either before or after paying the bill.

1195. Is there a time limit for submitting a Medicare claim?

Yes. In general, providers must file claims within one calendar year from the date of the covered service. In extremely limited circumstances (such as the delay being due to an error by Medicare or a beneficiary's retroactive Medicare entitlement), Medicare may waive the one-year time limit.

1196. Where does a physician or supplier send Part B (Medical Insurance) claims?

See *Appendix G* for the names and addresses of the Medicare Administrative Contractors (MACs) selected to handle Part B (Medical Insurance) claims in each state.

1197. What is a Medicare Administrative Contractor and what does it do?

A Medicare Administrative Contractor (MAC) is a private health care insurer that has been awarded a geographic jurisdiction to process Medicare Part A and Part B (A/B) medical claims or Durable Medical Equipment (DME) claims for Medicare Fee-For-Service (FFS) beneficiaries. CMS relies on a network of MACs to serve as the primary operational contact between the Medicare FFS program and the health care providers enrolled in the program. MACs are multi-state, regional contractors responsible for administering both Medicare Part A and Medicare Part B claims. MACs perform many activities including:

- Process Medicare FFS claims

- Make and account for Medicare FFS payments

- Enroll providers in the Medicare FFS program

- Handle provider reimbursement services and audit institutional provider cost reports

- Handle redetermination requests (1st stage appeals process)

- Respond to provider inquiries

- Educate providers about Medicare FFS billing requirements

- Establish local coverage determinations (LCD's)

- Review medical records for selected claims

- Coordinate with CMS and other FFS contractors

1198. Must Medicare claims be paid in a prompt manner?

Medicare Administrative Contractors (MACs),[1] previously known called "carriers" for Part B (Medical Insurance) and "intermediaries" for Part A (Hospital Insurance), must pay Medicare claims promptly. Not less than 95 percent of "clean claim" payments must be issued, mailed, or otherwise transmitted within specified time limits. A clean claim is a claim that has no defect or impropriety or particular circumstance requiring special treatment that prevents timely payment from being made. The deadline for payment of a clean claim is thirty calendar days.

If payment is not issued, mailed, or otherwise transmitted within thirty calendar days on a clean claim, interest must be paid for the period beginning on the day after the required payment date and ending on the date on which payment is made.

MACs are prohibited from issuing, mailing or otherwise transmitting payment for any electronic claims within thirteen days after claim receipt. This prohibition on paying claims is expanded to twenty-six days for claims not submitted electronically.

Appeals Procedure

1199. Does a beneficiary have the right to appeal a decision made on a claim?

Yes, if a Medicare beneficiary disagrees with a decision on the amount Medicare will pay on a claim or whether services received are covered by Medicare, the person has the right to ask for a review of the decision. The notice from Medicare tells the patient the decision made on the claim and what steps to take to appeal the decision. If a person needs more information about the right to appeal, he or she should contact the local Social Security office, the Medicare Administrative Contractor (MAC) that processed the initial claim, or the Quality Improvement Organization (QIO) in the beneficiary's state. See Appendix H for a list of Quality Improvement Organizations.

1200. Does a beneficiary have the right to appeal a decision made on a claim?

A Quality Improvement Organization (QIO) is a group of health quality experts, clinicians, and consumers organized to improve the quality of care delivered to people with Medicare.

---

1. What is a MAC https://www.cms.gov/Medicare/Medicare-Contracting/Medicare-Administrative-Contractors/What-is-a-MAC.html (Last accessed October 17, 2018).

There are two types of QIOs that work under the direction of the Centers for Medicare & Medicaid Services in support of the QIO Program:

1. ***Beneficiary and Family Centered Care (BFCC)-QIOs***

    BFCC-QIOs help Medicare beneficiaries exercise their right to high-quality health care. They manage all beneficiary complaints and quality of care reviews to ensure consistency in the review process while taking into consideration local factors important to beneficiaries and their families. They also handle cases in which beneficiaries want to appeal a health care provider's decision to discharge them from the hospital or discontinue other types of services. Two designated BFCC-QIOs serve all fifty states and three territories, which are grouped into five regions.

2. ***Quality Innovation Network (QIN)-QIOs***

    The QIO Program's fourteen Quality Innovation Network-QIOs (QIN-QIOs) bring Medicare beneficiaries, providers, and communities together in data-driven initiatives that increase patient safety, make communities healthier, better coordinate post-hospital care, and improve clinical quality. By serving regions of two to six states each, QIN-QIOs are able to help best practices for better care spread more quickly, while still accommodating local conditions and cultural factors.

1201. How does a person appeal a Part B (Medical Insurance) claim?

After the doctor or supplier or other provider submits the claim for payment to the appropriate Medicare Administrator Contractor (MAC), Medicare will send a notice of the decision made on the claim. If the patient disagrees with the decision, he or she can ask the MAC that handled the claim to review it. The patient has six months from the date of the decision to ask the MAC to review it. If the patient disagrees with the MAC's written explanation of its review decision and the amount remaining in question is $100 or more, the patient has six months from the date of the review decision to request a hearing before a hearing officer. The patient may combine claims that have been reviewed or reopened, so long as all claims combined are at the proper level of appeal and the appeal for each claim combined is filed on time.

If a person disagrees with the hearing officer's decision and the amount in question is $500 or more, the person has sixty days from the date he or she receives the decision to request a hearing before an Administrative Law Judge. Cases involving $1,000 or more can eventually be appealed to a federal court.

To determine whether an individual meets the minimum amount in controversy needed for a MAC hearing ($100) or administrative law judge hearing ($500), the following rules apply:

(1) The amount in controversy is computed as the actual amount charged the patient for the items and services in question, less any amount for which payment has been made by the MAC and less any deductible and coinsurance amounts applicable in the particular case.

(2)   A single patient may aggregate claims from two or more physicians/suppliers to meet the $100 or $500 thresholds. A single physician/supplier may aggregate claims from two or more patients to meet the $100 or $500 threshold levels of appeal.

(3)   Two or more claims may be aggregated by an individual patient to meet the amount in controversy for a MAC hearing, only if the claims have previously been reviewed and a request for hearing has been made within six months after the date of the review determination(s).

(4)   Two or more claims may be aggregated by an individual patient for an administrative law judge hearing, only if the claims have previously been decided by a MAC hearing officer and a request for an administrative law judge hearing has been made within sixty days after receipt of the MAC hearing officer's decision(s).

(5)   When requesting a carrier hearing or an administrative law judge hearing, the appellant must specify in the appeal request the specific claims to be aggregated.

Two or more patients may aggregate their claims together to meet the minimum amount in controversy needed for an administrative law judge hearing ($500).

The determination as to whether the amount in controversy is $100 or more is made by the MAC hearing officer. The determination as to whether the amount in controversy is $500 or more is made by the administrative law judge.

When a civil action is filed by either an individual patient or two or more patients, the Centers for Medicare & Medicaid Services may assert that the aggregation principles may be applied to determine the amount in controversy for judicial review ($1,000). Additional information is available at the CMS website.[1]

1202. How does a person request a review by the Medicare Administrative Contractor that handled the claim?

A reconsideration request must be made in writing and filed at a Social Security Administration or the Centers for Medicare & Medicaid Services office, or in the case of a qualified Railroad Retirement beneficiary, filed at a Railroad Retirement Board office. The request must be filed within six months of receipt of the notice of the initial determination, unless an extension of time for filing the request is granted.

The parties to a reconsideration determination are entitled to written notice specifying the reasons for the decision and advising them of their right to a hearing if the amount in question is $100 or more.

Subsequent review processes include:

- Redetermination by a Medicare Administrative Contractor (MAC)

- Reconsideration by a Qualified Independent Contractor (QIC)

---

1. https://www.medicare.gov/claims-and-appeals/ (Last accessed October 17, 2018).

- Administrative Law Judge (ALJ) Hearing or Review by Office of Medicare Hearings and Appeals (OMHA)

- Review by the Medicare Appeals Council (Council)

- Judicial review in U.S. District Court

1203. How does a person request a hearing with a Medicare Administrative Contractor hearing officer?

An individual who is dissatisfied with a reconsideration determination is entitled to a hearing if the amount in controversy is $100 or more. The request for a hearing must be made in writing and filed at a Social Security Administration or the Centers for Medicare & Medicaid Services office or, in the case of a qualified Railroad Retirement beneficiary, at a Railroad Retirement Board office. The hearing request must be filed within six months after the date of an individual's receipt of notice of the reconsidered determination, unless the deadline is extended.

1204. How does a person appeal a Part A (Hospital Insurance) decision made by a Quality Improvement Organization (QIO)?

Quality Improvement Organizations (QIOs) make decisions on the need for hospital care. Whenever a patient is admitted to a Medicare-participating hospital, the patient is given *An Important Message from Medicare*, which describes the individual's appeal rights as a hospital patient and supplies the name, address, and phone number of the QIO in his or her state. The hospital is also required to provide the patient with *How to Request a Review of the Notice of Noncoverage*, which includes a general statement about the posthospital services to which the patient is entitled.

To determine whether a patient meets the minimum amount in controversy needed for a hearing ($100), the following rules apply:

(1)   The amount in controversy is computed as the actual amount charged the patient for the items and services in question, less any amount for which payment has been made by the intermediary and less any deductible and coinsurance amounts applicable in the particular case.

(2)   A single patient may aggregate claims from two or more providers to meet the $100 hearing threshold and a single provider may aggregate claims for services provided to one or more patients to meet the $100 hearing threshold.

(3)   Two or more claims may be aggregated by an individual patient only if the claims have previously been reconsidered and a request for hearing has been made within sixty days after receipt of the reconsideration determination.

(4)   When requesting a hearing, the appellant must specify in the appeal request the specific claims to be aggregated.

Also, two or more patients may aggregate their claims together to meet the minimum amount in controversy needed for a hearing ($100).

The determination as to whether the amount in controversy is $100 or more is made by the administrative law judge.

If a hospital, without consulting the QIO, recommends against admission to the hospital, review of this decision by the QIO may be obtained by writing to the QIO and requesting a review. If the QIO participated in the preadmission denial, a reconsideration of the denial can be requested. If an expedited request for review is made within three working days of the denial, the QIO has three working days to respond.

The appeals process for determinations of noncoverage after a patient is admitted to the hospital is similar to the process for preadmission denials. The hospital cannot charge the patient for the cost of an additional stay unless

(1)   the hospital or its utilization review committee determines that hospital care is no longer necessary, or the QIO states in writing that hospital care is unnecessary, and

(2)   the patient receives written notice that charges will be made beginning the third day after receipt of the notice and the decision may be appealed by following procedures specified in the notice.

The hospital must have either the agreement of the physician or the QIO before giving a patient written notice of noncoverage. If the physician, but not the QIO, agrees with the hospital, the patient may make a telephone request to the QIO for review, with a simultaneous written confirmation to the QIO of the request for review. If the patient makes this request prior to noon of the day following receipt of notice of noncoverage, the patient cannot be liable for hospital charges until noon of the working day after receipt of the QIO's decision. The QIO must determine, within one full working day of the request (and receipt of pertinent information and/or records from the hospital), the appropriateness of the hospital's decision that the beneficiary no longer requires inpatient hospital care.

If the patient does not appeal, he or she will be liable for all hospital charges beginning the third day after receipt of the hospital's notice.

If the QIO, rather than the physician, agrees with the hospital's initial notice of noncoverage, the patient can request that the QIO reconsider its decision. If the QIO upholds its initial decision, the patient is liable for all charges beginning the third day after receipt of the hospital's notice of noncoverage.

The patient should request that the QIO review the hospital's notice of noncoverage as soon as possible. If the patient requests a review while in the hospital or within three days of notice of noncoverage, the QIO must render its decision within three working days.

The patient may request a review by the QIO at any time within sixty days after receipt of the hospital's noncoverage determination. The QIO will have thirty days to issue a decision (unless the request was made within three days of receipt of the noncoverage determination or while the patient was hospitalized).

If the HMO, rather than the hospital, makes the determination of noncoverage, the patient may request an immediate QIO review of the determination.

For the immediate QIO review process, the following rules apply:

(1)   the patient or authorized representative must submit the request for immediate review to the QIO that has an agreement with the hospital in writing or by telephone by noon of the first working day after receipt of the written notice of the determination that the hospital stay is no longer necessary,

(2)   on the date it receives the patient's request, the QIO must notify the HMO that a request for immediate review has been filed,

(3)   the HMO must supply any information that the QIO requires to conduct its review by the close of business of the first full working day immediately following the day the enrollee submits the request for review,

(4)   in response to a request from the HMO, the hospital must submit medical records to the QIO by close of business of the first full working day immediately following the day the HMO makes its request,

(5)   the QIO must solicit views of the patient who requested the immediate QIO review, and

(6)   the QIO must make a determination and notify the patient, the hospital, and the HMO by close of business of the first working day after it receives the information from the hospital, the HMO, or both.

The HMO continues to be financially responsible for the costs of the hospital stay until noon of the calendar day following the day the QIO notifies the patient of its review determination. But the hospital may not charge the HMO if it was the hospital (acting on behalf of the patient) that filed the request for an immediate QIO review, and the QIO upholds the noncoverage determination made by the HMO.

The patient may appeal a QIO reconsideration decision to an Administrative Law Judge within sixty days, provided the amount of the controversy is at least $200. Cases involving $2,000 or more can eventually be appealed to a federal court.

1205. How does a person appeal all other Part A (Hospital Insurance) claims?

Appeals of decisions on all other services (generally, those not relating to inpatient hospitalization) covered under Part A (Hospital Insurance) (skilled nursing facility care, home health care, hospice services, and some inpatient hospital matters not handled by QIOs) are handled by the Medicare Administrative Contractors (MACs). If a patient disagrees with the MAC's initial decision, the patient may request reconsideration. The request may be submitted directly to the MAC or through a Social Security office. Any Social Security office will help the patient request reconsideration.

If a patient disagrees with the MAC's reconsideration decision and the amount in question is $100 or more, the patient has sixty days from the date he or she receives the reconsideration decision to request a hearing by an administrative law judge. Cases involving $1,000 or more can eventually be appealed to a federal court.

1206. How does a person appeal a decision made by a Health Maintenance Organization (HMO)?

If a person has Medicare coverage through an HMO, decisions about coverage and payment for services will usually be made by the HMO. When the HMO makes a decision to deny payment for Medicare-covered services or refuses to provide Medicare-covered supplies requested by the patient, the patient will be given a *Notice of Initial Determination*. The HMO is also required to provide a full, written explanation of the patient's appeal rights.

If a patient believes that the decision of the HMO was not correct, the patient has the right to ask for reconsideration. The patient must file a request for reconsideration within sixty days after the patient receives the *Notice of Initial Determination*. The request for reconsideration may be mailed or delivered to the HMO or to a Social Security office.

The HMO must reconsider its initial determination to deny payments or services. If the HMO does not rule fully in the patient's favor, the HMO must send the patient's reconsideration request and its reconsideration determination to the Centers for Medicare & Medicaid Services (CMS) for a review and determination.

A patient may not proceed to the next level of administrative review until the HMO issues its decision or refers the matter to CMS.

An HMO must act on the patient's reconsideration request within sixty calendar days from the date of receipt of the request. If the reconsideration determination made by the HMO is entirely favorable to the patient, the HMO must notify the patient within the sixty-calendar-day period. If the HMO cannot make a decision that is fully favorable to the patient, the organization must submit the case file to CMS within the sixty-calendar-day period.

For good cause, CMS may allow exceptions to the sixty-day limit. "Good cause" is defined as unusual circumstances (such as natural disasters) which make it difficult or impossible for the patient to provide necessary information in a timely way. Failure of the HMO to provide the patient with a reconsideration determination within the sixty-day limit or to obtain a good-cause extension constitutes an adverse determination.

If the patient disagrees with the decision of CMS and the amount in question is $100 or more, the patient has sixty days from receipt of the decision to request a hearing before an administrative law judge. The amount in question can include any combination of Part A (Hospital Insurance) and Part B (Medical Insurance) services. Cases involving $1,000 or more can eventually be appealed to a federal court.

The rules regarding an immediate QIO review of a determination of noncoverage of inpatient hospital care by an HMO or hospital are discussed at Q 1204.

1207. What happens if an organization providing items or services to a person under Medicare ceases to continue providing those items or services?

An organization must provide assurances to the Centers for Medicare & Medicaid Services (CMS) that, in the event it ceases to provide items or services, the organization will provide or arrange for supplemental coverage of benefits related to a pre-existing condition. This coverage must be provided to individuals enrolled with the organization who receive Medicare benefits and must continue for the lesser of six months or the duration of the contract period.

MEDICAID

Overview

1208. What is Medicaid?

Medicaid (Title XIX of the *Social Security Act*) is a federal-state matching entitlement program that pays for medical assistance for certain vulnerable and needy individuals and families with low incomes and resources. The program became law in 1965 as a jointly-funded cooperative venture between the federal and state governments to assist states in supplying medical assistance to eligible needy persons. Medicaid is the largest program funding medical and health-related services for America's poorest people. Medicaid includes the District of Columbia, as well as U.S. Territories.

The Medicaid program is jointly financed by the federal and state governments and administered by the states. Within federal rules, each state establishes its own standards of eligibility, chooses eligible groups, types and ranges of services, payment levels for most services, and administrative and operating procedures. The nature and scope of a state's Medicaid program is described in the state plan that the state submits to the Centers for Medicare & Medicaid Services (CMS) for approval. The plan is amended whenever necessary to reflect changes in federal or state law, changes in policy, or court decisions. Persons eligible for Medicaid in one state may not be eligible for Medicaid in another, depending on standards set.

Federal responsibility for the Medicaid program lies with the CMS in the Department of Health and Human Services (HHS). Beginning in 2014, the Affordable Care Act expanded eligibility for Medicaid to all individuals under the age of sixty-five in households with income up to 138 percent of the Federal Poverty Level. This expansion would arguably eliminate any need to be in a designated group or the need to clear an "asset test". However, in 2012, the United States Supreme Court ruled that the expansion of eligibility was optional to each state – thus, some states have implemented the expansion, which others have not.

States are required to provide certain basic medical assistance services to eligible recipients. These mandatory Medicaid services include inpatient and outpatient hospital care, health screening, diagnosis and treatment to children, family planning, physician services and nursing facility services to individuals over age twenty-one. States may also elect to cover any of over thirty specified optional services, which include prescription drugs, clinic services, personal care services, and services provided in intermediate care facilities for the mentally retarded.

To qualify for Medicaid, applicants must have both incomes and assets below certain limits, which vary from state to state.

Within broad national guidelines established by federal statutes, regulations, and policies, each of the states:

(1) establishes its own eligibility standards;

(2) determines the type, amount, duration, and scope of services;

(3)   sets the rate of payment for services; and

(4)   administers its own program.

Medicaid policies for eligibility and services are complex and vary considerably even among similar-sized and/or adjacent states. Thus, a person who is eligible for Medicaid in one state might not be eligible in another state; and the services provided by one state may differ considerably in amount, duration, or scope from the services provided in a similar or neighboring state. In addition, Medicaid eligibility and/or services within a state can change during the year.

Medicaid serves as a supplement to health insurance coverage provided by Medicare. Medicaid pays for extended nursing home care for elderly people who cannot afford to pay for it themselves. For those who qualify, Medicaid pays Medicare premiums, as well as Medicare coinsurance and deductibles. It may even pay the full cost of some services not covered by Medicare.

1209. What portion of Medicaid expenses are paid by the federal government?

The federal government pays a portion of the medical assistance expenditures under each state's Medicaid program, known as the Federal Medical Assistance Percentage (FMAP). The FMAP is determined annually by a formula that compares the state's average per capita income level with the national income average. States with a higher per capita income level are reimbursed a smaller share of their costs. By law, the FMAP cannot be lower than 50 percent nor higher than 83 percent.

The federal government shares in each state's expenditures for the administration of the Medicaid program. Most administrative costs are matched at 50 percent for all states, with higher rates for certain activities (such as development of mechanized claims processing systems). The Medicaid statute does provide for higher matching rates for certain functions and activities.

Federal payments to states for medical assistance have no set limit (cap); rather, the federal government matches (at FMAP rates) state expenditures for the mandatory services plus the optional services that the individual state decides to cover for eligible recipients, and matches (at the appropriate administrative rate) necessary and proper administrative costs.

Federal and State Share of Medicaid Spending
By Percentage and Dollars

Location	Federal %	Federal $	State %	State $
US – Nationwide	62.80%	$334,168,553,471	37.20%	$197,909,871,310
Alabama	69.60%	$3,683,285,808	30.40%	$1,610,967,783
Alaska	58.70%	$834,877,061	41.30%	$586,795,835
Arizona	74.40%	$7,912,721,453	25.60%	$2,728,015,576
Arkansas	78.60%	$4,349,837,098	21.40%	$1,186,669,876
California	62.50%	$53,483,021,620	37.50%	$32,047,934,903

Location	Federal %	Federal $	State %	State $
Colorado	60.30%	$4,439,240,635	39.70%	$2,919,081,824
Connecticut	58.60%	$4,602,089,940	41.40%	$3,251,492,864
Delaware	60.00%	$1,116,368,801	40.00%	$745,627,374
District of Columbia	74.20%	$1,770,812,871	25.80%	$616,341,600
Florida	60.40%	$12,971,284,552	39.60%	$8,504,768,202
Georgia	67.50%	$6,583,762,079	32.50%	$3,166,394,656
Hawaii	64.00%	$1,287,199,014	36.00%	$725,219,136
Idaho	72.00%	$1,245,680,313	28.00%	$485,562,289
Illinois	60.10%	$10,233,645,818	39.90%	$6,805,531,402
Indiana	68.80%	$6,418,350,565	31.20%	$2,910,085,423
Iowa	63.80%	$2,911,040,985	36.20%	$1,652,129,751
Kansas	56.90%	$1,729,174,010	43.10%	$1,311,385,551
Kentucky	79.60%	$7,563,524,472	20.40%	$1,935,894,232
Louisiana	62.70%	$5,055,265,242	37.30%	$3,003,106,004
Maine	62.50%	$1,613,797,535	37.50%	$966,421,792
Maryland	59.80%	$5,715,856,385	40.20%	$3,837,077,571
Massachusetts	56.10%	$8,725,129,244	43.90%	$6,839,295,936
Michigan	72.70%	$11,592,262,917	27.30%	$4,356,845,440
Minnesota	58.40%	$6,388,362,214	41.60%	$4,547,395,155
Mississippi	74.10%	$3,821,647,803	25.90%	$1,334,941,062
Missouri	64.10%	$6,154,468,468	35.90%	$3,453,696,954
Montana	67.70%	$778,122,685	32.30%	$371,570,788
Nebraska	53.60%	$1,012,637,147	46.40%	$875,438,786
Nevada	75.30%	$2,355,114,580	24.70%	$772,423,136
New Hampshire	58.80%	$1,018,780,818	41.20%	$713,078,297
New Jersey	61.40%	$8,735,757,972	38.60%	$5,499,231,598
New Mexico	79.20%	$3,907,017,957	20.80%	$1,026,653,511
New York	54.70%	$32,722,952,884	45.30%	$27,083,184,664
North Carolina	66.20%	$8,922,363,531	33.80%	$4,560,944,905
North Dakota	60.90%	$509,325,597	39.10%	$327,027,702
Ohio	69.00%	$14,895,079,570	31.00%	$6,702,731,052
Oklahoma	63.50%	$3,171,087,216	36.50%	$1,825,880,609
Oregon	77.80%	$6,274,826,603	22.20%	$1,791,897,763
Pennsylvania	55.90%	$13,066,141,815	44.10%	$10,328,112,297
Rhode Island	59.20%	$1,537,154,263	40.80%	$1,061,289,853
South Carolina	70.80%	$4,221,308,050	29.20%	$1,742,497,893

Location	Federal %	Federal $	State %	State $
South Dakota	56.10%	$456,258,592	43.90%	$356,826,406
Tennessee	65.10%	$5,949,549,945	34.90%	$3,194,970,741
Texas	58.90%	$21,084,258,163	41.10%	$14,723,345,923
Utah	70.90%	$1,556,673,067	29.10%	$639,701,558
Vermont	60.40%	$987,854,213	39.60%	$646,768,005
Virginia	50.70%	$4,106,008,635	49.30%	$3,997,259,593
Washington	64.90%	$6,894,834,262	35.10%	$3,726,311,812
West Virginia	76.80%	$2,822,267,663	23.20%	$853,170,867
Wisconsin	58.80%	$4,691,345,487	41.20%	$3,283,601,055
Wyoming	51.00%	$289,125,853	49.00%	$277,274,305

Medicaid Eligibility

1210. What major groups are states required to cover?

States have some discretion in determining who their Medicaid programs will cover and the financial criteria for Medicaid eligibility. To be eligible for federal funds, states are required to provide Medicaid coverage for most individuals who receive federally assisted income mainte-nance payments, as well as for related groups not receiving cash payments. As part of the Patient Protection and Affordable Care Act (PPACA), Medicaid eligibility has been expanded to include more low-income adults. As previously stated, states do have some discretion in determining who their Medicaid programs cover, and as a result some states will not be expanding their Medicaid coverage to include the additional low-income adults who would otherwise be eligible under the PPACA (see Q 1213).

Examples of the mandatory Medicaid eligibility groups (called Mandatory Categorically Needy) include the following for which federally matching funds are supplied:[1]

- Individuals with limited income and have children and who meet the requirements of Aid to Families with Dependent Children (AFDC) that were in effect in their states on July 16, 1996.

- Supplemental Security Income (SSI) recipients (or in states using more restrictive criteria – aged, blind, disabled, and institutionalized individuals).

- Infants born to Medicaid-eligible pregnant women. Medicaid eligibility must con-tinue throughout the first year of life, so long as the infant remains in the mother's household and she remains eligible (or would be eligible if she were still pregnant).

- Children under the age of six whose family income is at or below 133 percent of the FPL. As of 2019, the Federal Poverty Level for a family of four is $25,100 making

---

1. 42 U.S.C. §1396a.

133 percent to be $33,383. (The minimum mandatory income level for infants in certain states may be higher than 133 percent, if as of certain dates the states had established a higher percentage for covering these groups.) States are required to extend Medicaid eligibility until age nineteen to all children in families with incomes at or below the federal poverty level.

- Pregnant women whose family income is under 133 percent of FPL. (The minimum mandatory income level for pregnant women certain states may be higher than 133 percent, if as of certain dates the states had established a higher percentage for covering these groups.) Services to pregnant women is limited to those related to pregnancy, complications of pregnancy, delivery and postpartum care. Once eligibility is established, pregnant women remain eligible for Medicaid through the end of the calendar month ending sixty days after the end of the pregnancy, regardless of any change in family income. States are not required to have a resource test for these poverty-level related groups. However, any resource test imposed can be no more restrictive than that of the AFDC program for infants and children and the SSI program for pregnant women.

- Infants born to Medicaid-eligible women, for the first year of life.

- Recipients of adoption assistance, foster care, and guardianship care under the Social Security Act.

- Supplemental Security Income (SSI) recipients in most states – or the aged, blind and disabled in states using more restrictive Medicaid eligibility standards that pre-date SSI.

- Certain Medicare beneficiaries. (See Q 1220.)

- All children under age nineteen, in families at or below the FPL. In 2019, the FPL is $25,100 for a family of four and is $31,380 in Alaska and $28,870 in Hawaii.

- Special protected groups who lose cash assistance because of the cash programs' rules, but who may keep Medicaid for a period of time. Examples are: persons who lose AFDC or SSI payments due to earnings from work or increased Social Security benefits; and two-parent, unemployed families whose AFDC cash assistance time is limited by the state and who are provided a full twelve months of Medicaid coverage following termination of cash assistance.

- Recipients of adoption or foster care assistance under Title IV-E of the Social Security Act.

Certain qualified aliens, including certain permanent residents, certain persons claiming asylum, certain refugees, certain aliens whose deportation has been withheld, and certain veterans and their spouses and dependents, are covered under Medicaid. (Persons claiming asylum, refugees, and deportees are only required to be covered by Medicaid for the first five years of their status in those categories.)

1211. What are Supplemental Security Income states (SSI States)?

Generally, the Social Security Act requires states to provide Medicaid benefits automatically to those receiving categorical welfare assistance. However, the Section 209(b) provision allows states to provide Medicaid benefits only to those persons who would have qualified for Medicaid on January 1, 1972, without adjustment for medical inflation rates. In most states, the Medicaid program includes ALL SSI recipients. These states are called "SSI States".

Other states, however, cover only those persons who are age sixty-five, disabled, or blind and meet the Section 209(b) means test, which is more restrictive than the SSI means test. These states are called "Section 209(b) states." Section 209(b) states include: Connecticut, Hawaii, Illinois, Minnesota, Missouri, New Hampshire, North Dakota, Ohio, Oklahoma, and Virginia. These ten states have elected to define disability more narrowly than the federal definition for SSI entitlement. Indiana was a Section 209(b) state but converted to automatic enrollment in 2014.

1212. Do states have the option of providing additional Medicaid coverage?

Yes, states have the option of providing Medicaid coverage for "Optional Categorically Needy" groups (as opposed to the Mandatory Categorically Needy described in Q 1210). These optional groups share characteristics of the mandatory groups, but the eligibility criteria are somewhat more liberally defined. Examples of the optional groups that states may cover as Optional Categorically Needy (and for which they will receive federal matching funds) under the Medicaid program include the following:

- Infants up to age one and pregnant women not covered under the mandatory rules whose family income is below 185 percent of the Federal Poverty Level (FPL) (the percentage is set by each state).

- Certain aged, blind, or disabled adults who have incomes above those requiring mandatory coverage, but below the Federal Poverty Level (FPL).

- Children under age twenty-one who meet what were the AFDC income and resource requirements in effect in their state on July 16, 1996 (even though they do not meet the mandatory eligibility requirements).

- Certain working-and-disabled persons with family income less than 250 percent of the Federal Poverty Level (FPL) who would qualify for SSI if they were not working.

- Children under age nineteen, or a younger age specified by the state, in households with incomes at or below 100 percent of the Federal Poverty Level (FPL). States may provide a full, continuous twelve months of eligibility for such children.

- Institutionalized individuals with incomes and resources below specified limits. The amount is set by each state – up to 300 percent of the SSI federal benefits rate.

- Persons who would be eligible if institutionalized but are receiving care under home and community-based services waivers.

- Aged, blind, or disabled recipients of state supplementary income payments.

- Tuberculosis-infected persons who would be financially eligible for Medicaid at the SSI income level (only for TB-related ambulatory services and TB drugs).

- Individuals in HMOs Guaranteed Eligibility.

- Individuals receiving Hospice Care.

- "Optional targeted low-income children" included in the CHIP program.

- Certain uninsured or low-income women needing treatment or screened for breast or cervical cancer through a program administered through the Centers for Disease Control and Prevention.

- Individuals age nineteen through sixty-four at or below 133 percent of the Federal Poverty Level (FPL).

- "Medically needy" persons (described below).

The option to have a "medically needy" program allows states to extend Medicaid eligibility to additional qualified persons who may have too much income to qualify under the Mandatory or Optional Categorically Needy groups. This option allows them to "spend down" to Medicaid eligibility by incurring medical and/or remedial care expenses to offset their excess income, thereby reducing it to a level below the maximum allowed by that state's Medicaid plan. States may also allow families to establish eligibility as medically needy by paying monthly premiums to the state in an amount equal to the difference between family income (reduced by unpaid expenses, if any, incurred for medical care in previous months) and the income eligibility standard.

Eligibility for the Medically Needy program does not need to be as extensive as the Categorically Needy programs. But states that elect to include the medically needy under their plans are required to include certain children under age eighteen and pregnant women who, except for income and resources, would be eligible as categorically needy. They may choose to provide coverage to other medically needy persons: aged, blind, and/or disabled persons; certain relatives of children deprived of parental support and care; and certain other financially eligible children up to age twenty-one.

States can expand Medicaid eligibility for children under the State Children's Health Insurance Program. To be eligible for federal funds, states must submit to, and obtain approval from, the Secretary for Health and Human Services for a State Child Health Plan. States that elect to use the child health assistance funds to expand Medicaid eligibility and meet conditions for participating in the program are eligible to receive an enhanced Medicaid match for "optional targeted low-income children." Coverage may start retroactive to any or all of the three months prior to application if the person would have been eligible during the retroactive period. Coverage stops at the end of the month in which a person's circumstances change. Most states have additional "states only" programs to provide medical assistance to specified poor persons who do not qualify for Medicaid. Federal funds are not provided for state-only programs.

Medicaid does not provide health care services for all poor persons. To be eligible for Medicaid, a person must belong to one of the designated groups listed above, as well as meet income and assets/resources tests. Even under the broadest provisions of federal law (except for a few emergency services for certain persons), the Medicaid program does not provide health care services, even for very poor persons, unless they are under age twenty-one, pregnant, aged, blind, disabled, or in certain AFDC-type families. The Patient Protection and Affordable Care Act (PPACA) did expand the eligibility for coverage under Medicaid; however, there are still states that have chosen not to include those who would be covered under this expansion. For more complete coverage of the PPACA expansion see Q 1210 and Q 1213.

1213. What effect does the Patient Protection and Affordable Care Act (PPACA) have on Medicaid eligibility?

Under the PPACA, Medicaid is set to expand its eligibility for coverage to include persons with income levels at or below 133 percent of the federal poverty level. In 2019, a standard 5 percent income disregard applies to most individuals, effectively increasing the eligibility level to 138 percent of the poverty level. For the first three years of Medicaid expansion, the federal government will pay for the additional cost.

States Adopting Medicaid Expansion

Alaska	Michigan*
Arizona*	Minnesota
Arkansas*	Montana[2]
California	Nevada
Colorado	New Hampshire*
Connecticut	New Jersey
Delaware	New Mexico
District of Columbia	New York
Hawaii	North Dakota
Illinois	Ohio
Indiana*	Oregon
Iowa*	Pennsylvania
Kentucky	Rhode Island
Louisiana	Virginia[3]
Maine[1]	Vermont
Maryland	Washington
Massachusetts	West Virginia

* Have approved Section 1115 waivers for the Medicaid expansion.

[1] Maine adopted the Medicaid expansion through a ballot initiative in November 2017 and the ballot measure requires submission of a state plan amendment (SPA) within 90 days and implementation of expansion within 180 days of the measure's effective date, but the Governor failed to meet the SPA submission deadline (April 3, 2018). The Governor complied with a Maine Supreme Judicial Court order to submit an expansion SPA to the federal government on September 4, 2018. However, the Governor also sent a letter to the federal government asking CMS to reject the SPA.

[2] Montana have approved Section 1115 waivers for the Medicaid expansion. They will vote on a measure on the November ballot that would eliminate the state's June 2019 expansion program sunset date and raise tobacco taxes to fund the state's share of expansion costs.

[3] Scheduled to begin Jan. 1, 2019.

The Supreme Court has ruled that states may "opt-out" of the Medicaid expansion. In the states that adopted Medicaid expansion, it became effective on January 1, 2014 except for the following states:

Michigan – April 1, 2014	Alaska – September 1, 2015
New Hampshire – August 15, 2014	Montana – January 1, 2016
Pennsylvania – November 1, 2015	Louisiana – July 1, 2016
Indiana – February 1, 2015	Virginia – January 2019

Currently, the following states have opted out of Medicaid expansion:

Alabama	Oklahoma
Florida	South Carolina
Georgia	South Dakota
Idaho*	Tennessee
Kansas	Texas
Mississippi	Utah[1]
Missouri	Wisconsin[2]
Nebraska*	Wyoming
North Carolina	

* Will vote on a measure on the November ballot that would adopt the ACA Medicaid expansion to 138 percent of the federal poverty level.

[1] The Utah Legislature passed, and Governor Herbert signed a bill on March 27, 2018 directing the state to seek federal approval to expand Medicaid to 100 percent of the federal poverty level (FPL) using the ACA enhanced federal match rate and add a work requirement for the expansion population. To date, CMS has not approved waivers to access the enhanced match rate unless a state implements the expansion to 138 percent FPL. In addition, Utah voters will vote on a measure on the November ballot that would fully expand Medicaid to 138 percent FPL.

[2] Covers adults up to 100 percent of FPL in Medicaid but did not adopt expansion.

If all states were to participate in this expansion, it is estimated that it would add fifteen million people to the Medicaid program. This expansion would continue to increase Medicaid participation to twenty-six million by 2020. From 2014 to 2016, the federal government covered 100 percent of the cost of Medicaid Expansion. From 2020 forward, the federal government will cover 90 percent.

The Kaiser Family Foundation provides a map indicating Medicaid expansion.[1]

1214. What are the proposed changes to the Kentucky Medicaid Expansion?

In January of 2014, the Commonwealth of Kentucky implemented a traditional Medicaid Expansion though the terms of the Affordable Care Act. Governor Matt Bevin, elected in 2015 with the promise to end the Medicaid Expansion. However, instead of attempting to eliminate the Medicaid Expansion, the Governor is proposing a Section 1115 Waiver entitled "Kentucky HEALTH" – "Helping to Engage and Achieve Long Term Health". The waiver application was

---

1. https://kaiserfamilyfoundation.files.wordpress.com/2016/07/current-status-of-the-medicaid-expansion-decisions-healthreform.png (Last accessed October 17, 2018).

officially submitted to the Centers for Medicare and Medicaid Services and is currently being reviewed. On July 3, 2017, Kentucky submitted an amendment seeks Section 1115 waiver authority to modify the current terms of Medicaid coverage by changing Medicaid in Kentucky as follows:

- Implementing premiums based on a sliding scale based on household (rather than individual) income, ranging from $1.00 per month for individuals with incomes below 25 percent FPL and up to a maximum of $15.00 per month in the first two years of enrollment for those from 100-138 percent FPL, increasing beginning in year three;

- Requiring payment of the first premium before coverage is effective for those from 100-138 percent FPL (coverage would be effective after sixty days for those below 100 percent FPL who do not pay a premium);

- Disenrolling those above 100 percent FPL for failure to pay a premium after a sixty-day grace period and barring re-enrollment for six months unless the beneficiary pays past due and current premiums and completes a financial or health literacy course;

- Coverage would be effective after sixty days for those under 100 percent FPL who do not pay a premium. Those above 100 percent FPL who fail to pay a premium after a sixty day grace period will be disenrolled and barring from re-enrollment for six months unless the beneficiary pays past due and current premiums and completes a financial or health literacy course;

- Requiring a certain number of weekly hours of employment activities as a condition of eligibility for most adults;

- Prohibiting beneficiaries who do not timely renew Medicaid eligibility from re-enrolling in coverage for six months unless beneficiary completes a financial or health literacy course;

- Waiving non-emergency medical transportation for expansion adults;

- Adding a high deductible health savings account (funded by the state) to existing capitated managed care coverage and offering an incentive account to purchase extra benefits, funded through completion of specified health-related or employment activities and/or up to half of any remaining annual deductible funds;

- Those in hospice, with HIV/AIDS or covered under SSDI would be considered "medically frail";

- Expanding Medicaid premium assistance to purchase cost-effective Employer Sponsored Insurance (ESI) after the first year of Medicaid enrollment and employment for adults and their Medicaid and CHIP-eligible children;

- Using federal Medicaid matching funds for short-term Institution for Mental Disease (IMD) services for non-elderly adults in certain counties;

- Requiring twenty hours per week of employment activities as a condition of eligibility can include volunteer work, employment, job search, job training, education, or caring for a non-dependent relative or person with a disabling chronic condition;

- Disenrolling beneficiaries who do not report changes to income or employment in a timely manner or who make false statements regarding work. Prohibits them from re-enrolling in coverage for six months unless they complete a health or financial literacy course; and

- Removing a proposed expansion of presumptive eligibility sites to county health departments and certain safety net providers, a provision originally included in the state's waiver application.

The Governor has indicated that if CMS does not accept the waiver, that Kentucky will drop the Medicaid Expansion entirely.

As of October 24, 2018, at the time of this book's printing, the status was still pending. Kentucky received CMS approval for the Kentucky HEALTH expansion waiver on January 12, 2018. On June 29, 2018, the DC federal district court issued a decision in Stewart v. Azar. The court invalidated the waiver approval and sent it back to HHS to reconsider the following provisions: the work requirement, monthly premiums up to 4% of income, coverage lockouts for failure to timely renew eligibility or timely report a change in circumstances, heightened cost-sharing for non-emergency ER use, and elimination of retroactive eligibility and non-emergency medical transportation. The separate "institution for mental disease" substance use disorder payment waiver continues.

Medicaid Services

1215. What basic services must be offered by Medicaid?

The Social Security Act requires that a state Medicaid program must offer medical assistance for certain basic services to most categorically needy populations. These services generally include the following:[1]

- Inpatient hospital services

- Outpatient hospital services

- Prenatal care and pregnancy related services including sixty days postpartum services

- Vaccines for children

- Physician services

- Nursing facility services for persons aged twenty-one or older

---

1. 42 U.S.C. §1396d.

- Family planning services and supplies

- Rural health clinic services

- Home health care for persons eligible for skilled nursing services

- Laboratory and x-ray services

- Pediatric and family nurse-practitioner services

- Nurse-midwife services

- Federally-Qualified Health-Center (FQHC) services, and ambulatory services of an FQHC that would be available in other settings

- Early and Periodic Screening, Diagnostic, and Treatment (EPSDT) services for children under age twenty-one

If a state chooses to include the medically needy population, the state plan must provide, as a minimum, the following services:

- Prenatal care and delivery services for pregnant women

- Ambulatory services to individuals under age eighteen and individuals entitled to institutional services

- Home health services to individuals entitled to nursing facility services

States may also receive federal matching funds for providing certain optional services. The most common optional Medicaid services include the following:

- Home health care services (eligibility does not depend on a need or discharge from a skilled nursing facility)

- Diagnostic services

- Clinic services

- Intermediate-care facilities for the mentally retarded

- Prescribed drugs and prosthetic devices

- Optometrist services and eyeglasses

- Dental care

- Hearing aids

- Nursing facility services for children under age twenty-one

- Transportation services

- Rehabilitation and physical therapy services

- Home and community-based care to certain persons with chronic impairments (this one is an option with an approved waiver).

States can use waivers to test new or existing ways to deliver and pay for health care services in Medicaid and the Children's Health Insurance Program (CHIP). Some of the items in the previous list as optional services would be included via these waivers. There are four primary types of waivers:

- Waivers for program flexibility to test new or existing approaches to financing and delivering Medicaid and CHIP

- Waivers to provide services through managed care delivery systems or otherwise limit people's choice of providers

- Waivers to provide long-term care services in home and community settings rather than institutional settings

- Simultaneously implementing two types of waivers to provide a continuum of services to the elderly and people with disabilities, as long as all Federal requirements for both programs are met

1216. Is AIDS covered under Medicaid?

Medicaid is the largest single payer of direct medical services for persons with AIDS.

States must provide the full range of Medicaid services covered in the state plan to eligible persons with HIV disease. States may also provide optional services that are often appropriate for people with HIV/AIDS (such as targeted case management, preventive services, and hospice care). All states cover FDA-approved prescribed drugs.

While Medicaid provides a range of health care services to people with AIDS and HIV, one of the most important is prescription drugs, an optional Medicaid benefit that all states have chosen to provide to their Medicaid populations. Under the Patient Protection and Affordable Care Act (PPACA), Medicaid eligibility expanded in 2014 to include many people with HIV who are not currently covered by the program. However, this coverage is still dependent on the state approving the Medicaid expansion plan. Many states have chosen to opt out of the expansion, or have not yet made a final decision about the expansion (see Q 1213). Individuals should contact their state Medicaid agency for state-specific criteria.

1217. What optional services may a state elect to provide?

States may elect to provide several other services for which federal matching funds are available.

Some of the most frequently covered optional services are:

- clinic services,

- medical transportation services,

- intermediate-care facility services for the mentally retarded,

- optometrist services and eyeglasses,

- prescribed drugs,

- case management services,

- prosthetic devices,

- dental services and dentures,

- podiatry services,

- physical therapy and occupational therapy,

- speech, hearing, and language disorder services,

- chiropractic care,

- hospice care,

- respiratory care services,

- private duty nursing services,

- services for individuals age sixty-five and older in an institution for mental disease,

- self-directed personal assistance services,

- TB related services,

- inpatient psychiatric services for individuals under age twenty-one,

- other diagnostic, screening, preventive and rehabilitative services, and

- home and community-based care for functionally disabled elderly persons.

Payment under Medicaid

1218. How are providers of health care services paid under Medicaid?

Medicaid operates as a vendor payment program, with states paying providers directly. Providers participating in Medicaid must accept Medicaid payment rates as payment in full. States may pay for Medicaid services through various prepayment arrangements, such as Health Maintenance Organizations (HMOs). Within federally-imposed upper limits and specific restrictions, each state generally has broad discretion in determining the payment methodology and payment rate for services. Generally, payment rates must be sufficient to enlist enough providers so that covered services are available, at least to the extent that comparable care and services are available to the general population within that geographic area. States must make additional payments to qualified hospitals that provide inpatient services to a disproportionate number of Medicaid recipients and/or to other low-income persons under what is known as the Disproportionate Share Hospital (DSH) adjustment. These payments are limited.

The federal government pays a portion of the medical assistance expenditures under each state's Medicaid program, known as the Federal Medical Assistance Percentage (FMAP). The FMAP is determined annually by a formula that compares the state's average per capita income level with the national income average. States with a higher per capita income level are reimbursed a smaller share of their costs. By law, the FMAP cannot be lower than 50 percent nor higher than 83 percent. In FY 2019, the FMAPs varied from a low of 50 percent in fifteen states to 76.39 percent in Mississippi, and averaged 58.82 percent overall. For children covered through the CHIP (formerly SCHIP) program, the Federal government pays states a higher or "enhanced" FMAP, which averaged 71.17 percent in FY 2019.

Federal Medical Assistance Percentages and Enhanced Federal Medical Assistance Percentages Effective October 1, 2018-September 30, 2019

	Federal medical assistance percentages	Enhanced federal medical assistance percentages	Enhanced federal medical assistance percentages with ACA 23 Pt Inc***
Alabama	71.88	80.32	100
Alaska	50	65	88
American Samoa*	55	68.5	91.5
Arizona	69.81	78.87	100
Arkansas	70.51	79.36	100
California	50	65	88
Colorado	50	65	88
Connecticut	50	65	88
Delaware	57.55	70.29	93.29
District of Columbia**	70	79	100
Florida	60.87	72.61	95.61
Georgia	67.62	77.33	100
Guam*	55	68.5	91.5
Hawaii	53.92	67.74	90.74
Idaho	71.13	79.79	100
Illinois	50.31	65.22	88.22
Indiana	65.96	76.17	99.17
Iowa	59.93	71.95	94.95
Kansas	57.1	69.97	92.97

	Federal medical assistance percentages	Enhanced federal medical assistance percentages	Enhanced federal medical assistance percentages with ACA 23 Pt Inc***
Kentucky	71.67	80.17	100
Louisiana	65	75.5	98.5
Maine	64.52	75.16	98.16
Maryland	50	65	88
Massachusetts	50	65	88
Michigan	64.45	75.12	98.12
Minnesota	50	65	88
Mississippi	76.39	83.47	100
Missouri	65.4	75.78	98.78
Montana	65.54	75.88	98.88
Nebraska	52.58	66.81	89.81
Nevada	64.87	75.41	98.41
New Hampshire	50	65	88
New Jersey	50	65	88
New Mexico	72.26	80.58	100
New York	50	65	88
North Carolina	67.16	77.01	100
North Dakota	50	65	88
Northern Mariana Islands*	55	68.5	91.5
Ohio	63.09	74.16	97.16
Oklahoma	62.38	73.67	96.67
Oregon	62.56	73.79	96.79
Pennsylvania	52.25	66.58	89.58
Puerto Rico*	55	68.5	91.5
Rhode Island	52.57	66.8	89.8
South Carolina	71.22	79.85	100
South Dakota	56.71	69.7	92.7
Tennessee	65.87	76.11	99.11
Texas	58.19	70.73	93.73
Utah	69.71	78.8	100
Vermont	53.89	67.72	90.72
Virgin Islands*	55	68.5	91.5
Virginia	50	65	88

	Federal medical assistance percentages	Enhanced federal medical assistance percentages	Enhanced federal medical assistance percentages with ACA 23 Pt Inc***
Washington	50	65	88
West Virginia	74.34	82.04	100
Wisconsin	59.37	71.56	94.56
Wyoming	50	65	88

1219. What is the amount and duration of Medicaid services?

Within broad federal guidelines, states determine the duration and amount of services offered under their Medicaid programs. They may limit, for example, the number of days of hospital care or the number of physician visits covered. But some restrictions apply: Limits must result in a sufficient level of services to reasonably achieve the purpose of the benefits. Limits on required (nonoptional) benefits may not discriminate among beneficiaries based on medical diagnosis or condition.

In general, states are required to provide Medicaid coverage for comparable amounts, duration, and scope of services to all categorically-needy and categorically-related eligible persons.

There are two important exceptions:

(1) Medically necessary health care services identified under the Early and Periodic Screening, Diagnostic, and Treatment (EPSDT) program for eligible children that are within the scope of mandatory or optional services under federal law must be covered, even if those services are not included as part of the covered services in that state's plan (i.e., only these specific children might receive that specific service).

(2) States may require "waivers" to pay for otherwise-uncovered Home and Community-Based Services (HCBS) for Medicaid-eligible persons who might otherwise be institutionalized (i.e., only persons so designated might receive HCBS).

States have few limitations on the services that may be covered under these waivers, as long as the services are cost-effective (except that, other than as a part of respite care, they may not provide room and board for recipients). With certain exceptions, a state's Medicaid plan must allow recipients to have freedom of choice among participating providers of health care.

1220. How does Medicaid help with Medicare coverage for the needy, elderly, and disabled?

Persons who are eligible for Medicare and whose income and assets fall below specified limits may also receive help from Medicaid. For persons who are eligible for full Medicaid coverage, the Medicare health care coverage is supplemented by services that are available under their state's Medicaid program. For example, depending on the state, supplies and services such as eyeglasses, hearing aids, and nursing facility care beyond the 100-day noncustodial-care limit covered by Medicare, may be provided by the Medicaid program. However, if a person is a Medicare beneficiary, payments for any services covered by Medicare are made by Medicare before any payments are made by the Medicaid program; Medicaid is always "payor of last resort." Individuals who are covered by Medicare and who also have full Medicaid coverage are often referred to as "dual eligibles".

In addition, there are four groups of Medicare beneficiaries who may not be fully eligible for Medicaid, but who do receive some help through their state Medicaid program. Most of the Medicare beneficiaries helped by Medicaid are those identified as:

(1)   Qualified Medicare Beneficiaries (QMBs);

(2)   Specified Low-Income Medicare Beneficiaries (SLMBs);

(3)   Qualified Individual (QI);

(4)   Qualified Disabled Working Individual (QDWI).

Qualified Medicare Beneficiary Program (QMB)

- Eligibility Criteria:

    - Must be *eligible* for Medicare Part A (even if not enrolled)

    - Income must be at or below 100 percent of the Federal Poverty Level (FPL)

    - Less than or equal to three times Supplemental Security Income (SSI) resource limit – this is adjusted annually in reference to the Consumer Price Index

- Coverage:

    - Medicaid pays the individuals Part A and Part B premiums

    - Medicare coinsurance and deductibles – subject to limits imposed by the state

Specified Low Income Beneficiary Program (SLMB)

- Eligibility Criteria:

    - Must be *enrolled in* Medicare Part A

    - Income must be greater than or equal to 100 percent of the Federal Poverty Level (FPL) but not more than 120 percent of FPL

    - Less than or equal to three times Supplemental Security Income (SSI) resources limit – this is adjusted annually in reference to the Consumer Price Index

- Coverage:

    - Medicaid pays the individuals Part B premiums

Qualified Individual (QI) Program

- Eligibility Criteria:

    - Must be *enrolled in* Medicare Part A

    - Income must be greater or equal to 120 percent of the Federal Poverty Level (FPL) but not more than 135 percent of FPL

    - Less than or equal to three times Supplemental Security Income (SSI) resource limit – this is adjusted annually in reference to the Consumer Price Index

- Coverage:

    - Medicaid pays the individuals Part B premiums

Qualified Disabled Working Individual (QDWI) Program

- Eligibility Criteria:

    - Medicare Part A benefits have been lost due to individual's return to work

    - Income must be less than or equal to 200 percent of Federal Poverty Level (FPL)

    - Less than or equal to two times Supplemental Security Income (SSI) resource limit – this is adjusted annually in reference to the Consumer Price Index

- Coverage:

    - Medicaid pays the individuals Part B premiums

Selection by states is on a first-come, first-served basis.

Long-Term Care

1221. Does Medicaid provide coverage for long-term care?

Yes. Medicaid provides long-term care coverage for eligible people age twenty-one and older in certain settings and as long as the individuals satisfy applicable resource and income limits. Long-term care coverage under Medicaid generally covers nursing home services for all eligible people and also covers home and community-based services for people who would need to be in a nursing home if they did not receive the home care services. Most long-term care services assist people with Activities of Daily Living (ADLs), such as dressing, bathing, and using the bathroom. Long-term care can be provided at home, in the community, or in a facility. For purposes of Medicaid eligibility and payment, long-term care services are those provided to an individual who requires a level of care equivalent to that received in a nursing facility.

In most states, Medicaid will also cover services that will help a person remain in his home, such as personal care services, case management, and help with laundry and cleaning. Medicaid will not pay for rent, mortgage, utilities, or food.

Medicaid does not cover assisted living – in most states. This would be the in-between stage before a nursing home, but when an individual is past independent living. This stage can be quite expensive and can last for quite a long time, so preparing in advance is important.

As with all Medicaid programs, eligibility for long-term care services will vary from state to state. Long-term care services that may be available to a person in one state may not be available in another state. For example, some states cover assisted living services, while others do not. An individual should contact their state Medicaid office to find out specific eligibility for that state.

State LTC Partnership Program

1222. What is a "qualified state long-term care insurance partnership?"

A qualified state long-term care insurance partnership is a state Medicaid plan amendment that provides for the disregard of assets or resources in an amount equal to the insurance benefit payments made to or on behalf of an individual who is a beneficiary under a qualifying Long-Term Care (LTC) insurance policy.

A qualifying LTC partnership policy must meet the following requirements:

1. The policy covers an insured who was a resident of the state when coverage first became effective under the policy.

2. The policy is a tax-qualified LTC insurance policy issued not earlier than the effective date of the state LTC partnership program.

3. The policy must meet the standards contained in the 2000 NAIC Model LTC Policy Act and Regulations.

4. The policy must contain the following inflation protection provisions:

    a. Buyers younger than age sixty-one – compound annual inflation protection

    b. Buyers ages sixty-one to seventy-five –some level of inflation protection

    c. Buyers age seventy-six or older – no inflation protection required

5. Agents selling the policy must receive appropriate training and demonstrate understanding of the policy.

6. The issuer of the policy must provide regular reports with information on policy benefits, claims, underwriting, terminations, and other information deemed appropriate.

7. The policy must not be subject to any state insurance mandates not applicable to all LTC insurance policies sold in the state.

Standards do exist (under the Deficit Reduction Act of 2005 (DRA)) for the uniform reciprocal recognition of LTC partnership policies, under which benefits paid by such policies will be treated the same by all states with qualified state LTC insurance partnerships. A state with a LTC insurance partnership is subject to the standards unless the state formally elects to be exempt from such standards.

Exempt Income and Resources

1223. Are certain income and resources exempt from the financial eligibility standards that govern Medicaid eligibility?

A single individual will not qualify for Medicaid in most states unless he has less than $2,000 in countable assets (although it may be higher in some states).

In determining whether applicants for Medicaid meet asset criteria, certain assets are considered "countable" and other assets are considered "exempt." Exempt assets include the following:

- The cash value of permanent life insurance policies up to $2,500 of face value, and all life insurance policies with no cash value (term insurance).

- Household furnishings (furniture, paintings, appliances, etc.), which are exempt only while used in the applicant's home.

- Burial funds up to $1,500 (reduced by the face value of any cash-value life insurance policies otherwise exempted and any amounts held in an irrevocable burial fund trust). There is no dollar limit if the burial plan is irrevocable.

- Property used in a trade or business.

- Burial space (grave site, crypt, mausoleum, urn, grave marker).

- One automobile of any value:

    (1) for a married couple where one spouse is institutionalized;

    (2) if equipped for a handicapped person;

    (3) if used to obtain medical treatment; or

    (4) if used for employment.

- This exemption is limited to $4,500 in all other cases.

- Up to $572,000 of equity in a home provided it is the person's principal place of residence. This includes the land on which the home sits and any adjoining property. States may choose to increase this amount up to $858,000.

- Property owned with one or more other individuals, if the other owners use the property as the principal place of residence and would be forced to move if the property were sold.

- Personal effects, including clothing, photographs, jewelry, etc.

The home is treated as a resource after the individual has been institutionalized for six months, unless the individual's spouse or minor, disabled or blind child continues to reside in the home, or it can be shown that the individual may be able to leave the institution and return home.

Exempt assets lose that status upon the death of the Medicaid recipient. Therefore, the state may claim reimbursement from the recipient's estate. Medicaid authorities are sometimes granted a lien against the home, collectible after the death of the recipient (or the death of certain relatives living in the home) to compensate for Medicaid benefits paid to the homeowner.

Medicaid applicants must also meet income tests that vary by state. It is important to note that rules do differ quite significantly from state-to-state. In some of the states, there is no upper income limit for persons in nursing homes. The remaining states have "income caps" in determining eligibility for nursing home coverage. If a person has income below the private cost of nursing home care in one of the states where there is no upper income limit, he meets Medicaid's income test. For example, if a person has monthly income of $2,500 and the private cost of nursing home care is $3,000 (and he has less than $2,000 in countable assets), he or she will qualify for Medicaid. He will be required to pay all of his income, except for a small "personal needs allowance," to the nursing home and Medicaid pays the balance of the bill.

Federal law requires states with "income caps" to set their "income caps" no higher than 300 percent of the Federal SSI benefit level ($771 in 2019). Thus, the "income cap" can be no greater than $2,313 in 2019 for a single person. The maximum SSI benefit level is $1,157 for an eligible individual with an eligible spouse, and $386 for an essential person. Not all of the states using "income caps" set their cap at the maximum allowable level (300 percent of the SSI benefit level). For example, if a person's monthly income is $1,550 in a state that sets its cap at $1,500, he does not qualify for Medicaid.

Spousal Impoverishment

1224. Are there guidelines regarding the amount of income the community spouse of a nursing home resident can maintain?

The expense of nursing home care can rapidly deplete the lifetime savings of elderly couples. Because of this there are specially mandated Medicaid eligibility rules for couples when one-member needs nursing home care. The rules protect income and resources for the other member of the couple. Under these rules a healthy spouse is not required to give up all of his income or property simply for the spouse in need of nursing care to be eligible through Medicaid. This set of rules, called "spousal protections" allow the spouse of a nursing home resident to keep enough income and assets to live a life outside the nursing home. As with all Medicaid programs, there is great variation among states' spousal protections rules, but the basic guidelines are the same in every state.

Under the rules, certain income, assets, and the couple's home are protected. The following guidelines remain true for all states:

- **Protected Income**. The income of the spouse of the long-term care patient is protected as well as some of the long-term care patient's income if it is needed to financially support the spouse. The money that a spouse may keep and that is exempt from the Medicaid eligibility calculation is called the Minimum Monthly Maintenance Needs Allowance (MMMNA). The MMMNA varies from state to state, but the federal government sets a minimum and a maximum periodically that is tied to poverty guidelines. For 2018, the minimum is $2,057.50 and the maximum is $3,090.00. This income is disregarded by the state Medicaid agency in evaluating whether the needy spouse is financially eligible for Medicaid.

- **Protected Assets**. The spouse of the long-term care patient is allowed to keep one-half of the couple's combined marital assets subject to state set minimum and maximum allowable amounts (within federal guidelines). The state will measure the resources of the spouse applying for Medicaid on the date that the spouse began a hospital or nursing home stay that lasted at least thirty days. The amount of resources that the healthy spouse, called the "community spouse" is allowed to keep is called the Community Spouse Resource Allowance (CSRA). The CSRA varies by state (within a federally established minimum and maximum CSRA).

  If a spouse living in the community needs more income than the MMMNA or more resources than the CSRA, the spouse can seek a court order allowing a variation from the state agency's standard.

- **Protection of Home**. Federal Medicaid rules protect a Medicaid recipient's home and property, which is an important protection for the community spouse. If a Medicaid recipient expresses intent to return to the home, the first $572,000 in equity is excluded as a resource when calculating whether the needy spouse is eligible for Medicaid. Some states choose to raise the equity limit to $858,000. States do have discretion about when they will disregard the value of a home in calculating eligibility; many states require that the recipient must be actually likely to return to the home, not just that the recipient intends to return to the home.

2019 guidelines will be issued during December of 2018.

1225. What are the resource eligibility requirements that apply to a community spouse?

The spousal impoverishment provisions apply where the member of the couple who is in a nursing facility or medical institution is expected to remain there for at least thirty days. When the couple applies for Medicaid, an assessment of their resources is conducted. The couple's resources are combined and exemptions for the home, household goods, automobile, and burial funds are taken into account. (See Q 1223 and Q 1224.) The result is the spousal resource amount. The spousal resource amount is the state's minimum resource standard ($24,720 in 2018 – figures are not available for 2019, or the spousal share, which is equal to one-half of the couple's combined resources (not to exceed the maximum permitted by the state ($123,600 in 2018.

In order to determine whether the spouse residing in a medical facility is eligible for Medicaid, a determination of the couple's total countable resources must be made. All resources held by both spouses are considered to be available to the spouse in the medical facility, except for the Protected Resource Amount (PRA). This PRA is the greatest of:

- the spousal resource amount;

- the state spousal resource standard, which is the amount that the state has determined will be protected for the community spouse;

- an amount transferred to the community spouse for her/his support as directed by a court order;

- an amount designated by a state hearing officer to raise the community spouse's protected resources up to the minimum monthly maintenance needs standard (150 percent of the federal poverty level for a household of two).

The remainder becomes attributable to the spouse that is residing in a medical institution as countable resources. If the amount of resources is below the state's resource standard, the individual is eligible for Medicaid. Once resource eligibility is determined, resources of the community spouse are not attributed to the spouse in the medical facility.

1226. What are the income eligibility requirements for Community Spouses?

The community spouse's income is not considered available to the spouse who is in the medical facility, and the two individuals are not considered a couple for these purposes. The state must use the income eligibility standards for one person rather than two. Therefore, the standard income eligibility process for Medicaid is used. (See Q 1223 to Q 1225.)

1227. What is the process for the post-eligibility treatment of income for Community Spouses?

This process is followed after an individual in a nursing facility/medical institution is determined to be eligible for Medicaid. The post-eligibility process is used to determine how much the spouse in the medical facility must contribute toward the cost of nursing facility/institutional care. The process also determines how much of the income of the spouse who is in the medical facility is actually protected for use by the community spouse.

Deductions are made from the total income of the spouse who is residing in the medical facility in the following order:

- A personal needs allowance of at least thirty dollars

- The community spouse's monthly income allowance – between $2,057.50 and $3,090.00 (in 2018) – as long as the income is actually made available to the spouse

- A family monthly income allowance

- An amount for medical expenses incurred by the spouse who is in the medical facility

The sum of these deductions subtracted from the income of the individual who is in the medical facility will result in the amount the individual must contribute to the cost of care.

1228. What Medicaid planning strategies can spouses use to help with eligibility?

As explained in preceding questions Medicaid will pay for nursing home care only for those who are eligible. While some safe-guards and asset protections remain in place for the community spouse, many people feel that these do not do enough to protect their assets. Since Medicaid will pay for nursing home care only for those with limited assets and will penalize those who give away assets to qualify for Medicaid, people have long used other strategies in to circumvent the rules penalizing gifts of assets. Some of the more popular strategies used for making gifts while avoiding a transfer penalty are listed here. However, take note that new rules have made these strategies either completely ineffective or very difficult.

- **"Half a Loaf" Strategy**. At one time, this strategy was one of the most commonly used gifting strategies. A senior who anticipated needing long-term care would gift half of his assets to those of his choosing (preserving "half a loaf") and use the rest to pay for Medicaid during the penalty period. Using the half a loaf strategy, people often made gifts to family members on a monthly or bimonthly basis, based on state law. Now that the transfer penalty does not begin to run until a person applies for Medicaid and all of the other qualifications are met for Medicaid, periodic gifting is no longer effective.

- **Annuities**. An annuity is when a person pays a lump sum of cash in exchange for a series of guaranteed future payments during that person's lifetime. The strategy of purchasing an annuity to qualify for Medicaid still works for married couples, but there has been refinement in the law causing most of the older methods to be ineffective. The key to using this strategy successfully is to convert an asset into a stream of monthly income for the spouse who does not need long-term care. This works because only the income of the applicant is considered toward eligibility; income of the community spouse is excluded. Purchasing an annuity turns an excess asset into income, so the asset is transparent for Medicaid purposes. The annuity payments must be completed before the end of the community spouse's life expectancy. This rule prevents the likelihood that there would be annuity payments left for the heirs after the community spouse's death.

1229. Can a spouse refuse to support a spouse who has entered a nursing home, causing Medicaid to pay for the nursing home?

Theoretically, husbands and wives have an equal duty to support one another. In many instances, the spouse with more income and assets gets sick and enters a nursing home first. However, it is perfectly possible that the sick spouse will have very limited personal income and resources. In that case, the question becomes, what is the obligation of the healthy, more affluent, community spouse?

Perhaps surprisingly, Federal Medicaid law generally takes a "just say no" position. State Medicaid agencies are not allowed to deny Medicaid benefits to patients on the grounds that their wealthier spouses refuse to support them or let any of their own income or resources be used.

However, part of the Medicaid application process is an agreement to assign support rights to the Medicaid agency. The Medicaid agency then has a legal right to sue the community spouse for nonsupport. Whether this is a meaningful threat to individual community spouses depends on the local policy. Some Medicaid agencies are very active in this matter, but most bring few nonsupport suits.

Community spouses who want to preserve their own financial position, but who do not want to engage in outright "spousal refusal" can enter into an agreement with the state Medicaid agency. Usually, offering 25 percent of the difference between the community spouse's actual income and the monthly maintenance allowance will be acceptable. Note that Medicaid benefits can be denied to the spouse of a healthy person who refuses to provide information about his financial situation, so make sure that potential community spouses provide disclosure, even if they want to make a spousal refusal.

1230. Is divorce a viable planning strategy for Medicaid purposes?

Generally, no. Medicaid rules favor married couples. Medicaid-motivated divorce (as distinct from couples who are genuinely unhappy, or where one partner wants to remarry) is usually inadvisable.

When a couple divorces, either their property is community property, which is equally divided between them, or it is marital property which must be "equitably" divided. There are many factors in equitable distribution, but the needs of the parties are considered more important than who owned the property originally, or who contributed the funds used to purchase it. Therefore, it is possible that a large percentage of the couple's property will be distributed to the sick spouse, with resulting negative consequences for Medicaid planning.

Also, divorce courts have the power to order spousal support, depending on the relative needs of the spouses. A person who needs extensive long-term care is incapable of self-support, so it is possible that the divorce court will order the healthy, and wealthier, spouse to provide income to the sick spouse.

Capacity is also a problem. Legal capacity is required to sue or be sued, and a person suffering from Alzheimer's disease or some other type of dementia may lack such capacity. If a guardian has already been appointed, the guardian may be able to handle the divorce. On the other hand, some states have taken the position that divorce litigation is so inherently personal that a guardian cannot take part in it. In those states, a demented person's marriage is effectively permanent, because there is no way to dissolve it by divorce.

Medicaid Transfer Rules

1231. Can a person transfer property in order to meet the eligibility requirements for Medicaid?

Transfers of property for less than fair market value prior to applying for Medicaid benefits can result in a denial of benefits. States' rules will vary significantly from state to state, however, states may delay eligibility for Medicaid benefits for a period of time whenever it is determined that a person institutionalized in a medical institution or nursing facility has disposed of resources for less than fair market value within sixty months before application for Medicaid benefits. A transfer is an outright gift, or an exchange for something worth less than the full value of the transferred property.

Certain transfers can be made within sixty months of the application without loss of Medicaid eligibility.

The family home may be transferred to:

(1) the community spouse (noninstitutionalized spouse);

(2) a child who is under age twenty-one, blind, or permanently and totally disabled;

(3) an adult son or daughter residing in the home and providing care that delayed the person's need for care in a medical institution or nursing facility for at least two years;

(4) a trust created solely for the benefit of disabled children of the applicant;

(5) certain trusts created for a disabled child or grandchild under age sixty-five; and

(6) a brother or sister who has an ownership interest in the house and who has been living in the home for at least one year immediately before the person's admission for care.

Also, eligibility is unaffected if the transferor can prove that the intent of the transfer was to dispose of the resources either at fair market value or for other valuable consideration, or the exclusive purpose of the transfer was not to qualify for Medicaid. States can also grant eligibility where denial would amount to undue hardship.

All transfers of jointly-owned property to others are deemed to the Medicaid applicant. This penalty applies when the action taken by a co-owner reduces or eliminates the Medicaid applicant's ownership or control of the asset.

Two ways to transfer assets to family members without disqualifying for Medicaid benefits are:

(1) by transferring the assets to family members more than sixty months before the person applies for Medicaid benefits; and

(2) if the applicant is already in a nursing home or about to go into one, by retaining enough assets to pay for sixty months of care, transferring the balance, and not applying for Medicaid until sixty months after the date on which the last asset transfer is completed.

Any planning for Medicaid eligibility should be done with a clear understanding of all the present rules on the federal level and for the state in which the person(s) reside. These rules vary significantly from state to state, and change frequently. Additionally, it should be noted that there is the threat of criminal penalty for any lawyer or adviser assisting clients with Medicaid planning.

1232. How is the penalty period determined after an improper transfer of assets?

The penalty period of ineligibility for an improper transfer – see Q 1231 – begins on the later of the first day of the month of the transfer or "the date on which the individual is eligible for medical assistance under the State plan…based on an approved application for such care but for the application of the penalty period." The penalty lasts for the number of months equal to the total value of transferred property divided by the average cost of nursing home care to a private patient in the state or community of the applicant (the average private-pay rate). All transfers made in the sixty months prior to the application date are aggregated in determining the length of the penalty period. There is no limit to the length of the penalty period.

For example, a Medicaid applicant who improperly transfers a house worth $350,000 in a state with an average cost of nursing home care of $3,500 a month will be penalized with 100 months of ineligibility for Medicaid ($350,000 ÷ $3,500 = 100). But if a person gives away a house worth $350,000 and then waits more than sixty months to apply for Medicaid, he or she does not have to report the transfer and will not incur the period of ineligibility.

The rules have been made more restrictive in recent years and mean that common gifting strategies involving "half a loaf" or consecutive monthly transfers no longer work. (See Q 1228.)

If both spouses enter a nursing home at or near the same time, states are required to apportion the penalty between the spouses so that only one penalty applies. For example, an improper transfer of $70,000 in a state with a nursing home cost of $3,500 will cause each spouse to be ineligible for ten months ($70,000 ÷ $3,500 = 20 ÷ 2 = 10).

A Medicaid applicant cannot have a portion of the transferred property returned to eliminate the transfer penalty. All assets transferred for less than fair market value must be returned in order to eliminate some or all of the penalty period.

Each state has procedures for waiver of the transfer penalty when the transfer penalty results in undue hardship.

1233. What are the rules under Medicaid regarding the purchase of annuities?

Under the *Deficit Reduction Act of 2005* (DRA), purchasing an annuity by or on behalf of an applicant is considered an improper transfer of assets (see Q 1228, Q 1231, and Q 1232) unless the annuity meets certain requirements.

The purchase of an annuity will not be treated as an improper transfer of assets if the:

1. state is named as the primary remainder beneficiary for at least the total amount of medical assistance paid by Medicaid on behalf of the applicant;

2. state is named as the secondary beneficiary after the community spouse or minor or disabled child;

3.   annuity is purchased inside, or with proceeds from, a retirement account (IRA, Roth IRA, SEP-IRA, etc.)

Any annuity purchased on behalf of a Medicaid applicant must be irrevocable, nonassignable, actuarially sound, and provide for payments in equal amounts during the term of the annuity, with no deferral and no balloon payments.

Annuities purchased prior to February 8, 2006 (the effective date of the DRA) are governed by state-specific provisions. At a minimum, pre-DRA annuities must be actuarially sound (meaning they do not pay out over a time period exceeding the life expectancy of the Medicaid applicant).

Trusts

1234. Can a trust be used to shelter a Medicaid applicant's assets?

There are considerable limits on the use of trusts to shelter a Medicaid applicant's assets. Trust assets created or funded by a Medicaid applicant or by his spouse are considered available to the applicant to the extent the applicant derives any benefit from the trust.

If an institutionalized person or spouse (or, at the option of a state, a noninstitutionalized person or spouse) disposes of trust assets for less than fair market value on or after the look-back date for trusts, the person is ineligible for Medicaid for the following time period:

- For an institutionalized person, the number of months of ineligibility is equal to the total of all assets transferred on or after the look-back date divided by the average monthly cost to a private patient of nursing facility services in the state at the time of application. Ineligibility begins on the first day of the first month during or after which assets have been transferred for less than fair market value.

- For a noninstitutionalized person, the number of months of ineligibility may not be greater than a number equal to the total value of all assets transferred on or after the look-back date, divided by the average monthly cost to a private patient of nursing facility services in the state at the time of application. Ineligibility begins on the first day of the first month during or after which assets have been transferred for less than fair market value.

The look-back period in the case of payments from a trust or portions of a trust that are treated as assets disposed of is sixty months before:

(1)   the first date on which an institutionalized person is both institutionalized and has applied for Medicaid; or

(2)   the first date on which a noninstitutionalized person applies for Medicaid or, if later, the date on which the individual disposes of assets for less than fair market value.

An individual is considered to have established a trust if assets of the individual were used to form all or part of the corpus of the trust and any of the following individuals established the trust other than by will:

- The individual

- The individual's spouse

- A person, including a court or administrative body, with legal authority to act in place of or on behalf of the individual or the individual's spouse

- A person, including any court or administrative body, acting at the direction or upon the request of the individual or the individual's spouse

In the case of a revocable trust:

(1)   the corpus of the trust is considered a resource available to the individual;

(2)   payments from the trust to or for the benefit of the individual are considered income of the individual; and

(3)   any other payments from the trust are considered assets disposed of by the individual.

Assets are defined as all income and resources of the individual and the individual's spouse, including any income or resources which the individual or the individual's spouse is entitled to but does not receive because of action:

(1)   by the individual or the individual's spouse;

(2)   by a person, including a court or administrative body, with legal authority to act in place of or on behalf of the individual or the individual's spouse; or

(3)   by any person, including any court or administrative body, acting at the direction or upon the request of the individual or the individual's spouse.

In the case of an irrevocable trust:

- If there are any circumstances under which payment from the trust could be made to or for the benefit of the individual, the portion of the corpus from which, or the income on the corpus from which, payment to the individual could be made is considered resources available to the individual, and payments from that portion of the corpus or income:

  ○ to or from the benefit of the individual, is considered income of the individual, and

  ○ for any other purpose, is considered a transfer of assets by the individual. (See preceding definition of "asset".)

- Any portion of the trust from which, or any income on the corpus from which, no payment could under any circumstances be made to the individual, is considered, as of the date of establishment of the trust (or, if later, the date on which payment to the individual was foreclosed), to be assets disposed of by the individual and the value of the trust is determined by including the amount of any payments made from such portion of the trust after that date.

A trust includes any legal instrument or device that is similar to a trust but includes an annuity only to such extent and in such manner as the Department of Health and Human Services specifies.

1235. Are there exceptions to the trust rules under Medicaid?

Yes. There are three exceptions. The following trusts are exempt from the Medicaid trust rules:

1. A trust established by a parent, grandparent, guardian, or court for the benefit of an individual who is disabled and under age sixty-five, using the individual's own funds.

2. A trust composed only of pension, Social Security, and other income of the individual, in states which make individuals eligible for institutional care under a special-income level, but do not cover institutional care for the medically needy.

3. A trust established by a disabled individual, parent, grandparent, guardian, or court for the disabled individual, using the individual's own funds, where the trust is made up of pooled funds and managed by a nonprofit organization for the sole benefit of each individual included in the trust.

In all of the above instances, the trust must provide that the state receives any funds, up to the amount of Medicaid benefits paid on behalf of the individual, remaining in the trust when the individual dies.

A trust will not be counted as available to an individual where the state determines that counting the trust would work an undue hardship.

1236. What is a Special Needs Trust (SNT)?

A Special Needs Trust (SNT) is a specialized legal document designed to benefit an individual who is disabled. A SNT is most often a stand-alone document, but it can also be created as part of someone's (such as the disabled person's parent) will. SNTs have been in use for many years, and were given an "official" legal status by Congress in 1993.

An SNT enables a disabled person, or an individual with a chronic or acquired illness, to have held in trust, for his or her benefit, an unlimited amount of assets. In a properly-drafted SNT, those assets are not considered countable assets for purposes of qualification for certain governmental benefits.

These benefits may include Supplemental Security Income (SSI), Medicaid, vocational rehabilitation, subsidized housing, and other benefits based upon need. For purposes of a SNT, an individual is considered impoverished if his or her personal assets are less than $2,000.

An SNT provides for supplemental and extra care over and above that which the government provides.

An SNT must be irrevocable. A properly-drafted SNT will include provisions for trust termination or dissolution under certain circumstances, and will include explicit directions for amendment when necessary.

An SNT can be used for supplemental and extra care over and above what the government provides. A properly-drafted SNT will work on a sliding scale; in the event that the government provides for 100 percent of the disabled beneficiary's needs the trust will provide nothing. If there are no governmental benefits available, the trust can provide 100 percent of what is needed.

A properly-drafted trust will address the issue concerning paybacks to Medicaid or other government sources. The law requires that repayment language must be included in all SNTs, whether repayment is required or not.

A SNT that is funded by parents or other third-party sources will not be required to pay back Medicaid. An SNT that is funded by a personal injury settlement that is properly court-ordered into the SNT will not be required to pay back Medicaid. The only assets within an SNT that are subject to the repayment obligation are those assets which originally belonged to the disabled individual that are transferred into the trust. This type of trust is a first-party trust because the money is considered to be the beneficiary's money as opposed to money that has been gifted.

Examples of assets which would belong to the disabled individual in the first place include earnings from a job, savings, certain Social Security back payments, and personal injury recoveries which are not court-ordered into the SNT.

1237. What are the three different types of Special Needs Trusts (SNT)?

There are three types of Special Needs Trusts (SNT):

(1)   a family-type trust;

(2)   a pooled trust; and

(3)   a court-ordered trust.

These trusts are described in the subsequent questions.

1238. What is a family-type Special Needs Trust (SNT)?

The most commonly used SNT is a family-type trust, which is set up by the parents. The parents provide the money for the trust, often by will, and sometimes by purchasing life insurance payable to the trust.

In most cases, the parents write a will giving money or a house to the disabled son or daughter. After the beneficiary has died, anything left over goes to other family members. The left-over is called the "remainder."

Some parents place their property in a "living" or "inter vivos" trust, and provide in the trust that the disabled son or daughter is the beneficiary. With that type of trust, there is no need to wait for the parents to die. The trust becomes effective immediately. This is a good idea for families where aunts, uncles, and grandparents might want to leave money for the trust. Anyone can give money to the trust, either by writing a check or writing a will.

The key to a family-type SNT is that the money cannot be used for housing, food, or clothing. Those are considered basic needs under the Medicaid laws. If the disabled person is receiving free housing, food, or clothing from someone else, including a family member or a trust, then the government benefits will be reduced or eliminated.

The trust can be used to purchase a home, and perhaps rent it to the disabled person. The trust can pay for repairs, utilities and taxes for a home; it can purchase furnishings for the home. It can pay for vacations, summer camp, or trips. It can buy bowling shoes or other sporting equipment. It can pay for medical costs not otherwise covered by Medicaid, such as vitamins. It can pay for funeral and burial costs. It can pay for a lot of things, but it does not have to pay for anything unless the trustee thinks it is a good idea.

The parents generally serve as trustee as long as they are alive. When they die, a successor trustee must be ready to take over. Some parents choose a bank to serve as trustee, but banks are expensive and do not keep track of the disabled person's individual needs. A responsible family member is usually a better choice, if one can be found.

1239. What is a pooled Special Needs Trust (SNT)?

This type of trust is commonly referred to as a (d)(4)(C) trust, after the code section that authorized it. Anyone can put money into a pooled trust, including parents, grandparents, or even the individual with a disability. The pooled trust has no age restrictions.

There are four major requirements to establish a Pooled Trust:

- The trust must be established and managed through a nonprofit association.

- The trust must maintain separated accounts for beneficiary, but can pool the funds for management and investment.

- Each trust account must be established SOLELY for the benefit of an individual who meets the definition of being "disabled" under the law. The Pooled SNT must be established either by the disabled individual, their parent, their grandparent, their legal guardian or the court.

- Any funds remaining at the death of the beneficiary must be retained by the pooled trust to help or used to reimburse Medicaid.

The cash is kept in a bank, but the nonprofit owns all the deeds to houses and other real estate, as trustee. Banks do not want to own real estate in trust because they are afraid of environmental problems.

A pooled trust can purchase a home for the beneficiary and rent it to him. Before the pooled trust is set up, the parents and other family members explain what they want the trust to pay for, and who should be consulted about these matters.

1240. What is a court-ordered Special Needs Trust (SNT)?

A court-ordered trust, also called a Type "A" special needs trust, is used only for special circumstances, such as where the person with a disability has inherited money, or received a court settlement.

Because the disabled person actually owns the money, the funds cannot be put into the usual Special Needs Trust such as parents usually set up.

The "A" comes from the last letter of the federal statute, 42 U.S.C. §1396p(d)(4)(A).

Only certain people are allowed to set up this type of trust:

- One or both of the disabled person's parent

- The disabled person's grandparent(s)

- The legal guardian of the disabled person

- A court of competent jurisdiction

To qualify, the disabled person must be under sixty-five years old and meet the disability standards of Social Security. Someone who is not disabled enough to qualify for Social Security cannot have this type of trust.

The trust must specify that after the disabled person has died, anything left over will pay back the state for whatever medical assistance the government provided to the individual after the trust was set up. As a practical matter, that means that any unspent money will go to the government. It is unlikely that after Medicaid is paid back, anything will be left over.

1241. Should a Special Needs Trust (SNT) be set up during the grantor's life or as part of the grantor's will?

Generally, it is better to set up a Special Needs Trust (SNT) during the lifetime of the grantor. The advantage is that if other family members or friends of the disabled beneficiary wish to provide for the disabled beneficiary they may contribute to the already existing SNT. Another advantage is that if a person is chosen to be a successor trustee this person can gain experience as a trustee by acting as a cotrustee. Also, a trust created during the grantor's lifetime can be a "standby" trust that remains unfunded until the death of the grantor. Then the will or another trust of the grantor can simply add funds to the SNT at the grantor's death.

Another reason to create an SNT during the grantor's lifetime is that life insurance policies and retirement accounts can name the SNT as beneficiary of these policies or accounts more easily.

1242. What is the future of Special Needs Trusts (SNT)?

A number of states are imposing restrictions on distributions from SNTs. Most of these restrictions have been on self-settled trusts. But some states are also restricting third-party trust distributions.

There have been numerous court cases challenging these state-imposed restrictions. Decisions have been made which have both upheld the restrictions and struck them down. Because of these different results, it is very important for individuals to seek legal advice when setting up SNTs.

The Special Needs Trust Fairness and Medicaid Improvement Act was introduced before Congress by Congressman Glenn Thompson, Republican of Pennsylvania. It was approved by the House and Senate and on December 20, 2016, President Obama signed into law the Special Needs Trust Fairness Act as part of the 21st Century Cures Act. The new act allows individuals who are mentally capable to independently establish their own special needs trusts (also known as self-settled special needs trusts).

Estate Recoveries

1243. Can a state recover nursing home and long-term care Medicaid expenses from the estate of a deceased Medicaid recipient?

States are required to recover the costs of nursing facility and other long-term care services furnished to a Medicaid beneficiary from the estate of the beneficiary unless undue hardship would result. The estate may include any real or personal property or other assets in which the beneficiary had any legal title or interest at the time of death, including the home. Different estate recovery provisions apply to individuals who purchase specified long-term care insurance policies in designated states.

According to the Centers for Medicare & Medicaid Services (CMS), "undue hardship" might exist when the estate subject to recovery is the sole income-producing asset of the survivors and the income is limited or is a homestead of modest value.

It is possible that a state may conclude that an undue hardship does not exist if the individual created the hardship by resorting to estate planning methods under which the individual divested assets in order to avoid estate recovery. A state may adopt a rebuttable presumption that, if the individual obtained estate planning advice from legal counsel and followed this advice, the resulting financial situation would not qualify for an undue-hardship waiver.

The estate-recovery rules apply only to the estates of Medicaid beneficiaries dying on or after October 1, 1993, only to benefits paid on or after that date, and only for costs for a Medicaid recipient who was age fifty-five or older at the time the costs were incurred. Recovery of Medicaid costs cannot take place while the surviving spouse lives.

Discrimination

1244. Does federal law require that Medicaid patients be admitted to any (and all) nursing homes?

There is no requirement that nursing homes participate in Medicaid. Nursing homes receive reimbursement for Medicaid patients but it is usually much lower than the rates nursing homes charge private-pay patients (those who use their own funds, insurance benefits, or a combination of the two). Most nursing homes participate in Medicaid, but the level of participation can vary. A nursing home can make all of its beds Medicaid beds, or it can have some Medicaid beds and some private-pay beds.

If a patient in a nursing home starts out paying privately, uses up all excess resources, and becomes eligible for Medicaid, the nursing home is prohibited by federal law from evicting the patient because the method of payment has changed from private payment to Medicaid. The patient can be evicted if he cannot pay the nursing home and is also ineligible for Medicaid.

The nursing home contract defines the rights and responsibilities of the nursing home and patient. There are limitations on certain contract provisions that affect Medicaid patients:

(1)   A nursing home contract may not force the patient to give up the right to receive Medicare or Medicaid. A nursing home must counsel patients about the availability of these benefits.

(2)   A nursing home contract may not force a relative or friend of the patient to guarantee payments in order to get the patient into the nursing home. A nursing home can require a person in charge of a potential resident's funds to commit those funds to the payment of nursing home bills.

(3)   A nursing home cannot require a person or a person's family to pay more than the Medicaid rate in order to have a Medicaid-eligible person admitted to the nursing home.

Managed Care

1245. How has managed care changed the original Medicaid program?

A significant change to the original Medicaid program is the managed-care concept. Under managed-care systems, Health Maintenance Organizations (HMOs), Prepaid Health Plans (PHPs), or comparable entities agree to provide a specific set of services to Medicaid enrollees in return for fixed periodic payments for each enrollee. Managed-care programs seek to enhance access to quality care in a cost-effective manner. However, there are complexities in this, and waivers of certain parts of the Social Security Act are required. These waivers provide states with greater flexibility in the design and implementation of their Medicaid programs.

Section 1915(b) of the Social Security Act allows states to develop innovative health care delivery or reimbursement systems. Section 1115 of the Social Security Act allows statewide health care reform demonstrations for testing various methods of covering uninsured populations, and testing new delivery systems, without increasing costs.

Medicaid managed-care programs are growing rapidly and several states have converted their entire Medicaid programs into managed care. Over 17.6 million Medicaid recipients are enrolled in Medicaid managed-care programs – which is more than 50 percent of all Medicaid enrollees.

States can restrict choice by offering a choice between at least two managed-care organizations or Primary Care Case Managers (PCCMs), or at least one plan and one PCCM. States must permit individuals to change their enrollment for cause at any time, without cause within ninety days of notification of enrollment, and without cause at least every twelve months thereafter.

States may provide up to six months minimum enrollment that covers all managed-care entities.

There is protection for Medicaid beneficiaries in managed care, including:

(1)   assuring coverage of emergency services;

(2)   protection of enrollee-provider communications;

(3)   grievance procedures;

(4)   demonstration of adequate capacity and services;

(5)   protecting enrollees against liability for payment; and

(6)   antidiscrimination.

APPENDICES

APPENDICES

APPENDIX A
SOCIAL SECURITY TABLES

TABLE 1 — BENEFITS AS PERCENTAGE OF PIA

RETIREMENT BENEFIT
  Starting at Normal Retirement Age (NRA)
    (gradually rising from 65 to 67)......................................PIA
  Starting age 62 or above (but below NRA) ....PIA reduced

DISABILITY BENEFIT...PIA

SPOUSE'S BENEFIT (husband or wife of retired or disabled worker)
  Caring for child (under 16 or disabled) ....50% of PIA
  Starting at NRA (gradually rising from 65 to 67).....................50% of PIA
  Starting age 62 or above (but below NRA) ....50% of PIA reduced

CHILD'S BENEFIT
  Child of retired or disabled worker ....50% of PIA
  Child of deceased worker ....75% of PIA

MOTHER'S OR FATHER'S BENEFIT (widow(er)
  caring for child under 16 or disabled) ....75% of PIA

WIDOW(ER)'S BENEFIT (widow(er) not caring for child)
  Starting at NRA (gradually rising from 65 to 67).....................100% of PIA
  Starting age 60 or above (but below NRA) ....100% of PIA reduced

DISABLED WIDOW(ER)'S BENEFIT
  Starting age 50-60...71½% of PIA

PARENT'S BENEFIT (dependent parent of deceased worker)
  One dependent parent ....82½% of PIA
  Two dependent parents ....75% of PIA (each)

TABLE 2
QUARTERS OF COVERAGE REQUIRED TO BE FULLY INSURED FOR RETIREMENT BENEFITS

Birth Year	Men	Women
1892 or earlier	6	6
1893	7	6
1894	8	6
1895	9	6
1896	10	7
1897	11	8
1898	12	9
1899	13	10
1900	14	11
1901	15	12
1902	16	13
1903	17	14
1904	18	15
1905	19	16
1906	20	17
1907	21	18
1908	22	19
1909	23	20
1910	24	21
1911	24	22
1912	24	23
1913	24	24
1914	25	25
1915	26	26
1916	27	27
1917	28	28
1918	29	29
1919	30	30
1920	31	31
1921	32	32
1922	33	33
1923	34	34
1924	35	35
1925	36	36
1926	37	37
1927	38	38
1928	39	39
1929 or after	40	40

TABLE 3
MINIMUM NUMBER OF QUARTERS OF COVERAGE NEEDED TO BE FULLY INSURED AT DEATH

Birth Year	2018	2019
1955 or before	40	40
1956	39	40
1957	38	39
1958	37	38
1959	36	37
1960	35	36
1961	34	35
1962	33	34
1963	32	33
1964	31	32
1965	30	31
1966	29	30
1967	28	29
1968	27	28
1969	26	27
1970	25	26
1971	24	25
1972	23	24
1973	22	23
1974	21	22
1975	20	21
1976	19	20
1977	18	19
1978	17	18
1978	16	17
1980	15	16
1981	14	15
1982	13	14

TABLE 4
YEARS IN WHICH PERSON REACHES AGE 21

Birth Year	Year Person Reaches Age 21
1938	1959
1939	1960
1940	1961
1941	1962
1942	1963
1943	1964
1944	1965
1945	1966
1946	1967
1947	1968
1948	1969
1949	1970
1950	1971
1951	1972
1952	1973
1953	1974
1954	1975
1955	1976
1956	1977
1957	1978
1958	1979
1959	1980
1960	1981
1961	1982
1962	1983
1963	1984
1964	1985
1965	1986
1966	1987
1967	1988
1968	1989
1969	1990
1970	1991
1971	1992
1972	1993
1973	1994
1974	1995
1975	1996
1976	1997
1977	1998
1978	1999
1979	2000
1980	2001
1981	2002
1982	2003
1983	2004
1984	2005
1985	2006
1986	2007
1987	2008
1988	2009
1989	2010
1990	2011
1991	2012
1992	2013
1993	2014
1994	2015
1995	2016
1996	2017
1997	2018
1998	2019
1999	2020
2000	2021
2001	2022

TABLE 5
NUMBER OF YEARS EARNINGS THAT MUST BE USED IN COMPUTING RETIREMENT BENEFITS
(less if person had an established period of disability)

Birth Year	Computation Age	Year of Computation	No. of Years	No. of Divisor Months
1915	62	1977	21	252
1916	62	1978	22	264
1917	62	1979	23	276
1918	62	1980	24	288
1919	62	1981	25	300
1920	62	1982	26	312
1921	62	1983	27	324
1922	62	1984	28	336
1923	62	1985	29	348
1924	62	1986	30	360
1925	62	1987	31	372
1926	62	1988	32	384
1927	62	1989	33	396
1928	62	1990	34	408
1929	62	1991	35	420
1930 or later	62	1992 or later	35	420

TABLE 6 — INSURED STATUS NEEDED FOR SOCIAL SECURITY BENEFITS

The worker must be FULLY insured to provide monthly benefits for:

... Retired worker (at age 62 or over)
... Spouse of retired worker (at age 62 or over)
... Spouse of retired worker (at any age if caring for a child)
... Child of retired worker
... Widow(er) of worker (at age 60 or over)
... Disabled widow(er) of worker (at age 50 or over)
... Dependent parent of deceased worker

The worker may be either FULLY or CURRENTLY insured to provide monthly benefits for:

... Child of deceased worker
... Widow(er) of worker (at any age if caring for child)

A disabled worker must be FULLY insured and (a) if disability began at or after age 31, must have worked in covered employment 5 out of the last 10 years, or (b) if disability began before age 31, must have worked in covered employment ½ of the quarters between age 21 and onset of disability (but not less than 6), to provide benefits for:

... Disabled worker (at any age)
... Child of disabled worker
... Spouse of disabled worker (at age 62 or over)
... Spouse of disabled worker (at any age if caring for a child)

A worker who is either FULLY or CURRENTLY insured qualified for the lump-sum death benefit if he is survived by (1) a spouse who was living with him at the time of his death, or (2) a dependent child or spouse eligible to receive social security benefits based on his earnings record.

TABLE 7 — MAXIMUM AIME FOR RETIREMENT, SURVIVOR, AND DISABILITY BENEFITS*
(for workers earning $132,900 or more in 2019)

Year of Birth	Normal Retirement Age	Death in 2019	Disability in 2019	Year of Birth	Normal Retirement Age	Death in 2019	Disability in 2019
1957	10,093	9,768	9,589	1976	10,836	10,525	10,239
1958	10,174	9,856	9,666	1977	10,857	10,548	10,258
1959	10,248	9,936	9,737	1978	10,876	10,562	10,275
1960	10,309	10,063	9,794	1979	10,893	10,565	10,291
1961	10,359	10,123	9,843	1980	10,912	10,614	10,310
1962	10,394	10,182	9,875	1981	10,928	10,647	10,324
1963	10,425	10,227	9,905	1982	10,907	10,589	10,305
1964	10,451	10,272	9,930	1983	10,936	10,581	10,332
1965	10,484	10,289	9,961	1984	10,955	10,609	10,351
1966	10,485	10,306	9,962	1985	10,962	10,635	10,357
1967	10,561	10,321	10,035	1986	10,969	10,694	10,363
1968	10,584	10,341	10,056	1987	10,969	10,723	10,363
1969	10,609	10,356	10,079	1988	10,969	10,876	10,363
1970	10,635	10,369	10,104	1989	10,969	10,875	10,363
1971	10,659	10,389	10,127	1990	10,969	10,958	10,363
1972	10,676	10,399	10,144	1991	10,969	10,958	10,363
1973	10,700	10,430	10,166	1992	10,969	10,958	10,363
1974	10,717	10,497	10,183	1993	10,969	10,958	10,363
1975	10,739	10,457	10,204	1994	10,969	10,958	10,363

*   Normal Retirement Age for unreduced benefits (PIA) increases by two months a year for workers reaching age 62 in 2000-2005; maintains age 66 for workers reaching age 62 in 2006-2016; increases by two months a year for workers reaching age 62 in 2017-2022; and maintains age 67 for workers reaching age 62 after 2022.

*   AIME calculations assume that the worker earned the Social Security maximum earnings base in all years up to an including, respectively, the year before normal retirement ($132,900 is used for 2019 and later years), the year of death, the year before disability.

APPENDIX A

TABLE 8 — AIME FOR WORKERS EARNING $7,000-$62,200 IN 2019*

Year Born	AIME	Current Annual Earnings					
		$7,000-16,200	$16,200-25,400	$25,400-34,600	$34,600-43,800	$43,800-53,000	$53,000-62,200
1957	Retirement	750	1,338	1,925	2,514	3,104	3,692
	Death	715	1,273	1,833	2,395	2,955	3,514
	Disability	700	1,253	1,804	2,354	2,906	3,454
1958-1962	Retirement	781	1,393	2,005	2,618	3,230	3,843
	Death	719	1,284	1,848	2,412	2,979	3,541
	Disability	707	1,260	1,815	2,366	2,922	3,476
1963-1967	Retirement	834	1,489	2,145	2,800	3,455	4,111
	Death	733	1,317	1,889	2,465	3,043	3,620
	Disability	719	1,284	1,848	2,412	2,978	3,541
1968-1972	Retirement	903	1,609	2,320	3,025	3,734	4,441
	Death	766	1,366	1,968	2,567	3,169	3,768
	Disability	746	1,334	1,918	2,505	3,089	3,678
1973 - 1977	Retirement	947	1,689	2,433	3,176	3,918	4,662
	Death	802	1,433	2,065	2,694	3,325	3,956
	Disability	775	1,382	1,994	2,600	3,210	3,817
1978-1982	Retirement	985	1,758	2,531	3,306	4,079	4,852
	Death	842	1,502	2,162	2,821	3,484	4,141
	Disability	802	1,433	2,064	2,694	3,323	3,952
1983-1987	Retirement	1,008	1,803	2,594	3,386	4,178	4,969
	Death	910	1,602	2,305	3,011	3,714	4,419
	Disability	835	1,494	2,148	2,803	3,460	4,118
1988-1992	Retirement	1,015	1,811	2,605	3,403	4,200	4,996
	Death	985	1,759	2,532	3,306	4,080	4,857
	Disability	879	1,567	2,255	2,944	3,634	4,322

* AIMEs are approximate and based on the assumption that the worker has had 6% pay raises each year through 2019. AIME calculations for retirement assume that the worker's current earnings stay the same until Normal Retirement Age. Match AIMEs with AIMEs closest to them in Tables 10, 11, and 12 to determine benefits.

TABLE 9 — AIME FOR WORKERS EARNING $62,200-$132,900 IN 2019*

Year Born	AIME	Current Annual Earnings					
		$62,200-71,400	$71,400-80,600	$80,600-89,800	$89,800-99,000	$99,000-108,200	$108,200-132,900
1957	Retirement	4,282	4,868	5,455	6,015	6,588	7,161
	Death	4,077	4,637	5,196	5,724	6,260	6,798
	Disability	4,009	4,558	5,107	5,624	6,147	6,678
1958-1962	Retirement	4,458	5,069	5,684	6,296	6,905	7,510
	Death	4,110	4,672	5,237	5,803	6,366	6,916
	Disability	4,032	4,587	5,141	5,694	6,249	6,785
1963-1967	Retirement	4,768	5,422	6,080	6,732	7,390	8,047
	Death	4,202	4,777	5,354	5,932	6,509	7,086
	Disability	4,109	4,672	5,237	5,802	6,370	6,932
1968-19721	Retirement	5,153	5,860	6,571	7,280	7,985	8,696
	Death	4,372	4,973	5,576	6,177	6,777	7,377
	Disability	4,265	4,851	5,437	6,024	6,611	7,197
1973 - 1977	Retirement	5,410	6,151	6,895	7,638	8,382	9,125
	Death	4,589	5,220	5,849	6,481	7,109	7,743
	Disability	4,429	5,038	5,647	6,256	6,863	7,473
1978-1982	Retirement	5,628	6,404	7,176	7,948	8,722	9,499
	Death	4,807	5,468	6,129	6,790	7,450	8,109
	Disability	4,585	5,216	5,845	6,477	7,106	7,737
1983-1987	Retirement	5,766	6,559	7,352	8,145	8,938	9,731
	Death	5,124	5,832	6,536	7,241	7,945	8,649
	Disability	4,775	5,431	6,088	6,745	7,399	8,057
1988-1992	Retirement	5,795	6,590	7,387	8,186	8,981	9,778
	Death	5,630	6,406	7,179	7,951	8,724	9,500
	Disability	5,015	5,701	6,392	7,084	7,772	8,460

* AIMEs are approximate and based on the assumption that the worker has had 6% pay raises each year through 2019. AIME calculations for retirement assume that the worker's current earnings stay the same until Normal Retirement Age. Match AIMEs with AIMEs closest to them in Tables 10, 11, and 12 to determine benefits.

TABLE 10 — WORKER'S AND SPOUSE'S RETIREMENT BENEFITS*

Average Indexed Monthly Earnings	Worker FRA (PIA)	Spouse FRA	Total FRA Benefit	Worker FRA - 3**	Spouse FRA - 3	Total FRA – 3 Benefit	Worker FRA and Spouse FRA-3
$9,700	2,912	1,456	4,368	2,330	1,165	3,471	4,077
$9,675	2,908	1,454	4,362	2,327	1,163	3,466	4,071
$9,650	2,904	1,452	4,356	2,323	1,162	3,462	4,066
$9,625	2,900	1,450	4,350	2,320	1,160	3,457	4,060
$9,600	2,897	1,449	4,346	2,318	1,159	3,453	4,056
$9,575	2,893	1,447	4,340	2,314	1,157	3,448	4,050
$9,550	2,889	1,445	4,334	2,311	1,156	3,444	4,045
$9,525	2,885	1,442	4,327	2,308	1,154	3,439	4,039
$9,500	2,882	1,441	4,323	2,306	1,153	3,435	4,035
$9,475	2,878	1,439	4,317	2,302	1,151	3,430	4,029
$9,450	2,874	1,437	4,311	2,299	1,150	3,426	4,023
$9,425	2,870	1,435	4,305	2,296	1,148	3,421	4,018
$9,400	2,867	1,433	4,300	2,293	1,147	3,417	4,014
$9,375	2,863	1,431	4,294	2,290	1,145	3,412	4,008
$9,350	2,859	1,429	4,288	2,287	1,144	3,408	4,002
$9,325	2,855	1,427	4,282	2,284	1,142	3,403	3,997
$9,300	2,852	1,426	4,278	2,281	1,141	3,399	3,992
$9,275	2,848	1,424	4,272	2,278	1,139	3,394	3,987
$9,250	2,844	1,422	4,266	2,275	1,137	3,390	3,981
$9,225	2,840	1,420	4,260	2,272	1,136	3,385	3,976
$9,200	2,837	1,418	4,255	2,269	1,135	3,381	3,971
$9,175	2,833	1,416	4,249	2,266	1,133	3,376	3,966
$9,150	2,829	1,414	4,243	2,263	1,131	3,372	3,960
$9,125	2,825	1,412	4,237	2,260	1,130	3,367	3,954
$9,100	2,822	1,411	4,232	2,257	1,129	3,363	3,950
$9,075	2,818	1,409	4,226	2,254	1,127	3,358	3,945
$9,050	2,814	1,407	4,220	2,251	1,125	3,354	3,939
$9,025	2,809	1,405	4,214	2,248	1,124	3,349	3,933
$9,000	2,806	1,403	4,210	2,245	1,123	3,345	3,929
$8,975	2,802	1,401	4,204	2,242	1,121	3,340	3,923
$8,950	2,798	1,399	4,198	2,239	1,119	3,336	3,918
$8,925	2,794	1,397	4,192	2,236	1,118	3,331	3,912
$8,900	2,791	1,396	4,187	2,233	1,117	3,327	3,908
$8,875	2,787	1,394	4,181	2,230	1,115	3,322	3,902
$8,850	2,783	1,392	4,175	2,227	1,113	3,318	3,897
$8,825	2,779	1,390	4,169	2,223	1,112	3,313	3,891
$8,800	2,776	1,388	4,164	2,221	1,111	3,309	3,887
$8,775	2,772	1,386	4,158	2,218	1,109	3,304	3,881
$8,750	2,768	1,384	4,152	2,215	1,107	3,300	3,876
$8,725	2,764	1,382	4,146	2,211	1,106	3,295	3,870
$8,700	2,761	1,381	4,142	2,209	1,104	3,291	3,866
$8,675	2,757	1,379	4,136	2,206	1,103	3,286	3,860
$8,650	2,753	1,377	4,130	2,202	1,101	3,282	3,854
$8,625	2,749	1,375	4,124	2,199	1,100	3,277	3,849
$8,600	2,746	1,373	4,119	2,197	1,098	3,273	3,845
$8,575	2,742	1,371	4,113	2,194	1,097	3,268	3,839
$8,550	2,738	1,369	4,107	2,190	1,095	3,264	3,833
$8,525	2,734	1,367	4,101	2,187	1,094	3,259	3,828
$8,500	2,731	1,365	4,096	2,185	1,092	3,255	3,823
$8,475	2,727	1,363	4,090	2,182	1,091	3,250	3,818
$8,450	2,723	1,361	4,084	2,178	1,089	3,246	3,812
$8,425	2,719	1,359	4,078	2,175	1,088	3,241	3,806

TABLE 10 — WORKER'S AND SPOUSE'S RETIREMENT BENEFITS* (cont'd)

Average Indexed Monthly Earnings	Worker FRA (PIA)	Spouse FRA	Total FRA Benefit	Worker FRA – 3**	Spouse FRA – 3	Total FRA – 3 Benefit	Worker FRA and Spouse FRA-3
$8,400	2,716	1,358	4,074	2,173	1,086	3,237	3,802
$8,375	2,712	1,356	4,068	2,169	1,085	3,232	3,797
$8,350	2,708	1,354	4,062	2,166	1,083	3,228	3,791
$8,325	2,704	1,352	4,056	2,163	1,082	3,223	3,785
$8,300	2,701	1,350	4,051	2,161	1,080	3,219	3,781
$8,275	2,697	1,348	4,045	2,157	1,079	3,214	3,775
$8,250	2,693	1,346	4,039	2,154	1,077	3,210	3,770
$8,225	2,689	1,344	4,033	2,151	1,075	3,205	3,764
$8,200	2,686	1,343	4,029	2,149	1,074	3,201	3,760
$8,175	2,682	1,341	4,022	2,145	1,073	3,196	3,754
$8,150	2,678	1,339	4,016	2,142	1,071	3,192	3,749
$8,125	2,674	1,337	4,010	2,139	1,069	3,187	3,743
$8,100	2,671	1,335	4,006	2,136	1,068	3,183	3,739
$8,075	2,667	1,333	4,000	2,133	1,067	3,178	3,733
$8,050	2,663	1,331	3,994	2,130	1,065	3,174	3,728
$8,025	2,658	1,329	3,988	2,127	1,063	3,169	3,722
$8,000	2,655	1,328	3,983	2,124	1,062	3,165	3,718
$7,975	2,651	1,326	3,977	2,121	1,061	3,160	3,712
$7,950	2,647	1,324	3,971	2,118	1,059	3,156	3,706
$7,925	2,643	1,322	3,965	2,115	1,057	3,151	3,701
$7,900	2,640	1,320	3,961	2,112	1,056	3,147	3,697
$7,875	2,636	1,318	3,955	2,109	1,055	3,142	3,691
$7,850	2,632	1,316	3,948	2,106	1,053	3,138	3,685
$7,825	2,628	1,314	3,942	2,103	1,051	3,133	3,680
$7,800	2,625	1,313	3,938	2,100	1,050	3,129	3,675
$7,775	2,621	1,311	3,932	2,097	1,049	3,124	3,670
$7,750	2,617	1,309	3,926	2,094	1,047	3,120	3,664
$7,725	2,613	1,307	3,920	2,091	1,045	3,115	3,658
$7,700	2,610	1,305	3,915	2,088	1,044	3,111	3,654
$7,675	2,606	1,303	3,909	2,085	1,042	3,106	3,649
$7,650	2,602	1,301	3,903	2,082	1,041	3,102	3,643
$7,625	2,598	1,299	3,897	2,078	1,039	3,097	3,637
$7,600	2,595	1,298	3,893	2,076	1,038	3,093	3,633
$7,575	2,591	1,296	3,887	2,073	1,036	3,088	3,627
$7,550	2,587	1,294	3,881	2,070	1,035	3,084	3,622
$7,525	2,583	1,292	3,875	2,066	1,033	3,079	3,616
$7,500	2,580	1,290	3,870	2,064	1,032	3,075	3,612
$7,475	2,576	1,288	3,864	2,061	1,030	3,070	3,606
$7,450	2,572	1,286	3,858	2,058	1,029	3,066	3,601
$7,425	2,568	1,284	3,852	2,054	1,027	3,061	3,595
$7,400	2,565	1,282	3,847	2,052	1,026	3,057	3,591
$7,375	2,561	1,280	3,841	2,049	1,024	3,052	3,585
$7,350	2,557	1,278	3,835	2,045	1,023	3,048	3,580
$7,325	2,553	1,276	3,829	2,042	1,021	3,043	3,574
$7,300	2,550	1,275	3,825	2,040	1,020	3,039	3,570
$7,275	2,546	1,273	3,819	2,037	1,018	3,034	3,564
$7,250	2,542	1,271	3,813	2,033	1,017	3,030	3,558
$7,225	2,538	1,269	3,807	2,030	1,015	3,025	3,553
$7,200	2,535	1,267	3,802	2,028	1,014	3,021	3,549
$7,175	2,531	1,265	3,796	2,025	1,012	3,016	3,543
$7,150	2,527	1,263	3,790	2,021	1,011	3,012	3,537
$7,125	2,523	1,261	3,784	2,018	1,009	3,007	3,532

TABLE 10 — WORKER'S AND SPOUSE'S RETIREMENT BENEFITS* (cont'd)

Average Indexed Monthly Earnings	Worker FRA (PIA)	Spouse FRA	Total FRA Benefit	Worker FRA – 3**	Spouse FRA – 3	Total FRA – 3 Benefit	Worker FRA and Spouse FRA–3
$7,100	2,520	1,260	3,779	2,016	1,008	3,003	3,527
$7,075	2,516	1,258	3,773	2,012	1,006	2,998	3,522
$7,050	2,512	1,256	3,767	2,009	1,005	2,994	3,516
$7,025	2,508	1,254	3,761	2,006	1,003	2,989	3,511
$7,000	2,504	1,252	3,757	2,004	1,002	2,985	3,506
$6,975	2,500	1,250	3,751	2,000	1,000	2,980	3,501
$6,950	2,496	1,248	3,745	1,997	999	2,976	3,495
$6,925	2,492	1,246	3,739	1,994	997	2,971	3,489
$6,900	2,489	1,245	3,734	1,992	996	2,967	3,485
$6,875	2,485	1,243	3,728	1,988	994	2,962	3,480
$6,850	2,481	1,241	3,722	1,985	993	2,958	3,474
$6,825	2,477	1,239	3,716	1,982	991	2,953	3,468
$6,800	2,474	1,237	3,711	1,979	990	2,949	3,464
$6,775	2,470	1,235	3,705	1,976	988	2,944	3,458
$6,750	2,466	1,233	3,699	1,973	986	2,940	3,453
$6,725	2,462	1,231	3,693	1,970	985	2,935	3,447
$6,700	2,459	1,230	3,689	1,967	984	2,931	3,443
$6,675	2,455	1,228	3,683	1,964	982	2,926	3,437
$6,650	2,451	1,226	3,677	1,961	980	2,922	3,432
$6,625	2,447	1,224	3,671	1,958	979	2,917	3,426
$6,600	2,444	1,222	3,666	1,955	978	2,913	3,422
$6,575	2,440	1,220	3,660	1,952	976	2,908	3,416
$6,550	2,436	1,218	3,654	1,949	974	2,904	3,410
$6,525	2,432	1,216	3,648	1,946	973	2,899	3,405
$6,500	2,429	1,214	3,643	1,943	972	2,895	3,401
$6,475	2,425	1,212	3,637	1,940	970	2,890	3,395
$6,450	2,421	1,210	3,631	1,937	968	2,886	3,389
$6,425	2,417	1,208	3,625	1,934	967	2,881	3,384
$6,400	2,414	1,207	3,621	1,931	966	2,877	3,379
$6,375	2,410	1,205	3,615	1,928	964	2,872	3,374
$6,350	2,406	1,203	3,609	1,925	962	2,868	3,368
$6,325	2,402	1,201	3,603	1,921	961	2,863	3,363
$6,300	2,399	1,199	3,598	1,919	960	2,859	3,358
$6,275	2,395	1,197	3,592	1,916	958	2,854	3,353
$6,250	2,391	1,195	3,586	1,913	956	2,850	3,347
$6,225	2,387	1,193	3,580	1,909	955	2,845	3,341
$6,200	2,384	1,192	3,576	1,907	953	2,841	3,337
$6,175	2,380	1,190	3,569	1,904	952	2,836	3,332
$6,150	2,376	1,188	3,563	1,901	950	2,832	3,326
$6,125	2,372	1,186	3,557	1,897	949	2,827	3,320
$6,100	2,369	1,184	3,553	1,895	947	2,823	3,316
$6,075	2,365	1,182	3,547	1,892	946	2,818	3,310
$6,050	2,361	1,180	3,541	1,888	944	2,814	3,305
$6,025	2,357	1,178	3,535	1,885	943	2,809	3,299
$6,000	2,353	1,177	3,530	1,883	941	2,805	3,295
$5,975	2,349	1,175	3,524	1,880	940	2,800	3,289
$5,950	2,345	1,173	3,518	1,876	938	2,796	3,284
$5,925	2,341	1,171	3,512	1,873	937	2,791	3,278
$5,900	2,338	1,169	3,508	1,871	935	2,787	3,274
$5,875	2,334	1,167	3,502	1,867	934	2,782	3,268
$5,850	2,330	1,165	3,496	1,864	932	2,778	3,262
$5,825	2,326	1,163	3,489	1,861	931	2,773	3,257

TABLE 10 — WORKER'S AND SPOUSE'S RETIREMENT BENEFITS* (cont'd)

Average Indexed Monthly Earnings	Worker FRA (PIA)	Spouse FRA	Total FRA Benefit	Worker FRA – 3**	Spouse FRA – 3	Total FRA – 3 Benefit	Worker FRA and Spouse FRA–3
$5,800	2,323	1,162	3,485	1,859	929	2,769	3,253
$5,775	2,319	1,160	3,479	1,855	928	2,764	3,247
$5,750	2,315	1,158	3,473	1,852	926	2,760	3,241
$5,725	2,311	1,156	3,467	1,849	924	2,755	3,236
$5,700	2,308	1,154	3,462	1,847	923	2,751	3,231
$5,675	2,304	1,152	3,456	1,843	922	2,746	3,226
$5,650	2,300	1,150	3,450	1,840	920	2,742	3,220
$5,625	2,296	1,148	3,444	1,837	918	2,737	3,215
$5,600	2,293	1,147	3,440	1,834	917	2,733	3,210
$5,575	2,289	1,145	3,434	1,831	916	2,728	3,205
$5,550	2,285	1,143	3,428	1,828	914	2,724	3,199
$5,525	2,281	1,141	3,422	1,825	912	2,719	3,193
$5,500	2,278	1,139	3,417	1,822	911	2,715	3,189
$5,475	2,274	1,137	3,411	1,819	910	2,710	3,184
$5,450	2,270	1,135	3,405	1,816	908	2,706	3,178
$5,425	2,266	1,133	3,399	1,813	906	2,701	3,172
$5,400	2,263	1,131	3,394	1,810	905	2,697	3,168
$5,375	2,245	1,122	3,367	1,796	898	2,694	3,143
$5,350	2,237	1,118	3,355	1,789	895	2,684	3,131
$5,325	2,229	1,114	3,343	1,783	891	2,675	3,120
$5,300	2,221	1,110	3,331	1,776	888	2,665	3,109
$5,275	2,213	1,106	3,319	1,770	885	2,655	3,098
$5,250	2,205	1,102	3,307	1,764	882	2,646	3,086
$5,225	2,196	1,098	3,295	1,757	879	2,636	3,075
$5,200	2,188	1,094	3,283	1,751	875	2,626	3,064
$5,175	2,180	1,090	3,271	1,744	872	2,616	3,052
$5,150	2,172	1,086	3,258	1,738	869	2,607	3,041
$5,125	2,164	1,082	3,246	1,731	866	2,597	3,030
$5,100	2,156	1,078	3,234	1,725	862	2,587	3,019
$5,075	2,148	1,074	3,222	1,719	859	2,578	3,007
$5,050	2,140	1,070	3,210	1,712	856	2,568	2,996
$5,025	2,132	1,066	3,198	1,706	853	2,558	2,985
$5,000	2,124	1,062	3,186	1,699	850	2,549	2,974
$4,975	2,116	1,058	3,174	1,693	846	2,539	2,962
$4,950	2,108	1,054	3,162	1,686	843	2,529	2,951
$4,925	2,100	1,050	3,150	1,680	840	2,519	2,940
$4,900	2,092	1,046	3,138	1,673	837	2,510	2,928
$4,875	2,084	1,042	3,126	1,667	833	2,500	2,917
$4,850	2,076	1,038	3,113	1,661	830	2,490	2,906
$4,825	2,068	1,034	3,101	1,654	827	2,481	2,895
$4,800	2,060	1,030	3,089	1,648	824	2,471	2,883
$4,775	2,052	1,026	3,077	1,641	821	2,461	2,872
$4,750	2,043	1,022	3,065	1,635	817	2,452	2,861
$4,725	2,035	1,018	3,053	1,628	814	2,442	2,850
$4,700	2,027	1,014	3,041	1,622	811	2,432	2,838
$4,675	2,019	1,010	3,029	1,615	808	2,422	2,827
$4,650	2,011	1,006	3,017	1,609	804	2,413	2,816
$4,625	2,003	1,002	3,005	1,603	801	2,403	2,804
$4,600	1,995	998	2,993	1,596	798	2,393	2,793
$4,575	1,987	994	2,981	1,590	795	2,384	2,782
$4,550	1,979	990	2,969	1,583	792	2,374	2,771
$4,525	1,971	985	2,956	1,577	788	2,364	2,759

TABLE 10 — WORKER'S AND SPOUSE'S RETIREMENT BENEFITS* (cont'd)

Average Indexed Monthly Earnings	Worker FRA (PIA)	Spouse FRA	Total FRA Benefit	Worker FRA – 3**	Spouse FRA – 3	Total FRA – 3 Benefit	Worker FRA and Spouse FRA–3
$4,500	1,963	981	2,944	1,570	785	2,354	2,748
$4,475	1,955	977	2,932	1,564	782	2,345	2,737
$4,450	1,947	973	2,920	1,557	779	2,335	2,726
$4,425	1,939	969	2,908	1,551	776	2,325	2,714
$4,400	1,931	965	2,896	1,545	772	2,316	2,703
$4,375	1,923	961	2,884	1,538	769	2,306	2,692
$4,350	1,915	957	2,872	1,532	766	2,296	2,680
$4,325	1,907	953	2,860	1,525	763	2,287	2,669
$4,300	1,898	949	2,848	1,519	759	2,277	2,658
$4,275	1,890	945	2,836	1,512	756	2,267	2,647
$4,250	1,882	941	2,824	1,506	753	2,257	2,635
$4,225	1,874	937	2,812	1,499	750	2,248	2,624
$4,200	1,866	933	2,799	1,493	747	2,238	2,613
$4,175	1,858	929	2,787	1,487	743	2,228	2,602
$4,150	1,850	925	2,775	1,480	740	2,219	2,590
$4,125	1,842	921	2,763	1,474	737	2,209	2,579
$4,100	1,834	917	2,751	1,467	734	2,199	2,568
$4,075	1,826	913	2,739	1,461	730	2,190	2,556
$4,050	1,818	909	2,727	1,454	727	2,180	2,545
$4,025	1,810	905	2,715	1,448	724	2,170	2,534
$4,000	1,802	901	2,703	1,441	721	2,160	2,523
$3,975	1,794	897	2,691	1,435	718	2,151	2,511
$3,950	1,786	893	2,679	1,429	714	2,141	2,500
$3,925	1,778	889	2,667	1,422	711	2,131	2,489
$3,900	1,770	885	2,654	1,416	708	2,122	2,478
$3,875	1,762	881	2,642	1,409	705	2,112	2,466
$3,850	1,754	877	2,630	1,403	701	2,102	2,455
$3,825	1,745	873	2,618	1,396	698	2,092	2,444
$3,800	1,737	869	2,606	1,390	695	2,083	2,432
$3,775	1,729	865	2,594	1,384	692	2,073	2,421
$3,750	1,721	861	2,582	1,377	689	2,063	2,410
$3,725	1,713	857	2,570	1,371	685	2,054	2,399
$3,700	1,705	853	2,558	1,364	682	2,044	2,387
$3,675	1,697	849	2,546	1,358	679	2,034	2,376
$3,650	1,689	845	2,534	1,351	676	2,025	2,365
$3,625	1,681	841	2,522	1,345	672	2,015	2,353
$3,600	1,673	837	2,510	1,338	669	2,005	2,342
$3,575	1,665	832	2,497	1,332	666	1,995	2,331
$3,550	1,657	828	2,485	1,326	663	1,986	2,320
$3,525	1,649	824	2,473	1,319	660	1,976	2,308
$3,500	1,641	820	2,461	1,313	656	1,966	2,297
$3,475	1,633	816	2,449	1,306	653	1,957	2,286
$3,450	1,625	812	2,437	1,300	650	1,947	2,275
$3,425	1,617	808	2,425	1,293	647	1,937	2,263
$3,400	1,609	804	2,413	1,287	643	1,928	2,252
$3,375	1,601	800	2,401	1,280	640	1,918	2,241
$3,350	1,592	796	2,389	1,274	637	1,908	2,229
$3,325	1,584	792	2,377	1,268	634	1,898	2,218
$3,300	1,576	788	2,365	1,261	631	1,889	2,207
$3,275	1,568	784	2,352	1,255	627	1,879	2,196
$3,250	1,560	780	2,340	1,248	624	1,869	2,184
$3,225	1,552	776	2,328	1,242	621	1,860	2,173

TABLE 10 — WORKER'S AND SPOUSE'S RETIREMENT BENEFITS* (cont'd)

Average Indexed Monthly Earnings	Worker FRA (PIA)	Spouse FRA	Total FRA Benefit	Worker FRA – 3**	Spouse FRA – 3	Total FRA – 3 Benefit	Worker FRA and Spouse FRA–3
$3,200	1,544	772	2,316	1,235	618	1,850	2,162
$3,175	1,536	768	2,304	1,229	614	1,840	2,151
$3,150	1,528	764	2,292	1,222	611	1,831	2,139
$3,125	1,520	760	2,280	1,216	608	1,821	2,128
$3,100	1,512	756	2,268	1,210	605	1,811	2,117
$3,075	1,504	752	2,256	1,203	602	1,801	2,105
$3,050	1,496	748	2,244	1,197	598	1,792	2,094
$3,025	1,488	744	2,232	1,190	595	1,782	2,083
$3,000	1,480	740	2,220	1,184	592	1,772	2,072
$2,975	1,472	736	2,208	1,177	589	1,763	2,060
$2,950	1,464	732	2,195	1,171	585	1,753	2,049
$2,925	1,456	728	2,183	1,164	582	1,743	2,038
$2,900	1,448	724	2,171	1,158	579	1,733	2,027
$2,875	1,439	720	2,159	1,152	576	1,724	2,015
$2,850	1,431	716	2,147	1,145	573	1,714	2,004
$2,825	1,423	712	2,135	1,139	569	1,704	1,993
$2,800	1,415	708	2,123	1,132	566	1,695	1,981
$2,775	1,407	704	2,111	1,126	563	1,685	1,970
$2,750	1,399	700	2,099	1,119	560	1,675	1,959
$2,725	1,391	696	2,087	1,113	556	1,666	1,948
$2,700	1,383	692	2,075	1,106	553	1,656	1,936
$2,675	1,375	688	2,063	1,100	550	1,646	1,925
$2,650	1,367	683	2,050	1,094	547	1,636	1,914
$2,625	1,359	679	2,038	1,087	544	1,627	1,903
$2,600	1,351	675	2,026	1,081	540	1,617	1,891
$2,575	1,343	671	2,014	1,074	537	1,607	1,880
$2,550	1,335	667	2,002	1,068	534	1,598	1,869
$2,525	1,327	663	1,990	1,061	531	1,588	1,857
$2,500	1,319	659	1,978	1,055	527	1,578	1,846
$2,475	1,311	655	1,966	1,049	524	1,569	1,835
$2,450	1,303	651	1,954	1,042	521	1,559	1,824
$2,425	1,295	647	1,942	1,036	518	1,549	1,812
$2,400	1,286	643	1,930	1,029	515	1,539	1,801
$2,375	1,278	639	1,918	1,023	511	1,530	1,790
$2,350	1,270	635	1,906	1,016	508	1,520	1,779
$2,325	1,262	631	1,893	1,010	505	1,510	1,767
$2,300	1,254	627	1,881	1,003	502	1,501	1,756
$2,275	1,246	623	1,869	997	498	1,491	1,745
$2,250	1,238	619	1,857	991	495	1,481	1,733
$2,225	1,230	615	1,845	984	492	1,471	1,722
$2,200	1,222	611	1,833	978	489	1,462	1,711
$2,175	1,214	607	1,821	971	486	1,452	1,700
$2,150	1,206	603	1,809	965	482	1,442	1,688
$2,125	1,198	599	1,797	958	479	1,433	1,677
$2,100	1,190	595	1,785	952	476	1,423	1,666
$2,075	1,182	591	1,773	945	473	1,413	1,654
$2,050	1,174	587	1,761	939	469	1,404	1,643
$2,025	1,166	583	1,749	933	466	1,394	1,632
$2,000	1,158	579	1,736	926	463	1,384	1,621
$1,975	1,150	575	1,724	920	460	1,374	1,609
$1,950	1,142	571	1,712	913	457	1,365	1,598
$1,925	1,133	567	1,700	907	453	1,355	1,587

TABLE 10 — WORKER'S AND SPOUSE'S RETIREMENT BENEFITS* (cont'd)

Average Indexed Monthly Earnings	Worker FRA (PIA)	Spouse FRA	Total FRA Benefit	Worker FRA – 3**	Spouse FRA – 3	Total FRA – 3 Benefit	Worker FRA and Spouse FRA–3
$1,900	1,125	563	1,688	900	450	1,345	1,576
$1,875	1,117	559	1,676	894	447	1,336	1,564
$1,850	1,109	555	1,664	887	444	1,326	1,553
$1,825	1,101	551	1,652	881	440	1,316	1,542
$1,800	1,093	547	1,640	875	437	1,307	1,530
$1,775	1,085	543	1,628	868	434	1,297	1,519
$1,750	1,077	539	1,616	862	431	1,287	1,508
$1,725	1,069	535	1,604	855	428	1,277	1,497
$1,700	1,061	530	1,591	849	424	1,268	1,485
$1,675	1,053	526	1,579	842	421	1,258	1,474
$1,650	1,045	522	1,567	836	418	1,248	1,463
$1,625	1,037	518	1,555	829	415	1,239	1,452
$1,600	1,029	514	1,543	823	412	1,229	1,440
$1,575	1,021	510	1,531	817	408	1,219	1,429
$1,550	1,013	506	1,519	810	405	1,209	1,418
$1,525	1,005	502	1,507	804	402	1,200	1,406
$1,500	997	498	1,495	797	399	1,190	1,395
$1,475	989	494	1,483	791	395	1,180	1,384
$1,450	980	490	1,471	784	392	1,171	1,373
$1,425	972	486	1,459	778	389	1,161	1,361
$1,400	964	482	1,447	771	386	1,151	1,350
$1,375	956	478	1,434	765	383	1,142	1,339
$1,350	948	474	1,422	759	379	1,132	1,328
$1,325	940	470	1,410	752	376	1,122	1,316
$1,300	932	466	1,398	746	373	1,112	1,305
$1,275	924	462	1,386	739	370	1,103	1,294
$1,250	916	458	1,374	733	366	1,093	1,282
$1,225	908	454	1,362	726	363	1,083	1,271
$1,200	900	450	1,350	720	360	1,074	1,260
$1,175	892	446	1,338	713	357	1,064	1,249
$1,150	884	442	1,326	707	354	1,054	1,237
$1,125	876	438	1,314	701	350	1,045	1,226
$1,100	868	434	1,302	694	347	1,035	1,215
$1,075	860	430	1,289	688	344	1,025	1,204
$1,050	852	426	1,277	681	341	1,015	1,192
$1,025	844	422	1,265	675	337	1,006	1,181
$1,000	835	418	1,253	668	334	996	1,170
$ 975	827	414	1,241	662	331	986	1,158
$ 950	819	410	1,229	656	328	977	1,147
$ 925	811	406	1,217	649	325	967	1,136
$ 900	798	399	1,197	638	319	957	1,117
$ 875	788	394	1,182	630	315	945	1,103
$ 850	765	383	1,148	612	306	918	1,071
$ 825	743	372	1,115	594	297	891	1,040
$ 800	720	360	1,080	576	288	864	1,008

* The retirement age when unreduced benefits are available will be increased to age 67 in gradual steps starting in the year 2000. If you were born in 1943-1954, your retirement age for full benefits is 66. If you were born in 1955-1959, your retirement age for full benefits is your 66th birthday plus two months for every year you were born after 1954. If you were born in 1960 and after, your retirement age for full benefits is 67.

** Benefits listed are 80% of the corresponding PIA, but age 62 benefits are reduced further if worker is born in 1938 or after. Ex: Benefits is 75% of PIA for workers born in 1943-1954 and 70% of PIA for workers born in 1960 and after.

TABLE 11 — SURVIVOR'S BENEFITS

Average Indexed Monthly Earnings	Worker's PIA	Surviving Spouse & 1 Child; or 2 Children	Surviving Spouse & 2 Children; or 3 Children	One Child (No Mother)	Widow or Widower Age 60	Widow or Widower FRA	Each of Two Parents	Sole Parent	Maximum Family Benefits
$9,700	2,912	4,368	5,096	2,184	2,082	2,912	2,912	2,403	5110
$9,675	2,908	4,362	5,089	2,181	2,079	2,908	2,908	2,399	5102
$9,650	2,904	4,356	5,082	2,178	2,076	2,904	2,904	2,396	5095
$9,625	2,900	4,350	5,075	2,175	2,074	2,900	2,900	2,393	5088
$9,600	2,897	4,346	5,070	2,173	2,071	2,897	2,897	2,390	5082
$9,575	2,893	4,340	5,063	2,170	2,069	2,893	2,893	2,387	5075
$9,550	2,889	4,334	5,056	2,167	2,066	2,889	2,889	2,383	5068
$9,525	2,885	4,327	5,049	2,164	2,063	2,885	2,885	2,380	5060
$9,500	2,882	4,323	5,043	2,161	2,061	2,882	2,882	2,378	5055
$9,475	2,878	4,317	5,036	2,158	2,058	2,878	2,878	2,374	5048
$9,450	2,874	4,311	5,029	2,155	2,055	2,874	2,874	2,371	5040
$9,425	2,870	4,305	5,022	2,152	2,052	2,870	2,870	2,368	5033
$9,400	2,867	4,300	5,017	2,150	2,050	2,867	2,867	2,365	5027
$9,375	2,863	4,294	5,010	2,147	2,047	2,863	2,863	2,362	5020
$9,350	2,859	4,288	5,003	2,144	2,044	2,859	2,859	2,359	5013
$9,325	2,855	4,282	4,996	2,141	2,041	2,855	2,855	2,355	5005
$9,300	2,852	4,278	4,991	2,139	2,039	2,852	2,852	2,353	5000
$9,275	2,848	4,272	4,984	2,136	2,036	2,848	2,848	2,349	4993
$9,250	2,844	4,266	4,977	2,133	2,033	2,844	2,844	2,346	4985
$9,225	2,840	4,260	4,969	2,130	2,030	2,840	2,840	2,343	4978
$9,200	2,837	4,255	4,964	2,128	2,028	2,837	2,837	2,340	4972
$9,175	2,833	4,249	4,957	2,124	2,025	2,833	2,833	2,337	4965
$9,150	2,829	4,243	4,950	2,121	2,022	2,829	2,829	2,334	4958
$9,125	2,825	4,237	4,943	2,118	2,020	2,825	2,825	2,330	4950
$9,100	2,822	4,232	4,938	2,116	2,017	2,822	2,822	2,328	4945
$9,075	2,818	4,226	4,931	2,113	2,015	2,818	2,818	2,324	4938
$9,050	2,814	4,220	4,924	2,110	2,012	2,814	2,814	2,321	4930
$9,025	2,809	4,214	4,917	2,107	2,009	2,809	2,809	2,318	4923
$9,000	2,806	4,210	4,911	2,105	2,007	2,806	2,806	2,315	4917
$8,975	2,802	4,204	4,904	2,102	2,004	2,802	2,802	2,312	4910
$8,950	2,798	4,198	4,897	2,099	2,001	2,798	2,798	2,309	4903
$8,925	2,794	4,192	4,890	2,096	1,998	2,794	2,794	2,305	4895
$8,900	2,791	4,187	4,885	2,094	1,996	2,791	2,791	2,303	4890
$8,875	2,787	4,181	4,878	2,091	1,993	2,787	2,787	2,300	4883
$8,850	2,783	4,175	4,871	2,087	1,990	2,783	2,783	2,296	4875
$8,825	2,779	4,169	4,864	2,084	1,987	2,779	2,779	2,293	4868
$8,800	2,776	4,164	4,858	2,082	1,985	2,776	2,776	2,290	4863
$8,775	2,772	4,158	4,851	2,079	1,982	2,772	2,772	2,287	4855
$8,750	2,768	4,152	4,844	2,076	1,979	2,768	2,768	2,284	4848
$8,725	2,764	4,146	4,837	2,073	1,976	2,764	2,764	2,280	4841
$8,700	2,761	4,142	4,832	2,071	1,974	2,761	2,761	2,278	4835
$8,675	2,757	4,136	4,825	2,068	1,971	2,757	2,757	2,275	4828
$8,650	2,753	4,130	4,818	2,065	1,968	2,753	2,753	2,271	4820
$8,625	2,749	4,124	4,811	2,062	1,966	2,749	2,749	2,268	4813
$8,600	2,746	4,119	4,806	2,060	1,963	2,746	2,746	2,266	4808
$8,575	2,742	4,113	4,799	2,057	1,961	2,742	2,742	2,262	4800
$8,550	2,738	4,107	4,792	2,054	1,958	2,738	2,738	2,259	4793
$8,525	2,734	4,101	4,784	2,050	1,955	2,734	2,734	2,256	4786
$8,500	2,731	4,096	4,779	2,048	1,953	2,731	2,731	2,253	4780
$8,475	2,727	4,090	4,772	2,045	1,950	2,727	2,727	2,250	4773
$8,450	2,723	4,084	4,765	2,042	1,947	2,723	2,723	2,246	4765
$8,425	2,719	4,078	4,758	2,039	1,944	2,719	2,719	2,243	4758

TABLE 11 — SURVIVOR'S BENEFITS (cont'd)

Average Indexed Monthly Earnings	Worker's PIA	Surviving Spouse & 1 Child; or 2 Children	Surviving Spouse & 2 Children; or 3 Children	One Child (No Mother)	Widow or Widower Age 60	Widow or Widower FRA	Each of Two Parents	Sole Parent	Maximum Family Benefits
$8,400	2,716	4,074	4,753	2,037	1,942	2,716	2,716	2,241	4753
$8,375	2,712	4,068	4,746	2,034	1,939	2,712	2,712	2,237	4745
$8,350	2,708	4,062	4,739	2,031	1,936	2,708	2,708	2,234	4738
$8,325	2,704	4,056	4,732	2,028	1,933	2,704	2,704	2,231	4731
$8,300	2,701	4,051	4,726	2,026	1,931	2,701	2,701	2,228	4725
$8,275	2,697	4,045	4,719	2,023	1,928	2,697	2,697	2,225	4718
$8,250	2,693	4,039	4,712	2,020	1,925	2,693	2,693	2,221	4710
$8,225	2,689	4,033	4,705	2,017	1,922	2,689	2,689	2,218	4703
$8,200	2,686	4,029	4,700	2,014	1,920	2,686	2,686	2,216	4698
$8,175	2,682	4,022	4,693	2,011	1,917	2,682	2,682	2,212	4690
$8,150	2,678	4,016	4,686	2,008	1,915	2,678	2,678	2,209	4683
$8,125	2,674	4,010	4,679	2,005	1,912	2,674	2,674	2,206	4676
$8,100	2,671	4,006	4,674	2,003	1,909	2,671	2,671	2,203	4670
$8,075	2,667	4,000	4,666	2,000	1,907	2,667	2,667	2,200	4663
$8,050	2,663	3,994	4,659	1,997	1,904	2,663	2,663	2,197	4655
$8,025	2,658	3,988	4,652	1,994	1,901	2,658	2,658	2,193	4648
$8,000	2,655	3,983	4,647	1,992	1,899	2,655	2,655	2,191	4643
$7,975	2,651	3,977	4,640	1,989	1,896	2,651	2,651	2,187	4635
$7,950	2,647	3,971	4,633	1,986	1,893	2,647	2,647	2,184	4628
$7,925	2,643	3,965	4,626	1,983	1,890	2,643	2,643	2,181	4621
$7,900	2,640	3,961	4,621	1,980	1,888	2,640	2,640	2,178	4615
$7,875	2,636	3,955	4,614	1,977	1,885	2,636	2,636	2,175	4608
$7,850	2,632	3,948	4,607	1,974	1,882	2,632	2,632	2,172	4601
$7,825	2,628	3,942	4,600	1,971	1,879	2,628	2,628	2,168	4593
$7,800	2,625	3,938	4,594	1,969	1,877	2,625	2,625	2,166	4588
$7,775	2,621	3,932	4,587	1,966	1,874	2,621	2,621	2,163	4580
$7,750	2,617	3,926	4,580	1,963	1,871	2,617	2,617	2,159	4573
$7,725	2,613	3,920	4,573	1,960	1,868	2,613	2,613	2,156	4566
$7,700	2,610	3,915	4,568	1,958	1,866	2,610	2,610	2,153	4560
$7,675	2,606	3,909	4,561	1,955	1,863	2,606	2,606	2,150	4553
$7,650	2,602	3,903	4,554	1,952	1,861	2,602	2,602	2,147	4546
$7,625	2,598	3,897	4,547	1,949	1,858	2,598	2,598	2,143	4538
$7,600	2,595	3,893	4,541	1,946	1,855	2,595	2,595	2,141	4533
$7,575	2,591	3,887	4,534	1,943	1,853	2,591	2,591	2,138	4525
$7,550	2,587	3,881	4,527	1,940	1,850	2,587	2,587	2,134	4518
$7,525	2,583	3,875	4,520	1,937	1,847	2,583	2,583	2,131	4511
$7,500	2,580	3,870	4,515	1,935	1,845	2,580	2,580	2,128	4505
$7,475	2,576	3,864	4,508	1,932	1,842	2,576	2,576	2,125	4498
$7,450	2,572	3,858	4,501	1,929	1,839	2,572	2,572	2,122	4491
$7,425	2,568	3,852	4,494	1,926	1,836	2,568	2,568	2,119	4483
$7,400	2,565	3,847	4,489	1,924	1,834	2,565	2,565	2,116	4478
$7,375	2,561	3,841	4,481	1,921	1,831	2,561	2,561	2,113	4470
$7,350	2,557	3,835	4,474	1,918	1,828	2,557	2,557	2,109	4463
$7,325	2,553	3,829	4,467	1,915	1,825	2,553	2,553	2,106	4456
$7,300	2,550	3,825	4,462	1,912	1,823	2,550	2,550	2,104	4450
$7,275	2,546	3,819	4,455	1,909	1,820	2,546	2,546	2,100	4443
$7,250	2,542	3,813	4,448	1,906	1,817	2,542	2,542	2,097	4436
$7,225	2,538	3,807	4,441	1,903	1,814	2,538	2,538	2,094	4428
$7,200	2,535	3,802	4,436	1,901	1,812	2,535	2,535	2,091	4423
$7,175	2,531	3,796	4,429	1,898	1,809	2,531	2,531	2,088	4415
$7,150	2,527	3,790	4,422	1,895	1,807	2,527	2,527	2,084	4408
$7,125	2,523	3,784	4,415	1,892	1,804	2,523	2,523	2,081	4401

TABLE 11 — SURVIVOR'S BENEFITS (cont'd)

Average Indexed Monthly Earnings	Worker's PIA	Surviving Spouse & 1 Child; or 2 Children	Surviving Spouse & 2 Children; or 3 Children	One Child (No Mother)	Widow or Widower Age 60	Widow or Widower FRA	Each of Two Parents	Sole Parent	Maximum Family Benefits
$7,100	2,520	3,779	4,409	1,890	1,802	2,520	2,520	2,079	4395
$7,075	2,516	3,773	4,402	1,887	1,799	2,516	2,516	2,075	4388
$7,050	2,512	3,767	4,395	1,884	1,796	2,512	2,512	2,072	4381
$7,025	2,508	3,761	4,388	1,881	1,793	2,508	2,508	2,069	4373
$7,000	2,504	3,757	4,383	1,878	1,791	2,504	2,504	2,066	4368
$6,975	2,500	3,751	4,376	1,875	1,788	2,500	2,500	2,063	4361
$6,950	2,496	3,745	4,369	1,872	1,785	2,496	2,496	2,060	4353
$6,925	2,492	3,739	4,362	1,869	1,782	2,492	2,492	2,056	4346
$6,900	2,489	3,734	4,356	1,867	1,780	2,489	2,489	2,054	4340
$6,875	2,485	3,728	4,349	1,864	1,777	2,485	2,485	2,050	4333
$6,850	2,481	3,722	4,342	1,861	1,774	2,481	2,481	2,047	4326
$6,825	2,477	3,716	4,335	1,858	1,771	2,477	2,477	2,044	4318
$6,800	2,474	3,711	4,330	1,856	1,769	2,474	2,474	2,041	4313
$6,775	2,470	3,705	4,323	1,853	1,766	2,470	2,470	2,038	4306
$6,750	2,466	3,699	4,316	1,850	1,763	2,466	2,466	2,035	4298
$6,725	2,462	3,693	4,309	1,847	1,760	2,462	2,462	2,031	4291
$6,700	2,459	3,689	4,304	1,844	1,758	2,459	2,459	2,029	4285
$6,675	2,455	3,683	4,297	1,841	1,755	2,455	2,455	2,026	4278
$6,650	2,451	3,677	4,289	1,838	1,753	2,451	2,451	2,022	4271
$6,625	2,447	3,671	4,282	1,835	1,750	2,447	2,447	2,019	4263
$6,600	2,444	3,666	4,277	1,833	1,748	2,444	2,444	2,016	4258
$6,575	2,440	3,660	4,270	1,830	1,745	2,440	2,440	2,013	4251
$6,550	2,436	3,654	4,263	1,827	1,742	2,436	2,436	2,010	4243
$6,525	2,432	3,648	4,256	1,824	1,739	2,432	2,432	2,006	4236
$6,500	2,429	3,643	4,251	1,822	1,737	2,429	2,429	2,004	4230
$6,475	2,425	3,637	4,244	1,819	1,734	2,425	2,425	2,001	4223
$6,450	2,421	3,631	4,237	1,816	1,731	2,421	2,421	1,997	4216
$6,425	2,417	3,625	4,230	1,813	1,728	2,417	2,417	1,994	4208
$6,400	2,414	3,621	4,224	1,810	1,726	2,414	2,414	1,991	4203
$6,375	2,410	3,615	4,217	1,807	1,723	2,410	2,410	1,988	4196
$6,350	2,406	3,609	4,210	1,804	1,720	2,406	2,406	1,985	4188
$6,325	2,402	3,603	4,203	1,801	1,717	2,402	2,402	1,981	4181
$6,300	2,399	3,598	4,198	1,799	1,715	2,399	2,399	1,979	4175
$6,275	2,395	3,592	4,191	1,796	1,712	2,395	2,395	1,976	4168
$6,250	2,391	3,586	4,184	1,793	1,709	2,391	2,391	1,972	4161
$6,225	2,387	3,580	4,177	1,790	1,706	2,387	2,387	1,969	4153
$6,200	2,384	3,576	4,171	1,788	1,704	2,384	2,384	1,967	4148
$6,175	2,380	3,569	4,164	1,785	1,701	2,380	2,380	1,963	4141
$6,150	2,376	3,563	4,157	1,782	1,699	2,376	2,376	1,960	4133
$6,125	2,372	3,557	4,150	1,779	1,696	2,372	2,372	1,957	4126
$6,100	2,369	3,553	4,145	1,776	1,694	2,369	2,369	1,954	4121
$6,075	2,365	3,547	4,138	1,773	1,691	2,365	2,365	1,951	4113
$6,050	2,361	3,541	4,131	1,770	1,688	2,361	2,361	1,947	4106
$6,025	2,357	3,535	4,124	1,767	1,685	2,357	2,357	1,944	4099
$6,000	2,353	3,530	4,119	1,765	1,683	2,353	2,353	1,942	4093
$5,975	2,349	3,524	4,112	1,762	1,680	2,349	2,349	1,938	4086
$5,950	2,345	3,518	4,105	1,759	1,677	2,345	2,345	1,935	4078
$5,925	2,341	3,512	4,097	1,756	1,674	2,341	2,341	1,932	4071
$5,900	2,338	3,508	4,092	1,754	1,672	2,338	2,338	1,929	4066
$5,875	2,334	3,502	4,085	1,751	1,669	2,334	2,334	1,926	4058
$5,850	2,330	3,496	4,078	1,748	1,666	2,330	2,330	1,923	4051
$5,825	2,326	3,489	4,071	1,745	1,663	2,326	2,326	1,919	4044

TABLE 11 — SURVIVOR'S BENEFITS (cont'd)

Average Indexed Monthly Earnings	Worker's PIA	Surviving Spouse & 1 Child; or 2 Children	Surviving Spouse & 2 Children; or 3 Children	One Child (No Mother)	Widow or Widower Age 60	Widow or Widower FRA	Each of Two Parents	Sole Parent	Maximum Family Benefits
$5,800	2,323	3,485	4,066	1,742	1,661	2,323	2,323	1,917	4038
$5,775	2,319	3,479	4,059	1,739	1,658	2,319	2,319	1,913	4031
$5,750	2,315	3,473	4,052	1,736	1,655	2,315	2,315	1,910	4023
$5,725	2,311	3,467	4,045	1,733	1,653	2,311	2,311	1,907	4016
$5,700	2,308	3,462	4,039	1,731	1,650	2,308	2,308	1,904	4011
$5,675	2,304	3,456	4,032	1,728	1,647	2,304	2,304	1,901	4003
$5,650	2,300	3,450	4,025	1,725	1,645	2,300	2,300	1,898	3996
$5,625	2,296	3,444	4,018	1,722	1,642	2,296	2,296	1,894	3989
$5,600	2,293	3,440	4,013	1,720	1,640	2,293	2,293	1,892	3983
$5,575	2,289	3,434	4,006	1,717	1,637	2,289	2,289	1,888	3976
$5,550	2,285	3,428	3,999	1,714	1,634	2,285	2,285	1,885	3968
$5,525	2,281	3,422	3,992	1,711	1,631	2,281	2,281	1,882	3961
$5,500	2,278	3,417	3,986	1,708	1,629	2,278	2,278	1,879	3956
$5,475	2,274	3,411	3,979	1,705	1,626	2,274	2,274	1,876	3948
$5,450	2,270	3,405	3,972	1,702	1,623	2,270	2,270	1,873	3941
$5,425	2,266	3,399	3,965	1,699	1,620	2,266	2,266	1,869	3934
$5,400	2,263	3,394	3,960	1,697	1,618	2,263	2,263	1,867	3928
$5,375	2,245	3,367	3,928	1,684	1,605	2,245	2,245	1,852	3895
$5,350	2,237	3,355	3,914	1,678	1,599	2,237	2,237	1,845	3881
$5,325	2,229	3,343	3,900	1,672	1,593	2,229	2,229	1,839	3866
$5,300	2,221	3,331	3,886	1,665	1,588	2,221	2,221	1,832	3851
$5,275	2,213	3,319	3,872	1,659	1,582	2,213	2,213	1,825	3837
$5,250	2,205	3,307	3,858	1,653	1,576	2,205	2,205	1,819	3815
$5,225	2,196	3,295	3,844	1,647	1,570	2,196	2,196	1,812	3805
$5,200	2,188	3,283	3,830	1,641	1,565	2,188	2,188	1,805	3794
$5,175	2,180	3,271	3,816	1,635	1,559	2,180	2,180	1,799	3783
$5,150	2,172	3,258	3,802	1,629	1,553	2,172	2,172	1,792	3772
$5,125	2,164	3,246	3,787	1,623	1,547	2,164	2,164	1,786	3761
$5,100	2,156	3,234	3,773	1,617	1,542	2,156	2,156	1,779	3750
$5,075	2,148	3,222	3,759	1,611	1,536	2,148	2,148	1,772	3739
$5,050	2,140	3,210	3,745	1,605	1,530	2,140	2,140	1,766	3728
$5,025	2,132	3,198	3,731	1,599	1,524	2,132	2,132	1,759	3717
$5,000	2,124	3,186	3,717	1,593	1,519	2,124	2,124	1,752	3706
$4,975	2,116	3,174	3,703	1,587	1,513	2,116	2,116	1,746	3695
$4,950	2,108	3,162	3,689	1,581	1,507	2,108	2,108	1,739	3684
$4,925	2,100	3,150	3,675	1,575	1,501	2,100	2,100	1,732	3673
$4,900	2,092	3,138	3,661	1,569	1,496	2,092	2,092	1,726	3662
$4,875	2,084	3,126	3,647	1,563	1,490	2,084	2,084	1,719	3651
$4,850	2,076	3,113	3,632	1,557	1,484	2,076	2,076	1,712	3640
$4,825	2,068	3,101	3,618	1,551	1,478	2,068	2,068	1,706	3629
$4,800	2,060	3,089	3,604	1,545	1,473	2,060	2,060	1,699	3618
$4,775	2,052	3,077	3,590	1,539	1,467	2,052	2,052	1,692	3607
$4,750	2,043	3,065	3,576	1,533	1,461	2,043	2,043	1,686	3596
$4,725	2,035	3,053	3,562	1,527	1,455	2,035	2,035	1,679	3586
$4,700	2,027	3,041	3,548	1,521	1,450	2,027	2,027	1,673	3575
$4,675	2,019	3,029	3,534	1,514	1,444	2,019	2,019	1,666	3564
$4,650	2,011	3,017	3,520	1,508	1,438	2,011	2,011	1,659	3553
$4,625	2,003	3,005	3,506	1,502	1,432	2,003	2,003	1,653	3542
$4,600	1,995	2,993	3,491	1,496	1,427	1,995	1,995	1,646	3531
$4,575	1,987	2,981	3,477	1,490	1,421	1,987	1,987	1,639	3520
$4,550	1,979	2,969	3,463	1,484	1,415	1,979	1,979	1,633	3509
$4,525	1,971	2,956	3,449	1,478	1,409	1,971	1,971	1,626	3498

TABLE 11 — SURVIVOR'S BENEFITS (cont'd)

Average Indexed Monthly Earnings	Worker's PIA	Surviving Spouse & 1 Child; or 2 Children	Surviving Spouse & 2 Children; or 3 Children	One Child (No Mother)	Widow or Widower Age 60	Widow or Widower FRA	Each of Two Parents	Sole Parent	Maximum Family Benefits
$4,500	1,963	2,944	3,435	1,472	1,403	1,963	1,963	1,619	3487
$4,475	1,955	2,932	3,421	1,466	1,398	1,955	1,955	1,613	3476
$4,450	1,947	2,920	3,407	1,460	1,392	1,947	1,947	1,606	3465
$4,425	1,939	2,908	3,393	1,454	1,386	1,939	1,939	1,599	3454
$4,400	1,931	2,896	3,379	1,448	1,380	1,931	1,931	1,593	3443
$4,375	1,923	2,884	3,365	1,442	1,375	1,923	1,923	1,586	3432
$4,350	1,915	2,872	3,351	1,436	1,369	1,915	1,915	1,580	3421
$4,325	1,907	2,860	3,336	1,430	1,363	1,907	1,907	1,573	3410
$4,300	1,898	2,848	3,322	1,424	1,357	1,898	1,898	1,566	3399
$4,275	1,890	2,836	3,308	1,418	1,352	1,890	1,890	1,560	3388
$4,250	1,882	2,824	3,294	1,412	1,346	1,882	1,882	1,553	3377
$4,225	1,874	2,812	3,280	1,406	1,340	1,874	1,874	1,546	3366
$4,200	1,866	2,799	3,266	1,400	1,334	1,866	1,866	1,540	3356
$4,175	1,858	2,787	3,252	1,394	1,329	1,858	1,858	1,533	3345
$4,150	1,850	2,775	3,238	1,388	1,323	1,850	1,850	1,526	3334
$4,125	1,842	2,763	3,224	1,382	1,317	1,842	1,842	1,520	3323
$4,100	1,834	2,751	3,210	1,376	1,311	1,834	1,834	1,513	3312
$4,075	1,826	2,739	3,196	1,370	1,306	1,826	1,826	1,506	3301
$4,050	1,818	2,727	3,181	1,363	1,300	1,818	1,818	1,500	3290
$4,025	1,810	2,715	3,167	1,357	1,294	1,810	1,810	1,493	3279
$4,000	1,802	2,703	3,153	1,351	1,288	1,802	1,802	1,487	3268
$3,975	1,794	2,691	3,139	1,345	1,283	1,794	1,794	1,480	3257
$3,950	1,786	2,679	3,125	1,339	1,277	1,786	1,786	1,473	3246
$3,925	1,778	2,667	3,111	1,333	1,271	1,778	1,778	1,467	3235
$3,900	1,770	2,654	3,097	1,327	1,265	1,770	1,770	1,460	3224
$3,875	1,762	2,642	3,083	1,321	1,260	1,762	1,762	1,453	3213
$3,850	1,754	2,630	3,069	1,315	1,254	1,754	1,754	1,447	3202
$3,825	1,745	2,618	3,055	1,309	1,248	1,745	1,745	1,440	3191
$3,800	1,737	2,606	3,041	1,303	1,242	1,737	1,737	1,433	3180
$3,775	1,729	2,594	3,026	1,297	1,237	1,729	1,729	1,427	3169
$3,750	1,721	2,582	3,012	1,291	1,231	1,721	1,721	1,420	3158
$3,725	1,713	2,570	2,998	1,285	1,225	1,713	1,713	1,413	3147
$3,700	1,705	2,558	2,984	1,279	1,219	1,705	1,705	1,407	3136
$3,675	1,697	2,546	2,970	1,273	1,213	1,697	1,697	1,400	3126
$3,650	1,689	2,534	2,956	1,267	1,208	1,689	1,689	1,394	3115
$3,625	1,681	2,522	2,942	1,261	1,202	1,681	1,681	1,387	3104
$3,600	1,673	2,510	2,928	1,255	1,196	1,673	1,673	1,380	3093
$3,575	1,665	2,497	2,914	1,249	1,190	1,665	1,665	1,374	3082
$3,550	1,657	2,485	2,900	1,243	1,185	1,657	1,657	1,367	3071
$3,525	1,649	2,473	2,885	1,237	1,179	1,649	1,649	1,360	3060
$3,500	1,641	2,461	2,871	1,231	1,173	1,641	1,641	1,354	3037
$3,475	1,633	2,449	2,857	1,225	1,167	1,633	1,633	1,347	3015
$3,450	1,625	2,437	2,843	1,219	1,162	1,625	1,625	1,340	2994
$3,425	1,617	2,425	2,829	1,212	1,156	1,617	1,617	1,334	2972
$3,400	1,609	2,413	2,815	1,206	1,150	1,609	1,609	1,327	2950
$3,375	1,601	2,401	2,801	1,200	1,144	1,601	1,601	1,320	2928
$3,350	1,592	2,389	2,787	1,194	1,139	1,592	1,592	1,314	2907
$3,325	1,584	2,377	2,773	1,188	1,133	1,584	1,584	1,307	2885
$3,300	1,576	2,365	2,759	1,182	1,127	1,576	1,576	1,301	2863
$3,275	1,568	2,352	2,745	1,176	1,121	1,568	1,568	1,294	2841
$3,250	1,560	2,340	2,730	1,170	1,116	1,560	1,560	1,287	2820
$3,225	1,552	2,328	2,716	1,164	1,110	1,552	1,552	1,281	2798

TABLE 11 — SURVIVOR'S BENEFITS (cont'd)

Average Indexed Monthly Earnings	Worker's PIA	Surviving Spouse & 1 Child; or 2 Children	Surviving Spouse & 2 Children; or 3 Children	One Child (No Mother)	Widow or Widower Age 60	Widow or Widower FRA	Each of Two Parents	Sole Parent	Maximum Family Benefits
$3,200	1,544	2,316	2,702	1,158	1,104	1,544	1,544	1,274	2776
$3,175	1,536	2,304	2,688	1,152	1,098	1,536	1,536	1,267	2754
$3,150	1,528	2,292	2,674	1,146	1,093	1,528	1,528	1,261	2733
$3,125	1,520	2,280	2,660	1,140	1,087	1,520	1,520	1,254	2711
$3,100	1,512	2,268	2,646	1,134	1,081	1,512	1,512	1,247	2689
$3,075	1,504	2,256	2,632	1,128	1,075	1,504	1,504	1,241	2667
$3,050	1,496	2,244	2,618	1,122	1,070	1,496	1,496	1,234	2646
$3,025	1,488	2,232	2,604	1,116	1,064	1,488	1,488	1,227	2624
$3,000	1,480	2,220	2,590	1,110	1,058	1,480	1,480	1,221	2602
$2,975	1,472	2,208	2,575	1,104	1,052	1,472	1,472	1,214	2580
$2,950	1,464	2,195	2,561	1,098	1,046	1,464	1,464	1,207	2558
$2,925	1,456	2,183	2,547	1,092	1,041	1,456	1,456	1,201	2537
$2,900	1,448	2,171	2,533	1,086	1,035	1,448	1,448	1,194	2515
$2,875	1,439	2,159	2,519	1,080	1,029	1,439	1,439	1,188	2493
$2,850	1,431	2,147	2,505	1,074	1,023	1,431	1,431	1,181	2471
$2,825	1,423	2,135	2,491	1,068	1,018	1,423	1,423	1,174	2450
$2,800	1,415	2,123	2,477	1,061	1,012	1,415	1,415	1,168	2428
$2,775	1,407	2,111	2,463	1,055	1,006	1,407	1,407	1,161	2406
$2,750	1,399	2,099	2,449	1,049	1,000	1,399	1,399	1,154	2384
$2,725	1,391	2,087	2,435	1,043	995	1,391	1,391	1,148	2363
$2,700	1,383	2,075	2,420	1,037	989	1,383	1,383	1,141	2341
$2,675	1,375	2,063	2,406	1,031	983	1,375	1,375	1,134	2319
$2,650	1,367	2,050	2,392	1,025	977	1,367	1,367	1,128	2297
$2,625	1,359	2,038	2,378	1,019	972	1,359	1,359	1,121	2276
$2,600	1,351	2,026	2,364	1,013	966	1,351	1,351	1,114	2254
$2,575	1,343	2,014	2,350	1,007	960	1,343	1,343	1,108	2232
$2,550	1,335	2,002	2,336	1,001	954	1,335	1,335	1,101	2210
$2,525	1,327	1,990	2,322	995	949	1,327	1,327	1,095	2189
$2,500	1,319	1,978	2,308	989	943	1,319	1,319	1,088	2167
$2,475	1,311	1,966	2,294	983	937	1,311	1,311	1,081	2145
$2,450	1,303	1,954	2,280	977	931	1,303	1,303	1,075	2123
$2,425	1,295	1,942	2,265	971	926	1,295	1,295	1,068	2102
$2,400	1,286	1,930	2,251	965	920	1,286	1,286	1,061	2080
$2,375	1,278	1,918	2,237	959	914	1,278	1,278	1,055	2058
$2,350	1,270	1,906	2,223	953	908	1,270	1,270	1,048	2036
$2,325	1,262	1,893	2,209	947	903	1,262	1,262	1,041	2014
$2,300	1,254	1,881	2,195	941	897	1,254	1,254	1,035	1993
$2,275	1,246	1,869	2,181	935	891	1,246	1,246	1,028	1971
$2,250	1,238	1,857	2,167	929	885	1,238	1,238	1,021	1949
$2,225	1,230	1,845	2,153	923	880	1,230	1,230	1,015	1927
$2,200	1,222	1,833	2,139	917	874	1,222	1,222	1,008	1906
$2,175	1,214	1,821	2,124	910	868	1,214	1,214	1,002	1884
$2,150	1,206	1,809	2,110	904	862	1,206	1,206	995	1862
$2,125	1,198	1,797	2,096	898	856	1,198	1,198	988	1840
$2,100	1,190	1,785	2,082	892	851	1,190	1,190	982	1819
$2,075	1,182	1,773	2,068	886	845	1,182	1,182	975	1797
$2,050	1,174	1,761	2,054	880	839	1,174	1,174	968	1775
$2,025	1,166	1,749	2,040	874	833	1,166	1,166	962	1753
$2,000	1,158	1,736	2,026	868	828	1,158	1,158	955	1744
$1,975	1,150	1,724	2,012	862	822	1,150	1,150	948	1724
$1,950	1,142	1,712	1,998	856	816	1,142	1,142	942	1712
$1,925	1,133	1,700	1,984	850	810	1,133	1,133	935	1700

TABLE 11 — SURVIVOR'S BENEFITS (cont'd)

Average Indexed Monthly Earnings	Worker's PIA	Surviving Spouse & 1 Child; or 2 Children	Surviving Spouse & 2 Children; or 3 Children	One Child (No Mother)	Widow or Widower Age 60	Widow or Widower FRA	Each of Two Parents	Sole Parent	Maximum Family Benefits
$1,900	1,125	1,688	1,969	844	805	1,125	1,125	928	1688
$1,875	1,117	1,676	1,955	838	799	1,117	1,117	922	1676
$1,850	1,109	1,664	1,941	832	793	1,109	1,109	915	1664
$1,825	1,101	1,652	1,927	826	787	1,101	1,101	909	1652
$1,800	1,093	1,640	1,913	820	782	1,093	1,093	902	1640
$1,775	1,085	1,628	1,899	814	776	1,085	1,085	895	1628
$1,750	1,077	1,616	1,885	808	770	1,077	1,077	889	1616
$1,700	1,061	1,591	1,857	796	759	1,061	1,061	875	1592
$1,675	1,053	1,579	1,843	790	753	1,053	1,053	869	1579
$1,650	1,045	1,567	1,829	784	747	1,045	1,045	862	1567
$1,625	1,037	1,555	1,814	778	741	1,037	1,037	855	1555
$1,600	1,029	1,543	1,800	772	736	1,029	1,029	849	1543
$1,575	1,021	1,531	1,786	766	730	1,021	1,021	842	1531
$1,550	1,013	1,519	1,772	759	724	1,013	1,013	835	1519
$1,525	1,005	1,507	1,758	753	718	1,005	1,005	829	1507
$1,500	997	1,495	1,744	747	713	997	997	822	1495
$1,475	989	1,483	1,730	741	707	989	989	816	1483
$1,450	980	1,471	1,716	735	701	980	980	809	1471
$1,425	972	1,459	1,702	729	695	972	972	802	1459
$1,400	964	1,447	1,688	723	690	964	964	796	1447
$1,375	956	1,434	1,674	717	684	956	956	789	1435
$1,350	948	1,422	1,659	711	678	948	948	782	1422
$1,325	940	1,410	1,645	705	672	940	940	776	1410
$1,300	932	1,398	1,631	699	666	932	932	769	1398
$1,275	924	1,386	1,617	693	661	924	924	762	1386
$1,250	916	1,374	1,603	687	655	916	916	756	1374
$1,225	908	1,362	1,589	681	649	908	908	749	1362
$1,200	900	1,350	1,575	675	643	900	900	742	1350
$1,175	892	1,338	1,561	669	638	892	892	736	1338
$1,150	884	1,326	1,547	663	632	884	884	729	1326
$1,125	876	1,314	1,533	657	626	876	876	723	1314
$1,100	868	1,302	1,518	651	620	868	868	716	1302
$1,075	860	1,289	1,504	645	615	860	860	709	1290
$1,050	852	1,277	1,490	639	609	852	852	703	1277
$1,025	844	1,265	1,476	633	603	844	844	696	1265
$1,000	835	1,253	1,462	627	597	835	835	689	1253
$975	827	1,241	1,448	621	592	827	827	683	1241
$950	819	1,229	1,434	615	586	819	819	676	1229
$925	811	1,217	1,420	609	580	811	811	669	1217
$900	798	1,197	1,397	599	571	798	798	658	1205
$875	788	1,182	1,379	591	563	788	788	650	1190
$850	765	1,148	1,339	574	547	765	765	631	1155
$825	743	1,115	1,300	557	531	743	743	613	1122
$800	720	1,080	1,260	540	515	720	720	594	1087

TABLE 12 — DISABILITY BENEFITS

Average Indexed Monthly Earnings	Disabled Worker	Disabled Worker Spouse and Children	One Child (No Spouse)	Spouse FRA-3
$9,700	2,912	4,368	1,456	1,092
$9,675	2,908	4,362	1,454	1,091
$9,650	2,904	4,356	1,452	1,089
$9,625	2,900	4,350	1,450	1,088
$9,600	2,897	4,346	1,449	1,086
$9,575	2,893	4,340	1,447	1,085
$9,550	2,889	4,334	1,445	1,083
$9,525	2,885	4,328	1,443	1,082
$9,500	2,882	4,323	1,441	1,081
$9,475	2,878	4,317	1,439	1,079
$9,450	2,874	4,311	1,437	1,078
$9,425	2,870	4,305	1,435	1,076
$9,400	2,867	4,301	1,434	1,075
$9,375	2,863	4,295	1,432	1,074
$9,350	2,859	4,289	1,430	1,072
$9,325	2,855	4,283	1,428	1,071
$9,300	2,852	4,278	1,426	1,070
$9,275	2,848	4,272	1,424	1,068
$9,250	2,844	4,266	1,422	1,067
$9,225	2,840	4,260	1,420	1,065
$9,200	2,837	4,256	1,419	1,064
$9,175	2,833	4,250	1,417	1,062
$9,150	2,829	4,244	1,415	1,061
$9,125	2,825	4,238	1,413	1,059
$9,100	2,822	4,233	1,411	1,058
$9,075	2,818	4,227	1,409	1,057
$9,050	2,814	4,221	1,407	1,055
$9,025	2,809	4,214	1,405	1,053
$9,000	2,806	4,209	1,403	1,052
$8,975	2,802	4,203	1,401	1,051
$8,950	2,798	4,197	1,399	1,049
$8,925	2,794	4,191	1,397	1,048
$8,900	2,791	4,187	1,396	1,047
$8,875	2,787	4,181	1,394	1,045
$8,850	2,783	4,175	1,392	1,044
$8,825	2,779	4,169	1,390	1,042
$8,800	2,776	4,164	1,388	1,041
$8,775	2,772	4,158	1,386	1,040
$8,750	2,768	4,152	1,384	1,038
$8,725	2,764	4,146	1,382	1,037
$8,700	2,761	4,142	1,381	1,035
$8,675	2,757	4,136	1,379	1,034
$8,650	2,753	4,130	1,377	1,032
$8,625	2,749	4,124	1,375	1,031
$8,600	2,746	4,119	1,373	1,030
$8,575	2,742	4,113	1,371	1,028
$8,550	2,738	4,107	1,369	1,027
$8,525	2,734	4,101	1,367	1,025
$8,500	2,731	4,097	1,366	1,024
$8,475	2,727	4,091	1,364	1,023
$8,450	2,723	4,085	1,362	1,021

TABLE 12—DISABILITY BENEFITS (cont'd)

Average Indexed Monthly Earnings	Disabled Worker	Disabled Worker Spouse and Children	One Child (No Spouse)	Spouse FRA–3
$8,425	2,719	4,079	1,360	1,020
$8,400	2,716	4,074	1,358	1,019
$8,375	2,712	4,068	1,356	1,017
$8,350	2,708	4,062	1,354	1,016
$8,325	2,704	4,056	1,352	1,014
$8,300	2,701	4,052	1,351	1,013
$8,275	2,697	4,046	1,349	1,011
$8,250	2,693	4,040	1,347	1,010
$8,225	2,689	4,034	1,345	1,008
$8,200	2,686	4,029	1,343	1,007
$8,175	2,682	4,023	1,341	1,006
$8,150	2,678	4,017	1,339	1,004
$8,125	2,674	4,011	1,337	1,003
$8,100	2,671	4,007	1,336	1,002
$8,075	2,667	4,001	1,334	1,000
$8,050	2,663	3,995	1,332	999
$8,025	2,658	3,987	1,329	997
$8,000	2,655	3,983	1,328	996
$7,975	2,651	3,977	1,326	994
$7,950	2,647	3,971	1,324	993
$7,925	2,643	3,965	1,322	991
$7,900	2,640	3,960	1,320	990
$7,875	2,636	3,954	1,318	989
$7,850	2,632	3,948	1,316	987
$7,825	2,628	3,942	1,314	986
$7,800	2,625	3,938	1,313	984
$7,775	2,621	3,932	1,311	983
$7,750	2,617	3,926	1,309	981
$7,725	2,613	3,920	1,307	980
$7,700	2,610	3,915	1,305	979
$7,675	2,606	3,909	1,303	977
$7,650	2,602	3,903	1,301	976
$7,625	2,598	3,897	1,299	974
$7,600	2,595	3,893	1,298	973
$7,575	2,591	3,887	1,296	972
$7,550	2,587	3,881	1,294	970
$7,525	2,583	3,875	1,292	969
$7,500	2,580	3,870	1,290	968
$7,475	2,576	3,864	1,288	966
$7,450	2,572	3,858	1,286	965
$7,425	2,568	3,852	1,284	963
$7,400	2,565	3,848	1,283	962
$7,375	2,561	3,842	1,281	960
$7,350	2,557	3,836	1,279	959
$7,325	2,553	3,830	1,277	957
$7,300	2,550	3,825	1,275	956
$7,275	2,546	3,819	1,273	955
$7,250	2,542	3,813	1,271	953
$7,225	2,538	3,807	1,269	952
$7,200	2,535	3,803	1,268	951
$7,175	2,531	3,797	1,266	949

TABLE 12—DISABILITY BENEFITS (cont'd)

Average Indexed Monthly Earnings	Disabled Worker	Disabled Worker Spouse and Children	One Child (No Spouse)	Spouse FRA–3
$7,150	2,527	3,791	1,264	948
$7,125	2,523	3,785	1,262	946
$7,100	2,520	3,780	1,260	945
$7,075	2,516	3,774	1,258	944
$7,050	2,512	3,768	1,256	942
$7,025	2,508	3,762	1,254	941
$7,000	2,504	3,756	1,252	939
$6,975	2,500	3,750	1,250	938
$6,950	2,496	3,744	1,248	936
$6,925	2,492	3,738	1,246	935
$6,900	2,489	3,734	1,245	933
$6,875	2,485	3,728	1,243	932
$6,850	2,481	3,722	1,241	930
$6,825	2,477	3,716	1,239	929
$6,800	2,474	3,711	1,237	928
$6,775	2,470	3,705	1,235	926
$6,750	2,466	3,699	1,233	925
$6,725	2,462	3,693	1,231	923
$6,700	2,459	3,689	1,230	922
$6,675	2,455	3,683	1,228	921
$6,650	2,451	3,677	1,226	919
$6,625	2,447	3,671	1,224	918
$6,600	2,444	3,666	1,222	917
$6,575	2,440	3,660	1,220	915
$6,550	2,436	3,654	1,218	914
$6,525	2,432	3,648	1,216	912
$6,500	2,429	3,644	1,215	911
$6,475	2,425	3,638	1,213	909
$6,450	2,421	3,632	1,211	908
$6,425	2,417	3,626	1,209	906
$6,400	2,414	3,621	1,207	905
$6,375	2,410	3,615	1,205	904
$6,350	2,406	3,609	1,203	902
$6,325	2,402	3,603	1,201	901
$6,300	2,399	3,599	1,200	900
$6,275	2,395	3,593	1,198	898
$6,250	2,391	3,587	1,196	897
$6,225	2,387	3,581	1,194	895
$6,200	2,384	3,576	1,192	894
$6,175	2,380	3,570	1,190	893
$6,150	2,376	3,564	1,188	891
$6,125	2,372	3,558	1,186	890
$6,100	2,369	3,554	1,185	888
$6,075	2,365	3,548	1,183	887
$6,050	2,361	3,542	1,181	885
$6,025	2,357	3,536	1,179	884
$6,000	2,353	3,530	1,177	882
$5,975	2,349	3,524	1,175	881
$5,950	2,345	3,518	1,173	879
$5,925	2,341	3,512	1,171	878
$5,900	2,338	3,507	1,169	877

TABLE 12—DISABILITY BENEFITS (cont'd)

Average Indexed Monthly Earnings	Disabled Worker	Disabled Worker Spouse and Children	One Child (No Spouse)	Spouse FRA–3
$5,875	2,334	3,501	1,167	875
$5,850	2,330	3,495	1,165	874
$5,825	2,326	3,489	1,163	872
$5,800	2,323	3,485	1,162	871
$5,775	2,319	3,479	1,160	870
$5,750	2,315	3,473	1,158	868
$5,725	2,311	3,467	1,156	867
$5,700	2,308	3,462	1,154	866
$5,675	2,304	3,456	1,152	864
$5,650	2,300	3,450	1,150	863
$5,625	2,296	3,444	1,148	861
$5,600	2,293	3,440	1,147	860
$5,575	2,289	3,434	1,145	858
$5,550	2,285	3,428	1,143	857
$5,525	2,281	3,422	1,141	855
$5,500	2,278	3,417	1,139	854
$5,475	2,274	3,411	1,137	853
$5,450	2,270	3,405	1,135	851
$5,425	2,266	3,399	1,133	850
$5,400	2,263	3,395	1,132	849
$5,375	2,245	3,368	1,123	842
$5,350	2,237	3,356	1,119	839
$5,325	2,229	3,344	1,115	836
$5,300	2,221	3,332	1,111	833
$5,275	2,213	3,320	1,107	830
$5,250	2,205	3,308	1,103	827
$5,225	2,196	3,294	1,098	824
$5,200	2,188	3,282	1,094	821
$5,175	2,180	3,270	1,090	818
$5,150	2,172	3,258	1,086	815
$5,125	2,164	3,246	1,082	812
$5,100	2,156	3,234	1,078	809
$5,075	2,148	3,222	1,074	806
$5,050	2,140	3,210	1,070	803
$5,025	2,132	3,198	1,066	800
$5,000	2,124	3,186	1,062	797
$4,975	2,116	3,174	1,058	794
$4,950	2,108	3,162	1,054	791
$4,925	2,100	3,150	1,050	788
$4,900	2,092	3,138	1,046	785
$4,875	2,084	3,126	1,042	782
$4,850	2,076	3,114	1,038	779
$4,825	2,068	3,102	1,034	776
$4,800	2,060	3,090	1,030	773
$4,775	2,052	3,078	1,026	770
$4,750	2,043	3,065	1,022	766
$4,725	2,035	3,053	1,018	763
$4,700	2,027	3,041	1,014	760
$4,675	2,019	3,029	1,010	757
$4,650	2,011	3,017	1,006	754
$4,625	2,003	3,005	1,002	751

TABLE 12—DISABILITY BENEFITS (cont'd)

Average Indexed Monthly Earnings	Disabled Worker	Disabled Worker Spouse and Children	One Child (No Spouse)	Spouse FRA–3
$4,600	1,995	2,993	998	748
$4,575	1,987	2,981	994	745
$4,550	1,979	2,969	990	742
$4,525	1,971	2,957	986	739
$4,500	1,963	2,945	982	736
$4,475	1,955	2,933	978	733
$4,450	1,947	2,921	974	730
$4,425	1,939	2,909	970	727
$4,400	1,931	2,897	966	724
$4,375	1,923	2,885	962	721
$4,350	1,915	2,873	958	718
$4,325	1,907	2,861	954	715
$4,300	1,898	2,847	949	712
$4,275	1,890	2,835	945	709
$4,250	1,882	2,823	941	706
$4,225	1,874	2,811	937	703
$4,200	1,866	2,799	933	700
$4,175	1,858	2,787	929	697
$4,150	1,850	2,775	925	694
$4,125	1,842	2,763	921	691
$4,100	1,834	2,751	917	688
$4,075	1,826	2,739	913	685
$4,050	1,818	2,727	909	682
$4,025	1,810	2,715	905	679
$4,000	1,802	2,703	901	676
$3,975	1,794	2,691	897	673
$3,950	1,786	2,679	893	670
$3,925	1,778	2,667	889	667
$3,900	1,770	2,655	885	664
$3,875	1,762	2,643	881	661
$3,850	1,754	2,631	877	658
$3,825	1,745	2,618	873	654
$3,800	1,737	2,606	869	651
$3,775	1,729	2,594	865	648
$3,750	1,721	2,582	861	645
$3,725	1,713	2,570	857	642
$3,700	1,705	2,558	853	639
$3,675	1,697	2,546	849	636
$3,650	1,689	2,534	845	633
$3,625	1,681	2,522	841	630
$3,600	1,673	2,510	837	627
$3,575	1,665	2,498	833	624
$3,550	1,657	2,486	829	621
$3,525	1,649	2,474	825	618
$3,500	1,641	2,462	821	615
$3,475	1,633	2,450	817	612
$3,450	1,625	2,438	813	609
$3,425	1,617	2,426	809	606
$3,400	1,609	2,414	805	603
$3,375	1,601	2,402	801	600
$3,350	1,592	2,388	796	597

TABLE 12—DISABILITY BENEFITS (cont'd)

Average Indexed Monthly Earnings	Disabled Worker	Disabled Worker Spouse and Children	One Child (No Spouse)	Spouse FRA–3
$3,325	1,584	2,376	792	594
$3,300	1,576	2,364	788	591
$3,275	1,568	2,352	784	588
$3,250	1,560	2,340	780	585
$3,225	1,552	2,328	776	582
$3,200	1,544	2,316	772	579
$3,175	1,536	2,304	768	576
$3,150	1,528	2,292	764	573
$3,125	1,520	2,280	760	570
$3,100	1,512	2,268	756	567
$3,075	1,504	2,256	752	564
$3,050	1,496	2,244	748	561
$3,025	1,488	2,232	744	558
$3,000	1,480	2,220	740	555
$2,975	1,472	2,208	736	552
$2,950	1,464	2,196	732	549
$2,925	1,456	2,184	728	546
$2,900	1,448	2,172	724	543
$2,875	1,439	2,159	720	540
$2,850	1,431	2,147	716	537
$2,825	1,423	2,135	712	534
$2,800	1,415	2,123	708	531
$2,775	1,407	2,111	704	528
$2,750	1,399	2,099	700	525
$2,725	1,391	2,087	696	522
$2,700	1,383	2,075	692	519
$2,675	1,375	2,063	688	516
$2,650	1,367	2,051	684	513
$2,625	1,359	2,039	680	510
$2,600	1,351	2,027	676	507
$2,575	1,343	2,015	672	504
$2,550	1,335	2,003	668	501
$2,525	1,327	1,991	664	498
$2,500	1,319	1,979	660	495
$2,475	1,311	1,967	656	492
$2,450	1,303	1,955	652	489
$2,425	1,295	1,943	648	486
$2,400	1,286	1,929	643	482
$2,375	1,278	1,917	639	479
$2,350	1,270	1,905	635	476
$2,325	1,262	1,893	631	473
$2,300	1,254	1,881	627	470
$2,275	1,246	1,869	623	467
$2,250	1,238	1,857	619	464
$2,225	1,230	1,845	615	461
$2,200	1,222	1,833	611	458
$2,175	1,214	1,821	607	455
$2,150	1,206	1,809	603	452
$2,125	1,198	1,797	599	449
$2,100	1,190	1,785	595	446
$2,075	1,182	1,773	591	443

TABLE 12—DISABILITY BENEFITS (cont'd)

Average Indexed Monthly Earnings	Disabled Worker	Disabled Worker Spouse and Children	One Child (No Spouse)	Spouse FRA–3
$2,050	1,174	1,761	587	440
$2,025	1,166	1,749	583	437
$2,000	1,158	1,737	579	434
$1,975	1,150	1,725	575	431
$1,950	1,142	1,713	571	428
$1,925	1,133	1,700	567	425
$1,900	1,125	1,688	563	422
$1,875	1,117	1,676	559	419
$1,850	1,109	1,664	555	416
$1,825	1,101	1,652	551	413
$1,800	1,093	1,640	547	410
$1,775	1,085	1,628	543	407
$1,750	1,077	1,616	539	404
$1,725	1,069	1,604	535	401
$1,700	1,061	1,592	531	398
$1,675	1,053	1,580	527	395
$1,650	1,045	1,568	523	392
$1,625	1,037	1,556	519	389
$1,600	1,029	1,544	515	386
$1,575	1,021	1,532	511	383
$1,550	1,013	1,520	507	380
$1,525	1,005	1,508	503	377
$1,500	997	1,496	499	374
$1,475	989	1,484	495	371
$1,450	980	1,470	490	368
$1,425	972	1,458	486	365
$1,400	964	1,446	482	362
$1,375	956	1,434	478	359
$1,350	948	1,422	474	356
$1,325	940	1,410	470	353
$1,300	932	1,398	466	350
$1,275	924	1,386	462	347
$1,250	916	1,374	458	344
$1,225	908	1,362	454	341
$1,200	900	1,350	450	338
$1,175	892	1,338	446	335
$1,150	884	1,326	442	332
$1,125	876	1,314	438	329
$1,100	868	1,302	434	326
$1,075	860	1,290	430	323
$1,050	852	1,278	426	320
$1,025	844	1,266	422	317
$1,000	835	1,253	418	313
$ 975	827	1,241	414	310
$ 950	819	1,229	410	307
$ 925	811	1,217	406	304
$ 900	798	1,197	399	299
$ 875	788	1,182	394	296
$ 850	765	1,148	383	287
$ 825	743	1,115	372	279
$ 800	720	1,080	360	270

APPENDIX B
FEDERAL EMPLOYEE TABLES

TABLE 1—GENERAL PAY SCHEDULE FOR FEDERAL GOVERNMENT WORKERS
EFFECTIVE IN JANUARY 2018
The 2019 schedule was not finalized as this 2019 edition went to press. President Trump issued an Executive Order freezing increases but an increase of 1.4% to 1.5% is being considered by Congress.

Step	1	2	3	4	5	6	7	8	9	10
GS-1	18,785	19,414	20,039	20,660	21,285	21,650	22,267	22,891	22,915	23,502
2	21,121	21,624	22,323	22,915	23,175	23,857	24,539	25,221	25,903	26,585
3	23,045	23,813	24,581	25,349	26,117	26,885	27,653	28,421	29,189	29,957
4	25,871	26,733	27,595	28,457	29,319	30,181	31,043	31,905	32,767	33,629
5	28,945	29,910	30,875	31,840	32,805	33,770	34,735	35,700	36,665	37,630
6	32,264	33,339	34,414	35,489	36,564	37,639	38,714	39,789	40,864	41,939
7	35,854	37,049	38,244	39,439	40,634	41,829	43,024	44,219	45,414	46,609
8	39,707	41,031	42,355	43,679	45,003	46,327	47,651	48,975	50,299	51,623
9	43,857	45,319	46,781	48,243	49,705	51,167	52,629	54,091	55,553	57,015
10	48,297	49,907	51,517	53,127	54,737	56,347	57,957	59,567	61,177	62,787
11	53,062	54,831	56,600	58,369	60,138	61,907	63,676	65,445	67,214	68,983
12	63,600	65,720	67,840	69,960	72,080	74,200	76,320	78,440	80,560	82,680
13	75,628	78,149	80,670	83,191	85,712	88,233	90,754	93,275	95,796	98,317
14	89,370	92,349	95,328	98,307	101,286	104,235	107,244	110,233	113,202	116,181
15	105,123	108,627	112,131	115,635	119,139	122,643	126,147	129,651	133,155	133,659

LOCALITY PAY ADJUSTMENTS
Combined national and locality pay adjustments for 46 locations in 2018 are listed below.

Albany	16.50%	Laredo	17.40%
Albuquerque	15.76%	Las Vegas	16.49%
Atlanta	21.16%	Los Angeles	30.57%
Austin	16.71%	Miami	22.64%
Boston	27.48%	Milwaukee	20.14%
Buffalo	19.18%	Minneapolis	23.37%
Charlotte	16.21%	New York	32.13%
Chicago	27.47%	Philadelphia	24.29%
Cincinnati	19.87%	Phoenix	19.03%
Cleveland	20.08%	Pittsburgh	18.35%
Colorado Springs	16.59%	Portland	22.53%
Columbus	18.97%	Raleigh-Durham	19.52%
Dallas	23.40%	Richmond	18.79%
Davenport	16.08%	Sacramento	24.86%
Dayton	18.11%	San Diego	27.88%
Denver	25.47%	San Francisco	39.28%
Detroit	26.25%	Seattle	25.11%
Harrisburg	16.15%	St. Louis	16.17%
Hartford	28.21%	Tucson	15.66%
Houston	31.74%	Washington	28.22%
Huntsville	18.49%	Rest of U.S.	15.37%
Indianapolis	16.23%	Alaska	28.02%
Kansas City	16.10%	Hawaii	18.43%

TABLE 2—BASIC MONTHLY RETIREMENT ANNUITY FOR CSRS EMPLOYEES

High-3 Annual Salary	Years of Service							
	5	10	15	20	25	30	35	40
$15,000	$97	$209	$337	$466	$594	$723	$851	$980
16,000	103	223	360	497	634	771	908	1,045
17,000	109	236	382	528	673	819	965	1,110
18,000	116	251	405	559	713	868	1,022	1,176
19,000	122	264	427	590	752	916	1,078	1,241
20,000	129	278	450	621	793	964	1,135	1,307
21,000	135	292	472	652	832	1,012	1,191	1,371
22,000	142	306	494	684	872	1,060	1,249	1,437
23,000	148	320	517	714	911	1,108	1,306	1,502
24,000	154	334	540	745	951	1,157	1,362	1,568
25,000	160	348	562	776	991	1,205	1,419	1,633
26,000	168	362	590	807	1,030	1,253	1,475	1,698
27,000	174	376	608	839	1,070	1,301	1,533	1,764
28,000	180	390	630	870	1,109	1,350	1,589	1,829
29,000	186	404	652	901	1,149	1,397	1,646	1,895
30,000	193	417	674	931	1,188	1,445	1,702	1,959
31,000	199	432	697	962	1,228	1,494	1,759	2,025
32,000	206	445	720	994	1,268	1,542	1,816	2,090
33,000	212	460	742	1,025	1,308	1,590	1,873	2,156
34,000	219	473	765	1,056	1,347	1,639	1,930	2,220
35,000	225	487	787	1,087	1,387	1,687	1,986	2,286
36,000	231	502	810	1,118	1,427	1,735	2,044	2,352
37,000	237	515	832	1,149	1,466	1,783	2,100	2,417
38,000	245	529	854	1,180	1,506	1,831	2,157	2,483
39,000	251	543	877	1,211	1,545	1,879	2,213	2,547
40,000	257	557	900	1,242	1,585	1,928	2,270	2,613
41,000	263	571	922	1,274	1,624	1,976	2,327	2,678
42,000	270	585	945	1,305	1,664	2,024	2,384	2,744
43,000	277	598	967	1,335	1,703	2,072	2,440	2,808
44,000	283	613	990	1,366	1,747	2,121	2,497	2,874
45,000	289	626	1,012	1,397	1,783	2,168	2,554	2,939
46,000	296	640	1,034	1,429	1,823	2,216	2,611	3,005
47,000	302	654	1,057	1,460	1,862	2,265	2,668	3,070
48,000	308	668	1,079	1,491	1,902	2,313	2,724	3,135
49,000	315	682	1,101	1,520	1,941	2,360	2,780	3,200
50,000	321	695	1,123	1,551	1,980	2,408	2,836	3,252
51,000	327	708	1,145	1,582	2,019	2,456	2,893	3,330
52,000	334	724	1,169	1,614	2,060	2,505	2,950	3,397
53,000	340	737	1,190	1,645	2,099	2,553	3,007	3,461
54,000	346	750	1,213	1,676	2,138	2,601	3,063	3,526
55,000	353	765	1,236	1,706	2,178	2,649	3,120	3,592
56,000	360	779	1,258	1,738	2,218	2,697	3,178	3,658
57,000	366	793	1,281	1,769	2,257	2,746	3,234	3,722
58,000	372	806	1,302	1,799	2,297	2,793	3,290	3,787
59,000	378	820	1,325	1,831	2,337	2,841	3,347	3,853
60,000	386	835	1,349	1,863	2,377	2,891	3,405	3,919
61,000	392	848	1,370	1,893	2,416	2,938	3,460	3,984
62,000	398	862	1,393	1,924	2,456	2,986	3,518	4,049
63,000	404	876	1,416	1,955	2,495	3,035	3,574	4,114
64,000	411	890	1,438	1,986	2,509	3,083	3,631	4,180

TABLE 2—BASIC MONTHLY RETIREMENT ANNUITY FOR
CSRS EMPLOYEES (cont'd)

High-3 Annual Salary	Years of Service							
	5	10	15	20	25	30	35	40
$65,000	$417	$905	$1,462	$2,019	$2,575	$3,132	$3,689	$4,246
66,000	425	919	1,484	2,050	2,615	3,181	3,746	4,311
68,000	437	947	1,530	2,112	2,694	3,277	3,859	4,442
70,000	450	975	1,574	2,174	2,774	3,373	3,973	4,573
72,000	463	1,002	1,619	2,236	2,853	3,470	4,086	4,703
74,000	476	1,030	1,664	2,298	2,932	3,566	4,199	4,834
76,000	488	1,058	1,710	2,360	3,011	3,663	4,313	4,964
80,000	514	1,113	1,799	2,485	3,169	3,855	4,541	5,225
83,000	534	1,155	1,867	2,577	3,289	4,000	4,710	5,422
86,000	553	1,198	1,934	2,671	3,408	4,144	4,881	5,618
90,000	579	1,253	2,024	2,795	3,566	4,337	5,108	5,879
93,000	597	1,294	2,091	2,888	3,684	4,481	5,278	6,074
96,000	617	1,336	2,159	2,981	3,804	4,626	5,448	6,271
100,000	643	1,392	2,249	3,106	3,962	4,819	5,676	6,532
110,000	707	1,532	2,473	3,416	4,359	5,300	6,243	7,186

NOTE: According to OPM's recent Profile of Federal Civilian Non-Postal Employees only 4.21% of active federal employees are under the CSRS plan while 91.49% are in FERS.

The CSRS annuity is computed based on length of civil service including unused sick leave if retiring on an immediate annuity and "high-3" average pay. The high-3 average pay includes locality pay and annual premiums for standby duty and availability if applicable. Other pay such as differentials, overtime, allowances and others are not included.

Determination of length of CSRS service - add all periods of creditable service, and the period represented by unused sick leave, then eliminate any fractional part of a month. The "high-3" average pay is the highest average basic pay earned during any 3 consecutive - years of service. The basic annuity cannot be more than 80 percent of "high-3" average pay, unless the amount over 80 percent is due to crediting unused sick leave.

TABLE 3—BASIC MONTHLY RETIREMENT ANNUITY
FOR FERS EMPLOYEES

High-3 Annual Salary	Years of Service							
	5	10	15	20	25	30	35	40
$15,000	$65	$129	$193	$257	$322	$386	$450	$514
16,000	69	137	206	274	342	411	480	548
17,000	73	146	219	291	364	437	510	583
18,000	77	154	231	308	386	463	540	617
19,000	81	162	245	326	407	488	570	651
20,000	85	172	257	342	429	514	599	686
22,000	95	188	283	377	471	565	660	754
24,000	103	206	308	411	514	617	720	822
26,000	111	223	334	445	557	668	779	891
28,000	120	240	360	480	599	720	840	959
30,000	129	257	386	514	643	771	900	1,028
32,000	137	274	411	548	686	822	959	1,097
34,000	146	291	437	583	728	874	1,020	1,165
36,000	154	308	463	617	771	925	1,079	1,234
38,000	162	326	488	651	814	977	1,139	1,302
40,000	172	342	514	686	856	1,028	1,200	1,370
42,000	180	360	540	720	900	1,079	1,259	1,439
44,000	188	377	565	754	943	1,131	1,319	1,508
46,000	197	394	591	788	985	1,182	1,380	1,576
48,000	206	411	617	822	1,028	1,234	1,439	1,645
50,000	214	429	643	856	1,071	1,285	1,499	1,714
53,000	227	454	682	908	1,135	1,362	1,589	1,816
55,000	235	471	707	943	1,178	1,414	1,649	1,884
57,000	245	488	733	977	1,221	1,465	1,710	1,953
60,000	257	514	771	1,028	1,285	1,542	1,799	2,056
65,000	279	557	836	1,113	1,392	1,671	1,949	2,228
66,000	283	565	848	1,131	1,414	1,696	1,979	2,262
68,000	291	583	874	1,165	1,457	1,748	2,039	2,330
70,000	300	599	900	1,200	1,499	1,799	2,099	2,398
72,000	308	617	925	1,234	1,542	1,850	2,159	2,467
74,000	317	634	951	1,268	1,585	1,902	2,218	2,536
76,000	326	651	977	1,302	1,407	1,689	1,970	2,251
80,000	342	686	1,028	1,370	1,714	2,056	2,398	2,742
83,000	356	711	1,067	1,422	1,777	2,133	2,489	2,844
86,000	368	737	1,105	1,473	1,842	2,210	2,578	2,947
90,000	386	771	1,157	1,542	1,928	2,313	2,699	3,084
93,000	399	797	1,196	1,593	1,992	2,390	2,789	3,187
96,000	411	822	1,234	1,645	2,056	2,467	2,878	3,290
100,000	429	856	1,285	1,714	2,141	2,570	2,999	3,426
110,000	471	943	1,414	1,884	2,356	2,827	3,298	3,770

NOTE: Computation is based on the following:

- 1 percent of high-3 average salary for each year of service if under age 62 at separation for retirement, OR age 62 or older with less than 20 years of service

- 1 percent of high-3 average salary for each year of service at age 62 or older at separation with 20 or more years of service.

NOTE: 91.94% of Federal employees are part of the FERS system.

TABLE 4
AMOUNT OF INSURANCE PROTECTION UNDER THE FEDERAL
EMPLOYEES GROUP LIFE INSURANCE ACT OF 1980 (P.L. 96-427)
EFFECTIVE OCTOBER 1, 1981*

Annual Pay		Basic Insurance Amount	Amount of Group Life Insurance				
Greater than –	But not greater than –		Age 35 and Under	Age 36 (1.9)	Age 37 (1.8)	Age 38 (1.7)	Age 39 (1.6)
$ 0	$ 8,000	$10,000	$20,000	$19,000	$ 18,000	$17,000	$16,000
8,000	9,000	11,000	22,000	20,900	19,800	18,700	17,600
9,000	10,000	12,000	24,000	22,800	21,600	20,400	19,200
10,000	11,000	13,000	26,000	24,700	23,400	22,100	20,800
11,000	12,000	14,000	28,000	26,600	25,200	23,800	22,400
12,000	13,000	15,000	30,000	28,500	27,000	25,500	24,000
13,000	14,000	16,000	32,000	30,400	28,800	27,200	25,600
14,000	15,000	17,000	34,000	32,300	30,600	28,900	27,200
15,000	16,000	18,000	36,000	34,200	32,400	30,600	28,800
16,000	17,000	19,000	38,000	36,100	34,200	32,300	30,400
17,000	18,000	20,000	40,000	38,000	36,000	34,000	32,000
18,000	19,000	21,000	42,000	39,900	37,800	35,700	33,600
19,000	20,000	22,000	44,000	41,800	39,600	37,400	35,200
20,000	21,000	23,000	46,000	43,700	41,400	39,100	36,800
21,000	22,000	24,000	48,000	45,600	43,200	40,800	38,400
22,000	23,000	25,000	50,000	47,500	45,000	42,500	40,000
23,000	24,000	26,000	52,000	49,400	46,800	44,200	41,600
24,000	25,000	27,000	54,000	51,300	48,600	45,900	43,200
25,000	26,000	28,000	56,000	53,200	50,400	47,600	44,800
26,000	27,000	29,000	58,000	55,100	52,200	49,300	46,400
27,000	28,000	30,000	60,000	57,000	54,000	51,000	48,000
28,000	29,000	31,000	62,000	58,900	55,800	52,700	49,600
29,000	30,000	32,000	64,000	60,800	57,600	54,400	51,200
30,000	31,000	33,000	66,000	62,700	59,400	56,100	52,800
31,000	32,000	34,000	68,000	64,600	61,200	57,800	54,400
32,000	33,000	35,000	70,000	66,500	63,000	59,500	56,000
33,000	34,000	36,000	72,000	68,400	64,800	61,200	57,600
34,000	35,000	37,000	74,000	70,300	66,600	62,900	59,200
35,000	36,000	38,000	76,000	72,200	68,400	64,600	60,800
36,000	37,000	39,000	78,000	74,100	70,200	63,300	62,400
37,000	38,000	40,000	80,000	76,000	72,000	68,000	64,000
38,000	39,000	41,000	82,000	77,900	73,800	69,700	65,600
39,000	40,000	42,000	84,000	79,800	75,600	71,400	67,200
40,000	41,000	43,000	86,000	81,700	77,400	73,100	68,800
41,000	42,000	44,000	88,000	83,600	79,200	74,800	70,400
42,000	43,000	45,000	90,000	85,500	81,000	76,500	72,000
43,000	44,000	46,000	92,000	87,400	82,800	78,200	73,600
44,000	45,000	47,000	94,000	89,300	84,600	79,900	75,200
45,000	46,000	48,000	96,000	91,200	86,400	81,600	76,800
46,000	47,000	49,000	98,000	93,100	88,200	83,300	78,400
47,000	48,000	50,000	100,000	95,000	90,000	85,000	80,000
48,000	49,000	51,000	102,000	96,900	91,800	86,700	81,600
49,000	50,000	52,000	104,000	98,800	93,600	88,400	83,200
50,000	51,000	53,000	106,000	100,700	95,400	90,100	84,800

AMOUNT OF INSURANCE PROTECTION UNDER THE FEDERAL EMPLOYEES GROUP LIFE INSURANCE ACT OF 1980 (P.L. 96-427) EFFECTIVE OCTOBER 1, 1981*

Amount of Group Life Insurance						Amount of Group Accidental Death and Dismemberment Insurance
Age 40 (1.5)	Age 41 (1.4)	Age 42 (1.3)	Age 43 (1.2)	Age 44 (1.1)	45 and Over (1.0)	
$15,000	$14,000	$13,000	$12,000	$11,000	$10,000	$10,000
16,500	15,400	14,300	13,200	12,100	11,000	11,000
18,000	16,800	15,600	14,400	13,200	12,000	12,000
19,500	18,200	16,900	15,600	14,300	13,000	13,000
21,000	19,600	18,200	16,800	15,400	14,000	14,000
22,500	21,000	19,500	18,000	16,500	15,000	15,000
24,000	22,400	20,800	19,200	17,600	16,000	16,000
25,500	23,800	22,100	20,400	18,700	17,000	17,000
27,000	25,200	23,400	21,600	19,800	18,000	18,000
28,500	26,600	24,700	22,800	20,900	19,000	19,000
30,000	28,000	26,000	24,000	22,000	20,000	20,000
31,500	29,400	27,300	25,200	23,100	21,000	21,000
33,000	30,800	28,600	26,400	24,200	22,000	22,000
34,500	32,200	29,900	27,600	25,300	23,000	23,000
36,000	33,600	31,200	28,800	26,400	24,000	24,000
37,500	35,000	32,500	30,000	27,500	25,000	25,000
39,000	36,400	33,800	31,200	28,600	26,000	26,000
40,500	37,800	35,100	32,400	29,700	27,000	27,000
42,000	39,200	36,400	33,600	30,800	28,000	28,000
43,500	40,600	37,700	34,800	31,900	29,000	29,000
45,000	42,000	39,000	36,000	33,000	30,000	30,000
46,500	43,400	40,300	37,200	34,100	31,000	31,000
48,000	44,800	41,600	38,400	35,200	32,000	32,000
49,500	46,200	42,900	39,600	36,300	33,000	33,000
51,000	47,600	44,200	40,800	37,400	34,000	34,000
52,500	49,000	45,500	42,000	38,500	35,000	35,000
54,000	50,400	46,800	43,200	39,600	36,000	36,000
55,500	51,800	48,100	44,400	40,700	37,000	37,000
57,000	53,200	49,400	45,600	41,800	38,000	38,000
58,500	54,600	50,700	46,800	42,900	39,000	39,000
60,000	56,000	52,000	48,000	44,000	40,000	40,000
61,500	57,400	53,300	49,200	45,100	41,000	41,000
63,000	58,800	54,600	50,400	46,200	42,000	42,000
64,500	60,200	55,900	51,600	47,300	43,000	43,000
66,000	61,600	57,200	52,800	48,400	44,000	44,000
67,500	63,000	58,500	54,000	49,500	45,000	45,000
69,000	64,400	59,800	55,200	50,600	46,000	46,000
70,500	65,800	61,100	56,400	51,700	47,000	47,000
72,000	67,200	62,400	57,600	52,800	48,000	48,000
73,500	68,600	63,700	58,800	53,900	49,000	49,000
75,000	70,000	65,000	60,000	55,000	50,000	50,000
76,500	71,400	66,300	61,200	56,100	51,000	51,000
78,000	72,800	67,600	62,400	57,200	52,000	52,000
79,500	74,200	68,900	63,600	58,300	53,000	53,000

AMOUNT OF INSURANCE PROTECTION UNDER THE FEDERAL EMPLOYEES GROUP LIFE INSURANCE ACT OF 1980 (P.L. 96-427) EFFECTIVE OCTOBER 1, 1981*

Annual Pay		Basic Insurance Amount	Amount of Group Life Insurance				
Greater than –	But not greater than –		Age 35 and Under	Age 36 (1.9)	Age 37 (1.8)	Age 38 (1.7)	Age 39 (1.6)
51,000	52,000	54,000	108,000	102,600	97,200	91,800	86,400
52,000	53,000	55,000	110,000	104,500	99,000	93,500	88,000
53,000	54,000	56,000	112,000	106,400	100,800	95,200	89,600
54,000	55,000	57,000	114,000	108,300	102,600	96,900	91,200
55,000	56,000	58,000	116,000	110,200	104,400	98,600	92,800
56,000	57,000	59,000	118,000	112,100	106,200	100,300	94,400
57,000	58,000	60,000	120,000	114,000	108,000	102,000	96,000
58,000	59,000	61,000	122,000	115,900	109,800	103,700	97,600
59,000	60,000	62,000	124,000	117,800	111,600	105,400	99,200
60,000	61,000	63,000	126,000	119,700	113,400	107,100	100,800
61,000	62,000	64,000	128,000	121,600	115,200	108,800	102,400
62,000	63,000	65,000	130,000	123,500	117,000	110,500	104,000
63,000	64,000	66,000	132,000	125,400	118,800	112,200	105,600
64,000	65,000	67,000	134,000	127,300	120,600	113,900	107,200
65,000	66,000	68,000	136,000	129,200	122,400	115,600	108,800
66,000	67,000	69,000	138,000	131,100	124,200	117,300	110,400
67,000	68,000	70,000	140,000	133,000	126,000	119,000	112,000
68,000	69,000	71,000	142,000	134,900	127,800	120,700	113,600
69,000	70,000	72,000	144,000	136,800	129,600	122,400	115,200
70,000	71,000	73,000	146,000	138,700	131,400	124,100	116,800
71,000	72,000	74,000	148,000	140,600	133,200	125,800	118,400
72,000	73,000	75,000	150,000	142,500	135,000	127,500	120,000
73,000	74,000	76,000	152,000	144,400	136,800	129,200	121,600
74,000	75,000	77,000	154,000	146,300	138,600	130,900	123,200
75,000	76,000	78,000	156,000	148,200	140,400	132,600	124,800
76,000	77,000	79,000	158,000	150,100	142,200	134,300	126,400
77,000	78,000	80,000	160,000	152,000	144,000	136,000	128,000
78,000	79,000	81,000	162,000	153,900	145,800	137,700	129,600
79,000	80,000	82,000	164,000	155,800	147,600	139,400	131,200
80,000	81,000	83,000	166,000	157,700	149,400	141,100	132,800
81,000	82,000	84,000	168,000	159,600	151,200	142,800	134,400
82,000	83,000	85,000	170,000	161,500	153,000	144,500	136,000
83,000	84,000	86,000	172,000	163,400	154,800	146,200	137,600
84,000	85,000	87,000	174,000	165,300	156,600	147,900	139,200
85,000	86,000	88,000	176,000	167,200	158,400	149,600	140,800
86,000	87,000	89,000	178,000	169,100	160,200	151,300	142,400
87,000	88,000	90,000	180,000	171,000	162,000	153,000	144,000
88,000	89,000	91,000	182,000	172,900	163,800	154,700	145,600
89,000	90,000	92,000	184,000	174,800	165,600	156,400	147,200
90,000	91,000	93,000	186,000	176,700	167,400	158,100	148,800

AMOUNT OF INSURANCE PROTECTION UNDER THE FEDERAL EMPLOYEES GROUP LIFE INSURANCE ACT OF 1980 (P.L. 96-427) EFFECTIVE OCTOBER 1, 1981*

Amount of Group Life Insurance						Amount of Group Accidental Death and Dismemberment Insurance
Age 40 (1.5)	Age 41 (1.4)	Age 42 (1.3)	Age 43 (1.2)	Age 44 (1.1)	45 and Over (1.0)	
81,000	75,600	70,200	64,800	59,400	54,000	54,000
82,500	77,000	71,500	66,000	60,500	55,000	55,000
84,000	78,400	72,800	67,200	61,600	56,000	56,000
85,500	79,800	74,100	68,400	62,700	57,000	57,000
87,000	81,200	75,400	69,600	63,800	58,000	58,000
88,500	82,600	76,700	70,800	64,900	59,000	59,000
90,000	84,000	78,000	72,000	66,000	60,000	60,000
91,500	85,400	79,300	73,200	67,100	61,000	61,000
93,000	86,800	80,600	74,400	68,200	62,000	62,000
94,500	88,200	81,900	75,600	69,300	63,000	63,000
96,000	89,600	83,200	76,800	70,400	64,000	64,000
97,500	91,000	84,500	78,000	71,500	65,000	65,000
99,000	92,400	85,800	79,200	72,600	66,000	66,000
100,500	93,800	87,100	80,400	73,700	67,000	67,000
102,000	95,200	88,400	81,600	74,800	68,000	68,000
103,500	96,600	89,700	82,800	75,900	69,000	69,000
105,000	98,000	91,000	84,000	77,000	70,000	70,000
106,500	99,400	92,300	85,200	78,100	71,000	71,000
108,000	100,800	93,600	86,400	79,200	72,000	72,000
109,500	102,200	94,900	87,600	80,300	73,000	73,000
111,000	103,600	96,200	88,800	81,400	74,000	74,000
112,500	105,000	97,500	90,000	82,500	75,000	75,000
114,000	106,400	98,800	91,200	83,600	76,000	76,000
115,500	107,800	100,100	92,400	84,700	77,000	77,000
117,000	109,200	101,400	93,600	85,800	78,000	78,000
118,500	110,600	102,700	94,800	86,900	79,000	79,000
120,000	112,000	104,000	96,000	88,000	80,000	80,000
121,500	113,400	105,300	97,200	89,100	81,000	81,000
123,000	114,800	106,600	98,400	90,200	82,000	82,000
124,500	116,200	107,900	99,600	91,300	83,000	83,000
126,000	117,600	109,200	100,800	92,400	84,000	84,000
127,500	119,000	110,500	102,000	93,500	85,000	85,000
129,000	120,400	111,800	103,200	94,600	86,000	86,000
130,500	121,800	113,100	104,400	95,700	87,000	87,000
132,000	123,200	114,400	105,600	96,800	88,000	88,000
133,500	124,600	115,700	106,800	97,900	89,000	89,000
135,000	126,000	117,000	108,000	99,000	90,000	90,000
136,500	127,400	118,300	109,200	100,100	91,000	91,000
138,000	128,800	119,600	110,400	101,200	92,000	92,000
139,500	130,200	120,900	111,600	102,300	93,000	93,000

AMOUNT OF INSURANCE PROTECTION UNDER THE FEDERAL EMPLOYEES GROUP LIFE INSURANCE ACT OF 1980 (P.L. 96-427) EFFECTIVE OCTOBER 1, 1981*

Annual Pay			Amount of Group Life Insurance				
Greater than –	But not greater than –	Basic Insurance Amount	Age 35 and Under	Age 36 (1.9)	Age 37 (1.8)	Age 38 (1.7)	Age 39 (1.6)
91,000	92,000	94,000	188,000	178,600	169,200	159,800	150,400
92,000	93,000	95,000	190,000	180,500	171,000	161,500	152,000
93,000	94,000	96,000	192,000	182,400	172,800	163,200	153,600
94,000	95,000	97,000	194,000	184,300	174,600	164,900	155,200
95,000	96,000	98,000	196,000	186,200	176,400	166,600	156,800
96,000	97,000	99,000	198,000	188,100	178,200	168,300	158,400
97,000	98,000	100,000	200,000	190,000	180,000	170,000	160,000
98,000	99,000	101,000	202,000	191,900	181,800	171,700	161,600
99,000	100,000	102,000	204,000	193,800	183,600	173,400	163,200
100,000	101,000	103,000	206,000	195,700	185,400	175,100	164,800
101,000	102,000	104,000	208,000	197,600	187,200	176,800	166,400
102,000	103,000	105,000	210,000	199,500	189,000	178,500	168,000
103,000	104,000	106,000	212,000	201,400	190,800	180,200	169,600
104,000	105,000	107,000	214,000	203,300	192,600	181,900	171,200
105,000	106,000	108,000	216,000	205,200	194,400	183,600	172,800
106,000	107,000	109,000	218,000	207,100	196,200	185,300	174,400
107,000	108,000	110,000	220,000	209,000	198,000	187,000	176,000
108,000	109,000	111,000	222,000	210,900	199,800	188,700	177,600
109,000	110,000	112,000	224,000	212,800	201,600	190,400	179,200
110,000	111,000	113,000	226,000	214,700	203,400	192,100	180,800
111,000	112,000	114,000	228,000	216,600	205,200	193,800	182,400
112,000	113,000	115,000	230,000	218,500	207,000	195,500	184,000
113,000	114,000	116,000	232,000	220,400	208,800	197,200	185,600
114,000	115,000	117,000	234,000	222,300	210,600	198,900	187,200
115,000	116,000	118,000	236,000	224,200	212,400	200,600	188,800
116,000	117,000	119,000	238,000	226,100	214,200	202,300	190,400
117,000	118,000	120,000	240,000	228,000	216,000	204,000	192,000
118,000	119,000	121,000	242,000	229,900	217,800	205,700	193,600
119,000	120,000	122,000	244,000	231,800	219,600	207,400	195,200
120,000	121,000	123,000	246,000	233,700	221,400	209,100	196,800
121,000	122,000	124,000	248,000	235,600	223,200	210,800	198,400
122,000	123,000	125,000	250,000	237,500	225,000	212,500	200,000
123,000	124,000	126,000	252,000	239,400	226,800	214,200	201,600
124,000	125,000	127,000	254,000	241,300	228,600	215,900	203,200
125,000	126,000	128,000	256,000	243,200	230,400	217,600	204,800
126,000	127,000	129,000	258,000	245,100	232,200	219,300	206,400
127,000	128,000	130,000	260,000	247,000	234,000	221,000	208,000
128,000	129,000	131,000	262,000	248,900	235,800	222,700	209,600
129,000	130,000	132,000	264,000	250,800	237,600	224,400	211,200
130,000	131,000	133,000	266,000	252,700	239,400	226,100	212,800
131,000	132,000	134,000	268,000	254,600	241,200	227,800	214,400
132,000	133,000	135,000	270,000	256,500	243,000	229,500	216,000
133,000	134,000	136,000	272,000	258,400	244,800	231,200	217,600
134,000	135,000	137,000	274,000	260,300	246,600	232,900	219,200
135,000	136,000	138,000	276,000	262,200	248,400	234,600	220,800
136,000	137,000	139,000	278,000	264,100	250,200	236,300	222,400
137,000	138,000	140,000	280,000	266,000	252,000	238,000	224,000
138,000	139,000	141,000	282,000	267,900	253,800	239,700	225,600
139,000	140,000	142,000	284,000	269,800	255,600	241,400	227,200
140,000	141,000	143,000	286,000	271,700	257,400	243,100	228,800

AMOUNT OF INSURANCE PROTECTION UNDER THE FEDERAL EMPLOYEES GROUP LIFE INSURANCE ACT OF 1980 (P.L. 96-427) EFFECTIVE OCTOBER 1, 1981*

Amount of Group Life Insurance						Amount of Group Accidental Death and Dismemberment Insurance
Age 40 (1.5)	Age 41 (1.4)	Age 42 (1.3)	Age 43 (1.2)	Age 44 (1.1)	45 and Over (1.0)	
141,000	131,600	122,200	112,800	103,400	94,000	94,000
142,500	133,000	123,500	114,000	104,500	95,000	95,000
144,000	134,400	124,800	115,200	105,600	96,000	96,000
145,500	135,800	126,100	116,400	106,700	97,000	97,000
147,000	137,200	127,400	117,600	107,800	98,000	98,000
148,500	138,600	128,700	118,800	108,900	99,000	99,000
150,000	140,000	130,000	120,000	110,000	100,000	100,000
151,500	141,400	131,300	121,200	111,100	101,000	101,000
153,000	142,800	132,600	122,400	112,200	102,000	102,000
154,500	144,200	133,900	123,600	113,300	103,000	103,000
156,000	145,600	135,200	124,800	114,400	104,000	104,000
157,500	147,000	136,500	126,000	115,500	105,000	105,000
159,000	148,400	137,800	127,200	116,600	106,000	106,000
160,500	149,800	139,100	128,400	117,700	107,000	107,000
162,000	151,200	140,400	129,600	118,800	108,000	108,000
163,500	152,600	141,700	130,800	119,900	109,000	109,000
165,000	154,000	143,000	132,000	121,000	110,000	110,000
166,500	155,400	144,300	133,200	122,100	111,000	111,000
168,000	156,800	145,600	134,400	123,200	112,000	112,000
169,500	158,200	146,900	135,600	124,300	113,000	113,000
171,000	159,600	148,200	136,800	125,400	114,000	114,000
172,500	161,000	149,500	138,000	126,500	115,000	115,000
174,000	162,400	150,800	139,200	127,600	116,000	116,000
175,500	163,800	152,100	140,400	128,700	117,000	117,000
177,000	165,200	153,400	141,600	129,800	118,000	118,000
178,500	166,600	154,700	142,800	130,900	119,000	119,000
180,000	168,000	156,000	144,000	132,000	120,000	120,000
181,500	169,400	157,300	145,200	133,100	121,000	121,000
183,000	170,800	158,600	146,400	134,200	122,000	122,000
184,500	172,200	159,900	147,600	135,300	123,000	123,000
186,000	173,600	161,200	148,800	136,400	124,000	124,000
187,500	175,000	162,500	150,000	137,500	125,000	125,000
189,000	176,400	163,800	151,200	138,600	126,000	126,000
190,500	177,800	165,100	152,400	139,700	127,000	127,000
192,000	179,200	166,400	153,600	140,800	128,000	128,000
193,500	180,600	167,700	154,800	141,900	129,000	129,000
195,000	182,000	169,000	156,000	143,000	130,000	130,000
196,500	183,400	170,300	157,200	144,100	131,000	131,000
198,000	184,800	171,600	158,400	145,200	132,000	132,000
199,500	186,200	172,900	159,600	146,300	133,000	133,000
201,000	187,600	174,200	160,800	147,400	134,000	134,000
202,500	189,000	175,500	162,000	148,500	135,000	135,000
204,000	190,400	176,800	163,200	149,600	136,000	136,000
205,500	191,800	178,100	164,400	150,700	137,000	137,000
207,000	193,200	179,400	165,600	151,800	138,000	138,000
208,500	194,600	180,700	166,800	152,900	139,000	139,000
210,000	196,000	182,000	168,000	154,000	140,000	140,000
211,500	197,400	183,300	169,200	155,100	141,000	141,000
213,000	198,800	184,600	170,400	156,200	142,000	142,000
214,500	200,200	185,900	171,600	157,300	143,000	143,000

* P.L. 96-427 revised the group term life insurance coverage available to civil service employees. The amounts of group term life shown in this table became effective October 1, 1981.

APPENDIX C
SERVICE MEMBERS AND VETERANS TABLES

TABLE 1—COMPARATIVE RANKS

Comparative Officer Ranks

GRADE	ARMY	AIR FORCE	MARINE CORPS	NAVY
COMMISSIONED OFFICERS				
O-10	General	General	General	Admiral
O-9	Lieutenant General	Lieutenant General	Lieutenant General	Vice Admiral
O-8	Major General	Major General	Major General	Rear Admiral (Upper Half)
O-7	Brigadier General	Brigadier General	Brigadier General	Rear Admiral (Lower Half)
O-6	Colonel	Colonel	Colonel	Captain
O-5	Lieutenant Colonel	Lieutenant Colonel	Lieutenant Colonel	Commander
O-4	Major	Major	Major	Lieutenant Commander
O-3	Captain	Captain	Captain	Lieutenant
O-2	First Lieutenant	First Lieutenant	First Lieutenant	Lieutenant Junior Grade
O-1	Second Lieutenant	Second Lieutenant	Second Lieutenant	Ensign
WARRANT OFFICERS				
W-5	Chief Warrant Officer 5	None	Chief Warrant Officer 5	USN Chief Warrant Officer 5
W-4	Chief Warrant Officer 4	None	Chief Warrant Officer 4	USN Chief Warrant Officer 4
W-3	Chief Warrant Officer 3	None	Chief Warrant Officer 3	USN Chief Warrant Officer 3
W-2	Chief Warrant Officer 2	None	Chief Warrant Officer 2	USN Chief Warrant Officer 2
W-1	Warrant Officer 1	None	Warrant Officer 1	(USN Warrant Officer no longer used)

Comparative Ranks—Enlisted Personnel

GRADE	ARMY	AIR FORCE	MARINE CORPS	NAVY
E-9	Sergeant Major/ Command Sergeant Major	Chief Master Sergeant	Sergeant Major & Master Gunnery Sergeant	Master Chief Petty Officer
E-8	First Sergeant & Master Sergeant	Senior Master Sergeant	First Sergeant & & Master Sergeant	Senior Chief Petty Officer
E-7	Sergeant First Class	Master Sergeant & First Sergeant	Gunnery Sergeant	Chief Petty Officer
E-6	Staff Sergeant	Technical Sergeant	Staff Sergeant	Petty Officer, First Class
E-5	Sergeant	Staff Sergeant	Sergeant	Petty Officer, Second Class
E-4	Corporal	Senior Airman	Corporal	Petty Officer, Third Class
E-3	Private First Class	Airman, First Class	Lance Corporal	Seaman
E-2	Private	Airman	Private, First Class	Seaman Apprentice
E-1	Private	Airman, Basic	Private	Seaman Recruit

TABLE 2—BASIC MONTHLY PAY RATES†
Effective January 1, 2018 to December 31, 2018
Note that 2019 numbers were not available as this 2019 edition went to press.
2 or Less Years through Over 10 Years

Pay Grade	2 or less	Over 2	Over 3	Over 4	Over 6	Over 8	Over 10
COMMISSIONED OFFICERS							
O-10	–	–	–	–	–	–	–
O-9	–	–	–	–	–	–	–
O-8	10,399	10,739	10,965	11,029	11,311	11,782	11,892
O-7	8,640	9,042	9,228	9,375	9,643	9,907	10,212
O-6	6,552	7,199	7,671	7,671	7,700	8,030	8,074
O-5	5,462	6,153	6,579	6,660	6,925	7,084	7,434
O-4	4,713	5,456	5,820	5,901	6,239	6,601	7,052
O-3	4,144	4,697	5,070	5,528	5,792	6,083	6,271
O-2	3,580	4,078	4,696	4,855	4,955	4,955	4,955
O-1	3,108	3,235	3,910	3,910	3,910	3,910	3,910
COMMISSIONED OFFICERS							
(with over 4 years active duty service as an enlisted member or warrant officer)							
O-3E	–	–	–	5,528	5,792	6,083	6,271
O-2E	–	–	–	4,855	4,955	5,113	5,379
O-1E	–	–	–	3,910	4,175	4,330	4,488
WARRANT OFFICERS							
W-5	–	–	–	–	–	–	–
W-4	4,282	4,607	4,739	4,869	5,093	5,315	5,539
W-3	3,910	4,074	4,241	4,295	4,471	4,815	5,174
W-2	3,460	3,788	3,889	3,958	4,182	4,531	4,704
W-1	3,037	3,364	3,452	3,638	3,858	4,182	4,333
ENLISTED MEMBERS							
E-9	–	–	–	–	–	–	5,174
E-8	–	–	–	–	–	4,235	4,423
E-7	2,944	3,214	3,336	3,500	3,627	3,845	3,968
E-6	2,547	2,802	2,926	3,046	3,171	3,453	3,564
E-5	2,333	2,490	2,610	2,733	2,925	3,126	3,290
E-4	2,139	2,248	2,370	2,490	2,596	2,596	2,596
E-3	1,931	2,053	2,177	2,177	2,177	2,177	2,177
E-2	1,836	1,836	1,836	1,836	1,836	1,836	1,836
E-1*	1,638	1,638	1,638	1,638	1,638	1,638	1,638

TABLE 2—BASIC MONTHLY PAY RATES† (cont'd)
Effective January 1, 2018
Note that 2019 numbers were not available as this 2019edition went to press
Over 12 Years through Over 26 Years

Pay Grade	Over 12	Over 14	Over 16	Over 18	Over 20	Over 22	Over 24	Over 26
COMMISSIONED OFFICERS								
O-10	–	–	–	–	16,804	16,885	17,237	17,848
O-9	–	–	–	–	14,697	14,909	15,214	15,748
O-8	12,339	12,467	12,853	13,411	13,925	14,268	14,268	14,268
O-7	10,517	10,822	11,782	12,592	12,592	12,592	12,592	12,656
O-6	8,074	8,533	9,344	9,820	10,296	10,567	10,841	11,373
O-5	7,690	8,022	8,530	8,771	9,009	9,280	9,280	9,280
O-4	7,404	7,648	7,788	7,869	7,869	7,869	7,869	7,869
O-3	6,580	6,741	6,741	6,741	6,741	6,741	6,741	6,741
O-2	4,955	4,955	4,955	4,955	4,955	4,955	4,955	4,955
O-1	3,910	3,910	3,910	3,910	3,910	3,910	3,910	3,910
COMMISSIONED OFFICERS								
(with over 4 years active duty service as an enlisted member or warrant officer)								
O-3E	6,580	6,841	6,991	7,195	7,195	7,195	7,195	7,195
O-2E	5,585	5,738	5,738	5,738	5,738	5,738	5,738	5,738
O-1E	4,643	4,855	4,855	4,855	4,855	4,855	4,855	4,855
WARRANT OFFICERS								
W-5	–	–	–	–	7,614	8,001	8,288	8,607
W-4	5,877	6,173	6,454	6,685	6,910	7,240	7,511	7,821
W-3	5,343	5,538	5,740	6,102	6,347	6,493	6,649	6,860
W-2	4,874	5,082	5,245	5,392	5,568	5,684	5,776	5,776
W-1	4,544	4,752	4,915	5,066	5,249	5,249	5,249	5,249
ENLISTED MEMBERS								
E-9	5,291	5,439	5,613	5,788	6,069	6,306	6,557	6,939
E-8	4,539	4,678	4,828	5,100	5,237	5,472	5,602	5,922
E-7	4,187	4,369	4,493	4,625	4,676	4,848	4,940	5,291
E-6	3,776	3,841	3,889	3,944	3,944	3,944	3,944	3,944
E-5	3,310	3310	3,310	3,310	3,310	3,310	3,310	3,310
E-4	2,596	2,596	2,596	2,596	2,596	2,596	2,596	2,596
E-3	2,177	2,177	2,177	2,177	2,177	2,177	2,177	2,177
E-2	1,836	1,836	1,836	1,836	1,836	1,836	1,836	1,836
E-1*	–	–	–	–	–	–	–	–

† See Table 1 for rank corresponding with pay rate. Rates are rounded to nearest dollar.
* Applies to personnel who have served less than 4 months on active duty.

TABLE 3—CSRS MILITARY MONTHLY RETIREMENT PAY
Effective January 1, 2018 to December 31, 2018

Note that 2019 numbers were not available as this 2019 edition went to press.

RETIREES WHO ENTERED SERVICE BEFORE
SEPTEMBER 8, 1980

Pay Grade* Over	50.00% 20 Yrs	52.50% 21 Yrs	55.00% 22 Yrs	57.50% 23 Yrs	60.00% 24 Yrs	62.50% 25 Yrs	65.00% 26 Yrs	67.50% 27 Yrs	70.00% 28 Yrs	72.50% 29 Yrs	75.00% 30 Yrs
O-10	$8,402	$8,822	$9,242	$9,662	$10,082	$10,503	$10,923	$11,343	$11,763	$12,183	$12,683
O-9	$7,439	$7,811	$8,183	$8,555	$8,927	$9,299	$9,671	$10,043	$10,415	$10,787	$11,159
O-8	$6,963	$7,311	$7,659	$8,007	$8,356	$8,704	$8,839	$9,400	$9,748	$10,096	$10,445
O-7	$6,296	$6,611	$6,926	$7,240	$7,555	$7,870	$7,993	$8,500	$8,814	$9,129	$9,444
O-6	$5,148	$5,405	$5,663	$5,920	$6,178	$6,435	$6,535	$6,950	$7,207	$7,465	$7,722
O-5	$4,504	$4,729	$4,954	$5,180	$5,405	$5,630	$5,719	$6,080	$6,306	$6,531	$6,756
O-4	$3,934	$4,131	$4,327	$4,524	$4,721	$4,918	$4,995	$5,311	$5,508	$5,704	$5,901
O-3	$3,371	$3,540	$3,708	$3,877	$4,045	$4,214	$4,279	$4,551	$4,719	$4,888	$5,057
O-2	$2,477	$2,601	$2,725	$2,849	$2,972	$3,096	$3,145	$3,344	$3,468	$3,592	$3,716
O-1	$1,955	$2,053	$2,258	$2,248	$2,346	$2,444	$2,482	$2,639	$2,737	$2,835	$2,933
W-5	$3,807	$3,997	$4,188	$4,378	$4,568	$4,759	$4,949	$5,139	$5,330	$5,520	$5,711
W-4	$3,455	$3,628	$3,801	$3,973	$4,146	$4,319	$4,492	$4,664	$4,837	$5,010	$5,183
W-3	$3,174	$3,333	$3,491	$3,650	$3,809	$3,968	$4,126	$4,285	$4,444	$4,602	$4,761
W-2	$2,784	$2,923	$3,062	$3,202	$3,341	$3,480	$3,619	$3,758	$3,898	$4,037	$4,176
W-1	$2,625	$2,756	$2,888	$3,019	$3,150	$3,281	$3,413	$3,544	$3,675	$3,806	$3,938
E-9	$3,034	$3,186	$3,337	$3,489	$3,641	$3,793	$3,944	$4,096	$4,248	$4,399	$4,551
E-8	$2,618	$2,749	$2,880	$3,011	$3,142	$3,273	$3,403	$3,534	$3,665	$3,796	$3,927
E-7	$2,338	$2,455	$2,572	$2,689	$2,806	$2,923	$3,039	$3,156	$3,273	$3,390	$3,507
E-6	$1,972	$2,071	$2,169	$2,268	$2,366	$2,465	$2,564	$2,662	$2,761	$2,859	$2,958
E-5	$1,655	$1,738	$1,821	$1,903	$1,986	$2,069	$2,152	$2,234	$2,317	$2,400	$2,483

* See Table 1, for rank corresponding to pay grade.

TABLE 4—RATES OF DEPENDENCY AND INDEMNITY COMPENSATION— SURVIVING SPOUSE AND CHILDREN OF VETERAN WHO DIED BEFORE JANUARY 1, 1993*
38 USC §1311
Effective December 1, 2017 through December 1, 2018

Note that 2018 numbers were not available as this 2018 edition went to press.

Pay Grade*	Surviving Spouse** Only	Surviving Spouse** and 1 Child	Surviving Spouse** and 2 Children	Extra Per Child
COMMISSIONED OFFICERS				
O-10	$2,739***	$3,057	$3,375	$317.87
O-9	$2,498	$2,815	$3,133	$317.87
O-8	$2,335	$2,653	$2,971	$317.87
O-7	$2,126	$2,444	$2,762	$317.87
O-6	$1,970	$2,287	$2,605	$317.87
O-5	$1,747	$2,065	$2,382	$317.87
O-4	$1,587	$1,905	$2,223	$317.87
O-3	$1,497	$1,815	$2,133	$317.87
O-2	$1,401	$1,719	$2,037	$317.87
O-1	$1,355	$1,673	$1,991	$317.87
WARRANT OFFICERS				
W-4	$1,504	$1,845	$2,163	$317.87
W-3	$1,421	$1,761	$2,079	$317.87
W-2	$1,381	$1,720	$2,038	$317.87
W-1	$1,328	$1,666	$1,984	$317.87
ENLISTED PERSONNEL				
E-9	$1,461****	$1,772	$2,083	$317.87
E-8	$1,401	$1,712	$2,023	$317.87
E-7	$1,327	$1,638	$1,949	$317.87
E-6	$1,283	$1,594	$1,905	$317.87
E-5	$1,283	$1,594	$1,905	$317.87
E-4	$1,283	$1,594	$1,905	$317.87
E-3	$1,283	$1,594	$1,905	$317.87
E-2	$1,283	$1,594	$1,905	$317.87
E-1	$1,283	$1,594	$1,905	$317.87

*   See Table 1, for rank corresponding to pay grade. Surviving spouses of veterans who die after January 1, 1994, receive a basic monthly DIC rate of $1283.11 in 2018. Each child is entitled to $317.87 a month in 2018. Surviving spouses of veterans who die before January 1, 1993, are entitled to the benefits listed above or the new formula, whichever provides the greater benefits.

**   Monthly rate for the surviving spouse is increased by $317.87 if he or she is a patient in a nursing home or is virtually helpless or blind.

***   If the veteran served as Chairman of the Joint Chiefs of Staff or Chief of Staff to one of the services, the surviving spouse's rate shall be $2,940.07.

**** The payment to a surviving spouse alone if the veteran was Sergeant Major of the Army, Senior Enlisted Advisor of the Navy, Chief Master Sergeant of the Air Force, or Sergeant Major of the Marine Corps, or Master Chief Petty Officer of the Coast Guard is $1,578.

TABLE 5—RATES OF DEPENDENCY AND INDEMNITY
COMPENSATION—PARENTS
Effective December 1, 2017 through November 30, 2018

Note that 2019 numbers were not available as this 2019 edition went to press. 2019 figures can be approximated by multiplying 2018 figures by 2.8%) for 2018 COLA

Annual Income Amount	1 Parent Only (1)	Each of 2 Parents Not Living Together (1)	Each of 2 Parents Living Together or Remarried Parent Living with Spouse (2)
$800	$634	$459	$431
900	626	451	431
1,000	618	443	431
1,100	610	435	420
1,200	602	427	417
1,300	594	419	414
1,400	586	411	411
1,500	578	403	408
1,600	570	395	404
1,700	562	387	400
1,800	554	379	396
1,900	546	371	392
2,000	538	363	387
2,100	530	355	382
2,200	522	347	377
2,300	514	339	372
2,400	506	331	367
2,500	498	323	361
2,600	490	315	355
2,700	482	307	349
2,800	474	299	343
2,900	466	291	337
3,000	458	283	330
3,100	450	275	323
3,200	442	267	316
3,300	434	259	308
3,400	426	251	300
3,500	418	243	292
3,600	410	235	284
3,700	402	227	276
3,800	394	219	268
3,900	386	211	259
4,000	378	203	252
4,100	370	195	244
4,200	362	187	236
4,300	354	179	228
4,400	346	171	220
4,500	338	163	212
4,600	330	155	204
4,700	322	147	196
4,800	314	139	188
4,900	306	131	180
5,000	298	123	172
5,100	290	115	164
5,200	282	107	156

TABLE 5—RATES OF DEPENDENCY AND INDEMNITY
COMPENSATION—PARENTS (cont'd)
Effective December 1, 2017 through November 30, 2018

Note that 2019 numbers were not available as this 2019 edition went to press. 2019 figures can be approximated by multiplying 2018 figures by 2.8%) for 2018 COLA

Annual Income Amount	1 Parent Only (1)	Each of 2 Parents Not Living Together (1)	Each of 2 Parents Living Together or Remarried Parent Living with Spouse (2)
5,300	274	99	148
5,400	266	91	140
5,500	258	83	132
5,600	250	75	124
5,700	242	67	116
5,800	234	59	108
5,900	226	51	100
6,000	218	43	92
6,100	210	35	84
6,200	202	27	76
6,300	194	19	68
6,400	186	11	60
6,500	178	5	52
6,600	170	5	44
6,700	162	5	36
6,800	154	5	28
6,900	146	5	20
7,000	138	5	20
7,100	130	5	12
7,200	122	5	5
7,300	114	5	5
7,400	106	5	5
7,500	98	5	5
7,600	90	5	5
7,700	82	5	5
7,800	74	5	5
7,900	66	5	5
8,000	58	5	5
8,100	50	5	5
8,200	42	5	5
8,300	34	5	5
8,400	26	5	5
8,662 – 14,974	5	5	5
14,974 – 19,673	0	0	5

(1)   Payment based on total annual income

(2)   Payment based on total combined annual income

If entitled to Aid & Attendance allowance add $343 to the monthly rate.

APPENDIX D
MEDICARE TABLES

TABLE OF HOSPITAL INSURANCE (PART A)
Effective January 1, 2019

Service	Benefit	Medicare Pays	A Person Pays
HOSPITALIZATION Semiprivate room and board, general nursing, and other hospital services and supplies.	First 60 days	All but $1,364	$1,364
	61st to 90th day	All but $341 a day	$341 a day
	91st to 150th day[1]	All but $682 a day	$682 a day
	Beyond 150 days	Nothing	All costs
SKILLED NURSING FACILITY CARE Semiprivate room and board, skilled nursing and rehabilitative services and other services and supplies.[2]	First 20 days	100% of approved Amount	Nothing
	Additional 80 days	All but $170.50 a day	$170.50 a day
	Beyond 100 days	Nothing	All costs
POST-HOSPITAL HOME HEALTH CARE Part-time or intermittent skilled care, home health aid services, durable medical equipment and supplies and other services.	First 100 days in spell of illness	100% of approved amount; 80% of approved amount for durable medical equipment	Nothing for services; 20% of approved amount for durable medical equipment
HOSPICE CARE Pain relief, symptom management and support services for the terminally ill.	For as long as the doctor certifies need	All but limited costs for outpatient drugs and inpatient respite care	Limited costs for outpatient drugs and inpatient respite care
BLOOD When furnished by a hospital or skilled nursing facility during covered stay.	Unlimited if medically necessary	All but first 3 pints per calendar year	For first 3 pints[3]

1. 60 Reserve days benefit may be used only once in a lifetime.
2. Neither Medicare nor private Medigap insurance will pay for most nursing home care.
3. Blood paid for or replaced under Part B of Medicare during the calendar year does not have to be paid for or replaced under Part A.

TABLE OF MEDICAL INSURANCE (PART B) BENEFITS
Effective January 1, 2019

Service	Benefit	Medicare Pays	Patient Pays
MEDICAL EXPENSE Doctors' services, inpatient and outpatient medical and services surgical services and supplies, physical and speech therapy, diagnostic tests, durable medical equipment and other services.	Unlimited if medically necessary.	80% of approved amount (after $185 deductible). Reduced to 50% for most outpatient mental health services.	$185 deductible, 1 plus 20% of approved amount and limited charges above approved amount.[2]
CLINICAL LABORATORY SERVICES Blood tests, urinalyses, and more.	Unlimited if medically necessary.	Generally 100% of approved amount.	Nothing for services.
HOME HEALTH CARE Part-time or intermittent skilled care, home health aide services, durable medical equipment and supplies and other services.	Unlimited but covers only home health care not covered by Hospital Insurance (Part A).	100% of approved amount; 80% of approved amount for durable medical equipment.	Nothing for services; 20% of approved amount for durable medical equipment.
OUTPATIENT HOSPITAL TREATMENT Services for the diagnosis or treatment of illness or injury.	Unlimited if medically necessary.	Medicare payment to hospital based on hospital cost.	20% of whatever the hospital charges (after $185 deductible).[1]
BLOOD	Unlimited if medically necessary.	80% of approved amount (after $185 deductible and starting with 4th pint).	For first 3 pints plus 20% of approved amount for additional pints (after $185 deductible).[3]
AMBULATORY SURGICAL SERVICES	Unlimited if medically necessary.	80% of predetermined amount (after $185 deductible).	$185 deductible, plus 20% of predetermined amount.

1. Once a person has $185 of expense for covered services in 2019, the Part B deductible does not apply to any further covered services received for the rest of the year.
2. A person pays for charges higher than the amount approved by Medicare unless the doctor or supplier agrees to accept Medicare's approved amount as the total charge for services rendered.
3. Blood paid for or replaced under Part A of Medicare during the calendar year does not have to be paid for or replaced under Part B.

APPENDIX E
WHAT MEDICARE DOES NOT COVER

Some of these items can be covered by Medicare under certain conditions. See text for more detailed information on items covered under special conditions.

Acupuncture

Most chiropractic services

Cosmetic surgery (except after an accident)

Custodial care (Long-term care)

Most dental care

Dentures

Most prescription drugs and medicines taken at home (except through Medicare Part D)

Eyeglasses and eye examinations for prescribing, fitting, or changing eyeglasses

First three pints of blood

Routine foot care

Coverage received outside of the United States

Hearing aids and hearing examinations for prescribing, fitting, or changing hearing aids

Homemaker services

Meals delivered to the home

Naturopaths' services

Immunizations and vaccinations, except vaccinations against pneumococcal pneumonia, hepatitis B, or influenza virus; and immunizations required because of an injury or immediate risk of infection

Injections which can be self-administered

Non-emergency transportation

Nursing care on full-time basis in the home

Orthopedic shoes unless they are part of a leg brace and are included in the orthopedist's charge

Personal convenience items that the patient requests, such as a phone, radio, or television in the room at a hospital or skilled nursing facility

Physical examinations that are routine and tests directly related to such examinations

Private nurse care

Private hospital rooms

Services performed by immediate relatives or members of the patient's household

Services that are not reasonable and necessary

Services for which neither the patient nor another party on his behalf has a legal obligation to pay

Supportive devices for the feet

War claims occurring after the effective date of the patient's current Medicare coverage

Copies of X-Rays

Services payable by any of the following:

- Workers' Compensation (including black lung benefits)

- Liability or no-fault insurance

- Employer group health plans for employees and their spouses

- Employer group health plans for people entitled to Medicare solely on the basis of end-stage renal disease

- Another government program

APPENDIX F
EXAMPLE OF MEDICARE BENEFITS

Mr. Smith is sixty-nine years old, retired, and covered by Hospital Insurance (Part A), Medical Insurance (Part B), and Prescription Drug Insurance (Part D). After suffering a heart attack at his home in January 2019, he is taken to the hospital for surgery. Mr. Smith spends fifteen days in the hospital and seven days in a skilled nursing facility for therapy. When he returns home, he requires the services of a nurse and physical therapist for a short time to continue treatment.

	Total cost	Mr. Smith pays	Medicare pays
Hospital bill: *(Patient pays the deductible amount)*	$3,500	$1,364	$2,136
Ambulance to hospital: *(Patient pays 20% plus amount higher than customary charge)*	$70	$14	$56
Surgeon: *(Patient pays $185 deductible and 20% of the remaining bill; Medicare pays 80% of the bill after the deductible)*	$2,000	$548	$1,452
Anesthesiologist: *(Patient pays 20%; Medicare pays 80%)*	$300	$60	$240
Skilled Nursing Facility: *(Patient pays nothing for first 20 days, then $170.50 a day for 80 days)*	$1,050	$0	$1,050
Home visits by nurse: *(Medicare pays for nurse required for medical reasons)*	$90	$0	$90
Home visits by physical therapist:	$80	$0	$80
Equipment rental (wheelchair): *(Patient pays 20%; Medicare pays 80%)*	$85	$17	$68
Prescription drugs at home: *(assuming standard $400 deductible).*	$200	$200	$0
Total Cost:	**$7,375**	**$2,203**	**$5,172**

APPENDIX G
MEDICARE ADMINISTRATIVE CONTRACTORS
AS OF APRIL 1, 2018

MAC Jurisdiction	Previous MAC Jurisdiction	Processes Part A & Part B Claims for the following states:	MAC
DME A	DME A	Connecticut, Delaware, District of Columbia, Maine, Maryland, Massachusetts, New Hampshire, New Jersey, New York, Pennsylvania, Rhode Island, Vermont	Noridian Healthcare Solutions, LLC, contract number HHSM-500-2016-M0001Z
DME B	DME B	Illinois, Indiana, Kentucky, Michigan, Minnesota, Ohio, Wisconsin	CGS Administrators, LLC, contract number HHSM-500-2015-M0030Z
DME C	DME C	Alabama, Arkansas, Colorado, Florida, Georgia, Louisiana, Mississippi, New Mexico, North Carolina, Oklahoma, South Carolina, Tennessee, Texas, Virginia, West Virginia, Puerto Rico, U.S. Virgin Islands	CGS Administrators, LLC, contract number HHSM-500-2012-M0011Z
DME D	DME D	Alaska, Arizona, California, Hawaii, Idaho, Iowa, Kansas, Missouri, Montana, Nebraska, Nevada, North Dakota, Oregon, South Dakota, Utah, Washington, Wyoming, American Samoa, Guam, Northern Mariana Islands	Noridian Healthcare Solutions, LLC, contract number HHSM-500-2015-M0031Z
5	5	Iowa, Kansas, Missouri, Nebraska	Wisconsin Physicians Service Insurance Corporation, contract number HHSM-500-2012-M0005Z
6	6	Illinois, Minnesota, Wisconsin ****HH + H for the following states:** Alaska, American Samoa, Arizona, California, Guam, Hawaii, Idaho, Michigan, Minnesota, Nevada, New Jersey, New York, Northern Mariana Islands, Oregon, Puerto Rico, US Virgin Islands, Wisconsin and Washington	National Government Services, Inc, contract number HHSM-500-2012-M0013Z
8	8	Indiana, Michigan	Wisconsin Physicians Service Insurance Corporation, contract number HHSM-500-2011-M0006Z

MAC Jurisdiction	Previous MAC Jurisdiction	Processes Part A & Part B Claims for the following states:	MAC
15	15	Kentucky, Ohio ****HH + H for the following states:** Delaware, District of Columbia, Colorado, Iowa, Kansas, Maryland, Missouri, Montana, Nebraska, North Dakota, Pennsylvania, South Dakota, Utah, Virginia, West Virginia, and Wyoming	CGS Administrators, LLC, contract number HHSM-500-2015-M0032Z
E	1	California, Hawaii, Nevada, American Samoa, Guam, Northern Mariana Islands	Noridian Healthcare Solutions, LLC, contract number HHSM-500-2012-M0012Z
F	2 & 3	Alaska, Arizona, Idaho, Montana, North Dakota, Oregon, South Dakota, Utah, Washington, Wyoming	Noridian Healthcare Solutions, LLC, Contract Number 75FCMC18C0029
H	4 & 7	Arkansas, Colorado, New Mexico, Oklahoma, Texas, Louisiana, Mississippi	Novitas Solutions, Inc, contract number HHSM-500-2012-M0001Z.
J	10	Alabama, Georgia, Tennessee	Palmetto GBA, LLC, contract number HHSM-500-2017-M0001Z
K	13 & 14	Connecticut, New York, Maine, Massachusetts, New Hampshire, Rhode Island, Vermont ****HH + H for the following states:** Connecticut, Maine, Massachusetts, New Hampshire, Rhode Island, and Vermont	National Government Services, Inc, contract number HHSM-500-2013-M0015Z
L	12	Delaware, District of Columbia, Maryland, New Jersey, Pennsylvania (includes Part B for counties of Arlington and Fairfax in Virginia and the city of Alexandria in Virginia)	Novitas Solutions, Inc, contract number HHSM-500-2012-M0010Z
M	11	North Carolina, South Carolina, Virginia, West Virginia (excludes Part B for the counties of Arlington and Fairfax in Virginia and the city of Alexandria in Virginia) ****HH + H for the following states:** Alabama, Arkansas, Florida, Georgia, Illinois, Indiana, Kentucky, Louisiana, Mississippi, New Mexico, North Carolina, Ohio, Oklahoma, South Carolina, Tennessee, and Texas	Palmetto GBA, LLC, contract number HHSM-500-2015-M0028Z
N	9	Florida, Puerto Rico, U.S. Virgin Islands	First Coast Service Options, Inc., contract number HHSM-500-2014-M0021Z

APPENDIX H
MEDICARE QUALITY INNOVATION NETWORK (QIN) QUALITY IMPROVEMENT ORGANIZATIONS (QIOs)

Quality Innovation Networks (QIN)-QIOs will be responsible for working with providers and the community on multiple data-driven quality initiatives to improve patient safety, reduce harm, engage patients and families, and improve clinical care at their local and regional levels. The QIN-QIOs and the states they cover are listed below.

Alliant Health Solutions
Georgia, North Carolina
1455 Lincoln Parkway, Suite 800
Atlanta, GA 30346
(678) 527-3000
www.alliantquality.org

Atlantic Quality Improvement Network
District of Columbia, New York, South Carolina
1979 Marcus Avenue
Lake Success, NY 11042-1072
(516) 326-7767
www.ipro.org

atom Alliance
Alabama, Indiana, Kentucky, Mississippi, Tennessee
3340 Players Club Parkway, Suite 300
Memphis, TN 38125
(800) 528-2655
www.atomAlliance.org

Great Plains Quality Innovation Network
Kansas, North Dakota, Nebraska, South Dakota
1230 O Street, Suite 120
Lincoln, NE 68508
(844) 877-0464
www.cimronebraska.org

Health Quality Innovators
Maryland, Virginia
9830 Mayland Drive, Suite J
Richmond, VA 23233
(804) 289-5320
www.hqi.solutions

Health Services Advisory Group
Arizona, California, Florida, Ohio, Virgin Islands
3133 East Camelback Road, Suite 100
Phoenix, AZ 85016-4545
(602) 801-6600
www.hsag.com

Healthcentric Advisors
Connecticut, Massachusetts, Maine, New Hampshire, Rhode Island, Vermont
235 Promenade Street
Suite 500, Box 18
Providence, RI 02908
(401) 528-3200
www.healthcentricadvisors.org

HealthInsight
New Mexico, Nevada, Oregon, Utah
756 E. Winchester Street, Suite 200
Salt Lake City, UT 84107
(801) 892-0155
www.healthinsight.org

Lake Superior Quality Innovation Network
Michigan, Minnesota,Wisconsin
2901 Metro Drive, Suite 400
Bloomington, MN 55425-1525
(952) 853-8536
www.lsqin.org

Mountain-Pacific Quality Health Foundation
Alaska, Commonwealth of the Northern Mariana Islands, Hawaii, Montana, U.S. Pacific Territories of Guam and American Samoa,Wyoming
3404 Cooney Drive
Helena, MT 59602
(800) 497-8232
www.mpqhf.org

Qualis Health
Idaho,Washington
10700 Meridian Ave N, Suite 100
Seattle, WA 98133
(800) 949-7536
www.qualishealth.org

Quality Insights Quality Innovation Network
Delaware, Louisiana, New Jersey, Pennsylvania, West Virginia
3001 Chesterfield Avenue
Charleston, West Virginia 25304
(304) 346-9864
www.qualityinsights-qin.org

Telligen
Colorado, Iowa, Illinois
1776 West Lakes Parkway
West Des Moines, Iowa 50266
(800) 383-2856
www.telligen.com

TMF
Arkansas, Missouri, Oklahoma, Puerto Rico, Texas
5918 West Courtyard Drive
Austin, TX 78730-5036
(800) 725-9216
www.tmf.org

APPENDIX I
MEDICARE BENEFICIARY AND
FAMILY-CENTERED CARE QUALITY
IMPROVEMENT ORGANIZATIONS (QIOs)

A Quality Improvement Organization (QIO) is a group of health quality experts, clinicians, and consumers organized to improve the quality of care delivered to people with Medicare.

BFCC-QIOs help Medicare beneficiaries exercise their right to high-quality health care. They manage all beneficiary complaints and quality of care reviews to ensure consistency in the review process while taking into consideration local factors important to beneficiaries and their families. They also handle cases in which beneficiaries want to appeal a health care provider's decision to discharge them from the hospital or discontinue other types of services. Two designated BFCC-QIOs serve all fifty states and three territories, which are grouped into five regions.

Beneficiary and Family Centered Care (BFCC)-QIOs manage all beneficiary complaints, quality of care reviews, EMTALA, and other types of case reviews to ensure consistency in the review process while taking into consideration local factors important to beneficiaries and their families.

The BFCC-QIOs are listed below.

Area 1

States included: Connecticut, Maine, Massachusetts, New Hampshire, New Jersey, New York, Pennsylvania, Puerto Rico, Rhode Island, Vermont and the US Virgin Islands
BFCC QIO Area One
Agency Name: Livanta
Address: 10820 Guilford Rd, Ste 202
Annapolis Junction, MD 20701
Helpline Phone Number (complaints and appeals): (866) 815-5440 (toll-free)
TDD: (866) 868-2289
Fax: (844) 420-6671

Area 2

States included: District of Columbia, Delaware, Florida, Georgia, Maryland, North Carolina, South Carolina, Virginia, West Virginia
KEPRO QIO
Agency Name: KEPRO
Address: 5201 W. Kennedy Blvd, Suite 900
Tampa, FL 33609
Helpline Phone Number (complaints and appeals): (844) 455-8708 (toll-free)
Fax: (844) 834-7129

Area 3

States included: Alabama, Arkansas, Colorado, Kentucky, Louisiana, Mississippi, Montana, North Dakota, New Mexico, Oklahoma, South Dakota, Tennesseee, Texas, Utah, Wyoming
KEPRO QIO
Agency Name: KEPRO
Address: 5700 Lombardo Center Dr., Suite 100
Seven Hills, OH 44131
Helpline Phone Number (complaints and appeals): (844) 430-9504 (toll-free)
Fax: (844) 878-7921

Area 4

States included: Iowa, Illinois, Indiana, Kansas, Michigan, Minnesota, Missouri, Nebraska, Ohio, Wisconsin
KEPRO QIO
Agency Name: KEPRO
Address: 5201 W. Kennedy Blvd, Suite 900
Tampa, FL 33609
Helpline Phone Number (complaints and appeals): (855) 408-8557 (toll-free)
Fax: (844) 834-7130

Area 5

States included: Alaska, Arizona, California, Hawaii*, Idaho, Nevada, Oregon, Washington and the Pacific Territories
* Hawaii includes the Pacific Territories of American Samoa, Guam and the Commonwealth of the Northern Marina Islands.
BFCC QIO Area Five
Agency Name: Livanta
Address: 10820 Guilford Rd, Ste 202
Annapolis Junction, MD 20701
Helpline Phone Number (complaints and appeals): (877) 588-1123 (toll-free)
TDD: (855) 887-6668
Fax: (855) 694-2929

APPENDIX J
DURABLE MEDICAL EQUIPMENT (DME)
MEDICARE ADMINISTRATIVE
CONTRACTOR (MAC) JURISDICTIONS

As required by Section 911 of the Medicare Prescription Drug, Improvement and Modernization Act of 2003 (MMA), CMS was required to re-procure the DME MAC contracts every five (5) years. The DME MACs are responsible for processing Medicare Durable Medical Equipment, Orthotics, and Prosthetics (DMEPOS) claims for a defined geographic area or "jurisdiction." CMS has established four DME MAC jurisdictions that perform numerous functions on behalf of Medicare beneficiaries and establish relationships with suppliers of Durable Medical Equipment, Prosthetics, Orthotics and Supplies (DMEPOS).

The table below identifies the four DME MAC Jurisdictions along with their assigned geographic states, territories and districts.

DME MAC TABLE

Jurisdiction	States
DME MAC A	Connecticut, Delaware, District of Columbia, Maine, Maryland, Massachusetts, New Hampshire, New Jersey, New York, Pennsylvania, Rhode Island and Vermont
DME MAC B	Illinois, Indiana, Kentucky, Michigan, Minnesota, Ohio and Wisconsin
DME MAC C	Alabama, Arkansas, Colorado, Florida, Georgia, Louisiana, Mississippi, New Mexico, North Carolina, Oklahoma, Puerto Rico, South Carolina, Tennessee, Texas, U.S. Virgin Islands, Virginia and West Virginia
DME MAC D	Alaska, American Samoa, Arizona, California, Guam, Hawaii, Idaho, Iowa, Kansas, Missouri, Montana, Nebraska, Nevada, North Dakota, Northern Mariana Islands, Oregon, South Dakota, Utah, Washington and Wyoming

Fact Tables about Durable Medical Equipment MAC Jurisdictions

Facts about DME MAC Jurisdiction A (JA) – Connecticut, Delaware, District of Columbia, Maine, Maryland, Massachusetts, New Hampshire, New Jersey, New York, Pennsylvania, Rhode Island and Vermont

- Total Number of Fee-for-Service Beneficiaries: 8,147,982 (as of 09/30/2017)

- Total Number of Suppliers: 19,271 (as of 09/30/2017)

- Total Annual Claims Volume: 19.4 percent of national DME Workload

Contract Implementation Status and Schedule

- Fully Implemented: July 1, 2016

- States impacted: Connecticut, Delaware, District of Columbia, Maine, Maryland, Massachusetts, New Hampshire, New Jersey, New York, Pennsylvania, Rhode Island and Vermont

- Outgoing contractor: NHIC, Corp.

- Incoming contractor: Noridian Healthcare Solutions, LLC

Facts about DME MAC Jurisdiction B (DME B) - Illinois, Indiana, Kentucky, Michigan, Minnesota, Ohio and Wisconsin

- Total Number of Fee-for-Service Beneficiaries: 6,781,251 (as of 09/30/2017)

- Total Number of Suppliers: 16,712 (as of 09/30/2017)

- Total Annual Claims Volume: 20.7 percent of national DME Workload

Contract Implementation Status and Schedule

- Fully Implemented: July 1, 2016

- States impacted: Illinois, Indiana, Kentucky, Michigan, Minnesota, Ohio and Wisconsin

- Outgoing contractor: National Government Services, Inc.

- Incoming contractor: CGS Administrators, LLC

Facts about DME MAC Jurisdiction C (DME C) - Alabama, Arkansas, Colorado, Florida, Georgia, Louisiana, Mississippi, New Mexico, North Carolina, Oklahoma, Puerto Rico, South Carolina, Tennessee, Texas, U.S. Virgin Islands, Virginia and West Virginia

- Total Number of Fee-for-Service Beneficiaries: 13,926,675 (as of 09/30/2017)

- Total Number of DME Suppliers: 32,252 (as of 09/30/2017)

- Total Annual Claims Volume: 38.6 percent of national DME Workload

Contract Award Information

- Solicitation on FedBizOpps (FBO): RFP-CMS-2011-0006, posted November 30, 2010

- Award Announcement: DME MAC Jurisdiction C Award on FBO, August 31, 2012

- Contract Awardee: CGS Administrators, LLC, contract number HHSM-500-2012-M0011Z

- DME MAC Jurisdiction C Award Fact Sheet (August 2012)

- Anticipated Contract End Date: March 2021

Facts about DME MAC Jurisdiction D (DME D) - Alaska, American Samoa, Arizona, California, Guam, Hawaii, Idaho, Iowa, Kansas, Missouri, Montana, Nebraska, Nevada, North Dakota, Northern Mariana Islands, Oregon, South Dakota, Utah, Washington and Wyoming

- Total Number of Fee-for-Service Beneficiaries: 8,997,116 (as of 09/30/2017)

- Total Number of DME Suppliers: 19,106 (as of 09/30/2017)

- Total Annual Claims Volume: 21.2 percent of national DME Workload

Contract Award Information

- Solicitation on FedBizOpps (FBO): HHSM-500-2015-RFP-0101, posted November 24, 2014

- Award Announcement: DME MAC Jurisdiction D award on FBO, September 10, 2015

- Contract Awardee: Noridian Healthcare Solutions, LLC, contract number HHSM-500-2015-M0031Z

- DME MAC Jurisdiction D Award Fact Sheet (September 2015)

- Anticipated Contract End Date: January 2024

APPENDIX K
INSURANCE COUNSELING — GENERAL INFORMATION

In addition to insurance counseling, these state health insurance assistance program offices can answer questions about Medicare bills, Medigap policies, and Medicare plan choices.

State Program	Phone	State Program	Phone
Alabama SHIP	1-800-243-5463	Montana SHIP	1-800-551-3191
Alaska SHIP	1-800-478-6065	Nebraska SHIIP	1-800-234-7119
Arizona SHIP	1-800-432-4040	Nevada SHIP	1-800-307-4444
Arkansas SHIIP	1-800-224-6330	New Hampshire SHIP	1-866-634-9412
California HICAP	1-800-434-0222	New Jersey SHIP	1-800-792-8820
Colorado SHIP	1-888-696-7213	New Mexico	1-505-476-4799
Connecticut CHOICES	1-800-994-9422	New York HICAP	1-800-701-0501
Delaware ELDERinfo	1-800-336-9500	North Carolina SHIIP	1-800-443-9354
District of Columbia HICP	202-739-0668	North Dakota SHIC	1-888-575-6611
Florida SHINE	1-800-963-5337	Ohio OSHIIP	1-800-686-1578
Georgia	1-800-669-8387	Oklahoma SHICP	1-800-763-2828
Hawaii	1-888-875-9229	Oregon SHIBA	1-800-722-4134
Idaho SHIBA	1-800-247-4422	Pennsylvania APPRISE	1-800-783-7067
Illinois SHIP	1-800-548-9043	Rhode Island SHIP	1-401-462-4444
Indiana SHIIP	1-800-452-4800	South Carolina I-CARE	1-800-868-9095
Iowa SHIIP	1-800-351-4664	South Dakota SHINE	1-800-536-8197
Kansas SHICK	1-800-860-5260	Tennessee SHIP	1-877-801-0044
Kentucky SHIP	1-877-293-7447	Texas HICAP	1-800-252-9240
Louisiana SHIIP	1-800-259-5301	Utah SHIP	1-800-541-7735
Maine SHIP	1-877-353-3771	Vermont SHIP	1-800-642-5119
Maryland SHIP	1-800-243-3425	Virginia VICAP	1-800-552-3402
Massachusetts SHINE	1-800-AGE-INFO (243-4636)	Virgin Islands VI SHIP	1-340-772-7368
Michigan MMAP	1-800-803-7174	Washington SHIBA	1-800-562-6900
Minnesota SHIP	1-800-333-2433	West Virginia WV SHIP	1-877-987-4463
Mississippi SHIP	1-800-948-3090	Wisconsin SHIP	1-800-242-1060
Missouri Claim	1-800-390-3330	Wyoming WSHIP	1-800-856-4398

State Program	Website
Alabama SHIP	http://alabamaageline.gov/assets/ship-brochure.pdf
Alaska SHIP	http://dhss.alaska.gov/dsds/Pages/medicare/default.aspx
Arizona SHIP	https://des.az.gov/services/aging-and-adult/state-health-insurance-assistance-program-ship
Arkansas SHIIP	https://insurance.arkansas.gov/pages/consumer-services/senior-health/
California HICAP	https://www.aging.ca.gov/(X(1)S(0rry5ak3zo2fblkjrryyaozx))/hicap/default.aspx?AspxAutoDetectCookieSupport=1
Colorado SHIP	https://www.colorado.gov/dora/division-insurance
Connecticut CHOICES	http://www.ct.gov/agingservices/cwp/view.asp?a=2513&q=313032
Delaware ELDERinfo	http://www.delawareinsurance.gov/DMAB/
District of Columbia HICP	https://dcoa.dc.gov/service/health-insurance-counseling
Florida SHINE	http://www.floridashine.org/
Georgia	http://aging.dhs.georgia.gov/georgiacares
Hawaii	http://www.hawaiiship.org/
Idaho SHIBA	https://doi.idaho.gov/shiba/
Illinois SHIP	http://www.illinois.gov/aging/ship/Pages/default.aspx
Indiana SHIIP	http://www.in.gov/idoi/2495.htm
Iowa SHIIP	http://www.shiip.state.ia.us/
Kansas SHICK	http://www.kdads.ks.gov/commissions/commission-on-aging/medicare-programs/shick
Kentucky SHIP	http://www.chfs.ky.gov/dail/ship.htm
Louisiana SHIIP	http://www.ldi.la.gov/SHIIP/
Maine SHIP	http://www.maine.gov/dhhs/oads/community-support/ship.html
Maryland SHIP	http://www.aging.maryland.gov/pages/statehealthinsuranceprogram.aspx
Massachusetts SHINE	http://www.mass.gov/elders/healthcare/shine/overview-of-councils-on-aging.html
Michigan MMAP	http://mmapinc.org/
Minnesota SHIP	http://www.mnaging.net/en/Advisor/InsFinBenefits/Health%20Insurance%20Counseling.aspx
Mississippi SHIP	http://www.mdhs.state.ms.us/aging-adult-services/programs-daas/services-for-seniors/
Missouri Claim	http://missouriclaim.org/
Montana SHIP	http://dphhs.mt.gov/sltc/services/aging/SHIP/ship
Nebraska SHIIP	http://www.doi.nebraska.gov/shiip/
Nevada SHIP	http://adsd.nv.gov/Programs/Seniors/SHIP/SHIP_Prog/

State Program	Website
New Hampshire SHIP	http://www.servicelink.nh.gov/medicare/index.htm
New Jersey SHIP	http://www.state.nj.us/humanservices/doas/services/ship/
New Mexico	http://www.nmaging.state.nm.us/
New York HICAP	http://www.aging.ny.gov/HealthBenefits/Index.cfm
North Carolina SHIIP	http://www.ncdoi.com/SHIIP/Default.aspx
North Dakota SHIC	http://www.nd.gov/ndins/shic/
Ohio OSHIIP	http://www.insurance.ohio.gov/Consumer/Pages/ConsumerTab2.aspx
Oklahoma SHICP	http://www.ok.gov/oid/Consumers/Information_for_Seniors/SHIP.html
Oregon SHIBA	http://www.oregon.gov/dcbs/insurance/SHIBA/Pages/shiba.aspx
Pennsylvania APPRISE	http://www.aging.pa.gov/aging-services/insurance/Pages/default.aspx
Rhode Island SHIP	http://www.dea.ri.gov/insurance/
South Carolina I-CARE	http://aging.sc.gov/contact/Pages/SHIPContactInformation.aspx
South Dakota SHINE	http://www.shiine.net/
Tennessee SHIP	http://www.tn.gov/
Texas HICAP	http://www.tdi.texas.gov/consumer/hicap/
Utah SHIP	https://daas.utah.gov/
Vermont SHIP	http://asd.vermont.gov/services/ship
Virginia VICAP	http://www.vda.virginia.gov/vicap2.asp
Virgin Islands VI SHIP	http://ltg.gov.vi/vi-ship-medicare.html
Washington SHIBA	https://www.insurance.wa.gov/contact-shiba
West Virginia WV SHIP	http://www.wvship.org/
Wisconsin SHIP	https://www.dhs.wisconsin.gov/aging/index.htm
Wyoming WSHIP	http://www.wyomingseniors.com/services/wyoming-state-health-insurance-information-program

APPENDIX L
STATE AGENCIES ON AGING

Note: State agencies on aging can provide information and assistance on a variety of Medicare, insurance, and elder care issues.

Alabama
Department of Senior Services
RSA Plaza
201 Monroe Street, Suite 350
Montgomery AL 36104
(877) 425-2242
(334) 242-5743
http://www.alabamaageline.gov
Ageline@adss.alabama.gov

Alaska
Commission of Aging
Department of Health and Social Services
150 Third Street, No. 103
P.O. Box 110693
Juneau, AK 99811-0693
(907) 465-3250
http://dhss.alaska.gov/acoa/Pages/default.aspx

Arizona
Department of Economic Security
Aging and Adult Administration
1789 West Jefferson Street, #950A
Phoenix, AZ 85007
(602) 542-4446
https://www.azdes.gov/daas/

Arkansas
Division of Aging & Adult Services
P.O. Box 1437, Slot S-530
700 Main Street, 5th Floor, S530
Little Rock, AR 72203-1437
(501) 682-2441
http://www.daas.ar.gov/

California
Department of Aging
1300 National Drive, Number 200
Sacramento, CA 95834-1992
(916) 419-7500
https://www.aging.ca.gov/

Colorado
Division of Aging and Adult Services
Department of Human Services
1575 Sherman Street, 10th Floor
Denver, CO 80203-1714
(303) 866-2800
https://www.agingcare.com/

Connecticut
State Department on Again
55 Farmington Avenue, 12th Floor
Hartford, CT 06105-3730
Phone (860)424-5274
Toll Free (in State) 1-866-218-6631
Fax (860)424-5301
http://www.ct.gov/agingservices

Delaware
Services for Aging & Adults with
Physical Disabilities
Dept. of Health & Social Services
Herman M. Holloway, Sr. Campus
Main Administration Building, First Floor Annex
1901 N. DuPont Highway
New Castle, DE 19720
1-800-223-9074
Fax: (302) 255-4445
http://dhss.delaware.gov/dhss/dsaapd/index.html

District of Columbia
Office on Aging
500 K Street, NE
Washington, DC 20002
(202) 724-5622
http://dcoa.dc.gov/

Florida
Department of Elder Affairs
4040 Esplanade Way, Suite 315
Tallahassee, FL 32399-7000
Phone: 850-414-2000
Fax: 850-414-2004
TDD: 850-414-2001
Email: information@elderaffairs.org
http://elderaffairs.state.fl.us/index.php

Georgia
DHS Division of Aging Services
Two Peachtree Street, NW
33rd Floor
Atlanta, Georgia 30303-3142
Phone: 404.657.5258
Fax: 404.657.5285
Toll Free: 866-55-AGING or 866-552-4464
http://aging.dhs.georgia.gov/

Hawaii
Executive Office on Aging
250 South Hotel Street, Suite 406
Honolulu, HI 96813-2831
(808) 586-0100
http://health.hawaii.gov/eoa/
eoa@doh.hawaii.gov

Idaho
Commission on Aging
341 W. Washington
Boise, Idaho 83702
Phone: (208) 334-3833
or 1-800-926-2588
http://www.idahoaging.com

Illinois
Department on Aging
Main Office:
One Natural Resources Way, Suite 100
Springfield, IL 62702-1271
1-800-252-8966
FAX: 217-785-4477
Chicago Office:
Michael A. Bilandic Building (also known as the
State of Illinois Building)
160 North LaSalle St., Suite N-700
Chicago, IL 60601-3117
312-814-2630
FAX: 312-814-2916
Senior HelpLine/Benefit Access Program
1-800-252-8966
aging.ilsenior@illinois.gov
http://www.state.il.us/aging/2aaa/aaa-main.htm

Indiana
FSSA Division of Aging
402 W. Washington St. W454, P.O. Box 7083, MS21
Indianapolis, IN 46207-7083
(888) 672-0002
(317) 232-7858
http://www.in.gov/fssa/2329.htm

Iowa
Department of Elder Affairs
Jessie M. Parker Building
510 East 12th St., Suite 2
Des Moines, IA 50319-9025
(515) 725-3333
https://www.iowaaging.gov/

Kansas
Department on Aging
New England Building
503 South Kansas Avenue
Topeka, KS 66603-3404
(785) 296-4986
Toll Free: 800-432-3535 (in Kansas only)
https://www.kdads.ks.gov/contact-us

Kentucky
Department for Aging & Independent Living
Cabinet for Health & Family Services
275 East Main Street, 3W-F
Frankfort, KY 40621
(502) 564-6930
http://chfs.ky.gov/dail/

Louisiana
Governor's Office of Elderly Affairs
Mailing Address: P.O. Box 61, Baton Rouge, LA
70821-0061
Office: 525 Florida Street, Baton Rouge, LA
(225) 342-7100

Maine
Office of Aging and Disability Services
Maine Department of Health and Human
Services
SHS 11
Augusta, Maine 04333
Voice: (207) 287-9200 or (800) 262-2232
Fax: (207)287-9229
TTY: Maine relay 711
http://www.maine.gov/dhhs/oads/

Maryland
Department of Aging
301 West Preston Street, Suite 1007
Baltimore, MD 21201-2374
(410) 767-1100
http://www.aging.maryland.gov/

STATE AGENCIES ON AGING

Massachusetts
Executive Office of Elder Affairs
One Ashburton Place, 5th Floor
Boston, MA 02108
617-727-7750
800-243-4636 (nationwide)
800-872-0166 (TTY)
617-727-9368 (FAX)
http://www.mass.gov/elders/

Michigan
Office of Services to the Aging
P.O. Box 30676
300 East Michigan Avenue, Third Floor
Lansing, MI 48909-8176
(517) 373-8230

Minnesota
Board on Aging
Department of Human Services
Minnesota Board on Aging
Mailing Address: P.O. Box 64976, St. Paul, MN
55164-0976 Office: Elmer L. Andersen Human
Services Building, 540 Cedar Street St. Paul, MN
55155
(800) 882-6262
(651) 431-2500
http://www.mnaging.net/
mba@state.mn.us

Mississippi
Council on Aging
Division of Aging & Adult Services
750 N. State Street
Jackson, MS 39202
(800) 948-3090
(601) 359-4929
http://www.mdhs.state.ms.us/
aging-adult-services/

Missouri
Division of Senior & Disability Services
Department of Health & Senior Sciences
P.O. Box 570
Jefferson City, MO 65102-0570
(800) 235-5503
(573) 526-3626
http://www.mdhs.state.ms.us/
aging-adult-services/

Montana
Office on Aging
Senior and Long-Term Care Division
Department of Public Health and Human Services
111 Sanders Street
P.O. Box 4210
Helena, MT 59604
(888) 706-1535 (406) 444-7788
http://dphhs.mt.gov/SLTC

Nebraska
State Unit on Aging
P.O. Box 95026
301 Centennial Mall - South
Lincoln, NE 68509-5026
(800) 942-7830
http://dhhs.ne.gov/medicaid/Aging/pages/
AgingHome.aspx

Nevada
Division for Aging Services
Department of Health & Human Services
3416 Goni Road, Building D-132
Carson City, NV 89706
(775) 687-4210 x226
http://adsd.nv.gov/

New Hampshire
Bureau of Elderly & Adult Services
129 Pleasant Street
Concord, NH 03301-3852
(603) 271-4394
http://www.dhhs.nh.gov/DCBCS/beas/index.htm

New Jersey
Division of Aging Services
New Jersey Department of Human Services
240 West State Street
P.O. Box 715
Trenton, NJ 08625-0715 (800) 792-8820
(609) 292-4027
http://www.state.nj.us/humanservices/doas/
home/

New Mexico
Aging and Long-Term Services Department
2550 Cerrillos Road
Santa Fe, NM 87505
Mailing Address
P.O. Box 27118
Santa Fe, New Mexico 87502-7118
(800) 432-2080
(505) 476-4799
http://www.nmaging.state.nm.us/

New York
State Office for the Aging
Two Empire State Plaza
Albany, NY 12223-1251
(800) 342-9871
(518) 474-7012
http://www.aging.ny.gov/

North Carolina
Division of Aging & Adult Services
2101 Mail Service Center
101 Blair Drive
Raleigh, NC 27699-2101
(919) 855-4840
http://www.ncdhhs.gov/divisions/daas

North Dakota
Aging Services Division
Department of Human Services
1237 West Divide Avenue #6
Bismarck, ND 58501
(800) 755-8521
(701) 328-4601

Ohio
Ohio Department of Aging
246 N. High St./1st Fl.
Columbus, OH 43215-2406 (800) 266-4346
(614) 466-5500
http://aging.ohio.gov/home/

Oklahoma
Aging Services Division
Department of Human Services
2401 N.W. 23rd St., Suite 40
Oklahoma City, OK 73107-2442
(405) 521-2281
http://www.okdhs.org/programsandservices/
aging/

Oregon
Seniors & People with Disabilities
Department of Human Services
500 Summer Street, N.E., E12
Salem, OR 97301-1073
(800) 282-8096
(503) 945-5811
http://www.oregon.gov/dhs/spwpd/pages/
index.aspx

Pennsylvania
Department of Aging
Forum Place
555 Walnut Street, 5th Floor
Harrisburg, PA 17101-1919
(717) 783-1550
http://www.aging.pa.gov/Pages/default.aspx

Puerto Rico
Governor's Office for Elderly Affairs
P.O. Box 50063
Old San Juan Station
San Juan, PR 00902
(787) 721-6121 (Local)
(787) 725-4300 (Fax)

Rhode Island
Department of Elderly Affairs
Louis Pasteur Building, 2nd Floor
57 Howard Avenue
Cranston, RI 02920 (401) 462-0501
http://www.dea.ri.gov/

South Carolina
Lieutenant Governor's Office on Aging
Bureau of Senior Services
1301 Gervais Street
Suite 350
Columbia, SC 29201
(803) 734-9900
(800) 868=9095
http://aging.sc.gov/Pages/default.aspx

South Dakota
Office of Adult Services & Aging
Department of Social Services
700 Governor's Drive
Pierre, SD 57501-2291
(605) 773-3165
https://dss.sd.gov/asa/

Tennessee
Commission on Aging & Disability
Andrew Jackson Building
500 Deaderick Street, Ninth Floor
Nashville, TN 37243-0860
(615) 741-2056
https://www.tn.gov/aging/

Texas
Department of Aging & Disability Services
John H. Winters Human Services Complex
701 West 51st Street
P.O. Box 149030
Austin, TX 78714-9030
(512) 438-3030
http://www.dads.state.tx.us/

Utah
Division of Aging & Adult Services
Department of Human Services
195 North 1950 West
Salt Lake City, UT 84116
(801) 538-3910
(800) 371-7897
http://www.dads.state.tx.us/

Vermont
Agency of Human Services
Department of Disabilities, Aging & Independent
Living
Weeks Building
103 South Main Street
Waterbury, VT 05671-1601
(802) 241-2401
http://dail.vermont.gov/

Virginia
Department for the Aging and Rehabilitative
Services
1610 Forest Avenue, Suite 100
Henrico, VA 23229
(800) 552-3402
(804) 662-9333
http://www.vda.virginia.gov/

Washington
Aging & Long-Term Support Administration
Department of Social and Health Services
P.O. Box 45600
Olympia, WA 98504-5600 (mailing)
640 Woodland Square Loop SE
Lacey, WA 98503-1045 (physical)
(360) 725-2300
https://www.dshs.wa.gov/altsa

West Virginia
Bureau of Senior Services
1900 Kanawha Boulevard, East
3003 Town Center Mall, Third Level
Charleston, WV 25305-0160
(304) 558-3317
(877) 987-3646
https://www.dshs.wa.gov/altsa

Wisconsin
Bureau of Aging & Disability Resources
Department of Health & Family Services
One West Wilson Street, Room 450
P.O. Box 7851
Madison, WI 53707-7851
(888) 701-1251
(608) 266-1865
https://www.dhs.wisconsin.gov/aging/index.
htm

Wyoming
Division on Aging
Department of Health
6101 Yellowstone Road, Suite 259B
Cheyenne, WY 82002-0710
(800) 442-2766
(307) 777-7986
http://www.health.wyo.gov/aging/index.html

APPENDIX M
SOCIAL SECURITY FORMS
AVAILABLE ON THE WEBSITE

Number	Title
CMS-40B	Application for Enrollment in Medicare - Part B (Medical Insurance)
CMS-L564	Request for Employment Information
CMS-L564S	Solicitud De Información Sobre El Empleo
HA-501-U5	Request for Hearing by Administrative Law Judge
HA-520-U5	Request for Review of Hearing Decision/Order
HA-539	Notice Regarding Substitution of Party Upon Death of Claimant
HA-539-SP	Aviso Sobre La Substitución De La Parte Interesada Tras El Fallecimiento Del Reclamante
HA-4608	Waiver of Your Right to Personal Appearance Before an Administrative Law Judge
HA-4631	Claimant's Recent Medical Treatment
HA-4632	Claimant's Medications
HA-4633	Claimant's Work Background
IRS SS-4	Application for Employer Identification Number
IRS W-4V	Voluntary Withholding Request
Online	Adult Disability Report
Online	Appeal a Recent Medical Decision
Online	Apply for Disability Benefits
Online	Apply for Retirement, Spouse's or Medicare Benefits
Online	Apply Online for Extra Help with Medicare Prescription Drug Plan Costs
Online	Change Address or Telephone Number
Online	Child Disability Report
Online	Get a Replacement Medicare Card
Online	Representative Payee Accounting Report
Online	Request a Form SSA-1099/1042 (Benefit Statement) for tax or other purposes
Online	Request a Proof of Social Security Benefits Letter
Online	Request Special Notices for the Blind or Visually Impaired
Online	Sign Up For or Change Direct Deposit
SF-1199A	Direct Deposit Sign-Up Form
SS-5	Application for a Social Security Card
SS-5-FS	Application for a Social Security Card (Outside of the U.S.)
SS-5-SP	Solicitud para una tarjeta de Seguro Social

Number	Title
SSA-1-BK	Application for Retirement Insurance Benefits
SSA-2-BK	Application for Wife's or Husband's Insurance Benefits
SSA-3	Marriage Certification
SSA-4-BK	Application for Child's Insurance Benefits
SSA-4-INST	Reporting Responsibilities for Child's Insurance Benefits
SSA-5-BK	Application for Mother's or Father's Insurance Benefits
SSA-5-INST	Reporting Responsibilities for Mother's or Father's Insurance Benefits
SSA-7-F6	Application for Parent's Insurance Benefits
SSA-8	Application for Lump-Sum Death Payment
SSA-10	Application for Widow's or Widower's Insurance Benefits
SSA-10-INST	Reporting Responsibilities for Widow's or Widower's Insurance Benefits
SSA-16-BK	Application for Disability Insurance Benefits
SSA-16-BK-SP	Solicitud para beneficios de seguro por incapacidad
SSA-16-INST	Reporting Responsibilities For Disability Insurance Benefits
SSA-21	Supplement to Claim of Person Outside the United States
SSA-24	Application for Survivors Benefits (Payable Under Title II of the Social Security Act)
SSA-25	Certification of Election for Reduced Spouse's Benefits
SSA-44	Medicare Income-Related Monthly Adjustment Amount - Life-Changing Event
SSA-88	Pre-Approval Form for Consent Based Social Security Number Verification (CBSV)
SSA-89	Authorization for the Social Security Administration To Release Social Security Number (SSN) Verification
SSA-89-SP	Autorización para que la Administración de Seguro Social Divulgue la Verificación de un Número de Seguro Social (SSN)
SSA-131	Employer Report of Special Wage Payments
SSA-150	Modified Benefits Formula Questionnaire
SSA-199	Vocational Rehabilitation Provider Claim
SSA-200	CBSV Enrollment Application
SSA-308	Modified Benefits Formula Questionnaire, Foreign Pension
SSA-437-BK	Complaint Form for Allegations of Discrimination in Programs or Activities Conducted by the Social Security Administration
SSA-437-BK-SP	Formulario Para Querellas De Alegaciones De Discriminación En Los Programas De La Administración Del Seguro Social
SSA-521	Request for Withdrawal of Application
SSA-545-BK	Plan for Achieving Self-Support
SSA-546	Worker's Compensation/Public Disability Questionnaire

Number	Title
SSA-561-U2	Request for Reconsideration
SSA-604	Certificate of Incapacity
SSA-623-F6	Representative Payee Report Not available online - contact your local Social Security office
SSA-632-BK	Request for Waiver of Overpayment Recovery or Change in Repayment Rate
SSA-640	Financial Disclosure for Civil Monetary Penatly (CMP) Debt
SSA-671	Railroad Employment Questionnaire
SSA-711	Request for Deceased Individual's Social Security Record
SSA-714	You can make your payment by Credit Card
SSA-721	Statement of Death by Funeral Director
SSA-753	Statement Regarding Marriage
SSA-754-F4	Statement of Marital Relationship
SSA-769-U4	Request for Change in Time/Place of Disability Hearing
SSA-770-U4	Notice Regarding Substitution of Party Upon Death of Claimant Reconsideration of Disability Cessation
SSA-773-U4	Waiver Of Right To Appear - Disability Hearing
SSA-781	Certificate of Responsibility for Welfare and Care of Child
SSA-783	Statement Regarding Contributions
SSA-788	Statement of Care and Responsibility for Beneficiary
SSA-789-U4	Request for Reconsideration - Disability Cessation
SSA-795	Statement of Claimant or Other Persons
SSA-820-BK	Work Activity Report (Self-Employed Person)
SSA-821-BK	Work Activity Report
SSA-827	Authorization to Disclose Information to the Social Security Administration
SSA-827-INST	Instructions for Completing the SSA-827
SSA-827-INST-SP	Instrucciones para completar el formulario SSA-827
SSA-1020-INST	General Instructions for Completing the Application for Extra Help with Medicare Prescription Drug Plan Costs
SSA-1020B-INST	General Instructions for Completing the Application for Extra Help with Medicare Prescription Drug Plan Costs
SSA-1020B-INST-SP	Instrucciones generales para llenar la Solicitud para el Benefi cio Adicional con los gastos del plan de medicamentos recetados de Medicare
SSA-1021	Appeal of Determination for Extra Help with Medicare Prescription Drug Plan Costs
SSA-1021-SP	Apelación de la determinación para recibir el Beneficio Adicional con los gastos del plan de medicamentos recetados de Medicare
SSA-1021-INST	Instructions for Completing the Appeal of Determination for Extra Help with Medicare Prescription Drug Plan Costs

Number	Title
SSA-1021-INST-SP	Instrucciones para llenar la apelación de la determinación para recibir el beneficio adicional con los gastos del plan de medicamentos recetados de Medicare
SSA-1026B-OCR-SM-INST	Review of your Eligibility for Extra Help
SSA-1026B-OCR-SM-INST-SP	Revisión sobre su derecho a recibir el Beneficio Adicional
SSA-1372-BK	Advanced Notice of Termination of Child's Benefits
SSA-1372-BK-FC	Advanced Notice of Termination of Child's Benefits (Foreign Claims)
SSA-1383	Student Reporting Form
SSA-1383-FC	Reporting to Social Security Administration by Student Outside the United States
SSA-1414	Credit Card Payment Form
SSA-1560-U4	Petition to Obtain Approval of a Fee For Representing a Claimant Before the Social Security Administration
SSA-1694	Request for Business Entity Taxpayer Information
SSA-1695-F3	Identifying Information for Possible Direct Payment of Authorized Fees
SSA-1696-U4	Appointment of Representative
SSA-1699	Registration for Appointed Representative Services and Direct Payment
SSA-1724-F4	Claim for Amounts due in case of a Deceased Beneficiary
SSA-1945	Statement Concerning Your Employment in a Job Not Covered by Social Security
SSA-2000-F6	Application for Special Benefits for World War II Veterans
SSA-2010-F6	Statement for Determining Continuing Entitlement for Special Veterans Benefits (SVB)
SSA-2032-BK	Request for Waiver of Special Veterans Benefits (SVB) Overpayment Recovery or Change in Repayment Rate
SSA-2512	Pre-1957 Military Service Federal Benefit Questionnaire
SSA-2519	Child Relationship Statement
SSA-2855	Statement of Funds you Received
SSA-3033	Employee Work Activity Questionnaire
SSA-3105	Important information about your appeal, waiver rights, and repayment options
SSA-3288	Consent for Release of Information
SSA-3288-SP	Consentimiento para divulgar información
SSA-3368-BK	Disability Report - Adult
SSA-3369-BK	Work History Report
SSA-3373-BK	Function Report - Adult

SOCIAL SECURITY FORMS AVAILABLE ON THE WEBSITE

Number	Title
SSA-3375-BK	Function Report - Child Birth to 1st Birthday
SSA-3380-BK	Function Report - Adult - Third Party Form
SSA-3381	Medical and Job Worksheet - Adult
SSA-3441-BK	Disability Report - Appeal
SSA-3820-BK	Disability Report - Child
SSA-3881-BK	Questionnaire for Children Claiming SSI Benefits
SSA-3885	Government Pension Questionnaire
SSA-4111	Certification of Election for Reduced Widow(er)'s and Surviving Divorced Spouse's Benefits
SSA-4162	Child Care Dropout Questionnaire
SSA-5665-BK	Teacher Questionnaire
SSA-5666	Request for Administrative Information
SSA-7008	Request for Correction of Earnings Record
SSA-7050-F4	Request for Social Security Earnings Information
SSA-7104	Partnership Questionnaire
SSA-7156	Farm Self Employment Questionnaire
SSA-7157-F4	Farm Arrangement Questionnaire
SSA-7160	Employment Relationship Questionnaire
SSA-7163	Questionnaire about Employment or Self Employment
SSA-7163A-F4	Supplemental Statement Regarding Farming Activities
SSA-8510	Authorization for the Social Security Administration to Obtain Personal Information
SSA-L706-F3	Letter to Custodian of Birth Records

These can be accessed at https://www.ssa.gov/forms/.

INDEX

(All references are to question numbers, unless otherwise noted.)

A

2019 Social Security & Medicare Facts

INDEX

N